ACLS History E-Book Project

Reprint Series

The ACLS History E-Book Project (www.historyebook.org) collaborates with constituent societies of the American Council of Learned Societies, publishers, librarians and historians to create an electronic collection of works of high quality in the field of history. This volume is produced from digital images created for the Project by the Scholarly Publishing Office and the Digital Library Production Service at the University of Michigan, Ann Arbor. The digital reformatting process results in an electronic version of the text that can be both accessed online and used to create new print copies. This book and hundreds of others are available online in the History E-Book Project through subscription.

Many of the works in the History E-Book Project are available in print and can be ordered either directly from their publishers or as part of this series. For information refer to the online Title Record page for each book. Inquiries regarding this series can be directed to info@hebook.org.

ACLS

HISTORY E-BOOK

http://www.historyebook.org

INDONESIAN TRADE AND SOCIETY

SELECTED STUDIES ON INDONESIA

VOLUME ONE

Published for
The Royal Tropical Institute – Amsterdam
Under a grant from
The Netherlands Organization
for the Advancement of Pure Research – The Hague

INDONESIAN TRADE AND SOCIETY

Essays in Asian Social and Economic History

by

J. C. van Leur

W. van Hoeve Publishers Ltd – The Hague

1967

THE HAGUE

Second edition 1967

PRINTED IN THE NETHERLANDS

Foreword

In a world becoming more and more a cultural unity, the diversity of languages is an ever greater obstacle to scholarly progress. And certainly scholarly work published in the language of such a small cultural area as the Dutch runs a great risk of eluding the attention of the international scholarly world. It was as a result of this consideration that in 1948 a committee was established for the editing of English translations of studies on Indonesia written in Dutch. Since 1952 the committee has been affiliated with the Royal Tropical Institute at Amsterdam.

As the first volume in the series of works to be published under its auspices, the editors let their choice fall on the work of a scholar who has made an important contribution – though one up to now little noticed outside the Netherlands – to a better understanding of Asian history and the historical relation between Europe and Asia: the late Dr van Leur.

Jacob Cornelis van Leur, who was born at Utrecht in 1908, spent a large part of his youth in the province of Zeeland, where even in his school years he manifested a great deal of interest in history, and especially in the rôle the Zeeland towns Middelburg, Veere, and Flushing had played in the past as centres of world trade.

In the years he spent in studying for the Netherlands East Indies civil service at the University of Leiden he had ample opportunity further to develop his broad interest in the cultural, economic, and social history of Europe, and of Asia as well.[1] His original, but often rather bold and heretical hypotheses several times brought him in opposition to his professors.

In his dissertation Van Leur made an attempt at analyzing early Asian society with the aid of the methodology of sociology and economic history developed by Max Weber – a methodology which at least for Indonesian history had not yet been applied. That Van Leur came to such surprising and often revolutionary conclusions lay not only in the method applied, however, but just as much in the broad, catholic knowledge and the sharply critical attitude regarding the theories current at the time which despite his youth he was able to bring to bear. When in his introduction he attributes "no value except that of a compilation"[2] to his dissertation, he is being extraordinarily modest. It is true the value of the work does not lie in the fulfillment of that traditional ideal of the student of history, the making available of new source material. But Van Leur has accomplished something in his dissertation that is at least as important. He has thrown the limelight of a new methodology on source material long since published and thereby enriched the historical discipline with a number of new hypotheses.

It was to be a long time before Van Leur's findings were to attract the attention in the Dutch scholarly world which they deserved, however. Alongside an amazing maturity his dissertation also exhibited a number of weaker aspects, some of them the defaults inherent in his good qualities – such as the tendency sometimes to state his new propositions and theories all too absolutely, – but some of them also having to do with his youthfulness. Not the least of these weaknesses, perhaps, was his style, on the one hand lapidary, on the other extremely circumlocutory, and along with it his tendency not to avoid a single sidepath but to carry the reader along with him in seven league boots through widely separated periods of history and from one end of the world to the other, all in one long concatination of catalogues and subordinate clauses.

Dr Van Leur had meanwhile become a civil servant in what was then the Netherlands East Indies. Nominated assistant *controleur* at Tulung Agung in eastern Java late in 1934, he was transferred in 1936 to the general secretariat of the governor-general at Bogor (then Buitenzorg) – an honour for so young an official. Working in the section for financial and economic affairs, he included in his circle of friends not only the small group of progressive Dutchmen, but – remarkably enough for a Dutch civil servant in Bogor in those pre-war days – also a number of Indonesians, several of whom now hold high posts in the country.

During his years in Indonesia Dr van Leur continued to be active in scholarly fields. He was one of a group of scholars who, under the guidance of Professor J. H. A. Logemann, made a study of Dutch East India Company sources to collect material on constitutional law, and in 1938 was one of the founders of the Historical Section of the Royal Batavian Society of Arts and Sciences,[3] of which he later served as secretary. From the Bogor period came also his shorter studies in the field of Indonesian history in which he attempted to give further foundation and verification to several of the hypotheses brought forward in his dissertation. As a part of a work on the history of the Dutch overseas, Van Leur wrote "De wereld van Zuid-Oost Azië" (The World of Southeast Asia), a study of the position of the Dutch United East India Company in the first half of the seventeenth century. Only two of the three chapters were published; the third did not reach the Netherlands before the German invasion on the tenth of May, 1940. In that year there also appeared under his name an interesting study of the Eighteenth Century as a category in the writing of Indonesian history. An attempt to have the complete text of "De wereld van Zuid-Oost Azië" published in Indonesia was thwarted by the Japanese attack in 1942.

The Pacific War was to have a much more disastrous consequence for Van Leur, however. He had volunteered for the navy as decoding officer. At the time of the battle of the Java Sea he was on board one of the ships of the Allied navy. His ship was torpedoed, and he, just past thirty-four years of age, was one of the victims.

One wonders whether he had a premonition of his early end. Some things give that impression – so great was the energy with which he attempted in his few years of scholarly productivity to outline the field for further research, and so well considered the course he took, that his work, fragmentary as it is, can still in a certain sense be seen as a unity in itself.

Van Leur did not survive to see his life work recognized, not even in the Netherlands. It was only after the war that his writings began to attract the attention of more than a very restricted circle of scholars.

In the past few years, however, a number of scholars carrying on research, some of them working independently, some making use of Van Leur's publications, have arrived at conclusions more or less in agreement with those he had reached. Professor Bosch, in his inaugural lecture at the University of Leiden on the problem of the Hindu colonization of the archipelago,[4] pointed out that Van Leur's sociological point of view was in very close harmony with the conclusions he himself had reached some years ago by means of an approach from the point of view of cultural history. The late Professor Schrieke in a manuscript left behind at his death, a translation of which is to appear as third volume in the series of which this book is the first, arrived at conclusions very close to those of Van Leur in regard to the causes of the process of Islamization in Indonesia. In his book *Asia and the West*,[5] Maurice Zinkin, probably without any knowledge of Van Leur's work, defended a point of view on the relation between Asia and Europe in the past in a number of essential aspects coinciding with the point of view of Van Leur.

Others scholars, for example Dr van Naerssen,[6] Dr Locher,[7] and Professor Coolhaas,[8] have in the past few years taken it upon themselves to dispute Van Leur's standpoint, at least in some of its often all too absolute forms. But, generally speaking, scholars in the Netherlands and Indonesia have become more and more convinced of the importance of his work. In 1948 Professor Wertheim gave a lecture on Van Leur's life work which was later published as the first essay in his book *Herrijzend Azië* (Asia Resurgent),[9] and he also saw to it that the ill-fated third chapter of Van Leur's "De wereld van Zuid-Oost Azië" finally achieved publication in 1947. Other scholars as well – for example Professor Bouman[10] of the University of Groningen and Professor Resink[11] of the University of Indonesia, both of whom had known Van Leur personally, and earlier than others had seen him for his true worth – at various occasions called attention to Van Leur's significance.

In the Dutch intellectual world, then, the name of Van Leur has by now penetrated to a fairly wide circle of scholars.[12] Outside the Netherlands it is another matter. One of the British experts on early Asia *par excellence*, Professor Boxer of the University of London, though he does not share Van Leur's point of view completely, has shown a high esteem for his work.[13] The following passage from a study by Sir George N. Clark of Oriel College, Oxford, gives evidence of the appreciation of another British scholar:

> ... much of his interpretation would have been accepted by the men of the seventeenth century themselves as a matter of course. ... Dr. van Leur's chief services are in his realistic view of the trade of the Far East, which he divests of much accretion due to reading back into the seventeenth century the promise of the later political and economic domination, and in his testing by this view the sociological doctrines of Max Weber.[14]

Professor Wertheim placed a great deal of emphasis on the importance of Van Leur's theories in his *Effects of Western Civilization on Indonesian Society*.[15]

As long as Van Leur's writings remained untranslated, however, it was a matter of course that his work would attract only a very limited amount of attention. Now that a large part of the work of Max Weber has become available to the English-speaking public through translation,[16] it would seem to be the proper moment to make Van Leur's research accessible to that same international public, based on Max Weber's methodology as the work is.

The basic principle followed has of course been that of reproducing Van Leur's writings as nearly as possible in the form in which he left them. Changes have been made in the text only in cases where it is obvious from Van Leur's own notes that he would have made them himself in a following edition, and in cases here and there where the text would have been incomprehensible to the non-Dutch reader without a certain amount of expansion or explanation. Many of the notes have been rechecked for accuracy, and they have been recast in a form enabling the foreign reader to use them with less difficulty than those in the original text. The quotations have been given from the published English texts and translations wherever possible, and references have in some cases been changed to the editions of standard works most easily available.

At the same time the occasion of translation has given the opportunity to make Van Leur's writings, and especially his dissertation, more readable. Without allowing the positive qualities of Van Leur's often very pithy manner of expression to be lost, the translators have attempted to make the dissertation into a more smoothly flowing whole. From a stylistic point of view the result will without doubt not be completely satisfactory to the English-speaking reader. But to achieve a more satisfactory English style would probably have meant completely rewriting the whole dissertation, and that on the other hand would have meant losing much of Van Leur's characteristic manner of expression as well as making the work of translation a completely Sisyphean task.

For inclusion in this edition of Van Leur's works, the editors have selected the following writings, which together give a more or less complete picture of Van Leur's theories and form something of a unity:

1 The dissertation repeatedly mentioned above. Published in Dutch under the title *Eenige beschouwingen betreffende den ouden Aziatischen handel* (Some Observations Concerning Early Asian Trade), this book is the most general and the most fundamental of Van Leur's writings, and therefore out of methodological as well as chronological considerations deserved to come first. The further writings all of them build more or less on the foundations laid down in the dissertation, and in some cases are a repetition or variation of themes in it.

2 A methodological essay originally entitled "Aanteekeningen

met betrekking tot de beoefening der Indische geschiedenis" (Some Notes Regarding the Study of the History of the Indies). In it Van Leur has attempted to outline a program for scholars occupied with Indonesian history and its problems.

3 "De wereld van Zuid-Oost Azië" (The World of Southeast Asia), in both form and content doubtless the most mature of all Van Leur's writings. The work was written in response to a request from Dr de Haan and Professor van Winter for a contribution to be included in a book they were editing under the title *Nederlanders over de zeeën* (Dutchmen Over the Seas). Characteristic for Van Leur is the introductory note he later wrote for the study:

> The editors requested a contribution on the overseas history of the Dutch in Asia treating the first voyages to the Indies and the East India Company up to 1650. For anyone who considers the true historical picture of those voyages and the early history of the Company it must be obvious that to speak here of a chapter in Dutch colonial history would mean an exaggeration.
>
> It is fundamentally incorrect to make Dutch colonial history begin on the twenty-third of June, 1596, unless one wishes to consider history as chronological whimsy.
>
> The first question ought to be whether the arrival of those few ships from around the Cape constituted a decisive factor in the course of history for the countries of southeast Asia. It is not the value of Dutch colonial history that is the most important thing, after all, but an evaluation within the framework of the general history of southeast Asia and Indonesia. The question alike arises whether in consideration of the above the date 1650 has any sense or significance as a point in time.
>
> Whoever wishes to write the history of the Dutch Company, then, will have to begin with a general description of the stage of Asian history in the sixteenth and seventeenth century. Whoever wishes to write the political history of Indonesia then will have to begin with the analysis of the general social and economic 'conditions' which helped to determine the course of those unique historical facts.
>
> The following study has been designed as an attempt at making a (comparative) description of those 'conditions' and at placing the first half century of Dutch activity in southeast Asia within the proper frame of reference. At the same time it has meant for the writer the elaboration of a point on a program he has repeatedly brought forward.[17]

The first two chapters of "De wereld van Zuid-Oost Azië" were published in the above-mentioned book, but without footnotes. The notes were to be found in the manuscript and in the proofs prepared for the ill-fated publication of the study in Indonesia, however, and are here published for the first time. There are also a number of minor variations between the text as here published, which is based on the manuscript and the Indonesian proofs, and the text published in *Nederlanders over de zeeën*. A page of the third chapter has unfortunately been lost from the manuscript as a result of war conditions.

4 A group of reviews written on the various volumes of the history of the Netherlands East Indies published under the editorship of Dr Stapel in the period just before the last war. The last of the articles, "Eenige aanteekeningen betreffende de mogelijkheid der 18e eeuw als categorie in de Indische geschiedschrijving" (Some Comments on the Possibility of the Eighteenth Century as a Category in the Writing of Indonesian History), is actually more an independent essay than a review. It constitutes a rather important supplement to Van Leur's longer works, in that, while in his dissertation he covered mainly the periods before the arrival of the Dutch, and in "De wereld van Zuid-Oost Azië" considered the first half of the seventeenth century, this essay gives an interesting consideration of a later period, the eighteenth century.

The translation has been made by Mr James S Holmes and Mr A. van Marle, the latter of whom was also entrusted with the task of preparing this volume. Publication has been made possible through the financial support of the Netherlands Organization for the Advancement of Pure Research (z.w.o.).

THE EDITORS

Amsterdam, Autumn 1954

Notes

1 During his student years Van Leur was also an active member and for a time secretary of the student indologists society. In 1930 he joined with a few other students of 'indology' – the course of study for persons training to become civil servants in the Indies – to found and edit the *Indologen Blad* (Indologists' Journal), the periodical of the society. The following year he served as one of the founders of the *Leidsch Universiteitsblad* (Leiden University Paper), and towards the end of his studies he was entrusted with seeing Professor van Vollenhoven's *Staatsrecht Overzee* (Constitutional Law Overseas) through the press.

2 See below, p. 7.

3 See below, pp. 155–156.

4 F. D. K. Bosch, *Het vraagstuk van de Hindoe-kolonisatie van den Archipel* (The Problem of Hindu Colonization of the [Indonesian] Archipelago), Inaugural lecture, University of Leiden, Leiden, 1946.

5 Maurice Zinkin, *Asia and the West*, London, 1951; revised edition, London, 1953.

6 F. H. van Naerssen, *Culture Contacts and Social Conflicts in Indonesia* (Occasional Papers of the Southeast Asia Institute, I, New York, 1947; translation by A. J. Barnouw of *Cultuurcontacten en sociale conflicten in Indonesië*, inaugural lecture, Wageningen Agricultural University, Amsterdam, 1946) especially 7, 11; "Het sociaal aspect van acculturaties in Indonesië" (The Social Aspect of Acculturations in Indonesia), *Zaïre*, II (1948), 625–638, especially 633; "De aanvang van het Hindu-Indonesische acculturatie proces" (The Beginnings of the Process of Acculturation in Hindu Indonesia), *Orientalia Neerlandica: A Volume of Oriental Studies* (Leiden, 1948), 414–422, especially 418.

7 G. W. Locher, "Inleidende beschouwingen over de ontmoeting van Oost en West in Indonesië" (Introductory Observations on the Meeting of East and West in Indonesia), *Indonesië* (Indonesia), II (1948–1949), 411–428, 538–555, especially 422–428.

8 W. Ph. Coolhaas, "Van koloniale geschiedenis en geschiedenis van Indonesië, van historici en taalambtenaren" (Of Colonial History and the History of Indonesia, of Historians and Philologist Civil Servants), *Bijdragen tot de Taal-, Land- en Volkenkunde* (Contributions to Philology, Geography, and Ethnology), CVIII (1951), 135–160, especially 151–153.

9 W. F. Wertheim, *Herrijzend Azië* (Asia Resurgent; Arnhem, 1950), 11–29.

10 P. J. Bouman, "Causaliteit en functioneel verband in de sociologie van Max Weber" (Causality and Functional Relationships in the Sociology of Max Weber), *Causaliteit en functioneel verband in de sociologie: Handelingen van de*

"*Nederlandsche Sociologische Vereeniging*", *December 1946* (Causality and Functional Relationships in Sociology: Proceedings of the Dutch Sociological Society, December, 1946; Amsterdam, 1946), 7–24, especially 24 (summary of discussion).

11 G. J. Resink, "Speelmans tweede rechtsschepping" (Speelman's Second Legal Creation), (*Indisch*) *Tijdschrift van het Recht* ([Indies] Law Journal), 1947, pp. 277–296, especially 279, 291–292, 294; "Over ons gemeenschappelijk verleden in het recht van vrede" (On our Common Past in the Law of Peace), *Gedenkboek uitgegeven ter gelegenheid van het vijfentwintigjarig bestaan van het rechtswetenschappelijk hoger onderwijs in Indonesië op 28 October 1949* (Memorial Volume Published on the Occasion of the 25th Anniversary of Higher Law Education in Indonesia on 28 October, 1949; Groningen, 1949), 250–257, especially 256; "Iets over Europacentrische, regiocentrische en Indocentrische geschiedschrijving" (Something on Europe-Centred, Region-Centred, and Indonesia-Centred Historiography), *Oriëntatie* (Orientation), xxxvii (October, 1950), 22–30, especially 26; "Tussen de mythen: Van koloniale naar nationale geschiedschrijving" (Between the Myths: From a Colonial to a National Historiography), *De Nieuwe Stem* (The New Voice), VII (1952), 346–355, especially 348, 353; "Passe-partout om geschiedschrijvers over Indonesië" (Writers of Indonesian History in Passe-Partout), *Indonesië*, VI (1952–1953), 372–379, especially 376; "Zakelijkheid en zekerheid in de Indonesische geschiedschrijving" (Objectivity and Certainty in the Writing of Indonesian History), *Weerklank op het werk van Jan Romein: Liber Amicorum* (Echoes to the Work of Jan Romein: Liber Amicorum; Amsterdam, 1953), 146–156, especially 148.

12 See also D. de Vries, "Indonesische Geschiedenis" (Indonesian History), *Oriëntatie*, iv (January, 1948), 27–31, especially 27 (reprinted in his *Culturele aspecten in de verhouding Nederland-Indonesië* [Cultural Aspects in the Relations Between the Netherlands and Indonesia; Amsterdam, 1948], 126–132, especially 126); J. G. de Casparis, "Twintig jaar studie van de oudere geschiedenis van Indonesia" (Twenty Years of Study of the Early History of Indonesia), *Oriëntatie*, xliv (January, 1954), 626–664, especially 646, 647–648, 651–652.

13 C. R. Boxer, review of Johan van der Woude, *Coen, koopman van Heeren Zeventien* (Coen, Merchant for the Gentlemen Seventeen), *The Far Eastern Quarterly*, X (1950–1951), 216–217; *The Christian Century in Japan: 1549–1650* (Berkeley, 1951), viii–ix; "Some Considerations on Portuguese Colonial Historiography" *Proceedings of the International Colloquium on Luso-Brazilian Studies, Washington, October 15–20, 1950* ... (Nashville, Tenn., 1953), 169–180, especially 171–172.

14 G. N. Clark and W. J. M. van Eysinga, *The Colonial Conferences Between England and the Netherlands in 1613 and 1615* (Bibliotheca Visseriana; two volumes, Leiden, 1940, 1951), II, 25.

15 W. F. Wertheim, *Effects of Western Civilization on Indonesian Society* (Institute of Pacific Relations International Secretariat Paper No 11, New York, 1950, soon to be published in expanded form by the Institute of Pacific Relations in cooperation with the publisher of this book), 1, 19–20, 34–35. See also his "Early Asian Trade: An Appreciation of J. C. van Leur", *The Far Eastern Quarterly*, XIII (1953–1954), 167–173.

16 See bibliography below, pp. 438–439, and also Hans Gerth and Hedwig Ide Gerth, "Bibliography on Max Weber", *Social Research*, XVI (1949), 70–89.

17 Written as a prefatory note planned to be published with the study in the journal *Djåwå.*

Bibliography of the Writings of J. C. van Leur

"Voorwoord van de Redactie" (Foreword by the Editors), *Indologen Blad* (Indologists' Journal), I, i (December, 1929), [1].

Review, A. D. A. de Kat Angelino, *Staatkundig beleid en bestuurszorg in Nederlandsch-Indië* (Political Policy and Administrative Supervision in the Netherlands East Indies), Part One – *Indologen Blad*. I, i (December, 1929), [1]–[3]; Part Two – *Indologen Blad*, I, ii (January, 1930), [3]–[5].

"Nederlandsch-Indonesisch Verbond Afdeeling Leiden †" (In Memoriam: The Dutch-Indonesian Association, Section Leiden), *Indologen Blad*, I, i (December, 1929), [3]–[5].

Notice, J. A. Eigenman, *Indië en de Ministerraad* (The Indies and the [Dutch] Cabinet), *Indologen Blad*, I, i (December, 1929), [6].

"Marionettendécor voor: Casanova in Amsterdam 1757" (A Marionette Setting for Casanova in Amsterdam, 1757), *Indologen Blad*, I, ii (January, 1930), [6]–[7].

Notice, *Rapport sur la préparation par le gouvernement soviétique des révoltes coloniales* (Report on the Preparation of Colonial Revolts by the Soviet Government), *Indologen Blad*, I, ii (January, 1930), [8].

"De economie in het studieprogramma der Vereenigde Faculteiten" (Economics in the Combined Faculties Program of Study [for 'Indologists']), *Indologen Blad*, I, vi (May, 1930), [5]–[6].

"De geschiedenis in het studieprogramma der Vereenigde Faculteiten", (History in the Combined Faculties Program of Study [for 'Indologists']), *Indologen Blad*, I, viii (September, 1930: wrongly numbered vii and dated June), [2]–[3].

Notice, C. Z. Klötzel, *Indien im Schmelztiegel* (India in the Melting Pot), *Indologen Blad*, I, viii (September, 1930), [6]–[7].

"De eenheid der Leidsche studenten" (Leiden Student Unity), *Indologen Blad,* II, ii (May, 1931), [1]–[2].

Review, M. V. Polak, *Inleiding in de economie* (Introduction to Economics), *Leidsch Universiteitsblad* (Leiden University Paper), II, iii (21 October, 1932), 7–8.

"De opleiding der Indische bestuursambtenaren" (The Training of Indies Civil Servants), *Koloniaal Tijdschrift* (Colonial Journal), XXI (1932), 577–585.

"'s Rijks Universiteit te Leiden als provinciaal instituut" (The State University of Leiden as an Institution of Provincial Importance), *Leidsch Universiteitsblad,* II, ix (17 January, 1933), 1–3.

With Ivo Samkalden, "Open brief aan de redactie ..." (Open Letter to the Editors ...), *Indologen Blad,* V, vi (15 April, 1934), 35.

Review, C. van Vollenhoven, *Staatsrecht Overzee* (Constitutional Law Overseas), *Leidsch Universiteitsblad,* III, xv (18 May, 1934), 2–3.

Eenige beschouwingen betreffende den ouden Aziatischen handel (Some Observations Concerning Early Asian Trade). Middelburg, 1934.

"P. A. Haaxman †" (In Memoriam: P. A. Haaxman), *Soerabaiasch Handelsblad* (The Surabaya Commercial News), 25 January, 1935.

"Internationale valuta-stabilisatie: Het aspect der economische omstandigheden" (International Stabilization of Currency: The Aspect of the Economic Circumstances), *Indische Courant* (The Indies News), 3 December, 1935.

"De Weltwirtschaft valt uiteen: Einde van het oude Europa" (The World Economy Falls to Pieces: The End of the Old Europe), *Indische Courant,* 4 December, 1935.

"De beteekenis der crisis: Een nieuwe tijd van nationale consolidatie" (The Significance of the Crisis: A New Period of National Consolidation), *Indische Courant,* 5 December, 1935. (This and the two preceding items were written originally as a single article entitled "Te simplistisch" [Oversimplified]).

"Indië's economische toekomst" (The Economic Future of the

Indies), Part One – *Indische Courant*, 24 December, 1935; Part Two – *Indische Courant*, 31 December, 1935.

"Samensmelting" (Fusion [of Budi Utomo and Persatuan Bangsa Indonesia]), *Indische Courant*, 14 January, 1936.

"Inheemsch volksleven: Contrasten te Soerabaia" (Native Life: Contrasts in Surabaya), *Indische Courant*, 18 January, 1936.

"Hervorming" (Reforms), *Indische Courant*, 29 January, 1936.

"Fascistische leuzen en waarheid: Resultaten van een almachtige regeeringspers" (Fascist Slogans and Truth: Results of an All-Powerful Government Press), *Indische Courant*, 14 February, 1936.

"Het boerenbolsjewisme in China: De richting van Moskou's invloed" (Agrarian Bolshevism in China: The Direction of Moscow's Influence), *Indische Courant*, 25 February, 1936.

"Opleving in Indië" (Recovery in the Indies), Part One – *Indische Courant*, 11 March, 1936; Part Two – *Indische Courant*, 31 March, 1936.

"Geboorte en doel van de 'New-Deal'" (Birth and Aim of the 'New Deal'), *Indische Courant*, 1 April, 1936.

"Groei en doel van de New-Deal" (Growth and Aim of the New Deal), *Indische Courant*, 6 April, 1936.

"New-Deal en Amerikaansche industrie" (The New Deal and American Industry), *Indische Courant*, 22 April, 1936.

"De New-Deal en het geldwezen" (The New Deal and Finance), Part One – *Indische Courant*, 6 May, 1936; Part Two – *Indische Courant*, 7 May, 1936.

"Amerika's New Deal" (America's New Deal), *Indische Courant*, 18 May, 1936.

"Enkele aanteekeningen met betrekking tot de beoefening der Indische geschiedenis" (Some Notes Regarding the Study of the History of the Indies), *Koloniale Studiën* (Colonial Studies), XXI (1937), 651–661.

"Wederom het geval 'Z'" (Once More the Z [entgraaff] Case), *Kritiek en Opbouw* (Criticism and Construction), I (1938–1939), 159–160.

"De muze van Jan Compagnie: Prospectus van dichtende kooplieden" (The Muse of John Company: Prospect of Poetizing Merchants), *Bataviaasch Nieuwsblad* (Batavia Daily), 22 March 1939. (Review, E. du Perron, editor, *De Muze van Jan Companjie.*)

Review, J. Th. Vermeulen, *De Chineezen te Batavia en de troebelen van 1740* (The Chinese at Batavia and the Troubles of 1740), *Tijdschrift voor Indische Taal-, Land- en Volkenkunde uitgegeven door het Koninklijk Bataviaasch Genootschap van Kunsten en Wetenschappen* (Journal of Indonesian Philology, Geography, and Ethnology Published by the Royal Batavian Society of Arts and Sciences), LXXIX (1939), 147–149.

Review, F. W. Stapel, editor, *Geschiedenis van Nederlandsch Indië* (History of the Netherlands East Indies), Volume One, *Djåwå* (Java), XIX (1939), 286–292.

Review, F. W. Stapel, editor, *Geschiedenis van Nederlandsch Indië*, Volumes Two and Three, *Tijdschrift voor Indische Taal-, Land- en Volkenkunde ...*, LXXIX (1939), 589–595.

"De wereld van Zuid-Oost Azië" (The World of Southeast Asia), Chapters One and Two, in J. C. de Haan and P. J. van Winter, editors, *Nederlanders over de zeeën* (Dutchmen over the Seas; Utrecht, 1940), 101–144.

"Positieve Nederlandsche cultureele politiek in Indië?" (A Positive Dutch Cultural Policy in the Indies?), *Koloniaal Tijdschrift*, XXIX (1940), 434–441.

"Eenige aanteekeningen betreffende de mogelijkheid der achttiende eeuw als categorie in de Indische geschiedschrijving" (Some Comments on the Possibility of the Eighteenth Century as a Category in the Writing of Indonesian History), *Tijdschrift voor Indische Taal-, Land- en Volkenkunde ...*, LXXX (1940), 544–567.

"Mahan op den Indischen lessenaar" (Mahan on the Indies Writing Desk), *Koloniaal Tijdschrift*, XXX (1941), 576–586.

"Ongepaste Critiek: II" (Improper Criticism: II), *Kritiek en Opbouw*, IV (1941–1942), 225–226.

"De wereld van Zuid-Oost Azië", Chapter Three, with introduction by W. F. Wertheim, *Tijdschrift voor Geschiedenis* (Historical Journal), LX (1947), 292–314.

Contents

Maps

On Early Asian Trade

The Dutch version of "On Early Asian Trade", published in book form in 1934 by Firma G. W. den Boer, Middelburg, under the title *Eenige beschouwingen betreffende den ouden Aziatischen handel* (Some Observations Concerning Early Asian Trade), was written by J. C. van Leur as his doctoral dissertation, and was defended by him on 5 October, 1934.

FOR MY PARENTS

FOR PEU

Introduction

On 22 June, 1596, after a long and unlucky passage around the Cape of Good Hope and northeast across the Indian Ocean, the four Amsterdam ships of the first Dutch 'Company for Afar' came to anchor before the Javanese town of Bantam, thus ending a voyage that had begun on 21 March, 1595, when they had set sail from Tessell. Then the accounts[1] change over from the hardly varying details of the sea journal and lead us into a lively, colourful world. The accounts of the first voyage transport us into the midst of everyday life in the town of Bantam – ceremonial visits are exchanged with the town authorities, the governor, and the *shahbandar;* nobles and merchants come on board:

> There came such a multitude of Javanese and other nations as Turks, Chinese, Bengali, Arabs, Persians, Gujarati, and others that one could hardly move.[2]

> ... they ... came so abundantly that each nation took a spot on the ships where they displayed their goods, the same as if it were on a market. Of which the Chinese brought of all sorts of silk woven and unwoven, twined and untwined, with beautiful earthenware, with other strange things more. The Javanese brought chickens, eggs, ducks, and many kinds of fruits. Arabs, Moors, Turks, and other nations of people each brought of everything one might imagine.[3]

An incident recorded in passing on one of the first days (10 July, 1596) sheds still more light on the busy trade of people from all sorts of places.

> ... the tenth many Turkish and Arab merchants came on board, whereunder one Kojah[4] Rayoan by name, who had earlier been to Venice and spoke fairly good Italian, who raised the point of sailing home with us in order to journey from there back to Constantinople, which was his country, because he could not travel over Achin, a town in Sumatra, since the king ... holds all merchants and had recently taken two Bantamese

> junks, consequently he had to stay at Bantam... He offered to lay in his goods along with ours, and make the ships' owners his heirs in case he should come to die on the voyage.[5]

In Bantam, then, one comes across a Turkish merchant, a 'wholesale dealer' from Constantinople whose trading expeditions, on which he went along with his goods himself, had taken him across routes from Venice to into the Far East. When Admiral van Neck's ship lay before Bantam in 1598, "a man of honourable countenance, ... old in years, [who] was well accompanied ...", came on board – a merchant born in Delhi, trading in cloves in the Moluccas. He pointed out the route there to Van Neck, "offering to go with us in person (as he had to be there) and to secure great amity of the kings and rulers of the land for us".[6] In 1605 on Banda Admiral van der Hagen met an African merchant from Fez.[7] The captains and clerks from Holland and Zeeland had arrived at ports where stopping-off places had been established in the ancient sea trade routes from the Far East to the region of the Mediterranean.

Many centuries have known that sea trade route. In the cultural history of Asia it has made its influence felt in various periods. The sea route linked India with the ancient world and China with the western and eastern parts of Indonesia and with India. It was one of the chief nerves in the body of early Islam stretched out from west to east. Along that sea route, in journeys lasting months and years, were brought the Eastern goods which found their markets in the Roman Empire, then in the Byzantine and Moslem lands and cities, and some of which – like crumbs falling from the table – made their way on into southern and northwestern European trade. Part of the journeying of Buddhist priests and pilgrims between China and India took place by sea. The culture of early Indonesia and early Indo-China bears the stamp of Brahmanism and Buddhism, and the sea routes carried the Indians there. Islam set out toward the East along the coast, following the sea route from port to port. In his "L'Arabie et les Indes Néerlandaises", Snouck Hurgronje has characterized this cultural sphere spanning the world from Morocco to Indonesia in a few very illustrative episodes. The awe-inspiring conquests of the Mongol khans in the thirteenth and fourteenth centuries created a second world empire beside that of Islam, one that stretched from China to the Black Sea.[8] In the fourteenth century one could meet merchants on the sea route from Genoa, Venice, and Pisa carrying on trade with China under the protection of the Mongol states;[9] in Canton one could find a colony of the Italian nation that had swarmed there 'on adventure',[10] as in the Far West regular Italian shipping had established itself at Bruges.

It appears from their embassies that already in very early times Indonesian states took part in the trade along the sea routes, trade providing the princes and lords with foreign wares for ambassadorial gifts. A last witness of Indonesian trade westwards is given in the establishment of Indonesian authority on Madagascar.[11] Reliefs on the Javanese temple Barabudur as well as tales in *The Thousand and One Nights* point toward the sea route.

The sea route has maintained its significance up to the present time. The changes that the nineteenth century brought, however, were both important and drastic. Industrialization of western Europe under modern capitalism set a mass traffic of goods in motion; the lands of an ancient Asian culture were mobilized as consumers' markets for the large industries of the West and (under colonial capitalism) fitted into the trade system as areas for supplying the raw materials and plantation products of modern colonial mining and agriculture. In the last forty years the appearance of Japan and America on the scene has multiplied and accelerated this trade system. Asian shipping, once master of the sea routes, has been repressed by the modern shipping of the capitalistic states, degraded to subordinate coastwise shipping, destroyed.[12] The chain of great Asian ports of the present day, from Suez to Kobe, preserves only a few old names, and even then the memory is only a sound, no tangible, appreciable remainder. In the dead towns of Zeeland and West

Friesland it is only with difficulty that one can realize a past of international shipping and world trade. If one goes along the inner dikes of the eastern polders at Walcheren, from Arnemuiden towards Welzinge, it will be hard for one to imagine that here in earlier times was the place where southern and northern European ships trading on Bruges and Antwerp anchored and wintered;[13] a bit to the south, on the Scheldt, modern trade goes on at the moment night and day; Middelburg lies far inland now; Arnemuiden is a poor fishing village in the midst of diked-in land. So it is too with the shabby remains of shipping trade and ancient fame in the East, in Achin, Malacca, Palembang, Bantam, and Tuban,[14] in Pegu and Cambay, in Hormuz and Macalla.

From two different points of view the history of the Asian sea route deserves attention. In the first place for defining its position in the general course of economic history. Whereas one has to start from the presence of the modern capitalism which at the moment gives its imprint to the existence of the whole world[15] (whether by an economic relationship of direct dependence or one of indirect exposure to the influences of variable, all-embracing business cycles), it is the business of economic history to determine how modern capitalism was built up, and in what times, where its foundations were laid, to what extent it was all the work of western Europe alone, and, furthermore, how the periods whose existence is characterized by different social and economic structures are marked off in relation to the period of modern capitalism, and what things are typical features of such other forms. All the material to be collected must serve again and again to bring to the fore the influence of modern capitalism (tremendous in dimensions, fatally decisive, all-dominating) and to contrast the other periods with it. Therefore it must be determined what the significance of the sea route was as regards the capacity of commerce and trade, the forms of their organization, and their importance for the material foundations of cultural history.

The history of the sea route deserves attention in the second place for determining its significance for the early history of Indonesia. There are important episodes in Indonesian political and cultural history which are closely linked to trade and the trade route. For reconstructing them accurately, data on the social and economic 'foundations' are indispensable, but extremely scarce. Perhaps some facts out of the history of the trade route can shed a bit of light there, and open up the possibility of exploring the economic history of the area.[16]

The study below has no value except that of a compilation. Only printed material has been used, and the treatment is only fragmentary. That even with such methods the study was undertaken may still be motivated. In the present tendencies among the Indonesian ethnic groups, in the struggle for the political and cultural forms of a modern Indonesian national life, one can see everywhere the endeavour to form an Indonesian cultural ideal which, as a glorification of the past, must be a source of strength for the times to come and a means of binding ethnic groups together. The endeavour finds expression especially in the paper noise of native journalism and the book-language agitation of the 'popular leaders',[17] but even so there can be no doubt that it also has deeper roots, in all those who appreciate the fact that their land, 'the land of their cradle, their love, their old age, and their grave', was in its historic past a part of the impressive whole of an earlier Asia – in all those who now want to make that past again a spiritual possession for the present generation of Indonesians. For a powerful cultural ideal no other motives are necessary. A first requirement for the non-Indonesian towards all this is to take an attitude of objectivity, for which historical research is necessary.

Furthermore, alongside the controversies about political reforms in the colonies which have attracted practically exclusive attention during the last fifteen years, with the complications of the world crisis in colonial lands the problem of the social and economic forms of the near future has recently come to the fore. The 'crisis of capitalism' has a special aspect in colonial areas –

that of building up economic forms in 'newly capitalistic' lands. Alongside the 'development' of natural resources and colonial peoples by the expansion of a modern capitalism revolutionizing everything that exists, other forms have been conceived, the prospect of building up a complex of national economies and trade spheres systematically has been opened, and undisguised doubts about the continued existence of capitalism in the future have arisen.[18] The determination of what has developed in the course of history plays an important rôle in the preparation of such a policy of planning; in a colonial land the major factor is the older, native element. Perhaps an historical elucidation of a fragment of older, native economic life can also form a contribution towards such a goal.

Chapter One

On Methodology and Theory

Three gigantic world-encompassing problems – that of the state, that of the people, and that of economy – force the thinking élite of the turbulent first half of the twentieth century A.D. to a fundamental redefinition. In all three fields in their interwovenness and division, general laws valid for every human group and laws pertaining to special aspects of life have to be laid down for the whole surface of the present earth, concatenated in population but yet not uniform. The whole range of world history from the very beginning on also needs to be reworked in this sense, from a critical distance. The world's economic history, above all, requires a new balance of world history and specialized history if valuable possibilities in understanding the human spirit are not to escape it.

Heichelheim, "Gesichtspunkte", 154.

I

The age of modern capitalism has put us in a position in which we make use of knowledge of the whole world every day. Business and trade have spread a cobweb net over the earth. Industries find all parts of the world opened to them and forced on them as prospective markets. The big-banking system has brought the interests of the most widely distant lands, cities, and ports, and mining, industrial, and agricultural areas within the sphere of investment and speculation, which in turn has extended its interests to all levels of society. Industry and banking have built up world concerns, as if to ridicule national borders and political entities. Modern communication has fitted the whole world into the system of stock exchanges and wholesale markets. And, finally, the present political system of the great powers and the international organization of states mean a consistent *Weltpolitik* in the most colossal form ever seen.

All interests are connected in a never-ending criss-cross. The repercussions of fluctuations in the world wheat price affect American and Argentine farmers and Indian peasants, grain silos and elevator systems in the Middle West and primitive barnsheds in the Punjab. The interests of railroads in Angola, China, and Canada are controlled in London. Germany and England are contesting for the Argentine and Chinese import markets; Japan is attempting to open up western and central European import markets. The front lines in the world trade war are incessantly shifting. The shipping columns in the daily papers give a review of all the ports and coasts of the world; the contents of the financial journals contain observations on conditions and prospects of enterprises spread all over the earth. Every land, every people is now brought together in one tremendous structure, an interdependence of the most fundamental basic interests, a constantly progressing uniformity in ways of living, a more and more perfect social and psychological mobilization of the masses down to the last man. That is the picture of the present-day world, the result of a century of modern capitalism. Modern capitalism has set the pattern of nineteenth and twentieth-century civilization.

2

This tremendous structure the whole world is still set to work on every day is not more than about a hundred twenty years old. The time of its beginnings was the time of the first fragile steam engines, the cumbrous steam paddle-wheelers, the family banking house of Mayer Amschel Rothschild,[1] the *Journal des Débats*, the Holy Alliance. In a hundred twenty years a gigantic world-wide structure has been built up from those paltry foundations.

Carried along in that rise, pushing and being pushed in turn at a thousand points, the arts and sciences in western Europe are irrevocably connected with the course of economic and political development. Intellectual patterns and currents and economic patterns and forms arose independently of each other, on their own strength; time has created a tightly interwoven fabric of the two, the civilization of the nineteenth century.[2]

As one of the social sciences, the historical discipline was also influenced by the spirit of the century, while the special circumstances of the times in the various European countries and the position of historians and intellectuals, too, made their influence felt. In Germany, under a conservative regime, Hegel ended the great age of German philosophy with the foundation of the historical discipline as a field of philosophy having its own laws.[3] Marx, revolutionary, an emigrant from Germany, was strongly influenced by the spirit, and borrowed from the method, of the eighteenth-century English and French essayists and Encyclopedists, rational and theoretical, polemical and political, and the early nineteenth-century French sociologists such as Comte and historians such as Guizot, Mignet, and Thierry. And, above all, he was impressed by the disturbed times of reform and consolidation under the modern bourgeois regime in France. In opposition to Hegel's, his view of history was economic and revolutionary, 'historical-materialistic'.

Progressing side by side with the economic and social transformations going on in Europe after 1848 – the triumph of modern capitalism and the formation of national states, – dogmatic historical materialism, linked to Marxism as a political movement, grew in importance and exerted its influence as far as into the sedate spheres of scholarship. Its influence is undeniable,[4] even though other historical traditions were perpetuated by such men as Ranke, Treitschke, Macaulay, Carlyle, and Fruin. Since then circumstances have changed. The expansive force of revolutionary Marxism was broken after fifty years, and the dialectical system of scientific Marxism, fallen back from the sphere of political agitation, has been put to another use and is being carried on by another sort of thinkers. The question – from the point of view of cultural history a central one – of 'superstructure' and 'basis', growing out of the Marxist view of things and stated in that classical example of demagoguery, the masterly pamphlet *The Communist Manifesto*, was gradually changed into the question of the 'functional relationships' of the social-economic field and other fields of culture.[5] Already, however, the passage of time has pushed forward new modes of historical thought, and the whole nineteenth-century heritage of 'positivitic' sciences of man is now being threatened by neo-romantic, biological and vitalistic, organological and anthropomorphistic theories such as those of Chamberlain, Spengler, and Spann which go back to the first opponents of the Great Revolution and to that antipode of the second half of the nineteenth century, Nietzsche.

3

The all-dominating significance of modern European history as the background for the theory and philosophy of history has retroacted on earlier history. The western European middle ages and the Renaissance, especially, have been fitted into the sequence of periods ancient, medieval, and modern,[6] a sequence already sketched in outline by eighteenth-century French historians and social theorists and by Herder, defined by Hegel, and used by Marx as the basis for his 'dialectical' scheme of progress, which was also extremely influenced by the contemporaneous development of capitalism from the 'forties to the 'seventies.

> Marx, like Hegel and practically all the moderns, is basically convinced of such development of the whole *as* whole in unlimited expansion, and measures that development with the expansion in productivity which makes possible an ample life and freedom for cultural activities for ever larger and more organized masses of people. From this, then, results the most essential problem of progress, that of maintaining productivity, expanded with the help of the sharpest class division and developed at the cost of the exploited class, but making the material results of it equally available to all members of society. In this sense one finds the idea of progress in world history also with him.[7]

Marx, once more following the main lines drawn by Hegel, limited this historical process geographically to the regions around the Mediterranean and in western and northwestern Europe. His tripartite division of the economic stages in world history is, it is true, actually quadripartite, with Asian, classical, feudal, and capitalistic phases. By the Asian phases he meant the ancient Oriental bureaucratic despotism founded on irrigation techniques, with its 'basis' in ancient Oriental (Indian) village institutions.[8] But it was only brought into the picture as a vague, shadowy concept. His consideration of actual historical processes begins only with the civilizations of the Mediterranean, and the transition from ancient Indian civilization to Near Eastern and their relationship to each other have been left in the dark.[9] The 'course of progress in world history', then, is based upon the actual preponderance of modern capitalism and the 'progressive' sequence of periods, ancient, medieval, modern. Up to now the schema has remained current and accepted, supported as it is by the still vital, driving concept of 'evolution', 'development', 'progress'.[10] This situation has also led to the hegemony of western European history and the hegemony of its terminology, whether theoretical or historical, economic or sociological.

4

World empires have been governed from Antioch, Rome, Baghdad, and Karakorum, from the Escurial and the Palace of St James. Yet how insignificant their power, how loose their bonds, compared to the grip in which London's City, New York's Wall Street, present-day Washington, and modern Moscow now hold the world. Bureaucratic machineries of government with an extravagance of officials were known to ancient Egypt and Peru as well as the modern civil-service state, yet never before has the complex, rationally organized level of 'time table precision', as Mannheim calls it, of the present-day state been reached.

But however much the absolute superiority in world history of the modern-capitalistic period may be recognized, there can be no doubt that in allowing it too great predominance scholars have made their interests too one-sided and have obscured the problems involved, without allowing the full, true light to fall on the other ages in the history of mankind. The hegemony of the concept of evolution expressed in the categories of western European history leads to inaccurate thinking and imprecise evaluation. This appears at once in the problem of the connection between the ancient and medieval periods, or that of the significance of the Byzantine and Islamic cultural sphere.

There is too much of a tendency to view the economic history of the Roman Empire – Hellas and especially the Hellenistic kingdoms are usually ignored in this regard – as the end of classical 'development' and at the same time linked to that of the early western European middle ages, thus putting the Roman colonial regime in northwestern Europe in a false light and blazing a convenient trail through the period of the Western migrations. Scholars seek for ages parallel with the modern period, even for cycles following similar courses,[11] or else they degrade the whole ancient period to being primitive in an economic sense and of no importance for modern times. One rarely finds the point of view that the ancient world deserves to be seen as a self-contained period moving along its own historical lines, with an historical course that has no evolutionary value for modern history, but at best a limited paradigmatic one. To say nothing of the distortion of facts of the Marxist scheme of things, in which the element of 'historical necessity' does so much damage.[12] But the usual view of economic history, also, too rarely shows a consciousness how much periods and cultural techniques can overlap each other without having to be bound by a 'trend of time'.[13] Probably too close a linkage to the historical development of Christianity has supported this incorrect point of view.[14]

Economic, social, and technical conditions in the days of the Roman Republic or Ptolemaeic Egypt could be 'more highly developed' than in the days of Otto I or Frederick II. Organizational forms, furthermore, can have an existence of their own, 'autonomous' in nature and growth, without there having to be any such thing as borrowing or continuity and without the 'newer' form having to have 'developed' out of the 'older'.[15] Max Weber has stated and recorded all this for the period in question the most pointedly, and in so doing he has indicated the way toward a true understanding of the periods of economic history.[16] It is highly significant that Weber used agrarian history as a starting point. For, alongside the objection that is to be made against many of the surveys of economic history – that legal history is too often confused with and held to be social-economic history, thus so-called sociological typology,[17] – a second objection can also be raised: that trade and business aspects are too often placed in the foreground (and the history of crafts and industry too often telescoped), while after all the lines of agrarian history are different from those of the history of business and trade, and agrarian conditions have a decisive influence on urban development and the machinery of government, on the general cultural and social level thus. The lines of agricultural history follow their own course. For one moment, in the age of 'high capitalism', it has seemed otherwise, but now already the events of the present day reveal the autonomous characteristics of agriculture. In all ages – and the period of modern, high capitalism should not make us lose sight of this – the agrarian element has predominated.[18] Thus Weber's survey gains in value. His genius, following the sure compass of time, guided him to a true understanding of the periods of history.

5

When one considers the age of the Islamic and the related Byzantine civilizations side by side with the western European middle ages, the same objections to the hegemony of categories bearing the stamp of modern western European economic history arise. Usually writers are content with a few short references, emphasizing religious differences;[19] sometimes even those are lacking. Social-economic history experiences the injurious repercussions of such an attitude.[20] Depicting the western European middle ages historians overlook the fact that the contemporaneous Byzantine-Islamic 'middle ages'[21] manifest traits many of which had a direct formative influence on the lands of western Europe,[22] while, along with a structure like that of the Western middle ages in only a few respects, those 'Eastern middle ages' show a broader design, one more important and more elaborate, all in all a more impressive whole than do the western European middle ages so often hypostatized into the basis for an absolute world order.[23] In the fields of business regulation,[24] of merchant and craft gild organization,[25] of city government,[26] of state bureaucracy and administration,[27] in the fields of currency system, banking, and fiscal affairs,[28] military and naval organization,[29] commercial regulation and law[30] – in all these one must conclude that the Byzantine-Islamic 'middle ages' manifest fully developed, mature forms, while in comparison the western European middle ages manifest only partially developed, immature parallel forms, lacking in richness and complexity. There was a distance between them such as that in modern-capitalistic forms of organization and culture – this time in reverse order historically – between the United States and the older Europe. A real insight into the economic history of the western European middle ages can only be gained by testing and assaying them in comparison with the Byzantine-Islamic 'middle ages'.[31] One result of such a change in angle of view is that it brings specific peculiarities of modern capitalism, along with the problem of the historical category 'capitalism' in general, more sharply into focus.

6

Capitalism, that is to say, the search for profit on the rationalized basis of money (capital) calculations, is as old as the urban history of mankind, and from its beginning on it has been a phenomenon of every age and every land, in dimensions varying from those of small handicraft patterns to the greatest imaginable. It can take the form of exploiting capacities for profit-making – on the basis of a rational system of 'accounting' – by means of trade (shipping), speculation in sorts of money, coining and printing of media of exchange, extension of credit for productive and consumptive ends; by means of financing wars and rebellions, colonial possessions (tributes and deliveries, sources of supply, mines, plantations), fiscal institutions (farming of taxes and offices), machineries of government. In every age, in every land, one encounters such forms of capitalism – in Babylon and Republican Rome as private enterprise reaching very large dimensions; in Egypt and Imperial Rome as 'quasi-public enterprise' and state enterprise reaching colossal dimensions;[32] in medieval Italy as well as in the China of the 'Contending States', the tyranny of Ch'in Shih Huang Ti, and the Han Dynasty (239 B.C.– 220 A.D.),[33] in India,[34] Japan,[35] Java,[36] and the caliphates[37] as well as in Holland under the stadtholder king[38] in the forms of supplies for army and government, tax-farming,[39] exploitation of monopolies, wholesale trade, speculation, usury.

All of that has little to do with modern capitalism as it has grown up in western Europe. The characteristic element of modern capitalism is its exploitation of the profit-making capacities of a rationalized organization for the mechanized mass production of goods built up with free labour and based on a free, specifically peaceful market for sales. Along with that organization goes a system of finance (investment of capital in stocks and bonds) oriented to the remunerativeness of such a type of organization, and a system of speculation on standardized stock-market equivalents of the masses of goods produced and on securities, the documents of the system of finance. Economic theory has been modelled on these forms of economic life; in a certain sense they are the only forms public opinion considers acceptable. Of the older forms of capitalism mentioned above some have been driven back from their positions as dominant figures in much of political (but not economic) history, some have disappeared completely. Another economic mechanism and another economic morality have come to prevail in the liberalistic forms of economic life of modern states and peoples, though older forms of capitalism continue to exist – interesting and important chapters in history could be compiled on modern 'political capitalism'[40] in the munitions industries, the oil interests, Tammany, the financing of the National Socialist Party in Germany, and so forth.

To relate all this to the criticism of the hegemony of western European economic history and its categories made above: in using that history as the only basis one loses sight of the multiformity of capitalism; in using its categories one applies false criteria to the facts in other lands and periods. Actually the books on economic history have recognized only two forms of capitalism, so-called 'mercantile capitalism',[41] and modern industrial capitalism with its unity of business, commerce, and finance and its basis of free markets and free trade. The scholars taking part in the controversy over capitalism in the ancient world merely applied the category modern capitalism, searching for big business, mass production of consumers' goods, rational organization of labour, free trade and free sales markets, and, at best, as a concession permitting the form of mercantile capitalism – capitalistically organized home 'industry' and handicrafts.

However much the ancient world was acquainted with the economic organization of trade and handicrafts (machine techniques were lacking), still in those forms there are no parallels to modern capitalism which can be carried through consistently. Free labour did not predominate – even though the trades and crafts were by no means exclusively worked by slave labour, that source of labour prevented the rational application of working power and the massive concentration corollary to it. Alongside each other stood the small businesses of freemen and those of *apophora*-bound slaves working on their own. The highest concentration of labour was to be found in *ergasteria* the size of larger master craftsmen's shops and medium-sized handicraft factories. The market was free but small. Transportation and communication were irregular. There was no mass market for producers' and consumers' goods. Production and consumption in the closed economies of town and countryside were largely taken care of by the inhabitants themselves; alongside those economies were the no less closed economies of the patriciate and the court in the cities and in the country; furthermore, the state provided for its own needs through state enterprises, also applying systems of monopoly for various goods.[42]

The use of the categories of western European economic history for the Byzantine-Islamic area encounters the same dangers.

There substantially the whole of ancient society continued its existence, at most refined and extended over new areas.[43] It seems to me that Brentano, in his article on Byzantine economy, has not escaped the dangers. Sketching the economic life of Byzantium as completely built up on capitalistic foundations, he fails to elucidate the special nature of that capitalism – state monopolism alongside unfree labour,[44] the absence of a mass market, various forms of 'irrational' political capitalism.

This cursory outline of the significance of the patterns of political capitalism and of modern capitalism (rational, technical, organizational, with labour as basis)[45] has no doubt shown sufficiently that, in the arrangement of material and the correct understanding of historical forms in time, full justice cannot be done to the economic history of other periods and areas when one uses the categories of western European economic history as the point of departure.

What has been said here of capitalism, as historically the most important category, holds also for other forms. In regard to the gilds no claim to completeness can be made if only the forms of the western and northwestern European middle ages are taken as the basis for categorization – the 'origin of the gilds' controversy, the controversy on whether the organization of the town grew out of that of the manor,[46] shows the too great limitation of the category. Nor does western Europe have any priority on the state fiscal and economic policy of mercantilism.[47]

The same thing holds true in regard to agriculture and village institutions. The relative power of the state and local proprietors, the development of village institutions – these cannot be grasped completely with feudalism and vassalage, soccage and commonage alone. The differences in agrarian structure resulting from the two agricultural methods, dry-field farming and irrigation farming, lead to two widely varying, equally important patterns in agrarian history, and they also provide the solution to a number of problems in political history, above all, those of the structure of the state and its system of taxation. Western Europe has known only the first form in its agrarian history. And the history of the gild, of the town, and of agriculture, even for western Europe, is not limited in time to the period between 1200 and 1500.

The same thing holds for mining.[48] When the so-called Industrial Revolution (the term is relative: the sixteenth century, already, had an 'industrial revolution') is introduced as the most important caesura in the history of modern capitalism in western Europe, it is often overlooked that the germ of modern capitalism did not lie in the textile industry with its whole system of branches and methods already specialized in the early-capitalistic period, but in the mechanical techniques of European mining. There began the great, all-dominating change, the revolutionization of Europe and the world through steam, coal, and iron – "the epic of iron, greater and grander than all the ancient epics".[49] Because the textile trades and crafts were predominantly urban forms and of old breeding places for social unrest and revolutionary eruptions, the place of the economic and technical history of those trades and crafts also predominates in the history of the class struggle.[50]

The list of categories could be extended much further. A primary requirement is a social-economic-historical system which in the structure of its concepts and the usability of its categories is applicable to all areas brought within its reach by world history. Again it is Max Weber who has pointed the way,[51] not only as regards sociology in general,[52] but also as regards social-economic theory and history specifically.[53]

7

On moving on to the regions of India, China, and Japan, one is immediately struck by the inadequacy of the western European view of history and its categories. The relationship between western European and Byzantine-Islamic history still makes at least some sense because of the historical links they both have to the ancient Roman world – links which, however, give no occasion for one to formulate an unbroken sequence: ancient history, medieval history, modern history. But no such links are present in the case of India, not to mention that of China. No political power nor cultural influence of a pronounced and lasting sort has been exerted there by western Europe. The contact of the Hellenistic Diadochian kingdoms with the kingdoms of India was a contact of great powers on the basis of equality, and that fact was not changed by shifts in power in the Iranian and Bactrian lands. There was a strong Hellenistic influence exerted by Graeco-Bactrian craftsmen and court artisans on the style of Indian sculpture of the age – best known is the Graeco-Buddhist so-called Gandhara art, one influence among many in the Indo-Scythian period.[54] But that does not justify overlooking the fact that in the fields of public administration, organization of the population, taxation, public works, and military affairs, the Indian kingdoms had from early times on been the compeers of the ancient Mediterranean and Hellenistic states. The routes from the classical world eastwards led not to colonial regions of barbarians like those north and northwestwards, but to lands and states with a social structure as complicated and as elaborately organized as its own. It is once more a question of religious or philosophical preference if one wants to place India in the rear guard of civilization, of which Hellas and Rome are supposed to have formed the phalanx.[55] In that way the same sort of error is committed as in regard to Islamic civilization.

The course of Indian history forces one to lay aside the western European historical schema for good. Whether it makes any sense at all to distinguish an ancient, a medieval, and a modern period of history for India is a question to which I cannot here give any definitive answer. (Weber's use of such categories for India is not clear to me – in practice he considers little more than the 'medieval' period.)[56] In any case, however, parallels with European history should be rejected. The conquests and settlements of the Aryan peoples in the plains of the Indian subcontinent, the rise and consolidation of the great kingdoms and the formation of the social system, the social-economic complications of history accompanying the great revelationist religious movements – all these point to a separate, autonomous historical picture. The earlier 'barbaric' invasions of the Afghans and Mongols had a different effect than had the migrations and conquests of the Germanic 'barbarians' in the West; the later Turco-Mongol invasions carried Islam to northern India; Indian Islam and the so-called Hindu Renaissance of the eighteenth century were once again factors with a completely 'Indian' significance. In the meantime the developing European colonial phase created the circumstances which up to the present day have accentuated very specially the cleavage between India and western Europe. India, like every other civilized state in the world, has known 'foreign regimes' in every age. But the 'foreign regime' of the western European powers overseas, accompanied by occupation of the overseas territories by modern capitalism, is one of a unique sort. Europe remained a colonial area for the Roman Empire and the Byzantine and Moslem states of the Near East up to the fifteenth century, when the Spanish and Portuguese voyages overseas introduced the beginnings of the expansion of European power already foreshadowed by Venice in the Mediterranean. Until deep in the middle ages Europe was a dependent 'colonial' area for everything that had to do with culture, religion, and economic and administrative techniques.[57]

As a first orientation and introduction to India, *The Hindu Social System* and the remainder of the second volume of Max Weber's studies in the sociology of religion should be mentioned before anything else. It is a work unfortunately too little known – as the work of that great master of the social sciences is in general too little known, especially in Dutch circles – but one more valuable and stimulating for the reader than the specialized publications of indologists on the subject. The indologists, still predominantly philological in their aims, work in the field of social-economic history chiefly with traditional, threadbare categories.[58] That they also treat 'comparative cultural history' before any surveying and clearing work has been done in the social-economic field is regrettable. With them one finds oneself on dangerous ground.

A systematic investigation and arrangement of the great mass of material on India was begun some time ago by the historian and ex-civil servant W. H. Moreland, who carried on that admirable English tradition, the tradition of Elphinstone, Raffles, and Yule. (A tradition existing here in Holland, differently oriented, but just as admirable, is that of Wilken, Liefrinck, Westenenk, Mallinckrodt.) Moreland, beginning his study with the period of the sixteenth and seventeenth-century Mongol emperors,[59] worked with Indian and western European sources (reports of trading voyages and company administrative reports of the Portuguese, English, and Dutch) alike. For earlier periods certainly no such rich harvest can be gathered. However, the sketch by Weber mentioned above gives an idea of how much the literary and philological material can yield when it is analyzed and digested according to the methods of economic history.[60] Perhaps, then, Moreland's pessimism is somewhat too strong,[61] even though the difficulties offered by the material must not be underestimated. Almost every time one reads one of Moreland's sound, excellent chapters, the questions arise: How did such technological and organizational forms come into existence? How did a system of credit instruments extending over areas greater than those of medieval and early-capitalistic western Europe originate? How did Indian fortunes as huge as the Fuggers' arise? How did the whole system of crafts, commerce, and overseas trade develop? And such shipbuilding techniques, and military techniques? If one considers the circumstances of the 'historical *milieu*', then it becomes apparent that they for the most part remained almost the same down through the centuries. In other words, the predisposition for the rise of such forms did not by any means date from the sixteenth or seventeenth century. On the contrary. The nature of the sources led Moreland to treat the data from the time of Akbar on, but, seen within the framework of Indian historical conditions, the starting point was arbitrarily chosen.

An accurate use of the phenomena encountered in other historical areas and periods for the purposes of orientation and illustration would, if defined sharply and with the proper respect for the historical *milieu* (environment, climate, land, people), lead to more important possibilities than 'caste system' or 'Indian philosophy' as vague general Indian dispositions. For instance, one of the most important phenomena in this regard is the agricultural system connected with the technique of field irrigation. The imprint which the irrigation system, together with the taxation system, stamps upon village institutions, social structure, and property conditions makes it a phenomenon of great importance in such a working method. But the conclusion should not be that of using 'parallels' blindly. Every paradigmatic application of early Germanic or pre-revolutionary Russian village institutional patterns to southeast Asia is, because of the difference in agricultural methods, dangerous.[62] A positivistic research into types, using the terminological system of general sociology and social-economic history and seeking the causes of historical development, could perform a preliminary work of great value.

Sharp distinction and historical definition are primary requirements for such research. Rouffaer, in his work on block and batik printing on the Coromandel Coast and Java, gives an extremely expert and detailed technological description of craft and trade methods.[63] But if, on reading it, one meets the following words:

> an Oriental people, living in communion with nature, effortlessly taking advantage to the full of the things provided by her, not seeking complexity, but content with the most simple, which so often is of the most worth ...[64]

and one considers that this characterization is from the pen of one of the best-trained historians of things early Indonesian and Indian – then it becomes clear what the requirement of sharp distinction and historical definition means. After all, the technique of that cotton-printing and wax-stencilling craft is by no means so simple; every pre-capitalistic and early-capitalistic technique all over the world, not by any means only the one under discussion, has taken advantage to the full of the provisions of nature; that "Oriental people, living in communion with nature", has built up a social structure of a very high degree of complexity. Such a terminology is confusing, and it is too vague, especially in its irritating use of the fallacy 'Oriental' – a fallacy, because only dilettanti with a very vague notion and a few ideological simplifications push such divisions ('Oriental' and 'Occidental') to the forefront as dominant, thereby overlooking the richness, the complexity, and the equal worth of organizational forms of culture and life which have reached maturity along 'autonomous' routes. Economic history and sociology need to have done with this confusion created by ideology, from the very beginning.[65]

What has been said in regard to India is in part also valid for Indonesia. The succeeding chapters are especially concerned with that area, so that these questions will be gone into more deeply there.

8

One can speak without reservation of the inapplicability of the western European historical method on turning to China. The unique fact of the continuance of a centralized state for nearly two thousand years within an area remaining practically the same territorially, and the continuance with and through that state of a uniform style and tradition of civilization – all this is a very singular course of events in social-economic history, and it presents a totally different picture from that offered by the Mediterranean and western and northwestern European historical complex. Hegel's remark that "China actually has no history"[66] is thus not only completely consistent but very characteristic. 'Ancient', 'medieval',[67] and 'modern' periods, with 'ancient' or 'medieval' predominating – that is out of the question in Chinese history.

From the eighth to the third centuries B.C., states were formed in the valleys of the middle regions of the Hwang-ho and the lower regions of the Wei-ho and the Fen-ho, with a few advance posts in the river basins of the Yangtze-kiang and the Han-kiang.[68] They were states on the old colonization basis of village and castle principality, states half patrimonial and bureaucratic (because of the river channelization and irrigation work: ancient Egypt offers an instructive example in this respect) and half feudal (because of the continuous defensive struggle against the 'barbaric' peoples of the mountains and the steppes to which ancient China, more than ancient Egypt, was forced to adjust itself).[69] The ancient Mesopotamian city kingdoms offer another illustration of such a coexistence of patrimonial bureaucratic authority and feudal military authority.[70] The castle principalities and city monarchies were then consolidated into territorial states,[71] after which the revolutionary tyranny of Ch'in Shih Huang Ti (246–210 B.C.) broke up the sometimes divided, sometimes confederated Contending States (239–221 B.C.) by force and founded a despotic unitarian state. The Han Dynasty (202 B.C.–220 A.D.) then established the authority of the bureaucratic civil-servant state, expanding the state's administrative machinery over the territory which from Ch'in Shih Huang Ti's conquests on was to form the traditional territory of the Chinese Empire, the eighteen provinces.[72] Dynasties succeeded one another, the bureaucratic superstructure and the agrarian basis of the empire alike underwent the most violent shocks and the most revolutionary experiments,[73] the government interfered in handicrafts and trade in every age, periods of strong military expansion on land and sea alternated with periods of defensive isolation. The inrush of 'barbarians' in the sixth and the following and the twelfth and thirteenth centuries from the northeast and northwest (the Tartars and Mongols) and in the seventeenth century from the northeast (the Manchus) had no ruinous results. The state continued to exist as a unity under foreign dynasties; the character of Chinese traditions of civilization and the structure of Chinese social and economic life kept on unimpaired.[74]

There exists even less of a general economic history for China than for India – or Indonesia. Miss Ping-Hua Lee's work *The Economic History of China* is unsatisfactory, even though it somewhat prematurely enjoyed the honour of being included in Weber's general bibliography[75] under one heading with the writings of Cunningham, Ashley, Levasseur, Beloch, and Meyer. A good economic history of China is not yet possible, because the material has not been adequately treated.[76] But another question is whether a typology of Chinese social-economic history is possible. For one who is not a sinologist and who has made only a limited survey of the sources to answer such a question must seem audacious. I may nevertheless comment that each acquaintance I make with another specialized study reveals once more how abundant is the material out of which an extensive though fragmentary systematization of social and economic life could be made. Only after such a systematization is made can a typology be determined. Esson M. Gale's edition of Huan K'uan's *Discourses on Salt and Iron*, from the time of the Han Dynasty;[77] Vissering's *On Chinese Currency*, based on Ma Tuan-lin's chronicle of monetary history written in 1321 and covering the ages from the Han Dynasty to the last of the Sungs; Hirth's *Ancient Porcelain: A Study in Chinese Mediaeval* [!] *Industry and Trade*; Morse's *The Gilds of China*; Nyok-Ching Tsur's "Die gewerblichen Betriebsformen der Stadt Ningpo";[78] Burgess' *The Guilds of Peking* – such studies as these provide material from widely varying periods. The large general works such as those of Franke and Grousset also contain a great deal of material.[79] Here too Max Weber's genius has blazed a trail, in the part on "Sociological Foundations" of his *The Religion of China*, with its chapters – "City, Prince and God"; "The Feudal and Prebendal State"; "Administration and Rural Structure"; "Self-Government, Law, and Capitalism".[80]

It is at once obvious that it is at the moment impossible to give a complete picture of the whole course of Chinese history in all its complexity. Such a complete picture, placed within an economic-historical framework, is not yet possible and feasible even for western Europe, to say nothing of the ancient Mediterranean world or that of Islam. It is necessary, however, for Chinese history to receive a structural form. That form can be built up by using as materials general sociological-historical categories which set Chinese history alongside the histories of the other Asian lands, the 'ancient world', and the lands of the West as a part of the history of mankind. After all, in China, too, irrigation farming was carried on, mines were dug, the pressure of taxation was burdened on the people, towns and strongholds were built, mania for profit and lust for power filled men, worldly love and luxury were pursued, monasteries were founded and temples and palaces erected, money was issued and overissued till there came a mass depreciation, overseas journeys were undertaken and caravans set out, war was carried on, hunger endured, rebellion roused. For that reason above all, then, the right of the philological sciences to consider those fields as reservations outside the territory of 'ordinary' 'general' history must be disputed. That the chances for setting up such a structural form do not have to be exactly in direct proportion to the amount of detailed material collected is shown by the work of Weber, just as in times gone by it has been shown by the work of Gibbon, of Ranke, of Burckhardt, of Mommsen.

9

In the case of Japan,[81] not only has the adjustment to a modern governmental system imported from western Europe and to modern capitalism formed a most highly important factor in the country's recent history and given rise to a series of interesting situations resultant from the establishment of modern capitalism there; for earlier periods also Japan offers rich material illustrative of an autonomous process of social-economic transformation, the course of its history being dominated by the strictly organized aristocratic state. By way of illustration one needs only to point to the eighteenth century, the great years of the Tokugawa shogunate (1573–1868). In western Europe the cultural aspects of the period are now quite well known, especially through the products of Japanese pictorial art; few periods of non-'Western' art present a more interesting panorama than it. Independent of the developments of the gradual 'evolution' of Western art, forms had arisen which one tends involuntarily to feel are closely related; and the subjects of that art, its preponderant 'secularity' and urbanity, too, cause it to be placed alongside seventeenth and eighteenth-century western European art. But as is usual in considerations of art and the history of art, the social and economic background of that culture remains in the dark. What a wealth of material still lies hidden away is shown by every study dealing with the social and economic history of Japan. It appears for example in the long series of Japanese cameral papers and ephemeral reports listed in the bibliography to Miss Takizawa's *The Penetration of Money Economy in Japan and Its Effects upon Social and Political Institutions.* At the same time, however, her book shows how much that material is mutilated by the use of historical categories which are strictly modern western European. The term 'capitalism' is carelessly applied. Miss Takizawa wastes valuable material[82] in order to demonstrate something that did not exist.

In the period from the seventeenth century to the nineteenth Japan exhibited the following process: a partial repression of the social power of the nobility,[83] a growth of that of the urban great merchants and money holders, a state of oppression in rural areas because of the burden of debts (debts exploited by the urban merchants and the nobility), migration away from the land, and growth of the mass of landless paupers in the cities.[84] With the restrictions mentioned above, then, this process in Japan forms a pendant to the pattern recurring throughout the whole ancient period in the Mediterranean: the burden of debts in rural areas, the system of usury on the money debts of the peasants carried on by urban groups. In that relationship lies the form of 'class struggle' of the ancient world.[85] And of Japan as well. A rise of 'capitalism' there in the sense Miss Takizawa would like to use it, that is, modern, rational capitalism with technological organization of labour, is out of the question. There is not even a hint of any form of mass production for an extensive sales market or for export, or of entrepreneurial forms such as manufacture or domestic industry capitalistically organized. What did grow and prosper was 'political' capitalism:[86] urban exploitation of the profit-making possibilities of usury, buying up, tax farming, and monopolization. Town and state governments were patrimonial and feudal; law, very uncapitalistically, was administered in a typically material order.[87] Miss Takizawa unjustly populates the cities with "proletarian masses" and "wage-workers, who constituted the masses of city population", and would like to find a modern-capitalistic class struggle.[88] Two mistakes in principle have made her disquisition a failure, incorrect use of the categories of social-economic history and identification of money economy with capitalism.[89] The roots of modern capitalism in Japan reach no deeper historically than the Meiji period.

Just as in regard to China, the question needs to be raised here – is a typology of organizational forms possible for Japanese social-economic history? In this case, too, it appears to me that the question can be answered in the affirmative,[90] provided that the method of general social-economic and sociological typology is used.[91] Certainly, such a typology would for the time being be far from complete; however, even in a fragmentary sketch it would be able to indicate in their true nature and concrete significance the vast quantity of materials and the abundance of different compositional possibilities appearing in the various periods in the history of man and the world. It would make it possible to construct the series of historical 'ideal types' needed in order to provide a basis for all historical and sociological study, and thus, above all, to open the way along which non-European history – 'history' in the broadest sense of the word, that of 'non-historical' areas such as Africa and northern and central Asia as well as of 'historical' ones such as India and China – could be transferred from the fields of philology, ethnology, and exotic curiosity to the field of legitimate general history. Research in cultural history needs to be preceded by sociological analysis and the construction of a sociological frame of reference.

10

This essay's point of departure was the fact that modern capitalism is the decisive issue for the present-day world. It spans the whole globe, invading every cultural sphere and setting its stamp on every organizational form of human society. Therefore, the central problem of all sociology and social-economic history is: how did modern capitalism arise? In order to capture the significance of that system in its specific characteristics and to delineate precisely from it periods with another structure, the material to be offered by a systematization of general economic history and sociology is needed. Large-scale, systematic exploitation of the profit-making possibilities of trade, banking and money matters, colonial possessions and monopolies; financing of wars and expeditions; exploitation of tax systems; control over the conditions of living of large masses of people; alliances of trade and finance with the state – all of them are as old as the history of civilization itself.[92] The characteristics peculiar to modern capitalism – pacification of world markets, political control of possessions and spheres of influence (*pax Britannica, pax Neerlandica*, and so forth), mobilization of the world as a market for sale and production of goods and raw materials, mechanization of big industry, rational organization of free labour and free capital – all of them remain unique. This sort of systematization of sociology and general economic history cannot be constructed with the categories of western European history; as has already been illustrated,[93] the pattern of western European history impressed on those categories makes them unsuitable.

The point of view can also be illustrated in another way. All history, as the history of mankind, is of equal value. To allow a religious, a philosophical, or a biological attitude to prevail means to bring in a value judgement. To have a Christian concept of history, or a humanist one, or a progressive, or a racist, means to abandon the exact, positivistic science of history. The technical objections to the 'universal' point of view adhered to above are frankly admitted – the necessity for studying from secondary sources, the often-existing inaccessability of various fields, the difficulty in working with the specialized disciplines. But they remain technical objections, not fundamental ones. The illustrative nature of all historical life demands the construction of a comprehensive series of historical categories. The same sort of interest and the same categorical relationships need to hold for the Hindu-Javanese court of the *Nagarakertagama* as for the world of Villehardouin, the same for Abul Fazl's *Institutes of Akbar* as for Commines, for the scenes in *The Thousand and One Nights* as for those in Boccaccio and Chaucer, for the Ukiyoye masters' portrayals of social life as for those of the Dutch Haarlem and Amsterdam schools.[94]

The following chapters, covering only a portion of one limited field in the history of southeast Asia, are designed on the basis of such a concept.

II

Coupled with the hegemony of the categories of western European history challenged above is a second, even more outspoken hegemony, that of the categories of theoretical economics. A few comments on the position of this second group of categories and the interrelationships of the two groups are perhaps in order.

Economic history was differentiated from general history only relatively recently, and became established as a separate historical discipline in the latter half of the nineteenth century. Actually, economic history has been completely worked out and consolidated only for western Europe. The same results are being approached for the ancient world. For the other areas only a beginning has been made up to now; the lines of research in ethnology and legal history have very often led to the special field of economics, however.

A thing that must give occasion for amazement is the fact that research in economic history is not on very good terms with the study of theoretical economics. However, it can be established without much difficulty that while studies of theoretical economics keep far removed from the historical in the ordinary sense of the word, if the historical becomes involved the categories of theoretical economics prove to be very remote from those of history. The whole of economic theory seems to be estranged from historical reality. There, too, the hegemony of western European categories wreaks vengeance. Modern economic theory has been modelled on the economic structure of developing modern capitalism, absolutizing the tendencies which appeared there historically, rationalizing them to the extreme, and, under the influence of nineteenth-century natural scientific thought, moulding them into a system of laws expressing the inherent workings of society in the social-economic field. Historical study has shaken off the bonds of the nineteenth-century influence of the natural sciences and the eighteenth-century Anglo-French utilitarian, rationalistic thought related to it. (Only the militant 'Marxist science' – disappearing in western Europe, flourishing in the USSR but without representing any intrinsic value for western Europe any more – carries on this point of view.) But theoretical economics is for the most part still under such influences. Especially deeply rooted is the proposition that theoretical economics must be a discipline based on laws, and the most dangerous consequences can grow out of such an interpretation of the term 'economic laws'. (The concept of 'laws'[95] is modelled on that of natural scientific laws, which are completely unhistorical, in existence and at work in the same way in the time of Archimedes as in the time of Hertz and Joule.) The paradox has arisen that such terms, by their nature completely 'universal', have proved to be practically worthless when applied to historical facts. Reduction to 'general tendencies' means such a stripping bare of every historical phenomenon that the characteristic, the time-bound, definitively historical of the situation is lost. The same applies even to contemporary history, actually. The impressive magnitude of modern economic life – of industry and banking, imperialism, and modern governmental economic policies – is not to be found recaptured in the theoretical studies. For it one needs to go to the biographies of the great personalities of economic life, to historical monographs and journalistic literature.[96]

12

Political economy – the term, still being used, is curious, dating back as it does all the way to the sphere of cameralistic mercantilism – is, as the study of the 'search for the satisfaction of wants', based on the whole system of exchange in society, 'commercial activities', in Pierson's words, or, in a more refined, modern form of expression, 'disposition of goods', by members of society. Analysis takes place in the form of a search for the laws or rules which define the course of social-economic events in such an exchange between groups of individuals, covering the activities in all the different organizational forms of mankind.[97] The economically relevant is separated from the irrelevant. And the nature of the laws – in the most modern point of view; alongside it older points of view of laws-in-the-natural-scientific-sense continue their existence – is seen as a functional relationship of a permanent regularity. In the words of Schumpeter:

> The explanation our theory gives is a description of functional relationships between the elements of our system by means of the shortest and most universally valid formulae possible. We call these formulae laws.[98]

In the words of Pareto, whose point of view is carried through with the most extreme consistency:

> Thanks to the use of mathematics the whole theory is now based only on an experimental fact, *i.e.* on the determination of the quantities of goods which form identical combinations for each individual. The theory of the economic discipline thus acquires the rigour of rational mechanics; it deduces its results from experience without allowing any metaphysical entity to intervene.[99]

Or in the words found in a recent Rotterdam School of Economics dissertation:

> Economics is an empirical discipline. The content of what we observe is constantly changing. The empirical material which provides its object is thus historically quite relative. If the discipline wishes to maintain the universal validity of its propositions, it must deduce them from a form free of every element of historical relativity. From the material, constantly subject to change, it must then isolate only those elements which are to be found in every form of economic life.[100] The definition of the object of economics amounts to this, then – we must ascertain which are the elements that will be encountered in every form of economy and thus constitute the general conditions of economic life. Once the general conditions are established, we will be able to find them in every form of economy we come across in reality. Otherwise it is a proof that in the group of conditions constituting the object of economics elements are still included which are peculiar only to certain forms of economic life.[101]

Thus, research in economic theory reveals itself to be the worst enemy of research in social-economic history. The application of universal categories ends up in the destruction of unique historical forms. Such an irreconcilable opposition of two disciplines by nature so closely related in the sort of problems considered and the material worked with is unacceptable. Beside a system of universal categories for social-economic history there needs to be a system of categories for economic theory essentially 'similar and equal'. Theoretical economics, as a branch of the economics of society, makes up a part of the social sciences. And the social sciences, including also the discipline of history,[102] need to be strictly separated from the field of the natural sciences as well as that of philosophy and metaphysics, as a division of the humanities.

13

Economics is concerned with all human activities having to do with providing the necessities of life,[103] seen in the context of the social-historical forms within and through which those activities take place.[104] All those forms, the whole of 'style' and 'type' of motives and fulfilment in which a certain pattern in cultural history places human activities in providing necessities of life, need to be involved as 'economically relevant':[105] the harvest, feast, and game ceremonials in early agrarian societies, or, more generally, all the ritual forms with which agriculture and handicrafts have been invested; the payment in rice made by a Japanese *daimio* to his *samurai* retinue in exchange for armed service; the connection between farm ownership and ability to bear arms among the Teutons; citizenship, land ownership, and ability to bear arms among the Hellenes; possession of rice and other fields and services to village, headman, and prince on Java and Madura; monastery and temple communities and church organizations and their links to governmental authority and economic life in ancient Egypt, the Islamic world, medieval western Europe, India, Tibet, the colonial Jesuit state Paraguay. In modern society, art dealing, the cinema, political publishers, and party organizations (Tammany, the former German Socialist Party, the Italian Fascist one, the Communist Party of the U.S.S.R., and so forth) need just as much to be included. A narrow 'economic' interpretation of the 'search for the provision of the necessities of life' excludes such things. Interpretations on the basis of a 'search for the satisfaction of wants' garble the facts.

By stating the problem in this way – 'understanding' (in the Weberian sense) the nature and actual, *i.e.*, historical, structure of social activities as they take place in connection with and growing out of the forms for providing necessities – the subject economics, as a unity of historical and theoretical categories, becomes a branch of the social sciences.[106]

14

The historical categories involved are the same as have been treated in the first sections of this chapter; they are inseparably linked to the categories of theoretical economics. The close relationship of the two arises from the nature of the social sciences as a humanistic discipline. The structure of categories in the humanities is in sharp distinction to that of categories in the natural sciences.

In the natural sciences categories are used for analysis of empirical phenomena and research on generality, *i.e.*, conformity to law, without regard for historical significance or environment. The flashes of lightning on Mount Sinai or day-before-yesterday's summer thunderstorm are electrical phenomena of equal value as research material. Problems of mechanics are posed in the construction of an ancient Egyptian pyramid or that of a New York skyscraper alike. The storm in *The Tempest* and the air streaming through the ventilator in Lyon's Corner House can be reduced to the same sort of atmospheric phenomena. Graphic images of life and the world – water, the wind, sunlight, the odour of flowers – are concepts a natural science cannot use;[107] they only become usable material upon being reduced to atoms and electrons and being schematized into 'forces', 'force fields', and so on.

In the humanities, categories are formed in the opposite way. There the thousandfold uniqueness of historical forms of life and the inexhaustible richness of their sequence remain the primary thing.

> For the natural sciences ... the material is given and defined, open to observation, arrangement, and experiment. For history the material – certain events from a certain past – is not given. It does not exist any more in the sense in which nature exists. In order to be able to think of it as existing the historian must carry on a laborious work of research and verification, of sieving and sifting on tradition, before he comes to know the raw material of his activity, the 'facts'. ... The gaining of historical insight is not a process which follows critical treatment of the raw material, it is constantly being acquired in the work of 'digging' itself. Scholarship is not realized in the individual only in synthesis, but in analysis already. No true historical analysis is possible without the constant interpretation of meaning. In order to begin analysis, there must already be a synthesis present in the mind.[108]

Thus, then, the categories in the humanities are the recapitulative, constructive expression of the caught essence of cultural phenomena; the general, theoretical categories of the natural sciences, on the other hand, are arrived at by means of mechanically reductive analysis.[109] The concept 'plough' does not have to do with a reduction of the wood of the frame or the steel of the blade to molecules, but with the nature of the special function that implement has in its use by man. The concept 'cathedral' does not have to do with the quality, construction, or spatial proportions of the complex of wood and stone, but with the essential function of that institution in the complex of religious forms in cultural life. The general characteristics making up the essence of the category 'place of worship' are not to be arrived at by omitting the special characteristics of all the forms of offering places, temples, mosques, and basilicas known in history and reducing them to a general unit, perhaps supplemented by and combined with such units as ritual, priestship, sources of income, and community of believers arrived at in the same way. They are to be arrived at by the opposite way, by determining the 'synthetic' (in Huizinga's term), the 'aprioristic' (in Sombart's) 'church', the recapitulative, constructive expression of the essence of that cultural phenomenon. Thus, if the category 'warrior' is posited, then the various forms in which historical reality has expressed itself – the Athenian marine, the warrior of the Dyak tribe, the European conscript, the Scottish mercenary, the Prussian territorial – receive their content against the background of the category.[110]

> While thus, as one could say, all general concepts of things natural are nominalistic concepts of order, all general concepts of things cultural are realistic concepts of essence which are only afterwards also used as generic concepts in as far as more limited concepts are subordinated to them.[111]

15

The nature of social-economic 'law' is to be defined in the same way: as a certain regularity in the forms for providing necessities as they occur within the complex whole of a civilization. The nature of these forms as such fixes certain limits and courses within and along which lie bound together certain proportional relationships (wage funds, surplus value, land rent), certain structural relationships (business trends, booms, slumps, production cycles), and certain complexes of purposeful, rationally arranged and motivated activities (the 'law'-governed relationship of supply and demand, activities oriented to marginal utility, Gresham's 'law' as the social effect of such activities, and other such 'laws').

Such a complex of cultural phenomena arises from and consists of activities of people in relationship with other people (a purchase, a religious service, a marriage, a military expedition) and in connection with natural objects and materials (agriculture, shipping, fortification, housebuilding). The motives of the enactors are the causes of human activities;[112] the activities can be put in order by 'accounting' them to the motives. The motives are bound up in the whole 'thinking activity' of man, which in all its forms constantly undergoes the influence of culture;[113] thus they constantly appear in the phenomenological forms of culture as 'causal relations'.

The regularities manifested by certain complexes of activity find a limitation in the nature of such phenomenological forms. The explanation of such regularities, or 'laws', becomes, then, an explanation of a sum of individual causal cases occurring in a definite 'complex of meaning'. That 'complex of meaning' needs to be taken completely into account: the causality behind the general term is always to be found in individual motives. There cannot be any transition to a general mechanical causality such as the natural sciences operate with; there cannot be any emancipation of a set of economic 'key activities' from others 'economically irrelevant'.[114]

What, then, is the value of economic 'law'? The theory can only have the pretension of being a collection of schemata of the courses of certain phenomena (always historical) which are logical in proportion and structure, as well as – and this is the most important part of the 'law' question – of the courses of rational economic activities, *i.e.*, rational activities within the complex forms for providing necessities.[115] The schemata are fixed as 'ideal types',[116] that is to say, instead of being 'deduced' from the empirical reality of the phenomena, they are 'purposefully' constructed – here the spectre of the natural sciences rears its head – under the most rational conditions calculable in order to describe the courses of the most rational activities possible. Such schemata, as 'laws', do not in any sense implicitly contain the essence of economic activities, the general conditions for economic life over against which what is left of the phenomena would be only irrelevant economically, like the squeezed out rind of a lemon. Schemata are aids in the sense that they can be of use as orientations in ordering reality and as means in understanding the interrelationship of phenomena, in 'accounting' to their motives factors woven inseverably together, in defining the probable outcome of a certain complex of historical – also contemporary historical – activities.

> The theory of marginal utility, and in general every economic theory, ... tries to 'understand' certain 'adaptations' in the outward behaviour of man to a very special kind of conditions of existence lying outside his

> reach... ...it is always attempted to make the 'adaptation' to them understandable under the heuristic assumption made for the purpose that the activity studied by the theory runs a strictly 'rational' ... course.[117]

That is all the significance 'law' can have in economic theory. Far from dominating economic theory as natural law and lowering social-economic history to drayman service, economic 'law' or 'science' is only an auxiliary, a dependent branch of the subject of economics, one built "on pragmatic foundations, *i.e.*, using the categories 'ends' and 'means'",[118] and possessing no ontological validity in itself.

16

It is in such a way that a 'universal' economic theory 'applies', inextricably bound to the categories of social-economic history and in essence subordinated to them as it is. The field of theory, being modelled on the economic course of modern capitalism, has been loaded down with a collection of 'laws' the heuristic value of which is limited for other periods of history and for areas that have not been reconstructed from the very foundations by modern capitalism. What is needed is the dethronement of the categories of theoretical economics now exercising hegemony and a search for working hypotheses for the 'accounting to' and 'understanding' activity of research in social-economic history more adjusted to the nature and structure of other ages and forms of civilization.

It is an incontrovertible fact that the determination of prices in Indonesian village economy or in indigenous Indonesian trade, crafts, or agriculture does not conform to the conditions and outcomes prescribed by the theory to the same extent as the determination of prices for products of European colonial agriculture and mining, or the determination of prices in the various sections of western European and American economic life. Just as it is possible to speak of the theory as 'inapplicable' in the determination of prices for Frisian trade during the Carolingian period or for German mining in the middle ages. However, it would be an error to conclude that in the whole of phenomena of economic reality – *i.e.*, economic-historical reality: 'today', as 'yesterday', is already history – there should be an area where the theory 'works' and one or more where it does not. The theory is valid only as a collection of orientative, schematic ideal types of a rational structure in the field of provision of necessities, aids in understanding the content, form, and interrelationship of economic phenomena. Thus, the theory 'works' just as much – or, what is the same thing, just as little; there is no question of a natural validity: it is an 'as if' construction,[119] a logical, not an ontological question, with suitability decided in practice – in the determination of prices on the Javanese village markets as on the commodity markets of Chicago and New York. The two sorts of 'markets' have nothing more than their outward name in common.[120] That the theory 'applies' to the second sort of 'market' is a unique fact in cultural history, a result of the development of modern capitalism, the order of which has – or should one say had – the tendency to achieve such a degree of rationality in its forms that economic reality and a rational, maximally theoretical schema coincided. If the theory proves to have no applicability, then one must look around for other theoretical schemata to use as heuristic means.[121] Social-economic history and the 'theoretical economics' related to it, as branches of the social sciences, must use the categories of cultural history which are 'universal' in validity, based on the same sort of methodology, regardless of whether the material concerned is from the time of Charlemagne or Wallenstein, of Werner Siemens, Rathenau, and Mussolini or the Tokugawa shogunate or Dandolo, of King Açoka or Emperor K'ien Lung.

17

The illustrative nature of all historical life was raised earlier as an argument for the proposition that the categories of social-economic history must have a general validity. This illustrative nature should also be considered in planning specifically economic research as it needs to take place, using heuristic, theoretical means. The example Werner Sombart gives of the working method to be followed is too lucid and impressive not to be taken over completely. Because of the illustrative nature of phenomena of reality, because of their historical shapes and colours, economic research needs to trace 'complexes of meaning' and thus proceed from complex to complex, building up phenomena by historical analysis, piece by piece.

> ... Let us take for example the observation of a boxcar which I see rolling along past me loaded with coal, and which I can give a place in the following complexes of meaning:
>
> 1 Complex of meaning: The car is part of a train pulled by a locomotive – steam engine, rails, railroad; thus it belongs in the technological (if one likes) totality railroad.
>
> 2 Complex of meaning: The organization of the railroad – state railway, board of directors, schedule, station, conveyance of goods.
>
> 3 Complex of meaning: The systeem of shipping rates – coal shipping rates, classes of rates, rate policies.
>
> 4 Complex of meaning: The coal is being transported from the mine. Thus, the removal – miner, shaft, tunnels, establishment for the extraction of coal, etc.
>
> 5 Complex of meaning: The company the mine belongs to – corporation, foundation, board of trustees, board of directors, shareholders, aim: realization of dividends, etc.
>
> 6 Complex of meaning: The coal syndicate of which the mining company is a member – trust agreement, quota system, sales, pricing office, price policy, etc.
>
> 7 Complex of meaning: The destination of the car, the *terminus ad quem* – the coal has to be used. Complex: steam and technology, use of coal for providing steam.
>
> 8 Complex of meaning: If the enterprise for which the coal is to be used is *e.g.* a cotton mill, regarding factory organization – use of steam power for running spinning machines, cotton, processing, hiring of people, factory regulations.
>
> 9 Complex of meaning: The cotton mill, now as enterprise.
>
> 10 Complex of meaning: The cotton milling industry as trust.[122]
>
> The primary complexes in which the individual phenomenon is given a place are, in the example chosen, predominantly basic complexes. That is in accord with the nature of the object and would be true in most cases. Only the secondary and tertiary complexes are stylistic and interrelational complexes.[123]

> Now, the placing of phenomena in such complexes is the next problem arising for the expert economist. In solving this problem, however, he will have to be prepared to undertake such placing wisely. That can only be done if he undertakes it within the framework of a system. The system is available to him... It is shaped above all by the configurational concept of the economic system,[124] the function of which now becomes completely clear to us. All complexes of meaning of a lower order can be given a place within those of a higher order, and finally within the complexes supreme in the economic system. Thus national economy takes shape.[125]

If one imagines this method brought to bear on the reality around us and on historical 'reality' as it is depicted in word, form, and image in all the existent documentary material of civilization: to give a few examples, in Backhuysen's painting *The Dock and the Storehouses of the East India Company in Amsterdam* and Van Everdingen's *Gun Foundry in Södermannland, Sweden*, in Caspar and Jan Luyken's etchings of the crafts, in *The Money Counters* (attributed to Quinten Massijs) and Van Valkenborch's *Mining Industry*, in Faed's *The Statute Fair*;[126] if one considers the sequences of scenes as they come to the fore in the travel books of earlier and later times, of Herodotus and Marco Polo, of the first Dutch voyage to the Indies, of Bernier and Du Halde[127] (one could go on almost indefinitely) – then it becomes obvious how hopeful and fruitful the work of research in general economic history, projected as has been illustrated in a few methodological and theoretical points in this chapter, can be.

Chapter Two

Trade and the Trade Routes

> *"However, do tell me who you are and where you come from. What is your native town? Who are your people? ... what kind of vessel brought you here? How did the crew come to land you in Ithaca, and who did they claim to be? ..."*
>
> *"... As for my arrival in Ithaca, I came with my own ship and crew across the wine-dark sea. We are bound for the foreign port of Temese with a cargo of gleaming iron, which we mean to trade for copper. My ship is not berthed near the city, but over there by the open country, in Reithron Cove, under the woods of Neion. ..."*
>
> *The Odyssey*, I, 169–172, 182–186, translated by E. V. Rieu.

I

The 'second renascence' of the western European cultural community sent the arts and sciences on new, far-reaching paths. A new European civilization of bourgeois democracy took form, in the ebbing stream of absolutism, ecclesiastical hierarchy, oligarchy, and baroque already fixed on a firm foundation. Its exponents created new patterns and established a new tradition: English nature description, bourgeois moral description (Thomson, Young, Richardson), historical romanticism (Percy, *Ossian*), new schools of painting, a new theatre, before long (amidst the decisive political complications, even) a new music,[1] French sociological theories (the Encyclopedists, Rousseau), German neo-classicism (Winckelmann, Lessing) – the whole stream of new art forms and social views which, merging with the stream of political movements and finally with economic changes, came to make up the Nineteenth Century.

Not only did investigation of older, traditional values take freer flight. Equipped with new methods of scholarly research the eighteenth century gradually took spiritual possession of the areas of the world already first laid open by merchant fleets and navies, then acquired territorially by the conquests of trading companies and states. Not only did an intensified element of cosmopolitanism come to mark art and world view (Herder, Georg Forster, Goethe's veneration of the *Sakuntala*, his *West-Eastern Divan*, Natchez romanticism, the influence of early Chinese cameralism on the Encyclopedists, especially Quesnay[2]), but sturdier foundations were laid as well, those of Oriental studies and ethnology. The humanities, liberated from the pressures of the baroque tradition, began the rise which was to make them appear in the nineteenth century as the compeer of the sovereign natural sciences. Alongside the older branch of Semitic studies,[3] now too in a new ascendancy, the branch of Indian studies appeared (William Jones) and the work of sinology was transferred to Europe (De Mailla). Then, already, Alexander von Humboldt could offer a synthesis,[4] and akin to it is the totality of Hegel's world picture.

The course of scholarly research led much further still, however. In the nineteenth century began the rediscovery of the remains of the ancient Hellenic and Near Eastern civilizations (Schliemann, Botta, Layard) and of their epigraphic and literary heritage (Champollion, Rawlinson, Oppert); the same process also began for other parts of Asia, as the series *Sacred Books of the East* impressively bears witness.[5] New branches were added to philology, theology, comparative law, before long comparative history. This work of material and spiritual rediscovery – work carried on by scholars of the whole world, in dozens of places, in the schools and in the field – has continued up to the present day, as the excavations at Doura-Europos and Mohenjo-Daro and the recent work in Mesopotamia, Turfan, and East China give evidence. The work of prehistory, too, has expanded its scope, all over the world. This work of the humanities on the past of man is now being carried out on a larger scale than ever. It is work on a tower which grows *because* of multiplicity of tongues and dispersion over the whole face of the earth.[6]

2

Wherever the problem at hand is systematic study of the picture of life in all that past, social-economic history, as a social science, has an important rôle. (Though the work carried out is completely dependent on the preparatory work done by philology.) The aim of the work cannot be to interpret the meaning of events nor to render those events in any ideological form, but only to perform the 'technical' work of systematizing the relationships within and between historical forms of social life, of fixing the nature of those components of history. Thus, not the moral or aesthetic meaning of the Olympic games, but their organization as an Hellenic social and political whole. Not the architectural beauty of the edifices on the Acropolis, but the organization for their construction as related to the organization of the *polis*. Not the philosophical value or significance of the Indian soteriologies, but the phenomenon of hierocracy and monastery and temple organization in Indian and other Asian states. Not the inward value of the Chinese *literati* civilization, but its significance as expression of a bureaucratic officialdom. And so on. Not orientation to any 'general trend', but orientation to the historical autonomy and value of each individual phenomenon.

There does not appear to be any 'formative power' proceeding from such a discipline. However, neither the last word in questions of the times nor the historical legitimation of any ideology is the affair of history and sociology. For them the factor of personality, might, or – what is the same thing – right exerted is decisive. What 'formative power' does procede from such a discipline is that of a system of sociological and historical categories[7] and, later, of those ideal types with which an 'optimal accounting to' in regard to the past as well as the present can be achieved. More than that history cannot 'teach'.[8] Whereas every controversial opinion and ideology defends itself with and for history, the humanities can only be preserved by maintaining a 'trained view of disregard' and a strict neutrality. This does not lead to the inactivity of historism, for the free, 'creative' activity of man is maintained. (Whether it is 'free' or 'unfree' is a point for metaphysical debate.) To be neutral is more honourable for the humanities than to render fawning services to an ideology. And only in that way will it be possible to treasure for the future the work carried out.

3

In Oriental studies, alongside the philological work a great deal of historical work has been done, and as a result a substantially complete historical chronology of the countries of Asia has been established, and linked to the chronologies of the Mediterranean and Near Eastern world and that of medieval western Europe. And thus – despite Troeltsch's objection[9] – it has become possible to speak of the history of Asia, a part of the history of mankind.

The construction of a chronology, however, has the immediate and important consequence that it introduces the question of historical categories. As has been pointed out above, that consequence cannot be rejected. That the histories which have been written regarding the lands of Asia stand apart "somewhat exotically..., with the predominance of philology which has lasted up to the present day",[10] is an evil which should not be perpetuated.

More has been done for the Mediterranean and Near Eastern world in this regard than for the other regions. There the retrospective influence of the sovereign history of western Europe has made itself felt, and the work in historical sociology (in practice the task of 'economic history') has been pretty much completed, that is to say, arranged in a – still disputable – schema.[11] Byzantine studies and more recent Islamic studies have accomplished a great deal for the Near East. For the other regions, however, the work of analysis and synthesis has not yet been carried out to such an extent. Weber set to work on it in its full range for India and China.[12] But for Indonesia, alongside a flowering of philological study, practically everything else is still undone.[13]

4

The problem of historical categories has been taken up from a completely different angle, however – not, it is true, consciously and methodically as such, – namely, in the literature on the geographical works and accounts of travels that appeared in the West and in Asia regarding each other. In those works, too, where the pictures given and the commentary on them are completely contemporaneous, the need for a clearly formulated series of historical categories makes itself felt. Practically all the study carried on in connection with such works considers only problems of a philological and a purely geographical sort, however. Is it absolutely impossible to bring the aspect of economic history more to the fore? However that may be – the question is laid aside for the time being, – in this field, too, the problem has not been clearly and consciously put.

What accounts on the Orient have come down from the ancient world have been collected as one series in the editions of McCrindle.[14] Works by Moslem scholars and accounts of travellers from the Moslem world of the caliphates also consider the Middle and Far East.[15] From the Chinese world come accounts of the travels of Buddhist pilgrims who journeyed from China to India and Ceylon overland *via* Turkestan and Bactria and overseas *via* Indonesia.[16] A number of accounts of travels in eastern Asia – from adventurers, from merchants, from monks and priests – reached Europe in the middle ages. The period of the great Mongol khans, from the end of the thirteenth century through the fourteenth, linked Asia from the furthest parts of China with Europe, and sent missions and trade on new routes. (Those were, however, routes which before that had already been travelled from the early West, especially in the missionary activities of Nestorianism, which had followed the routes of Buddhist missions and set out its posts over the whole of central and eastern Asia in an organization encompassing regions more outstretched than those of the Christendoms of Rome and Byzantium.) Most of these accounts have been made available in new editions, above all through the work of the Hakluyt Society.[17] The important work done by Yule is linked most of all with this period.[18] The official reports of Chinese functionaries contain a great deal of material[19] (just as various functionaries in the caliphates made their knowledge as officials the basis for geographical work).[20] For the first period after the great voyages overseas around Africa, when the Portuguese and Spanish, and then the Dutch and English footholds and conquests were still "only coastal towns and ports, pin-points on the map" and the chronology of colonial history had not yet become that of Asian history proper, the accounts of the Portuguese and those who journeyed with them to Asia and of the Hollanders and Zeelanders and others who sailed for Asia from the United Provinces are actually to be counted as the same sort of material.[21]

Thus there are accounts covering more than two thousand years offering information on states, peoples, religions, handicrafts, and trade in the early Asian world, accounts giving a picture of life in many different times, one of a great richness, not so much in regard to the chronologies of dynasties and the canons of religions as to life in the streets of the cities, on the ships, along the land routes, and in the marketplaces.[22] But precisely because of that they pose the important problem of historical structure.

Furthermore, just as there are great differences in time and morality both between Tacitus, Qazwini's informants, Guiccardini, and Arthur Young themselves and between their accounts on Europe that need to be taken into consideration, so there are for the series of accounts listed above and their authors. Herodotus of Halicarnassus, contemporary of Pericles and Thucydides; Marco Polo, 'Illustrious Citizen of the City of Venice' and contemporary of Dante, gentleman commander of one of the Venetian galleys in the naval battle near Curzola; Abu Abdallah Mohammed, called Ibn Battuta, Moslem, native of Tangier in Morocco; Chau Ju-kua, chief of the Imperial Chinese customs, inspector of trading junks, in the city Chuanchow; Jan Huyghen van Linschoten, factor at Goa for the Fuggers and the Welsers of Augsburg, later treasurer of the town Enkhuizen – these belong just as much to different worlds. Is it too bold to state that a clearly formulated series of historical categories is required for all this?

5

From the very beginning Oriental studies have carried on the work of determining what contact there was between various parts of the early Asian world, making use of philological and geographical material. In the nineteenth century, after the spirit of the times, a search for the interrelation of Asian civilizations was linked up with that work.[23] Since the ideas of totality and synthesis to be achieved by way of 'scientific objectivity' have been laid aside, however, the search has been abandoned.[24]

What remains, then, is 'the history of trade' from the earliest times on. In it there is naturally a closer relationship to general history and its categories. Even so there is an important objection to it which requires further discussion.

The true history of trade[25] is often replaced by the history of technical developments in shipping. Since trade history has followed the traditional pattern and limited itself to the world of the Mediterranean and Near East and the later world of the European Atlantic states, the tendency can be accounted for. Alongside that, the impression made by modern capitalistic technology has been decisive. In the light of nineteenth-century technical development – for the older writers the early Cunard (1840) and North German Lloyd (1857) steamers sailing to what is for us a completely outdated America, the America of De Tocqueville, were the ultimate; later developments made them into museum-pieces – shipping and trade have been fitted into a scheme of 'evolution' from the boat fashioned out of a tree trunk with fire and a stone chisel to the ocean liner of modern times.[26] But the category 'trade' is affected detrimentally by being linked together with the history of technology. All the laws, all the characteristics peculiar to it are shoved into a corner – the nature of trade, its extent (the emphasis constantly falls on the movement of goods across great geographic distances, the concept of 'world trade', with the many misunderstandings it arouses, thus also appearing on the scene), its importance for the communities existing at the time concerned, its organization of merchants, if any, the 'economic spirit' of the traders, its money and payment system, and so on. All this has only a very distant relationship to the historical 'evolution' of technology.

Some of these points are returned to below. Here it needs only to be mentioned that the significance of the voyages across the Atlantic would seem to be overrated. Their chief emphasis lay in their political import – those conquests to the west and the south represented the West's first new accomplishment on a European scale in history – much more than in their economic and technical (nautical) significance. This point, too, is further developed below.

Because of the present approach to the history of trade, the general history which makes use of it derives little benefit from it, either from its directive principles or its categories. Its directive principles are oriented to its Mediterranean and western European periods: the Phoenicians, the Greeks, Carthage, Rome, North Sea and Hansa shipping, Atlantic shipping; such periods have little or no value for Asia. Its categories are lacking in accurate, clearly defined historical content.[27]

6

More recent workers in prehistorical research have collected a great deal of material which points up the shortcomings of the traditional history of trade, forming as it had done the link in the schema of evolution between the data from the ancient Mediterranean and Near Eastern world and ethnological hypotheses. Both geographical and historical limitation and arrangement in progressive stages distort the picture of trade history, and that of economic history in general. It was Heichelheim who, summarizing the most important material of the investigations, recently brought prehistory within the sphere of economic history,[28] and at the same time, especially in his rewarding methodological point of departure,[29] indicated a new path to follow. The 'civilizations of the great historic rivers' are forms of a civilization already stabilized for thousands of years. Research in prehistory has uncovered the existence of a form of civilization in which man was sedentary and carried on farming, as hoe culture, later on holding livestock as well, a form in which crafts were pursued, both as domestic tasks and as independent occupations, one in which the sedentary form of settlement was integrated by a social structure. Under the influence of the geographical *milieu* there could be a transition from hoe culture to 'horticulture' with river or hillside irrigation; in other places, accompanied by the use of domesticated livestock, it could develop into the forms of dry-field cultivation, sod farming followed by rotation and fallowing. Intensive and extensive systems of agriculture, thus. Prehistorical chronology gives the period from 15,000 to 10,000 B.C. as the age of formation for such 'agrarian' or 'plough' civilizations.[30] From about 7000 to 5000 B.C. they have existed throughout the world.

The concept of 'agrarian civilization' – because of the diversity of agricultural methods, it seems to me that this term must be given preference – has more importance than that of being the characteristic of one of the oldest forms of social existence for mankind. Heichelheim himself also makes a broader use of the concept. 'Agrarian civilization', used as a category in the sense of an ideal type, happily breaks through the schema of 'stages of civilization' theories constructed with data from ethnological research now largely outdated. With it in place of the concept of evolutionary law there is given an historical concept – the autonomous, 'unique' course of forms of social life.[31]

Heichelheim's work is of great value for the methodological treatment of economic history. The category 'agrarian civilization' enters into a fruitful interaction with Sombart's categories in his schematization of pre-capitalistic economic systems.[32] Besides economic history, such disciplines as ethnology, philology, and the history of law also use categories of historical evolution more or less directly in their research. It could be of value to look at such categories more closely in their relation to economic history. In regard to the development of law and the legal community, for example,[33] the concept of evolution is no longer tenable as a regular generality. As Heichelheim points out emphatically, 'agrarian civilization' formed the basis of all civilized life up to the time of modern capitalism, and outside the orbit of regions directly dependent on capitalism still forms it up to the present day. The oldest urban civilizations, which at the same time were the '*oikos* civilizations' [34] of the oldest sacred and secular dynasties, were established on the foundations of agrarian civilization. It is chiefly with them that the documentary material of human history makes a beginning.[35]

Prehistory reveals migrations which extended over areas covering the whole of the three continents Asia, Europe, and Africa. From the earliest times on trade traffic went on side by side with the migrations. In the agrarian civilization the social organization offers the possibility for a series of commercial forms to arise – sale, share-cropping, wages, debt relationships, rent. Money trade is by no means a necessary requirement. The differentiation of 'village' or 'market' trade and foreign trade is a relative one: a 'high stage of economic development' is not necessary for the existence of the second form, and both are in actual practice 'peddling trade'. Trade as a secondary occupation, whether accompanying farming or independent crafts, alongside trade as a self-sufficient profession, and both forms mixed up with the antithesis 'local trade' and 'long-distance trade' – agrarian civilizations such as those of Russia and Java still possessed all this at the time of nineteenth-century research, while historical research on the origins of modern capitalism in the traditionally capitalistic countries has revealed the same sort of forms in pre-capitalistic and early-capitalistic periods there.

Early trade moved over regions as far-flung as did the trade of later times, and was just as much 'world trade'.

> Long-distance trade transported valuable weapons, tools and utensils, materials for tools, finery, and foreign varieties of plants and types of livestock along the overland routes (illustrated for research in the discoveries of trading depots) and the overseas routes along all the coasts from the Atlantic Ocean to the Indian.[36]

'International trade', thus, and trade in valuable, high-quality products.

7

Just as trailblazing as Heichelheim's historical and prehistorical work is Malinowski's work in ethnology. In his *Argonauts of the Western Pacific*, the excellent monographic treatment of a part of the ethnographic material he gathered in his field work among the 'savages' of southeastern New Guinea and the archipelago to the east of it,[37] Malinowski builds up the pattern of commercial and ceremonial 'potlatch' forms of trade (primarily interinsular trade) which binds the populations of that far-flung island world together in a great community (in turn strictly subdivided) of participants in the magic, ceremonial exchange of certain objects fixed by tradition in a strictly regulated series of transactions carried on in fulfilment of obligations on the one side and in receipt of outstanding 'claims' on the other, from region to region, from hand to hand: the Kula.[38] Recent ethnology has called attention to the deep-rooted irrationalities and magical elements in all the forms of social organization. What is being carried on by ethnology primarily in research among 'primitive peoples' is also being carried on by modern social analysis for the 'most highly developed' groups of mankind.[39] All of life's forms, basic activities and everyday legal relationships and the highest expressions of religion and government alike, are closely circumscribed by magic.[40] There is no 'magical period' in the past of mankind, over and done with. Magic continues to live as the taproot of even the highest forms of civilization. The category 'trade', too, shares to a large extent its imprint.

Aside from the general methodological part of Malinowski's book, excellently formulated and carried through,[41] the most important aspect of it is that it recounts in such detail the elaborate social structure of the peoples studied in all its complexity and refinement[42] that the term 'primitive', laden with value judgements as it is, is clearly shown to be foolish and indefensible.[43]

Malinowski's chief field of research was on the island of Boyowa, one of the main islands in the northwestern part of the archipelago,[44] where the social structure is strongly marked by an aristocratic authority – in contrast to that of the majority of the other regions, where a weak 'republican' regime controlled by elders,[45] the typical Papuan and Melanesian system of authority, prevails.[46] The aristocratic authority puts its stamp on the Kula transactions in this part of the circle,[47] as well as on the other commercial activities[48] with which the Kula is interwoven as one thread among many, along with barter trade, sale of craft products, and interinsular shipping.[49]

The non-economic, magical and ritual exchange of Kula gifts plays a preponderant rôle in the social organization of the peoples. But the position of trade in general is also an important one,[50] with large interinsular trading expeditions despite a mutual 'foreignness' of peoples[51] and an almost undeveloped sailing technique. The expeditions are either undertaken as voyages of village companies[52] or as voyages in which the noble village chiefs and chiefs of the sub-clans[53] hold dominant positions. That dominance takes a magical, ritual form within the frame of the Kula – the right to have a larger amount of gifts for exchange, the right to act as a partner in the Kula system, a general position of reverence – as well as a general economic form – ownership of boats, the equipping of them, leadership of the expedition. The voyages were great interinsular expeditions[54] with at the same time a large list of merchandise for trading[55] and a very limited trade turn-over.[56]

Here, then, is a social organization – of 'savages', it must constantly be remembered – with the traits characteristic for an 'agrarian civilization': village organization and the whole 'communal' agrarian organization of labour connected with it, differentiated crafts and specialized craft villages, overseas expeditions and overseas commercial relations, all under a clearly defined aristocratic authority,[57] which in the case in question takes the form of shipowning, organization of expeditions, and the chief rôle in the barter trade carried on. The same sort of pattern will come up again later. And, without making any attempt at fitting this 'primitive stage' into an evolutionary 'scheme of development' in history, I should like to point out that the surprising analogy with the distant world of seas and ships of the earliest days along the Aegean coasts indicated by Malinowski through the parallel with the Argonauts in the title of his work is certainly justified from the point of view of economic history.[58]

The Kula system has been cited here as an illustration. Is the difference between such proa expeditions and much of the earlier history of trade really so great as is suggested by the separation of 'primitive' and 'civilized' peoples?[59] The fact is well enough known that potlatch transactions are a phenomenon to be found all over the world, and as 'rudiments' also in 'later' periods.[60] The sea trade–potlatch enterprise of these peoples has therefore been called to attention. Are there not analogous patterns hidden in the trade history of the ancient world? The standard point of view on the history of trade, still considering such material rationalistically and evolutionistically, 'from barter to world trade', gives no thought to such things.[61]

8

Three patterns dominated the social-economic history of the ancient world, the world of the Mediterranean and the Near East – agrarian civilizations, the cities, and the *oikos* states. In reverse order, the three patterns have each in turn been decisive at crucial moments in history.

The oldest 'civilizations of the great historic rivers', Egypt and Mesopotamia, consisted of great organizations of the whole economic and social life of agrarian civilizations under monarchies; mass domestication made possible by river and canal irrigation farming formed the basis for control of the population by the officialdom of the ruler. All subjects were required to render service to the authority, and that service was organized and directed bureaucratically by an administrative apparatus. The chief rôle of the cities was that of being royal seats – *kraton* towns, thus –

in which levies in kind were brought together from the whole country, and royal storehouses in which the levies were stocked and from which the host of officials, the army, and the royal household were provided. The same system was used for lower administrative units. Large-scale planned projects of agrarian colonization were undertaken, and with the services of the subjects monumental building activities were accomplished. They were forced-labour states, soccage states or liturgical states. The legal status of the agrarian population could vary from that of free-holders to that of serfs and slaves brought into the state by predatory war, purchase, or subjugation and established in agrarian colonies. So far as the power of the patrimonial, bureaucratic despotism was concerned the status made little difference economically. The bureaucratic regime provided the framework for the 'economic development' of the 'civilizations of the great historic rivers'. The prosperity of the whole complex depended on the proper functioning of the central authority, as is shown in its full significance by the account of the seven fat years and the seven lean years in the forty-first chapter of *Genesis*. There were periods of greater 'freedom' when the central authority was pushed aside by the aristocracy or through a greater strength of the priesthood and temple organizations. Nevertheless the mechanism had to keep on functioning in the same way, though on a smaller scale; the bonds holding the whole complex of bureaucratic organization could not be broken except under penalty of anarchy and economic ruin. The penetration of money into the natural organization of the systems of agriculture and taxation did not mean any essential change in the structure, though it is true that with the money system (non-intensive as it was, of course) the exploitation of the taxation system was able to lay heavier burdens on the agrarian civilizations. The agrarian and bureaucratic forms remained essentially the same. The dominant groups and their cultures could decay and change, but in the empires of the pharaohs, the Ptolemies, the Assyrian, Persian, and Moslem rulers there is the same basis to be found.

The cities formed a second historical pattern. Such castle principalities as Mycene are a type apart; that they must have controlled a powerful organization of serfdom and forced labour is evidenced by their building activities.[62] Another type is represented by the early Hellenic city monarchies, aristocratic groups at the head of a social system constructed on a genealogical and territorial basis.[63] Such settlements had much less a 'bourgeois' character than did the royal seats of the great patrimonial, bureaucratic states. Piracy and expeditions for conquest, as well as trade, helped to build up the fortunes of the ruling aristocratic groups. The basis of such city states was provided by agrarian civilizations on the one hand and groups of freemen and serfs attached to the aristocratic settlements on the other.[64] Control of land property always remained the most important thing; the 'commercial' element was subordinate to it and irregular in nature. The independent city, whether an aristocratic city state or a castle principality, could become the basis of a patrimonial, bureaucratic regime on a smaller scale the equivalent of that of the *oikos* empires. The Jewish state of King Solomon[65] and the castle principality of Mycene are both of that type. On the northern coasts of the Mediterranean, however, the aristocratic city states remained scattered and independent,[66] the extraordinarily broken coastline of the Aegean basin playing a very prominant rôle in the situation. In that region the aristocratic city state developed through a series of historical transformations into the *polis* of the Hellenes and the Romans.[67] Military and war circumstances were more than the interests of trade and transportation the decisive factors in the transformation. The course of development was not the same in Greece and in Rome. In Greece, with the change brought about in military technique, aristocratic power was pushed aside by the 'democracy' of the hoplite,[68] the militant landed citizen whose war equipment was provided for out of his own property. With the development of naval power as the most important element in the fighting organization of various Hellenic cities, including Athens, the military service of the landed citizenry was replaced by a general service of all citizens in the navy. In the *polis* Rome the peasantry called to arms was the strength sustaining military expansion until late in the Republican period. Different from in Greece, where radical democracy and demagogical power succombed before the assault of the Macedonian monarchical aristocracy, in Rome the hegemony of the urban patriciate was maintained, and with the steady expansion of Roman territory it developed into monarchical, patrimonial forms.[69] The change in military organization – with the undermining of the agrarian economic basis of the peasantry its service in the army lost in importance and was superseded by the use of mercenaries – made the generals an independent political force, and that force, along with the formation of factions among the aristocracy, brought about the establishment of the principate and the military monarchy.

The Macedonian monarchy in settling its conquests used the Hellenic *polis* as the colonizational basis of its power and spread it as far as the hills of Afghanistan and the plains of the Oxus. The *polis* came to be a characteristic of the Macedonian regime.[70] The development in the Roman Empire was different. The late republican period had already shown that the strength of the *polis* Rome lay in markedly patrimonial forms; the empire brought the patrimonial, bureaucratic organization to full development. An example for this had already been set by the Hellenistic states in the Near East, and the Egyptian organization, especially, influenced the Roman imperial one.[71] The political power of the *polis* was broken – one can find this movingly pictured in the words of the 'town clerk' of Ephesus given in *Acts of the Apostles*.[72] The gravitational point of power shifted from city stronghold to territorial organization. From a coastal power the Roman state became a 'world' power; the whole of the ancient world was politically united in its *orbis terrarum*. In the course of the following centuries of peace the state intervened in social-economic life more and more. The territorial organizations of the regions of the Near East, the coastal cities, the agrarian civilizations of southwestern, northwestern, and central Europe – all of them were bound together into a colonial-military and bureaucratic-administrative state, a state of forced labour and serfdom, a new *oikos* of gigantic dimensions.

What patterns of economic 'development' can be found in all this? The trade carried on by the agrarian civilizations[73] continued in the same forms, and the complex of agrarian civilization, however battered, remained the basis of social-economic life. The *oikos* state carried on trade – the central authority had trading expeditions and overseas voyages undertaken, often by serfs and slaves. With greater freedom, trade, established in the cities, was able to earn an important place for itself[74] in the form of powerful wholesale commerce and banking. It formed one of the chief means of existence for the seaport cities.

All this trade covered extensive areas and was 'international' trade, 'world' trade. However, it is not possible to establish any 'evolution' in the order of the periods of trade. Two factors always continued to determine its patterns – the wealthy money-holders on the one hand and the travelling pedlars on the other.[75] For the first trade was a matter of occasional investment of capital; for the second it was an occupation – peddling. Forms such as royal trade – in Egypt, for example – consisted of occasional trade or wholesale trade under royal direction; to view such forms as merely being an 'exchange of gifts' would be biased. The oldest forms of 'private' international trade, in Babylon, already revealed the pattern: royal, hierocratic, and private bourgeois holders of money and goods who carried on international wholesale trade by investing in *commenda*,[76] over against travelling groups of traders who actually carried out the transporting of goods. The pattern also provides the key to Greek trade. In the oldest aristocratic city states the groups in power combined trade under their direction with expeditions for piracy and war, both of which were 'aristocratic expeditions'. In later periods the aristocracy dominated trade not as *entrepreneur* or merchant but as financier and sometimes occasional trader; the actual trade was carried on at a lower level, as peddling trade. Furthermore, not 'bourgeois' economic life but war, booty, and political tribute dominated in the classical *polis*; and not a 'bourgeois' class[77] but, especially in the democratic city, the landed citizenry kept on a war footing, and the ship's company.[78] The Roman aristocracy dominated the fields of conquest, colonial expansion, and international trade, once again not as a modern entrepreneurial class[79] but by means of moneyholding, occasional trade, and political-capitalistic exploitation – *commenda*, bottomry, speculative wholesale trade, exchange of money, farming of offices and taxes, exploitation of slaves and serfs. Beneath this level, once again, there came handicraft trade, peddling, shipping carried on as a trade.

The 'world economy' of the ancient world, then, had nothing in common with modern conditions. There was no 'free trade', no 'world market', no 'export industry', no 'proletariat';[80] instead, handicrafts and trades formed the basis of social-economic life, and political and economic power were controlled by the landed citizenry, the aristocracy, and the more-or-less plebeian 'aristocracy of wealth'. What there was of a market system was extremely unstable; war was always one of the chief nerves of economic life. What could grow to gigantic forms was political capitalism, but in the time of the empire, with *pax Romana* dominating the whole region, that variety of capitalism shrivelled away. The state took away the sources of profit, interfered a great deal in economic life even in times of peace, gradually 'socialized' parts of overseas trade and of distribution, and bound the tradesmen hereditarily to their trades, the peasants to the land, the armies to the frontier provinces. What remained was an inter-related system of trade and handicrafts in a state based on soccage and serfdom.[81]

The next phase in the historical process was the downfall of the western half of the empire and its return to agrarian civilization, with mere remnants of colonial urban civilization (most clearly illustrated by the ruins in the frontier regions, in Trier, in Gaul, in the Balkans) remaining; and alongside that the continued existence of the eastern parts of the empire, within constantly contracting borders, as a unit – also economically[82] – inside the framework of the same rigid bureaucratic regime, with a direct continuity of administrative traditions. The new flourishing of the Near East after the Moslem conquests, in which the old agrarian civilizations built upon flooding and irrigation and the old urban civilizations once again became the bases of 'world states', continued the pattern down to the eleventh century of the Christian era. By a false parallel the whole of that Moslem civilization is characterized as 'medieval', while in essence its continuation of the pattern of the ancient world is the most remarkable fact about it. In the case of Egypt, for example, that continuity has been clearly shown.[83]

There can be no question of any dynamic tendency toward continuous economic progress in the pattern of the ancient world. Trade and industry were held fast in traditional handicraft forms.[84] Every trace of mechanization was lacking.[85] The market was either extremely unstable,[86] threatened and upset by constant plundering and war, or it was kept in restraint by the regulations of a dominating liturgical administration. Furthermore, the geographical distances show that trade was international, a 'world trade' even, from the earliest historical times on. The structure of the trade, its place in the whole complex of political and economic power relationships, was that of occasional capital investment and trade by widely divergent propertied groups alongside handicraft trade, peddling trade. Royal treasuries as well as every nobleman, official, or merchant could provide finance and be involved in the series of trade transactions being carried on more or less continuously.[87] On the other hand the trade was actually carried on as peddling trade involving multitudes of people – the traders from Nineveh, for example, of whom there were more than the stars of heaven[88] – grouped together in foreign lands according to the nation and the place they came from, forming the foreign quarters in the cities, the colonies, courts, and *fondachi*,[89] the 'streets' of Israelites in Damascus and Syrians in Samaria mentioned in the *First Book of Kings*.[90]

There are very few data on the amount of goods transported in the ancient world, and what there are are not very reliable. However, what is revealed by excavations regarding the size of cities and royal treasures, what is shown by the forms of agrarian civilization still in existence, what can be learned from analysis of technological parallels in history – all these together provide justification for endorsing what Max Weber has said: trade was international, and the goods traded make up a long list including precious metals, jewelry, fabrics, earthenware, but also base metals and many raw materials for handicrafts and *ergasterion* industry, thus not only trade exclusively in valuable, high-quality products. There was no question of a trade in mass quantities of goods; whenever shipments of large quantities occurred the immediate cause was usually a political one. This can be seen in the case of the imports of grain in Athens and Rome, two examples best known in history, though, as has been said, one may not draw any conclusions for trade in general from them.[91]

> Such trade is completely incomparable to modern exchange. It was about the same as if now only champagne, silk, and such things were traded in.[92]

The profits of such a peddling trade in expensive goods were high, as that was the only possibility of covering the high costs of transport from foreign lands in journeys lasting months, even years. Even so for a true historical picture one must link that trade with the poor remnants of the international peddling trade still to be encountered in Europe in the venders wandering from door to door and the hawkers at fairs selling rugs and worthless trinkets. Their goods-in-trade are now for the most part by-products of modern industry, and their trade is a miserable business of begging. Nevertheless it is there the related forms are to be found.

9

The Mediterranean and Near Eastern world was linked by trade with the world of southern Arabia and India. The excavations at Mohenjo-Daro in Sindh and Harappa in the Punjab have made it certain that trade linked the urban civilizations of Mesopotamia with those of northwestern India in the third millennium B.C.[93] References to ship expeditions to southern Arabia organized by Egyptian rulers go back to the eleventh dynasty (2350 B.C.);[94] part of the goods obtained in southern Arabia – it is not of decisive importance whether by barter or with a special measure of value, 'money' – and taken back to Egypt had come from other lands, very probably some from India.

The expansion of the Aryan peoples over the plains of northern India,[95] in the course of which the established Sumerian-Dravidian society was damaged and subjugated but not destroyed, brought the establishment of a new aristocracy dominating over a tremendous complex of agrarian civilization newer than that of the Near East. In comparison to that of the Mediterranean and Near Eastern world, Indian history is extraordinarily meagre in chronology.[96] In attempting to summarize the situation in early India, one arrives at a picture such as the following: an agrarian civilization in village settlements in the great river plains, one not so strictly bound to irrigation farming as those of the arid areas of Egypt and Mesopotamia; aristocratic regimes with the village or a group of villages as basis;[97] 'cities' in the same sense as the monarchical city states in *Genesis*; a patrimonial, bureaucratic monarchical state which, not always with lasting success, attempted to keep the aristocratic regimes in check and bind them together (a course of events the reverse to the one in Egypt during the twelfth and thirteenth dynasties, when the class of prebendary officials became independent and set themselves up as a 'feudal' aristocracy); true cities, typical royal seats; a system of soccage side by side with urban groups; an urban patriciate comparable to that of Babylon at the time of Hammurabi; and beneath it the lesser folk.[98] These forms, it would seem, need to be considered as having arisen autonomously, not as having been 'imported' from the West.[99]

The bipartite picture of the Mediterranean and Near Eastern world – coastal areas, the city states; and inland areas, the 'civilizations of the great historic rivers'; and the historical interconnections of the two – is not applicable in the same measure to India. Both aspects were present: there were great territorial states in the plains of northern India, cut off to the north and the east by high mountain chains, and in the river plains and coastal plains of southern and southeastern India, and there were coastal states of a limited size, especially on the western coast, where the mountains come very close to the sea along the whole coast. But the lay of the coasts, the unindented coastline, the insurmountable difficulty of the monsoon winds over the whole region, along with the great open seas around India and the isolation caused by the high mountains, made it impossible for a parallel situation to develop. And in the field of political history every parallel must be abandoned completely.

Research in ethnology and prehistory shows that there had been migrations over great distances in those regions, by sea as well as by land. For example, those of the Indonesians through southeast Asia, eastwards and westwards (and from anthropological and technological data – the use of the single-outrigger proa – regarding the peoples of the south coast of India around the Gulf of Manaar, Hornell for instance has deduced a Polynesian migration from the east).[100] In all such migrations there will have been elements of 'trade'. Because of its contacts by land and by sea, northwestern India belonged to the trading area of the 'ancient world' already very soon after the beginning of the historical era.

In historical times the geographical position of India made overseas trade its most important sort of trade, and along with that made the coastal city the first and foremost form to be connected with it. Cities, trading cities included, have been known throughout Asian history from the earliest times on. The sequence of historical development which Weber formulated as:

> certain stages of organization which in some degree appear to have repeated themselves for each of those classical peoples from the Seine to the Euphrates who have known urban development at all...[101]

can also be of use for regions further east.[102]

Such cities depended on trade. That applies to the earliest cities of northwestern India, to the ports on the west coast and the south coast in Hellenistic and Roman times, and to such powerful coastal city states as Calicut later. The trade, carried on westward to Egypt and Mesopotamia and south and eastward to Indonesia and China (dating from the beginning of the Christian era, according to the most reliable accounts), covered distances many times greater than those of the 'ancient world'. It was 'world trade', international trade in the full sense of the term.

What is the key to a true understanding of that trade? The trade route ran from port town to port town, as though over many stages.[103] There was an interplay between trade and the towns. But here one comes upon a point of the utmost importance: such trade had nothing in common with 'bourgeois', commercial forms of trade, however much many historical philologists may wish to establish the reverse. The coastal principalities, independent urban monarchical or aristocratic regimes,[104] dominated trade, interfering not only by levying tolls and requiring compulsory stapling, but also by carrying on trade and shipping of their own, regulating prices, claiming the right of pre-emption, acting as the financiers of trade. The ruling class was the chief owner of land (which was usually leased out to small farmers for rent in money or kind), had political control of the city, accumulated its chief movable wealth from trade,[105] owned ships, possessed money, carried on occasional trade, sometimes exploited craftsmen working in 'putting-out industries'. There could also exist an urban patriciate on a level with the politically dominant group as far as the size of possessions was concerned, though more or less widely separated from it in 'class' traditions; economically the two groups operated in alliance with each other.

Between these groups and the trade they dominated there was a great distance, both socially and economically. The actual trade[106] was handicraft trade, peddling trade, the work of the mass of merchants; the structure and 'economic mentality' of such an international trade must be thought of in terms of handicraft forms. One is constantly struck by the large number of traders, the bustle on shipboard and in the harbours, the trading voyages with hundreds of merchants. In every port town there were foreign quarters, colonies, courts, *fondachi*. Trade, still imbedded in the age-old forms of mutual aid, involved many people grouped according to city and region of nativity and ancestry. The long duration of the voyages made settlements necessary at the 'stages' in foreign lands.[107]

The aristocracy and the patriciate were 'passive' so far as the profession of international trade was concerned – that is to say, they were its financiers, they invested occassionally in *commenda* and bottomry.[108] The 'active' ones were the handicraft traders undertaking journeys with *commenda* money or *commenda* merchandise, and, alongside them, the independent handicraft traders, among them pedlars travelling with packs on their backs, journeying individually or in company as pedlar caravans. Shipping, too, manifested the same forms, the commander and crew carrying on trade on their own account alongside the transport of people and goods.

There were, then, the royal court, the aristocracy, and the urban patriciate on the one hand, and the great mass of pedlars and craftsmen[109] on the other. It would be completely incorrect to visualize for that peddling trade the picture of poverty it evokes at the moment. Though the trade was a trade in craft forms, in was international trade in valuable high-quality products;[110] though there were comparatively few transactions involving comparatively little merchandise, the value of the turn-over was very high.[111] Jan Huyghen van Linschoten had such trade in mind when he wrote from Goa in 1584:

> I should be much inclined to travel into China and Japan, which are the same distance from here as Portugal, that is, he who goes thither is three years on the road. If I only possessed two or three hundred ducats they could easily be converted into six or seven hundred. ... but to enter on such a thing with empty hands I thought folly: one must start tolerably provided to make profit.[112]

With that is provided the key to the true nature of 'Oriental' trade.[113]

A further problem in this connection is the way the 'historical development' of that trade should be pictured. It seems to me that the picture sketched above had undergone little or no change for at least two thousand years up to and into the seventeenth century. For from around the beginning of the Christian era on this can be stated with certainty. The accounts of trade between Rome and India show a trade in Asia developed to the same level technologically as that in the 'ancient world'. It is apparent from the valuable Indian craft goods exported, especially fabrics, from the way the traders from the Roman Empire settled in Indian ports, from the data on navigation given by Pliny and the author of the *Periplus*, from the settlement of Indian traders in Alexandria, from the service of Roman troops as mercenaries for Indian harbour princes.[114] Weber, in this case following Kanakasabhai,[115] gives a description of the Tamil harbour town Kaviripaddinam, on the Coromandel Coast, as it was shortly before the Christian era. In the royal part of the city were the patricians, who were the landlords, and the fine craftsmen, Brahmins, doctors, astrologers, singers, actors, and musicians; in the commercial part were the warehouses, which also served as shops, the common crafts, and the quarter for foreigners, including Western merchants. Between the two lay the market square.[116]

10

In the time of the western European middle ages Islam gained a great deal of ground in the Indian ports, and Moslem trade – by no means identical with Arab trade[117] – occupied an important place in the whole of trade in Asia, even though Indian trade was not supplanted at any single point. Did Moslem trade signify a new 'stage of evolution' in Indian and Oriental trade? From such a question there arises another – what was the nature and the significance of Moslem trade, which in the time of the western European middle ages either shared the power of Indian trade or dominated alone in southern Asia?

The sphere of Moslem trade, the territory of the caliphates – at their zenith the whole region from extreme northwestern Africa and southwestern Europe to the Punjab – plus the other regions associated with them commercially, coincided to a very large extent with the sphere of trade of the ancient world. As early as the time of the Roman Empire[118] trade extended to Lake Chad and to Senegambia, from where caravan trade was carried on northwards to Numidia and Mauretania (a trade carried on earlier by the *polis* Carthage) and eastwards to the Upper Nile (Kordofan, Darfur, and the Axumite Kingdom).[119] Trade with northwestern Europe had already been opened by the Greeks, through Massilia;[120] trade with northeastern Europe (where even prehistorical trade routes have been traced)[121] by Greek colonies on the Black Sea, as the coins from Thasos and Olbia discovered in East Prussia and western Russia bear witness.[122] Macedonian political colonization as far east as the Pamir established connections between India and the Near Eastern and Mediterranean world in the Hellenistic period;[123] in the time of the Roman Empire further expansion eastwards took place by means of the 'official' connection of the silk route protected by the respective governments and passing across the Pamir and through Turkestan to the China of the Han Dynasty.[124] From Ptomelaeic Alexandria the age-old shipping to India and on to Ceylon[125] and into the Indonesian seas was maintained and expanded, part of it organized by the rulers. Southern Arabia also took part in the shipping and trade.[126] At the time of the Roman Empire there was a flourishing caravan trade to the east from Syria, as the glory of the city Palmyra gives evidence.[127] Egyptian, Greek, and Roman shipping, along with Indian and Arabian, maintained trade on the east coast of Africa. It is highly probable, after all, that monsoon shipping was known to the Indians long before the 'discovery' by Hippalos.[128] The routes for trade on eastern Africa, too, had already been travelled in earlier times: the Indonesian sphere of expansion reached to Madagascar. Northern Madagascar and the mouth of the Rovuma River were the terminal points for the sea trade of the ancient world.[129]

The 'world trade' of the Roman Empire, then, did not have any 'nationally Roman' quality as trade;[130] it was a trade in which the most divergent peoples took part, while the Roman regime derived the profits.[131] It covered the area of practically all the known world; if *pax Romana* was fatal for the 'free' political capitalism of the ancient world, it worked to the advantage of this quiet, pacific peddling trade. The possibility of 'development' lay primarily in a quantitative consolidation of trade, not in a qualitative transformation of it. In the growth and flourishing of trade there was no question of a configuration of dynamic progress, but only of a greater confluence of amorphous elements. And the bases of social-economic life continued to be the massive agrarian civilizations, essentially self-sufficient; the crafts and trades, lacking all technological ability and essentially traditionalistic; the cities, in many ways bound to 'social monopolism'; and finally the bureaucratic state with its serfdom and soccage, constantly interfering more and more. It seems to me it is impossible to indicate how trade at the time of the Roman Empire was 'more highly evolved' than in previous ages. The letter of credit was developed in the Hellenistic period; the first elementary forms of monetary exchange, which were brought to further development in Byzantine and Moslem trade, also date from the Hellenistic period.[132] Furthermore there is a great distance in time between the first appearance of such a form of exchange and its usage as a dominant form. And here too the economic mentality needs to be taken into account – when last comes to last, the corollary to a banking system or a wholesale trade with credit instruments is not necessarily capitalism, let alone modern capitalism.

The disintegration of the empire and the disturbances accompanying it caused this fabric of 'world trade' to decay and fall asunder, until with the formation of the new Moslem states a new 'world trade' was created, this time as 'Arab', or better (however much that term too needs restriction) as 'Moslem'. Moslem trade covered practically the same regions as trade in the time of the Roman Empire. The areas of the old northwestern European provinces now belonged to the sphere of the Germanic states which had resulted from the migrations; in regard to trade, however, their relation to the world of the Mediterranean and the Near East was not changed.[133] There Jewish and Syrian trade, along with Moslem, dominated.[134] Byzantine trade, just as ancient Roman trade, was trade carried on by foreigners.[135] In other areas the Moslem sphere of influence spread out over what had been that of the Roman Empire and extended its borders to the north and east in Europe and Asia and to the south in Africa. In this process three things need to be distinguished: the organization of power in the Moslem states, the caliphates; the missionary activities of Islam; and trade.

After the centre of temporal authority was transferred from Mecca to Damascus, the chief area of Moslem political power consisted of the age-old urban civilizations[136] of Syria, Mesopotamia, Egypt, and the former Roman provinces in northern Africa and Spain. The ancient machinery of the bureaucratic state and the urban regime continued to exist exactly as they had been;[137] there, too, the pliable mass of subjects not involved in politics[138] made up the fiscal basis of the state. In this regard the Moslem regime did not introduce any new elements. The way in which the taxation system, the backbone and nervous system of the state, was operated in mass forms – tax farming, with all the forms for exploiting the fiscal strength of the population connected with it – was nothing new. All this was conducted by a group of high officials, foreigners, and army commanders[139] and linked by them to the other familiar forms of political capitalism:[140] trading enterprises, colonial predatory expeditions, exploitation of *ergasteria* and plantations with semi-free or unfree craftsmen and workers. And alongside those, the characteristic investments of capital in *commenda* and bottomry, with a trade and production in craft forms in the background. The banking and wholesale dealing in money found in elaborate forms in the caliphates[141] were always much more directly linked to political capitalism and mass fiscal operations[142] than to trade, let alone 'industry'.

The Byzantine Empire and the caliphates, with their administrative bureaucracy, their urban civilizations, their taxation system and military organization, were 'highly developed',[143] especially in their money economy,[144] in comparison to the agrarian civilizations of the western European states of the middle ages early and late, with their 'natural economy', their agrarian feudal hierocracy and secular authority, and only the first beginnings of urban forms in a small number of towns.[145] If one transfers the periodization of western European history to the Near East and speaks of the 'Moslem middle ages', then the category 'middle ages' no longer has any content. None of the elements making up the social-economic picture of the western European middle ages found an equivalent in the Moslem states. Their 'level of development' should be measured in terms of the preceding period, that of the ancient world, not that of the western European middle ages.

The first onslaught of Islam was a combination of military power and religious fanaticism. Its conquests established a nominally Moslem regime as a superstructure above the existent one.[146] The religions already to be found in the area, although reduced to submission, were maintained or at least left unmolested. Alongside that, however, Islam developed a great missionary power among the people politically subjugated; Moslem missions, soon also including new converts from the whole area of the ancient world falling under Moslem political domination, carried on their work of proselytization far beyond the caliphates, northwards into Europe, eastwards across the Pamir along the missionary route of the preceding world religions Nestorianism and Buddhism as far as into China, and southwards to the African peoples.

The Moslem 'knight of the spirit'[147] and the Moslem merchant missionary are the sociological types of the disseminator of Islam,[148] the latter emanating more strength than the former, and over a longer period of time. With the consolidation of the patrimonial, bureaucratic caliphates, the belligerent aristocratic groups and clan organizations of the first period of Moslem expansion were replaced by standing armies, often consisting of purchased slaves. With the flourishing of commerce accompanying the formation of the great Near Eastern states, it was above all through international trade that Islam spread, with the traders and along the trade routes.

Not that Islam as such had a direct influence on that trade, on commercial forms and the organization of merchandising. Religion and trade need to be kept apart in this respect. 'Moslem world trade' as a commercial system was a continuation of forms and complexes already in existence. Trade was able to expand under the protection of Moslem political power,[149] but it remained as before peddling trade in which Arabs took a place (to what extent is a moot question) alongside Jews, Persians, Greeks, Nestorians, Indians, and so forth. The division according to religions is a different affair, and has no direct significance commercially and economically. There was no more a national Moslem trade than there was a national Roman trade. The forms of Arab – or rather Moslem – commercial law were those of Greek and Hellenistic law. The system of credit instruments (bills of exchange, letters of credit, orders)[150] may have been perfected in the Moslem period, but considering the internationality of trade, even in the caliphates, it remains to be seen to what extent it was the work of Arabs, or even Moslems. Furthermore, the influence of trade in the true sense of the word was not necessarily preponderant in that process of perfecting, for banking and trade in money were linked most closely of all to fiscal exploitation by political means and to political capitalism. It is therefore not clear to me where a 'higher level of economic development' is to be found in the Islamic period. Political capitalism was an age-old pattern, by no means specifically Moslem. The complex of urban civilizations, too, was a heritage from the ancient world; city organization, trades and manufactures, merchant gilds, shipping, and transport systems were none of them new creations of Islam. The element of free handicrafts was perhaps more important than in the ancient world, and slave labour less so. But that, too, remains to be seen. The gilds were just as much under the control of the bureaucratic administration as in Byzantium.[151] A course of political development such as that in southern and western Europe – where first the citizenry under the domination of the urban patriciate and lords united in *conjurationes* to constitute the urban authority, and later the gilds as revolutionary organizations of the citizenry captured that urban authority from the feudal, hierocratic, and/or patrimonial lords of the towns who constituted the urban patriciate and the nobility-within-the-cities[152] – is lacking. Still, just as the course of political events in the Hellenic cities exerted little direct influence on 'economic development' in the sense of progress, even so the regime of the revolutionary gilds had little to do with the 'economic development' of Europe; in its fully developed form as the economic regime in power it had a stagnating effect, even, which is why it was broken by the modern European monarchical state in the later middle ages.[153] The rise of modern capitalism had no direct connection with the gild system.[154]

To what extent Islam may have been able to influence the economic mentality towards modern capitalism has not yet been investigated.[155] In my opinion there cannot have been a great influence. Islam either remained to a large extent bound to tradition and magic; or else as *virtuoso* religiosity it was carried by social groups which stood outside active economic life as a more or less organized hierocratic power (compare Catholicism, the influence of which also has been small on the formation of the modern capitalistic mentality), or in lower middle-class 'orders' and 'brotherhoods' (compare the brotherhoods of the mysteries in the ancient world) took an unwordly, pietistic direction, and not the direction of an 'inner-worldly asceticism' of 'vocational holiness' as an ethical rationalization manifested by representatives of seventeenth and eighteenth-century Calvinism.[156]

The achievement of Islam in the fields of literary and humanistic culture had as such no direct relationship to the complex of social-economic organization, let alone any influence on it. It was too much bound to tradition for that; the social distance between the learned and the merchants and tradesmen was too great and the nature of learning too scholastic. This should be kept in mind in considering Moslem achievements in the fields of geography and nautical science; those achievements never had a decisive influence on the level of organization of trade and shipping. The work of the learned was primarily a continuation of Greek and Roman erudition on a theoretical basis, supplemented empirically as of old by scattered verbal reports of contemporaries and material collected from the encyclopedic scholarship of the time.

In the East, Moslem 'world trade' linked India, Indonesia, and

China to the ancient world. The only development in that Oriental trade through the long ages of the Roman Empire and then after the formation of the Moslem unit of power was one of an irregular course of increase and decrease in quantity of international peddling trade based primarily upon urban capital investments often politically determined. The 'market' continued to be small and unstable, regulated by political aims, burdened by the enforced stapling required by the political authority. There, too, the only 'industrial' production for the market was that of the *ergasterion* and the master's workshop.[157] The merchandise traded was still for the most part the same sort of valuable high-quality products as of old. For such reasons a configuration of dynamic progress was as much out of the question there as in the case of Roman 'world economy'.

II

That, as has been said, Moslem trade did not at all mean Arab trade was true for the lands further east as well as other regions. Moslem trade to the east, dependent on the ports of northwestern and southeastern India, was, in its age-old character of trade carried on by foreigners, the trade of Islamized Indians. It has already been pointed out that the Islamization of India had no direct relation to commercial and economic affairs. Furthermore the fact that trade in money and wholesale trade in goods were in the hands of certain highly respected Hindu castes and that the forms of the system of credit instruments, the fiscal system, the craft system, and so forth were Indian shows that India reached social-economic maturity and historical greatness along autonomous lines – but at the same time that there, too, the general characteristics of the configuration for periods earlier than that of modern capitalism are completely applicable.[158]

The structure of trade and the town has already been sketched. There was not any essential change in the structure: the Kaviripaddinam of Greek and Roman times[159] presented the same picture as the Calicut of the sixteenth century, the Bantam of 1596, the Mocha of the seventeenth century (especially important as a port-of-call for Indian trade), the harbour principality Macalla in 1931. A detailed sketch of the port of Mocha is given in the records of the Dutch Company reprinted by Terpstra. Indian trade brought goods there which were then transported further northwards in the traditional way, part of them finding a market in Arabia and part on the opposite coast in Africa. With the monsoon winds the ships came in from the Indian and Indonesian ports, and the Arabian coasters as well. The goods brought were the traditional valuable high-quality products: pepper, gum lac, benzoin, cotton cloth, tobacco, cinnamon, nutmeg, cloves, mace, camphor, porcelain, sandalwood, musk, diamonds, indigo, drugs, tin, iron, steel, the perfumes and gums of southern Arabia. The exchange trade came from Suez in the form of a single ship filled primarily with money, but also with coral, woollen cloth, Italian goods, camlet, and so forth. The market was extremely small and unstable:

> The big ship that comes each year from Suez has not come yet, that is long tardy and is a great loss for all the ships lying here, for by lack of buyers they have to give their goods so cheap that they cannot stand it...[160]

> At the moment [1621] there are nothing but sellers here and each one seeks only to get rid of what he has in order to leave here with the monsoon and not stay over.... They cannot collect the debts they have however diligently they may try; it all is waiting for the coming of the ships from above.[161]

The tolls were levied in money or merchandise. The pasha controlled the trade, with rights of pre-emption, enforced stapling, extortions, and trade on his own account (usually as incidental trade).

> The ship from above... has come now at last but without any money, because all the merchants lent most of their money to the new pasha and they have not got any payment from him yet.[162]

The merchants travelled with their wives and children.[163] The ship's companies were large: on two ships from Dabhol there were respectively two hundred and a hundred fifty Lascars.[164] The traders lived in colonies in Mocha. Those from Dabhol were highly esteemed there, "were and are called the makers-of-trade in the Arabic tongue, keep a house here, and pay less toll than is granted us ..."[165] On this international market, the transit port of a world trade, commerce was carried on as peddling trade:

> ... A Chinese *datching* [hand-scales] on which two picul or thereabouts can be weighed is needed to be sent because we have no way to know how to deal with weights; we weigh with a set of stones and change every day ...[166]

The trade of travelling pedlars – and alongside it the personal overseas trade of rulers, whether carried on in private ships with a private cargo (a ship belonging to the ruler of Golconda setting sail from Masulipatnam for Mocha),[167] or in partnership with merchants, the goods being placed on board ship side by side (at Cambay the factor of the prince Asaf Khan, brother-in-law of the grand mogul, put some silverwork and 3,055 gold ducats, or around twenty-four hundred pounds, on board a ship setting sail from the city of Chaul;[168] as a comparison, another ship coming into Chaul carried a cargo with a value estimated at a hundred thousand pounds).[169]

All this can be compared to a description made in 1931 of the harbour principality of Macalla, the chief port of Hadramaut, a sultanate with a small area of land and living from trade. The town, with twelve thousand inhabitants, has fortifications, palaces, a handicrafts quarter, a trading quarter, and a slave quarter (slaves being used as soldiers). The corps of officials includes many foreigners from India, the trade in money is in their hands, and they also have an important share in the town's international commerce. There are orchards and tobacco plantations owned by the sultan, the regent, and the wealthy townsmen, the tobacco being exported to Egypt. There is a local fishing industry, and local shipping for the plantations of guano fertilizer, which is transported further inland by camel. Trade is carried on with the interior of Hadramaut by caravan. Food – rice – is imported from Bengal. Local trade, probably of a quite primitive sort, is carried on with the bedouins from the desert.[170]

Trade, then, was international,[171] carried on over a system of stages, the coastal harbour states, and as such a thin but golden thread binding the Asian world across great distances. So far as India was concerned, the system consisted of a few coastal settlements scattered along a shoreline more than fifteen hundred miles long from the Ganges round Cape Comorin to the Indus, small foci of trade and crafts, for the most part politically isolated from the great inland areas. (The immediate hinterland, even, could remain untouched by all this, as is still illustrated today in the 'tribal areas', the 'backward tracts' lying along the Kalingga Coast.)

The pattern of political capitalism, also, was international. In his study of the influence of Islam on the foundations of Jewish banking, Massignon gives a lively sketch of the Jewish financiers of the time, worthy forefathers of Süsz and Rothschild. The forms of financial exploitation were no exclusively Jewish affair, however. Von Kremer's excellent description of the Abbassidic revenues reveals forms of political capitalism practised by high officials of the caliphate of Arab and perhaps of Persian origin which were completely the match of those practised by Jews;[172] and the lust for profit of the wealthy Indian merchants has often been compared to that of Jewish merchants. A few illustrations of some aspects of Indian political capitalism may be given – as everywhere, adventure and the exploitation of political power played a leading rôle in it.

The Arab family At-Thaibi, or Thibi, occurs in the records at the end of the thirteenth century. Malik-ul-Islam Jamaluddin Ibrahim At-Thaibi, farmer-general of Fars, lord of Kais and other pearl islands in the Persian Gulf, governor of Shiraz in 1306, was holder of a large share in the rich export trade in Arabian horses. (How that trade, pre-eminently a trade in luxury products, was carried on appears from other data. The Arabian ships were weakly constructed, without any ironwork, held together by rope and wooden nails, with the most simple rigging, lacking even a deck; the cargo stored in the ship was covered with hides, and then the horses were put on top. These ships, seemingly little seaworthy, had much earlier been recorded in the

Periplus; they have also been mentioned by a Chinese in an account from the end of the eighth century, by Marco Polo, and by an eye-witness from the middle of the nineteenth century.[173] Political-capitalistic exploitation does not at all mean 'economic development' in the modern-capitalistic sense.) Jamaluddin's son, Fakruddin Ahmed, was governor of Hormuz and ambassador to the grand khan of China (1297–1305). Takiudin Abdurrahman became regent of the state of Çola in Tanjore at the end of the thirteenth century, and was succeeded in the office by his son Surajuddin and his grandson Nizamuddin.[174]

The middle of the seventeenth century provides the example of the regent of Golconda, Mir Jumla, a merchant risen from the dregs of the earth, as regent also shipowner, sea trader, controller of a large part of the Coromandel shipping on Persia, Basra, Mocha, and Pegu.[175] (The rise of persons from the lowest classes of the populace to high and the highest positions in the administration was a very common occurence in those patrimonial, bureaucratic states large and small where there was not, or not any longer, a strong aristocratic tradition dominant. This applied even for slaves.)[176]

Also of the seventeenth century is the perhaps Tamil family Malaya, in Pulicat, carrying on shipping and overseas trade, moneylending and trade in money. One of the heads of the family, who exploited various offices farmed out to him, was as well a commander of troops in war – thus leading a seigneurial way of life.[177]

All these are illustrations of political capitalism, in their nature and form the same as those of the ancient world, for example the power of the Carthaginian family Barca, with private colonial possessions in Spain, silver mines, slaves working there and on plantations, slave armies, trade;[178] or the colonial exploitation and financial operations of the aristocracy in the Rome of the late republic.[179] A Crassus might be mentioned alongside the Jews Yusuf Ibn Pinehas and Harun Ibn Imran of Baghdad,[180] alongside a Jamaluddin Ibrahim At-Thaibi; or a Manik Chand alongside the Peruzzi and the Fuggers.[181]

12

China offers a different political picture. At the time when shipping from the Indian ports first reached southern China *via* the coasts of Indonesia and Indo-China, around the beginning of the Christian era, the borders of Chinese imperial authority had already been extended as far as the South China coast and into Tonkin. In that far south the empire found itself on conquered territory: up to the time of the tyranny of Ch'in Shih Huang Ti and the first imperial dynasty, the Han, the territory of China had been primarily the regions of Shensi, Shansi, and Honan, with a constantly expanding area of colonization in the lower plains of the Hwang and the Yangtze. The southern parts of the empire will certainly have been looked upon as conquered areas during the first dynasties. Part of the trade and shipping on South China was probably carried on by Indonesians, and perhaps some of it by foreigners from the west, that is to say, India, as well: a possibility that constantly existed because of the intermingling nationality of ships and merchants, the more so considering the peddling character of international trade. At any rate, the trade which linked the chief provinces of China lying to the north with the seas to the south needs to be looked upon as being in the same sort of position as the trade in the Roman northern border regions on the mouths of the great rivers and along the Channel, a trade attaching itself to military conquests, one mainly carried on by foreigners, no 'national' Roman trade. In the course of the centuries the great process of Chinese colonization which Granet has described for the old northern region must have expanded southwards until it had filled the valleys of the coastal rivers from Kwangtung to Chekiang and had built up there the impressive complex of farms and villages and towns which has never failed to fill every foreigner with awe.[182] Imperial authority was always maintained through the course of the whole process. It was, then, a course of events which could to a certain extent be compared to the one which began to unfold itself in the provinces of the Roman Empire under the protection of the colonial regime but was interrupted there by the retreat of the Roman armies and the contraction of the imperial borders. The imperial authority was that of a bureaucratic, civil-servant state, but one in which the Confucian *literati* class, which had made sure of its power during the period of the Contending States, had set a characteristic Chinese imprint on bureaucratic forms. Chinese civilization was a typically urban civilization: the Chinese cities revealed a pre-eminently 'urban bourgeois' character,[183] and the organizations of the urban population were manifold and powerful. But even so the cities as well as the villages remained under the control of the imperial authority. No struggles for political autonomy arose – the political development of the *polis* was lacking, and the various phases in the development of the revolutionary municipality in southern and western Europe just as much. Imperial authority, urban civilization, and agrarian civilization seem to have remained the same throughout the long ages of the empire's existence, however turbulent that existence may have been.

In 166 A.D., the so-called Roman embassy from Marcus Aurelius arrived in China, and in the same period Indian and Indonesian embassies, following the sea route, also came to the Celestial Kingdom.[184] At that time there was already a Chinese regime established, perhaps an urban stronghold, in Tonkin.[185] The authorities of the central government figured in every record, regardless of the schisms in the empire and the divisions into hostile dynasties. What was lacking in China was the politically independent harbour principality, the partition into inland territories and independent coastal regions. Everywhere in the mighty Chinese port towns there were to be found a subdued population and, as masters with political and military power, the officials of the central government. What records there are throw a flash of light on the port towns and their trade. The great period of the T'ang Dynasty, a period of peace and mass colonization, seems also to have been beneficial to the southern ports and to international trade. Canton and Chuanchow[186] date from that period as great port towns.[187] (The imperial capital still lay in Old China, at that time at Hsianfu, in Shensi.) It was once again the central authority which through its bureaucratic regime of civil servants dominated trade: in the eighth century, "or probably somewhat earlier", was established the Bureau of Trading Junks, with a varying number of offices in the different port towns which registered incoming ships, collected the high port and toll fees (and according to Chang also freight charges, however that governmental intervention may have taken place), exercised strict customs and stapling regulations, served as the shipping board, and furthermore were concerned with patrolling the coast and with the reception of embassies and arrangements for their further travel.[188] Marco Polo's thirteenth-century description of the city Hangchow throws that city, the imperial capital of the Sungs until 1276 when it was captured by the Mongols, "the great city Kinsay", the "famous rhapsody of the Manzi capital", in full light.[189] And since then down through the centuries it has not changed in a single essential point. All the characteristics of the Chinese port town were gathered together there: tremendous multitudes (Hangchow is considered to have been the largest city in the world at that time),[190] great international trade, a dominating central government with an extensive machinery of officials controlling trade and crafts.[191]

The historical accounts there are of Chinese trade and the elements related to it are without exception disappointing, because they fail in any way clearly to limit and define the category 'trade' historically. The leading position occupied by the imperial government through its body of officials leads one to suspect the possibility that state trade and state shipowning existed. Chinese trade, too, was acquainted with the bipartite division of on the one hand a moneyholding urban patriciate investing intermittently in trade and on the other an itinerant trade in handicraft forms and the many 'lower middle class' organizational forms of companies and societies related to it. The Chinese merchant class was highly peaceable, approximating closely the 'bourgeois' groups characteristic for the ancient world, which were without rights politically. Did a 'middle class' develop as dominant in Chinese trade? Political capitalism, which was powerful in ancient China at the time of the Contending States, was pulled down by the imperial authority of the Chinese humanistic government so far as its belligerent political forms were concerned. Patrician merchant gilds having great power comparable to the *Richerzeche*, the gild of the rich merchants in Cologne, were to be found in China,[192] and there were merchants with tremendous fortunes.[193]

The problem of the history of Chinese trade is a part of the problem of the general economic history of China. From the unification of ancient China into the empire after the period of the Contending States, the civil service system had been in operation over cities and provinces which also had a continuous existence through the ages. A net of inter-communicational forms spread out over town and country; crafts and highly differentiated manufactures employing many workers, such as mining and metalworking, were developed. That does not mean that there was any definite, critical break in Chinese history, however. In periods of longer or shorter duration a certain historical peripeteia – for example an inflation of money with its ruinous results – sometimes made itself felt to the full; besides that great national catastrophes – floods, crop failures, and so forth – gave an irregular rhythm of disintegration and consolidation to the agrarian basic structure of the empire, and thus to the whole structure; and there were furthermore the foreign invasions and migrations, sometimes connected with dynastic changes, sometimes not. With all this there does not appear to have been a transformation in quality, not even a gradual one. Recovery seems to have come about in the same forms as were traditional; the framework of the bureaucratic civil-service system protecting and preserving the political and fiscal organization and the cultural heritage always remained. Consequently in the Chinese economic society, which would seem to have offered so many possibilities for it, high capitalism never arose, despite the overabundance of commercial and social-economic organizational forms – wholesale trade, finance, banking and money exchange, 'heavy industry' in forms surpassing those of early-capitalistic western Europe, manufactury, exploitation of crafts by means of the putting-out system, and economic relations covering many provinces, over distances that would have been 'international' in western Europe.

In view of all this, a question arises regarding Chinese trade. Has one there, too, to reckon with an historical constant, more or less from the beginning on? Even the latest study of Chinese trade[194] does not give any answer to the question.

In Chinese trade there were periods of great overseas expansion alongside periods of passivity and mass 'embargo'. To what extent was that a stereotype of official Chinese historiography? The periods are linked with the course and position of the imperial government, but in how far do they directly coincide with reality? Economic motives cannot be given in explanation of them.[195] Krause goes even so far as to say that Chinese trade retreated as soon as the trade carried on by foreigners actively extended to China:

> For the Chinese were never a seafaring people and for the purpose of trade they always went to meet their customers only for the time until those customers had advanced further themselves and came to their country.[196]

The internationality of peddling trade together with the lack of direct commercial and economic interest on the part of the bureaucracy and the patriciate make such a thing within certain limits possible – that is to say, a heavy trade carried on by foreigners was of just as much value for the bureaucracy of the ports and of the empire as a fiscal and commercial aim as a 'national' trade would have been, and with the complete internationality of peddling trade commercial investments were just as feasible in a trade of foreigners. But despite this the economic periods of Chinese trade in my opinion remain as a whole unexplained.

From the rather small amount of information furnished by the sources it seems to me it must be accepted that from the time when the process of Chinese colonization in South China was completed, Chinese trade contained the developed forms shown by later detailed sources, to which the accounts by Marco Polo and Ibn Battuta provide an introduction.[197] That is to say, the craft trade[198] of groups of pedlars travelling in foreign countries, whether with *commenda* investments or in joint-stock companies; shipowning, whether by craft gilds or shipping gilds or by urban lords, patricians, and officials; private trade and/or occasional trade by the latter groups,[199] and the possibility of a system of factors overseas. A peddling trade involving many people is indicated by the Chinese trading colonies in other lands as well as by the foreign settlements in China – colonies of Persians, Arabs (or Moslems in general?), Jews, Armenians, and Indians, but surprisingly enough not of Indonesians, are mentioned by name in this respect.[200]

There in eastern Asia just as much as along the western trade routes and in the ancient world peddling trade was a trade in valuable high-quality products; Gibbon's 'mordant aphorism' that "the objects of oriental trade were splendid and trifling" is also completely applicable to Chinese trade.[201]

Technical data on navigation, too, throw little light on Chinese trade. However, one needs to remember in the first place that ship construction develops to a much higher level in connection with and dependence on warfare than within the commercial framework. In the present connection it seems to me that there should not be a high value attached to figures. Data fix the time of the voyage from Canton to Çriwijaya in the seventh century A.D. at twenty days, a month, and more than a month;[202] in the ninth century a few weeks;[203] the tenth century a month.[204] In the eleventh century it was thirty-nine days from Palembang to Canton;[205] in the seventh century it was fourteen days from Jambi to Kedah, and from there to Negapattinam thirty days.[206] In the thirteenth century it was thirty days from Brunei to Champa, forty days to Palembang, and forty-five days to Java.[207] In the fourteenth century from Chuanchow to northern Achin it was a hundred twenty-one days,[208] from Canton to Annam twenty days, from Tonkin to the Tenassirim region forty days,[209] and from the Ganges ports to Java forty days.[210] In the fifteenth century from Ceylon to northern Achin it was twenty days, from there to Malacca seven days, and to Tenassirim sixteen days.[211]

In 1615 the length of the voyage of Chinese junks from South China to Bantam was sixteen, seventeen, eighteen, or twenty days, in 1622 from South China to Batavia forty-three days.[212]

Not only are such figures possibly inaccurate; they can furthermore have reference to widely varying types of ships, even though the same type of ships may be assumed for periodical commercial travel on the main routes. Even where there is some possibility of a controlled comparison, however,[213] no further light is thrown on the situation. A Chinese text from the first century A.D. gives a duration of twelve months for the outgoing voyage from Tonkin to India, and ten months for the return voyage. The itinerary of an embassy from South China to the Indian ports on the Ganges in the second century A.D. gives a duration of ten to twelve months. In the beginning of the eleventh century an embassy from southern India arrived in China over the sea route after a voyage of two hundred forty-eight days.[214] One is thrown off the track when faced by such consistency. Ferrand annotates the data: "With an interval of a dozen centuries, these data can be considered as concordant with each other..."[215] On the basis of these and similar figures one must come to the conclusion also in regard to technical data on navigation that no 'development' can be indicated in the field; from that, then, the hypothesis of an historical constant may possibly be confirmed.

The ships built were of innumerable types, from the simplest fishing canoes to the great junks for overseas navigation described extensively at the end of the thirteenth century by Marco Polo.[216] The great junks, with bottoms reinforced with iron, four fixed masts, a deck, watertight bulkheads in the hold, a two-hundred to three-hundred man crew, fifty to sixty cabins,[217] are considered by Yule to have been in their time the greatest ships at sea anywhere in the world.[218] But such ships had already appeared in the accounts of Asian shipping centuries before,[219] and they appeared also in the notices dating from the sixteenth and seventeenth centuries,[220] and those from in the nineteenth.[221] Among their hundreds of passengers one must visualize tens and hundreds of traders, each one coming on board with his bales and packs[222] in the same way as the steerage passengers of the present day on the emigrant ships and in Asia the pilgrim ships to Mecca – the result of the large number of people involved in the trade on the one hand, and on the other of the limited opportunity for travel because of the periodicity of sailings in connection with the half-yearly winds controlling all shipping.

13

Trade, then, can be viewed as an 'historical constant'. No qualitative transformations can be indicated in the course of history; the basis, which was determined by the fixed rhythm of arrival and departure with the changing yearly monsoons, remained the afflux of larger or smaller crowds of pedlars of expensive and valuable high-quality products, and the only alterations were quantitative ones within the given framework. There could be variations in the state of trade: the markets could be crowded; ships could fail to come because of war, piracy, shipwreck, famine or epidemics in the ports or on the way; the volume of trade could increase or decrease; the rhythm of turnover could speed up or slow down somewhat – these are all of them always 'tendencies' in connection with which the 'market' has to be visualized in the most tangible sense of the word, the market square, on the beach, before the town ports, the narrow shop and warehouse streets in the town (the Hellenic *deigma*, the Moslem bazaar), the transactions in bargaining and selling taking place beside the supply of goods, in the booth, from person to person.[223]

An 'international trade', thus, a 'world trade'. Viewed in the forms advanced here as a hypothesis, the wondrous picture is explained of a trade which went its way from the one end of the world to the other, handling and transporting expensive merchandise, closing sales in royal courts and in patrician dwellings, winning riches, and at the same time exposing itself to perilous adventure[224] and suffering a wanderer's existence – a trade which was an affair of princes and lords and at the same time a powerless thing, a trade which seems to have been trifling and at the same time involved many people.[225] The cultural and historical value of that trade[226] is usually assessed as ten times higher than its economic value. It would, however, be incorrect to do as usually is done – to draw from its value for cultural history any conclusion as to an equal importance for economic history.

Chapter Three

INDONESIA AND THE TRADE ROUTE

To want to approach this world with such terms as 'Our Orient', 'the Netherlands East Indies', 'the Netherlands in the Tropics', and the like is to fail to appreciate the fact that it existed and was alive before a single Dutchman appeared in the tropics.

Colenbrander, *Geschiedenis*, II, 45.

I

The comparatively regular coastline of southern Asia trails off in the southeast into the world of the Indonesian Archipelago, abundantly irregular. One could draw a parallel – however halting a one – with the comparatively regular coasts of the western basin of the Mediterranean as set against the island world and the shores surrounding it in the eastern basin of the Aegean. The racial pattern of importance for southeast Asia in historical times has been formed by Indonesian ethnic groups. Migrating from the mainland of southeast Asia, they gradually gained control of the whole area as a region for colonization and domination.[1]

Earlier peoples had preceded them; migrations westward may also have taken place earlier. (Research in prehistory and anthropology will probably lead to further information on this.) An estimate based on geological and prehistorical material has fixed the date 2000 B.C. as the time the Indonesians arrived in the archipelago.[2]

The migrations must have taken place for a great part by sea. Sailing will undoubtedly have played an important rôle in organizing the colonization and providing means of existence. Despite the dangers inherent in drawing comparisons, I should like here to refer once again to Malinowski's description of the island region to the east of New Guinea as an illustration of the complexity with which a social structure and social-economic existence characterized by magical power – a society of 'savage' Papuas – can be interrelated, with navigation, interinsular communication, and shipowning.[3] And, after all, how close those sailors of the Kula are to the sailors of the earliest periods in the ancient Mediterranean world.

The 'historical development' of Indonesian colonization through the whole archipelago is a difficult subject even for historical hypothesis. Especially important historically, however, is the fact that the Indonesian sphere came to lie to the east of the mighty Indian sub-continent with its states, ports, shipping, and trade, while – probably about the beginning of the Christian era – the Chinese Empire had extended its borders into the plain of Tonkin. Even though the dates in history cannot be given with perfect precision, it can be assumed without any danger that about that same time the Indonesian Archipelago was reached by Indian trade – that is to say, the same trade already considered above especially in its relations with countries to the west: the powerful, wealthy, extensive overseas trade of the Indian coastal towns.[4] In my opinion there must have been Indian trade in the archipelago earlier than Chinese trade[5] – there were ports on the coast of India with a shipping actively involved in international trade long before there were on the south coast of China.[6] In Indonesia, as elsewhere, the trade was one in valuable high-quality products. In it spices, drugs, expensive sorts of wood, forest products, animal products, and exotic birds and other curiosities were shipped out from Indonesia and similar Indian and Near Eastern wares were brought in. There, as elsewhere, it was a trade "splendid and trifling".[7]

In the cultural history of Indonesia there are a number of very important problems linked to that trade, in the first place the problem of the influence of Indian civilization in Indonesia, an influence so important that a large part of Indonesia's early history is called Hindu-Indonesian history. Those ages were followed by a period of Islamic expansion, and colonial circumstances have changed the whole picture fundamentally, but the impressive temple remains of Barabudur and Angkor Wat are still standing in Indonesia and southern Indo-China as monuments of that past, and a remembrance of it lives on in various cultural forms on the island of Bali.

2

Various explanations of the influence of Indian civilization on Indonesia have been offered by way of hypothesis. Mookerji, who constructs a Hindu imperialism occupying the shores and hinterlands of Farther India and Indonesia through the course of the centuries from the fourth century A.D. up to the time of the Moslem invasions and conquests in India, goes the furthest in nationalistic self-exultation.[8] His view of things is not very clear, but in general tends to be an account of a process of colonization in the sense ascribed to Hellenic colonization from the middle of the eighth century to the end of the sixth century B.C.: organized migration of ethnic and/or class groups for political and belligerent purposes.[9]

This view has not been taken over by Dutch historians, but has been reinterpreted in the sense that:

> ...the adoption of Hindu civilization by leading [Indonesian] circles was a result of pacific penetration carried on by traders who after settling permanently perhaps had intermingled with the indigenous peoples and then perhaps had incited more countrymen, including non-traders, to follow their example.[10]

> ...a gradual infiltration by means of trade...[11]

Professor Berg would like to give a larger place to the belligerent element once more, and calls especial attention to the Indian aristocratic groups alongside or instead of the Indian traders as the leading transmitters of Indian civilization, and particularly as its representatives in Indonesia.[12]

None of these hypotheses seems to me satisfactory, at least none completely. In what follows a new view of the matter – but new only in the arrangement of material already available, for no new facts have been added – is developed.

3

Through trade Indonesia was linked with the Indian ports and later also became the trading area for the Chinese. (To what extent Indonesian shipping played an active rôle is a question never raised!) Trade connected the outstretched coasts of Indonesia with the west, and later with the north, as though by means of a gossamer, golden thread. The goods brought in and shipped out, together with the traders and the ships, converged at various larger and smaller stages on the trade route – settlements in Indonesia under an Indonesian government where peddling trade was crowded together around the staple. One must picture the trade of foreigners, chiefly Indians, in Indonesia as being carried on in the same way as the trade of foreigners, Phoenicians, under the shadow of the Hellenic noble or royal castle.[13] With regard to social-economic life, and thus with regard to trade – and international trade, the key to all that has been said above on the history of trade – the predominant position of rulers and lords ('headmen', in the colourless official Netherlands Indies terminology) should be taken as a starting point. This is also true with regard to the history of Indonesian trade. The dominant economic and political position of the ruling princes and aristocratic groups is a certainty for the whole early period of Indonesian history; it would appear to be the case just as well for later times, in the seventeenth and eighteenth centuries. Commercial domination was expressed in a number of forms: levies and tolls, enforced stapling, monopolization, exploitation of some kinds of production for sale in trade, occasional trade, shipowning, and *commenda* investments, and the practising of salvage rights and piracy as well. Only the definitive establishment of the Dutch colonial, military regime everywhere in the archipelago carried out in the nineteenth and twentieth centuries was able to break the dominating position of 'headmen' and 'native rulers'.[14] By that act of cutting off the Indonesian states large and small from independent international trade and independent shipping one of those states' chief sources of strength was drained away.

4

What should be understood by the 'primitive' society with which Indian and perhaps other traders travelling eastwards came in contact? In this point lies what is practically the key thesis of the following disquisition. There is too much uncertain in the premisses of the hypotheses put forward up to now.

Research regarding the Indonesian society of early historical times is still in a preliminary stage.[15] The research on the cultural situation on Java before the spread of Indian civilization undertaken by Brandes – a philologist! – in 1889 still served as the starting point for Krom's observations in 1926 and 1931.[16] Part of Brandes' Ten Points[17] have been contested, and part have appeared to be incorrect. Krom summarizes the 'pre-Hindu' cultural situation as follows:

> ... the settled population ... somewhat organized politically, applying the wet-field method of rice-growing with the complex system of irrigation accompanying it, possessing knowledge of navigation and the stars, working metals – bronze, copper, iron, and gold, – and probably holding domesticated cattle. On a part of Java the dead were entombed in megaliths of coffin and cromlech shapes; everywhere on the island terraces were built up or hacked out in the mountains as places of worship, probably ancestor worship especially, in which rough statues and piles of stones played a rôle. For the rest one may form something of a picture of the mental condition of the people from what ethnology indicates as general Indonesian; the early sources, however, are silent in that regard. Sumatra must in general have shown traits closely related to those of Java, even though there are also traces of yet other combinations and completely non-Javanese remains to be found.[18]

With that there is much said, very much, and at the same time little. Points of prime importance such as political organization, irrigation agriculture, navigation, and metalworking are supposed to have existed, to have been 'pre-Hindu', but their nature is not further examined. Judging from the evidence of these few stray forms, the 'pre-Hindu' communities would seem to have been already in essence on the same level as what is still encountered in social structure and social-economic life in many regions of Indonesia at the present time. From the existence of irrigation farming and the administrative system connected with it can be deduced the existence of patrimonial, bureaucratic states conceived on a larger or smaller scale,[19] and at the same time the most highly developed forms of village organization, with a nucleus of founding families, and village elders, a supervisor of lands, and perhaps patrimonially nominated headmen. From the existence of navigation can be deduced trade and the forms of social structure, inter-communication, and authority connected with it. From the existence of metalworking in well-organized villages under a stable authority can be deduced crafts, and a resultant multiformity in organization of communities and peoples.[20]

All this remains hypothesis, of course.[21] It finds support from two sides, however. In the first place, through nineteenth-century research in the Indonesian Archipelago there has come to light the abundant variety of organizational forms of peoples, political institutions, and social-economic life there, a variety which nevertheless has left the picture of an Indonesian ethnic unity intact. (An 'evolutionary' arrangement according to a system using the concept of 'stages' needs, of course, to be rejected.)[22] Although determining the antiquity of such organizational forms is a precarious affair,[23] they are in any case to be accepted as autochthonously and historically Indonesian, however much they may have been transformed or damaged by miscegenation and colonization, struggles between ethnic and class groups, catastrophes occurring in the course of history, and so forth. This basis of what is historically general Indonesian should be used as the starting point for all observations. No one would think of considering the organization of the Indonesian villages, the basis of the whole of Indonesian agrarian civilization, as an 'import' from elsewhere. And just as little the hundreds of special forms of social structure and social-economic organization in Indonesia. The system of family, clan, village, and village federation organizations in Minangkabau; the tribal groupings of Ceram; the class organizations on Leti and Timor; the complex of *gaukang* societies in southern Celebes and the class structure corollary to it; the institution of land supervisor on the islands of East Indonesia;

the form of nuclear villagers;[24] the Balinese irrigation association system; *sawah* cultivation outside Java (Palembang, Minahasa, Timor, the Karo region) are matters of a local, indigenous sort.[25] The interwovenness of systems of family law and social structure – the forms of authority and government in Minangkabau and the matriarchal system; such forms on Bali and the patriarchal system;[26] such forms on Timor and parental systems, both matriarchal and patriarchal – indicate just as many different processes of indigenous historical development. The occurence alongside each other of 'republican', 'monarchical', and 'oligarchical patrician' forms of government – 'republican' in the traditional indigenous tribal authority, and in village government in Minangkabau; 'monarchical' in the states of the Malays and on Timor; 'patrician' in the aristocratic societies of southern Celebes – also shows to what extent those forms of authority have developed individually and indigenously in history, each one under the prevailing tensions and balances of power of the groups involved.

Many another thing could be added to such a series. There can only be one conclusion, however – the Indonesian peoples, scattered over the islands of the archipelago, each group in its own historical and geographical *milieu*, have exhibited processes of long-lasting, independent historical 'development' in a multiplicity of forms of governmental, legal, and social organization and social-economic life, forms the inner power of which could vary according to circumstances, but which in the course of history have been subjected to the greatest tests of strength and have proved to have power of resistance.[27]

In the second place, though various forms of foreign culture and various world religions have successively exerted their influence on the region of Indonesia, the opinion is generally shared that these influences have remained weak despite centuries-long operation. They did not bring any fundamental changes in any part of Indonesian social and political order. The sheen of the world religions and foreign cultural forms is a thin and flaking glaze; underneath it the whole of the old indigenous forms has continued to exist – with many sorts of gradations appearing, of course, according to the cultural level. Magic and belief in spirits continued to exist under Hinduism and Islam; Indonesian popular law did not give way to Hindu or Moslem scholarly law. Furthermore, the circles which were 'conscious' representatives of foreign cultures and world religions were always small and limited. Krom and Berg agree on this as far as the sphere in which Indian civilization operated is concerned.[28] (As I shall discuss further below, it would be incorrect to think that it was always only the highest circles which must have been the representatives of such cultural forms.)

By way of summarizing this and bringing it into connection with the observations on Brandes' Ten Points, it occurs to me that in any discussion of the 'pre-Hindu' cultural situation in Indonesia – or at least on Java – the term 'primitive' needs to be discarded as suggesting a completely fallacious assumption and saying nothing.[29] One certainly would not have found oneself in the midst of savages.[30] Much more, even: the Indonesian social and political organization existed in all its multiformity and strength,[31] a strength which was nourished by the autonomous, indigenous order of things, a strength which was and remained sufficient unto itself.[32] The transformations which unmistakably took place in the traditional indigenous order followed their own fated course, quite separate from the course of foreign cultures and religions.[33]

5

The Aryan conquest and colonization of northern India resulted in the establishment of a number of states in the river plains, the old indigenous inhabitants of which were kept in a state of subjugation. From the position of the dominant groups as conquerors, the inter-ethnic relationship, and the Aryan aristocratic society divided into classes there grew the complex of ethnic and social structure which in India developed to such an unheard-of height of articulation and sharp division, the so-called caste system. In it the position of the ancient Aryan priesthood, the Brahmins, became an all-dominating one, growing in the course of the centuries, and especially in those just after the beginning of the Christian era.[34] This Aryan occupation did not expand further than to the plains of northern India as colonization. The Deccan Plateau and the southern Indian coastal regions remained Dravidian, traditional and indigenous in their whole complex of ethnic structure and regal authority. Indian civilization, however, continued to move further southwards.[35] The chief disseminator of the process of 'Indianization' was the Brahman priesthood; the aim of the 'Brahman mission' was not the preaching of any revealed doctrine of salvation, but the ritualistic and bureaucratic subjugation and organization of the newly entered regions.[36] Wherever the process of 'Indianization' took place, 'religious' organization was accompanied by social organization – division in castes, legitimation of the ruling groups, assurance of the supremacy of the Brahmins. The colossal magical, ritualistic power of the Brahman priesthood was the most characteristic feature of early Indian history. The rationalistic, bureaucratic schooling of the priesthood as the intellectual group, which went to make up its great worth, its indispensability even, for any comprehensive governmental organization, was there (as elsewhere in the world in organized hierocracies) interwoven with the sacerdotal function. The Brahman priesthood developed high qualities in that field as well, but its decisive influence came from the magical, ritualistic power of domestication which it in the absoluteness of its power was able to develop.

Under such conditions Indian civilization expanded over southern India:

> As the Slavic princes of the East called into their lands German priests, knights, merchants, and peasants, so the kings of the East Ganges plain and of Southern India from the Tamils to the southern tip called upon Brahmans trained in writing and administration. Their services were enlisted to assist the prince in the formal organization, in the Hindu manner, of his patrimonial bureaucratic rule and status structure and to consecrate the prince as a legitimate Raja or Maharaja in the sense of the Hindu Dharmashastras, Brahmanas, and Puranas. Telling documents of land-grants, issued occasionally to dozens, even to hundreds,

of obviously immigrant Brahmans at once, are found dispersed throughout India.[37]

The process of Hinduization was going on for southern India around the beginning of the Christian era.[38] It continued through the centuries, so that now the whole social structure of southern India is that of the caste system, in that not intrinsically different from northern India, the classical home of Indian civilization.

Southern India was the trading region for Indonesia;[39] the shipping to the east went especially from the southern Indian ports. By means of that trade, whether carried on as Indonesian shipping[40] or through the intermediacy of Indian shipping, the Indonesian rulers and aristocratic groups came in contact with India, perhaps seeing it with their own eyes. In the same sort of attempt at legitimizing their interests involved in 'international trade' (in the first place *vis-à-vis* Indian traders themselves), and (though this was probably of secondary importance) organizing and domesticating their states and subjects, they called Indian civilization to the east – that is to say, they summoned the Brahman priesthood to their courts.[41]

6

There were, then, no 'Hindu colonization' in which 'colonial states' arose from intermittent trading voyages followed by permanent trading settlements; no 'Hindu colonies' from which the primitive indigenous population and first of all its headmen took over the superior civilization from the west; and no learned Hindus in the midst of Indian colonists as 'advisers' to their contrymen.

Trade and the trader have been viewed as the supreme disseminators of Hindu culture. It is ominous that that trade has not anywhere been defined in detail historically, neither by Krom, nor Rouffaer, nor Berg. If that had been done, the impossibility of traders having figured in such a rôle would have appeared. The majority of the traders in the peddling trade belonged to the lower social groups, and foreigners from all sorts of countries were intermingled with them.[42] The same thing held for the crews of the ships, often African negroes and slaves. It is impossible for such people to have been administrators of ritual, magical consecration and disseminators of rationalistic, bureaucratic written scholarship and wisdom.[43] As can be seen in the case of Çriwijaya in the seventh century and Bantam in the sixteenth, Indian trade, with its populous 'caravan' forms and its participants from all the shores of India as well as from other lands, established itself in villages or city quarters – *kampongs* in the colourless Netherlands Indies terminology – or in the neighbourhood of royal seats or cities with aristocratic courts and quarters. The traders were as far separated from the ruler and his court as were the subjects of the ruler.[44] This does not exclude the transference of a number of cultural influences:[45] precisely because of the dominant position the rulers and nobles held in international trade, the most prominent of the foreign merchants will have always gone to court,[46] the same as the officials of the rulers and the nobles, and if necessary the latter themselves, will have gone to the market to carry on trade, to make purchases, or to obstruct trade for the benefit of their own transactions.[47] A large amount of cultural influence will have been transmitted by trade and the traders in this way. But as regards the specifically Indian cultural forms – in which, as even the oldest inscriptions extant unanimously bear witness,[48] what was involved was the ritualistic, magical legitimation of the ruler, the offerings, the consecration formulae, the classical, mythological genealogy of the ruling house[49] – it must be considered completely out of the question that traders, even if they had been rich merchant gentlemen, should have participated in such things repeatedly and in a way defined in so much detail. It can only have been the work of Brahmins.[50] But the Brahmins were just as far removed from the traders as were the Indonesian rulers and lords,[51] and they must have stressed that more than ever in their contacts with the Dravidian population of Hinduized southern India to which the traders for the most part belonged.[52] A view of the situation such as that of Krom therefore seems to me to be inaccurate to the core.[53]

The whole concept of a Hindu colonization and the rise of a ruling 'half-breed' Hindu-Indonesian class as a result of 'miscegenation' between the representatives of Hindu culture, chiefly traders, and the 'highest levels' of Indonesian society needs to be abandoned.[54] Such a concept is unhistorical, above all because of the inaccurate use of the category 'trade'. (Remarkably enough, the anthropological element has never been further elucidated – if the representatives of Hindu culture were southern Indian in origin, then it should be possible to make out a fairly strong admixture of Dravidian elements through the centuries. Has such a possibility ever even been considered?)

7

The concept of Hindu colonization – with its corollary that new reserves from India were constantly replenishing the higher ranks of the Hindu-Indonesian organization through the centuries, so that when Islam (or in some versions the Portuguese) came to 'dominate the seas' and no new crossings of emigrants could take place any longer, the 'half-breed' regime weakened and then decayed and collapsed[55] – seems improbable when seen in the light of Indonesian migration and colonization forms.[56]

Indonesian migrations were numerous, and of every sort.[57] There were three main types. First of all, colonization by large groups, emigrants from one region who settled down in another. Trade could play a dominant rôle in such migrations, but it goes without saying that the groups always took along the other forms of their social organization as well: family law, crafts, land law, and so forth – which, it goes again without saying, underwent changes in the region where they settled. There were, for example, the Minangkabau and Malay colonies to the north and the south on the west coast of Sumatra, in the river valleys of the Jambi region, to the east of the highlands of Minangkabau, on the Malay Peninsula, on Madagascar, perhaps on Timor, and on many another island in the archipelago;[58] the Buginese settlements in central and northern Celebes and on Riau;[59] the migrations in the islands of East Indonesia.[60] Chinese colonization in Indonesia also belongs in this category.

The second type was the emigration of individuals. The settlement of foreign traders is above all related to this type. The foreigners formed 'colonies' or 'quarters' – *kampongs*, – had their own administration and authorities and their own law, and, to put it grandiloquently, enjoyed a certain degree of exterritoriality.[61] The Indonesians in other countries[62] and – on exactly the same footing – the Indians, Arabs, and Chinese in Indonesia and elsewhere were examples of the type. The forms of settlement have already been discussed.

The third type, in this connection of great importance, was that of establishment of authority in foreign regions – for example, that of the Malay coastal states on Borneo, the Buginese states in eastern Sumbawa and western Flores and on the islands of Riau and Lingga, and the Balinese control of Lombok.[63] And, in connection with that, colonial occupation and the subjugation of overseas and inland regions – the system of 'representative headmen', the form of Achinese supremacy over the Gayo, Alas, Karo, Simelungun, and Toba Batak regions; the provincial governors from the Malay coastal states of Sumatra in the hinterlands; the 'state commissioners' of Siak over the Minangkabau colonies there; heads of provinces of the Malay states held in apanage on Borneo and their Malay tax collectors over the Dyak tribes (along with the Malay village settlements there with their Malay village headmen, examples of the first type); the authorities from the small coastal states in the southern curve of the Gulf of Tomini over the mountain tribes of Torajas; the 'intermediary heads' and state representatives of Ternate and Tidore on Halmaheira, Buru, and the coast of New Guinea.[64]

There is a definite historical basis for these types, however much uncertainty there may be regarding exact historical dating.[65] They reveal the historical forms of colonization and colonial conquest as they appear in the few rare data from early Indonesia and as they are familiar from elsewhere in history: in the Hellenic colonization overseas to the west and the north, the Norse colonization of Iceland, the German migrations to the east in the middle ages, the *conquista* from Spain and Portugal to the west and the southwest.[66] In surveying the Indonesian forms one is constantly struck by the survival and strength of the traditional indigenous organizational forms, by the clear and colourful configurations wherever other forms by might and main superimposed themselves on the existing ones[67] and under the tension of new adjustments created a new pattern, and by the durability of the forms when transferred outside Indonesia. Indonesian customs, forms of administration, law, and material culture have continued to exist, and though they have manifested changes in changed circumstances, their continuity has remained a certainty.

With this schema of Indonesian and other historical relationships in mind, let us look once more at the concept of 'Hindu colonization'. It is not possible to believe that there could have been a political invasion from India arriving by way of the trade route (which continued to be heavily travelled, perhaps constantly more heavily travelled, down through the ages), without its having left relics or lasting after-effects, documentary remains[68] or a deep imprint on the land and people of Indonesia. One must therefore reject the idea of an Indian political imperialism.[69]

Nor is it possible to believe that there could have been colonization by large groups of Indians following the trade route and keeping in constant contact with India *via* it, without their having brought with them all the forms of their own cities and countrysides: their caste system (the real one, including all levels of society), their crafts, their house[70] and town building, their vernacular language,[71] traditional law,[72] and political organization. There is not a trace of such a thing to be found.[73] Furthermore, such group colonization does not necessarily lead to political expansion in a foreign country and supremacy over it, as is proved by the situation of Chinese group colonization in Indonesia.

There remains the other form, the emigration of individuals, the colonies of traders and other foreigners. Such colonies still exist in the present day, those of Indians too, but the *kampong keling*, the *pekojan*, with its own way of life, its own customary law and habits, its completely indigenous Indian cultural pattern,[74] had next to no contact with Indonesian life.[75] And it is precisely in the *kampong keling* that Indian international trade must be sought;[76] there were located the transit point, the market, the harbour. And this was true in Semarang in 1898 – even though it was a dead settlement with the international trade wasted away, not because of Islam but because of modern-capitalistic trade and shipping – just as well as in Bantam in 1596, in Malacca in 1511, in Çriwijaya in 900,[77] and in the Indonesian ports of the fifth century and earlier when the first epigraphic and sacral relics indicate Indian cultural influence in Indonesia. But no decisive Indian cultural influence on the courts of rulers and nobles originated from the trading quarters and foreign quarters.[78] No power to recite consecration formulas and issue royal edicts and charters of consecration, all of them in the sacral language, and to supervise sacral building, with all its systematic magical, geomantic ritual, came from there. Krom's reasoning that "such cultural influences can be satisfactorily explained from trade relations"[79] therefore seems to me incorrect. There cannot and should not be any causal connection made between trade relations and the sort of writing used for charters of consecration.[80]

8

The initiative for the coming of Indian civilization emanated from the Indonesian ruling groups, or was at least an affair of both the Indonesian dynasties and the Indian hierocracy.[81] That cultural influence had nothing directly to do with trade.[82] The course of events amounted essentially to a summoning to Indonesia of Brahman priests, and perhaps alongside them of Indian *condottieri*[83] and Indian court artificers[84] (whose position in the court can probably best be imagined by the analogy of the culdees in the period of early medieval architecture in northern Europe, as artificers a branch of the famed Irish missionary church).[85]

This process took place in southern India, Ceylon, and Farther India as well as in Indonesia and southern Indo-China.[86] The

Indian priesthood was called eastwards – certainly because of its wide renown – for the magical, sacral legitimation of dynastic interests and the domestication of subjects, and probably for the organization of the ruler's territory into a state. Alongside the priesthood, Indian artifice came to the royal courts,[87] and the architectural activities of the rulers and the official religious activities of those overseas states alike show the unmistakable imprint of Indian civilization on Ceylon, Indonesia, Farther India, and southern Indo-China.

One must imagine that southeast Asia was 'Hinduized' in the same way the German civilization of the middle ages extended its influence far beyond the limits of German group colonization, in the same way the Graeco-Byzantine hierocracy set its stamp on the civilization of Russia.[88] It was, as Huber has stated it, a "...Brahmanic civilization ... in its conquest of the Southern seas..."[89]

9

None of the facts of Hindu-Indonesian history are opposed to such an hypothesis: on the contrary, only with it is the historical picture clarified.

Some of the oldest epigraphic remains in Indonesia found up to the present time come from regions which have never occupied an important place in later periods. In others, however, the forms appear which were to dominate early Indonesian history – the Javanese states, with a focal point shifting from central to eastern Java, and the Sumatran state Çriwijaya, on the Palembang River. Here the untenability of the colonization hypothesis – trade shipping, a permanent trade settlement or colonization, formation of colonial states by means of peaceful penetration – appears clearly. Here are two clearly outlined forms in opposition to each other. On the one hand the Javanese states, centred in the interior regions in the plains between the volcanoes, difficult to reach from the coast, their power and wealth based on the Indonesian agrarian civilization of those regions, from the time of the earliest data on revealing the type of an *oikos* state, a state based on levies and soccage, with an administrative machinery expanding in patrimonial, bureaucratic forms, a state with a hierarchy of officials.[90] On the other hand the Sumatran state, a coastal state, a 'commercial power', a 'sea power'[91] lying open on the river close to the sea, basing its might and wealth on the stapling of the international trade of southeast Asia, an expansive maritime power, revealing in its structure certainly not the picture of a patrimonial, bureaucratic hierarchy, but – insofar as the scarce data make any picture possible – a closed aristocratic community as the backbone of royal authority.

In this connection the following details regarding Çriwijaya are certain. The royal authority based its power on the compulsory stapling it enforced upon the international trade of southeast Asia. Military and maritime force was used without hesitation to maintain that power. There were tributary overseas possessions, and overseas predatory expeditions.[92] Ships were owned by the ruler, perhaps by him alone. Military power was supplied by the nobility, perhaps in conjunction with the ruler's own troops. The trading section of the town revealed forms characteristic for an international peddling trade carried on by a multitude of people from countries everywhere.[93]

The following hypothesis may serve to explain the origin of Çriwijaya. The ruling Indonesian authority would seem to have arisen in the way sketched several times above – a group of people under the authority of an aristocratic community ('headmen') took up navigation and trade. It was the same process the stages of which can be traced later in Indonesia. The ability of the aristocratic community to amass wealth from personal trade, levies on transit trade, war, and plunder was the chief mobile basis of its power.[94] The fighting forces of the state, consisting of a 'militia' equipped by the nobility alongside the ruler's own troops, made up a military organization which formed a basis for a relationship similar to that between ruler and nobles in the ports of northern Java in the fifteenth and sixteenth century. The notice written in 1226 by Chau Ju-kua should be seen in that light:

> When they are about to make war on another state they assemble and send forth such a force as the occasion demands. They (then) appoint chiefs and leaders, and all provide their own military equipment and the necessary provisions.[95]

The Arabian account of the 'streets' with merchants and traders and the 'streets of moneychangers' where eight hundred moneychangers exercised their profession is characteristic for the trade concentrated in the city, huddled around the staple. The number may be apocryphal, but one account such as this calls to mind with a single stroke the familiar picture of handicraft trade, trifling, splendid, international. The chief sphere of power for Çriwijaya was the river and the sea. The hinterlands of Sumatra had been subjugated, but they did not form the heart of the state. Because of its political and social structure as a coastal settlement with a non-intensive exercise of authority, Çriwijaya despite fabulous wealth did not possess the power, the 'manpower', posessed by the states of the Javanese interior, which was expressed especially in the building of monuments. Only a bureaucratic hierarchy can collect and exploit the economic and technological capacities of a great agrarian civilization. Coedès points in that direction in his comment:

> If it [*i.e.*, Çriwijaya] left behind only an insignificant number of archeological monuments and inscriptions, that is clearly because its kings were more occupied with supervising the trade of the straits than with constructing temples or having their praises engraved in stone. In this regard the nearness of Java, completely covered with archeological remains, certainly put it at a disadvantage in the eyes of history.[96]

But in the Çailendra period on Java, when the interior central Javanese state was under the supremacy of Çriwijaya, it was possible for great edifices – Barabudur, Chandi Mendut, the Chandi Sewu complex – to be constructed there to the glory of the doctrine of Buddhism, and of the Mountain Lords, its protectors in southeast Asia. Krom's reasoning in this regard[97] seems to me incorrect. The fact that a Barabudur arose on Java and not on Sumatra is linked to the fact that the concentration of labour needed could be achieved on Java, in a state with soccage and an officialdom, and not on Sumatra, either in the city on rafts on the Palembang River or in the sparsely populated highlands of the interior.[98] The relationship of the supreme authority on Sumatra and the subordinate authority on Java, where the machinery of the patrimonial, bureaucratic state was maintained intact – in the following period, when 'independence' was regained, it mobilized the labour to build the just as great Çiwaitic complexes – can be thought of as being analogous to that of the *polis* Rome and its province Egypt. Here opposing each other geographically and historically are two powerful indigenous Indonesian types of authority the process of formation of which must have stretched over centuries. (Probably the Javanese type must be considered the older.)[99] It is impossible to bring a colonization by traders into any relation with this.[100]

10

In consideration of the nature of power relationships and economic structure as well as the nature of Indian culture overseas, the road from the settlement of 'Hindu' traders – after all a meaningless term – to the royal court must be deemed an impossible one. Trade was to be sought in the quarter of traders and foreigners, the *kampong keling*. Indian culture was to be sought at the royal court and in the temples, monasteries, and hermitages. And because of the sociological structure of the groups representative of Indian culture and Indian trade, there was no link at all between the two phenomena. What expressions of Indian civilization there were in early Indonesia were without exception sacral, either as ritual or as literature. As Krom has said, "...the things of the spirit are of Indian origin..."[101]

Krom, using the 'colonization' hypothesis once more to explain the situation in early central Java, comments with reference to Brandes' theory that "a new emigration of Hindu colonists" had taken place there:

> the assumption of such a new influx [seems] indeed the most probable one. There would not even have had to be so many individuals, but there

would have had to be disseminators of culture *par excellence*, persons from whom a great spiritual power radiated. Political authorities are certainly out of the question; the organization in Farther India as well as on Java has remained in innumerable ways far too 'native' for that.[102]

Such a view of things approaches almost to the point of identity the hypothesis defended here: a Javanese state, a Javanese court at which the Indian higher clergy moved, fulfilling sacral and bureaucratic functions.

With reference to a charter of a Çiwaitic foundation in central Java dating from 760, Krom remarks:

... the elaborate ceremonial with its priests skilled in the *Rig Vedas* and its various sorts of offerings belongs to a society thoroughly Hinduized, at least as far as the outward forms of religion are concerned...[103]

With the exception that the 'society' was not Hinduized, but that an Indonesian dynasty on Java was legitimized sacrally by an Indian hierocracy, this fits perfectly into the picture developed above as an hypothesis.

With reference to the early central Javanese inscription from Changgal, dating from 732, on the foundation of a Çiwaitic sanctuary by the ruler, which reports the establishment of a *linga* and alongside eulogies for prince and country gives information on the Indian origin of the Çiwa cult adhered to on Java, Krom adds the following reasoning:

In any case King Sanjaya and his followers traced their worship of Çiwa back to that of Kunjarakunja, and with that point of origin for the ancestral religious practice a point of origin for the very coming of those ancestors is also given. Since the family is not traced further than the king's father it would seem that it did not reach back further and that that father, possibly a participant in the new influx of Hindus [see above], was the first of the dynasty on Java; opposed to that, however, is the fact that according to the Chinese the central Javanese Ho-ling had already long been in existence and would continue to be known under the same name. But, whether it should be dated earlier or later, Kunjarakunja at last gives a name, a clue to the origin of the Hindu immigrants, and fortunately there is no longer any doubt as to the identity of the region. It is an area in southern India appearing as Kunjaradari and mentioned in the *Brhatsamhita* (24:16) as between Kach and Tamraparni. The mountain to which that region owes its renown is located exactly on the

> border of Travancore and Tirunelveli, for there on the Podiyan stands the hermitage of the great seer Agastya, who once carried Hindu civilization to southern India and is still deemed to have his dwelling there. Therefore it is to be expected that a cult of Çiwa originating from there would also include worship of Agastya; thus, then, Agastya will have been the Brahmin who functioned as the ... intermediary at the investiture of the king and in any case it is certain ... that Java worshipped Agastya. Thus, alongside the data discussed earlier pointing toward southern India as the origin of the Hindu colonists, on the authority of the Changgal inscription there is now added the certainty that people in 732 were well aware of having received their cult of Çiwa from the land of Agastya, also in southern India.[104]

Here one is once more struck by the historically and sociologically irresponsible construction of trading colonies of Dravidians out of which a Dravidian ruler of Java was to have sprung, alongside an Indian hierocracy, in this case a most distinguished sect of Çiwaites, probably descendants of Aryans from northern India. However, if one lets drop the whole colonization hypothesis and considers the Indonesian ruler on Java as a person who had royal investiture conferred on him – what a powerful sacral legitimation in the eyes of persons coming overseas from India, in the eyes of strangers and perhaps of southern Indian rulers! – and a mythological Indian genealogy assigned to him[105] by the Indian priesthood, in this case the important southern Indian Çiwaitic sect of Agastya, and who for his part endowed the hierocracy with prebends out of the plenitude of his power: then the whole picture is explained not only more accurately, but in much clearer historical forms.[106]

II

The ruler, for his part, guaranteed the economic existence of the hierocracy.[107] And authority and hierocracy, both of them based on the power to exploit the Indonesian agrarian civilization and/or international trade, dominated early Indonesian history politically and culturally. The Javanese states were examples of the first type; Çriwijaya of the second. The great differences between these two types of states, added to the differences in geographic *milieu*, should make one shrink from applying the theory of colonization to them, left utterly lacking in precision as it has been. Schrieke, going in the direction of precision, comments:

> The forms of the 'caste system' which the Hindu immigrants introduced to the inhabitants of the archipelago were not primarily theoretical schemas of the lawbooks, but forms corresponding to the social structure of their Indian homeland. Therefore a knowledge of the social structure in Coromandel and Gujarat at the time of the emigration is indispensable for determining the nature of that foreign influence.[108]

In this hypothesis a shift has already been made from trading settlement (the first type listed above) to group colonization (the second type), while on the one hand not a trace of group colonization is to be found through all the long centuries of continuous Indian trade and Indian-Indonesian civilization, and on the other hand the Indian cultural influence in Indonesia had no sociological basis at all in colonization, but was an affair of the hierocracy. It can be seen to what an *impasse* further elaboration of the colonization hypothesis leads.

The whole early Indonesian culture was a courtly one, the creation of the rulers, the possession and exclusive craft of the hierocracy: monuments (sanctuaries, monasteries, hermitages, burial temples, tower temples, bathing places), literature, theological writings, and the study of law.[109] The whole culture of prince and priest stood towering far above the Indonesian population.[110] It was not its cultural possession.[111] Its function was only to render service and to pay levies.[112] The recollection of the ancient Near Eastern and Indian soccage state or liturgical state constantly comes to mind. The continuity of Indonesian history, or at least of the patrimonial, bureaucratic structure, is an established fact.[113] (To qualify the Hindu-Javanese era as 'medieval' or to distinguish a period 'middle ages' in it therefore seems to me a perverse usage of such an historical category. No use is ever made of other periods of history taken over by analogy.)

12

Linked to the preceding question is a second question related to the trade route – the question of how Islam was spread. Here too it seems to me that in consideration of the nature of international Asian trade a new hypothesis can be substituted for the existing ones.

Through the ages international trade bound the various parts of Asia together and linked them to the shores of the Near East as though with gossamer, golden threads. With the changes in dynasties and religions trade went on, carrying many cultural elements in its train. The preceding sections of this chapter have been an attempt at laying the proper historical relation between the trade route and Brahmanic culture in southeast Asia. That cultural influence was one of several which took ship and went overseas in something of the same way the Apostle Paul undertook his journey from Caesarea to Rome first in an Adramyttian ship and then in a grain ship from Alexandria. In the course of the centuries Buddhist pilgrims, Arab and Persian traders, and Franciscan and Dominican missionaries[114] travelled along the same eastern trade route. And Islam, too, followed the route to the east.

Arab and Persian shipping appears as a rule not to have made its way further than the ports of western and southern India. Arab and Persian traders, however, followed the trade route all the way to the Chinese ports. There seems to have been an Arab trading colony established in Canton as early as the fourth century.[115] Settlements of Arab traders were mentioned again in 618 and 626.[116] In later years the colonies carried on Moslem religious practices and were under Moslem control. The Arabs were one group among several: Persians, Jews, Armenians, Nestorian Christians.[117] It goes without saying that there were also Moslem colonies to be found at the intermediary stations on the long trade route in southeast Asia.[118] That there are allusions to Arab settlements or colonies on the west coast of Sumatra as early as 674 A.D.,[119] and that Arab tombstones dating from 1082 on Java and 1039 in Champa have been discovered[120] are therefore nothing out of the ordinary as evidence of settlements of Arab traders, perhaps with their families.[121] The complete internationality of trade from earliest times on is certain.

There had, then, been Moslem trade involved in the traffic of the Indonesian ports for centuries without there having been question of missions and conversions to Islam to any appreciable degree. Toward the end of the thirteenth century a change began to take place, however, a change which developed rapidly in the fourteenth century and became the dominating phenomenon in Indonesia in the fifteenth and sixteenth centuries.

Trade itself did not play an independent rôle in the change. The trade of the Moslems was no more directly related to the conquests of Islam in southeast Asia than Indian trade had been related to the expansion of Brahmanic culture there. In this case, too, trade and faith need to be kept separated. Nor did Islam bring 'economic development' to Indonesia. The Islamization of Indonesia was a development determined step for step by political situations and political motives.

At the end of the thirteenth century rulers of some newly-arisen coastal states in northern Sumatra adopted Islam.[122] With the political decline of the ports across the straits, on southern Sumatra,[123] the new trading settlement Malacca developed quickly and was nourished in its growing strength by the powerful trade movement of the fifteenth century. Its dynasty[124] then adopted Islam[125] and used it as a political instrument against Indian trade – in which the Moslem trade from the ports of northwest India was at that time taking a chief position,[126] – against Siam and China, and against the Hindu regime on Java. The ruler was thus assured of the backing of powerful allies in the west[127] and was given admittance to the unity of Islam, the political influence of which was then expanding into Indonesia.[128] In India, as a result of the constant wars between Moslem and Hindu princes and Moslem dynasties among themselves, anarchy reigned. Through the course of events in India the influence of Brahmanic civilization as a political and ideological factor in southeast Asia must have decreased steadily. The decline in Brahmanic political and hierocratic power reached its end with the establishment of Mogol authority in 1526 and the fall of the kingdom of Vijayanagar in 1556. All that together gave Islam its chance in Indonesia.

From Malacca it reached the coastal ports of northeastern Java. Rising with the overseas trade, the Javanese aristocratic families there had grown in power,[129] owning ships, carrying on personal trade, investing in *commenda*, exploiting and monopolizing the staple trade from and to East Indonesia and Malacca. They had their own slave troops, perhaps already using the new military technique of firearms.[130] The antithesis between the aristocratic families and the central authority of Majapahit, and the aspirations of the families to exercise their own supreme authority over the state,[131] made Islamization into a political instrument. Like the dynasty of Malacca, but for Javanese political motives, the aristocratic communities striving upwards accepted Islam out of opposition to the Hindu central authority. Later a new factor appeared in the arrival of the Portuguese in the Far East, leading to the fall of Malacca in 1511. With that Islam and political and military motives become completely entangled with each other, and the great struggle between Moslems and Christians was then carried from one end of Asia to the other.

13

The most important point in this connection, however, is the sociological structure of Islamic missionary activities. It has already been touched upon above that it is dangerous to make a comparison between 'Moslemization' and 'Hinduization'. Krom treats the two processes in the same way:

> Traders from India and Malacca settled on Java, just as in turn a large Javanese colony lived in a quarter of Malacca at the beginning of the sixteenth century. Marriages of the foreigners with maidens of the country had the same results as earlier with the establishment of Hinduism, and as far as religion is concerned the effect must have been even more immediate, since the wife of a Mohammedan must after all have embraced Islam herself.[132]

Leaving out of consideration for the moment its historical value for Indian civilization, the argument advanced regarding Hinduization, that of the 'higher civilization' of the traders in opposition to the 'primitiveness' of the Indonesians, does not apply to the

Indonesians of the time of Moslem missionary activities. Even if it should be accepted that the Moslem traders from India and Persia[133] were 'highly civilized' – a supposition very much open to doubt, – they still had over against them, or rather above them, the aristocratic Indonesian families of the port towns of Java, who were at least as highly civilized, moreover maintaining strong patrician and feudal traditions. The acceptance of Islam on Java had nothing to do with the transmission of a 'higher civilization'. Javanese political motives and tactical considerations of the aristocracy brought about Islamization.

There is something more, however. The great mistake in the reasoning of Krom and other historians lies in the fact that the Indian ritual and literary sacral culture of Hinduism transmitted by the powerful groups of the Brahmanic priesthood – certainly not by overseas traders – had nothing to do with 'religion' in the sense that Islam is a religion. Islam is a prophetic doctrine revealing the way to salvation and redemption – in that bearing intact the stamp of the Jewish and Christian doctrines of revelation which served as examples for it, – and through its eschatological and soteriological nature it bears the characteristics typical of an expansive missionary religion. Along with that also comes the fact that Islam does not have an exclusive, magical *charisma* of the priest such as that of Catholic Christianity, but has remained a missionary community in the early Christian sense. Because of the expansive, missionary nature of Islam, every Moslem is after all a propagandist of the faith. That is why the trader from the Moslem world was the most common 'missionary' figure in foreign regions. That is why in this case the faith was certain to follow the routes of trade.

Hinduism is as completely the opposite to that as is imaginable. In the first place it did not possess an expansive soteriological and prophetic mission – at least not in the periods here under discussion – and the bearers of its doctrine possessed an extremely powerful exclusive, magical *charisma*, a *charisma* reinforced by the ritual, hereditary group divisions of the caste system. For that reason Hinduism never followed the routes of trade in the sense that traders were its missionaries. They could not have been: that task was reserved for the Brahmins alone.[134]

For a better understanding of the historical position of Islam in an Indonesia of a Brahman culture, the parallel might be drawn – in its consequences admittedly a dangerous one – that Islam was a Calvinistic mission of simple preachers like the first Reformed preachers in northern Europe, directing itself against the Roman Catholic hierarchy of a Hindu-Indonesian hierocracy: it was Datheen and Hembyse against Granvelle. The Javanese aristocracy, who wished to gain control of the central power, used the new religion for political motives: Van Brederode and Jan and Philips van Marnix against the Brussels government.

To what extent Moslem missionary activities brought about 'conversions' is not clear from the source material. It is no more to be believed for Indonesia than for elsewhere that they were directed at the masses of the people.[135] Commercial and other motives of Gujarati Moslems[136] regarding the trade of the Javanese ports and the lords of the trade there, the Javanese patriciate; political motives of that patriciate regarding the international trade and the government of Majapahit – those two factors together brought about the Islamization of Indonesia. In the disturbances of the sixteenth century, with first the state of constant war against the Christians and then the hard struggle against the Dutch Company dominating social, economic, and political life in Indonesia, Islam became entirely a political affair, and exclusively an affair of the aristocracy, the people in political power.[137]

Islam did not bring a 'higher civilization'. On the contrary; that was already excluded by the position of the 'missionaries'. That much of the Hindu-Indonesian cultural tradition has been preserved is to be explained by the position of the Javanese aristocracy-turned-Moslem as the dominant group from the ranks of which the rulers and the officials of the new Moslem central government came, so that the Indian-Indonesian cultural heritage of the inland states was preserved in the patrimonial, bureaucratic structure of the administrative state.[138]

Nor did Islam bring 'economic development'.[139] The trade and transportation forms remained the same as they had been traditionally. It is impossible to indicate any economic form or any form in commercial law that may have come to Indonesia with Islam as a new and more highly developed phenomenon. Furthermore Chinese trade continued to dominate an important part of Indonesian commerce, so that Chinese commercial forms were valid in that sphere. No influence of Arabian or any other Near Eastern customary law can be traced in Indonesian law. Moslem law remained scholarly law with a very limited validity and lacking any influence on cardinal points.

Chapter Four

Indonesian Trade and the Coming of the Europeans

I

In 1498 the ruler of Melinde had supplied the seafarers on the Portuguese ships of Vasco da Gama, lying offshore, with a pilot for the voyage to Calicut, and the pilot, a Moslem from Gujarat, had come aboard. When Da Gama showed him his astronomical instruments, among them some wood-and-metal astrolabes, "The Moor did not manifest any astonishment at seeing such instruments..."[1] This incident is characteristic of the whole position of the European shipping newly come to Asian waters. After journeying through the inhospitable seas of southern Africa the Portuguese ships had come into regions where there was a complex of shipping, trade, and authority as highly developed as the European:[2] forms of political capitalism as least as large in dimensions as those of southern Europe, and probably larger; shipping in bottoms many of them carrying more than those used in European merchant shipping; a trade in every conceivable valuable high-quality product carried on by a great multitude of traders; merchant gentlemen and harbour princes wielding as great financial power as did the merchants and princes of Europe. By conquering the chief strategic points on the Asian sea routes, the Portuguese succeeded in establishing a colonial domain in that world, a weak empire[3] which nevertheless was able to maintain itself with great vitality for a century. The Portuguese colonial regime, built by and upon war, coercion, and violence, did not at any point signify a stage of 'higher development' economically for Asian trade. The traditional commercial structure continued to exist,[4] however much damaged by religious wars breaking out between Moslems and Christians. Trade did not undergo any increase in quantity worthy of mention in the period.[5] The commercial and economic forms of the Portuguese colonial regime were the same as those of Asian trade and Asian authority: a trade relatively small in volume, conducted by the government as a private enterprise,[6] and all further exercise of authority existing only to insure the financial, fiscal exploitation of trade, shipping, and port traffic,[7] with the higher officials and religious dignitaries recruited from the Portuguese aristocracy. Official exploitation, the economic policy of the colonial regime, was feudal, then, not bourgeois commercial.[8] The farming of revenues on a large scale in practice transferred the exploitation to the Indian and Persian Moslem wealthy merchants. The ordinary Portuguese 'free burghers' – to use the Dutch Company term – carried on their handiwork, shipping, and craft trading side by side with and together with Asians.[9] Ethnic intermixture took place on a large scale.

The Portuguese colonial regime, then, did not introduce a single new economic element into the commerce of southern Asia. The forms of political and economic domination – monopolies, financial exploitation, 'fiscalization' of the government – all of them originated in the caliphates and Byzantium, and were transferred to Portugal, and perhaps carried on there, by Jews and Italians.[10] The political power of the Portuguese, based on their military superiority, now made possible the large-scale application of those forms in Asia. That military superiority was the only thing the Portuguese carried overseas to Asia as a new and European element.[11] Though the Portuguese period was the first of the European colonial periods which from then on were to decide the fate of Asia, this fact serves to separate it from the following, second period, that of Dutch and English overseas voyages and colonial settlement, and to link it in spirit and forms to the previous periods, those of purely Asian trade.[12] The Portuguese regime only introduced a non-intensive drain on the existing structure of shipping and trade. The next period would in its time organize a new system of foreign trade and foreign shipping, it would call into life trenchant colonial relationships, and it would create new economic forms in Europe – not perhaps as a direct result but rather as a parallel development bolstered by the system. Not Lisbon and Seville, but Amsterdam, Middelburg, Enkhuizen, and London were among the heralds of a new era.

2

Such, in cursory outline, were the main features of the Portuguese regime. The original plan of this study was to sketch the picture of international Asian trade and the trade route from Portuguese sources, later to compare that sketch with the material to be found in the literature from and about the first voyages of the northwest European trading companies and the period immediately following. It has proved impossible to do this. Research in the Portuguese sources has had to be put aside, and research on the Dutch and English voyages and settlements has had to remain merely fragmentary. Only a selection from the printed materials – chiefly those of the first Dutch voyage edited by Rouffaer and IJzerman, the series of sources edited by De Jonge and Van Deventer and later continued by Tiele and Heeres, and Colenbrander's edition of documents from the period when Coen was governor-general – has been gone through, and the remarks below can be and should be supplemented by the studies in the fields of colonial history and the history of missions, and above all by the material in the as yet unprinted Dutch Company records in the Netherlands State Archives. From those records especially the picture sketched below could be enriched at every point in tenfold measure.[13]

As regards this chapter, however, the chief point is whether the method followed in collecting and applying these data can gain approval, admitted that by going on in the way sketched above, by conducting research first of all in Portuguese records, more could be reached. The material employed has up to now been used especially for the national, colonial history of European states in Asia. It has a second aspect, however. That colonial history is after all one complex of events within the rich and turbulent world of the Far East. For colonial history that world was only an opponent and a background; in the course of time, with the genesis of western European global power and the consolidation of modern capitalism, that world receded further and further and was enfeebled more and more. But there is a possibility of reconstructing the picture of it fragmentarily from the earlier data of colonial history, to the benefit of economic history and history in general. And that is a work which, it appears to me, is at least as important as writing colonial history.

From the nature of things the available material applies first of all to commercial economic relations. A few fragments have here been collected for Indonesia, serving as they do to elucidate further what has been stated in the two preceding chapters and to supplement it with some statistical material which, however incomplete it may be, gives a firmer, more concrete basis to the hypotheses proposed there. Only with a greater wealth of data would it be possible to realize completely the task set in the introduction, that of determining the place of the history of the Asian sea route in the general course of social-economic history. Whoever wishes to undertake such a task will be moving in the field of what is really the general history of mankind. What sort of methodological requirements in the use of historical categories arise in that connection has been briefly indicated in Chapter One.

3

The general picture of trade in Indonesia around 1600 has already been sketched a number of times, so that little needs to be said here regarding it. Indonesia was at the same time a stage for trade in transit (a dangerous term if not further defined) and an objective of trade in itself.[14] Indian and Burmese shipping and trade and the travelling trade from the Persian, Arabian, and Turkish towns came to the Far East from the Indian ports and the Moslem states to the west of them. Junk shipping with its traders and its emigrants swarming out from the ports of South

China, in the period under consideration chiefly from Chuan-chow (Zaitun), was directed toward the ports and shores of Farther India and Indonesia. The Indonesian products – cloves, nutmeg, mace, pepper, sandalwood, sapanwood, gold, tin, precious stones, drugs and medicinal products, and rarities such as birds, tortoise shell, and so forth – were shipped to the north and the west, traded in exchange for Indian and Persian textiles, slaves, money, and uncoined metal, and for Chinese goods – silk and silk cloth, porcelain, lacquered objects, copperwork, paper, medicinal products, sugar, sumptuous handicraft goods – the largest part of which latter were reshipped to the west from the Indonesian staple ports. What little Japanese shipping there had developed – when it had begun is not certain – did not usually reach further than the ports of the Gulf of Siam. Siamese shipping to Indonesia, regulated by royal monopoly, was just as rare. Malay and Javanese shipping transported the Indonesian goods to the staple ports; besides that, foreigners carried on their own trade and shipping along the Indonesian ports. An extensive shipping of foodstuffs from the Javanese ports both to the east and the west in Indonesia was linked up with the shipping on the staple ports.

The semi-annual monsoon winds governed all ship movements and all trade. The west-northwestern winds carried the Indian and Chinese ships to Indonesia and the Indonesian ships to the spice islands and the sandalwood islands. The length of time the prevailing winds continued determined the length of time for trade; when the winds turned trade was over and the ships began their return voyages.

The picture of trade and shipping around 1600 is not the inviolate picture of early Asian trade. The Portuguese had interfered in the trade by then, carrying on trade directly from India to China and Japan *via* Malacca and taking out part of the spices from Indonesia and bringing in part of the Indian textile goods. All that was largely royal monopoly shipping, supplemented by a certain amount of shipping by Portuguese merchant adventurers. In eastern Asia the changes were greater. Because of the settlement of the Spanish on the Philippines and the import of Mexican silver from Acapulco, there arose a completely new, important Chinese trade on Manila,[15] and Japanese trade also turned in that direction. The whole Manila trade was a new creation; for the rest the traditional framework of trade remained the same as it had been. The Portuguese regime partially supplanted Oriental trade, but, though it did not stimulate it, it left it for the most part intact.[16] The results of the Dutch and English expeditions to Asia were much more drastic: the traditional structure of trade was twisted violently awry. The war between Spain and Portugal and the Republic of the Seven Provinces, transferred to Asia, rained blow after blow on 'Moorish' and Chinese trade alike, for they were time and again the object of plunder and reprisal. The conquest of the spice islands by the Dutch East India Company put a stop to a complete branch of traditional trade and thus disorganized the whole of it. The furious competitive struggle in the pepper regions disrupted the pepper market and made the prices shoot up. The trading companies, too, took over a part of Asian trade.[17] With the more highly developed military techniques of the Europeans, privateering, blockading, and open war struck hard. Religious war, which had already broken out between Islam and Catholicism with the coming of the Portuguese, now became a three-cornered struggle between those two and Calvinism. All this needs to be taken into consideration in judging the data on Asian trade given in the records of the first Dutch voyages and of the United Dutch Company. The older Portuguese data would therefore be of greater value for the purpose.

4

The spices were obtained from the small, scattered islands of Ambon, Ceram, and the northern Moluccas (cloves), and the Bandas (nutmeg and mace). There was one crop of cloves per year, with a large harvest about once every four years. For nutmeg there were three crops per year.[18]

The clove yield of the northern Moluccas can be set at an average of three thousand *bahar* per year,[19] the yield on Ambon at eleven hundred *bahar*.[20] The annual harvest in the Banda Islands can be estimated at 2500, 600, and 400 hundredweight (calculated at 113 pounds per hundredweight) of mace and 2825, 678, and 452 *bahar* of nutmeg.[21] Altogether the annual spice export, calculated in ship's tons of fifteen hundred pounds, will have amounted to around 2700 ton.

In 1621 the total annual sale of spices in Europe was estimated by the Dutch Company at:

1400 quarters of cloves at 350 lb. = 490,000 lb.
1000 quarters of nutmeg at 450 lb. = 450,000 lb.
600 quarters of mace at 300 lb. = 180,000 lb.[22]

Sales on the Eastern market, that is to say the market in China, Patani, Siam, India, Persia, and Arabia (Aden and Mocha) were set by Coen at:

286–429 quarters of cloves = 100,000 to 150,000 lb.
444 quarters of nutmeg = 200,000 lb.
100 quarters of mace = 30,000 lb.[23]

It is certain that the Company set its aims extremely low for its Asian trade. And it is certain that the amount of spices produced in Indonesia was larger than the amount carried by the Dutch Company alone, the rest being transported by Portuguese, Indian, and Indonesian interlopers and marketed in the Middle East. The amount of spices sold on the Eastern market must therefore be increased by at least a third.

The proportion of the spices shipped to Europe to those shipped to India, the Middle East, and the Far East was thus about two or three to one. The hand-over-hand increase in the wealth of Europe due to the shipment of precious metals from America, the profits from Oriental trade, and the expansion of early capitalism on the one hand, and the impoverishment of the caliphates under military dictatorships, the heavy struggle with the Christian national states of Europe (the Hapsburgs once more), and the loss of their monopoly of Moslem intermediary trade[24] on the other hand caused such a division in the sale of spices. It seems to me that the total consumption of spices for the preceding period, the heyday of the caliphates in the Moslem world, must be set at least a third higher, and the division of the spices between the caliphates and Europe calculated at the proportion of three to one. The total spice consumption could then be fixed at around two million two hundred thousand pounds, that is to say around 1470 ship's tons. Such a calculation is on the conservative side. Taking into account the loss of cargoes at sea, the tempo of trade, the distances on the sea route, and the stock-piling at the staple points, such a figure corresponds reasonably with the estimate given above of the amount of spices exported annually from Indonesia.

5

It appears that the pepper shipped from Indonesia went primarily to China. India supplied the pepper for shipping to the west from its own yield. The Indonesian pepper transported directly to the west must have made up only a small amount before the appearance of Dutch and English shipping. Portuguese pepper shipments, at any rate, primarily involved pepper from the ports on the Malabar Coast.[25] Indonesian pepper will have become a market product for China after Chinese shipping withdrew from India and established the staple of its trade in the Indonesian ports.[26]

In 1621 the total amount of pepper sold in Europe was estimated by the Dutch Company at twenty thousand bales, at three hundred fifty pounds per bale, making up fifty-eight thousand picul or a hundred sixteen thousand bags,[27] that is to say, approximately 4670 ton.[28] Portuguese shipments formed about a fifth of it – four thousand bales. As far as Indonesian pepper was concerned, the figures from around 1600 must be considered as being far above normal. On the one hand Indian shipping from the Malabar ports carried away a part of the Indonesian pepper; on the other the irregular competition of the Portuguese, the Dutch, and the English – and the French and the Danes as well – sent the amounts brought to the isolated markets shooting upwards.[29]

The following figures can be given for that time: forty-five thousand bags shipped per year from the ports on the east coast of Sumatra, fifty thousand bags from the west coast, ten thousand from the peninsular Malay ports, and fifty thousand from Bantam; the total, a hundred fifty-five thousand bags.[30] In the fifteenth and sixteenth century Chinese trade was the only purchaser of pepper. In my opinion the amount shipped to China can at best be set at fifty thousand bags per year,[31] and the total Indonesian pepper yield at sixty thousand bags, or two thousand four hundred ton. Such an estimate is on the liberal side.

Pepper from the plateaus of Sumatra came to market in the ports of the west coast – Selebar, Indrapura, Priaman – and of the east coast – Jambi, Indragiri, Kampar; pepper from western Java was marketed in Bantam, and that from the peninsula in the northern Malay ports – Patani, Ligor, Sengora. Pepper from Sumatra and perhaps elsewhere[32] also arrived on the markets in the ports of northern Java – Japara, Grise – and in Achin.

6

Sandalwood was the most important article in Chinese trade with the exception of pepper, and the amount of it shipped can be estimated at three to four thousand picul, or two hundred forty to three hundred ton, per year.[33]

As far as the other Indonesian products are concerned, the amount of drugs and medicinal products the Dutch Company was able to put on the market was small: fifty or sixty thousand pounds of camphor per year, six, eight, or ten thousand pounds of benzoin, thirty or forty thousand pounds of tumeric, and forty or fifty thousand pounds of radix China.[34] These figures may give some indication of the total amounts of such products produced. If the same basis of comparison for these and similar products is taken as was used above for the market in the caliphates and India as compared to the market in seventeenth-century Europe, the total amount of them shipped cannot be fixed higher than two or three score ton per year.

7

The amount of raw silk brought to Bantam per year was three or four hundred picul.[35] Important quantities of it were also carried to Malacca and Manila, from whence it was shipped to the Middle East and Europe by the Portuguese and Spanish. Considering this it seems to me that the amount traditionally carried from China to the west by Indians, Persians, and Arabs is to be fixed at fifteen hundred to two thousand picul, or a hundred twenty to a hundred sixty ton.[36]

A few thousand pieces of silk, damask, and satin cloth were shipped by the Dutch Company.[37] The amount traditionally imported to Indonesia can be set at ten to twenty thousand pieces.

There is a little material on the amount of porcelain imported. In 1620 the Company requested the shipment of:

> 4000 double butter dishes, 12000 pieces single butter dishes, 12000 fruit bowls, 3000 half fruit bowls, 4000 caudle cups, 4000 half caudle cups, 500 of the largest dishes, 2000 a size smaller, 4000 a size still smaller, 1000 bowls, 2000 half bowls, 8000 saucers, 8000 dinner plates...[38]

In 1622 it requested:

> 4000 pieces dishes of the largest size, 2000 pieces one size smaller, 4000 a size still smaller, 4000 double butter dishes, 25000 single butter dishes, 9000 fruit dishes, 3000 half fruit dishes, 8000 caudle cups with turned up edges, 1000 bowls, 2000 half bowls, 8000 saucers, 5000 dinner plates...[39]

In comparison to any modern figure such a shipment is a mere trifle, but seen in the light of the time it was an important overseas export of a valuable high-quality product and indicates the high development of porcelain manufacturing in China.[40] Making allowances for the other purchases, one may fix the total amount of porcelain absorbed by early Asian trade at six or seven thousand *corges*.[41]

As for the other Chinese trade goods – sugar, rock candy, ginger, musk, radix China, ambergris, some metals, lacquered objects, and other curiosities, – they were all of them shipped and traded in small quantities, a fact especially for the craft products partly determined by the nature of production in China.

8

The chief product carried eastwards by the Indians to exchange for Indonesian products was the cotton cloth from Coromandel and Gujarat. The organizational forms of the 'international export industry' producing it have already been referred to. A few notes on the 'mass export' involved should be made in this connection.

In 1619 the Dutch Company estimated its annual sale of Coromandel cloth in Indonesia at 3,650 *corges*.[42] If one figures that in 1619 the Company controlled a fourth of the total Coromandel cloth trade with Indonesia, as against three-eighths held by the Portuguese and three-eighths held by the 'Moors', then the total sale in Indonesia of cotton cloth from Coromandel would amount to about fourteen thousand *corges*, or two hundred eighty thousand pieces. The 'Information on Divers Lands and Islands Lying Towards the East Indies for Trading There Successfully, and What Merchandise is Available and What is Best Liked There'[43] dating from 1603 advises the purchase of a total of 1832 *corges* of Coromandel cloth and 466 *corges* of Gujarati. Advice is lacking for a number of sorts of cloth; supplementing proportionally one arrives at a total purchase of two thousand five hundred *corges*. If one calculates that in 1603 the Dutch trade made up an eighth of all the cloth trade on Indonesia, then there will have been a total sale of twenty thousand *corges*, or four hundred thousand pieces, in Indonesia per year.[44]

Alongside that the amount of tapestries and light textiles imported from Persia[45] and the Chinese cloths[46] were of practically no importance, and the amount of Javanese and Balinese cotton cloth brought on the market can be estimated at a few thousand pieces at the most.

9

The shipping from the other Malay and Javanese ports to the stapling ports of the international trade carried the spices there and took the Indian cloth and Chinese products away. At the same time, it also supplied the spice islands to the east and the ports to the west – Bantam and Malacca and the other Malay ports on the peninsula and both coasts of Sumatra – with rice and slaves. Besides rice, the foodstuffs trade,[47] which was primarily Javanese, transported salt, coarse sugar, coconuts and coconut oil, garlic, onions, and so forth. "Several hundred junks"[48] were involved in the trade. There are some figures regarding this sort of shipping on Malacca. Balthazar van Eyndhoven's 'Demonstration of the Situation of the Mataram Emperor of Java, and of the Trade that Might Be Done at Japara',[49] written in 1615, states that fifty junks sailed from Japara to Malacca every year; alongside that came the ships going to Jambi, Johore, Pahang, and so on. In 1617 there is mention of a hundred twenty Javanese junks filled with rice sailing for Malacca.[50] The total amount of ships sailing to the west each year can be set at two hundred junks averaging a hundred ton apiece.[51]

The way the spice islands were furnished with food is an interesting case of food provision across long distances overseas. Up to 1621 the population of Banda was about fifteen thousand people;[52] that of Ambon and the northern Moluccas at the time a hundred fifty thousand.[53] Sago was the staple food for the people of the region; in Ambon and the northern Moluccas it was supplemented by the products of *ladang* farming: tubers, ground-nuts, and rice. Plus the rice imported. If a full ration of rice is set at thirty-six pounds per person per month,[54] and if it is assumed that on Banda two-thirds of the population had a rice ration of twelve pounds per person per month (the many slaves and poor free peasants will have had to live chiefly if not completely on sago and fish), then 1,440,000 pounds of rice were needed for Banda each year. If it is figured that on Ambon and in the northern Moluccas one-third of the population would use eighteen pounds of rice per person per month (there was more sago available there, more locally-grown rice, and many slaves), then the amount used there would have been 10,800,000 pounds. Together, then, a total of 12,240,000 pounds, or 8100 ton[55] – that is to say, the import of about a hundred thirty or forty junks carrying cargoes averaging sixty ton per junk.

The total Javanese trade in food supplies within Indonesia will thus have amounted to a shipment of around twenty-eight thousand ton of rice[56] in around three hundred thirty or forty junks averaging from sixty to a hundred ton.[57]

10

In the preceding section a transition was already made from the goods shipped to the ships themselves. Let us now consider more closely the ships and their relation to the goods shipped. From the estimates made above it is apparent that there was only one product, rice, which was transported in anything like mass quantities, and that in a total amount which is only of small importance when compared to the capacities of modern mass trade transportation. None of the other products – spices, pepper, drugs, cotton cloth, porcelain and other craft goods, silk – were shipped in more than small quantities.

Moreland estimated the capacity of the Portuguese trade carried on from India to China at three thousand ton per year, to the spice islands at a thousand,[58] and to Pegu at five thousand; the Indian trade from Coromandel at ten thousand ton, and that on Achin at three thousand; and the Chinese trade on Bantam at two thousand ton.[59]

The Indian trading ships averaged around two hundred ton[60] – in consideration of Moreland's statement that his estimates are on the liberal side[61] one should perhaps figure a hundred fifty to a hundred seventy-five ton. That would mean, then, eighteen to twenty ships for the trade on Achin.[62] Of the sixty or sixty-five ships which according to this estimate would have made up the capacity of Coromandel trade, a part went to the Middle East, a part to Bengal and Pegu, and perhaps thirty or forty at most to Indonesia.[63] There was one ship each year from Pegu to Bantam.[64] In times of peace an average of eighteen or twenty junks went from China to Manila and the Indonesian ports to the south and west each year.[65] Leaving the new trade on Manila out of consideration, one arrives at the figure of eight to ten ships, large vessels of from two hundred to four hundred ton, for the traditional Chinese trade.[66] The number of ships involved in the internal Indonesian spice, slave, and foodstuffs trades was above calculated at around three hundred thirty or forty junks, medium-sized vessels. Besides those there were small coasters and fishing ships.

The Indian and the Indonesian trade both had to yield a part of their tonnage to the Portuguese. When adding that tonnage to the Asian trade, one should calculate the number of ships over which it was distributed as larger than a strict division would indicate, for the Portuguese trade was a centralized royal trade, and in the Indian trade, on the other hand, shipowning will have been distributed among Indian lords and merchant gentlemen and partnerships of them, and perhaps among shipping and trade gilds as well. Therefore at a liberal estimate there need to be around fifty ships added to the Indian trade, and around ten to the Indonesian.

Figured liberally, with no allowances made for losses due to navigation or piracy or disablement from action in other ways, southeast Asia's international commerce, a 'world trade', was carried on as a sea-going trade[67] with a total of four hundred eighty ships, large and medium-sized vessels. The trade linking Indonesia to China and the parts of Asia to the west amounted to around a hundred fifteen ships. These figures depict the state of trade in the fifteenth and sixteenth centuries, when it reached its highest level as independent, 'autonomous Asian' trade.

II

Alongside figures on shipping, the way in which trading was carried on in Indonesia should also be considered. The characteristic of trade pointed out again and again above is the large number of people involved – the multitudes of traders, the colonies of merchants abroad, the settlements of foreign 'nations', the separate sections of towns, the *fondachi*, the turbulent trade in the trading quarters.

> The heathenish Indians that dwell in Goa are verie rich Marchants, and traffique much, there is one streete within the towne, that is full of shops kept by those Heathenish Indians, that not onely sell all kindes of Silkes, Sattins, Damaskes, and curious works of Porselyne from China and other places, but all manner of wares of velvet, Silke, Sattin, and such like, brought out of Portingall,[68] which by meanes of their Brokers they buy by the great, and sell them againe by the peece or elles, wherein they are verie cunning, and naturally subtill. There are in the same street on the other side,[69] that have all kindes of linnen, and shirts, with other clothes ready made for all sortes of persons, as well slaves as Portingales, and of all other linnen worke that may be desired. There are [in another street] Heathens that sell all kindes of womens clothes, and such like wares, with a thousand sorts of clothes and cottons... There is also another street where the Benianes of Cambaia dwell, that have all kind of wares out of Cambaia, and all sortes of precious stones, and are very subtill and cunning to bore and make holes in all kinds of stones, pearles, and corrals [and the like], on the other side of the same street dwell other heathens, which sell all sortes of bedsteedes, stooles and such like [turned] stuffe, very cleverly covered over with Lacke [of all colours], most pleasant to behold, and they can turne the Lacke into any coloure that you wil desire. There is also a street full of gold and Silver Smithes that are heathens, which make all kinde of workes, also divers other handicrafts men, as Coppersmithes, Carpenters, and such like occupations, which are all heathens, and every one a street by themselves. There are likewise other Marchantes that deale all by great, with Corne, Rice, and other Indian wares and Marchandises, as wood and such like....[70]
>
> There is in every place of the street exchangers of mony, by them called Xaraffos, which are all Christian Jewes.[71] They are very readie and expert in all manner of accounts, and in knowing of all sorts of money, without whose help men dare not receave any money, because there is much counterfet money abroade, which is hard to bee knowne from the good, were it not for these Xaraffos, which can discerne it with halfe an eye. ...[72]
>
> The Canaras and Decaniins ... many of them dwell in Goa, where their wares and shops are, of all sorts of Velvets, Silkes, Sattins and Damaskes, which they buy by great of the Portingales, also al kinds of cotton linnen, porselyne, and all kindes of wares and marchandises of Cambaia, China, Bengalla, etc. which they likewise buy of the Portingales, and other nations, and sell it againe by retaile: for the which

> purpose they have brokers of their owne Countrimen, which looke for all kindes of wares and commodities.[73]

In Malacca alone there lived a thousand traders from Gujarat, and three or four thousand were constantly journeying between the ports of northwest India and that Indonesian staple port.[74] Then there were the traders from Coromandel, whose trade on Indonesia was more important than that from northwest India, and the other foreigners, the 'Hindus',[75] Persians, and Arabs, as well as the Chinese settlement and the quarter or quarters of Indonesian merchants from elsewhere.[76] An estimate of from ten to fifteen thousand traders at Malacca in the heyday of its staple would be a conservative one.

Bantam, a staple port of a smaller size, presented the same sort of picture.[77] "In the towne there is a great resort of divers Countries and nations..."[78] Indians from every part of the subcontinent, people from Pegu and Siam, Persians, Arabs, Turks, Chinese, and people from elsewhere in Indonesia: Malays, Ternatans, Bandanese, Banjarese, Buginese, Macassarese. Each 'nation' had its quarter or suburb inside or outside the walls.[79] And the spice trade carried hundreds of Indonesian and foreign traders to the east; in 1609 there were fifteen hundred Javanese traders on Banda alone.[80]

It was the same picture in every port. The traders swarmed out by dozens and hundreds along every coast and throughout the whole world of Indonesia and southeast Asia, flocking together by thousands at the stapling points. Yet the figures on these many traders should be considered alongside the figures on the movement of ships and goods. The traders arrived by hundreds, there were only a tenth as many ships. Taking a very conservative figure of eight thousand traders from India and the Moslem countries further west and a thousand from China travelling overseas to Indonesia each year, if one apportions the amounts of goods to the traders then there are a few picul of silk and sandalwood per trader, a single chest with a few dozen pieces of silk cloth, a few *corges* of porcelain, a few dozen bags of pepper, a few *bahar* of cloves and nutmeg, a few hundredweight of mace. Whatever inaccuracies there may be in the estimates made in the preceding sections, it is impossible that they could change this general picture. The international trade of southeast Asia was a small-scale peddling trade.[81] The traders, shipping out with their goods by dozens[82] on long voyages the periodicity of which was governed by the semi-annual monsoon winds, were pedlars with valuable high-quality products.[83] They went out either as independent pedlars, perhaps in companies, or as traders on *commenda*.[84] True 'wholesale trade', 'passive' investment trade, was vested in the merchant gentlemen of the port towns, alongside whom other wellborn persons – nobles, members of the *noblesse de robe*, temple functionaries – could appear as financiers. Compare the pedlars' packs of the travelling traders with the power of the merchant gentlemen in Masulipatnam who could deliver cotton cloth in thousands of *corges* at a time, or of the Chinese monopoly trader Simsou who alone had an annual turnover of eight hundred picul of silk.

The antithesis is here sharply formulated. In reality, of course, there were gradations. Merchants of position and wealth could go on trading journeys themselves;[85] a system of factors sent out on journeys and/or placed at staple ports could exist alongside *commenda* investment in peddling trade, or even replace it.[86] But all that does not change the fact that there appears to be only one conclusion regarding the international Asian trade carried on along the great sea route. It was a small-scale peddling trade, a trade in valuable high-quality products.[87]

12

That that trade was not of a 'bourgeois commercial' sort has already been indicated in the previous chapters. The financiers of trade were often princes, religious dignitaries, and nobles. The merchant gentlemen, as *popolo grosso*, led a seigneurial way of life when compared to the *popolo minuto*, the masses of craftsmen and 'actual' traders. Furthermore, the princes and lords were themselves often merchants, moneylenders, and shipowners. Their trade could be occasional or regular. The former could result in sudden obstruction of markets, forced purchases, temporary monopolization;[88] the latter could develop in a series of possibilities from that of possessing the right of regular pre-emption on incoming trade to that of holding a complete monopoly on trade and shipping and carrying on shipping in self-owned ships. The royal sea-trade monopoly in Siam has already been mentioned.[89] The ruler of Achin introduced a pepper monopoly, drawing pepper from the ports on the west coast of Sumatra under his dominion, investing his own money, and pushing through sale of his pepper on the market before the free pepper. (It does not seem to me impossible that this pepper monopoly should be viewed as a means of defending the Moslem Achinese-Indian trade against the trade of the foreign Europeans; the Gujarati and Arab buyers were given preference.) The royal pepper amounted to from a fourth to a third of the total quantity handled.[90] The export of Mataram rice from Japara was a royal monopoly in the hands of the *tumenggungs* of Kendal and Tegal.[91] The ruler of Macassar had an 'agent' on Banda for the spice trade whom he:

> supplies every year with rice, pieces of cloth, and everything that is liked there, in order to gain as much mace for his country as possible, and thus to lure some merchants to him; is also able to have great quantities bought up; also knows how to make presents to the Bandanese priests..., so that it works to great advantage to him there...[92]

There are some data on the trade of Indonesian lords: the Patani *orang kaya* Sri Maharajah Indra, shipping arrack to the Moluccas, apparently in someone else's ship;[93] the *shahbandar* and the *datuk besar* of Patani, owning ships and carrying on freight shipping;[94] the rulers of Achin, Johore, Jambi, Surabaya, and Macassar, the lords in Bantam, Jambi, Jakarta, Ternate, and Macassar, the governors of Demak, Kendal, and Sukadana, the *shahbandar* of Grise, all of them owning ships and carrying on trade; and foreigners, the *daimios* of Nagasaki and Arima and the lords of Siam, sending out junks.[95] The queen of Patani lent money to the Dutch Company, and the English attempted to borrow money from the governor of Bantam.[96]

13

Trade came and went with the alternating semi-annual winds, and the nature of the trade staying over was just as much determined by that periodicity. It was spread out over the many markets of Indonesia and concentrated at a few stapling points. The markets were isolated from each other and showed important variations in structure, while the amount of goods turned over was small, even at the largest of them. The trade of the Sumatran ports was based on the export of gold and a few thousand bags of pepper, that of East Indonesia on a few thousand *bahar* of spices. A part of the trade was trade of the royalty and nobility. The sale of cotton cloth needs to be thought of as divided over dozens of markets – that is to say, at the most a few thousand *corges* were sold at each important market, and those were taken from there to the final consumers by traders at second-hand, and perhaps third or fourth.[97] Trade took place between the pedlars arriving in caravans and the local traders, who then either carried the goods further themselves or – as wholesale traders and merchant gentlemen – stored the goods and at the opportune time sold them on the local market, shipped them further, or gave them out in *commenda*. Thus went the trade in both directions, in the rhythm of the prevailing winds. The annual movement of the masses of travelling pedlars governed the market – when they had departed trade was at a standstill. The market tendency was the opposite of dynamic: what came on the market had to be sold, and the goods disappeared with the traders, or if the trading failed, traders and goods stayed over. Prices fluctuated very sharply with the periods, a wholesale trade which took over the goods and thus kept them off the market and regulated prices was of little significance.[98]

The trade on the market was a person-to-person bidding and bargaining over the lots of goods; the purchases took place in many small quantities. One should read the account of the peddling activities of the factor Karel in Bantam during the first Dutch voyage. And such a peddling trade took place with the

Javanese nobles and the leading Moslem merchants, 'wholesale traders', as Rouffaer calls them.[99] Chinese merchants offered amounts of pepper for sale: one, two, or three hundred bags.[100] Chinese and other foreign merchants sold their goods on the ships "just as though they were on a market".[101]

Exporting took place *via* the municipal weigh-house. Each lot was taken there and was only freed for export after it had been weighed and the many taxes large and small which encumbered purchasing had been paid.[102] That is to say, international trade was regulated in the same forms as those of trade in the western European middle ages,[103] or, if one prefers, those of present-day trade on a local market, for example the cheese trade in Dutch towns such as Alkmaar and Leiden.

With trade spread out among many isolated markets there was a wide variation in weights and measures. To mention only the chief measure of 'wholesale' trade, the *bahar* of the Moluccas amounted to 600 pounds, that of Bantam to 495, that of Malacca to 530 or 540, and so forth. The kinds of money varied just as much. On Java, and probably in the ports on which Javanese ships traded, circulated the lead cash imported from China, thousands of which, threaded on a string through a hole in the center of them, counted for one real of eight; and alongside it there were Spanish and Portuguese money, Chinese trading money of bar silver, Persian *larrins*, small silver bars the shape of horseshoes. In Achin people reckoned in taels of gold; on the west coast of Sumatra trade took place primarily as direct barter on the basis of money calculations; the same thing was true of Banda, but on the basis of nutmeg weights; on Ambon there was money calculation and money trade; on Sumbawa gold and silver bracelets served as money; on Bima barter exchange was carried on with small stones; in Jambi light pepper served as small change; on Buton pieces of cotton were means of exchange and measures of value.[104] With such a diversity and so much dispersion of the markets, with such a superficial money economy, it goes without saying that:

> ...moneys among the nations of the Indies are not considered nor regarded as an evaluated currency, but after the manner of merchandise rising and falling according to the need for them...[105]

14

In the preceding sections the most important aspects of trade, shipping, and marketing in Indonesia have been considered in turn. In closing a summary may be given in the form of a brief reconstruction of the whole picture of international trade in Indonesia around 1600 at two chief points, the staple port Bantam and the spice islands – this especially with an eye to finding reflected in the Indonesian situation around 1600 some of the historical processes discussed in Chapter Three.

However much the staple at Bantam around 1600 was of importance for international Asian trade, it is a pity from the point of view of cultural history that the Dutch accounts have not furnished the wealth of material for one of the ports of eastern Java that they have for Bantam. The centre of Javanese political and maritime power lay after all in such towns as Tuban, Jaratan, Grise, Surabaya, Demak, and Japara.[106] Bantam, originally a port of little significance under the control of the Hindu-Sundanese inland state of Pajajaran, was in 1527 forceably occupied together with the region around Jakarta by the Moslem zealot Faletehan in the name of the sultan of Demak. It was planned to use it as a Moslem outpost against the Portuguese, who, having conquered Malacca in 1511, had gained Sunda Kalapa (Jakarta) as a foothold in Java by a treaty with the ruler of Pajajaran. With the struggle for the central power in the later period of the Javanese disturbances, the vassal of the sultan of Demak made himself independent.[107] The Javanese colony of Bantam – it seems to me after all that Bantam's position can best be given as that of daughter city to Demak[108] – was thus a rather recent settlement compared to the cities of eastern Java.

The accounts from the first Dutch voyages reveal the picture of an aristocratic city surrounded by gated walls. The position of the ruler was sustained by the might of the nobility, and means of power were in their hands.[109] Each of the nobles exercised control over a section of the city,[110] and in his court[111] each maintained his armed retinue of warriors, mercenaries, and slaves.[112] The general authority was in the hands of a council of ruler and lords.[113] Administrative intervention in shipping and trade, at the boom and at the weigh-house, was in the hands of the *shahbandar*,[114] whose position was a 'bourgeois' one, in Bantam as elsewhere often held by foreigners – Indians or Chinese.[115] The nobles and the ruler based their chief power on agrarian possessions: subject villages and apanages and their settlements of slaves in the country.[116] They also had slaves in the city, *apophora*-bound, working in crafts, fishing, and probably trade.[117] Shipowning – trading junks and war proas – and regular and occasional trade were further sources of income. And probably also ownership of land and/or houses in the city.[118]

The political power which the nobility wielded over the city of Bantam is beyond doubt, as appears also from their seigneurial position.[119] A 'bourgeois' patriciate was formed by the merchant gentlemen, the 'wholesale traders'. In Bantam, the southern staple port of Chinese trade, Chinese merchants made up an important part of the patriciate.[120] They too dwelt in stately houses, owned warehouses and ships, and held slaves.[121] They sent slaves with *peculium* on sea trade,[122] and they employed their means in *commenda* given out to independent peddling traders. The merchants settled at Bantam sent their money to China for trading,[123] as in the other direction, and perhaps on a greater scale, the Chinese merchant gentlemen gave out money in *commenda* for the trade on Indonesia. It is not clear whether there was a direct consignment trade as well.[124] The wealthy Chinese in Bantam also exercised the business of moneylending and usury.[125] There is unfortunately no mention of it, but it is very probable that the farming of taxes and duties was in their hands: the example of Jakarta–Batavia, where the Dutch Company after only a few years began to farm out its sovereign levies one after the other almost exclusively to Chinese, is nearly as much as a guarantee of it.

Around 1600 Bantam was also acquainted with Indian patricians, such as the *keling* Chetty Maluku who, perhaps in connection with his trade on the Moluccas,[126] possessed a court in the city, an armed retinue, and trading ships.[127] Also mentioned as a citizen of prominence was Andamohi Keling, "Andemon, one of the most excellent"; one can find "The Court of Andemoin" on Lodewycksz.'s plan of the city.[128] The Turkish, Persian, and Arab merchants also held a dignified position and were to be found in the company of the great.[129] Nothing is mentioned concerning their housing. Perhaps the Moslem trade-from-afar was more mobile, much more a rich peddling trade, voyaging and trekking.[130]

The Chinese traders lived in a quarter within the walls, the other foreign traders in the suburbs.[131] A part of them will have sought *pied à terre* at Bantam periodically with the prevailing winds, to journey away again with the new season; another part will have stayed settled at Bantam[132] alongside the local trading class. Gujarati, Coromandelese, Bengalese, and 'foreign Indonesians' – Buginese, Bandanese, Banjarese, people from Ternate, Macassar, and eastern Java – were to be found settled in the suburbs.[133] It appears to me that there the great mass of travelling peddlars found shelter, on an equal footing with local traders and craftsmen, together making up the whole lower-class group of Indonesians and foreigners.[134] Merchants of importance lodged within the city by their colleagues the 'wholesale' merchants.[135]

On the one hand were the *shahbandar*, the 'principal Chinese', and the 'nobleman' Chetty Maluku with whom the captains, commissioners, and admirals of the Company fleets and later on the Company lodge consorted, and on the other the mass of traders carrying their valuable goods on board ship or selling the commissioners a few bags of rice, pepper, or spices on the market, the Chinese buyers:

> going inland into the villages with their weights in hand, weighing first how much there was there and then bidding according to what money they think the people need...[136]

The two, the nobles and merchant gentlemen on the one hand and the mass of pedlars,[137] craftsmen, peasants, and slaves on the other, were very widely separated socially and economically. But the nobles furthermore dominated the class of merchant gentlemen and the whole of trade, holding the power to exercise authority as they did.

The 'chief market' of Bantam, the morning market held on the market field to the east of the city outside the gates, gives a clear picture of peddling trade. All the local market trade of the town[138] and all the peddling trade in goods imported to the stapling point from overseas were to be encountered on the same footing there – all sorts of foodstuffs (of which rice and salt, for example, came from overseas, and may perhaps have been vended by the Javanese who had transported them), pots, pans, pepper bags, spices, Gujarati and Bengali with painted articles and trinkets, Persians and Arabs with jewels, rows of Chinese shops (like the 'streets' of the 'heathenish Indians' in Goa) with all their expensive goods: damask, velvet, satin, silk, gold thread, cloth of gold, porcelain, lacquered work, copperwork, woodwork, medicinal products, and the like.[139] The trade carried on there was not a market trade with sales to the inhabitants of Bantam for local consumption, but the international Asian trade of the stapling point Bantam, carried on as peddling trade.

It was also there on the market field, however, that the "centre of the Bantam wholesale trade"[140] was to be found:

> the great market which is also the Exchange, where one sees many nations walking...[141]
>
> the merchants and ships' captains... who trade and sail in every region...[142]
>
> the merchants and adventurers...[143]
>
> the merchants who have all sorts of cloth and other wares *en gros* for sale and give out money for voyages[144] for a double return if the voyage succeed, but if the ship be wrecked, the merchant loses the capital or the money lent...[145]

Here, then, was the exchange, the meeting place of merchant gentlemen and ship's captains.[146] The fair of the western European middle ages and the exchange of the western European early-capitalistic period were as it were brought together on the market field at Bantam. But – differently from in western Europe at the time, where the predominant power of international trade already rested under the arches of the exchange buildings[147] and the traditional fair had fallen from the ranks of an annual market to that of an amusement fair or at best retained only a local and rural significance – in Asia, as the staple port here illustrates, the fair remained dominant in international trade as an 'annual market' lasting half a year, and the exchange was absorbed in it.

15

The spices came from a few small groups of islands spread out over East Indonesia. The populations of the islands, whose existence was put an end to more or less radically by the carrying through of the Dutch Company monopoly in the first part of the seventeenth century (1621–1656), around 1600 had social organizations of a characteristic sort. The people of the Banda Islands lived in a few fortified villages on the inaccessible, rocky heights,[148] and for their existence had to depend almost completely on the importation of their staple foods, sago and rice. The people of the islands of Ambon and the northern Moluccas were also settled in fortified villages high up on the rocks,[149] but grew a larger share of their own food, cultivating tubers and rice on dry forest fields. Everywhere, however, sago was imported from the Kai and Aru Islands lying to the east, from Ceram, and from Sula and the Banggai Islands to the west,[150] and rice was brought in with the food supply trade coming chiefly from the Javanese ports. The wealth of the inhabitants of the islands was concentrated in their possession of orchards and forests of clove and nutmeg trees.

In these widely scattered islands – from Ternate to Ambon it is about three hundred seventy-five miles, from Ambon to Banda another hundred fifty – shipping naturally played a large rôle. The shipping of the inhabitants was carried on almost exclusively in great galleys, the *kora-koras*, planked outrigger proas up to more than fifty yards in length, paddled by over a hundred rowers. Commercial shipping was of less importance than military and predatory expeditions, in which taking the heads of the defeated enemies was the custom. The people of Banda, especially, give the impression of having been bellicose. The qualification 'Argonauts of East Indonesia' enters the mind as one becomes acquainted with the leagues and factions uniting and dividing those seafaring islanders with each other and among themselves – the Pela League linking the islands of Ambon and Hitu to those of Banda,[151] and the Uli-lima and Uli-siva factions found on all the islands.[152]

The political structure on Banda and Ambon was 'patrician republican', with a staunchly unitary society under a rigidly exclusive aristocratic regime: *orang baik versus orang kaya.*[153] The free population was poor and subservient to the nobility; slaves were held chiefly by the nobles. As regards the spice trees, the clove forests on Ambon and the nutmeg orchards on Banda,[154] the largest share of those, too, fell to the nobles – besides levying tithes[155] and exploiting their own forests and orchards with their own slaves[156] they monopolized the buying up of the rest of the spices so that the trade with the incoming Indonesians and other 'outlanders' went chiefly through their hands.[157] One should not imagine a 'wholesale trade' here: the nobles weighed the spices themselves in their own houses,[158] and the figures on ships, traders, and goods given earlier establish beyond doubt the picture of a multitudinous peddling trade.[159] The Javanese junks – with their holds divided into small compartments into which the many traders each of them stored his cargo[160] – brought the food supplies, the cotton cloth, the copperwork (especially gongs from Patani), the slaves, and so forth which were sold in the peddling trade at the small stapling points of the spice islands.[161]

The lion's share of the import will have fallen to the nobles, because of their monopoly position and the power of their wealth, which also gave them the benefits of anchorage money, tolls, and trading permit rights. It is true that there was a permanent intermediary trade of foreigners – Gujarati, Arabs, probably Javanese[162] – established in East Indonesia, but considering the rhythm of trade the significance of that trade at second, or rather third, hand cannot have been predominant.

The islands' harvests were limited, altogether around four million pounds, or thirty or forty thousand 'man-burdens',[163] which is not so small in comparison to the total population. If one calculates that there came around a hundred forty junks with some six thousand traders,[164] then there were only a few *bahar* exported per trader, with a value of from a hundred fifty to two hundred reals.[165]

In contrast to Banda and Ambon, the northern Moluccas had a monarchical rule with a somewhat centralized regime. The structure of the state of Ternate was that of an aristocratic state with its ruler as chief among peers;[166] there the regime was more burdensome on the inhabitants of the widely scattered islands, requiring participation in military expeditions, sago voyages, galley duties, and forced relocation of people.[167] Governors were established by the rulers of Ternate on the coasts of Ceram and on Ambon,[168] thus around three hundred seventy-five miles from the centre of the realm; their rôle was limited economically to that of levying tolls, delivering products,[169] and controlling the ports. For the rest the clove trade of the Moluccas – of which Makian was the richest in cloves – was in the hands of the nobles.[170]

The most interesting of the things taking place in East Indonesia around 1600 was the missionary activity of Islam. The expansion of Islam into that 'farthest East' was something emanating from the Javanese traders, who were there truly pedlar missionaries.[171] The youth and thus their families were pushed toward the new doctrine *via* what must have been very defective instruction in the religion and the holy tongue Arabic. What is most important in this connection is that with that process the authority of the nobility remained the same – more strongly put, that Islamization took place under its protection.[172] Religion and authority remained separate fields,[173] though it is true that there too Islam was used as a political weapon, in this case against the Calvinism of the Dutch Company. (One wonders whether it was also aimed against Portuguese Catholicism there.) The Moslem religious teachers, guided especially by the Ternatese governors,[174] carried on a continuous struggle with the Calvinists for the still heathen population. There too, then, the process of Islamization was determined by political motives, and therefore its sociological structure needs to be considered quite separately from any possible cultural or political results.

On the Study of Indonesian History

The Dutch version of this article was originally published under the title "Enkele aanteekeningen met betrekking tot de beoefening der Indische geschiedenis" (Some Notes Regarding the Study of the History of the Indies), in *Koloniale Studiën* (Colonial Studies), XXI (1937), 651–661.

On the Study of Indonesian History

Whoever approaches the history of Indonesia enters into an unknown world. The expression should not be taken too absolutely – in that world too, in the series of historical situations, one is again and again struck by phenomena and configurations calling up images from the familiar history of the Mediterranean and western European areas. But on closer examination what had seemed historical parallels are seen to assume a complete historical autonomy that makes it practically impossible to carry through any comparison of phenomena. The comparison of the Germanic mark village with the Javanese *desa*, often suggested and just as often opposed, says enough in this respect. Viewed as a whole Indonesian history remains a new and unknown world: as much by the autonomy of its historical perspectives as by the nature of its historiographic treatment.

Let us briefly survey how the historical material is treated, allowing the subject of periodization to serve as a starting point.

A prehistory, 'international', like every prehistory of a national history, leads up to a period of 'ancient' history, an age which is hardly considered to fall within the borders of historical study, but has remained the field for ethnological research, the object of more-or-less bold hypotheses. The work of Perry, Kruyt's hypotheses regarding the sequence of development in central Celebes,[1] the question, still half in the darkness, of the structure of pre-Hindu Indonesian (or Javanese) society may together illustrate the character of the period, still unfixed and completely undefined methodologically.

The 'real' historical epoch begins, then, with the Hindu-Indonesian period, which merges into the Islamic, while that in its turn is succeeded by 'colonial history', a history which must be considered to have continued up to the present day, but from which the contemporary part falls practically completely outside the study of history. It has been the subject of all sorts of ideological and political interest; De Kat Angelino as well as Sutomo and Sukarno have used it as such. But is has hardly been the subject of real historical research at all – for a parallel with the Netherlands, where the railroad strike of 1903 has been the subject of a dissertation,[2] one will search in vain for Indonesia.

These historical periodizations together appear to be a bundle of very heterogeneous indications for certain periods of time. On closer inspection such indications prove to have very little value in defining the nature and the course of Indonesian history. By itself that would not need to weigh too heavily, but such a system of periodization perpetuates a great deal that is imperfect and incorrect, and it is therefore injurious to the understanding of Indonesian history, and that of history in general, from the very outset. This can be clarified with a few illustrations.

From the first centuries – that is, of the Christian era – till into the fifteenth century, Hindu culture is said to have dominated in Indonesia. It was imported from India. Whether it was a process of actual colonization is a question not to be considered here (the authorities are not united in their opinions on this cardinal point); it is enough to point out there is general agreement on the fact that that Hindu culture touched only the top layer of Indonesian society, and even then only in certain aspects of life. But from the village to the court of the prince, true Indonesian society as an Indonesian organization is left in the background. The nature of the source materials (of which more later) unsupplemented by a broader synthesis of, among other things, meticulous historical research on agriculture, is largely the cause of this one-sidedness. Under closer examination that true Indonesian society appears to be the source of all technological achievements, from *sawah* cultivation to temple construction, from metalwork to overseas trade.

Hindu-Indonesian society was brought to a crisis by Islamic missionary activities and the unrest in various Indonesian states coincident (perhaps largely accidentally) to them. The age of political transition before the establishment of the new religion on Java (the hegemony of the dissident coastal princes and the fall of Majapahit), makes up the contents of the so-called Islamic period, which found a conclusion in the establishment of a new central inland authority on Java at Pasar Gede and later at Mataram. The starting point for the period is the beginning of the spread of the new religion in Indonesia; it is ended with a temporary resolution to a series of political entanglements on Java which it is true were related to the new religion, but in no sense determined by it only.

Islamization penetrated deeper and political tensions between the states created further entanglements, but in the meantime the voyages around Africa for trade and warfare had begun from western Europe. Thus opened the period of colonial history. The engrafted slip of European outpost, at first of limited political significance and practically without economic importance for the East, gradually grew irremovably fast to the tree of Asian civilization. However, from the point of view of its own 'internal' development as well as from that of the history of Asia, the 'colonial' period has remained undifferentiated. It includes an early commercial-capitalistic phase (it is a question by itself whether in the Portuguese period the 'Asian' forms of political capitalism were not completely equal to those of the newcomers)[3] and a modern industrial-capitalistic phase, without the significance of that all-important structural change ever receiving its due in historical study.

Seen in the framework of 'Oriental' history, colonial history appears to be at the same time much more and much less than 'colonial'. The qualification is of little value in distinguishing questions of the structure and course of historical processes. Take for example the Dutch East India Company in the first century of its existence. Not only did the Company build its fortified stronghold of Batavia with Chinese labour and Chinese construction techniques, but it handed over the exploitation of town finances to Chinese tax farmers. It carried on trade at the many trading points everywhere in the archipelago in the same way as

Oriental traders and on the same footing, buying cloves on Ambon from the Ambonese *orang kaya* in his house, on the scales of the nobleman, as the Javanese trader did; buying pepper in Jambi alongside the Chinese small engrossers from men come down from Minangkabau, buying on no larger a scale than the Jambi court lords and the Javanese, Malay, and Chinese traders coming there. In Achin and in the ports on the western coast of Sumatra controlled by Achin it was subjected to the imposition of a toll by the *panglima* just the same as everyone else. It fitted its ships with Japanese rigging; it obtained the metal for guns and ironwork and the ingredients for its gunpowder and other ships' necessaries from Japan.

Again and again we encounter Asian historical traits standing beside European as of equal value in the process of contact between 'East' and 'West'. All such 'Oriental' traits result from autonomous sequences of historical development; at the same time they are just as much moot points for research in Indonesian history. It would appear that the siege of the new Batavia threatened by armies from Mataram in the 1620's can by no means be characterized with tales in the style of the well known one regarding the Javanese attack on the redoubt Hollandia. It was no performance of a disorderly gang of natives put to the sword by a small, resolute piquet of armed soldiers; the Javanese troops appear to have possessed not only discipline and ability in organized military manoeuvring, but also technical knowledge in throwing up siege and trench works. New questions arise in relation to the military science of those large armies, and in relation to their firearms technique as well.

Roundabout the activities of the Company, other historical processes continued their development in this period of 'colonial' history. Islamization went on: the conversion of Macassar to the new faith was at least as important as that of Java. New Chinese colonization movements set in, it would seem in connection with the troubles at the end of the Ming dynasty.

Also in the sixteenth century must have come the conquest of Madagascar, a remarkable expression of Indonesian power overseas after Majapahit, one of the many aspects of the enigma of Madagascar, which probably will for the time being remain an enigma to history.[4] All this is enough to indicate that early colonial history is of more importance as a source of knowledge of the Oriental Indonesian world of the time than as a source for the history of European positions overseas.

Knowledge of the Oriental Indonesian world to be gathered from the Company's historical source materials can also be used for clarifying the important question of what the significance of that evidence is within the frame of reference of Indonesian history. What place did the seventeenth century take in the succession of perspectives in Indonesian history? Which phase is represented by the development of the toll system and the existence of the political agent, such as those of Achin on the western coast of Sumatra? How and when did the system of tax-farming arise, for example as it existed at Bantam? What was the significance of the commercial shipping of the Indonesian lords in the many coastal towns? How did nautical and military techniques develop? What is the significance of seventeenth-century evidence for, for example, the Majapahit period? What is the relationship of the economic and political structure of Bantam in 1596 or Jambi in 1624 to that of Çriwijaya? How did the patrimonial system of bureaucracy in the Javanese inland states develop, and what are the evolutionary traits which may have brought it about? Is it possible to measure the technical capacity of the early empires in regard to, for instance, their building activities (Barabudur, Prambanan) on the basis of seventeenth-century population data?[5]

All these questions converge on the main problem, that of 'evolution' in Indonesian history as basis for building up a view of Indonesian history from the successive structures of historical situations. A second problem, almost as important, is closely related to it – that of what historical categories should be used to indicate those historical situations and historical patterns. The historical categories borrowed from Mediterranean and western

European history are not usable as they stand, any more than the criteria for defining the broader divisions of history, 'ancient', medieval', 'modern', and 'recent' history with their transitional periods. Categories such as nobility, village, bureaucratic central authority, town, bourgeoisie, handicrafts, prebend, church need to be given another content if they are to be used. In Indonesia the imported world religions have acquired a different structure and direction and have interwoven themselves in the fabric of the society in a different way. A system of categories of its own, built up with the available historical factual material, is a chief requirement for a correct view of Indonesian history.

A check of how these points are handled in the historical studies now in existence shows that either, in the most cases, such things have not been taken into account,[6] or that they have been dismissed with the admission that the content of such categories must result from the autonomous evolutionary process of Asian history and the negative assurance that the categories in use elsewhere cannot be applied. The positive work still needs to be done: the question of historical terminology, the determination of historical categories in a broader relationship. By those who up to now have devoted themselves to the cultivation of Indonesian history the work on the plot 'historical method' has been left undone. The field lies fallow.

Going on in this critique from the periodization and terminology of Indonesian history to its students, one again finds a great heterogeneity, with separations determined not primarily by a rational division of fields of work but chiefly by factors lying outside history. The first periods are the field of prehistorians and ethnologists; the Hindu period is chiefly that of archeologists and philologists, the Islamic that of philologists alone; and colonial history is the foster child of Dutch historians, scholars most of whom have remained unfamiliar with Asian history and who, furthermore, study the subject primarily as the history of the Dutch overseas – which means a near mutilation of the rich sources of that history, of at least as much importance in an

'Asian' context. The otherwise excellent biography of Speelman by Dr Stapel is only one illustration of this point. Admitted that a biography of Speelman should first of all follow the Rotterdammer in his richly checkered career through the Company's hierarchical system – but both Speelman and the Company were rising in the Indonesian world by means of a hard struggle with the existent powers. Why, then, does more light not fall on that world? Why is it only seen as the antagonist; why does it all remain so grey and undifferentiated? In this case lack of sources cannot apply: Dr Stapel himself lists Speelman's accounts of Coromandel, Macassar, and Mataram affairs.[7] Thus in the work of one of the best colonial historians can be seen the one-sidedness and thereby the incompleteness of colonial history of the traditional sort.

The sources of Indonesian history are as heterogeneous as its periodizations. There is not much value in a comparison with for example Dutch history, where there is a much smaller difference in types of sources (and their languages), as well as a much larger quantity and a great deal more intensive and specialized study of them. A comparison would be unfair to the Indonesian sources. The study of those sources is in many ways only in an initial stage; the materials are still indeterminate, aspects change again and again. To pass judgement on them is as unnecessary as it would be unfair. What is to be objected to is that such isolated studies maintain incorrect periodizations and classifications and keep the sources for the most part within their own field, and that the isolated groups of specialists, though in many cases they are not even primarily historians, hold the history of certain periods as a monopoly. Thus have arisen the heterogeneity of the whole study of Indonesian history and the impoverishment of the study of history in general. With a full recognition of the necessity of the existing method of work, one could desire that a closer contact were brought about between such specialists and both philologists and historians. It is to be desired because thus valuable material once studied by trained historians could enrich not only the periods involved and Indonesian history as a whole, but also history in general. In determining general historical categories an interaction among the various groups could be expected, to the mutual inspiration and enrichment of their research. After all, the demarcation of areas of study is far from rational. The major historical themes cross over the borders; the configurations of important patterns often cut across two of them. Materials of the same kind are to be found in different fields, and the working hypotheses and analogous situations demand an exchange of data. Different from the study of European history, where the existing specialization is the result of a unity of discipline and a differentiation of field, the study of Indonesian history demands more cooperation in order to attempt to achieve recognition of the unity of the historical discipline.

The work of determining historical categories is in no sense a high flown work lost in the clouds, but more fairly one of constructing a set of tools for working historical materials in a more general context. It is the task first of all of sociologically trained historians, working in cooperation and interaction with specialists as briefly outlined above. The work of Max Weber could provide a guide in this regard.[8] Putting the various data of early Indonesian history into proper relationship is just as necessary for that task as working with more modern material. What material is furnished by documents from the Hindu-Javanese period can be related not only to what is provided by seventeenth and eighteenth-century Company sources but also – in the field of agrarian history, for example – to what Sloet's research on land rights or the research on the 'declining prosperity' of Java has produced.[9] Historical material can be brought together from a number of places. It is buried in a book such as Dr Pijper's *Fragmenta Islamica* as well as Dr Duyvendak's study of the Kakean order.[10] Dr Kruyt's hypotheses on the history of Celebes fall under it, and Dr Vroklage's work, with its attempt to achieve a morphology of cultural history.[11] Reciprocal testing of such material is a premise for arriving at a valid analysis of it.

It is necessary that the history of Indonesia be seen by its students as a methodological unit, and, though the individual nature of the various fields of study should be acknowledged, at the same time because of the proximity of those fields the need for establishing cooperation – to the enrichment of Indonesian history in general, and in the service of the formation of it – must also be recognized.

Such cooperation could find expression in an organization of the specialized students of history – the archeologists, the philologists, and the historians. Out of the foregoing there arises a first premise that such an organization must be inclusive. Limitation to the students of colonial history, as was suggested in an earlier stage of the discussion on the establishment of an historical section of the Batavian Society of Arts and Sciences,[12] would be a limitation as impractical as incorrect, for a division based on the traditional periodization of history is contradictory to the nature of Indonesian history, which, to the benefit of its general treatment, breaks through that periodization in its major themes. The first requirement is not that of organizing specialists but that of bringing various groups of them together in the cause of historical work to be carried on cooperatively on a more extensive basis.

Indonesian history is an international history. Both ethnological and documentary studies show it to be dominated by the coming of peoples and ideologies from elsewhere – ancient Indonesian immigration, Hinduism, Islam, Chinese cultural influences, European overseas voyages. It is therefore all the more remarkable that there is no systematic coordination of the study of Indonesian history with that of the history of lands nearby. The work carried on in history in India, the Malay Peninsula, Indo-China, China, and Japan, work frequently touching upon Indonesian history, does not become generally known. In the field of philology contacts are maintained (for example, between the Kern Institute at Leiden and l'Ecole Française d'Extrême Orient at Hanoi), but they hardly reach outside that limited field. The objection holds just as much in regard to European historical studies. For instance, with regard to what is carried on in the field of research on early capitalism and in that on more recent economic history, not everything of importance for the course of affairs in the Indies – the Indies of Van Imhoff as well as the Indies of Van der Capellen and Van Tuyll van Serooskerken[13] – is well enough read and assimilated in Indonesia. If desired, the field could be expanded still further and the Greek colonization of the Mediterranean areas, the Danish colonization of Iceland, and the Genoese *maone* taken into consideration, to the benefit of comparative colonial history. Such a thing is a point in itself.

It is desirable, then, to establish contact between the various groups of specialists working on Indonesian history, to the benefit of its study in a broader context. It hardly seems necessary to argue the point that such contact can best take place under the auspices of the Batavian Society. For the time being it is not necessary to decide whether it should take place informally or in the shape of a new historical section to be established. Contact with the Society is very much to be desired – for one reason because most of the historians concerned are already members of the institution, and for another because only the Society can provide the means for supporting some of the various activities properly. One thinks, for example, of contact with other institutions, in Asia (branches of the Royal Asiatic Society, historical societies in India, the school at Hanoi) as well as in Europe (the Dutch State Commission for the Publication of Historical Documents, the Amsterdam Economic History Archives, the Dutch Historical Society).[14] Some of the results of mutual consultation could be, for example, a plan for the publication of various sources, the study of various historical topics, the collection of various materials. Such publications can only be undertaken under the direction of the Society. Giving publicity to the results of research in history elsewhere insofar as it is considered to be of importance to Indonesia, another point regarding which such consultation can be productive, could also best occur under the patronage of the Society. Finally, with the constant changing of persons in the group – the evil of the Indies – the Society can form an element of continuity, a guarantee that things will go on, which after all cannot be underestimated as a psychological factor in such a plan of cooperation.

The World of Southeast Asia: 1500–1650

Dr van Leur's second longer study, written, under the title "De wereld van Zuid-Oost Azië", in the years immediately preceding the Second World War, was to have been published in a volume on Dutch 'colonial history' being edited by J. C. de Haan and P. J. van Winter. With the occupation of the Netherlands by Germany, in May, 1940, however, only the first two chapters of the study were received by the editors, to be included, somewhat revised and without footnotes, in the volume *Nederlanders over de zeeën* (Dutchmen Over the Seas; Utrecht, 1940).

In Indonesia, meanwhile, Dr van Leur, doubting that the book planned by Dr de Haan and Professor van Winter would be able to appear under German censorship, regained rights to his study and arranged for its publication in the journal *Djåwå* (Java). This plan, too, was frustrated with the invasion of Indonesia by Japan and the consequent cessation of the journal.

It was only after the war that the third chapter was to achieve publication, edited with a brief introduction by Professor Wertheim, in *Tijdschrift voor Geschiedenis* (Historical Journal), while the notes of the first two chapters have remained unpublished up to the present time. This translation, based on the original manuscript and the printer's proofs prepared for the journal *Djåwå*, presents Dr van Leur's study in nearly complete form (one page of the manuscript of the third chapter has unfortunately been lost) for the first time.

Chapter One

I

The Level of Asian Technology: 1500

In 1498 the Portuguese ships under the command of Vasco da Gama, after having sailed around the southern point of Africa, lay off Melinde, on the eastern coast, and the ruler of the port town gave them two of his pilots to go on the crossing to Calicut on the western coast of India. When on board, Da Gama showed his nautical instruments, including wood-and-metal astrolabes, to one of the guides, a Moslem from the northwest Indian coastal region of Gujarat. The 'Moor' did not show a single sign of astonishment: the use of such nautical aids was also known to shipping on those routes.[1]

In 1511, when D'Albuquerque attacked the Malay port town of Malacca, the artillery battle carried on by the two sides showed that the Indonesian city was just as well acquainted with the use of big guns as the European seafarers. With the fall of the stronghold three thousand pieces of artillery, including two thousand bronze cannon, most of them of small calibre, fell into the hands of the conquerors.[2] And in the same year Malays also went along to tend the guns on D'Abreu's Portuguese ships in the first voyage further east toward the Moluccas.[3]

In the struggle between the state of Achin and the Portuguese of Malacca in 1564, the Ottomans, the masters of Egypt and the ports on the Red Sea, sent the sultan auxiliary troops, skilled artillery men, and a large quantity of guns and ammunition.[4] In one of the later sieges of Portuguese Malacca by Johore, the ruler of Achin according to the account of Jan Huyghen van Linschoten sent to the ruler of Johore:

> a peece of Ordinance, such as for greatnes length and workmanship, the like is hardly to bee found in all Christendome [or so well wrought]...

> ... which I have purposely set down to let you know that they have other kindes of Mettals, and know howe to handle them.[5]

Legaspi, coming to the Philippine – thus, Indonesian – island Cebu in the first Spanish voyage across the Pacific, found there in 1565 a Moslem trader, factor of the sultan of Brunei in North Borneo, and on Luzon and off Mindoro Moslem, Chinese, and Japanese merchants and ships (1565, 1570–1572). With the attack made by the Spaniards on Manila in 1570, the place was burned; one thing that went up in flames was a house where artillery was cast, and in which twelve pieces were still to be found.[6]

After they had sailed around the Cape and crossed the Pacific, then, the Portuguese and Spaniards encountered nautical and military techniques which were on an equal footing with European. The Islam which the Portuguese and Spanish nobility had driven back from their own borders southwards into Africa they encountered here once more, from the eastern coast of Africa to the very rim of the Pacific. Christian chivalric war for honour and spoils, carried on here as a sea struggle, brought all the Asian coasts in fire and flame and caused leagues to be formed between the Oriental rulers and requests for support to be sent out reaching from the sultan of Achin to the Ottomans and from Malacca to the court of the Ming Dynasty in Peking (in 1512 and 1520 embassies from the expelled Malay ruler, to whom the seal of vassalage had been given by the emperor of China, came to the court seeking support against the 'Franks').[7]

2

The Nature of Asian Trade

When Legaspi was in the Philippines in 1565 and came to speak of trade, he was given to understand that it was true that copper, tin, Chinese porcelain, benzoin, Indian cloth, cast-ironwork, and steels were carried from Brunei to the southern Philippines, but that the valuable goods he had brought with him from New Spain could not be sold there in ten years' time; if on the other hand he should go to Brunei or Siam everything would be got rid of in eight days.[8]

The traveller Barthémy wrote of Malacca that more ships were harbouring there than in any other place in the world and that every sort of spice and an immeasurable amount of other wares were marketed there.[9] In 1511 D'Albuquerque expostulated with his naval council, which was in dissention over whether to continue the attack on Malacca, that if the city were wrested from the Moors Cairo and Mecca would become completely impoverished and Venice would become dependent on the spice trade from Lisbon.[10] Van Linschoten, writing of the trade in Canton, was willing to:

> say and affirme that in the Haven and ryver of Canton, there are alwaies more ships and barkes, then are in the whole countrie of Spain...[11]

The criterion applied shows how powerfully he was impressed.

Barbosa recounted how Indian cloth and bronze gongs were buried by the inhabitants of the Molucca Islands as treasure.[12] *Patola* (cloth from Cambay), porcelain, and gongs still played a large rôle in the payment of court fines there centuries later.[13] The recent discoveries of rare and costly Chinese ceramics in Indonesia, which have brought to light pieces of porcelain dating from the time of the Han Dynasty, around the beginning of the Christian era, on up to the times of the Ming and Manchu emperors,[14] have confirmed the richness of the *pusaka* treasures built up from the merchandise of foreign trade.

The abundance of Oriental products at Malacca, on the other hand, is measured realistically in the estimate made by Dirck Gerritsz. Pomp alias China, who had sailed with the Portuguese:

> ...Malacca, where all exquisitenesses are..., yea, even if one wanted to load a ship of six hundred ton with them...[15]

The Portuguese sent out one carack per year on the valuable trade on China. The voyage took three years. The king of Portugal had the captaincy at his disposal, and awarded it to persons of great distinction. The trade brought a profit of from a hundred fifty to two hundred thousand ducats, that is to say fifty to sixty-five thousand pounds.[16] In a Portuguese estimate of the amount of spices transported during the fifteen-thirties it is figured that around eighty ton were shipped by the Portuguese around the Cape to Europe, as against twelve hundred eighty ton that went by way of India to the caliphates and the Mediterranean.[17]

A picture thus of wealth and rarity, small quantities and distances spanning continents.

3

The Internationality of Asian Trade

On 22 June, 1596, the first Dutch ships of the Amsterdam 'Company for Afar', coming to anchor off the western Javanese port town of Bantam after having crossed from Madagascar and through the Sunda Straits, were surrounded by that same international trade:

> There came such a multitude of Javanese and other nations as Turks, Chinese, Bengali, Arabs, Persians, Gujarati, and others that one could hardly move.[18]

> ...they ... came so abundantly that each nation took a spot on the ships where they displayed their goods, the same as if it were on a market. Of which the Chinese brought of all sorts of silk woven and unwoven, spun and unspun, with beautiful earthenware, with other strange things more. The Javanese brought chickens, eggs, ducks, and many kinds of fruits. Arabs, Moors, Turks, and other nations of people each brought of everything one might imagine.[19]

And a few days later, on 10 July, 1596, appeared the connection Venice and the Mediterranean continued to have with the Far East in spite of the threat contrived by D'Albuquerque:

> ...the tenth many Turkish and Arab merchants came on board, whereunder one Kojah[20] Rayoan by name, who had earlier been to Venice and spoke fairly good Italian, who raised the point of sailing home with us in order to journey from there back to Constantinople, which was his country, because he could not travel over Achin, a town in Sumatra, since the king ... holds all merchants and had recently taken two Bantamese junks, consequently he had to stay at Bantam... He offered to

> lay in his goods along with ours, and make the ships' owners his heirs in case he should come to die on the voyage.[21]

In 1598, when the ship of Admiral van Neck of the Old Amsterdam Company lay off Bantam, there came an Indian merchant from Delhi, "a man of honourable countenance, ...old in years, [who] was well accompanied...", offering to go along with him on the voyage to the Moluccas, "(as he had to be there) and to secure great amity of the kings and rulers of the land for us".[22]

In 1605 Van der Hagen, admiral of the United Company fleet of 1603, met a Moslem merchant, originally from Fez, on Banda.[23] In 1602 the merchants Hans de Wolff and Lafer, sent out to Surat by the factory established in Achin by the expedition of three Zeeland ships under the admiralty of Van Spilbergen, went to northeast India on an Achinese ship;[24] Van Spilbergen himself found the chief of Mohelli, one of the Comoro Islands to the north of the Mozambique Channel, able "to point out all the places of the East Indies" on the globe shown him, "and was well conversant with the Red Sea".[25]

4

Portuguese and Spanish Power

From the very beginning the Dutch had to face up to the Spanish and Portuguese in Asia with the force of arms: it was the war of independence against the Hapsburg monarchy, transferred to the Far East and the Middle East. Malacca had been in the hands of the Portuguese since 1511; they possessed a fortified point on Ambon (first established in 1522, and after that moved on the island several times); the fortress on Ternate had been lost in 1576, but another had been won on Tidore two years later; Dominican missions had established a pair of fortifications on Solor and Flores in 1566 and 1570. The mighty Portuguese Macao, won in 1557, a self-governing city under a senate, linked Malacca and the outpost on Hirado, off the coast of the Japanese island of Kyushu. To the west, the Portuguese strongholds on

Ceylon commanded the sea passages to the Gulf of Bengal and Sumatra and to the Malabar Coast. And there were other outposts at Negapattinam on the Coromandel Coast, at Goa (the seat of the viceroy), Cochin, Quilon, Damao, and Diu on the west coast of India, and at Muscat and Hormuz at the entrance to the Persian Gulf, and there were strong forts on the east coast of Africa. The Spanish castle of Manila formed a naval station and arsenal in the Philippines, with a long line of communication to New Spain.

Based on an armament which did not differ significantly from that of India, China, or Indonesia in technology, but was most of the time able to keep the upper hand because of greater striking power and better navigation, Portugual's might was primarily maritime and as such was able to maintain its importance in the *histoire de bataille* of all southern and southeastern Asia year in and year out. That was less the case with the Spanish settlement in the Philippines, which could develop little military strength against China. The years were filled with piracy and naval warfare by the Portuguese, defense against assaults and attacks on trading ships, war fleets, and fortresses, guerilla warfare with a strong element of vendetta to it. Even so that aggressive display of power was in the last instance a factor of rather limited import for the thousands-of-miles-long trade routes. The Portuguese regime was of little significance commercially or economically.

The scanty amount of shipping on the route Japan–China–Malacca, the transport of Indonesian spices in a single freighter per year, the limited amount of trade carried on by the independent Portuguese and mestizo merchant adventurers, the low frequency of ships in the trade on the Middle East and the monopoly on export from Goa (which was usually farmed out) all of them argue this. On the other hand Asian trade continued inviolate everywhere. Politically, China as well as the Moslem powers continued to resist the Christian regime.

In trade the belligerent activity of the Portuguese had become one thread more in the fabric of the international exchange of goods carried on in those lands, from Suez to Nagasaki. A monopoly was never carried through anywhere. In the royal trade on the Moluccas there was an average of four hundred *bahar*[26] of cloves transported per year – that is to say, a hundred fifty ton – out of a total clove yield of an average of three thousand *bahar* on the islands of Ternate, Tidore, Moti, Makian, and Batchan in the northern Moluccas.[27] It was the same with other products. In quantity Portuguese trade was exceeded many times by the trade carried on by Chinese, Japanese, Siamese, Javanese, Indians from Coromandel, Gujarat, and Malabar, and Arabs.

5

The Asian Sea Route

Despite the existence of Portuguese and Spanish strongholds in southern and eastern Asia, that world was not a colonial one in the sense that the Europeans were in a dominating position. The international Asian character of trade was maintained, while the political independence of the Oriental states remained practically uninfringed upon by European influence. The great intra-Asian trade route retained its full significance.

The route along which Kojah Rayoan had travelled from Venice to Bantam was the age-old route which had been of importance throughout the whole of early Asian history. The sea route linked India *via* many stages to the ancient world, and later to the Moslem caliphates, where under a new regime the highly developed complex of ancient urban civilization was preserved in essence; it linked Indonesia[28] to India and that wonderland of bureaucratic power, China. It was one of the chief nerves in the body of traditional Islam outstretched from west to east. Brahmanism and Buddhism had gone southeastwards from India along the sea route and set their imprints on the civilizations of Indonesia and the southern part of Farther India. The conquests of the Mongol khans in the thirteenth and fourteenth century – Peking in 1215, Canton in 1278, Bukhara and Samarkand in 1220, the Punjab in

1222, Baghdad in 1258, Liegnitz in 1241 – had brought China within the reach of the Western world; in the fourteenth century Genoese, Venetians, and Pisans were to be met on the sea route, carrying on trade under the protection of the Mongol states as far as into China, and there was in Canton a settlement of the Italian nation swarmed out on adventure, just as there was a terminus for Italian trade in the far west, the land behind the dikes of Witsand and Bruges of which Dante speaks.[29]

6

Early Indonesia

The sea route left its trace through all of early Indonesian history – a history at least as ancient as that of western Europe. Excavations in western Java and southern Sumatra have unearthed Chinese ceramics from the period of the Han Dynasty – around the time of the birth of Christ – which must certainly be considered as having had a sacral function (grain urns, rice wine vases, offering dishes, and so forth) and undoubtedly point toward firmly established settlements of Chinese in those regions[30] – settlements connected with the same kind of overseas and interinsular trade which was familiar in all the later ages at many a point in the archipelago, settlements of a sort which has continued up to the present day. The impressive central Javanese temples, Kalasan, Barabudur, Prambanan, and so on, are contemporary to the Carolingian period; the glory of Majapahit is contemporary to the Avignon episode of the papacy, the revolts of the Flemish gilds, and the victory of the Turks at the Battle of Kosovo.

However, although the chronology of early Indonesian history has already been very much enriched, the course of Indonesian historical development still lies for an important part in darkness. It is certain that there was a strong imprint of influences from India on the civilization. Countless variants of the Indian magical and soteriological doctrines Brahmanism and Buddhism appear in the inscriptions and monuments, and they were so strong an influence that the era from *circa* 200 or 300 A.D. to the fifteenth century is usually spoken of as Hindu-Javanese and Hindu-Indonesian history. What the nature and the form of the Indian civilization which went overseas to southeast Asia was has up to now been a moot point. The concept is losing in influence that Indian civilization was carried by colonization (peaceful, according to some) of Hindu traders – colonial history *avant la lettre*, thus – and that it was the main stimulus for the development of Indonesia, forming states, introducing organization, in fact even interfering in the age-old basis of all culture, agriculture, by instituting wet-field rice farming.[31] Especially through the results of recent prehistorical research it is becoming clearer and clearer that the basis of Indonesian civilization was laid in the neolithic period and the bronze age there, and that it developed upon that indigenous basis.[32] The existence of *sawah* farming in a few areas, especially, must point toward a very long process of development there. The length of time needed for the development of wet-field rice farming and the phenomena related to it – irrigation and terrace-construction, and special forms of social organization in the village, the region, and the royal court with its corps of officials – needs to be measured in ages.[33]

Given such a frame of reference, the conditions for an influence of Indians through colonization are completely lacking. Neither the firm transplantation of culture on the basis of war of Greek colonization which built up Massilia (Marseilles) and Malucha (Malaga) as Greek colonial cities overseas with the appearance and organization of a *polis* in Hellas, nor the construction of military and civil works of the Roman colonial regime appears to have been a characteristic of Hindu colonization in Indonesia. Nor was there a transplantation of a folk culture which set its stamp on the land, the way of building, the language, the folklore in the way the Germanic farmstead civilization with the great migrations took root in northern France, England, and the Scandinavian countries. The Hindu cultural influence involved only things of a sacral and magical sort: religious activities, ritual, literature, administrative techniques, and architectural work carried on for exclusively religious purposes. Therefore the hypothesis is more probable that Hinduization was a matter of the Indian hierocracy coming from the powerful Hindu states of southern India (with which there was no doubt contact by ship, in the same way as there was contact with South China at that time) to the Indonesian courts, scribal priests combining governmental skill and sacral legitimation. It was a process in many respects comparable to the first stages in the expansion of the power of the Roman and Byzantine churches in northern and eastern Europe; the introduction of Church Latin and Church Slavic, vehicles for the foreign religion and the court chancellery, also found a parallel in the expansion of Sanskrit writing in Indonesia.

A second imprint on Indonesian civilization was made by Islam. Islam was a missionary community in the early Christian sense, with every believer a potential missionary for spreading its doctrine. However, though it had already been present for centuries in the foreign colonies in the East – on the west coast of Sumatra *circa* 674,[34] in China arriving along the sea route in the seventh century,[35] in Java and Farther India known from tombstones dated from the years 1082 and 1039,[36] – Islam began to exert wider influence only in the fourteenth century. It prevailed in some small harbour principalities of northern Sumatra at the end of the twelfth century; the rulers of the newly founded Malacca accepted it in the fourteenth century. On Java it gained a firm footing in the courts of the coastal urban aristocracy; at the same time the central state Majapahit disintegrated, certainly not because of a religious war, but because of the power of the regional authorities in the coastal provinces: it was a process which had taken place earlier and was to be repeated again later. Islamization proceeded further eastwards to the Moluccas, antedating the Portuguese there.[37] In the seventeenth century, in 1606, the state Goa, including Macassar, went over to the new doctrine.

The expansion of the new religion did not result in any revolutions or any newly arrived foreign colonists coming to power – the Indonesian regime did not undergo a single change due to it. It is not clear what the causes were that the great proselytization for the new gospel in southeast Asia began only in the thirteenth century though it had already been known for centuries. Perhaps it was a repercussion of the Mongol wars and the threat to the Moslem caliphates, perhaps too more forceful counter-propaganda arose as a result of the coming of Christian missionaries during the rule of the Mongol khans.[38] The expansion of Islam later gained strength through the eruption of the struggle with the Portuguese in Asia, after which the Moslems consciously counteracted every Christian influence. The political significance of the support Moslem rulers gave each other is thus easily understandable. Furthermore, the continued conquests of the now Moslem Mongols in India, the establishment of the Mogol Empire in 1526, and the fall of the southern Indian Hindu kingdom of Vijayanagar in 1565 meant the end of the far-reaching secular power of the Brahmins, the constant decline of which will not have failed to exercise influence overseas as well.

Nor is there any question of a deeper influence of a cultural sort. Islam did not bring a single innovation of a 'higher level of development' to Indonesia, socially or economically, either in state polity or in trade.

Both these world religions were only a thin, easily flaking glaze on the massive body of indigenous civilization. Indonesia's relations with the rest of Asia were established at a time when the independence of the Indonesian states was unshaken and the primacy of Indonesian civilization unchallenged.

7

Nobles and Tax Farmers: The Portuguese Regime

As has already been indicated, and as will appear more clearly from what follows, the penetration of the Portuguese and the Spanish overseas did not determine the character of the sixteenth century in southeast Asia. The Dutch seafarers did not arrive in a Portuguese Asia, neither a Portuguese India nor a Portuguese

Indonesia, but in regions in which the position of the Portuguese was militantly held in check or repulsed. Portuguese power was typically medieval in character, a fact which helps to explain its limited effectiveness. There was not much unity to the scattered territory of port settlements spread out over thousands of miles, despite the centralized royal shipping from Goa to Europe. There was no hierarchy of officials with a distinction between civil and military administration, but a conglomeration of nobles and *condottieri* each with his own retinue of henchmen bound to him by a vassal's loyalty or a lust for gain; often the officials in authority provided their own equipment and carried out exploitation for their own benefit by means of offices bestowed on them, frequently on a short term basis. Portuguese power sought its strength, then, not in taking over Oriental trade or establishing a territorial authority, but in acquiring tribute and booty. Non-economic motives – lust for plunder, not lust for profit – played the chief rôle in the overseas expansion. In connection with this the forms for farming out the trade on the Indies, in which among others the Fuggers and the Welsers had a share, and for farming out the collection of pepper, forms which meant the handing over of the most important aspects of commercial exploitation to private persons in exchange for a fixed income, were characteristic. They were forms typical of political and fiscal capitalism, in which Asian trade and Asian wealth, too, were assigned their functions anew, for the benefit of the Portuguese authorities' revenues.[39]

8

Asia in the Sixteenth and Seventeenth Centuries

Under Sultan Selim (1512–1520) the Egyptian caliphate of the Mamelukes fell into the hands of the Ottoman sultans pressing in from the north. Under Suleiman (1520–1566), contemporary of the Hapsburger Charles V, Mesopotamia was added to the Ottoman state – in the west in the same period Algeria was conquered and Hungary occupied, – thus bringing the shores of the Red Sea and the inner end of the Persian Gulf under Turkish rule. The Moslem Mongols under Babur began the conquest of India, crossing the Hindu Kush from Samarkand in 1519; the plains of the northern Ganges were won with the battle near Panipat in 1526; the great struggle with the Rajput and Hindu states of interior India (Mewar, Vijayanagar) was begun, to be ended for the time being to the advantage of the Mongols with the fall of Chitor in 1568. The Moslem states Gujarat, Bengal, and Orissa followed (1573, 1576, and 1592 respectively), and the might of the Indian Mogol Empire was established, with the brilliant names of its rulers: Akbar (1556–1605), Jahangir (1605–1628), Shah Jehan (1628–1658), and Aurangzeb (1658–1707). There remained only a few national Indian states in the south of the subcontinent, among them the powerful harbour principality Calicut on the Malabar Coast, while the Buddhist-Cingalese state of Kandy maintained its independence on Ceylon.

In China the emperors of the Ming Dynasty defended themselves against the increasingly stronger attacks of the Mongols from the northwest, strengthening the fortifications of the northern cities in 1564 and the Great Wall in 1600. From the sea the Japanese made attacks on the Chinese coast, plundering Ningpo in 1523 and besieging Nanking in 1555, and piracy grew, a base for it being created on Formosa. Burma and Siam appeared as conquerors from the south in Yunnan. The Japanese attacked again in 1592, this time in Korea, but they were repelled by China. In the meantime the Tungus tribe of Manchus settled on the Amur began to go on the move and slowly penetrated southwards, controlling the whole Liaotung Peninsula by 1623 and conquering Korea in 1637. Weakened internally by rebellions, the empire could not hold the northern borders any longer; the Manchus pushed through and in 1644 occupied Peking. The new dynasty was enthroned and a long struggle was begun by the Ming rulers fled to the south; one of the strongest figures in the defense of the nation was Admiral Cheng Cheng-keng – Koxinga, as he was called in the Dutch records – to whom the Dutch outpost on

Formosa fell prey in 1662. The Manchus – the Tartars of the Dutch Company accounts – carried on the conquest; the last great resistance, that of the Ming general Wu San-kwei from 1673 to 1682, was beaten down; in 1683 followed the occupation of Formosa by the Manchus, and the southern border of China was brought under the new central authority and closed.

Japan was dominated by division and rivalry between the great landlords, the *daimios*, with their noble vassals, the *samurai*, and a struggle of the political authorities against the well-organized Buddhist monastic hierarchy, so that the Jesuit missions of the Portuguese were able to enter the land in 1549, valued as a counter-force against Sinaizing influences. The country was reunited by Toyotomi Hideyoshi (1536–1598), and by his successor, Tokugawa Ieyasu (1542–1616), consolidated into the shogunate, the imperial major-domoship of his family. Hermetically sealing off Japan from the rest of the world in the time of the third shogun, Iyemitsu (1623–1649), not long after the persecution of Catholic Christians had been begun with fire and sword in 1614, the shogunate created that wondrous social-economic entity of a directed and regulated feudal and bourgeois state which lasted up till 1868.

9

Indonesia in the Sixteenth and Seventeenth Centuries

In Indonesia the nominal power the Javanese state Majapahit had exercised over the rest of the archipelago (1330–1400) was repulsed, and the state was further weakened through the defection of its dependencies on Java itself. As many times before, the aristocratic groups of the northern coastal towns took up arms against the administrative hierarchy of Majapahit; this time Islam also played a rôle in the opposition, though not a predominant one. According to Indonesian tradition, Pati Unus, a Moslem who from Japara had made an unsuccessful attack on Portuguese Malacca in 1513, around 1520 as ruler of Demak put an end to the Hindu dynasty of Majapahit, the remains of which continued a precarious existence in eastern Java (Pasuruan, Panarukan, Balambangan) until 1639, then to be transferred to Bali. The regalia of Majapahit went over to Demak. Around 1550 rival groups wrested the power from Demak and transferred it to the central Javanese Pajang. In 1582 and the following years one of the state officials at Jogja, Senopati, an adventurer of low origin, was able to usurp the rule of the state and in 1586 shifted the seat of government to the age-old heart of the central Javanese region, Mataram, bringing the provincial governors and vassal princes from eastern Java to the western borders of the state at Cheribon under his authority or in alliance with him. For the powerful coastal towns taking part in international trade, towns such as Japara, Tuban, Sedayu, Grise, Jaratan, Surabaya, Pasuruan, and Panarukan, the link with the inland state was still often nominal. The new central state could develop a new administrative machinery superior to the local authorities only to a limited degree. Under Sultan Agung (1613–1645) the central regime exerted more power: the coastal towns were brought under the rule of the state by force and the regional native aristocracy was replaced by a corps of officials. Meanwhile, in 1628–1629 the struggle was begun with the Dutch stronghold of Batavia, which underwent two sieges. For years afterwards the coast of Java stayed closed to Dutch trade, so that even the rice supply of the central naval station and warehouse of the Dutch Company had to be carried overseas from Farther India, Siam, Burma, India, and Japan. A treaty of peace, by which free Javanese trade on Ambon, Banda, and Ternate and on the west beyond Malacca was allowed only for ships with a pass from the Company, was concluded only in 1646.

The coastal principality of Bantam – founded as a state in the sixteenth century by Moslem Javanese swarming out from Demak, before that along with other ports, including Sunda Kalapa or Jakarta, under the control of the independent inland Sunda state of Pajajaran – remained independent. In 1522 a Portuguese ambassador from Malacca effected an alliance with Pajajaran in

Sunda Kalapa; in 1527, however, Bantam captured the harbour town and sealed off the coast for the non-Moslem Sunda lands.

After the Portuguese conquest of Malacca in 1511, the sultanate removed its seat to the island of Bintang and later to Johore on the mainland of Malaya, carrying on guerilla warfare against Portugal from there but maintaining only a small trade within the reach of Portuguese control, though continuing to exercise suzerainty over the Malay lands on the east coast of Sumatra (Deli and Siak).

The trade route, mobile just as every traditional non-modern-capitalistic movement of trade was, with multitudes of people, a small turnover, and undeveloped technical means, was governed by Portuguese Malacca only to a small extent, and shifted primarily to Achin and Bantam for Indian and Chinese trade respectively. The states on the north coast of Sumatra had already long been ports of call on the trade route. Islam had therefore found its first political expansion there. Certainly under the influence of the new political constellation the power of the Achinese court and its followers grew. The state established control ports having authority to levy tolls and demand tribute from trade along the west coast of Sumatra as far as into the Indrapura region. The name of Sultan Mansur I (1567–1585) is linked to that expansion of power. Influence was also exercised on the west coast of the peninsula of Malaya, among other places in Perak, tributary for delivering tin.

The northern coast of Malaya was in Siam's sphere of political influence (Patani, Sengora, and Ligor), while at the same time Chinese cultural influences made themselves strongly felt there.

In southern Sumatra, beyond the power of Achin, lay Jambi and Palembang, dominating the Batang Hari and Musi Rivers. (The trade going to Minangkabau, the nucleus of traditional Malay culture and earlier royal power, reached there chiefly *via* the river from Jambi.) Their political influence did not extend far. Both were independent, and oriented to Java rather than to the Malay Peninsula; as were the village leagues in the Lampong region, an area without a royal authority of its own, part of it coming under the suzerainty of Bantam. Fringes of partly Malay and partly Javanese colonization on the shores of Borneo had resulted in coastal kingdoms at the trans-shipment points on the river mouths, Brunei, Sukadana, Kota Waringin, Martapura (Banjarmasin), Pasir, and Kutei being the chief of them. The Dyak hinterlands remained unknown.

The two large states in the extreme east of Indonesia, Ternate and Tidore, had wide spheres of suzerainty. Based on small island strongholds, they – and especially Ternate – were masters and tribute lords of the spice islands. Their political authority had been established over the manifold and widespread island communities and smaller states divided into the great leagues – or perhaps totem clans – of Uli-siwa and Uli-lima, and over the shores of New Guinea. The authority of Ternate extended over northern, eastern, and central Celebes including inland areas (the Toraja region, Poso), Buton, and parts of the Lesser Sunda Islands, and, nearer by, northern Halmaheira, Buru, Ceram, Ambon and the Uliasa Islands, and Banda. The southern part of Halmaheira and the shores of New Guinea recognized Tidore as suzerain. The Macassarese and Buginese states in southwestern Celebes were in comparison of the second class. Achin, Mataram, and Ternate were the three leading Indonesian powers of the sixteenth century.

10

Dutch Trade on Adventure

After the most difficult years in the war of independence against the Hapsburgs – who had just turned back the Turks in 1571 in the sea battle of Lepanto, – the merchants of the towns in Holland and Zeeland with the help and under the stimulus of the rich immigrants from the southern Netherlands within a brief period changed over to transoceanic trade. Thus the Dutch intra-European commerce which had slowly grown out of medieval trade, with its fishing and its early crafts for export (clothmaking, brewing), was expanded at a very rapid rate into world commerce. Trade with Guinea and Brazil was being carried on in the 1590's, and was quickly followed by the most appealing voyage on adventure, that around the Cape to Asia.

In 1595 the first Amsterdam company for trade on the Indies sent out a fleet of four ships under Cornelis de Houtman; three ships returned to Tessell on 14 August, 1597. In the meantime a second company had been formed. The first company bought up the second, and on 1 May, 1598 the enlarged 'Old Company' sent out a fleet of eight ships under Jacob van Neck, Jacob van Heemskerck, and Wybrand van Warwyck. From Flushing the merchant De Moucheron sent two ships toward the East in March, 1598, and the same month a Middelburg company had three ships set sail, one of which was wrecked before getting any further than Dover. In June of the same year a Rotterdam enterprise fitted out five ships under Mahu and De Cordes, themselves partners in the enterprise, to sail around South America to war on the Spanish colonies and then go on to Asia. In September Olivier van Noort also set out from Rotterdam with four ships of the Magellan Company, he too fixing his course for the Straits of Magellan.

A third fleet of the Old Company, three ships under Steven van der Hagen, set out to sea from Amsterdam in April, 1599; a fourth, four ships under Wilcken, in December, 1599; a fifth, six ships under Van Neck, in June, 1600. A new Amsterdam enterprise, the Brabant Company, in which the immigrant Le Maire exerted the leading influence, sent out four ships under Both and Van Caerden in December, 1599 and two ships on a second voyage in June, 1600.

In 1601 a coalition of the two Amsterdam companies took place, along with a similar fusion of the two Zeeland enterprises into one Middelburg company. A fleet of four vessels set out for the Middelburg shipowners in February, 1601, while a fleet of thirteen ships under Jacob van Heemskerck and Wolfert Harmensz. was sent out by the Amsterdammers in April. In May three more ships, sailing from Veere, went out under Van Spilbergen, sponsored by De Moucheron and his group, who had stayed out of the Middelburg company. New undertakings were being contemplated in other towns – Delft, Hoorn, Enkhuizen.

In the meantime the authorities stepped in. Judging it more serviceable and profitable for the state of things in general and for the inhabitants of the United Netherlands in particular that the various enterprises be united and trade and shipping thus given a basis, order, and polity, the grand pensionary of Holland was able to carry through an amalgamation into a United Company, and on 20 March, 1602, the new company obtained from the States General a charter valid for twenty-one years granting exclusive rights for trade, shipping, and exercise of authority in the territory between the Cape of Good Hope, the meridian a hundred miles east of the Solomon Islands, and the Bering Straits. The consolidation of the independent groups in various towns fitting out their own voyages into one body with one capital for general equipping of ships was without doubt a piece of statesmanship of the first order. The object pursued was more a political than an economic one. Most of the voyages from 1594 to 1602 either had been profitable or gave prospects of being so; in 1602 mention was made of:

> many ships fitted out and sent thither from time to time which have come back again with no mean successes reckoned all in all...

There was no need for 'reorganization', nor was a 'concentration' in the hands of one dominating group of traders, moneylenders, and shipowners the aim. Rather, the government – and in this it followed the general line of governmental theory of the time – strove for the establishment of a political and military instrument able to bring force to bear against the Spanish monarchy. National political creations of the sort were characteristic for the growing strength of the northwestern European states in the time. The influence of Stadtholder Maurice in unifying the clashing urban groups shows what a central monarchical authority might have been able to achieve even in the loosely confederated provinces of the Dutch Republic. The process was not continued, however, and the chances were allowed to go by. As far as the economic aspect is concerned, no noticeable increase in the capacity of trade took place. The capital of the various companies which had undertaken the earlier voyages added together amounts to a sum that is not much lower than the capital of the United Company (a little over five hundred thousand pounds, which had to be deposited in three equal annual parts, on 1 October, 1602, 1603, and 1604).[40] The form in which the chartered monopoly company began its existence was essentially the same as that of the companies for individual voyages, though a change later appeared in the growing amount of fighting equipment the ships had to carry in a time when a state navy hardly existed. To define the Company's character at the outset as that of "the first large joint-stock company the world's history has known" [41] would seem to be going too far. One should rather speak of it as a company in the meaning of the word at the time, a partnership on adventure owning ships on a long-term basis and enjoying a monopoly and wielding political authority. This character of the enterprise will be returned to further on.

II

A Survey of the Dutch Voyages

The first fleet of the Amsterdam company of 1594 opened trade at Bantam but became involved in conflicts with the authorities there and the Portuguese, who from Malacca incited the Javanese regents of the city against the Hollanders. The voyage further eastward to the Moluccas was given up east of Java, and then the journey home was begun *via* the Bali Straits. The 1598 fleet of the Old Company traded at Bantam, and part of it went on to the Moluccas, where the first Dutch spice trading was begun. Trade took a turn for the worse on Ambon; factors were left behind on Ternate, Bandaneira, and Bandalontar; no fighting occurred. The ships of De Moucheron's company became involved in a conflict in Achin and hardly any trading was done. The Middelburg company of 1598 tried to obtain trade at Bantam.

The Rotterdam ships under Mahu and De Cordes became separated beyond the Straits of Magellan. One ship turned back after endless difficulties, one ship was delivered over and sold to the Spanish authorities in Valparaiso after some unfortunate warfare on the west coast of South America, one ship sank in the Pacific, one ship was placed under arrest in Japan, the fifth was taken by the Portuguese off Tidore. Van Noort had to unload one ship and burn it on the Argentine coast; after the passage through the Straits of Magellan one ship got lost from the others, completing the crossing westwards after a warring expedition along the west coast of South America, only to be shipwrecked on the coast of Ternate; Van Noort himself, having completed the crossing of the Pacific after making raids on the west coast of America, lost another ship in the Philippines in a naval battle with the Spaniards, and in 1601 returned with a single ship by way of Brunei, Jaratan in eastern Java, and the Bali Straits to the Netherlands.

The 1599 Amsterdam ships, the Old Company's third fleet, went to the Moluccas, where they were not able to subdue the Portuguese fort on Ambon, but erected a fortress of their own, the Castle Afar, and closed some contracts for the delivery of spices. The fourth Amsterdam fleet, also sent out in 1599, could not obtain any trade in Achin and had to vacate the Castle Afar on Ambon. The fifth, sent out in 1600, traded in Bantam and on Banda and Ternate, but attempted in vain to overmaster the Portuguese stronghold at Tidore. Missing Patani, they repaired to South China, where an unsuccessful struggle with the Portuguese was carried on at Macao; returning, they obtained trade with Patani and left a factor there. The ships of the Brabant Company of 1599, too, failed to obtain trade at Achin, and carried on trade at Bantam. That company's second voyage, in 1600, was unsuccessful in its attempts to trade on the west coast of Sumatra, and then it, too, limited itself to trading at Bantam. The ships of the United Zeeland Company of 1601 gained a factory in Achin, found Bantam blockaded by the Portuguese, did not obtain any trade on Ambon, and finally traded at Patani, where a factory was established. A part of the 1601 fleet from Amsterdam, under Wolfert Harmensz., attacked the Portuguese off Bantam and broke the blockade; clove trade was obtained at Ternate, and in 1602 monopoly contracts were made at Banda for the nutmeg trade of Bandaneira, Bandalontor, Rozengain, and Ai. The other part of the fleet, under Heemskerck, carried on trade at Achin and Bantam, and in 1602 established a lodge at Grise and traded at Patani. In 1603 a factory was established at Johore, where the annual Portuguese freighter from Macao to Malacca was taken prize off shore. The Zeeland ships under Van Spilbergen went to Batticaloa on Ceylon, whence contact was made with the ruler of Kandy and conversations were carried on regarding a league against the Portuguese who had a firm hold on the west coast of the island. (On a following visit, however, Vice-Admiral de Weert of the United Company's first fleet, of 1603, was murdered in a Cingalese raid.) Van Spilbergen also traded in Achin, and, together with the English admiral who was there at the same time, in 1602 captured the annual Portuguese freighter from Coromandel to Malacca, and finished by trading in Bantam before sailing home.

12

With the Dutch East India Company at War

From this brief survey it is clear that before the United Company there was very little attempt made by the Dutch to establish power in Asia. To achieve such power, to establish a naval station and a naval base, to erect central warehouses, and from there first of all to attack the hereditary enemies Portugal and Spain, were the chief aims for which the new company was established. After the consolidation of the separate companies there arose the system of an annual voyage from Holland and an annual return voyage as well as a regular movement of ships travelling some routes in Asia to collect products for the return ships.

Consequently military exploits against the Portuguese and

Spaniards formed the chief activity of the following years. In 1603 the second United Company fleet attacked Mozambique and Goa, without success; on Ambon, however, the Portuguese Fort Victoria was conquered in 1605; Tidore went over to the Dutch but, left without a garrison, was occupied from Manila by the Spanish in 1606. The third fleet, sailing in 1605, blockaded Malacca, but did not reach any final result; attacks on the Spanish forts on Ternate and Tidore failed; a Dutch stronghold, the Redoubt of Malayu, later christened Orange, was established on the northern part of Ternate; Van Caerden, the commander of the fleet, was taken captive by the Spaniards in the occupation of the spice island Makian. The fourth fleet, the fleet of 1607, once again made unsuccessful overtures against Mozambique and Goa; nor was anything accomplished against Malacca. The first attempt at ensuring the nutmeg monopoly by force was made in attacking Banda and establishing Fort Nassau on Bandaneira. Admiral Verhoeff met his death in 1609, but the contract remained, renewed by Simon Jansz. Hoen; the Spanish fort on Batchan was taken and garrisoned with Dutch troops.

Then in Holland there was a change-over to a new policy: a governor-generalship was established, which meant a greater centralization of the administration and a reinforcement of it when compared to the changing admiralties. In 1610 the fifth fleet sailed out with the first governor-general, Both; a central administrative council, the Council of the Indies, was instituted to function along with him as the governing authority. The foundation of a fixed point for arsenals and warehouses, a 'central rendezvous', now stood as a directive in the instructions;[42] in the meantime the Dutch lodge at Bantam, the oldest of the strongholds, became to some extent the centre, with the establishment of a general accounting office for the Indies there. The choice of a central rendezvous was left between Johore, Bantam, and Jakarta. The idea of a conquered Malacca as the rendezvous, earlier foreseen in a treaty with the ruler of Johore in 1606,[43] was abandoned. The choice fell on Jakarta, as being the place of the three where the Indonesian adversary was weakest, a nobleman ruling over a small coastal town without much trade and a small hinterland which could yield only a limited amount of pepper.

English shipping in the Indonesian seas was by then becoming a second problem of importance alongside the problem of the might of the Portuguese and Spanish, the struggle against which was not suspended with the Twelve Years' Truce (1609–1621) inasmuch as the truce was disregarded overseas. The East India Company of London founded in 1600, a regulated company, a gild of merchants such as for example the older English Levant Company, sailed the Asian seas at the same time as the Dutch. In various ports, with their limited market trade, intrigues with the Indonesian authorities concerning the trade in spices worked to the disadvantage of both the Dutch and the English. English lodges were established in Bantam, Ambon, Macassar, and Jakarta, with a presidency at Bantam; a fortress on Pulau Run in the Banda Islands followed in 1616. The more belligerent Dutch shipping became, the stronger the opposition grew. On Banda the English supported the inhabitants against the Dutch in the growing tension resulting from the strict maintenance of the nutmeg monopoly of 1609.

After new reinforcements of the English fleet had arrived from Europe, in 1618, during the governor-generalship of J. P. Coen, the conflict began. There had not been much progress made in establishing the Dutch central rendezvous at Jakarta: the lodge there had been rebuilt and expanded to a fortress with the regent of the city disapproving but not interfering. With the opening of hostilities Coen retreated to the Moluccas for reinforcement after an indecisive sea battle off Jakarta; the fort underwent a siege and capitulated to the English on 1 February, 1619, but a deployment of Bantamese troops caused the execution of the capitulation to be suspended. The Bantamese expelled the regent of Jakarta and then the English also retreated. With the beginning of the east monsoon the Dutch governor-general's fleet returned from the Moluccas with reinforcements and appeared before the city late in May; landing forces drove back the Bantam besiegers and took the city. The fort, on conquered ground, was occupied as a free territory under the sovereignty of the Company. In keeping with the instructions of the directors of the Company, it was given the name Batavia – an exceptional and peculiar manifestation of nationalism through which was preserved the memory of the ancient Batavians as the people from which the Dutch had sprung. Coen took the leadership, and the English forces were repulsed: the lodge at Bantam was isolated and in a hunt for English ships prizes were taken in the Sunda Straits, off the west coast of Sumatra, and off Patani.

The turn events then took is an amazing one. With the end of the Twelve Years' Truce European political considerations brought the States General to an agreement with England regarding the warfare overseas. On 9 February, 1619, cooperation between the two companies was regulated at London. The English company would hold a third of the spice trade, the Dutch two-thirds; the pepper trade at Bantam was to be shared equally. The question of the right of the English to build fortresses was for the moment left undecided. A Council of Defense alternately under English and Dutch chairmanship was given the highest authority overseas, with a joint fleet for defense.

Attempts of the fleet against Spanish Manila and Portuguese Goa followed in 1620 and 1621. A venture against Macao carried out by the Dutch as an attempt to capture the China trade failed. As a belated result, however, came the foundation of Fort Zeelandia on Formosa in 1624. When it proved impossible for the English to take a larger share in the fleet for defense, Coen undertook in 1621 to ensure the nutmeg monopoly on Banda; there was violent resistance, followed by the complete subjugation of the inhabitants of the islands.

> The contracts have been violated so many times that one cannot hope for anything certain from that nation unless they be once and for all brought under control by warfare...[44]

The contracts on Ambon were sworn to anew in a general assembly of the Indonesian headmen presided over by Coen; the English outpost remained on Ambon alongside the Dutch. In 1623 the personnel of the English lodge, with their Japanese bodyguards,[45] were seized and sharply examined as being suspected of a murderous plot against the Dutch stationed at Fort Nassau. Confessions followed, some under torture, some without. The case was ended on 9 March, 1623 with the execution of ten Englishmen, nine Japanese warriors, and the chief of the slave quarter. The incident was taken very seriously in English diplomacy and in the struggle of those years between the English and the Dutch it took a fixed place in the pamphlet literature of popular politics. With the Treaty of Westminster in 1654 a payment was made to some of the heirs of the people executed, by way of recompense. But the conflict did not bring any change in the state of affairs in southeast Asia. Though in Europe the kingdom of England was growing in power on land and sea, its power in Asia was and remained limited. The English withdrew from Batavia to the island of Lagundi in the Sunda Straits, close to the Lampong coast, where illness devastated the settlement and what few people were left had to be taken back to Batavia again in Dutch Company ships. There remained a small English lodge at Bantam. No new trade or armed action at all took place.

The ventures against Portugal and Spain remained for the time being without important results, though their routes were disturbed by the Dutch ships sent out on patrol – two hundred off Malacca, for example, a blockade carried on for years, – and the Portuguese fort on Solor was conquered by the Dutch in 1613, so that after the Moluccas the Lesser Sundas too were lost to the Portuguese.

In 1628 and 1629 followed the attacks of Mataram on Batavia, and the Indonesians then came to the fore as enemies. For the position of Mataram, the fortress in the west was certainly more serious than the first interference with freedom of trade and shipping in the Moluccas (Banda) had been. The Javanese expeditions both of them ended in failure, it is true, but not before the new city had been pressed to the utmost. A state of war continued and was only ended with a treaty of peace in 1646. In 1642 the superiority of the Dutch at sea brought Palembang over to an alliance with Batavia. Bantam, the old trading centre and since

1619 an open enemy, was held in a state of constant, more or less effective blockade the same as Malacca. An attempt was made to force a large part of Chinese trade from there to Batavia with cruisers and cutters; a treaty of peace was agreed upon in 1645.

The struggle with the English and the Javanese sultanate and the subjugation of Banda fell in the years of Coen's governor-generalship (1619–1623, 1627–1629). The great struggle with Portugal was fought out chiefly under Governor-General Van Diemen (1636–1646). Begun against the Portuguese possessions under the Spanish crown, it was ended against a Portugal once more (in 1640) become independent. Goa was patrolled; after a treaty with the Cingalese ruler in 1638 the Portuguese castles on Ceylon were attacked; Malacca too was attacked, and fell in 1641 after a heavy siege, the first large military action of the Dutch on land; most of the Portuguese outposts on Ceylon were subjugated in a campaign of siege and blockade continued for several years – Batticaloa was won in 1638, Trincomalee in 1639, Negombo in 1640, lost again, and reconquered in 1644, Galle in 1640. In 1641 a ten years' truce was closed in Europe between Portugal and the Dutch Republic, by which hostilities overseas would cease a year after the exchange of ratifications. Attacks on Colombo failed, but in 1642 Negapattinam capitulated, after which in 1644 a treaty regarding Ceylon was concluded in Goa. In it the Cingalese cinnamon lands were demarcated and the conquered outposts were left in the hands of the possessors of the moment.[46]

13

The Penetration of the United Company in Asia

> *But in my opinion we cannot exist in the Indies without authority and power, mingled with agreeable apposite means and reasonings...*
>
> Coen to the Gentlemen Seventeen, 22 October, 1615 (Colenbrander, *Coen*, I, 128).

That the outcome of the war was advantageous to the Dutch Company is clearly shown in what has already been written above: a general rendezvous established, fortresses and military control vigorously continued, and the original inhabitants of Banda deported and exterminated, so that the nutmeg monopoly became a complete one, the stronghold of Malacca and sturdy castles on Ceylon taken, a blockade continued, now of Goa, a fort set up on the Coromandel Coast, English trade practically driven out of Indonesia, the incidental French and Danish shipping liquidated without great difficulty, the power of the Spanish in Manila put on the defensive after the Treaty of Munster (in 1642 the Spanish fort of Kelang on northern Formosa went over to the Dutch Company). On the sea route to Holland, furthermore, Mauritius was held from 1638 on, while from 1647 on settlements at the Cape of Good Hope were attempted and in 1652 accomplished and secured by the establishment of a fort.

Is this enough to justify one's speaking of the rise of a Company Indies? It would appear premature. The control of a few points on the intra-Asian trade routes had also formed the power of the Portuguese. The fortified outpost in western Java, which became the terminus of the transoceanic route and the Dutch routes in Asia, was new. The fort of Zeelandia was established on Formosa, facing Macao, but the Dutch were not admitted to the trade on China, the provincial Chinese authority in Fukien being strong enough to exclude them. The Dutch in Japan had always lived in very limited freedom; during the Tokugawa shogunate the outpost from being limited became completely isolated with the transfer in 1647 of the Company lodge from Hirado, where it had been established in 1609, to the island of Deshima, close to Nagasaki, where the Japanese exercised a strict control on the departure and wintering of the ships and on the markets and prices of goods. Dutch trade on Patani lapsed after the foundation of Batavia, and in November, 1622 the office was closed. Trade was undertaken on Siam, Cambodia, Annam, and Tonkin, and lodges were established there in 1607, 1620, 1636, and 1637 respectively, but the course of trade was slow. The lodge established in 1610 in Arakan, at the extreme southwestern point of the coast of Burma, was closed in 1617. On the Coromandel Coast of India the Company was able to obtain the privilege of transforming the lodge at Pulicat, founded in 1610, into a stronghold, Fort Gelria, in 1613. There had been an office in Masulipatnam since 1604; trade was carried on in Tegenapatnam and Tiruchirapalli from 1608[47] and 1610 on, respectively, and at Hooghly, in the delta of the Ganges, from 1634 on. After a visit earlier by factors of the Zeeland company, a lodge had been established in Surat in 1604, and was renewed in 1616 after a conflict with the authorities. A number of offices in the other Gujarati ports and the inland empire of the mogul – Broach, Cambay, Ahmadabad, Burhanpur, Sharkej, Agra, Baroda, Jalalpur – were in turn linked to it. Trade on Persia was opened up in 1623 under a special grant of the ruler, a share in the mighty international silk trade being carried on under the royal monopoly. The Company also came to trade at Shihr on the coast of Hadramaut in 1614, at Aden in the same year, at Mocha in 1616, and in 1620 even in Mecca. With the fall of Hormuz, the key fortress on the Persian Gulf, in 1622, after a siege by the Persians and the English, the power of the Portuguese in those regions was greatly weakened. With the loss of Muscat to Arab hands in 1648 it was weakened even more. The political power of the Dutch Company in the regions was insignificant, however. The Portuguese sea power based at Goa was still by no means negligible in Indian and African waters and made continuous heavy armament necessary, and the might of the Mogol rulers and governors, the Persian court, and the Turkish governors in Arabia as well was too substantial to oppose.[48] Fort Gelria at Pulicat was a welcome haven for Dutch trade on the Coromandel Coast, which was often quite seriously harassed by the continual wars the Hindu and Moslem rulers of the Deccan were forced to carry on with the Mogols. No offensive power emanated from the fort, which had been granted the Dutch by a privilege from the Hindu ruler of Chandragiri, descendant of the rulers of Vijayanagar.[49]

14

Dutch Power in Asia: 1650

The power of the Dutch, then, was concentrated chiefly in Indonesia. What sort of power it was has been sketched briefly above. It did not constitute any political preponderance in the archipelago. The might of the Javanese and the Achinese was still too unshaken for that.[50] The might of Ternate had been reduced, injured in the struggle the Europeans had fought out there, through the fortresses on the clove islands and the blockade fleets and punitory expeditions going out from them and through the fall of Banda. The governorships over Ambon and Ceram held by Ternate were abolished in 1643 after repeated resistance and warfare. Still it would be wrong to assume that the spice trade thus came completely into the hands of the Dutch. A part of the spices continued to be carried in Malay and Javanese ships and, in the latter part of the period, when a portion of the trade which had gone to Malacca and Bantam was directed to the port on southern Celebes, in Macassarese ships – albeit violently opposed by the Company, which forced its subjects and allies to render heavy armed service and galley service. The pepper trade, due to Company shipments turned primarily toward Europe, but before then very probably directed chiefly toward China,[51] continued. Chinese junks went to the Indonesian-controlled ports as well as to Batavia and the ports on Formosa. The shipping from Achin on India went on. The Company now had a share in the transport of cloth from Coromandel, one of the most remarkable branches of international Asian trade, and a similar position in the trade on northwestern India and in the land trade in the Mogol Empire, in Persia, and in Turkish Arabia.

A distinction must be made between the economic and the political element in the development of Dutch power in Indonesia. Dutch political influence depended on armed power: the Company's technology in the arts of war appears to have been in general superior to that of the Indonesians, both on water and on land. In that region the defensive power of the Orient seems to have become weaker comparatively. (There does not appear to have been a clear inferiority of the Indonesians to the Portuguese technologically, nor does there seem to have been a clear superiority of European armaments to that of the Turks, the Indians, the Chinese, and the Japanese.) The heart of the whole matter lies in its military aspect – the progress of Dutch power must be attributed not to more diplomatic insight, to greater courage and greater impetuosity, to greater economic reserves, but to the sturdier rigging and the greater speed of the ships, the more powerful cannon-royal, the greater mobility of armed troops. The modern idea that political domination in colonial lands is based on the preponderance of a more highly developed economic system, is in fact even the instrument of it, needs here to be discarded. The pattern of the seventeenth century belongs in another configuration as far as economics is concerned. The Dutch Company's profits – which were not sufficient for financing its outposts in the Indies, its servants, and its ship personnel, and for keeping the rotating commercial capital up to the mark – and the goods for the Company's return fleets were both obtained from Asian trade, for a small part under pressure but for the largest part in free commercial exchange. Coined money, mostly silver, had to be shipped from Europe to Asia every year. And as is illustrated statistically below, there was no question of a European preponderance in trade, either in volume or in organization. It cannot be said forcefully enough that in order to gain objectivity one needs here to abandon the idea of modern-capitalistic trade mobilizing mass quantities of goods and supplying raw materials for mechanized industries and industrial products in demand for everyday consumption. One should call to mind the old trade in valuable high-quality products and hand-made craft products moving from market to market over routes lasting many months and years in a slow turnover through weigh-houses, treasuries, and warehouses – a trade in its extensiveness and infrequency also different from the staple trade of the towns in Holland and Zeeland, in which with a large number of ships travelling over short routes salt and wine, wool and dried fruits, grain and wood, copper and iron, trinkets, linen, and dairy products were turned over in a high frequency, enlivening and stimulating factories, handicrafts, and trades.

Chapter Two

I

The Oriental Trade Goods

Indian cloth and Indonesian spices, precious stones and perfumes, medicinal products and varieties of wood were carried from the east along the sea routes and caravan routes from the earliest history of the great states of northern Africa and the Middle East on. For example, the caravan of Ishmeelites to whom Joseph was sold by his brothers, "their camels bearing spicery and balm and myrrh, going to carry it down to Egypt";[1] or the traders from Sheba, Asshur, and Chilmad, "merchants in all sorts of things, in blue clothes, and broidered work, and in chests of rich apparel, bound with cords, and made with cedar"[2] – Oriental merchandise, thus. This sort of trade was to be found in every state, under every dynasty. One of the sources of the wealth of Solomon's great kingdom was the organization of such caravan trade, and Solomon's ships, sailing out from Ezion-geber on the shore of the Red Sea to Ophir,[3] probably reached the Malabar Coast.[4] In the Alexandrian book on trade and shipping during the first century A.D., the *Periplus*, pepper, betel nuts, ivory, pearls, and cloth are listed as Indian products, and the Indian ports Muziris (Mangalore) and Broach are mentioned. Pliny's statement that the amount of twenty-five million sestertia of silver was drained out of the Roman Empire each year in its trade with India is well known.

The same complex of trade was to be encountered in Byzantium and the Moslem caliphates, where the urban civilizations and forms of government of the ancient world were continued. Europe was then, as in Roman times, still a market of little importance, a source of sales in very small quantities to the courts of secular and religious dignitaries. Gradually, with the development of towns in northern Europe, the market for Asian merchandise there was expanded; it remained small compared to those of southern Europe and the Near East and India, however. The new Portuguese shipping *via* the Atlantic was not able off-hand to divert the course of Asian trade; the small amount mentioned above of spices shipped to Lisbon in the 1530's is therefore understandable. With the developments of the sixteenth century the level of sales in northern and western Europe was sent climbing upwards, and the market for spices around the beginning of the seventeenth century was maintained by the Dutch Company on the same level for decades.

Through the centuries trade was constantly carried on between Indonesia and China – a trade which for the dimensions of the empire and the distances of the voyages was also small. The Chinese court chroniclers have noted down the trade goods and gifts brought into the ports by merchants and ambassadors during the successive dynasties. The sending of embassies from the Indonesian states to China as a symbol of an as a rule nominal political allegiance took place down through the centuries; later the embassies of the Dutch Company travelling from Batavia were received by the Chinese authorities of the Manchu Dynasty on the same basis. In the first century of the Christian era, silk goods, precious stones, and pearls were listed as trade goods[5] (excavations have brought to light the costly Han Dynasty porcelain of that period in various places in Indonesia); in the tenth century ivory, frankincense, rose water, dates, preserved peaches, white sugar, crystal rings, glass bottles, naphtha, coral, cotton cloth, rhinoceros horn, perfumes, condiments;[6] in the time of the Sung Dynasty (960–1279) gold, silver, anice, pepper, areca nuts, sulphur;[7] ambassadorial gifts from Majapahit in the last quarter of the fourteenth century were black slaves, pearls, pepper.[8] (In the same way the ruler of Arakan sent a gift of ten slaves with an embassy to the governor-general of the Dutch Company in 1623,[9] and pepper, birds, and edible birds' nests were part of the gifts of an embassy from the coast of Palembang to Batavia in 1637.)[10] The trade of which these ambassadorial gifts are a reflection was the same sort of trade as that in Bantam in 1596.

2

Indonesia and the Eastern Sea Route

For all the shifts in political power and cultural forms, then, the general course of Asian international trade remained essentially unchanged. Indonesia was at the same time a stage for trade in transit and an objective of trade in itself. From the Indian ports and the Moslem states Indian and Burmese trade and shipping and the travelling trade from the Persian, Arabian, and Turkish cities came to the Far East. From the ports of South China, primarily Canton and the cities in Fukien, junks with Chinese traders and emigrants in exodus – an age-old movement of colonization, one which had certainly increased with the final struggle of the Ming rulers and their adherents against the Manchus – set out for the shores and ports of Farther India and Indonesia. The Indonesian products cloves, nutmeg, mace, pepper, sandalwood and sapanwood, camphor, cinnamon, wax, resin, gold, precious jewels, drugs and medicines (rhinoceros horn), rarities such as birds and tortoise shell, tin, and so forth were exported to the north and the west, where they were traded for Indian and Persian textiles, indigo, slaves, iron and steel, and money and materials for money, and for such Chinese goods as silk and silk cloth, porcelain, lacquered work, copperwork, paper, medicinal products, sugar, hand-made luxury products, and Japanese silver, the largest share of which were re-shipped from the Indonesian ports on to the west. Malay and Javanese ships conveyed the Indonesian products to the chief ports; besides that, foreign ships travelled along the Indonesian ports carrying on their own trade. Linked to the conveyance of spices and other products was an extensive shipping in rice, salt, and other food supplies from the Javanese ports both eastwards and westwards in the archipelago. Japanese ships most of the time did not travel further than the ports in the Gulf of Siam. Siamese ships were infrequent in Indonesia, regulated as they were by a royal monopoly. The shipping from Spanish Manila to Mexico, which brought about an increase in Chinese trade on the Philippines, was something new; Portuguese trade and shipping followed the old routes.

The semi-annual winds of the tropical seasons controlled all movement of ships and all trade. The west-northwestern winds prevailing from December to March carried the Indian and the Chinese ships to Indonesia and the Indonesian to the spice islands and the sandalwood islands. The length of time the prevailing winds lasted determined the length of time for trading; with the turning east-southeastern winds from April to September trade ended and ships began the return trip toward India and China. And in later times the Company's fleets returning to Holland would set out through the Sunda Straits with the northwest wind around the end of December.

3

The Travelling Foreign Traders

Many an example of the rôle in trade of foreigners carrying along goods of their own, taking goods to market as factors of an owner of merchandise, or setting out with money or goods on *commenda* is also to be found in the European trade of the middle ages. There were for instance the house of the Scottish staple in Veere and the 'Steelyard' of the Hanse in London, colonies which had their own law and were governed according to their own customs. At the time of the shipping trade on the Roman Empire from Muziris, the Roman colony there owned a temple dedicated to Augustus.[11] In the eight century Islam with its mosques arrived with the traders from the caliphates forming colonies in Canton and other Chinese cities.

The trade involved great multitudes of people moving from place to place, and there were colonies of foreigners everywhere. A thousand traders from Gujarat lived in Malacca before it fell in 1511, and three or four thousand were constantly travelling between India and there.[12] To those numbers should be added the Indian traders from Coromandel, the foreigners from Persia and

Arabia, the Chinese settlement, and the quarter or quarters of the 'foreign Indonesians', chiefly Javanese – altogether surely ten to fifteen thousand traders. It was the same picture at Bantam, a smaller size staple port: "In the towne there is great resort of divers Countries and nations..."[13] There were people from every part of India and from Pegu and Siam, Persians, Arabs, Turks, and Chinese, as well as 'foreign Indonesians' – Malays, Ternatese, Bandanese, Banjarese, Macassarese, Buginese – each 'nation' living in its quarter inside the wall or its suburb outside.[14] It was the same situation on the spice islands: in 1609 there were fifteen hundred traders for the purchase of the spice crop on Banda alone,[15] and there was a Gujarati quarter there.[16]

It is the same picture in every port. The traders swarmed out by tens and hundreds along every coast on the whole route in southeast Asia, flocking together by thousands at the staple points. Handicrafts, moneychanging, and permanent settlement were linked to the market trade. In a certain sense the Chinese and Arab *kampongs* of the Indonesian towns are remnants of such foreign quarters, now greatly changed and disintegrating.

In Scania in southern Sweden, the centre of herring fishing in the middle ages, there were trading colonies from most of the various towns in the Netherlands – Kampen, Harderwijk, Zutphen, Stavoren, Hindelopen, Groningen, Nijmegen, Zierikzee, Maastricht, and Bois le Duc.[17] The metalsmiths from Nuremberg appeared with their wares at Scania in the same way they went to Frankfurt to trade at the fairs.[18] Traders who had come on the ships from Leiden set up their booths in Scania and sold Leiden cloth by the whole piece or cut to size.[19]

In the same way the Javanese traders went to Banda, pulling their junks on shore, carrying the cargo to booths set up there, and selling their wares the rest of the season, until the winds turned.[20] The preparations for setting out on the spice trade from Macassar in 1624 have been described:

> ... all the Malay and other foreign traders, being more than six hundred strong, prepare themselves to go out again with the beginning of the coming western monsoon, most of them with small vessels [usual for

> the spice trade] to Amboyna and the surrounding regions, with as great a capital as they can bring together, some of it rice, but most of it cash, through last year's profits being made keen and fed with a great hope of making still more this year; [it is said that] the king for his part will send two chiefs over them, with the express charge that in case the inhabitants of Amboyna or thereabouts request any help or assistance they shall perform that same completely, according to their ability...[21]

(This last is a sign of the waxing power of Macassar and in a certain sense a prototype of a 'consular function' such as the towns of southern Italy had also developed earlier in the Mediterranean.) Forty junks went from Macassar to Ambon and Ceram for the clove trade with the western monsoon of 1624–1625.

> Those who sailed the junks were ... most of them Malays from Patani, from Johore, and other places, who lived in many thousands in Macassar, and who controlled most of the shipping in every direction...[22]

In the western monsoon of 1630–1631:

> 32 or 33 junks large and small, having 30 to 70 persons on them, had left Macassar again for Luhu and Kambelo [western Ceram]...[23]

– a total of sixteen hundred people, more or less, on the ships, thus, traders and crew together.

The Portuguese colony at Macassar at the time was estimated to be five hundred man strong; "...the king there suffers that they may exercise their religion in that land...",[24] a fact which is surprising in the recently Islamized Macassar, but one fitting completely into the general picture of the internationality of trade, in which in foreign states other peaceful sects were left unmolested. There were Hindus in Moslem Malacca and Moslems in Confucian China. Only with the religious wars of the Portuguese did there come a change, but as in the Moslem caliphates Jews were employed as publicans[25] and Nestorian monks as officials,[26] and good relations were maintained with the Jewish court bankers,[27] in the same way in Catholic Goa taxes were farmed out to the Hindu wholesale traders and moneyholders there for the sake of efficiency,[28] and the Dutch Company farmed out the city taxes of Batavia to Chinese there. In Goa, further, all foreign sects were tolerated:

...the Portingales... dwell in the towne among all sorts of nations, as Indians, Heathens, Moores, Jewes, Armenians, Gusarates, Benianes, Bramenes, and of all Indian nations and people, which do all dwell and traficke therein, everie man holding his own religion, without constrayning any man to doe against his conscience...[29]

4

The Pedlars

In 1360, with the settlement of a dispute between shippers trading on Flanders and the local small traders regarding the sale of oil within Rostock, the municipal council of the city made a distinction between the oil brought in from overseas regions and that from Lübeck, Stralsund, and neighbouring places. The traders on Flanders were allowed to sell *en détail* only the oil imported from overseas.[30] In the same way the peddling shippers from Leiden stood in their booths in Scania to sell Leiden cloth cut to small sizes. It was a peddling trade coming from a long distance away, the traders travelling with their goods and selling them retail. In 1428 an edict of the duke of Burgundy prohibited the import of English woollen cloth and yarn in the Netherlands. On the basis of the prohibition the goods of a citizen of Utrecht coming from overseas were seized in Dordrecht in 1432. The goods consisted of cloth, tinware, and a hundred ten pounds of woollen yarn which the man "had bought in a village [in England] from the mayor for 7 nobles". The captain had a share of two and three-quarters nobles in the yarn, and the ship's crew one of a noble and a half.[31]

There was the same sort of trade in Asia. The Chinese who brought raw silk, silk cloth, and porcelain on board the first Amsterdam ship in Bantam had come from the north three thousand miles overseas in order to carry on small trade in the Javanese ports.

...these small pedlars, who take money on interest and bottomry in China and go trading to Bantam and Patani with it, have to sell dearer or cannot remain solvent...[32]

– that is to say, they had to carry on their trade in the season before the wind turned, because their small means did not allow them to stay over and await a better sale in a new season. The large Chinese junks of hundreds of tons of which Marco Polo had earlier preserved accounts, ships often larger than the great East Indiamen, carried hundreds of traders to Indonesia, and besides them also emigrants who frequently had to earn their passage by indenturing their bodies:

> the Chinese who come by thousands from China each year [and] have to care for their freight and costs often pawn their bodies therefor...[33]

In 1625 the Chinese fleet trading on Batavia – five junks, most of them six or eight hundred ton; a total tonnage thus as large as or larger than that of the whole return fleet of the Dutch Company – arrived with four hundred eighty, five hundred, one hundred, and five hundred persons.[34] In 1626 there were junks of eight hundred ton with five hundred, five hundred, and four hundred fifty persons on board.[35] In 1627 there were five junks, three of them with four hundred, three hundred fifty, and five hundred persons respectively.[36] The trade on Batavia was only one branch of the important Chinese overseas trade. It was estimated in 1626 that from the ports of Fukien four junks would go out to Batavia, four to Cambodia, four to Cochin China, three to Siam, one to Patani, one to Jambi, one to Jaratan (Grise), and around a hundred smaller junks on the shorter overseas route to Manila.[37] There was the same sort of picture in 1631: five junks to Batavia, two to Patani, one to Sengora, five to Cambodia, two to Siam, five to Cochin China, and seventy or eighty to Manila[38] – an exodus overseas, thus, of around six or seven thousand persons.

The same sort of trade was carried on by Indonesians, and Chinese settled in Indonesia, going to China with the returning junks. A list has been preserved of the bottomry money which traders from Jambi sent to China in a Chinese junk in 1636 for trading. From the list appears the large amount of participants in such trade as well as the small amount of money each of them (with one exception, perhaps a merchant gentleman) invested in it:

The following Chinese residing in Jambi have demonstrated to the [Company] merchant Lucas de Vogel that ... 1247 reals of 8 in specie were sent to their friends in China with the Chinese junk last year, to wit:

Bingouw . . .	700 reals
Piesjangh . . .	50 „
Gochie	90 „
Hockhum . . .	30 „
Cambingh . .	80 „
Inretullus . . .	50 „
Gecko	47 „
Jan Peck . . .	45 „
Chiactin . . .	40 „
Pettingh . . .	20 „
Chily Kitchil .	20 „
Inretullus . .	20 „
Tingpat	20 „
Sico	20 „
Sambayangh .	25 „

Account in total 1247 reals [actually 1257].[39]

Sums of from four to eight pounds were sent out three thousand miles away for making profit in overseas trade. It would be hard to find a more characteristic illustration of peddling trade.

Small traders, each shipping out with his goods for a peddling trade having a value of a few pounds. The following situation, showing how a mass of hundreds of such people sailing on a Chinese junk melted away, is another illustration of the same sort. A Chinese food supply ship seized by the Dutch Company in its blockade of Manila in 1616 and taken to Banda was disposed of by a resolution of the president and councillors of the lodge at Bantam (4 March, 1617) as follows:

> As the Chinese with the junk conquered by the *Black Lion* have jumped overboard and run away in large groups numbering 80 each day and the rest are also resolved to it through fear so they said that they will be used on galleys or otherwise for slaves in Amboyna or Banda, notwithstanding that it has been attempted to turn them away from that wrong opinion with all good reasons, [they] still persist stubbornly and desperately thereby, it is approved, in order to avoid further accidents as well as the scandal of the Chinese and Javanese in Bantam, that the aforesaid captured Chinese shall be given their choice that those who

remain voluntarily shall keep their goods in order to be able to benefit from them to their own advantage as free persons in Amboyna or Banda, and those who are not disposed to do such shall have all their goods taken prize and be set on shore here...[40]

Linked to this overseas trade involving small sums of money and correspondingly small cargoes there was a purchasing and market trade set up on essentially the same footing. The Amsterdammers who sought trade in Bantam in 1596 peddled goods in a rented house and went out to buy pepper on the *pasar*, the market. The small everyday business is given a lively description in the letters from the commissioner Jan Jansz. Karel in Bantam to the authorities on the ships riding at anchor offshore.

[6 August, 1596] Tomorrow I shall go to the *pasar* and look for the anice and other herbs, and if You desire to have pepper bought on the *pasar* will You kindly advise me so...

[7 August] These morning hours I have gone to the *pasar*, but have not carried out anything special...

[10 August] ...further yesterday received 20 measures of old pepper, weighing 58 lb. net, for a thousand cash the measure, was very dry; have today inquired after the price of pepper on the *pasar*, would not have less than 1100 cash now... ...[it] is necessary to speak with the governor [the regent of Bantam] ... about pepper, the sooner the better, for if he stores it then we shall not see any quantity coming on the *pasar* yet...

The same day we had a merchant who offered 2 bags of pepper per ell for a piece of madder-red cloth the which cost seven shillings, and it was left to him at 2½; would have let him have it if he had offered ¼ more, as the interpreter approved of the sale...[41]

A trade in small measures with the cash, the Chinese lead coin with a square hole in the middle so it could be threaded on a string, around a thousand of which had something like the same value as fourpence. All this is on the same level with the trade carried on by the Chinese pepper buyers at Bantam:

going inland into the villages with their weights in hand, weighing first how much there was there and then bidding according to what money they think the people need...[42]

5

The Merchant Gentlemen

It would be an incomplete description to say that this trade was carried on only by small traders, however. Alongside the Dutch ships trading on Scania and the ships from Rostock trading on Flanders, carrying on peddling trade, there were great merchant gentlemen to be found in many towns, combining merchandise trade with money investment and money trade, 'bankers' and 'capitalists', well-born men most of the time staying at home. There were the many great names of the Italian towns (the Peruzzi and the Bardi, the Scali and the Amieri, and so forth), the Vicko van Gelderses of Hamburg, Mandual of Marseilles, Jehan Boine Broke of Douai.[43] There was the same situation in Asia.

Alongside the small traders, merchants arrived in Indonesia with cargoes worth thirty or forty thousand reals, that is to say from fifty-five to seventy-five hundred pounds,[44] on five junks with cargoes having a total value estimated at three hundred thousand reals.[45] (It should be borne in mind that the largest investment in the Dutch United Company of 1602, that of Le Maire, amounted to £ 8100, Lyntgens' investment to £ 5000, and Jacques de Velaer's to £ 4800.) The Turkish merchant Rayoan in 1596 planned his return to Europe with the Amsterdam ships as the same sort of voyage. Such large sums were not necessarily sent out from the hands of one person: the merchant could take money given him in *commenda* or bottomry by persons staying at home. Even so the difference between the pedlars and the merchant gentlemen remains striking.

The merchant Bingouw of Jambi who sent seven hundred reals of eight to China for trade invested ten or twenty times as much as the rest of the traders. The Chinese wholesale trader at Bantam Simsuan, dealer in pepper and sandalwood, owner of ships sent out to trade, large landowner and squire,[46] debtor to the Dutch Company for hundreds of pounds advanced on products to be delivered, was pressed for payment by a resolution of the president and councillors of the lodge at Bantam (1 July, 1616):

> As Simsuan, a Chinese merchant residing here, is indebted to the general Company a good lot of pepper and as it appears it will not be possible to collect much of his outstanding debts, it is approved that he shall be ordered and forced to have a good sum of the means sent by him to China brought hither next year to pay us, as also that it shall be publicly declared and announced that if the friends of the said Simsuan be negligent in this we will avail ourselves of whatever persons and goods we may be able to lay hold of at Simsuan's and their cost...[47]

Another merchant, Aytuan, was in 1616 said to be "very bad off for many thousands".[48]

After the establishment of Dutch trade on Formosa the Chinese government granted a monopoly of imports to the merchant gentleman Simsou, who shipped goods with five junks at a time and held tens of thousands of pounds of Company funds advanced for the purchase of silk. The total annual turnover in silk ran to eight hundred picul, that is to say, two or two and a half times as much as the total amount of silk carried by the Chinese ships trading on Bantam annually.[49] The wealthy in China – the *commenda* moneylenders, who were not necessarily professional traders, as well as the merchant gentlemen – who sent the small traders out to trade with their money and merchandise so that if one wanted to harm them one would have to take violent possession of the pedlars, body and goods, were the subject of Coen's speculations sent to the Gentlemen Seventeen 20 June, 1623:

> It is my opinion that even if Your Excellencies should send ten hundred thousand pieces of eight and more to the king and regents of China as a gift [in the hope of opening up trade in China], nothing would be gained, not because of their ancient regulations, with which they seek to excuse themselves, but mainly out of regard for the inequably higher damage we cause them by preventing the trade on Manila, which is principally an affair of the Chinese lords. The Chinese say that [the risk of] losing the goods will not make them abandon the trade on Manila, but that if we want to keep them from there we will have to imprison or kill all the people we get hold of in order to make the fear of losing life and property greater for the poor than the hope of making profit, for as long as the poor are not in bodily danger the rich will always venture the goods...[50]

This, then, is the counterpart to the peddling trade described above.

The commanders of the Chinese junks were also merchant gentlemen, and overseas they were treated as of high rank.[51] In 1625 in Batavia the *nakoda* or ship commander Wangsan offered to deliver in Formosa one thousand to fifteen hundred picul of silk with a total value of two to three hundred thousand reals, thus forty to sixty thousand pounds, which meant a tenth of the total capital of the Dutch Company.[52] In 1632 in Persia a whole Company cargo was handed over to one of the merchants of the royal silk monopoly for ten thousand *toman*, or around thirty-five thousand pounds, seventy per cent. in goods and thirty per cent. in cash, all in order to obtain silk.[53] In the Mogol lands as well, in 1637, whole cargoes were traded to Moslem merchants in single contracts, to be settled:

> three months from the following new moon, being the following 24th April, in gold pagodas of good alloy and current money...[54]

In the cities of the Coromandel Coast – Masulipatnam, Pulicat, and so forth – there were great merchant families such as the Hindu Malayas, who carried on shipping as far to the west as Aden and the regions around Mecca and as far to the east as Indonesia, conducted trade and banking, and led a seigneurial way of life; members of the family held governmental posts, while the office of commander of the army was also occupied by one of them.[55] And there was the 'Moorish' (actually Persian Moslem) merchant gentleman Mirocomaldy of Masulipatnam, also carrying on shipping with his own vessels eastwards and westwards,[56] but sending out goods on Dutch Company ships with a slave or a factor as well.[57] The merchant gentlemen played an important rôle in the Coromandel cloth trade, which through its putting-out system interfered on a large scale in the clothmaking industry carried on primarily by semi-rural weavers and wood block and wax colour printers. In 1619 the Dutch Company's total sale of cotton cloth was estimated at three thousand *corges* (each of twenty pieces) per year; the merchants of Masulipatnam offered the fabrics for sale a thousand *corges* at a time.[58] In this period the town government of Surat was farmed out by the Mogol administration to members of the *haute bourgeoisie*, seigneurial in their way of life, in return for the sum of twenty *lakh mamudi*, or around sixty thousand pounds, per year.

In this class of merchant gentlemen there was a scale of possible independent activities ranging from that of carrying on one's own trade, owning one's own ships, and having one's own factors to that of investing in bottomry and *commenda* completely passively, whereby either shippers or small traders took the money or had it taken to be used in trade. To judge from a passage in the accounts of the first Dutch voyage to the East, the latter form seems to have predominated in Bantam:

> The merchants who are wealthy in general stay at home, then when some ships are ready to leave they give those going with them [the shipper-passengers; often the crew also took part in trade] a sum of money to be repaid doubly, [the amount] more or less according to the length of the voyages, of which they make an obligation, and if the voyage is prosperously completed then the giver is paid according to the contract, and if the drawer cannot pay the money because of some misfortune then he must give his wife and children in pledge for the whole time until the debt is paid, unless the ship be wrecked – then the former loses the money he lent...[59]

6

The Lords of the Land

Towering high above the masses of small traders as *popolo grosso* above the *popolo minuto*, patricians leading a seigneurial way of life, merchant gentlemen though not always wholesale merchants by profession – the wealthy merchant class was allied to the mighty who exercised social and political authority. In some places, as in Surat, the wealthy merchant class held political power themselves; in others authority remained exclusively in the hands of the related class of nobles and high royal officials, independent governors, and collegiate bodies. Hierarchies of officials made their influence felt from Yemen to Nagasaki, in the political systems of the Turkish sultanates, Persia, Mogol and Hindu India, Siam, Cambodia, China, and Japan, and in Indonesia as well. Levies on imports and exports, taxes, regulations on travel and trade, and so forth fell within their province. The exploitation of official positions by farming them out or by operating them oneself as a source of income might lead to a lack of constancy in the way authority was exercised, sometimes even to a lack of integrity on the part of the functionaries, but the idea that corrupt and despotic regimes invariably worked disruptively everywhere certainly goes far beyond reality. Some of the centrally directed corps of officials had a greater sphere of operation as a technical apparatus than could be found anywhere in Europe at the time. The most impressive example was that of China, but the statement holds just as well for India or Persia, where officials exercised authority over cities most of them larger than any in Europe,[60] supervised a system of post roads with stages and public hostels extending over greater distances than any national road net in Europe, and so forth. The strict supervision exercised by the authorities in Japan had an evil reputation everywhere, but as a form of bureaucratic regime in the sixteenth and seventeenth centuries it has not become the less remarkable and progressive thereby.

The mighty of the earth, the rulers, the princes and the high officials, the nobles and the military officers too, took part in the large-scale trade on adventure. Here also there was a range of possibilities varying from monopoly to occasional trade and shipping, and from personal trade, whether for the benefit of the state treasury or for private gain, to investment of money in the trade enterprises of others. Market trade, in which the backing of authority made possible the formation of 'pools', the regulation of prices, and pre-emption, was included in the operations carried on. Most of the time, however, the trade pursued by the mighty will have been a sideline, one facet in the power of their wealth, and as such it will have shown the characteristics of occasional trade. The governor of Nagasaki, a high dignitary, constantly referred to as 'Excellency' by the Dutch Company, regularly sent money (up to thirty thousand tael, or more than seven thousand pounds) in trade, receiving silk and silk cloth and so forth from China for the money invested.[61] One of his junks sailed to Siam in 1631.[62] There was a junk belonging to the lord of Arima trading on Manila in the same year,[63] and junks of the lord of Hirado traded on Cambodia.[64] There is mention of bottomry given out by the "Japanese lords and merchants" of Hirado in the Chinese trade on Formosa,[65] and the mandarin of Changchow in Fukien carried on trade on Batavia.[66] Royal ships from Arakan went to Pulicat, but on the other hand two servants of the king's supreme *capado* or eunuch arrived in Batavia with two packs of cloth![67]

In Siam a considerable part of the trade was a royal monopoly, the king's factors dealing in sapanwood, tin, birds' nests, ray skins, and so forth and royal junks trading on Batavia, Japan and China, and, going out from Tenasserim, on the Coromandel Coast.[68] Alongside that, merchandise was shipped on other vessels. There is also mention of a royal trading junk from Cambodia.[69] The mogul carried on trade on Mocha and Aden from Surat.[70] His brother-in-law, Prince Asaf Khan (whose factor sent 3,055 gold ducats, or around fourteen hundred pounds, and some silver work from Cambay to Arabia in the ship of the city of Chaul) and the governor of Surat traded on Balsora (Orissa) and Aden.[71] The governor of Ahmadabad, too, carried on overseas trade.[72] The ruler of Golconda carried on trade and shipping, his ships sailing from Masulipatnam to Mocha.[73]

With the Dutch Company's liquidation of the English ships in Indonesia after the conquest of Jakarta, several vessels were captured off Tiku on the west coast of Sumatra in September, 1619. On one of them, the *Dragon*, along with Achinese and other Gujarati traders there was a Gujarati called Malinshiary, pilot for the prince Sultan Khurram, the later Mogul Shah Jehan.

> Whereas on the English ship *The Dragon* captured before Tiku we have taken a Gujarati named Malinshiary, being a pilot of the prince Sultan Khurram, the youngest son of the grand mogul in Surat, who importunes us much and troubles us to have reparation and retribution for the cloths and other merchandise which were laden in the English ships won by

> us off Tiku for the account of the aforesaid his prince Sultan Khurram, according to his declaration handed over for that purpose amounting to 13000 pieces of eight, moreover in *The Dragon* the value of 300 pieces of eight for his private account – it has been approved to give him an honourable accomodation at Jakarta until by time and tide the occasion shall present itself that we can transport him back to Surat with our or other ships; and with regard to his request, to announce to him that as his prince or lord is our good friend and we are of the intention to send a fleet to Surat at an opportune time, we ourselves shall settle the affair in amity with his lord...[74]

There was the same situation in Indonesia. Ships belonging to the ruler of Achin went to Masulipatnam, carrying:

> eleven head of elephants and further laden with pepper, tin, sulphur, benzoin, camphor, aloe wood, Achinese silk...[75]

There were ships belonging to the queen of Patani going to Palembang,[76] and ships belonging to the ruler of Johore.[77] The export of rice from Mataram *via* Japara became a royal monopoly in the hands of the *tumenggungs* of Kendal and Tegal.[78] The ruler of Macassar had a factor on Banda for the spice trade, whom he:

> supplies every year with rice, pieces of cloth, and everything that is liked there, in order to gain as much mace for his country as possible, and thus to lure some merchants to him; is also able to have great quantities bought up...[79]

The governor of Jambi owned ships and carried on trade[80] – as did the *shahbandar* and the *datuk besar* of Patani,[81] the nobles of Bantam and Jakarta,[82] the *shahbandar* of Grise, the governor of Demak,[83] and the governor of Sukadana. In 1637 a *pangeran* of Palembang sent ten picul of pepper (not quite a single ton) to Batavia in a junk, "going consigned in the hands of one Chinese called Jucko";[84] in the same year the governor of Martapura (near Banjarmasin) sent a junk with twelve *koyan* of pepper (more than twenty-five ton, figuring the *koyan* at three thousand two hundred pounds) to Cochin China.[85]

Such trade could be supplemented by an extensive market trade. The pepper on the west coast of Sumatra was bought up by the agents of the ruler of Achin among others, and the ruler's share made up around a third to a half of the total export of the crop.[86] Closing the market could be a following step:

> [1632] ... the trade in the regions of Gujarat also turned out to be small, as in Baroda and Ahmadabad we and all other foreign traders are publicly denied the purchase of cloth, which is all bought up on behalf of the king [the mogul], and there is reason to fear that such prohibitions will follow in Broach and also Surat itself...[87]
> [1633] The anil and salt-petre stored in Burhanpur last year by order of the king...[88]
> [1607, Patani] ... the great knavery of the *mantris* who every other day forbid our men the purchase of pepper or something else, seeking to buy up everything themselves in order that thereafter whatever is wanted would have to be got from their hands...[89]
> [1599, Bantam] ... and when they [the town authorities] believe that they will gain more in selling than the common folk imagine, they buy the pepper from them, then make agreements with the foreign traders, to whom they have [the pepper] delivered which they had bought from the poor at a lower price the day before. In this way they earn a great deal of money without having to face any risk of loss, or taking any trouble thereunto...[90]

In Nagasaki the market prices for silk were established by the Japanese authorities independently after they had consulted with the most prominent merchants in the five imperial cities – the so-called *pancado*.[91]

7

The Products

From Portuguese and Dutch figures an estimate can be made of the amounts of various products coming on the market in Indonesia.

Spices – cloves, nutmeg, and mace – were obtained on the tiny islands of the northern Moluccas, Ambon, and Ceram (cloves) and the Banda Islands (nutmeg and mace). There was a clove crop once a year with a bumper crop around once every four years, and three crops of nutmeg each year. The clove yield on the northern Moluccas averaged three thousand *bahar* per year,[92] and on Ambon eleven hundred *bahar*.[93] The annual spice yield on the Banda Islands amounted to twenty-five hundred plus six hundred plus four hundred hundredweight of mace and twenty-eight hundred plus six hundred plus five hundred *bahar* of nutmeg.[94] Converted into tons of fifteen hundred pounds, there was thus a total yield of around twenty-nine hundred ton.

Pepper, grown on Java, Sumatra, Malaya, and Borneo, was taken to Bantam, the ports on the west coast of Sumatra, Jambi, Indragiri, Kampar, Achin, Patani, Ligor, Sengora, and Martapura and other ports in southeastern Borneo, and from the latter ports was also shipped to Grise and Japara and other ports in central and eastern Java. The amount brought into Bantam can be fixed at fifty thousand bags of sixty pounds per year,[95] in Achin and the ports on the west coast of Sumatra also fifty thousand bags, in the east coast ports – primarily Jambi – forty-five thousand bags, and in the ports on the peninsula ten thousand.[96] A total of a hundred fifty-five thousand bags, or around sixty-two hundred ton.

Around three or four thousand picul of sandalwood – two hundred forty to three hundred twenty ton – were brought on the market each year.[97] The amount of drugs and medicinal products – camphor, benzoin, sarsaparilla, and curcuma – was at best a few ten thousands of pounds, thus a few dozen ton.[98]

Along with salt, sugar, coconuts and coconut oil, garlic, and onions, the mainstay of the Javanese food supply trade to the east and the west was rice. In 1615 it was figured that fifty rice junks from Japara went to Malacca each year;[99] alongside that came the shipping on Bantam, Johore, Jambi, Palembang, and Patani. There is mention of a hundred twenty Javanese rice junks for Malacca in 1617.[100] The total shipping to the west can be set at two hundred junks averaging a hundred ton each.

The spice islands, with little agriculture of their own, lying in East Indonesia (the rest of which was accustomed to the much more primitive diet of sago) and importing rice from abroad, provide an interesting case of supplying of food over long distances overseas. Banda before it was subdued had a population of fifteen thousand;[101] Ambon and the northern Moluccas numbered a hundred fifty thousand.[102] If it is calculated that two-thirds of the population on Banda and one-third on Ambon and the northern Moluccas consumed rice (slaves and the poor will have had a diet primarily of sago) and if the rations are set at eighteen to twenty pounds per month (a complete rice ration, one *kati*, or a pound and a fifth, per person per day, would amount to thirty *kati* or thirty-six pounds per month), then the total amount of rice needed per year would be around thirteen million pounds, or eight thousand eight hundred ton – that is to say, the import of around a hundred fifty sixty-ton junks. The total Javanese food-supply trade would thus have amounted to around thirty thousand ton of rice per year transported by around three hundred seventy-five junks of sixty to a hundred ton.

Around three to four hundred picul (of a hundred thirty-three pounds each) of raw silk were brought into Bantam each year.[103] As has already been mentioned, the total amount exported from China to the south amounted to much more. The whole amount shipped southwards can safely be put at two or three thousand picul, that is to say, around a hundred sixty to two hundred ton. The amount of silk cloth shipped can be figured at ten to twenty thousand pieces per year.

In proportion the amount of porcelain imported for use by Indonesians and Chinese in Indonesia, for saving as treasure (the valuable pieces), and for trans-shipment westwards was impressive. This has been confirmed time after time by the finds made in the excavations still being carried on in Indonesia. It is difficult to estimate the size of it. In 1622 the Dutch Company requested the shipment of:

> ...4000 double butter dishes, 12000 pieces single butter dishes, 12000 fruit bowls, 3000 half fruit bowls, 4000 caudle cups, 4000 half caudle cups, 500 of the largest dishes, 2000 a size smaller, 4000 a size still smaller, 1000 bowls, 2000 half bowls, 8000 saucers, 8000 dinner plates...[104]

As an illustration of industrial export, chiefly of the highly-developed manufacture of porcelain in the Kiansi province, these figures are a mere trifle. If one multiplies them tenfold and calculates an average of twenty pieces to the *corge*, one arrives at an annual import of from six to eight thousand *corges* in Indonesia.

The chief trade product going from India eastwards was the cotton cloth from Coromandel and Gujarat. In 1619 the Company estimated its annual sale of Coromandel cloth in Indonesia at 3,650 *corges*.[105] If it is figured that a fifth of the whole cloth tradewas held by the Dutch at the time, then the whole export to the east would amount to around eighteen thousand *corges*, or three hundred sixty thousand pieces. In an estimate made in 1603 it was calculated as desirable that the Company purchase 1832 *corges* of cloth from Coromandel and 466 *corges* from Gujarat.[106] If it is figured that in 1603 the Hollanders and Zeelanders held an eighth of the whole cloth trade and if allowance is made for cloth coming from elsewhere, then there will have been an annual sale of around twenty thousand *corges*, or four hundred thousand pieces, in Indonesia. It was calculated by the Company that in 1619 a capital of twenty-five thousand pounds and in 1621 forty-two thousand pounds was needed for Coromandel cloth, and in 1623 from forty-two to forty-eight thousand for Coromandel and Gujarati cloth.[107]

It is obvious that any idea of an industry meeting mass demands was out of the question. The large local village and town weaving crafts supplying cloth for the craftsmen, their families, and a limited group around them went on unchanged. Indian cloth was distributed over extensive regions with populations of millions in a trade carried on in various towns and points involved in international commerce, predominantly as luxury goods supplied to the mighty, the wealthy, the higher classes. The organization of the weaving, colour printing, and batik trades in India – semi-rural, traditionalistic (probably divided according to castes), decentralized in its manufactury, lacking mechanical power – also indicates a craft which was widely practised by many people but nevertheless one working within very limited capacities on a handicraft level.

The Dutch Company took too limited a part in the Japanese and Chinese trade and the Indian, Persian, and Arab trade for one to be able to form a picture of the whole from a calculation of its commerce.

8

The Ships

The tonnage of Chinese shipping southwards has already been indicated. Exclusive of the trade on Manila, there were fifteen junks averaging six hundred ton, or a total of nine thousand ton. The shipping from Siam can be set at around three to four thousand ton, that from the rest of Farther India at four thousand.

The Indian shipping from Coromandel was calculated by the English historian Moreland at ten thousand ton, that on Achin at three thousand, and that on Pegu and Arakan at five thousand. He has also estimated Portuguese trade on the route Malacca–China–Japan at three thousand ton and on the spice islands at a thousand.[108] The trade from northwest India on Persia and Arabia can be set at ten thousand ton at the least. Javanese shipping has been estimated above at thirty thousand ton; probably another twenty thousand ton can be added for the rest of Indonesian large-scale shipping, thus giving a total of fifty thousand ton. The shipping on the Indonesian seas with their countless interinsular possibilities involved by the nature of things a larger number of vessels than that along the fairly unbroken shores of the mainland of southeast Asia.

If the size of the Chinese junks is estimated at an average of six hundred ton, the Siamese ships at five hundred, the ships from Tonkin, Annam, and Cambodia at four hundred, the Indian ships at two hundred, and the Indonesian junks at a hundred ton, that would mean that there were fifteen ships involved in the seagoing trade on Indonesia from China, eight from Siam, ten from the rest of Farther India, fifty each from Coromandel and northwestern India, fifteen on Achin, and twenty-five on Pegu and Arakan, while the interinsular trade in the Indonesian Archipelago was carried on with five hundred medium-sized vessels.

Besides that there are twenty-five large junks to be calculated for trade on Japan, and for the trade from Japan around thirty.

Let us consider the movement of ships at Batavia. The *Dagh-register* for 1636, for example, gives the following figures on vessels arrived. (It must be borne in mind that every vessel arriving at the Boom, the port and port-tax office, was recorded, down to the smallest outrigger proas and five-man dinghies; small ships of not more than five or six ton have been omitted here.)

I From elsewhere on Java			
Charingin	1	Batang	3
Bantam	61	Kaliwungu	1
Krawang	1	Demak	5
Indramayu	3	Japara	36
Cheribon	9	Lasem	2
Losari	6	Jaratan	19
Tegal	19	Surabaya, Grise	15
Pekalongan	14		
II From Sumatra and environs			
The Lampong region	6	Bangka	2
Palembang	5	Bengkalis	2
Indragiri	5	The west coast	10
III From Borneo			
Sukadana	2	Martapura	3
Kota Waringin	2	Elsewhere	2
IV From the Lesser Sunda Islands			
Bima	3	Bali	1
Lombok	1		
V From outside Indonesia (junks, *wangkangs*, and *balangs*)			
Patani	1	Annam	1
Cambodia	2	Formosa	1
China	6		

It can be assumed that the Javanese ships trading on Batavia, or at least those from Japara and nearer, may have made two trips per year, and the ships from Bantam, considering the shortness of the voyage, even three. Furthermore, in consideration of the fact that there were a very large number of small proas supplying the market of the town and the fort of Batavia with vegetables, rattan, charcoal, and so forth, it can be assumed that only half of the ships were sea-going. If these allowances are made, one finds that there were some seventy-two sea-going Javanese junks involved in the shipping on Batavia, as well as some forty-four vessels large and small from the rest of Indonesia and eleven ships large and small from other countries in Asia. Such figures check well with the estimates given above, and at the same time form an illustration of the fact that Dutch Batavia did not develop into the natural staple point for Indonesian and Asian shipping any more than Portuguese Malacca had been able to do.

9

The Markets

A large number of pedlars with small cargoes and a small capital, a limited number of ships and a resultant overabundance of 'shipper-passengers', products in small quantities, long trading periods, as many markets as there were towns and ports, each one with its own money, its own weights, its own measures, its own customs: from these few factors alone the character of international Asian trade can be determined. Some quotations from Dutch Company records will serve to illustrate the nature of the markets.

Japan – a notice from the *Daghregister* for 1624 reads:

> From a missive from Nieuroode [merchant-in-chief of the Dutch Company in Japan] it is understood that this monsoon a large quantity of silk and silk goods was brought from Macao with Portuguese *navetas* [Portuguese-rigged junks of around a hundred to a hundred fifty ton] as well as from China with 30 or 40 small junks, likewise from Cochin China with a Japanese junk together with one from Tonkin and other places to a slack market in Japan...[109]

In 1633 the silk price in Japan fell sharply:

> ...because of the Japanese and Chinese junks which with the previous southern monsoon arrived in great numbers at Nagasaki, in Satsuma, and the Ryukyus from Tonkin, Cochin China, Changchow, and Fu-ch'ing [the region of the Fukien ports] and brought around 2500 picul of raw Chinese and Tonkinese silk, as well as out of respect for the *pancado* which the councillors of state [the officials of the shogunate] had

> enforced on the Company restricting our former freedoms, and had moreover ordained ... that [we] should also not be allowed to sell any other goods ere and before the price had been set by the *pancado*...[110]

Some notices on Siam read:

> [1624] 3 Japanese junks have departed for Siam, so that it appears there will not be much for our Company to do in the trade in deerskins there...[111]

> [1631] The cloth trade was extremely poor there, also through being spoiled by the triennial import of the [Batavian] free burghers Van Haps, Meerwyck, and their partners, who now on the 21st of August last arrived in Siam from Tenasserim with a cargo of 160 to 170 packs of cloth from the [Coromandel] Coast worth around 30 or 40,000 reals of 8, whereby not only the market for cloth, benzoin, and other products is spoiled, but also caused the monopoly [of the Siamese court dignitaries for restricting the market], to the excessively great loss of the Company...[112]

> [1636] There arrived in Tenasserim from Coromandel three Moorish ships with cloth, which have made the price of it decrease very much...[113]

Tonkin – a report of the lodge of Japan in 1636 gives an account of the course of Japanese trade in Tonkin, describing its strict regulation, which began with taking inventory of ship, cargo, and capital, unloading the ship into river barges and transporting the merchandise to the capital on a license of the court and under the guidance of a mandarin. The cargo was unloaded in the town and inspected by the customs, the Japanese were lodged in a special quarter, and the day for free trade announced. In order to be able to buy up silk, the Japanese had the silver they had brought with them melted down in Tonkin and transformed into the alloy current there. "When their trade is finally carried out and the cargo brought with them sold" there followed the delivery of the royal silk, the preparations for leaving, and the departure seawards to the junks which had been left there.[114] In 1637, before the arrival of three Portuguese junks, the price of silk had dropped to forty-five tael per picul, "and after their coming rose to 60 tael..."[115]

Arakan – in 1637:

> The ship of Mangelis, a famous Moorish merchant, had also arrived there from Achin with around 90 *bahar* [or about twenty-five ton] of pepper – through which Arakan was filled with pepper, and the Company's ... was still unsold...[116]

Patani – in 1632 Caẹn, commander of the fleet patrolling Macao and Manila, wrote:

> Whereas the Chinese junk that had been there [in Patani] last year and now had departed, as well as one Berent Pessaert, burgher at Batavia, had transported most all the pepper from there, ... there was little pepper..., [I] decided to leave without removing any pepper...[117]

Coromandel – in 1632:

> The president [of the lodge at Pulicat] advises ... that not only is the trade in cloth on the coast aforementioned being spoiled, but that we will hardly be able to get our [the Company's] requirements for cloth [annual orders given to putting-out merchants], as the English and other great [Indian] merchants from Viziapur, Berhampur, and surrounding places who are wandering around the Coromandel Coast with their large supplies of capital are buying up the cloth and fine fabrics without regard to length, thickness, and breadth, and far above their usual price...[118]

Aden – another Company notice reports that on 14 September, 1635 there arrived at Surat:

> ...a frigate belonging to a banian merchant coming from Shihr [in Hadramaut], bringing from there 30 bales of *soulge* or red dye, [and] a lot of chalkstone, with which tidings came that the traders with their cloth, cotton, tobacco, etc. found a very bad market in Shihr and they had lost as much as 40 or 50 per cent. In Aden there lay more than 24 ships from various regions, by which ships was brought such an abundance of cloth and other merchandise that the place remained so overcrowded with them the merchants could not get rid of their goods except with great loss. Through these great losses and misfortunes which the Moors and banians have met and suffered with their goods in Mocha, Aden, as well as in Shihr, many Moorish and banian merchants in Surat and the regions roundabout have gone bankrupt, through which the price of cloth has fallen throughout the whole region of Hindustan...[119]

The counter-trade in those extreme western outposts of Asian sea trade came from Egypt. In 1621 in Mocha, as the factor of the Dutch Company wrote, the Egyptians – usually with a single ship – failed to come:

> The big ship that comes each year from Suez has not come yet, that is long tardy and is a great loss for all the ships lying here, for by lack of buyers they have to give their goods so cheap that they cannot stand it...
>
> At the moment there are nothing but sellers here and each one seeks only to get rid of what he has in order to leave here with the monsoon and not stay over. ...They cannot collect the debts they have however diligently they may try; it all is waiting for the coming of the ships from above.[120]

And on the market there, an important link in the international commerce between Europe and Asia, trade was conducted on the basis of peddling. Thus there came a request to Batavia from the Dutch factor:

> ...a Chinese *datching* [hand-scales] on which two picul or thereabouts can be weighed is needed to be sent because we have no way to know how to deal with weights; we weigh with a set of stones and change every day...[121]

Martapura – the merchant Gerrit Corssen, who was trading in pepper on Borneo during the western monsoon of 1633–1634:

> ...on arriving in Martapura... had collected and negotiated with all energy and industry without having been able to sell the remainder of the cargo he had brought along or acquire any amount more than ... 100 ton of pepper, partly because of the undesired assortment of the said remainder, partly because of the bad crop of the previous pepper season and the late harvest of the present one, but especially because the king not only had admitted into his country the 4 Macassarese and 13 Javanese small junks which had also arrived there this year to procure pepper and had acquired a good lot of pepper through the favour of the principal *orang kayas* of Martapura, but also had permitted and allowed them to contract and export pepper, against his last year's promises...[122]

The west coast of Sumatra – in 1634:

> ...the ship *Den Brack* [which] departed from here [Batavia] on the 12 March was prosperously arrived in Selebar [on the Benkulen Coast] on the 24 following, ...finding there lying ready to sail two Chinese junks from Batavia which had collected and bought up everything that had come and been brought there the previous western monsoon, and the merchant Jan Tombergen had not been able to trade and negotiate more

than a remainder of 33 *bahar* of pepper from his arrival in Selebar up to the 6 of April last. And as that place was therewith utterly cleared of pepper the said Tombergen had resolved to sail to Benkulen with the ship *Den Brack* and there also [they] have traded and contracted at least 35 to 40 *bahar* of pepper, which was also left there by the aforesaid junks, after that to depart for Salido [near Painan on the Padang Coast, one of the sources of gold] with the intention of collecting a lot of gold and pepper there, and to wait for the coming harvest of pepper more at ease...[123]

Jambi – 1636:

The Chinese junk [which] arrived in Jambi the end of March last ... is buying up the pepper for high prices up to 8 and 9 reals for the picul with its capital of Chinese merchandise brought along worth about twenty thousand reals of eight, moreover making great presents [to the local officials and nobles] and getting them on board [the ships] by various means ... In the same way the aforesaid junk is also amassing all the cash that there is by the Jambinese, etc. for Chinese wares they sell to them, so that the Jambinese in place of buying our [the Company's] cloth with their money now spend everything on the aforesaid Chinese merchandise, whereby they even sail upriver [the Batang Hari] with small proas in order to procure pepper. The proas coming down from above appearing in Jambi say that they will not sell their pepper yet, and in the meantime they deliver for great profits to the junk, so that our people sit idle most of the time...[124]

Bantam – in 1615 Coen wrote to the Gentlemen Seventeen:

...and do not be surprised that the people of the junks [the Chinese ships trading on Bantam] are selling better silkware than ours a third cheaper on the market than ours is priced at on the bill, for time and need are law for all such people. ...and because we and the English have lacked money this year the Chinese are left with most of their ordinary silk cloth on their hands, so that it is possible to get it for cash more than a hundred per cent. cheaper than last year, and the porcelain for much less even...[125]

Achin – in 1636:

...various vessels were come to Achin, and more than have been seen in many years, namely:

3	three from the Coromandel Coast that brought more than 500 packs of cloth on the market	
1	one from Pegu	All laden with cloth, cotton *roucou* dyed, etc., and the Dabhol ship brought two fine horses as a gift for the King
1	one from Surat	
1	one from Dabhol	
1	one from the Malabar Coast	
7	seven ships.	

In that way, as has been said, Achin being filled with merchandises so that they have dropped in price by almost the half.[126]

10

Summary

Countless markets, lying isolated from each other and varying greatly from one another in structure. A few hundred *bahar* of spices, a few thousand bags of pepper, a few hundred packs of cloth, a few dozen *corges* of porcelain, a few dozen picul of wood products on each market. An international trade of person-to-person haggling and retail sales with hand scales or *via* the town weigh-house or the government toll house, carried on in the periods when trade was concentrated in the towns because of the favourable winds and the harvests there. When the traders were gone and the money brought along had been put to use or spent, trade came to a standstill.

If the facts and figures given above on pedlars, products, ships, and markets are fitted together, then in the great overseas Asian trade there comes to each pedlar on one of the few dozen ships an average of a few picul of silk and sandalwood, a few dozen pieces – a single chest – of silk cloth, a few *corges* of porcelain, a few bales of cotton cloth, a few dozen bags of pepper, a few *bahar* of cloves and nutmeg, a few hundredweight of mace. With one or two traits of large-scale monopoly trade, trade *en gros*, and extensive occasional trade, the general commercial picture remained that of a small trade in costly products carried on by a multitude of pedlars from Suez to Nagasaki. Considering such trade, Van

Linschoten, writing from Goa in 1584, could rightly hope for profits from a long journey with forty pounds:

> I should be much inclined to travel into China and Japan, which are the same distance from here as Portugal, that is, he who goes thither is three years on the road. If I only possessed two or three hundred ducats they could easily be converted into six or seven hundred. ... but to enter on such a thing with empty hands I thought folly: one must start tolerably provided to make profit.[127]

– for in that predominantly cash trade with a small turnover, a long-term trade carried on within limited, isolated market spheres, a high percentage of profit was not only traditional but necessary in order to cover costs and possible because of the great rarity of the limited quantities of goods. On the other hand the traditionality was assured by the handicraft character of trade, which could not be upset by wholesale trade and occasional trade, but which could, even so, be tilted far off-balance by small modifications.

> The gentlemen [wrote Coen to the Seventeen] will understand that no places in the Indies ... are supplied properly without money in cash, even if they be supplied with a tenfold cargo in merchandise; what is more, there are many places which the more they are supplied with merchandise the more serious it is, if they do not have money in cash besides, for in all the Indies there cannot be more turned over than is retailed every day, which is the cause of the extraordinary rising and falling in the prices of merchandise, for there are nowhere great or rich, daring merchants to be found such as one encounters in Europe who at the same time have the power and the right to buy up an excellent portion and reserve it for retailing ...[128]

The last part of this quotation is definitely painted too darkly. But it is true that neither merchant gentlemen, lords, nor princes played a continuous, dominant rôle in trade. The power they had over market, weigh-house, and boom may have been firmly established; it was the pedlar who carried the wares trading on adventure.

Chapter Three

I

Dutch and Asian Bureaucracy

In the preceding chapters have been sketched the Asian states and the outstretched net of international Asian trade in which after 1600 the flags of the Dutch republic, provinces, and companies also appeared. Lodges, treaties, fortresses, and after 1619 a fortified Dutch town bore witness to the might of the Dutch overseas. The series of Company stations, unprotected and protected, continued to expand up to 1650.

How the political situation developed has been touched upon in the first chapter; how trade progressed, in the second. Especially the European archives have provided documents on Asian trade; those of the East itself to a lesser degree. The bureaucratization of the Company's business overseas is impressive; the facts and figures from every trading post were assimilated by the general direction, from 1613 on in Bantam, and later in Batavia Castle. All the cargoes brought in and shipped out, with lots ranging in value from a few dozen pounds to hundreds of thousands, the chain of fortresses, the crews of the ships, things worth knowing about dozens of foreign lands and ports – everything was recorded and kept up to date by a corps of clerks. Seen in the light of their time, the general reports to Holland made by the central administration at Batavia, with their extensive appendices treating every trading post, are impressive in size.[1] Did Asian trade in contrast escape such a mania for accountancy and registration; was it unacquainted with such statistical exactitude? Or was there any fundamental difference to be found between European and Asian trade in regard to such things? It would seem certain there was not. Even in case the extensive machinery of the Company's system of ships, outposts, and fortresses was not equalled in all its complexity by the machinery of Asian trade, there is ample evidence that the lands of the Orient were just as much acquainted with 'paper work', especially in government bureaucracies. The comment of the traveller Pyrard on the court bureaucracy of the *zamorin* of Calicut is illustrative:

> ... I have ofttimes wondered to see the great number of men with no other duty or work all day but writing and registering. These posts are of much honour ... Some make entry of all goods arriving for the king; others, the dues and taxes paid day by day; others, the expenditure of the king's household; others, the most notable incidents of each day, both what happens at court and in the rest of the kingdom; in short all news, for he has everything registered; and each clerk has his separate room. They keep also a register of all strangers who come there, taking their names and nationalities, the time of their arrival, and the business that has brought them, and so they did with us. It is a wondrous thing to observe their number and the perfect order that exists among them, and how fast they write... The king hath the like writers in all towns, ports, harbours, and frontier passages of his kingdom, who render account to those of the palace, all being well organised and in obedience one to another, each having his proper superior. Throughout the whole Malabar Coast there is the same manner of writing and the same ordering thereof.[2]

Here is one of the many counterparts to the clerical activity at Batavia. An arrest of the Company's ships at Hirado in Japan was executed and then lifted again with no less precision than that of any European procedure.

> ... the flute *Warmondt* with the person of Sir Pieter Nuyts arrived in Japan on the 12th September last [1632], and like other ships of the Company was taken into custody, stripped of guns, rudder, and sails, and the merchandise being stored in a warehouse under the seal of the governors of Hirado.
>
> Likewise that our people in Hirado were written through the person of the agent Willem Jansen and on the 7th December were told by the governors of Hirado that the emperor and state council of Japan understood and had with certainty learned that Sir Pieter Nuyts, formerly governor in Taiwan, was sent to Japan and was arrived in Hirado with the flute *Warmondt*, in order, on being delivered to His Majesty, to account for the affronts taken by His Majesty from the actions of the said Governor Nuyts in Taiwan; and that the arrested ships, people, and goods of the Company had been released on the 22nd November

last on the decision of Their Excellencies in Yedo [the seat of the central government under the shogunate] and restored their former freedom after they had taken over in their custody the aforesaid Pieter Nuyts, whom they accomodated in a gentleman's house under the same guard by which the lodge had been kept during the arrest.[3]

The value of royal letters is illustrated below.

2

Dutch and Asian Traders

The record of the Company's trade has been preserved even to details. It ranged from the small trade of pedlars to the large-scale trade of merchant gentlemen. But in the whole range of transactions there was always an Asian in a counter-rôle, and of him, unfortunately, it would seem almost no documents have been preserved. The person facing the commissioner Jan Jansz. Karel bargaining over the exchange of a piece of red madder-dyed cloth worth seven shillings for two bags of pepper per ell was a Chinese or Indonesian pedlar. In 1637 the merchant Lucas de Vogel, at the lodge at Jambi, took in the following amounts of pepper on which advances had been given:

From the free burgher Francisco Pinto	248 picul 68 *kati*
From Jurutulis [scribe – to whom?]	114 picul 10 *kati*
From Jecko } Chinese buyers	133 picul 13 *kati*
Piusjangh } Chinese buyers	187 picul 50 *kati*
From Cantjus and Masjuda	35 picul 83 *kati*
	719 picul 42 [actually 24] *kati*.

– while the sub-merchant higher up the Jambi River:

promoted the collection of the remaining debts by every possible means – who up to now has reached little. Some even deny their debt and others are impoverished so that the Company will apparently suffer great loss thereby; one Chiaetin, Chinese, who is indebted 524 reals to the Company and was on the point to come hither, poisoned himself without leaving anything but his wife and child, who were accepted by the Company and will be sold ere long, and as nothing else is to be expected from them, the said De Vogel requests the rest of the debt to be written off...[4]

In order to counteract extensive short-weighing in the pepper market at Martapura, the merchant-in-chief Cramer applied to the ruler of Banjarmasin with the request either to increase the measure for pepper or to grant permission for him to weigh with the Chinese scales, the *datching*, when buying pepper – to which was answered that people were accustomed of old to selling by measure and:

> ... that the introduction of weighing would have caused a great confusion among the peasants (who are still almost savage and brutal people [were they Malay colonists or Dyak uplanders?]) and consequently we would have to be contented with the old custom of receiving pepper by measure ...[5]

The episode is characteristic for the size of Company trade as well as for the way the Banjarmasin market was bound by tradition.

The 1598 fleet of the Old Company arrived in Banda for the trade in nutmeg and cloves in 1599 too late to buy from the nobles and had to collect spices from the small growers:

> I [Van Heemskerck] could not wish otherwise than that the nobles here had much merchandise of nutmeg and mace, for everything is in demand by them. Then we would lightly obtain our cargo and at a good price. But there is not much. It all has to be bought from the inhabitants here by the pound ...[6]

The nobles on Ambon traded their cloves themselves; the sales took place on the scales in their own homes. During a conflict between the Dutch and an English clove buyer in 1613:

> ... an *orang kaya* Ticos, who is a very proud man and has been long a great ally of ours has hung scales in his quarters and sold and had sold a lot of cloves to the English ...[7]

On the other hand on the Malabar Coast a Hindu merchant from the banian caste in 1637 proposed closing a transaction by which the following Company goods would be purchased:

500 to 1000 *man* lead at 1½ pagodas	
1 to 2000 do tin at 3 pagodas	
50 to 100 do mace at 30 pagodas	
1 to 2000 do copper at 3 pagodas	} in Deccan *man*
150 to 200 do Chinese silk at 35 pagodas	
200 *man* sarsaparilla at 5 pagodas	
1000 do sapanwood at 5 pagodas	

4 to 500 pieces damask at ¾ pagoda
4 pieces red cloth at 3 pagodas the ell
4 to 5000 packs madder at 22 pagodas the piece.

Offering in exchange to deliver annually 2000 *candy* pepper at 22 pagodas the *candy* of 500 Dutch pounds [plus a considerable supplement in money]...[8]

Converted at the rate of twenty-six pounds to one Deccan *man* – the standard weight there[9] – and ten shillings to the pagoda, this meant a purchase of goods worth around fifty to seventy-five thousand pounds and a delivery of pepper twenty-two thousand pounds in value and a million pounds, or 667 ton, in weight. A comparison of this with the total purchase value of the cargoes on the fleets returning to Holland, which amounted to from a hundred fifty to two hundred fifty thousand pounds on the average, gives an idea of the commercial and financial power of a merchant of this sort. No further evidence is needed that over against European trade forms there were trade forms certainly equal to them, very probably more powerful. In 1633 the Dutch Company lodge at Surat had taken up a money loan amounting to twenty-five thousand pounds for the financing of trade; the English office there was burdened with a loan of around sixty-seven thousand pounds at twenty-four per cent. per year.[10] The merchant gentlemen of Surat, then, had a sum of ninety-two thousand pounds which was lent to the two lodges; in the same decade the Company had taken up loans in Holland amounting to around eight hundred thousand pounds for the general financing of the whole enterprise.

In 1628 the chief mandarin of Amoy proposed to the Dutch Company a three years' commercial contract for the annual delivery of:

1400 picul raw silk at 140 tael [10 tael = 13½ reals] per picul
5000 picul sugar at 3 reals per picul
1000 picul confitted ginger at 4 tael per picul
5000 pieces silk goods at 14 and 19 mas [1 mas = 1/10 tael = 8 d] per piece

– the total for a sum of three hundred thousand reals of eight. In payment the Company was to deliver three thousand picul of pepper at eleven reals the picul and to pay the rest (thus 267,000 reals or £ 55,600) in cash.[11] Here too was a transaction bringing a great part of the Company's trade in the hands of a single Asian, in this case not a merchant but a political authority carrying on occasional trade on a large scale.

In the same way in 1625 the Chinese *nakoda* Wangsan offered in Batavia to deliver in Taiwan a thousand to fifteen hundred picul of raw silk at a hundred forty to a hundred sixty tael per picul, that is to say, reckoning a tael at six shillings eightpence, a transaction of a value of fifty-five to seventy-five thousand pounds. The whole raw silk import in Bantam at the beginning of the seventeenth century amounted to three or four hundred picul per year;[12] in 1619 the Dutch Company estimated the total sale of raw silk in Europe at six hundred picul.[13]

3

'Western' versus 'Eastern'

Should it be said of these two parties in trade that they lived in separate worlds, that their 'economic mentalities' were different, 'Western' *versus* 'Eastern', furthermore that the Western commercial spirit was more advanced, more highly developed than the Eastern? It would appear to be out of the question. In power to command merchandise and money Eastern trade was actually superior. The objectives, the methods of profit-making, and the techniques of trading revealed no differences worthy of mention, except for those resulting from the nature of the organization of the Company, in which, in divergence from the Eastern system of individual trade and trade by factors, people on *commenda*, and pedlars, the merchants were employed officials. If one should search there for elements of nascent modern capitalism – understanding modern capitalism as enterprise exclusively aimed at making profit on capital, completely oriented to a free sales market, rational in its techniques and organization – one would seek in vain. European overseas trade was driven by a desire for profit and a lust for gain, and was carried on as international trade over distances greater than those in Europe. But in its activities it adjusted itself to the same criteria valid for Asian trade; it did not introduce any new elements or create any differences in level. If the development of modern capitalism – which was indisputably dominant in the nineteenth century – is to be applied as *leit-motif* for the economic history of the whole modern period from 1492 on, then it needs to declared that in the first half of the seventeenth century the trade of the overseas companies showed no characteristics of any new capitalistic development. An accumulated capital of several hundred thousand pounds, an extensive commercial organization, world-wide overseas shipping, and profits up to a hundred and two hundred per cent. are not of themselves indicative of a modern-capitalistic structure.

The ideological antithesis between Protestant Christianity and Islam, the 'Moordom' of the 'descendants of Ham', created mutual distrust, veiled contempt, and aggression in the field of politics. But in the social-economic field the Calvinist version of reformed Christianity which was the official religion of the Dutch Republic and of the Company administration in Asia did not set its stamp on the Company's commercial affairs. The rationalization in attitude towards life by means of the legalism of 'inner asceticism' which Max Weber has pointed out in Calvinism as one of the roots of the spirit of modern capitalism is not to be found either in the enterprise in Holland or in the actions of the authorities and directors of the trade overseas.

4

The Company's Capital in Asia

The Company began its trade with a capital of no more than some five hundred thousand pounds. The trade was a belligerent trade, and the war soon required large sums: running expenses for pay, arms, and food, and expenses in a lump sum for building forts and reinforcing outposts. The trade was unilateral: no craft goods from Europe were taken to Asia to be sold – they could not possibly have competed with Asian craft goods, – but just as in Roman trade on Asia, silver was transported in coin and bar,[14] and besides it, food supplies, naval equipment, and arms.

Everything was set down in a simple single-entry system of mercantile bookkeeping, with money, merchandise, foodstuffs, and debts outstanding to the Company as credits and the expenditures for garrisons and ships, a reserve for bad debts, and outstanding debts of the Company as debits. The balance thus did not include the capitalized value of fixed properties. In 1622 the general report of the Company listed a little less than three hundred fifty thousand pounds in cash, merchandise, foodstuffs, and debtors. In Batavia it was figured that seventy-five thousand of that was needed for foodstuffs and other provisions for the Company apparatus, and twenty-five thousand for creditors.[15] A little less than two hundred fifty thousand pounds was left over for buying products for the return fleets and for taking part in intra-Asian trade. Coen's ideal was to regain the total cost of the Company's operations in Asia from intra-Asian trade, so that the capital invested in Asia would stay at the same level and the money sent out from the Netherlands could all of it be spent on goods for the return fleets[16] and eventually even such goods could be purchased with sums advanced from the profits made on intra-Asian trade.[17] The ideal was not realized: while the prices of those spices under the monopoly and the contracts remained low, the purchase prices (of pepper, among other things) on the open market and the expenses of the Company machinery rose. The Company ate into its funds in the sense that a part of the money sent out from Holland had to be spent on operation costs,[18] and it lagged behind in the sense that the Asian account closed with a loss. The Company balance grew slowly: set at three hundred forty thousand pounds in 1622, it was put at seven hundred ninety thousand in 1640 and a million fifty thousand in 1650, with a profit in Asia of a little less than a hundred thousand pounds in 1640 and about a hundred seventy thousand in 1650.[19]

That was no large capital for a company in Asia: the capital invested by a single Asian merchant gentleman in regular or occasional trade sometimes amounted to a very large percentage of the Company's total means. There is a figure in Coen's correspondence which is too remarkable not to be mentioned. Pointing out to the Gentlemen Seventeen the limited amount of capital they had sent, he reproaches them:

> the Spaniards and Portuguese are using more than 500 tons of gold for the trade on the Indies...[20]

The figure seems reliable. It gives an indication of the amount of capital circulating in the whole of Asian trade, in which the Dutch Company had only a small part. In 1621 the Portuguese return fleet, two caracks, carried along, besides seven thousand five hundred quintals of pepper and 635 quintals of salt-petre, diamonds having a purchase value of more than six hundred thousand ducats, or a hundred thousand pounds. The total value of the fleet exceeded that of the Dutch return fleets of that time,[21] and the Portuguese and Spanish trade fleets generally exceeded the Dutch in the period. Two hundred fifty thousand pounds was the value of the Portuguese imports in Nagasaki from Macao in 1621.[22] The shipments from New Spain to the Philippines in the same period had a value of two million three hundred thirty thousand pounds.[23] "Sundry millions" of reals circulated in the Portuguese western Asian trade and return trade.[24] In comparison, the sums Batavia could send out for trading were at best forty-two thousand pounds to Surat, and around the same amount to Coromandel.[25] And if one considers the limited significance of even Portuguese trade in Asia, the proportional value of Eastern trade can be surmised.

5

The Character of the Company in the Netherlands

Trading in partnership, the form of enterprise in which the overseas voyages of the 1590's were undertaken, was no new form for Holland and Zeeland, nor were the separation of ship owners and captains, the staying at home of traders, the accumulation of capital, the participation of non-traders as shipowners. The merchants sending out ships together could accumulate the sum needed for the voyage – for ship, goods, and cash – by taking 'parts'. It was customary for the parts to be resold in smaller portions to interested persons who were seeking a profitable investment for their money and thus became partners in the voyage. A mania for profits, for large profits – the same which forty years later brought on the tulip craze – introduced a strong element of risk to partnership in the initial voyages to the Indies and gave the first companies the character of speculative affairs.[26] Onto the part each shipper held there hung a swarm of enterprising speculators.[27] Such investments in bottomry – for that is how they are to be qualified – had nothing to do with investments in shares of an enterprise. Bottomry, or *commenda*, is a form as old as the civilized world, and one spread everywhere. It was to be found in Bantam in 1596:

> ...the merchants who have all sorts of cloth and other wares *en gros* for sale and give out money for voyages for a double return if the voyage succeed, but if the ship be wrecked, the merchant looses the capital or the money lent...[28]

It appears to have been one of the chief means by which overseas trade from South China was financed, and in Japan, too, it was the form for investing money in overseas commerce.[29] *Commenda*, with its separation of financiers and executors, gave a shipping enterprise the appearance of being a modern limited company. But that is of necessity quite out of the question in a situation where there were no continuous turn-over of capital, no account of the return on sums invested, no account of profits from the capital account contemplated or set up: where money was given out "for a double return". There was merely a balance made of the equipment and voyage accounts, and the remainder was paid out.

This system was also the basis for the new United Company of 1602, not as before for one voyage but with an account to be rendered every ten years:

everyone may be at liberty to depart thereout and take his money unto himself. But also everyone will again be allowed to enter therein anew.

Thus from being moneylenders and private shippers the participants became moneylenders to the chambers of the Company. The capital of the different chambers was kept separated. Now the voyages were undertaken in series. Liquidation after the separate voyages was changed into dividends on the amalgamated voyage accounts. At the subscription a condition was set that from the time of deposit to the time risk began with the departure of the fleet for the equipment of which the deposit was to serve, rent would be paid on the basis of eight per cent. per year – an arrangement quite the same as was customary for bottomry in the separate voyages.

The first decennial account, which should have been rendered in 1612, did not take place, nor did the second in 1622. In 1623 the States General established a quadrennial account to be rendered "with open doors and windows after affixing bulletins" In 1647 the quadrennial rendering of the account was moved behind closed doors.[30]

The transformation of the one-voyage account into decennial accounts and the later periodization in quadrennial accounts did not bring any essential change in the Company's plan of bookkeeping. The accounting of the unwieldy capital in the journal and the cash book and the setting of dividends without relation to capital and capital yield remained. The original working capital of 1602 remained until 1795. Around it there grew up a series of money manipulations of a completely different sort.

For fitting out ships for the successive voyages fresh money was required, and was not obtained through supplementary investments of the participants in the Company, but through the acceptance of deposits on interest. Before the sale of the goods brought in, the incoming fleets returning from the Indies were financed by money borrowed in anticipation, "to be paid back from the moneys resulting from the sales" – a practice found elsewhere only at a later time. With the renewal of the charter in 1623 it was stipulated that, "the debts and burdens being beforehand settled or properly deducted", the Company was required:

> to make an annual repartition to the participants, whether in merchandise suitable thereto or in cash, of 10, 15, 20, or as much more per cent. as be found [available] beyond the necessary equipment on land and elsewhere...[31]

Such repartitions are certainly not to be considered as payments of dividends on capital invested made after due calculation of the revenue account, but as payments from the present yield of an annual return cargo minus a part in cash deducted for new capital for trade or for liquidation of deposits.[32] There was no connection between capital and profit. The building and equipping of ships, and construction of works overseas (which became a completely new factor not at all fitting into the original commercial shipping accounts as the Company began to establish outposts in Asia and create a system of factories and fortresses) were financed as running expenses, together with salaries, military pay, and gifts, and the total profits made in the trade back and forth between the various offices in Asia, and none of them were brought into a capital account. The Asian offices, which had current accounts with the general office at Batavia, made yearly accounts in their respective trade books which through the inclusion of the estimated value of the immovable properties had to a certain extent the character of balance sheets, but they were not intended as capital accounts.

The capital of the original shares of 1603 remained the basis for the repartition in the rendering of the first decennial account. A policy of dividends in proportion to the return on the capital invested therefore became impracticable, impossible even. A single example:

> When in July, 1628 [it] was on the point of being resolved by agreement to make a repartition of twenty-five per cent. in money on the first of January then following, [it] was proposed by the delegates of the Amsterdam Chamber ere and before the votes were collected that though the condition of the Company would rather require that no payment was made both because of the high burden of the moneys on interest with which the Company was encumbered and the large amount of equipment required at the time by the situation in the Indies, even so, in order to

make the participants as content as feasible without weakening the body general of the Company too much they would agree in place of twenty-five per cent. to 12½ in money, on the said 1 January following; and that if after the arrival of the three ships at that time under arrest in England [because of suspicion of carrying contraband for Spain] and the drawing up of the Company's account, it might be found that aforesaid 12½ per cent. could be increased to 25, the said Chamber would be able to conform to the aforesaid 25 per cent. upon the declaration that no other repartition besides that would be allowed nor made. After the release of the three aforesaid ships from arrest and their arrival in this country, the aforesaid repartition was unanimously consented to and confirmed.[33]

Thus the general account of the Company, drawn up annually, cannot in any sense be considered as the balance sheet of an enterprise, but rather ought to be viewed as an annual inventory of goods and moneys, and of receipts and payments. It is impossible to determine the condition of the enterprise from the credit and debit balances. This system of accounting – which furthermore was and remained completely secret, – the separated finances, equipment, and sales of return cargoes of the six chambers, their completely autonomous position and the perilous balance in the College of Gentlemen Seventeen, the strictly limited freedom in trading shares, which were registered per chamber, the inclusion of the high offices of the Company in the oligarchical political system of the *haute bourgeoisie* and the accompanying complete lack of say of the participants over against the authorities – all these are so many points justifying the view that Sombart's characterization:

one [is] often in doubt whether or not one should consider [such] a company as a joint-stock company in the narrow sense, even if it issued shares, the special characteristics are expressed in it so defectively and indistinctly, so many things are taken from other societal forms...[34]

is completely applicable to the United Dutch Company.

The history of the development of modern capitalism – something completely different from the history of the acquisition of wealth in general, and colonial wealth in particular – has very little directly to do with the history of the Company as an entrepreneurial form, unless it would be in the fields of financial and banking affairs in later Company times. As a commercial enterprise the Company represented an old-fashioned, extremely conservative type. Nor do the speculation and lust for gain which found expression in the voyages to the Indies in the 1590's and up to 1602 – two of the most powerful factors in the expansion of Dutch influence over the world – intrinsically have anything to do with capitalism, let alone modern capitalism.

As a bureaucratic organization, the Company meant a point of higher development than the feudal, medieval forms of government of the Portuguese overseas. The separation of the property of the Company from that of the Company's servants, the payment of salaries according to a fixed scale from the highest overseas authorities to the lowest ship's boy, the maintenance of a relatively extensive corps of civil and military servants with hierarchies and promotions, and the establishment of a large staff in the Netherlands as well – all these made up an important point in history from the organizational point of view.

In the same way in the field of technology: the construction for overseas shipping and the equipment and armament of ships and military units brought about deliveries which can have been of influence on the formation of a larger market for manufactured products, even though it needs to be added that most of the Company's orders were fitted into the just as conservative machinery of Dutch 'industry' or were cared for under the Company's own management.

6

Dutch and Asian Shipping

What was actually the relative significance of the Company's shipping in the whole of Asian shipping of which an estimate was given in Chapter Two? In 1620 there were thirty-eight ships and yachts and seven sloops and frigates of the Company in the Indies.[35] In 1622 there were fifty-two ships, eighteen yachts, and thirteen frigates;[36] in 1628, sixty-one ships large and small.[37] If one figures the 1620 fleet as divided in five ships of eight hundred ton, ten of six hundred, ten of four hundred, and thirteen of two hundred, then the total tonnage at that time will have been around sixteen thousand. If ships in 1622 are figured at an average of four hundred ton and frigates at a hundred twenty ton, the total tonnage will have run to around twenty-four thousand. The ships were spread out from Mocha and Surat to Japan, and among them were those for patrolling and – this deserves especial attention – those for the return voyages to Holland, which for a large part stayed at anchor off Batavia. The total tonnage of the ships travelling regularly in Oriental waters over the widespread routes between the far-flung offices may have totalled, at a liberal estimate, twelve to fourteen thousand ton. It is clear, then, that in comparison to Indonesian shipping of around fifty thousand ton, Chinese and Siamese shipping of eighteen thousand ton, Achinese shipping of three thousand, or Coromandel shipping of ten thousand ton, the relative significance of Dutch shipping remained limited. As a whole complex with a central administration, however, it was extremely important.

How much Batavia was a Company station and not an Oriental commercial emporium can be seen if one compares the 1636 list of ships given above with the figures on Company ships.

Let us look first at international shipping.[38] The state of trade was as follows:*

If one considers the trade traffic of the Company broken down according to the various routes,[39] then it becomes clear that the tonnage available for each route was rather small, usually totalling at best a few hundred ton.[40] The small volume of shipping on the Moluccas is characteristic; in comparison to Asian trade on China and Japan, that of the Company was of a very modest size. On the other hand the significance of the centralized shipping to Europe of three to four thousand ton annually is clear. Even though such quantities of goods were often traded by Indian

* The following page of the manuscript is missing. [Editorial note]

and Chinese merchant gentlemen and high officials, the Company certainly was in that respect one of the great merchants of the Orient.

The shipping carried on by the European free burghers was insignificant. In the year 1636 six yachts belonging to free burghers arrived in Batavia – one from Bali, three from Ambon *via* Bali, two from Martapura, – and seven departed – three to Bali, one of them *via* Balambangan, and four to Ambon, two of them *via* Bali, one *via* Banjarmasin, and one direct.

7

Dutch Civilization Overseas

It is already clear from the above that the overseas personnel of the Company consisted of officials, soldiers, and ships' crews. The civilian element, furthermore, was also primarily oriented to warfare and military command. The governors-general themselves (Coen and Van Diemen) went to war; the members of the government had command of expeditions. And the strongholds in the spice islands and at Batavia were designed to be ready and willing to fight. The whole Company world was oriented to warfare and hostility.

Under the protection of Batavia Castle, established in 1619, a fortified Dutch town was laid out, part of it consisting of the area of the old Indonesian *kota* of Jakarta. Governor-General Specx was the builder of the eastern part of the town; Governor-General van Diemen of the part west of the Chiliwung.[41] The core of the town was formed by Indonesians from elsewhere and Chinese, however, with a number of Portuguese and mestizos and a very few Dutch free burghers.[42] The free trades and crafts, business, and commerce in the town were in Chinese hands; alongside them, in isolation, were the Company trades of the wharf and the castle, operated by Dutch manpower. Money was held almost exclusively by the Chinese, and the farming out of town taxes, contracts for supplies, loans and usury, possession of houses in town, and the first exploitation of the idle hinterlands behind Batavia all took place under their leadership.

Batavia inclusive of the castle and the garrison had a population of around six thousand persons in 1623, eight thousand in 1632, and twelve thousand (perhaps inclusive of the crews on Company ships) in 1638.[43] How much the population must have depended on the Company and its institutions can be seen by comparing the two sets of figures given earlier showing the relatively small significance of Asian trade and the predominant significance of the Company's central rendezvous for Batavia. Economically the Chinese retained their position alongside and under the Company, and the Chinese element was able to develop more strength in Batavia than in any town under Indonesian control.

Aside from the military ceremonies of the Company such as the reception of foreign ambassadors:

> Monday, New Year's Day [1624] the two Chinese ambassadors from the governor of the province Fukien sent to His Excellency the General were honourably escorted into the fort here ... The said ambassadors were conveyed by the bailiff of this town and some members of the town council together with the receiver-general of revenues of this kingdom as well as the *shahbandar* and 3 or 4 merchants-in-chief from their lodgings to the gate of the fort with 4 elephants and 10 or 12 horses, where having descended and been amicably welcomed and escorted in by the president of the honourable executive council, the treasurer, and some delegates from the aforesaid council, further passed in between two rows of armed soldiers from the gate on to the chamber where the said council assembles daily, where being led in by the aforesaid president and entertained around a half hour with refreshments, further being fetched from there by two councillors of the Indies and taken to the chamber before His Excellency the General. And after reciprocal compliments the said ambassadors have with proper respect handed over to His Excellency the General a letter written on a broad [paper]board in Chinese (coming from the governor of the province of Fukien) ...[44]

the Chinese festivals will have been the chief public ceremonies:

> ... their public and private sacrifices and offerings of swine, tubers, pastry, and all sorts of edible wares, likewise the burning of lamps, candles, incense, the producing of comedies and spectacles and especially their solemn processions, stately displays, and carrying around of their idol under silk parasols ...[45]

Indonesian culture did not display itself in the distant, hostile coastal town.

The Company authorities could not very well lead a 'seigneurial way of life' in the tiny fortified town. For the Chinese, Japanese, Indians, and Middle Easterners, the grim fortifications of Batavia may merely have summoned up the memory of strongholds and castles in their own lands. The Company lodges in the large Indian cities were not different from the *fondachi* of the other foreign nations. Zeelandia Castle on Formosa will not have aroused any surprise in the eyes of the Chinese and Japanese traders and officials, for it had the same structure as many fortifications in their own countries. But for the Indonesians the sturdy Italian-style castle structures, stronger than the more old-fashioned Portuguese fortresses, and much stronger than their own structures for defense, must have been something ominously new. The fortresses on the spice islands and the constant agression of their garrisons against the inhabitants of the islands and the foreigners coming to trade there must have become the objects of widespread hostility and hatred.

These images at the same time illustrate the cultural significance of the Dutch strongholds in the first half of the seventeenth century. The warring Company, with its military regime over the spice islands, its privateering in all the seas of Asia, and apart from that its trading on the Asian markets as one among many, exerted little or no influence of a cultural sort. For that it held too small an area and its position was too much a defensive one. The enforced conversions to Calvinist Christianity on the spice islands were a purely political phenomenon, perhaps accepted by the Indonesian federations – such as the general diet of Ambon, – allied to the Dutch castles, as a means of political cohesion. The many foreigners and Dutch dissenters in the service of the Company kept the Calvinists always a minority, and because of the great tolerance of the authorities made necessary by the circumstances the official religion did not produce much effect. In the Company East, as in the Netherlands, the presbytery as a rule stood in opposition to the castle.

8

1650: Retrospect and Prospect

How logical is it to close this survey with the beginning of the second half of the seventeenth century? For Java the end of the 1640's meant something of an interlude, with peace between Batavia and both Mataram and Bantam. But elsewhere the course of development went on unbroken. The struggle with Portugal for India and Ceylon was begun and ran on into the 1650's; the situation in western Asia did not undergo any change. In China the shadow of the struggle between the retreating adherents of the Ming Dynasty and the Manchus fell across the Company's position. In Japan the Company officials lived on just as before in isolation on the island Deshima, off Nagasaki. In Indonesia itself, Achin, Macassar, and Ternate stood beside Mataram[46] as important powers, and the Company's regime in the spice islands went on under menacing tensions of the inhabitants held in subjugation by force. The pacification of the regions by Governor-General van Diemen in the years 1636–1639 was followed within a decade by uprisings and war and a violent suppression of the rebellion under Governors Demmer and De Vlamingh van Oudtshoorn, and the struggle continued to rage till the years 1655–1656. The trade was small enough in size that every encroachment on the monopoly could be felt. And it is food for thought that the activities of the Portuguese still impeded and damaged Dutch shipping there.

A picture of the general position of the Dutch Company in Asia is given in the new 'Instructions for the Government in the Indies' drawn up by the Gentlemen Seventeen in a meeting at Amsterdam, 26 April, 1650.[47] It represented a conclusion to the early years of Dutch penetration in Asia in its consolidation of the organized machinery of government, and at the same time it gave a survey of the different positions the Company held in the various countries in Asia. In it, it is easy to ascertain where there was power exercised and where unsupported settlement. The Company's trade was of three sorts:

1 Trade from the region it had conquered: *e.g.* the Banda Islands.

2 Trade carried on under monopoly contracts with Ternate: the Moluccas and Ambon.

3 Trade with various other Oriental kings and princes on the basis of agreements reached as well as on the basis of free trade alongside other nations.

The Company's spice monopoly decreased the export of products from the Moluccas considerably. Its policy in the Moluccas was that its servants should not so much exert themselves to obtain a great deal of cloves as above all keep watch and take care that the cloves were not shipped away by the inhabitants or by foreign nations.[48] The islands of Ambon produced more cloves per year than all the world could consume;[49] the Banda Islands in the same way produced more nutmeg and mace than the whole world could use.[50] The extirpation of the plantations in the regions not directly policed by the Company was a logical consequence. The circle had not been so completely closed in any of the previous periods; the monopolization of the spice regions aimed at and in the course of time with force and violence accomplished by the Dutch Company was a completely new factor which began to delineate itself around 1650.

But elsewhere the Company appeared as one among many. The lodge at Macassar needed to be maintained:

> besides for the small trade of the Company there, to hear and to see what passes there and may serve the Company...[51]

Solor needed to be watched:

> to check the Portuguese there and give them no occasion to settle at Macassar from there, which would only result in more evil and greater infringement of Company trade...[52]

The Achinese trade needed "with great discretion and farsighted wisdom" to be increased more and more, especially with an eye to the trade on the tin regions:

> consequently there is no better means to gain admission to the aforesaid trade on advantageous conditions than to win the good grace and favour of the queen [Thapiatodin] and the lords of the court with annual presents...[53]

In order to corner the pepper, trade also needed to be carried on at Jambi, and it was better to buy dear there than to give up competition, "in consideration of the free access of other European nations there the which cannot be prevented by us..."[54] There ought also to be trade on Palembang:

> as long as most of the pepper is not taken by the Chinese and other Indian nations from there to Batavia, to which for long good hope was given, but up to now has not been followed by the proper success...[55]

War was not to be made on Martapura (Banjarmasin), Cambodia, and Annam, "notwithstanding the lawful and valid reasons..."; it was more advisable "to contrive means to be able to gain profits from the said nations by new access..."[56] Just satisfaction was to be given the ruler of Arakan for the robbing of his ship going to Coromandel, in order to be able to open up trade again.[57] On the Malabar Coast pepper was to be traded for:

> ...in order not to leave it alone for the Portuguese and other foreign nations, as well as in order constantly to observe the actions and trade of the Portuguese on aforesaid coast...[58]

The pressure of the Mogol government and the city administration of Surat was heavy; however, there was to be no war made against it "putting a certain trade at peril in the hope of a better (but with an uncertain result)...", but the difficulties arising were to be met with wisdom and understanding and settled:

> in which discreet directors can achieve the most, who get along well with the Moorish governors, caress them, and at the proper opportunity know how to treat them with what is pleasant to them, wherewith peace then can probably be preserved without estrangement...[59]

The naval demonstration begun against Persia was to be abandoned; an attempt was to be made to hold a share in the important silk trade by peaceful means:

> and to consider that the Company must never imagine that it will exercise its trade in Persia completely without any encumbrance of ship and road tolls, as that nation, being superb, courageous, and very desirous, [in exchange] for the benefit and profit the Company derives from its trade in the kingdom of Persia will want to be acknowledged, whether by presents to the king and the lords of the kingdom, or by contracting with the king for freedom from ship and road tolls at a certain reasonable price, at least 3 or 400 bales of Persian silk per year...[60]

Regarding Siam:

> in order to continue trade there with reputation and to be able to capture the favour of the lords, the king and Berguelang [one of the leading court dignitaries] must be greeted with annual presents pleasing to them; the costs of which, in consideration of the great commodity resulting to the Company therefrom, are expended for profit, and therefore you may not be too sparing therein...[61]

Because of the Indian trade in cotton cloth on Tenasserim, there was little for the Dutch to do there:

> however, you may not hinder them therein, in order to avoid all estrangement with that kingdom [Siam], being most damaging to the Company, as we may not set the law for everyone and should fall short everywhere...[62]

> In order to increase the ... trade on Taiwan it must be especially observed to entertain the Chinese well and not to do injustice in accepting their merchandise, but to pay them the reasonable price on delivery, according to the soundness of each specie...[63]

In Japan:

> our ministers have no other instruction to take there except to look to the wishes of that brave, superb, precise nation in order to please it in everything, and by no means to think on anything the which might cause greater antipathy to us... That consequently the Company's ministers frequenting the scrupulous state each year must above all go armed in modesty, humility, courtesy, and amity, always being the lesser...[64]

In Tonkin:

> trade ... being obtained for the Company with the greatest difficulty, our ministers must above all watch themselves not to give the king and the mighty of the state any least offense, but to complace the same and win their favour with annual presents and courtesy, the frequency of Portuguese, Japanese, and other nations already having provided great obstacles in the aforesaid trade...[65]

In Coromandel the Company's servants:

> must see to hold the great merchants in trade as friends, without ever thinking to come in estrangement with them through small quarrels and vexations...[66]

It would be wrong to brand these instructions with faintheartedness and unwarranted reserve. They reflect accurately the true state of affairs, the balances of power, and the possibilities. A Company regime with forts, garrisons, policing vessels, and auxiliary troops could be maintained in the small areas of the Moluccas, by making use of the traditional indigenous feuds and factions. In the Company's own town, Batavia, also. Elsewhere the Dutch had to depend on ships at sea and a small amount of ordnance in states much more powerful economically, administratively, and militarily, and the thing that mattered was the valuable trade:

> the peaceful trade throughout the whole of the Indies the kitchen at home must smoke of...[67]

> Company trade over the whole of the Indies [must] be based on the common right of all peoples, consisting in freedom of commerce, the which being granted in neutral places by free nations where We find laws and do not have to bring them, We may not appropriate the aforesaid trade according to our own ideas and constrain such nations thereto by force, just as the Company could not consider it that other nations would desire to prescribe law for the way of trading in places under its territory...[68]

> ...trade always entails that the one tries to prevent another's advantage, against which there is nothing else to do but to repay others with the same coin without giving thought to actual resistance, especially in places where we have no say but have to adjust ourselves according to the laws of those lands as far as trade is concerned...[69]

With the Company carrying on trade from Persia and southern Arabia to Formosa and Japan, warring against Portugal and the Javanese states, maintaining ships at sea, and expanding forts, with the costs rising and the returns to Europe staying the same at the will of the Gentlemen Seventeen, the expansion of trade in Asia and its becoming more tightly interwoven in the net of intra-Asian connections were the only possibility for increasing the profits there had to be to meet the expenses in Asia. But the Company had to make its way with difficulty in that Asian trade, so tightly bound to Oriental balances of power and state politics, not holding any advantage in any way, either in capital, in navigation, or in organization.

In his 'Remonstrance Regarding the Present State of the General Dutch Chartered East India Company'[70] dated from Amsterdam, 8 September, 1655, and directed to the Gentlemen Seventeen, Rijckloff van Goens, former first merchant-in-chief of Batavia Castle and member extraordinary of the Council of the Indies now returned to Holland, gave his comment on the state of the Company, in it more or less following the order of the Instruction of 1650 with his own information on the Indies. The retrogression in trade, the recession in the amount of capital employed, the necessity for attacking the Oriental states and princes by force made up the themes of his disquisition. In it – despite his apologetic denial:

> It appears from this account as though I incline completely toward war, but I assure Your Excellencies of the contrary...[71]

> It is not unknown to me how little the situation of the Company allows it to make use of warfare everywhere, and God be my witness that I should never advise thereunto except in necessity...[72]

– the demand for offensive force was raised against the policy of peaceful free trade of the Gentlemen Seventeen. But as regards Company affairs in Asia the sketches drawn in 1650 and in 1655 coincide. From the two of them together one can form a total picture of the condition of the Company – and conclude that one should beware of the idea that mid-way in the Golden Age of Dutch politics an empire had already been won in the Indies. As Van Goens wrote:

> [All] the offices of the Indies [are] taxed with one or another difficulty: Amboyna with a dangerous war whereon the Moluccas and Banda depend, Solor and Malacca with burdens and no profit, Mocha and Balsora with trade and no gain, Surat, Persia, Coromandel, and Bengal encumbered and annoyed by Moorish trade, and also Tonkin spoiled by the Chinese; Taiwan seems through divers accidents to be oppressed by God's hand; Japan through lack of capital cannot accumulate any capital; and Batavia is smothering in its own expenses and the burdens of all the offices, besides the losses at sea, now, may God improve it, having been several years extraordinary.[73]

Against the conservative peace policy of the Gentlemen Seventeen in Holland, a faithful reflection of the limited state of the

Dutch in Asia, Van Goens proposed his policy, certainly that of the 'progressives' of the regime at Batavia Castle, defensive in its protection of that limited state, but containing an element of expansion and a possibility of further shifts in power in its advocacy of war and the chances of war:

> ... the Christian maxims which Your Excellencies have continually followed, to pursue the trade of the Illustrious Company in peace and amity with all the mighty of the Indies, are being evilly interpreted... by them – there being no one in all the Indies who wishes us well, yea [we] are deadly hated by all nations – for even if we seek to win everyone over with right, moderation, and justice, still the general opinion of everyone is particularly to ruin us ... so that in my judgement earlier or later war will once have to be the arbiter...[74]

The second half of the century began under the sign of that grim, uncertain war, a greater struggle than had already been fought out, one which would eventually result in the laying of a firmer basis for the domination of the Castle and Port of Batavia and the expansion of the Dutch East India Company of 'laudable and redoubtable name'.

A History of the Netherlands East Indies: Three Reviews

The three articles here brought together were originally published as reviews of various volumes of the history of the Netherlands East Indies edited by F. W. Stapel under the title *Geschiedenis van Nederlandsch Indië* (five volumes published, Amsterdam, 1938–1940). The Dutch version of the first article, reviewing Volume One of the history, was published in the journal *Djåwå,* XIX (1939), 286–292; that of the second, reviewing Volumes Two and Three, appeared in the *Tijdschrift voor Indische Taal-, Land- en Volkenkunde* (Journal of Indonesian Philology, Geography, and Ethnology), LXXIX (1939), 589–595. The final article, revised from a paper read before the thirteenth session of the Royal Batavian Society of Arts and Sciences (Koninklijk Bataviaasch Genootschap van Kunsten en Wetenschappen) Historical Section on 18 April, 1940, was published in the *Tijdschrift voor Indische Taal-, Land- en Volkenkunde,* LXXX (1940), 544–567 under the title "Eenige aanteekeningen betreffende de mogelijkheid der 18e eeuw als categorie in de Indische geschiedschrijving" (Some Comments on the Possibility of the Eighteenth Century as a Category in the Writing of Indonesian History), and finds its basis in a consideration of Volume Four of the history edited by Dr Stapel.

One

The historian and the novelist are able to reconstruct nations or individuals in all the truth of their customs, on the basis of the remains of their public monuments or on the examination of their domestic relics... A mosaic reveals a whole society, in the same way the skeleton of an ichthyosaurus presupposes a whole creation. In either case everything is a part of a series of things, everything is linked together. The cause leads one to divine an effect, just as every effect enables one to return to a cause.

Hippolyte Taine

If the reader of the initial volume of the new *Geschiedenis van Nederlandsch Indië* (History of the Netherlands East Indies)[1] appearing under Dr Stapel's editorship has not before that succumbed from using the unmanageable volume with its pulpit Bible format and exhausting, extravagant print, by the time he reaches Dr Krom's contribution on Hindu-Javanese history[2] he will have finished reading Dr van der Hoop's summary of the prehistory of Indonesia.[3] That summary, after a survey of the chronology of the preceding unmeasured epochs, closes with a reference to more historical times: "And then, in the first centuries after the birth of Christ, the Hindu immigrants must have arrived".[4] The reference is taken over by Krom at the beginning of his study: "The history of what would one day become the Netherlands East Indies commences with the coming of the Hindus".[5]

The coming of the Hindus, then, – Hindu immigration, Hindu colonization – is made the *leit-motif* for the actual history of the region, which history in that way becomes a history *avant la lettre* of migration and colonization although in this case, different from in the case of later, true colonial history, there are still questions on the most cardinal points, and the whole basis for such an historical view, even, remains debatable.

To make a detailed criticism of this study, contributed by the leading authority in that area of history as a part of a popular reference work, could not be my intention, and in any case I lack the specialized knowledge in the field of epigraphy which would be needed. Now that the standard picture has once more been set down for a larger public, probably for a longer period and, considering the prestige of the contributors, authoritatively, in a general history of the Netherlands East Indies, the aim of the notes below is rather that of formulating a few questions, examining a number of data more closely in the light of what has been done in related fields of research, and, above all, confronting the results of such specialized work with some historical patterns of a more general influence.

Questions of method are not as yet often raised in the study of Indonesian history. Argument over planning in the craft of history would appear to be a waste of energy when there are so few hands in the workshop and work is more than abundant. Yet it needs to be stated on the other hand that a few lost arguments can no doubt be of value, for with all the hands in the workshop specialists, many of them not recruited from the branch of scholarship really competent, it is even harder than in other fields for a more general tone to make itself heard.

The real history of Indonesia "commences with the coming of the Hindus". Few things remain vaguer than that all-predominant fact, however. The Hindu period covers an era of fifteen centuries:

> it is the period of the assimilation of a higher civilization, the formation of states, the flourishing of trade, the period which made the archipelago into what it was when it first entered within the ken of Europe.[6]

If one then asks how such a Hindu immigration took place, what such a colonization and its sphere of influence actually were, then the complete vagueness of the concept becomes apparent.

It was not – even if one makes every restriction regarding the minuscule numbers commonly involved in events so extremely important historically[7] – a mass migration overseas. It was not a political conquest: neither an expansion by a national army going out in search of booty (as in the Greek conquests overseas), a marauding expedition (as those of the Norsemen), nor territorial expansion for political purposes (sometimes with a professional army, as in the Rome of the later Republic or in Venice). The immigration and colonization in Indonesia were in actuality not any such things: what came was not a influx of a large group of people (always with the reservation just made) but a series of cultural forms, a cultural revolution bringing a higher civilization and the formation of states as a result of a peaceful penetration primarily of traders.[8]

The cultural forms seem to have been of a very special sort. The work of Hindu colonization in Indonesia does not appear to have been carried on as the sort of cultural transference *en bloc* which built up Massilia and Malucha into colonial Greek cities overseas with the whole lay-out and organization of the Hellene *polis*, nor the sort that raised heavy military fortifications in the forests of the Rhine and on the barren heaths of the Tyne and made Trevirorum and Eburacum into cultural enclaves as colonial Roman cities. Nor does it appear to have been the transference of a popular culture putting its stamp on the soil from which it wrestled its existence, on the lay-out of fields, the construction of houses, the community forms of public life, the language, traditions, and folklore in the way Germanic farmstead culture enrooted itself in northern France, England, and Scandinavia with the great migrations. Hindu cultural influence had to do only with things sacral – religious rites and ritual, and also literature and governmental techniques, which had a consecrated, magical character.

Cultural elements do not always need to be transmitted by the people whose property they originally were. In such things the level of civilization plays the decisive rôle. It is true the spread of medieval architecture took place largely through the dispersal of skilled master craftsmen, just as the cultural influence of early Christian missions found its physical basis in the meagre cultural treasures of the missionaries from Ireland or the South. But the Renaissance was not spread by the dispersion of Italians northwards as far as Scandinavia, nor was the Italian journey of Northerners the decisive factor – Vondel never went south of the Alps and Shakespeare probably never left the shores of England. That process, however, took place in a society in which due to the means of transportation and communication, and especially the art of printing, cultural influences could spread in another fashion. In pre-capitalistic Europe that was impossible. And, as I believe I may state, just as impossible in pre-capitalistic early Indonesia.

The 'trader' who by means of long residence and intermarriage is supposed to have brought a higher civilization remains a dubious figure.[9] In pre-capitalistic commerce the traders because of their origin and status held a position which did not in the least allow them to fulfil at once the function of transmitters of culture *vis-à-vis* the rulers of the coasts they touched upon. Such a thing is almost completely out of the question for the small trader because of mutual 'foreignness' and mutual 'magical exterritoriality', and even for the rich merchant and the factor of noblemen overseas it is difficult enough. A figure such as Louys de Geer, dominating Sweden and spreading Dutch culture, is something out of a completely different sort of world.

The sort of culture transferred to Indonesia was first of all a complex of Brahmanic soteriology, esoteric as few others, magical and tabooed to the highest degree, the property of a *virtuoso* class which had isolated itself to the extreme from the other social classes – the Brahmins. There was no way of bridging the gap between merchant and Brahmin.

The wide diversity in the earliest epigraphic remains of itself already pleads little for a Hinduism having travelled by means of trade, but even more important is the fact that Indian civilization is to be encountered in the states in the interior of the main Indonesian island, Java. Those states were shut off to the south by jungles and an inhospitable sea, and natural and artificial circumstances combined to make them completely isolated from the coastal regions to the north. One has only to read the accounts of how the Dutch Company agents De Haen[10] and Van Goens[11] penetrated into the state of Mataram, accounts which call up vividly the idea of an entrance into a forbidden state and a forbidden city. How then is it possible to imagine the situation in which foreign pedlars might find their way to the royal courts to prepare the establishment of a new social order, the way for a higher civilization? And in a world in which all contact must undoubtedly have been even more intermittent and rare than in the seventeenth century, the mutual foreignness much greater still?

The Hinduization of Javanese civilization – and Indonesian civilization in general – was, then, an affair of the royal court and the hierocracy. How it could have been a result of pacific penetration with trade blazing the trail remains nothing less than an enigma.

Let us turn to the second component, the recipient civilization, early Indonesia.

If one reads the absorbing opening chapter of the first volume of Stapel's history through to the finish, one finds that the recapitulative survey of the prehistorical remains in Indonesia ends in front of the blank wall of Hindu Indonesia, before which one is supposed to trace the footprints of Hindu immigrants who effected the great transformation. Once one has got on the other side of the wall, one suddenly finds oneself, in Krom's contribution, in a completely different world. The early Indonesia of the new stone age and the bronze age has receded into obscurity and in the background of Krom's Indonesia there is another 'original' Indonesia for the reception of Hindu civilization, one which seems to have a different structure from that sketched by Van der Hoop.

The course of circumstances has caused scholars to approach the history of Indonesia *via* the great eighteenth-century Sanskrit studies while comparative philology has gone its own way. The dominance of Sanskrit in its various artistic forms and transformations on the epigraphic remains has given its students the weight of authority in studies of early Indonesia. Alongside those studies is to be found the first working hypothesis on the Indonesian migrations, that of Kern, drawn up on the basis of philological research. In 1889, also on the basis of philological research,

Brandes formulated his ten points on the cultural heritage of pre-Hindu Java, and that survey still served in Professor Krom's book as the *pièce de résistance*.[12]

Now prehistory, the youngest historical discipline, a lonely outpost in the no man's land of history, has sketched its picture of early Indonesia. Even though the attempt has been made to clarify the picture of Hindu Indonesia through the use of ethnographic material (the latest eloquent example is Dr Stutterheim's study of pre-Hindu burial practices),[13] the light which still can be shed on the civilization of the Hindu period by the data collected in prehistorical studies is surprising.

Prehistory is a matter of a great deal of fantasy, of such a degree of imagination that it sometimes appears questionable whether a sociologically and historically reliable construction of the facts can be made. The experts build a civilization around a potsherd, irrespective of whether the potsherd could have been a part of the possessions of a pedlar or an exile, a village of farmers or one of rain conjurors. More important, however, is the cultural inventory scholars in the discipline consider they are justified in attributing to certain prehistoric civilizations on the basis of findings and comparison of techniques. The nature and power of the neolithic civilization make its development and maturing just as great in significance as the transition from the age of handicrafts and empirical techniques to the machine age.[14] The neolithic age, it appears from the findings, was familiar with stone agricultural instruments, including *pachuls*,[15] which means that the cultivation of rice on *sawahs* was then already known.[16]

Call to mind for a moment what other things can be linked to this detail of neolithic civilization: *sawah* farming–water supply and distribution; organization of the farmers–irrigation units–farming on fixed plots–fixed seasons of harvest; calendar–authority–government; district–province–state. Present-day Java is still based on the use of the *pachul*: the transition from stone to iron is of relatively little importance. To what extent was the picture of agricultural Java in historical times as land of *sawahs* and *desas* already its picture in the neolithic age?[17]

The arguments that have already been used to dispute the significance of the imported characteristics in Hindu-Indonesian (or Hindu-Javanese) civilization at various points now acquire a new importance in the light of the findings of the prehistorians. Van der Hoop warns against an underestimation of the value of Indonesian civilization, the early cultural forms of the archipelago which were developed out of the civilization of the new stone age and the bronze age:

> The biggest mistake that can be made in regard to this Indonesian civilization is to underrate it. In general ... the faulty opinion that the Hindus were the bearers of culture here and the pre-Hindu inhabitants were a sort of savages ... is still all too dominant...[18]

Krom's view of that Indonesian civilization is set in something of a minor key:

> ... one certainly does not need ... to imagine an extraordinary civilization which might have been able to stand up to that of the Hindus as an equal. It is certain, however, that the latter did not arrive in the midst of savages...[19]

A highly negative pronouncement!

The key to a proper appreciation of Hindu cultural influence in Indonesia can only be found in a correct estimate of the significance of early Indonesian civilization in the broadest sense of the term. The statements of the archeologist-historians remain extremely vague on this point. The hypothesis of colonization as the vehicle of cultural transference is, as has been indicated in a few points above, hardly admissible – and certainly not if it is to be accepted that such deep-rooted matters as government, state organization, and dynastic positions had their origins in such a Hindu influence. This can be illustrated with a few examples.

Considering the Taruma inscription,[20] Krom maintains, on the basis of the fact that the construction of an irrigation conduit and a sacrifice of cattle at a place far from the coast are related in the inscription, that one cannot have to do with a Hindu adventurer, but with a permanent authority, either of a Hindu who has made himself king or of a 'Hinduized' Indonesian. The fact that the difference between a Hindu adventurer and a Hindu who has made himself king is not a great one need not be considered here: the core of Krom's argument lies in his evaluation of the sort of situation which may lead to the construction of an irrigation system on royal order. Such a situation presupposes a certain level of civilization, a development over a quite considerable period, a long-term evolution of government and people. The patterns of smaller and larger bureaucracies connected with irrigation systems offer material for deciding the question how slowly such an organization grows, how high a level of development such a state with a central government, a population performing soccage for the ruler, and a system of irrigation already presupposes. And it is such a pattern one must conclude existed in that upland region above Jakarta. It is impossible for such things to have been achieved in the course of even the twenty-two year reign mentioned in the inscription. They need to be thought of in terms of decades and centuries. But then the date of Hinduization has no fundamental relation to the state of affairs in the kingdom. It remains an arbitrarily chosen point in time. And this must hold to a very much greater degree for the large kingdoms isolated in the interior of central Java, probably the 'heartland' of the island's civilization from earliest times on.

Heichelheim, in an article written in 1932,[21] pointed out the significance of prehistoric civilization as the foundation for later urban civilization and in general as the basis for all formation of cities and states. As 'agrarian civilization' it has perpetuated its existence into the heart of historical times, up to the present day. Just as it formed the basis for the Chinese Contending States and the Mesopotamian city states, it seems to me to have formed the basis for Indonesian civilization and, especially in its largest single complex, that on Java, to have supported a highly organized political structure the unchanged existence of which has to be taken into account in earlier and later Indonesian history.

The pattern of the states as they came to the fore in the Hindu-Javanese period – a central royal authority with a sacral significance and a patrimonial bureaucracy, based on a population strictly domesticated, in villages and carrying on *sawah* farming on the plains; political and social life determined by the harvest and a taxation system of crop tithes in kind – can only have arisen in a formative process of ages and ages and can only be viewed as the outgrowth of the Indonesian civilization of the new stone age and bronze age.[22] It is technologically impossible for any colonization by Hindus, whether of traders or Brahmins, to have been able to accomplish anything in this field in the short period their presence there is proved by documents. The complex of governmental technique and sacral organization can only have risen slowly on an indigenous Indonesian basis.

The rôle of Hindu civilization appears to have been a much more modest one, in fact. Krom spoke of 'spiritual advisers' for the Hindu colonies.[23] If one overlooks the terminology, which rather leads one to think of confessional labour unions, the concept serves to indicate the autonomous rôle of the Brahman priesthood, which can without forcing be fitted into the picture of 'Brahmanic missions',[24] the 'Brahmanization'[25] of southeast Asia: a tranference of certain elements of a very exclusive soteriology by a caste of religious *virtuosi* surrounded by the aura of the glorious name of the great land of India. After the Brahmanization of southern India[26] that mission made its way along the sea route – probably already known for centuries – to the states on the islands of southeast Asia and the mainland of Farther India. It is not impossible the Brahmins came of their own will, though in Indonesia as elsewhere there may have been summonses for them, for which there are parallels in the Christian missions in Europe. Such Indian strangers became of influence only by virtue of the will and the desire of Indonesian rulers, however. Their work in Indonesia, as in India, was above all the legitimation of the ruling dynasty – *vis-à-vis* India, or possibly China, – the provision of mythological sanction to genealogy and tradition. Probably few in numbers, they were in reward guaranteed the benefit of the prebends which the patrimonial bureaucracy by its nature could award them.[27] Chancellory activities will have appeared alongside these – although it would be curious to have to accept the idea that the Javanese bureaucracy had carried on its regime without any scribal work. It is in these areas that the actual elements of the Hindu influence must be sought: sacral legitimation, chancellory techniques, and architectural techniques (in the field of stone construction). There would seem to be no place alongside this for a cultural influence in any broader sense.

The importation of new devotional forms, documentation, and the construction of buildings are favourite affairs of an absolute rule.[28] In consideration of the taboo nature of such skills and techniques practised as secret magic in the rigid and hierarchical state of the 'soccage and *kraton* kingdoms', it is – once again – nonsensical to try to perceive a way in which peddling traders from afar, humble worldlings, could spread in such high circles Hindu civilization, a soteriology of a very esoteric sort, and one laden with a powerful taboo.

In considering Hindu-Javanese history, there is a second point requiring comment. The system of periodization according to ages of development and decline determined chiefly from decorative and stylistic elements has led to the concept of a waning of cultural strength leading to disintegration in the fifteenth century.[29] The rise of missionary Islam as the dominant religion of the courts has then been taken as the basis for the periodization of the following age. As regards the completely static picture of the patrimonial agricultural states socially and economically, this procedure is probably justified. Other elements come into the picture, however, as soon as one turns to consider the towns and, in relation with them, the transformations in economic life connected with overseas trade. In doing which it should be remembered that everywhere in the world such overseas trade, with the accumulation of capital (that of the already established lords and mighty, whose wealth and power have their original basis in agrarian and social privileges, not that of the traders) made possible by it, has always been one of the most important factors in the process of social and economic transformation of classes and civilizations.

Due to the documentation on the ports on northern Java in the accounts of the first Dutch voyages, we possess a detailed picture of the coastal town carrying on international trade. It was a true town, with collegiate kingship (compare the Malay form of government, as well as the Buginese-Macassarese state councils), with pre-capitalistic handicraft trade on an international scale and with the first forms of capitalistic development, found everywhere in the world: *commenda*, commission contracts, letters of credit, merchant gentlemen, and royal private trade.[30] When did all this arise? Bruges and Rostock in the Europe of the Hanseatic League reveal another structure from that of the Roman Noviomagus and the Carolingian Dorestad. The (re-)development of early-capitalistic trade intervenes. Does the picture of Bantam and Tuban around 1600 hold also for the fourteenth, the thirteenth, the tenth century? Does it hold for the Çriwijaya of the Çailendras and the time of Chau Ju-kua? The lists of goods traded, with which one usually has to make do in the field of commercial history, are not enough: pre-capitalistic and early-capitalistic trade were both trade in luxury goods or at best in consumers' goods lacking any semblance of mass trade; pearls, rhinoceros horn, pepper, and gold can be exchanged in intertribal trade (in the Kula, for example) and in handicraft peddling trade as well as in a capitalistic form with an ordered, rational system of accounting based on letters of credit, bills of exchange, and a capital turnover.

To what extent it might be possible to trace the line of development, and of what significance it might have been for early Indonesia, what indirect repercussions it may possibly have had on the states of the interior – all that remains to be answered.

To return to the quotation from Taine in the headnote: it must be remembered that history, as the journal registering the course of the complex life of men as individuals and members of society, reveals only a limited number of phenomena in all the different forms of human society. Such things as agriculture, farmstead, village, royal court, monastery, fortress, boat, battle chariot, town hall, bridal procession, and grave occur in cultural configurations in a limited number of variations only. Up to now the piecing together of those phenomena for the history of early Indonesia has, generally speaking, remained still undone. Yet, so it seems to me, there lies a rewarding field of labour. The field for working hypotheses does not lie in tracing down the course of the decorative sacral motif and the detail of an inscription, it lies among such things as the neolithic *pachul* and the obligation for overseas trade in Bantam written on *lontar* with "a stiletto or iron bodkin"[31] – in the midst of everyday objects belonging to a single, continuous history of early Indonesia.

Two

The second and third volumes of the *Geschiedenis van Nederlandsch Indië*, edited by Dr Stapel, have appeared. Covering the sixteenth and seventeenth centuries, they are made up of contributions by Professor Berg on 'Javanese Historiography', Father Wessels on 'The Portuguese and the Spaniards', Dr Terpstra on 'The French and the English' and 'The First Dutch Companies',[1] and Dr Stapel himself on 'The Establishment of the United East India Company' and 'The Dutch East India Company in the Seventeenth Century', two contributions which together form the whole third volume.[2]

Professor Berg's study is related to the material of the first volume, which dealt with Indonesian prehistory and early history. Absorbingly written and all of a piece, it forms a noteworthy counterpart to Professor Krom's contribution on the historical aspect of the same period. If for Krom Hindu colonization and its effects on the Indonesian (Javanese) element is the *leit-motif*, Berg sees a much stronger national Javanese character which adapted foreign cultural elements and amalgamated them yet definitely maintained the primacy of Indonesian elements throughout the period. It appears there are antitheses in this area which cannot be reconciled until more study has been done.

In this work, too, in recording the course of history the fatal jump is taken to the overseas voyages of the Europeans and the offensive for colonial power. The Indocentric point of view is held for the preceding centuries, when Hindu civilization came from India and that of Islam from the world of the caliphates. But with the arrival of ships from western Europe, the point of view is turned a hundred eighty degrees and from then on the Indies are observed from the deck of the ship, the ramparts of the fortress, the high gallery of the trading-house. There lingers something highly unsatisfactory here.[3]

In this regard it is impossible to overrate the significance for early Indonesian history of Portuguese source materials, for they give a picture of the Indonesian world before any European influence was really at work. The materials from the first Dutch voyages and from the Dutch East India Company in the early seventeenth century have a significance of the same sort. For the eighteenth century, when the might of the Illustrious Company was expanding from that of coastal fort, port-of-call, and spice guard station to that of a landed power with territorial influence, a real power among the Oriental states, the atrophy of the Indonesian world becomes a question,[4] and at the same time the relative importance of the Company's history increases. But in any case in the seventeenth century the Oriental element, not the colonial, was dominant.

The questions how the threads making up the rich fabric of the cultural pattern of sixteenth-century Indonesia were spun, what the design of the fabric as a whole looked like – these are the questions that first come to mind when one considers the Portuguese period. They are more important than the course of Portuguese trade, conquest, and settlement in itself. The activities of the Portuguese had for the archipelago only a limited significance, despite the conquest of Malacca. Privateering, which had always clung to the sea routes from the Far East to the Near like a swarm of hornets, was increased ten times by their activities.

If one considers for example the significance attached to the level of development in artillery technique and usage in western European history, it is provocative to ask what significance such things had for Indonesia. Gunpowder, the manufacture of guns, and the use of artillery existed independently there. The figures on the guns captured on the fall of Malacca are telling.[5] The Malay town's resistance in the siege was one equal to the military technique of the Portuguese. Countless episodes from the everlasting sea struggle show how at sea, too, the use of fighting forces was on the same level. There was parity also in the field of shipbuilding. The Javanese ships' carpenters that D'Albuquerque took back with him from Malacca to Goa in 1511 are excellent illustrations of the fact.

In matters of trade, the same sort of comment. There was no superiority in trading method on the Portuguese side. The 'economic mentality'[6] of the Portuguese nobles and commoners was of the same sort as that of the Indonesian princes, courtiers, notables, and merchants. What is important for the colonial chapter of history is the great difference in the organization of the Portuguese and that of the Hollanders and Zeelanders. In comparison to the Portuguese method of aristocratic military exploitation in trade and establishment of authority, the thorough organization of the Dutch Company constitutes an institution of a considerably higher development, with its completely carried-out separation of merchant officials and goods and strongholds, its centralization of affairs, its bureaucracy, for that time elaborate. But even so it should not be forgotten that that chartered company was of itself in no way a modern-capitalistic institution.

Under Father Wessel's treatment the Portuguese period has remained rather meagre and sketchy, with too great an emphasis on the missionary element. Though figures may be considered out of place in a work such as the one under consideration, even so this author has been most chary of them. De Barros' data regarding the export of pepper from western Java are some of the few.[7] More were needed. The figures Tiele gives on production and shipment of spices are more valuable than pages of description.[8] They show how in the 1530's twenty ton of spices per year were shipped from the Moluccas around the Cape, while on the other hand 320 ton were transported to Hormuz and from there to the caliphates and the Mediterranean.

Dr Terpstra is very detailed in his treatment of the English and French voyages. Does all this belong in a history of the Dutch East Indies? The same question arises in regard to the treatment of the Dutch voyages to the northeast and the elaborate description of the economic and political transformation of the United Provinces around the end of the sixteenth century, leading up to the first trading companies. All of this belongs in a history of the Dutch overseas written from the point of view of the United Provinces, but rather less in a history of the Indies, unless one wishes the emphasis to fall without reserve on its colonial character.

Dr Terpstra's detailed account brings a happy order to the confused story of the first companies' ships, voyages, admiralties, outposts, and contracts.[9] There cannot be enough tables like those on pages 324 and 325.[10] More of them were to have been expected in these volumes. It is disappointing, though, when Dr Terpstra, recapitulating events in a more general relationship, comes to no further comparison than this:

> ... [the first companies] exhibit a more modern commercial form than the medieval merchant gilds – while in those the members carried on trade individually, here we see joint enterprises. The merchants do not accompany their commercial goods themselves any more, but send out others; their chief concern is no more simple maintenance of life, but the acquisition of large amounts of capital.[11]

For late sixteenth-century trade, even before the Dutch renunciation of the sovereignty of the Spanish king, this opposition is inadequate. Throughout the whole of the sixteenth century numerous more developed forms were growing out of the medieval institution – which furthermore had always known the form of the individual large-scale merchant 'on adventure' side by side with it. The Spanish De Hiniosas, De Castros, and De la Palmas and the French Caignart brothers in early sixteenth-century Middelburg, for example, were prototypes of the modern merchant, and their concerns already knew the beginnings of rationalization and documentation.[12] Cunertorf, the Kampen commercial house at Lisbon the records of which have been published by Nanninga Uitterdijk, also exemplified a more modern type.[13] And also in Oriental trade the figure of the merchant sitting at home, investing money in *commenda* and sending out goods to distant markets by factors, is known. The adventure trade of the towns in Holland and Zeeland expanded far beyond peddling of handicrafts, it is true, but, even in its very strongly developed element of speculation, it was not an absolutely new form in 1595.[14]

In Volume Three Dr Stapel gives a running account of events in the seventeenth century, from the establishment of the United East India Company to beyond the great age of Van Goens and

Speelman.[15] One must ask oneself what character this work actually was intended to have. Only a 'popular' history? Its price and its design do not imply it. A 'general' history for everyone outside the circle of specialists? In any case it is a pity that none of the volumes have been given a name or subject index. There is especially a need of one in the third volume, which contains the important developments of the seventeenth century in the archipelago, along with the treatment (absolutely necessary) of India, the Western Quarters, and the Cape, and Indo-China, China, and Japan. The post in Cambodia is mentioned on page 191, then again on pages 382 and following; Taiwan on pages 221 and following, 269, and 365 and following. This makes looking up details extremely difficult.

Reading Dr Stapel's account is a disappointment. More was to have been expected from the editor of Van Dam's *Beschryvinge van de Oostindische Compagnie* and an editor of *Corpus Diplomaticum*. The question already touched upon above returns emphatically here: is it correct to take the history of the Company as the frame of reference for the history of Indonesia in the seventeenth century? Does that history have to be treated as a part of Dutch history? If so, one necessarily arrives at the epic of mariners and warriors. Indonesian history was not merely that and nothing more. The preponderance of the Oriental element was at that time still too strong. Furthermore nothing is less desirable than a history shot through with controversial value judgements. Colonial history, even more than European, will remain so. There is a second point linked to this. The chief concern cannot be only to describe the history of the Dutch in Indonesia. With all respect for national tradition, that is not the most important thing. More important is the question what place overseas shipping and overseas trade took in the development of early capitalism in the Netherlands. How did the accumulation of colonial wealth proceed, and what extent did it reach? How did it compare to the general accumulation process of Dutch commercial capitalism? These are questions just as much of general European history as of Dutch. The point of the organization of the East India Company touched upon above is a part of the same problem. And furthermore, what was the make-up of the Indonesian economic structure in the seventeenth century? Dr Stapel's few comments in his twelfth chapter, on 'The Company and the Native',[16] actually should have formed the chief theme of the whole work. Only these and similar questions give value to history; the field appears to be still almost completely untilled.

Dr Stapel's history of the Indies doggedly follows the path of rise, flourishing, and decay of seventeenth and eighteenth-century Dutch history. It is not promising to note down his few comments in this regard. Of Brazil and Formosa: "The history of these two lost territories proves that also in its age of greatest glory a people has weak moments now and then".[17] One can perceive the epic, with all the value judgements in their worthlessness as heuristic principles along with it. This is not history, but national catechism. On Camphuys' regime[18] as an introduction to the old age of the Company:

> We do not at all wish to make a plea for war here, far from it, but still we must state as an historic fact that in the Indies as in the motherland the failure to reach quickly for the sword went paired with an increase in moral enervation, which in the Indies expressed itself in the circles of the 'qualified' chiefly in an increase in private trade and other frauds by officials, and in nepotism and the duplicity and lip-service inseparably connected with it. Although Camphuys himself was a completely honourable man, still the first signs of the 'wig era' and the oligarchy manifest themselves during his regime.[19]

Here the general significance of the eighteenth century, as well as its significance for Holland and Indonesia, is, it would seem, grossly wronged. The ineradicable theme of the 'wig era' appears, with all its grotesque train. And to present the loss of the moral courage of the pioneering era set over against the growth of interest in arts and sciences is a distortion – a distortion because in that way one loses sight of the steady growth in pacification of the world along with the growth of bourgeois civilization, which in the 'wig era' laid the foundations of our modern civilization. This is all an appendix to Dutch history. It does not give a very promising starting point for the account of Indonesian history in the eighteenth century to be undertaken by Professor Godée Molsbergen in Volume Four.

Both volumes under review are richly illustrated. The cumbersome format does not increase usability, but once more compels admiration.

Three

ON THE EIGHTEENTH CENTURY AS A CATEGORY IN INDONESIAN HISTORY

In the series of volumes edited by Dr Stapel under the title *Geschiedenis van Nederlandsch Indië*, the fourth volume, from the hand of the late Professor E. C. Godée Molsbergen, deals with the eighteenth century.[1] It is somewhat surprising to see such a periodization proposed, but on further consideration it gains a broader background. While actually up to now the only chronology of Indonesian history for that era has been the one begun by J. P. I. Du Bois in 1763[2] and followed by De Jonge and Van Deventer[3] as well as H. T. Colenbrander[4] – the succession of governor-generalships, – in Professor Godée's work the eighteenth century is seen as having a certain coherency, as being a certain unity. The theme is introduced on page seven with the happy images which recur on page 391 to close the account: the legends on the two faces of the medallion the East India Company struck in commemoration of its first centenary in 1702, *In altera saecula pergo* and *Invia nulla via favente Deo*.

Traditionally in the writing of Indonesian history the eighteenth century has merely been a sequel to the seventeenth in the series of governor-generalships continuing up to the fall of the Dutch Republic in 1795. After that the periodization would go on either in the same way or with differentiation according to the many transformations in political system in the motherland (the Batavian Republic, with, successively, its directory, its state government, and its council-pensionary; the Kingdom of Holland; the departments annexed to the French Empire) and consequently in the Indies (successively a colony under the republic, the kingdom, and the empire, then a territory under British administration – interim administration, as it could later be happily called), transformations finally ending in the restored authority of the sovereign prince, later king of the Netherlands.

Now Professor Godée has consciously chosen the eighteenth century as an historical whole. It is apparent from the definition in the opening words of his first chapter:

> Just as during the growth of every living organism there are transitional forms, the eighteenth century is such a form in the history of the development of the Netherlands as a colonial power, differing [from the seventeenth century] in its structure, political system, morality, sense of responsibility.[5]

Thus is called up the image of a closed historical unity (with characteristics, however, the heuristic value of which cannot be highly rated), the Eighteenth Century. Just as the categories *quattrocento* and *cinquecento*, the Eighteenth Century, the *dixhuitième*, is an historical category, an expedient perhaps, not a concept, but "laden with meaningful speculation".[6]

Actually it is a category for the periodization of time borrowed from western European and North American history. In the eighteenth century the coming-of-age of seventeenth-century civilization took place. It was the world of baroque and old-fashioned classicism, of conservative kingship and official church power, of the old oligarchies in states and factions, of political capitalism and early capitalism – the world of Louis XV, Maria Theresa, Stadtholder William IV, Van Slingelandt, Walpole, the *fermiers généraux*, the colonial companies, John Law, the world of Abbé Prévost, Swift, Pope, Holberg, Fontenelle, Marivaux, Boucher, and Bach. But at the same time the new bourgeois civilization was taking shape, the modern democratic movement, constitutional kingship on the continent, secularization and the lessening of the coercive power of the dogmas, modern capitalism, the new classicism, the first cosmopolitanism. Thus was it also the world of Louis XVI, Joseph II, Washington, the Encyclopedia, Rousseau, Voltaire, Priestley, Price, Franklin, Van der Capellen, Pieter Paulus, Arkwright, Stephenson, Adam Smith, Richardson, Diderot, Aagje Wolff and Betje Deken, Alfieri, Bishop Percy, Sir William Jones, Georg Foster, Herder. The turning point came around 1760. Even so a definite unity within this sharp division is indicated in the concept Eighteenth Century. Notwithstanding all the internal political and dynastic differences, the concept can pass the test of being applied to the history of every state. In Dutch history, for example, the movement from one pole to the other within this cultural whole is illustrated by the relationship regarding the stadtholdership of Lieven de Beaufort to Van Slingelandt in the thirties, or of Van der Capellen to Van de Spiegel in the eighties.[7]

Professor Godée is therefore consistent when he relates his use of the Eighteenth Century as a category in Indonesian history to its use in European history,[8] "The history of the Company in the eighteenth century is the reflected image of that of its mother country, in fact of the Europe of that day" – with the addition, "sometimes more fiercely lighted by the tropical sun, and influenced by the almost legendary distance that lay between the Netherlands and the archipelago".

Thus the history of Indonesia is fitted into the framework of eighteenth-century cultural history. Thus, furthermore, as the last quotation witnesses, it is fitted into the framework of the history of the Dutch East India Company. When one considers this, the question immediately arises whether it is correct. Can the category Eighteenth Century, then, be used for Indonesian history? Is it possible to write the history of Indonesia in the eighteenth century as the history of the Company?

I have already indicated regarding the seventeenth century[9] that the history of Indonesia definitely cannot be made equivalent to the history of the Company, that it is incorrect to make a break in describing the course of history upon the arrival of the first scattered seafarers, merchants, and privateers from northwest Europe[10] and change over to the point of view of the small, oppressed European fortress, the stuffy trading-house, and the armed ship riding at anchor. The theme needs to be taken up again, this time for the eighteenth century.

One should call to mind the picture of the over-all political situation in eastern and southeastern Asia during the eighteenth century – and of the position of the Company and the other European powers there.

First, the Oriental states, scanned from west to east, as was done in the general reports of the governor-general in Batavia to the members of the Company in Holland. The immeasurable technical progress of the nineteenth century has introduced the exotic element into literature concerning the East, and along with it at the same time the picture of decaying Oriental states and lawless despotisms, in contrast to the driving power, the perfection, and the liberality of the Christian states of the West. Commencing with Turkey, political and missionary literature has applied such a configuration all the way from Persia to China and Japan.[11] In general one without the necessary acquaintance with and use of contemporary literature on the Orient must be wary of this picture of decay projected backwards from the nineteenth century. This is especially true for the eighteenth century. One has only to think of the habit, originated in later times and practised most of all by Marxist class ideologists, of painting the miseries of France before 1789 and of England under the first stirrings (actually still so modest) of modern capitalism.[12]

Persia, then, was in the eighteenth century a country still intact. In India the establishment of local, even regional power by France and England did not disturb the power of the Mogol Empire more than fleetingly. Burma and Farther India harboured inviolate states. The excellent organization of the mandarin bureaucracy in Annam and Tonkin[13] was to disappear only with the colonial wars of the French under the Second Empire. Under the Manchu emperors, eighteenth-century China reached a pinnacle of political power and cultural achievement. Emperor K'ang Hsi (1662–1723) once more extended the military influence of the empire as far as into West Turkestan and placed Tibet under Chinese suzerainty. Emperor Ch'ien Lung (1736–1796) made the distant western borders secure, drove Nepal out of Tibet back over the Himalayas, and gained recognition of Chinese suzerainty from Burma (1769) and Annam (1789).

> Never, not even under the T'angs, were such vast regions in Mongolia and Turkestan so completely annexed to the empire. ... Never in all history had China's power and supremacy seemed to be so securely safeguarded.[14]

In Japan the shogunate remained unshaken. The new development of more influence shifting to a 'bourgeois' class of rich merchants, speculators, and money-holders[15] did not affect the existent order of things; the reverses through volcanic eruptions, floods, droughts, and crop failures[16] were of a completely static nature.

Also deserving consideration is the social and economic significance of the great masses of population: from sixty or eighty to a hundred million people in China,[17] twenty-six million in Japan,[18] a hundred million in India[19] – as opposed to the number of people in France, the most heavily populated European country: nineteen million at the end of the seventeenth century and twenty-three million at the end of the eighteenth (England counted only six million inhabitants; with Scotland, seven).[20] Such a comparison has a far-reaching validity in a world whose means of subsistence were practically equal technically in Asia and in Europe.

Then, on the other hand, one should look at the position of the European outposts in Asia. Russia had pushed across Siberia to the Sea of Okhotsk, but it remained completely peripheral in relation to China (as is shown by the treaties of 1688 and 1724) as well as to Japan. Nor had it yet begun its central Asian conquests. In the older strongholds in southeast Asia, did a change take place, did the balance shift and the Western element come to dominate? In the seventeenth-century political picture the Asian element had dominated completely when compared to that of the tiny outposts the Europeans had established. Was a balance struck later, and did the scales tip the other way in the eighteenth century? Certainly not for China, Japan, Indo-China, India, and Persia.

Not even for India. The beginning of British territorial control dated from Plassey, 1757. But after all Clive's battle was really only one against a provincial authority, the nawab of Bangal; the first territory gained was a zemindari apanage, the twenty-four

Parganas, granted by a firman from the nawab and later, in 1759, confirmed by the mogul. The expansion over Bihar and Orissa in 1765 took place in the form of a grant of the right to establish a divan for farming land taxes, completely in Mogol style. So strong was the influence of the Irano-Indian bureaucracy, superior to the English colonial one. It was not the first retinue of aggressive foreigners thus brought within the framework of the central power. Nor did the wars that came to India with Hastings establish English supremacy. That happened only in the nineteenth century. Though Plassey, like the capture of the town of Jakarta in 1619, may be a landmark in the light of later history, at the moment of the military feat itself it held no preponderant significance, and there was no drastic change as a result of it. There was not yet a Near East serving England as a basis for an Asian policy; that concept became a living one only with Napoleon's enormous plans of 1799, though there was a hint of what was coming in the trade agreement France reached with Egypt in 1785, stipulating free transit of Indian goods to Europe *via* Egypt.[21] The English settlements in India were still isolated transoceanic points.

The France of the *ancien régime*, with its superior organization of army and navy, held only a temporary position as a colonial power in Asia: the Dupleix episode did not last. Spain continued to exert its chief power in its American lands, using the Philippines mainly for trade with China, and hardly at all for exercising political power in southeast Asia. Portugal only retained control of its scattered outposts on the coasts of Africa, India, and China, without exercising any military or economic power.

In the eighteenth century, too, the Dutch East India Company maintained the most widely extended power and carried on the most distant active relations of all: on Ceylon, on Java, in Macassar, from Surat to Deshima, from the Cape to Ternate. In comparison to that net of strongholds, stations, and trading posts, the activities of the English were definitely more limited. The Dutch trading posts in Arabia and Persia were abandoned, in 1755 and 1766. Those in India lost in commercial significance for the Company; territorial significance they had never had. The hold on Ceylon became more certain. The outpost in Tonkin was liquidated in 1700, that in Siam in 1762. Formosa had been lost in the seventeenth century, and trade with China remained closed. The factory at Deshima carried on a profitable trade, but it was completely under the regulation of the central and municipal authorities in Nagasaki and had no power in its own right.

In Indonesia, the importance of the Sumatra and Borneo ports for the Company was diminishing. The spice islands remained under its occupation and administration. Its interests were being concentrated on Java, and it was there its power expanded. In colonial campaigns of the utmost difficulty – it would be worth the trouble to compare their military significance to that of the campaigns carried on at the same time in China, as well as in India and Siberia – the Company subdued the princes and lords, intervened in dynastic disputes, and pacified popular uprisings, until the arrangement in 1755 and 1757 for the tripartition of the former empire of Mataram into the realms of the *susuhunan* of Surakarta, the sultan of Jogjakarta, and the Mangkunagara gave the government at Batavia a predominant political influence – albeit a precarious one – over the course of affairs on Java. On the whole, then, Dutch influence in southeast Asia undoubtedly diminished. But in Indonesia, though an interinsular authority was not achieved, influence was growing on Java. The threads coming together at Batavia stretched far and wide, but they were fragile and often without political significance.

A general view of the whole can only lead to the conclusion that any talk of a European Asia in the eighteenth century is out of the question, that a few European centres of power had been consolidated on a very limited scale, that in general – and here the emphasis should lie – the Oriental lands continued to form active factors in the course of events as valid entities, militarily, economically, and politically.

If one looks at Indonesia more closely, the question of a moment ago can be stated more specifically. The Company was a political power in the archipelago: Batavia, town and castle, gave irrefutable evidence of it. What was the importance of the Oriental opponent? Did the general rule of continuing equality militarily and economically, which in the case of India and China spoke out so clearly, hold also for the Indonesian states?

Here we are pinched by the scarcity of material. De Jonge's great edition of sources moves quickly from the consideration of the rise of control in the whole of the East Indies to a similar consideration for Java only, and others have not completed his work for eighteenth-century episodes in the outer islands. The many studies of the outlying posts in the seventeenth century throw light on countless aspects of all southeast Asia, but such studies for the eighteenth century are almost completely lacking. Even if the outlying posts had become of secondary importance in the trade of the Company, that is by no means meant to imply that the Outer Quarters declined in significance in a general sense.[22] For the posts in the Middle East that is at once obvious. But for the posts in Indonesia it still has to be investigated. Here are a few tentative comments aiming in that direction.

If one pictures in one's mind the palaces and fortifications and strong Mogol castles of the Persian and Indian towns, the might of the Chinese cities, the fastnesses of the Japanese, the moving image of town and land as it is rendered by the Japanese artists of the eighteenth century, inspiring profound familiarity – then if one compares images from Indonesian lands, *kampong* and *kraton* towns such as Surabaya, Surakarta, Palembang, and Martapura, the result of the comparison seems unfavourable for the latter. Neither in power nor extent, in refinement nor diversity do the images of Indonesian civilization seem to excel. Even taking into consideration all the environmental and climatic factors which make different demands in subtropical and temperate zones than in tropical, they seem inferior to the images of continental Asian civilizations. On the other hand, if one calls to mind the complexity of the Javanese governmental machinery, or if one looks at the graceful aristocratic figures shown (for the first, time, actually, as they were) in the prints to Sir Stamford

Raffles' *History of Java*, one will immediately savour their exceeding refinement, their matchlessness.

A civilization[23] of as great dimensions and as great validity as that of Europe? Stapel has touched on the question.[24] Writing over the Company's blockade of the Indonesian coasts for monopoly purposes, he finds a gradual impoverishment of the populace – to be inferred, for example, from the decline in the sale of Indian cloth. Even before the end of the seventeenth century, supposedly, the money of the populace had flowed away and poverty arisen. Thus is created the concept of an impoverished, enfeebled Oriental world, economically undermined, politically second-rate. Is it correct?

Even without knowing further details, it seems to me inaccurate to dispose of such Indonesian states as Palembang, Siak, Achin, or Johore with the qualifications corrupt despotisms, pirate states, and slave states, hotbeds of political danger and decay. Inaccurate, if for no other reason, because despotism, piracy, and slavery are historical terms, and history is not written with value judgements. To choose examples from the field of Dutch history, the town of Flushing based its existence in the seventeenth and eighteenth centuries in no small measure on privateering and smuggling, and Middelburg's renowned trading company of 1720 occupied itself with privateering, smuggling to and from Spanish America, and slave trade,[25] which activities must have supplied the funds for building many of the fine mansions of Zeeland's capital.

The chief point is something else: what was the power – political, maritime, economic – of the harbour principalities? For source materials in usable form on the subject one will, so far as I can find, search in vain.[26] For Java the question is applicable in another relation. If one makes an attempt to measure Javanese military might in the wars of the eighteenth century – the imperial troops plus the Madurese units on the Company's side, that really impressive force of resistance – then, it seems to me, one will quietly set aside the possibility that the native element there was one without first-rate political significance, without any power at all equivalent to that of the Europeans. War is a rough measuring stick of degree and value, but nevertheless a very important one.

Are the criteria of the seventeenth century – when an Ala ed-din and an Iskander managed to impress the admirals and the crews of the Dutch ships in Achin with their power and princely grandeur, when the regent of Tuban sent his retinue with nobles on horseback and with elephants out of the city to welcome Heemskerck and Warwyck, the commanders of the second Dutch expedition to the Indies, when Batavia watched in alarm the besieging works of the *susuhunan*'s troops growing around the new town, – are these criteria still valid in the eighteenth century, or is that all changed, diminished, decayed?[27]

In answer to this, among others the following things should be pointed out. In the period before the conquest of Java Sir Stamford Raffles established himself at Malacca in 1810 as agent of the British governor-general for the Malay States, and from there he spun his intrigues for undermining the Franco-Dutch rule on Java.[28] The Balinese princes, and those of Mataram, Madura, Sumbawa, Bantam, the Lampong region, Palembang, Pontianak, Mindanao, all of them were spun into his net of correspondence.[29] This points out the significance of these lands as political factors: otherwise Raffles, whose discrimination in Oriental affairs cannot be denied, would not have included them as points in his program of action. And related to this was Leyden's and Raffles' concept of re-establishing the Indonesian unity of Majapahit, a congress of Indonesian princes:

> like the old Ban of Burgundy or the later one of Germany – a General Parliament of the Malay States, like the Amphictyonic Council of the Greeks.[30]

Is this a figment of his imagination, or is it a concept giving evidence of a deep feeling for politics, based upon the political significance of the Indonesian states at the time? I believe the latter.

It is true that in 1810 Raffles also speaks of the restoration of Indonesian states, "some of them weakened and impoverished by the ungenerous policy of the Dutch".[31] But countless notices plead against retrogression. These notices can only receive their full value once they are tabulated and placed in relation to each other,[32] but even incidental figures give reason for doubt. For example, Dirk van Hogendorp calculated in 1799 that with prosperity and a good government Java could export twenty thousand *koyan* of rice per year.[33] On the basis of shipping data from the years 1600 to 1610 I have made a rough estimate that in the beginning of the seventeenth century approximately twenty-eight thousand ton of rice per year were exported from Java east and west. The estimated figures, with two hundred years between, lie close by each other. The relative smallness of the interinsular trade is a trait common to all pre-capitalist and early-capitalist trade.[34]

Decay through fossilization of culture? Rouffaer and Juynboll have given their opinion for Javanese culture in this regard in sensitive remarks most precisely formulated in some passages of their book *De batik-kunst in Nederlandsch-Indië*.[35] For them the time when the court was at Kartasura should be considered as the Byzantine period of Javanese *kraton* civilization, the period in which late Javanese court etiquette and court language were polished and perfected, a period of increasing rigidity, but even so one able within that rigid framework to produce the late Javanese literature and, "as the last, noble expression of true Javanese artistry", the mid-Javanese school of batik colouring.

> ... born in the Kartasura period, it saved the late Javanese spirit from the reproach of having become sterile. On the contrary, whatever stately warmth, whatever noble ardour there was alive in Javanese nature poured itself, so to speak, into that last creation of the post-fifteenth-century Javanese spirit ...[36]

Further on Rouffaer and Juynboll return to this theme:

> Javanese plastic skill, which had become very decadent in the so-called Majapahit period (1300–1500), was after 1500 more and more suppressed and truncated by Islam and dry dogmatic concepts corollary to it.[37]

It seems to me that this quotation points the way toward a disputable premise, the influence of early Islam on Javanese culture. It could be mentioned that Professor Hazeu sees in the nineteenth-century court *pujangga* Rangga Warsita (1803–1873) the final apotheosis of medieval Javanese literary activities, thus shifting the accent even further forward in time.[38] But the problem can be still more closely approached from another way. Professor Romein has pointed out the relationship between the Byzantine style in art and the structure of the state – the imperium, the church connected with it, and the Eastern Roman bureaucracy, – and he has shown how this structure of the state is based upon continuity and unchanging stability and how the arts, courtly as they were, had to follow the same maxim.[39]

> It was their style, which to them could not but seem perfect, without competent rivals as they were in their own eyes, these heirs of the Roman world empire whose pride made them group their neighbours together under the name 'barbarians'; their style, which was indeed the perfect expression of their state; their state, which measured by ideal criteria was everything except perfect, but which showed a degree of stability that makes it understandable those taking part in it should have believed it to be perfect.[40]

I believe that in this direction lies a fruitful working hypothesis, the relationship between the structure of the Javanese state and the courtly arts. But then the argument of rigidity and fossilization seems to be refuted, replaced as it is by the concept of closed continuity.

If the economic situation of the Indonesian regions is to be measured by the Company's trade, its use of monopoly rights, and its application of shipping embargos, then the image of the dead seas of eighteenth-century Indonesia seems to make sense. But such a picture is incomplete. In the economic history of the eighteenth century in Indonesia the fact of 'smuggling' on a very extensive scale must be taken into account. The never-ending complaints about the corrupt body of Company officials, clandestine trade, private business, camouflaged shares in trading and shipping – all these can be explained as an attempt to complement insufficient salaries. But the other side of the coin is that Indonesian markets were ready and able to receive more goods and ship more wares. Thus the level of trade rose wherever the

Company thought it could suppress it. Side by side with such 'smuggling' was the extensive violation of the monopoly area, in the eighteenth century especially by English trade, and later by American as well. As early as 1784 the freedom of the Eastern seas had to be granted in the Treaty of Versailles.[41]

Even before the period of the steam engine and the triumphal march of Lancashire cotton goods, the export position of England was improved by an increase in production of piece-made goods. Sombart gives some figures.[42] In 1700 the value of England's exports to Asia amounted to £ 100,283, one and a half per cent. of the total value of its exports. In 1780 it amounted to £ 909,033, or six per cent. This illustrates, in the first place, Sombart's finding that markets in Europe, North America, and the West Indian slave colonies had a relatively greater significance for English trade than markets in the Asian lands, with their highly developed civilizations and their own exports, manufactures, and handicrafts. These Asian handicrafts were to be destroyed only by modern capitalism. But a figure of approximately nine hundred thousand pounds for the English export of goods to Asia in 1780 is interesting enough in itself. For the Dutch Company in those years, there was an average yearly shipment to Asia of £ 225,000 in merchandise, provisions, and company necessities, and £ 415,000 in gold and silver bullion and specie.[43] Dutch exports were already lagging behind English. Furthermore, the English controlled the Bombay, Bengal, and China trade – which means that the most valuable parts of the internal Asian trade had slipped away from the Company.

But this all means on the other hand that Asia, and Indonesia, were absorbing that increasing export of goods without the Dutch Company's having a part in it. Side by side with the history of the monopoly trade the historian of the Company must include, as of completely equal value, the history of the 'smuggling' of European and Asian export goods, which made up an integral part of the economic order and deserves also to be taken into consideration in evaluating the economic situation of Indonesia in the eighteenth century. According to modern concepts this seems impossible. But it needs to be considered that trade with Spanish America from smuggling stations in the Antilles was carried on as an honourable business during the whole of the eighteenth century. And if such a thing is considered incompatible with modern conditions, the enormous amount of smuggling carried on by Japanese traders *via* North China in the first stage of the China incident, a complete, romantic business with caravans of trucks protected by *ronins*, has shown that a highly developed modern-capitalistic apparatus actually can keep that old-fashioned, romantic offshoot alive. It seems to me that, until explained otherwise, these facts are in opposition to the concept of a languishing, retarded Indonesian world and an all-dominating Company.

Western trade with Asia was always a one-sided movement of goods in the sense that costly merchandise was received in exchange for coin and certain metals in ingot. The handicrafts of the Asian civilizations never left any important place for a sale of European craft goods. And European factory products found no admittance in Asia before the advent of steam and chemical techniques was able to bring about the beginning of a mass production of consumers' goods in western Europe and convert the basis of economic life from wood to iron, before the disintegration of the old, tradition-bound patterns of European life in class, town, and state was able to open up markets for mass sales to an amazingly fast-growing population. Colonial production was mobilized chiefly in the slave colonies, from which came Europe's sugar and tobacco. Also in the shipping from Indonesia, which in the seventeenth century had known only one product that could relatively be called a mass-export product, pepper, the emphasis shifted in the eighteenth century to the new mass-export products from Java, sugar and coffee. The question whether the cultivation of these new products upset the existent agricultural pattern excessively has not to my knowledge been answered:[44] the products were obtained by means of the traditional pattern of compulsory labour supervised by local officials for the benefit of lords and princes. Coffee was a newly imported crop; the cultivation of sugar had been indigenous from ancient times. Is it here, with the imposition of quotas and delivery obligations, that the exhaustion of village society, the basis of Javanese civilization, and thus the exhaustion of that civilization began? Tea, the next mass-export product, was supplied by China, a powerful agrarian and industrial unit, and was not significant for Indonesia as such. Of the other goods exported to Europe by the Company – Cingalese cinammon, Malay tin, indigo, salt-petre, sapanwood, camphor, spices – none of them increased noticeably in volume shipped. In 1621 the Company calculated the annual sale of spices in Europe at 1400 quarters (of 350 lb.) of cloves, 1000 quarters (of 450 lb.) of nutmeg, and 600 quarters (of 300 lb.) of mace, respectively thus 490,000 lb., 350,000 lb., and 180,000 lb.[45] In 1795 the commissioners-general calculated that respectively 250,000 lb., 320,000 lb., and 100,000 lb. of the same three spices had been shipped.[46] The significance of the new products coffee and sugar, shipped in millions of pounds, contrasts sharply with this, but such figures by their nature cannot but compare favourably with those of spices, produced on a small scale.

The pattern of Asia in the eighteenth century was still one with a closed, indigenous village society as social and economic basis. Though intra-Asian trade provided the market with imported goods (cloth from India, earthenware and iron and steel products from China), such goods were not for everyday, large-quantity sale. They could not be, considering the closed character of home and village structure and the handicraft character of the production centres and the trade system transporting the goods (which, rather, casually supplied the markets with relatively costly wares, many of which were stocked up as sacrosant heirlooms or financial investments) – considering, furthermore, the limited amount of money in circulation and the extremely slow turnover in trade. This is all so little different from Europe. Already arguing against economic retrogression is the fact that two of the largest branches of intra-Asian commerce, the Indian trade to the east and the Chinese trade to the south, went on throughout the eighteenth century. If one goes on to consider that trade in the eighteenth century furthermore moved nothing except very limited quantities of goods in a highly traditional agrarian world still based completely on self-sufficiency, with little independent city life, then the concept of economic retrogression becomes a highly dubious one, and it is up to those who maintain its validity to produce further evidence.

Thus, as soon as one has freed oneself of a Company-centred point of view, the Indonesian picture seems to fit without contradiction into the general Asian picture. There is a gradually ascending line, a curve, climbing throughout the eighteenth century, climbing even more rapidly because of the infusion of a stronger trade from Europe in the second half of the century. The line keeps on climbing over into the nineteenth century. When does it stop? Was it the destruction of Indian cloth production, the upheaval of the wars in India, Java, and Sumatra, the turn of affairs in China that changed the picture? Was it the increasing pressure of modern-capitalistic exports, and the stronger power of the modern military apparatus that went to support the 'peaceful trade' of Europe everywhere in Asia with threats and intervention? Were there internal factors that influenced the traditional indigenous society? For the eighteenth century, at any rate, it would seem that no such factors can be detected. Economically there was no ascendancy, no preponderance; militarily the same can be said regarding land power, though perhaps there was European superiority in some seas (whether also in those around India and China is a question). Politically the power of the Oriental states remained unshaken.

Also in conflict with the idea of a slow decline is the picture of Batavia as it appeared in 1816. The history of the Company and its trade on Indonesia is rather unclear for the second half of the eighteenth century. In 1816, with Dutch history breathing more easily in the air of the restoration, there would appear to have been an open centre for trade at Batavia: a bourgeois trade, strongly English, with other foreigners from America, Europe, and elsewhere in Asia, and moreover with Dutch commercial houses and independent firms for import, export, and shipping.[47]

Was this only filling the vacuum created by the disappearance of Company trade? Or, during the time of English rule (or earlier), had Java, too, been fitted into place in the expanding trade which before long would nourish Singapore as well as Batavia? What, for example, should be the evaluation of Van Hogendorp's data that "a multitude of vessels", bottoms of from thirty to four hundred ton, were being constructed by Chinese shipbuilders on Java at the end of the eighteenth century?[48] It should be noticed that it was the Asian trade which immediately took possession of the new port of Singapore. According to Colonel Farquhar's account of 31 March, 1820:

> Nothing can possibly exceed the rising trade and general prosperity of the infant colony; indeed, to look at our harbour just now, where upwards of *twenty* junks, three of which are from China, and two from Cochin China, the rest from Siam and other quarters, are at anchor, besides ships, brigs, prows, etc. etc., a person would naturally exclaim, Surely this cannot be an establishment of only a twelve months' standing! One of the principal Chinese merchants here told me, in the course of conversation, that he would be very glad to give five hundred thousand dollars for the revenues of Singapore five years hence. Merchants of all descriptions are collecting here so fast that nothing is heard in the shape of complaint but the want of more ground to build on. ... In short, this settlement bids fair to become the emporium of Eastern trade, and in time may surpass even Batavia itself.[49]

Once more intra-Asian trade appears alive and active, the chief vehicle of commercial prosperity.

To summarize, then, the course of Indonesian history, when checked in regard to a few episodes and economic concepts, does not appear to have coincided with that of the Dutch Company, no more so than the history of any European political foothold in Asia in the eighteenth century directed the general course of Asian history. Furthermore, there is an unbroken unity in the state of Asian civilization from the seventeenth century through the eighteenth and into the nineteenth. This makes the category Eighteenth Century useless as an instrument for ordering the facts in that historic landscape. Moreover, none of the essential elements of the category in Europe find any reflection in Asia. Two equal civilizations were developing separately from each other, the Asian in every way superior quantitatively.

The equality remained as long as the magic poison of modern capitalism had not yet enchanted Europe and northeastern America to produce steam, mechanics, and grooved cannon. If the American colonies with their settlers, the West Indian colonies with their plantations and slaves, the Spanish colonies, and the Dutch Cape Colony were all of them drawn into the eighteenth-century bourgeois movement and led on to revolution, Asia was not touched by it all. Tippo Sahib used the Jacobins as a political instrument against the English, as his predecessors had used the noble French adventurers and military commanders. The December Movement of 1795 in Batavia did not bring about a single social or political change.

In the introduction to the tenth volume of De Jonge's *De opkomst van het Nederlandsch gezag in Oost-Indië*, the last volume under his own editorship, there is a noteworthy comment which briefly sketches the general historical background and his own point of view on it. As such it is extremely valuable. Closing a survey of the events round about the year 1764, he writes, "...the old East India Company, along with the old improvident society of the eighteenth century, went slowly but inevitably to meet its doom".[50] Thus there, too, the link with the Eighteenth Century, the *ancien régime*, is made. General comments such as this one are rare with De Jonge, however indispensable for a correct understanding of history they may be. Yet, is it correct? Is the *milieu* of the Indies in the eighteenth century a reflection of the European world of the *ancien régime?*

It seems to me not. In the eighteenth century, along with the strengthening of the Company's control on Java, came the establishment of a colonial European society. It was a Dutch society only to a limited extent, because of the large number of foreigners and of the stronger, older Portuguese element in the culture of the lower groups, but above everything else because of its character, interlaced to a large extent with fragments of Oriental folkways and social forms. Thus had developed the opulent life of the higher classes in the Indies, with their country seats, their pomp and ceremony, their retinue of slaves and serfs – a life linked to that of the Javanese nobility more than to any other. On the other hand the officials in the lower ranks of the European administration followed a *kampong* way of life, in the cities living side by side with Orientals, Indonesian and Chinese. There was no antithesis Eastern–Western; there was only the antithesis higher classes–lower classes. This colonial civilization – for it definitely had a cultural style of its own, as the Batavian manor-houses witness[51] – consolidated itself in the eighteenth century and continued intact through the nineteenth. Only the twentieth century saw its decay, quick and complete.

The Indies of the Company lived a life completely their own. In the second half of the eighteenth century it found expression politically in the glorious period of Van der Parra's governor-generalship, of which the prints of Rach preserve the memory.[52] That some elements of the Enlightenment manifested themselves (for example, in the founding of the Batavian Society of Arts and Sciences)[53] has no deeper significance. There was no undercurrent of bourgeois political aspirations with a revolutionary, or even merely a reformistic, tinge. How different it was from the movement on the Cape, like that in the American colonies clearly established on an ideological basis. Nor was there a single element of any insurgent non-European movement ideologically nourished, like that of San Domingo. The seigneurial rule of the Company in close alliance with the princes and lords of Java did not contain any seeds of unrest or disintegration. Therefore the year 1795 does not mean a break in the history of the Indies.

The Company fell. In the Netherlands because of a remarkably conservative system of accounting and market operations, so it could be said – unjustly. It fell primarily because of its political links to the *ancien régime*. Its downfall in the Netherlands was more than anything else a political affair. Amsterdam's loss of its general staple market to London and Hamburg did not as such affect the Company fundamentally. By switching over to the basis of consignment trade and discount exchange of merchandise – a less stable basis, it is true – Amsterdam was able to keep on directing colonial trade, as after 1824 the Dutch Trading Company[54] was able to do under ten times less favourable circumstances.

The Company's downfall in Indonesia was certainly not in the first place an economic affair. As a great centre for the shipment of Asian goods to Europe it held its own up to the moment of the last convoy homeward. No more do internal Indonesian political causes seem to have brought about its fall. The reason for it was to be found more than anywhere else, if not exclusively, in the Company's maritime impotence (probably not at all in its military organization: the colony's army created in 1811 to resist the English invaders was by no means badly organized). At sea there was an absolute superiority for England. There the political impotence of the Dutch directors manifested itself, and for that the officials in the Indies were not responsible, or only quite obliquely so. Maritime impotence, which the government attempted insufficiently and without perseverance to redress, seems solely responsible for the Company's downfall.

Certainly the 'atmosphere of corruption' was not. That is the Dutch refrain also sung to the finale in Dr Godée's volume, but how unjustly. One does not write history with value judgements. If the officialdom of the Company actually was corrupt in the sense that that very extensive apparatus tolerated a great deal within and beside its by-laws, and that it derived advantage from a number of things partly by mixing private and official revenues and partly by gaining illicit earnings from official positions, even then there is no judgement passed on the regime. A modern, strict officialdom was only created with the Napoleonic state. Criticism of the integrity of eighteenth-century officials is thus *ex post facto* criticism. How did matters stand regarding the integrity of the officialdom in, for example, the Dutch Republic, an officialdom by far not so extensive as that of the Company? Furthermore, such corruption did not necessarily impair the efficiency of the administration. Not a single element predetermining destruction was contained in it. Such a regime could possess the full power to exist (to keep silent regarding its 'right to exist': that is not an historical question, but a political and ethical one, a value judgement) and to act.

Did there actually develop a species of officials in the eighteenth century lesser in everything than the 'great' ones of the seventeenth? It seems to be very doubtful. The achievements of a Hartingh, a Von Hohendorff, a Mossel, a Van der Parra, and, on the Indonesian side, of a Mangkubumi, a Mas Sahid, a Chakraningrat are certainly on a par with those of a Speelman, a Van Goens, and an Aru Palaka. The contention appears to me to be a result of the Dutch fable of the 'weak' eighteenth century, a legend spun by the revolutionary Patriots of 1795 to use politically against the *ancien régime* and by the nineteenth century national romantics to use literarily in favour of the 'Golden Age'. That the eighteenth century in the Netherlands produced no Vondel-esque dramas and no Rembrandt-esque paintings of Biblical heroes and guardsmen causes it to be overlooked that the period performed the great work of laying the foundations of modern bourgeois culture. In the Indies the situation was again different. The political achievement of the Company in the struggle for Java is one equivalent to the most important achievement of the seventeenth century, that of gaining control over Malacca, Ceylon, and Macassar. Therefore, if amended chronologically, Busken Huet's comment that in the history of Dutch expansion (conquered) Java holds one of the two most prominent positions does not seem groundless.[55]

In this regard Van Hogendorp is a poor witness. His *Berigt van den tegenwoordigen toestand der Bataafsche bezittingen in Oost-Indië* and his other writings as well give abundant evidence of his doctrinaire attitude and his lack of appreciation for the real nature of Oriental life as well as for the acquired rights of the Company. Along with that there was a strongly coloured personal animosity against the regime at Batavia as a source of his abundance of invectives: "the present nonsensical system of administration" and "the miserable and oppressive government" count among the milder of them.[56] Factional passion and personal hatred were allowed to discolour the picture of the government in Batavia at the end of the century. Here too Dutch history has not been able to rise beyond the fable and the pamphlet. The writing of the real history has still to begin.

To summarize, these few comments clearly show the inadequacy of the concept Eighteenth Century in regard to Indonesian history. In the eighteenth century that history is just as little a sequel to Dutch history as in the seventeenth, and the dates for beginning and ending periods in the course of Indonesian cultural history need to be different ones. Furthermore, also in that period of the establishment of a colonial empire, the 'colonial' antithesis, especially the antithesis 'East–West' – the fate of lands overseas in our time – is to be sought in vain.

Recently, in a passage of his reply to the provisional report of the Second Chamber regarding the 1940 budget for the Indies, the Dutch Minister for the Colonies, with a slight historical touch, sketched this picture in relation to education for Indonesians:

> The education which the East knew long before the coming of the Westerners and which still is widespread there is of a completely different character – its aim is not that of imparting intellectual knowledge, but that of spreading and deepening religion and theology. Such an education has its own cultural value; it is harmoniously developed out of the civilization of the Oriental peoples and is in response to their deepest needs. It is the education of peoples who did not know modern Western life, who shut themselves off from active, hurried life, from world trade and a world economy, by an isolation defending their mental and spiritual life, an isolation forming a stronger bulwark than a Chinese wall.[57]

Such an East, retiring into isolation, standing to one side along the path of the West, the path of hurried activity, world trade, world economy, modern life, seems to have been foreign to the eighteenth century. That century did not know any superior Occident, nor any self-isolating Orient no longer progressing with it. It knew a mighty East, a rich fabric of a strong, broad weave with a more fragile Western warp thread inserted in it at broad intervals.

Notes

Full titles of books and articles, referred to in the notes by short keywords, will be found in the bibliography below.

On Early Asian Trade

INTRODUCTION

1 In Rouffaer & IJzerman, *Schipvaart*. See also Purchas, *Pilgrimes*, V, 195–201.

2 Rouffaer & IJzerman, *Schipvaart*, I, 74.

3 *Ibid.*, II, 293.

4 *Kojah or khojah*, from the Persian *chòjah* or *khwàjà*, a designation of respect for rich merchants. The word means 'Sir', 'Honourable', and was and is still applied especially to Europeans in the Arabic-speaking Near East as an equivalent to *monsieur*. In Turkey, where it is pronounced *khòja*, it has the meaning of scribe or wearer of a turban; in India it refers to Ismalilites, the followers of the Aga Khan (see Polo, *Book*, I, 146 n. 1), and in a few rare places (outside the Indonesian Archipelago) it is applied to eunuchs (Van Vollenhoven, *Adatrecht*, II, 117).

5 Rouffaer & IJzerman, *Schipvaart*, I, 83–84. "...some ... had beene in Constantinople, Venice and Rome, and one of them said, hee had foure monethes past [an incorrect translation: it should read 'for four months'] seene their Lad [misprint for 'Lord'] and God (meaning the Pope) whom they answered that they were Christians, and cared not for the Pope" (Purchas, *Pilgrimes*, V, 196, translated from Pontanus' *Rerum et urbis Amstelodamensium historia*, or Montanus' Dutch translation). See also the statement: "...the money of the Arabs lying deposited in banks in this town [Amsterdam]..." (Colenbrander, *Coen*, IV, 382–383).

6 Van Neck, "Reisverhaal", 254–255.

7 Van der Chijs, *Vestiging*, 26.

8 See Kotwicz, "Mongoles", 199–204. *Cf.* also Polo, *Book*, I, 14 n. 1, 28 n. 1, 454 n. 2†; II, 477 n. 1; *cf.* Fischel, *Jews*, 91–92.

9 Polo, *Book*, II, 212 n. 12.

10 Yule, *Cathay*, I, 167, 170–171.

11 Van Vollenhoven, *Adatrecht*, III, 583 ff.; *cf. ibid.*, II, 122, and Krom, *Geschiedenis*, 41 n. 3.

12 See Yule in his foreword to *Cathay*, I, x–xi.

13 See De Waard, "Walcheren", 140 ff.; Sneller, *Walcheren*, 1–9.

14 In 1930 proa shipping accounted for only 1% of all shipping in the Netherlands East Indies (*Bijlagen Volksraad*, article 7, p. 8).

15 See Weber, *Ethic*, 13–31.

16 "... the aim of all cultural history [is] to get to know man as he carries on his everyday life..." (Brugmans, *Leven*, I, viii).

17 See, *e.g.*, *Gedenkboek*, the political speeches of the nationalists M. Hatta and Sukarno at their trials (Hatta, "Indonesië", and Sukarno, *Indonesië*), Blumberger, *Beweging*, 213, 410, 434, and the remarkable news report from *Bintang Timoer* in *Nieuwe Rotterdamsche Courant*, 11 December, 1933. For the scholarly concept of Indonesian history in connection with the projected Faculty of Letters in a University of the Netherlands East Indies, see Brugmans, "Geschiedenisonderwijs".

18 See Sombart, "Wandlungen" (and the discussion following it, pp. 42–155), and *Future*. 'Planning' and 'development': the scaffoldings for the structures of national planned economies are already erected everywhere, in England (textiles and coal) and the United States (the system of NIRA codes, intended to become permanent) as well as in Italy and Germany – even in the Netherlands, where regulation after regulation is promulgated which, put in effect as a 'temporary crisis measure', time after time introduces into a liberal economy a piece of organization marked by another spirit, the spirit of a conscious, all-embracing interventionism. "The economic period we have entered into thus bears the imprint of a time of transition: it is the late period of the dominant economic system, the early period of a system striving for power" (Sombart, "Wandlungen", 41). A few words concerning the planned economy of the USSR are necessary in this regard. Despite all the 'atrocity propaganda' and all the reports (certainly true) of occasional serious mismanagement by government and industrial leadership, it needs to be stated that the Five Year Plans for economic development of the Soviet Union are accomplishing the gigantic task of:

(1) Systematically building up industry and developing raw materials and natural resources.
(2) Revolutionizing agriculture and village institutions while preserving the elements of value the old native organization of agriculture and village have to offer (see Van Vollenhoven, *Adatrecht*, I, 654).
(3) Developing a social and cultural policy of colossal dimensions for the urban and rural population.

The advantages of a planned economic and cultural development of the Soviet Union become obvious if one considers what the course of events would have been in case Russia had been 'developed' by Western capitalism as a semi-colonial land. (The first traces of such a process were already manifest in the years 1890–1910.) Then there would have been unbridled financial exploitation by foreign capital; unsystematic development of natural resources under the pressure of a foreign 'development fever'; drainage of the profits from development; slow – or perhaps even quick – destruction of old native village institutions; exploitation of the peasant masses by industrial capital on the one hand and the kulaks on the other, for which Stolypin's measures laid the foundations (like Fransen van de Putte's agrarian law of 9 April, 1870, *Staatsblad van Nederlandsch-Indië* [Gazette of the Netherlands East Indies], 1870, no 71, which would have led to the same result in Java); and driving of the pastoral and agricultural peoples of eastern, southern, and western Siberia – the 'colonial task' of the Soviet Union – towards destruction. And no social and cultural policy for the great masses of the poor (and then certainly still more impoverished) population. Violent criticism, based chiefly on a difference in world view, should keep these sober ecomomic facts in mind. The question needs to be put to the religious adversaries of the regime now in power in Russia whether the position of the Russian Orthodox Church would be better and more hopeful under a system in which the interests of Russia were not controlled in Moscow or Petrograd but by the stock markets and high finance in New York, Paris, and London. It appears that China is now to go the sorrowful way of 'free' industrialization. The threat that the USSR does constitute for the more-than-two-thousand-year-old cultural tradition of Europe is undoubtedly real. Proletarian Marxist technocracy offers no possibility for western Europe with its complex organization. But judgement of the results of capitalistic exploitation in Russia must be kept apart from that. One should reflect on the conditions in Central and South America.

I: ON METHODOLOGY AND THEORY

1 See Byron, *Don Juan*, Canto XII, v–vi (1823).

2 It is a Marxist distortion of the facts to link the triumph of modern capitalism closely to the series of bourgeois revolutions (and, carried further as wish-image and prophecy, the triumph of socialism to proletarian revolutions). They are the revolution legend and the mythology of revolution Marx created (see Sombart, *Sozialismus*, II, 331–341). The fact of the historical origin of modern capitalism in England, which does not bear the imprint of the Great Revolution, teaches otherwise. (In 1935 the Labour Party still could speak about the abolition of tithes as desirable!: see *The Times* [London], 4 October, 1935, p. 8.) So too does the fact of the retrogression of the first capitalistic 'colonization' in France from 1789 up to the 1830's. (See Knowles, *Revolutions*, 8, 9, 26, 35–36; Sombart, *Kapitalismus*, II, Part One, 13–15.) The construction of the French governmental organization and juridical system in Napoleonic France actually has nothing to do with the emergence of modern capitalism in France. A bureaucratic spirit does not need a capitalistic one for creating a state – compare Diadochian Egypt (and see Van Vollenhoven, "Administratief recht", 63–64, 69). And there is the

opposition of the strict limitation of the Roman juridical system and the unbridled licence of the later Republic's 'political capitalism'.

3 See Troeltsch, *Probleme*, vii–ix.

4 See Sombart, *Kapitalismus*, III, Part One, xviii–xxii; Weber, *Methodology*, 105.

5 "Liberated as we are from the antiquated notion that all cultural phenomena can be *deduced* as a product or function of the constellation of 'material' interests, we believe nevertheless that the analysis of social and cultural phenomena with special reference to their economic conditioning and ramifications was a scientific principle of creative fruitfulness and with careful application and freedom from dogmatic restrictions, will remain in such for a very long time to come. The so-called 'materialistic conception of history' as a *Weltanschauung* or as a formula for the causal explanation of historical reality is to be rejected most emphatically. The advancement of the economic *interpretation* of history is one of the most important aims of our journal." (Weber, *Methodology*, 68 – the study served as an introduction to the journal *Archiv für Sozialwissenschaft und Sozialpolitik* [Journal of Social Science and Social Policy] when it first came under the editorship of Jaffé, Sombart, and Weber: see *Methodology*, iii–iv). "... there remains a philosophical and generalizational spirit in such research, a tendency toward a dynamic, living concept of separate totalities and a developing, dynamic inter-relationship, above all a focus of attention on the significance of the social-economic basis for all these movements and configurations. All that stems from Marxism. But even so in such an attitude the Marxist concept of universal history moves to the background. Development becomes development of individual phenomena. Comparison of such phenomena no longer leads to universal history, but to sociology, in which the scientific elements of Marxism are now generally beginning to dissolve themselves." (Troeltsch, *Probleme*, 361; see also Blom, "Marx", 84).

6 See Troeltsch, *Probleme*, 764, 767.

7 *Ibid.*, 356.

8 See Weber, *Essays*, 411–412.

9 But see Wittfogel, *Wirtschaft*, I, viii, xiii–xvii, 683 and n., 700, 702 and n. 55, 727 and n. 148. Wittfogel works out the 'Asian' phase further, especially in regard to China. In this connection Metchnikoff's remarkable work *Fleuves* deserves to be mentioned first of all.

10 See Huizinga, *Werken*, VII, 49–50; also Wensinck, "School", 81, 88, 92; Van Vollenhoven, *Adatrecht*, II, 773 bottom; *Découverte*, 157–158.

11 See *e.g.* the controversy on whether 'capitalism' existed in the ancient world (Weber, *Sozialgeschichte*, 7 ff.; Meyer, *Schriften*, the chapters on 'Economic Development in the Ancient World' and 'Slavery in the Ancient World'; and, more recently, Bolkestein, *Leven*).

12 See Wittfogel, "Ursachen". On the stagnation of economic life in the later empire, he writes: "A specific constellation of productive powers, from

the directive significance of their natural elements, had led to an organization of the productive powers of society which crippled every essential evolutionary activity. A basic retrogression in the social conditions of the elements of production had to follow; the course had first to be steered out of the blind alley of slavery into colonate and economy-in-kind, in order to make possible the later rise to the different forms of production in the European middle ages under completely changed conditions" (*ibid.*, 603).

13 *Cf.* the statement: "Thoughtlessly used, without taking into account what the logical content of the concept is, the [word 'evolution'] is losing the heavy consistency of its rich imagery and becoming a vague substitute for ascertained causation in general" (Huizinga, *Werken*, VII, 50).

14 See Troeltsch, *Probleme*, 707. Goetz, too, commits this error: "...the appearance of the Germanic tribes in the west and the Slavs in the east as dominant powers in Europe and the western Mediterranean not only brought about the beginning of a new development in cultural history and thus in commerce as well, but also a permanent expansion of the area in which ideas and goods were exchanged on related principles. From then on throughout the course of the next five or six centuries northern and eastern Europe came within the orbit of the civilized world regenerated by Christianity. Civilization reached those peoples only in a Christianized form. Thus, while the dissolution of the Roman Empire had also brought about the dissolution of the great intercommunicational unit formed by its many territories, the aforementioned peoples found in and through religion an element in common linking them with each other and the previous bearers of civilization. In the similar moral world views spread by Christianity an important basis for the realization of intercommunication from people to people was given this tribal world, the development of such intercommunication in no sense being dependent only on technical and social factors of the parties concerned, but also on moral factors. Moreover, they had an outward bond in common in the hierarchy, which was organized on an international scale..." (*Verkehrswege*, 517; *cf.* also 569, 585–587, 598, 606–607, 628, 643–644, 666, 668). How false this proposition is in its generality is shown by the picture of Indonesia as an historical missionary territory for Islam and Christianity. The bare fact of Islamization or Christianization did not of itself mean a single transformation of a social or economic sort. The strong international orientation of Islam did not effect any direct economic shifts and transformations in areas involved. For a correction of Goetz' standpoint see Weber, *Sozialgeschichte*, 308–311; Sombart, *Kapitalismus*, I, Part One, 117 ff.

15 See Huizinga, *Werken*, VII, 57, 73.

16 In "Agrarverhältnisse im Altertum" (The Agrarian Institutions of the Ancient World), *Sozialgeschichte*, 1–288 (the article is not limited to material on agrarian history, but makes up a complete social-economic history of the ancient period), and in "Die sozialen Gründe des Untergangs der antiken Kul-

tur" (The Social Causes of the Decline and Fall of Ancient Civilization), *Sozialgeschichte*, 289–311.

17 "Neither Cunningham nor Levasseur, Inama-Sternegg nor Kowalewsky are essentially anything else but legal historians" (Sombart, *Kapitalismus*, I, Part One, 23). Kötschke's new work, *Wirtschaftsgeschichte*, suffers from this evil also. And for a crass example see Chen, *Confucius*, II, 506–507; *cf.* Lee, *China*, 144–145.

18 On the instigation of Simkhovitch, Miss Lee also wrote her *China* "with special reference to agriculture" (*q. v.*, 13–17, 137–138).

19 See *e.g.* Kötschke, *Wirtschaftsgeschichte*, 458–498.

20 See *e.g.* Schaeder, "Ausbreitung", 244–246 (summary).

21 The term is dangerous – such an historical concept presumes a previous history (ancient period) and a later history (modern period). For Byzantium and the caliphates the facts are different. One can see here the dangers in the use of western European historical categories. Wensinck uses the neutral term "the East during the middle ages" ("School", 82). Goetz uses alongside each other 'middle ages' and 'Orient' – a chronological and a geographical category of history! (see *Verkehrswege*, 636). *Cf.* Yule's reference: "the three great branches of mediaeval civilisation – European, Saracenic, and Chinese" (Polo, *Book*, II, 161 n. 3), and Fischel's statement: "Though the terms 'Middle Ages' or 'Mediaeval' taken over from European history are scarcely exact in this connection, they are retained here as a matter of convenience" (*Jews*, viii; *cf.* 72–73, 78 n. 3).

22 See Burckhardt, *Renaissance*, 2–3, 45. *Cf.* Weber, *Theory*, 291, *History*, 109, 223–224, 258; Le Bon, *Arabes*, 310, 316–318, 474, 531–532, 560–561, 614, 618, 633 ff.; Hartmann, *Kapittel*, 19–20, 22–23; Diehl, *Venise*, 12 ff.; Kantorowicz, *Frederick*, 216 ff., 280–281, 282 ff.; Fitzler, "Handelsgesellschaften", 211, 248–249.

23 See Troeltsch, *Probleme*, 118, 609 ff. The richness and totality of the social-historical picture of the Islamic world and its outward resemblance to various aspects of medieval western Europe cannot be traced back alone – or perhaps it is better to say can be traced only to a very limited degree – to the related revealed religions and philosophical currents which, especially in the prophetic stamp of their soteriologies, lend more than one characteristic in common to the culture and popular concepts of the Christian, Jewish, and Moslem peoples.

24 See Brentano, "Volkswirtschaft", 16–17, 26–27.

25 See Stöckle, "Zünfte"; *cf.* Le Bon, *Arabes*, 162.

26 See Stöckle, "Zünfte", 55, 63, 123.

27 See Stein, *Geschichte*, 141–160; *cf.* Kremer, *Einnahmebudget*, 14, 25, 62–63.

28 See Kötschke, *Wirtschaftsgeschichte*, 465–468, 489–490.

29 See Hartmann, *Kapittel*, 21.

30 See De Goeje, "Handelsverkeer", 268–269.

31 Insufficient knowledge prevents me from testing this statement in the field of cultural history as well, but I should like to maintain it without reservation for the field of social-economic history. In this regard I can only point to the not yet definitely decided question of the significance of Byzantine and Moslem scholarship for the revival and purification of humanism in western Europe (see Pleßner, *Geschichte*). If one considers the characteristics with which Burckhardt wished to construct his Renaissance types and patterns, then there is also the possibility of identifying and sketching such types and patterns in the East of an earlier time (see Fueter, *Historiographie*, 94; Neumann, *Weltstellung*, viii–ix, 81 ff.; Troeltsch, *Thought*, 114–116, 140–142; De Haan, review).

32 See Weber, *Sozialgeschichte*, 1–288 ("Agrarverhältnisse"), and *History*, *passim*.

33 See Granet, *Civilisation*, 103, 135–137, 141, 477–478, 482–483, 486; Huan K'uan, *Discourses*, xxiv, xxvii (Gale).

34 See Jain, *Banking*, 15, 39, 50; Terpstra, *Westerkwartieren*, 204, 206–207 (Appendix VI); Van Linschoten, *Voyage*, I, 259; Moreland, *Aurangzeb*, 85–86, 145, 148–149, 292; Polo, *Book*, II, 332 ff. n. 1 and subn. † (333).

35 Rathgen, "Volkswirtschaft", 177; Takizawa, *Penetration*, 103 (Miss Takizawa's study must be read critically, but the case in question is a documented statement).

36 See De Jonge, *Opkomst*, V, 199–200, VI, 160, 172–173, 184, VII, 141, 203; Van Neck, "Reisverhaal", 250–251. *Cf.* also Colenbrander, *Coen*, III, 826–827; Van Vollenhoven, *Adatrecht*, I, 472 (regarding Bali).

37 See Von Kremer, *Einnahmebudget*, *passim*; *cf.* Terpstra, *Westerkwartieren*, 253 (Appendix XXV).

38 *E.g.* the Sephardic Jews Machado and Pereira, to whom the responsibility for army provisions was farmed out (Muller, *Eeuw*, 536). And to what extent such figures as De Moucheron and De Geer?

39 On tax farming in Ghent in the thirteenth and fourteenth centuries, see De Roover, review, 90; on farming out of feudal financial rights in the east of the Netherlands in the sixteenth century before the Revolution, see Van Gelder, "Bailleul", 208.

40 'Political capitalism': the term is taken over from Max Weber, who first fully elucidated the great significance of the pattern in social and economic history. In the sketch following, his schematic summary in *Theory*, 255–257 (§ 31), has been used as point of departure.

41 Thus *e.g.* Wittfogel, too, qualifies the political capitalism of the Contending States only as 'mercantile-capitalistic' (see *Wirtschaft*, 502, 704, 760, 762). The vicious thing is that then in the term the commercial in the narrow sense of the word comes to predominate (see *ibid.*, 645, for a special form, 'putting-out capitalism') and thus as an historical category the term tends to be

applied wrongly. Trade proper remained for a large part outside the field of political capitalism. It went on predominantly in handicraft forms, with political capitalism intervening irregularly as occasional trade, 'crisis' trade, 'war profiteering'.

42 See Weber, *Sozialgeschichte*, 1–288 ("Agrarverhältnisse"), and *History*.

43 See Hartmann, *Kapittel*, 22; Kötschke, *Wirtschaftsgeschichte*, 60, 467, 490; Brentano, "Volkswirtschaft", 19, 50.

44 See Stöckle, "Zünfte", 123 ff.

45 See Weber, *Ethic*, 185, n. 2.

46 See Treub, *Hoofdstukken*, 12–13.

47 See Hartmann, *Kapittel*, 9, 22–23.

48 See the interesting quotations on Chinese mining in the "Wetenschappelijke Berichten" (Science Notes) in the *Nieuwe Rotterdamsche Courant*, 4 March, 1933 and 1 November, 1933; Wittfogel, *Wirtschaft*, 526–558.

49 The quotation is from Kellermann. *Cf.* Karl Kautsky (in the chapter on 'Capital and Labour in the Mining Industry') in Bernstein, *Geschichte*, I, Part One, 88, 94.

50 "The woollen industry was the most revolutionary urban craft of the later middle ages, and its workers, too, were revolutionary" (Kautsky in Bernstein, *Geschichte*, I, Part One, 102). See also Weber, *Religionssoziologie*, II, 345; Brentano, *Gilds*, 52–53, 56–57, 72, 79–80, 103.

51 "The doctrine of basic concepts in the field of the humanities is the most typical point in Weber's logic of history. The elucidation of their specialness, above all in the field of the social sciences, occupied him in almost all his logical studies, and with the help of that doctrine he later on constructed his sociology" (Marianne Weber, *Weber*, 327; *cf. ibid.*, 691, and Jaspers, *Weber*, *passim*).

52 In *Wirtschaft* together with the three volumes of *Religionssoziologie* (for parts translated into English see the bibliography below).

53 In *History* (the German edition of which was published posthumously, adapted from notes of Weber's lectures on the subject given at the University of Munich, Winter Semester, 1919–1920: see Marianne Weber, *Weber*, 683) together with the theoretical studies collected in *Wissenschaftslehre*, especially "Roscher und Knies und die logischen Probleme der historischen Nationalökonomie" (Roscher and Knies and the Logical Problems of Historical National Economy), 1–145; "Die Objektivität sozialwissenschaftlicher und sozialpolitischer Erkenntnis" (translated as "'Objectivity' in Social Science and Social Policy", *Methodology*, 50–112), 146–214; "Kritische Studien auf dem Gebiet der kulturwissenschaftlichen Logik" (translated as "Critical Studies in the Logic of the Cultural Sciences", *Methodology*, 113–188), 215–290; "Die Grenznutzenlehre und das 'psychophysische Grundgesetz'" (The Doctrine of Diminishing Returns and the 'Fundamental Law of Psycho-Physics'), 360–375; "Über einige Kategorien der verstehenden Soziologie"

(On Some Categories of Interpretative Sociology), 403–450.

54 See Hunter, *Empire*, 163–164, and *e.g.* Stier, *Pergamonaltar*, 58–60, 128, 130, 183–184.

55 See Troeltsch, *Probleme*, 694–722. The Propyläen history of the world undertaken in recent years by Walter Goetz and others (*Werdegang*) gives in its design a very clear illustration of this objection. In the first volume, *Das Erwachen der Menschheit* (The Awakening of Mankind), alongside the treatment of prehistory, earliest human history, and the influence of race, land, and climate as historical factors (chapters by Behn, Weidenreich, Hertz, and Vogel), the 'History of Eastern Asia Before Its Political Contact with Europe' is treated by Krause. Then in volume three, *Das Mittelalter* (The Middle Ages), a place is found for a 'History of India' by Kirfel. In volume nine, *Die Entstehung des Weltstaatensystems* (The Rise of the System of World Powers), come 'The Islamic World Since the Eighteenth Century' by Schaeder and 'The Modern Development of Eastern Asia' by Krause. Indian history is treated incidentally by Schaeder; in limiting his view chiefly to Moslem dominion, he gives an unsatisfactory treatment of eighteenth and nineteenth-century southern Asian history (see Lavisse, *Histoire*, VII, Chapter Six).

56 See Weber, *Essays*, 399; *System*, 64, 75, 77–79, 86, 89, 92, 95, 98, 122; *Religionssoziologie*, II, 322, 327, 353, 359.

57 Thus at least the standpoint of Le Bon, in *Arabes* – a bit too absolutely formulated perhaps, though in general having my approval.

58 See Masson-Oursel, *Inde*, 94.

59 *Akbar*; *Aurangzeb*; *System*.

60 Such works as Smith's *History* and Grousset's *Histoire* give the general frame of reference, but do not trace the lines of economic history specifically. Differentiation in the writing of history is only in its beginnings, and the application of a sociological criterium and use of social-economic categories ('economic history') is a work still to be done. For the history of western Europe this differentiation and application has for the most part already occurred, and the proper balance between the fields of economic and cultural history has been struck.

61 "...there is, I fear, little prospect that adequate materials for a similar study of earlier periods will ever become available..." (*Akbar*, v).

62 Lette's work, *Grondbezit*, does not seem to me to have escaped this danger completely.

63 Rouffaer & Juynboll, *Batik-kunst*.

64 *Ibid.*, I, 7 [translated from the Dutch text]. This antithesis between the excellently pictorial, affectionate, and extremely minute treatment of data (Rouffaer's pre-eminent skill) and the inaccuracy of the general social and economic terminology appears in many places in the book. Regarding the techniques of the early Indian larger shops (and manufacturies? – see Moreland, *Akbar*, 192–193) in making cloth for overseas export (see *Batik-kunst*,

260, 394, 422–423, 499, 523), Rouffaer speaks of "the industrial hurry which has urged [this craft] on since at least as early as 1500" (*ibid.*, 528, *cf.* 5). How matters stood with that 'industrial hurry' appears from his own report (on the investigation he organized in 1901) on the batik craft in Coromandel. For example, "the weavers in Kumbakonam, dwelling in special streets around a temple, according to caste" (254), "the printing blocks made by the craftsmen themselves" (256), etc. It is clear that here the way leads to different forms of craft techniques and methods. Snouck Hurgronje's account of an Achin trader in Negapattinnam in the 1870's is also instructive (reported by Rouffaer & Juynboll, *ibid.*, 521).

65 See *Religionssoziologie*, II, 374–375. It should be commented in passing that the term *orientalisch* often occurring in German writings chiefly concerns the Near East, the Lesser Asian and Egyptian territory of the former Roman Empire, the whole area of Islamic states and culture, not India and lands further east. See, *e.g.*, Goetz, *Verkehrswege*, 517, and *cf.* 606–607 and 636 ("...in the middle ages and in the Orient...").

66 "In that sense, China actually has no history. ...here before us we have the oldest state, and yet no history, but a state that exists today as we have learnt to know it in ancient times." (*Weltgeschichte*, II, 278). For Ranke, China was one of the "eternally stationary peoples" (*Weltgeschichte*, I, vii); see also Krause, *Geschichte*, I, 22.

67 But Van Orsoy de Flines could still speak of "Chinese ceramics from the middle ages" in his annual report "Verzameling", III, 209.

68 Granet, *Civilisation*, 80–83.

69 *Ibid.*, 90–99.

70 Weber, *History*, 57, 321.

71 One should constantly keep in mind with what a small number of people the older history of humanity was enacted. With the mention of the great early Mediterranean, Indian, and Chinese states, the epic pictures of those hosts, numerous as the sands of the sea, comes easily to mind: "By reason of the abundance of his horses their dust shall cover thee: thy walls shall shake at the noise of the horsemen, and of the wheels, and of the chariots, when he shall enter into thy gates, as men enter into a city wherein is made a breach" (*Ezekiel* 26: 10). But for the reality of history see Delbrück, *Kriegskunst*, I, 7–24 on the size of armies. The Visigoths who broke across the border of the Roman Empire near Durostrorum in 376 were 15,000 fighting men strong – with families, slaves, and wagon trains 40,000 head (Kötschke, *Wirtschaftsgeschichte*, 89; *cf.* Pirenne, *Mahomet*, 19–20). In 256 B.C., the state of Chou numbered 30,000 people spread over 36 towns (Granet, *Civilisation*, 475). The cultivated area in ancient Egypt consisted of only 29,150 square kilometres and thus was not even the size of present-day Belgium (Speck, *Handelsgeschichte*, I, 305 – in modern Egypt between 32,000 and 35,000 square kilometres are tilled). Caught within the sphere of such small numbers, such

limited environments, restricted to the measure of man, were the earlier and later epic and lyric forms of expression. When Nestor, on the beach before Pylos, tells the tale of the trials and adversities of the Trojan war – "Nor is *that* the full count of what the Achaean chivalry endured at Troy. There is no man on earth who could unfold to you the whole disastrous tale, not though you sat and questioned him for half a dozen years, by which time your patience would be gone, and you yourself be home." (*The Odyssey*, III, 113–117, tr. E. V. Rieu) – then one must remember that it is a military and naval expedition of perhaps a few hundred Hellenes that is involved. When P. C. Hooft makes the Princess of Orange complain over the battle before Bois le Duc –

'k Hoor alle daeghs van versche dooden
Gevelt in hol oft galery.
Elk overlijdt aan eighe looden;
Maer aller koeghels moorden my.

(I hear each day of newly dead
Felled in trench or gallery.
Each passes on of his own lead;
But ev'ry bullet murders me.)

– then one must call to mind the nature of wars and sieges in 1629. Thus also with the nationalistic pathos of *e.g.* Theodor Körner in 1815 and the Leiden Rifles in 1831. Modern civilization, which has multiplied all this in dimensions a thousand times and accelerated it all to a dizzy pace by modern techniques, has caused every measure defined by man to disappear, and thereby has largely destroyed the frame of reference for human forms of artistic expression that have existed down through the ages.

72 Granet, *Civilisation*, 119. But *cf.* Wittfogel, *Wirtschaft*, 33, 219–223, 287 & nn. 304–305, 290, 487–489 & nn. 101–102 & 109; Goetz, *Verkehrswege*, 304–305, 503. Because of Marco Polo's trip to the extreme southwest of the empire in the service of the Mongol regime (1277–1280), the situation in those 'outer possessions' comes sharply to the fore in his account. See in that regard the notes in Polo, *Book*, II, 35 n. 2, 48 n. 5, 57 n. 4, 59 n. 7, 67 n. 1, 79 n. 1, 81 n. 4, 88 n. 2, 91 n. 4, 96 n. 8, 117 n. 1, 120 n. 1, 123 n. 1, 124 n. 2, 127 n. 1, 128 n. 6, 228 n. 3, 243 n. 6, 298 n. 5, 301 n. 2.

73 If the experiment in agriculture and fiscal administration made by the Sung Dynasty premier Wang An-shih (1021–1086) had been continued and completely carried out, a revolutionary measure leaving those of Solon in Athens and the Gracchi in Rome far behind would have been realized – one whose significance could only be compared to that of the Russian Revolution

of 1917–1919 or (if they are carried through consistently) President Roosevelt's plans for economic 'recovery' in the United States. (See Krause, *Geschichte*, I, 159–161.)

74 *Cf.* Van Vollenhoven, *Adatrecht*, II, 6.

75 In *Wirtschaftgeschichte*, 18 (not reprinted in the English translation, *History*).

76 A statement made to the writer by Professor Duyvendak, 16 June, 1933.

77 See xix, xxi, xxvi there.

78 See Wittfogel, *Wirtschaft*, 645 n. 574.

79 Franke, *Geschichte*; Grousset, *Histoire*. A work such as Wilhelm, *Wirtschaftspsychologie* is practically worthless. Wittfogel gives a treasure of material in his overabundant footnotes. A bibliography was to have appeared in the second volume, which has never been published.

80 *China*, 3–104. It seems to me that a proof that Weber's work was aimed in the right direction is to be found in the fact that his typology of the ancient Chinese period of the Contending States and feudal aristocracies, the sketch of someone not a sinologist, dating from the years 1911–1913 (see Marianne Weber, *Weber*, 346, 349) was confirmed in all essential points by the work of the sinologist Granet (*Civilisation*) in 1929. Granet appears not to have known Weber's work, having limited himself to specialist publications.

81 See Weber, *Religionssoziologie*, II, 295–308, 367–368.

82 There are practically no translations of this Japanese economic literature. See Feenstra Kuiper, *Japan*, 296 (under Klapfroth).

83 Not of social esteem or political influence. The feudal military tradition in Japan has continued to exist up to the present time; even modern capitalism, with all its accompanying phenomena (democratization of way of life through education, parliamentary system, and civil power) has not been able to repress it, as it has been able to do in western Europe.

84 The total population remained constant throughout the eighteenth century. In 1721 it was 26,065,425; in 1846, 26,907,625 (Honjo, "Population", 65).

85 Weber, *Wirtschaft*, 514–601 ("Die Stadt" – The City); Bloch, *Kämpfe*. *Cf.* Wittfogel, *Wirtschaft*, 726–734, 746–747.

86 In my opinion, then, there was political capitalism during the Tokugawa period, despite the lack of the great stimuli war and foreign trade. This in opposition to Weber (see *Religionssoziologie*, II, 298–299).

87 See *e.g.* Takizawa, *Penetration*, 45–49, 103. *Cf.* Wittfogel, *Wirtschaft*, 755; Moreland, *Aurangzeb*, 154–155, 280, 295.

88 Takizawa, *Penetration*, 98, 105, 107, 120. "Modern socialism was born out of the discipline of the factory. Everywhere, in every age and in every land in the world there has been socialism of the most diverse natures. Modern socialism in its special form is only possible on that basis." (Weber, *Sozialpolitik*, 501).

89 *E.g.*, this passage: "...money was transforming the castle-town into a modern city" (Takizawa, *Penetration*, 71).

90 See Feenstra Kuiper, *Japan*, 291–299; Fukuda, *Japan*; Rathgen, "Volkswirtschaft".

91 America, Africa, the nomadic and the so-called 'primitive' peoples (How to draw the border between 'primitive' and 'civilized' peoples? Are inhabitants of Nias and Flores primitive, those of Java and Madagascar civilized?) are as a matter of fact just as much involved in this. Sociology must build with the materials of ethnology as well as with those of cultural history. And nomadic peoples (the Scythians, the Mongols, the Seljuks) have often played a very important rôle in cultural history.

92 See the passage by Sombart, here of central significance: "Europe's economic civilization had apparently attained the same point of development which up to then had been reached by every civilized people and had not been surpassed by any of them. Whether we look at China or India, Egypt or Babylonia, Greece or Rome, everywhere we find the same final state of affairs as that in which European economic life found itself at the end of the period of early capitalism – a state of affairs characterized by the following traits: a far-reaching exploitation of foreign peoples, and important trade in merchandise connected with it, a developed system of moneylending and high finance, a flourishing tax-farming economy, and along with them, on a limited scale, the beginnings of big industry on an organic basis. None of the peoples in the past had got beyond that situation; their fate carried them from there either toward decay or toward a closed economy of quiet small-scale farming. In either case capitalism broke down; the child was smothered in the cradle. None of the peoples in earlier history had known modern capitalism – and especially industrial capitalism, the central point of all modern capitalism – as it was experienced in the nineteenth century (but not earlier) by Europe." (*Kapitalismus*, II, 1154; *cf.* Troeltsch, *Probleme*, 719). It should be commented in this regard that Sombart does not use the word 'development' in the sense of evolution or progress, but in the sense of the coming to full growth of the forms and the spirit of a certain 'economic system'; the order of such economic systems is in no way linked to a general historical 'evolution' (see his *Ordnung*, 4–5, 30–32). In his research into the historical elements of modern capitalism, Sombart does not reach the degree of precision and deep-going analysis characteristic of Weber, especially in the first of the latter's studies in the sociology of religion, *Ethic*. Very much of what are indicated in Sombart's *Quintessence* ('A Study of the History and Psychology of the Modern Business Man', as its subtitle reads) as 'sources of the capitalistic spirit' cannot hold as specifically modern-capitalistic (see Weber, *Ethic*, 17–25, and *History*, 352–364).

93 The illustrations given are from the field of the methodology of history. Alongside them in our time stand the conjunction and the fusion of modern

capitalism with the forms of society in other parts of the world. The knowledge of those cultural areas, thus, becomes timely in another way – in the organization of national and international law, the establishment of a social policy, the determination of methods of economic development for areas now colonial or semi-colonial. The problems are there alike in modern Turkey, in Siam, in the Netherlands East Indies, in China, in central and southern Africa. But for such practical work, too, theoretical reflection is necessary, and thus also from such a starting point the problem of methodology is raised. This is the background of Van Vollenhoven's work in the fields of the history and description of law. Beginning with Indonesian law, he has extended his work to the legal systems of the whole world (see his *Adatrecht*, III, 121–122, 126–128, 172, 582, 621, 664, 666, 690, 719, 727, 739–740, 805–806, 819–820). Due to the lot of modern political history as well as due to the study of history as such, my standpoint as set out so far in this chapter ends up in opposition to that of Troeltsch, as he has summarized it: "...[the] limitation of general history to that of the peoples of Europe [is], because of the vastness of sources and facts as well as the understanding of far-reaching structural differences, demanded by historians nowadays – if they do not go even further in their limitations. Such is the constant, ever-recurrent result of research and reappraisal up to now. As a consequence historical thought has become ever more nearly identical with historical realism. That is the quintessence of our work in history. With the preponderance of philology which has lasted up to the present day, the study of the languages and history of other cultural areas stands apart somewhat exotically." (*Probleme*, 704–705, *cf.* 708, 710, 726). Troeltsch, it is true, recognizes the importance of a general sociology. "But such a sociology, then, is plainly not history and not philosophy of history, but a generalizational auxiliary discipline to both, very instructive and interesting, but still very undeveloped" (*ibid.*, 715). In such a way the study of history is too tightly bound to the study of the philosophy of history and the value of the auxiliary discipline sociology in constructing a frame of reference for history is underestimated. Where Troeltsch ends in limitation, one needs first to begin in comprehensiveness.

94 None of this has any relation to a 'cultural synthesis'. What is aimed at is a purely factual inventory of history for the sake of a general systematization of sociology and social-economic history supporting a purely causal, positivistic study of history – a universality which is already practised in modern ethnology and social psychology. In almost every case where the need for 'synthesis' appears, metaphysics or politics plays a rôle (see Troeltsch, *Probleme*, 697 n. 370, 699–700). Where a 'synthesis' is projected, the facts of history are distorted and the historical view is immobilized by the arrangement of patterns as stage properties in setting the scene for the 'total view' – *cf.* Troeltsch's statement on "... the violation of empirical history always committed thereby" (*ibid.*, 111).

95 The pragmatic weakening of the concept to 'tendencies' should not cause one to lose sight of the fact that the philosophical background of natural scientific thought is consciously or unconsciously maintained.

96 The books of Zola, Sinclair, Ehrenburg; *cf.* Kellermann. See also Sombart, *Quintessence*, 376 n. 156.

97 At least the basis must be expanded thus; it is true some theorists advocate a limitation of the general system of economics to the areas of western Europe and America, *i.e.*, the areas of modern capitalism. However, it seems to be logically included in the nature of a general doctrinal system that it should extend itself universally, unencumbered by territorial or historical limitations – thus C. A. Verrijn Stuart, Cassel, Menger, Pareto (see Boeke, *Economie*, 6–7).

98 Schumpeter, *Wesen*, 43. *Cf.* also Amonn, "Dynamik".

99 Pareto, *Manuel*, 160.

100 The consistent 'universal' point of view.

101 Aboetari, *Verhouding*, 148–149. *Cf.* "...the general in an empiric phenomenon ... is valid for phenomena still unknown as well as for those already known" (*ibid.*, 95).

102 See Weber, *Theory*, 99–101; Huizinga, *Werken*, VII, 76–77.

103 'Providing necessities', not 'seeking the satisfaction of wants'. The tendency of the second concept comes from eigteenth-century Anglo-French utilitarian, rationalistic thought; it presumes 'economic man'. The first concept bases itself rather on *Genesis* 3:19. *Cf.* Sombart's statement: "The thing that interests us in the problems of exchange is that material things enter into a certain exchange relationship to each other, and that finally immaterial things also are materialized in gaining exchange value. It is always *der Erden rest, zu tragen peinlich* [the earthly portion, heavy to bear] that makes us, also, take upon ourselves the trouble of carrying on economic activities." ("Objekt", 657).

104 See Mannheim, *Man*, 79–80.

105 See Hunger, "Geschenken", especially the last paragraph.

106 *Cf.* the letter by Meijer Ranneft, summary.

107 Psychology, planned as a natural science, arrives at grotesque images in its attempts at explaining human symbols, concepts, and actions by reducing them to consistent patterns and general basic elements. This is also the disappointing background of Freud's masterly hypotheses in the sociology of religion and the sociology of civilization, for example in *Future* and *Civilization*. *Cf.* Max Weber's critique of psychoanalysis as an auxiliary discipline to the humanities, made in 1907: "... [there] can be no doubt that Freud's thought may become very important for the interpretation of whole series of phenomena in cultural history, especially in the history of religion and morals" (Marianne Weber, *Weber*, 379; see the whole passage, 378–384).

108 Huizinga, *Werken*, VII, 43; *cf.* 76.

109 Compare the following quotations. "In the cultural sciences the knowledge of the universal or general is never valuable in itself to us" (Weber, *Methodology*, 80). "All knowledge ... is always knowledge from *particular points of view*" (*ibid.*, 81). "Thus, if one accordingly puts oneself at the historical pole, then for that person the fundamental category is the category of individual totality, as opposed to the element and the abstract general law into which in their interaction natural scientific analysis converts those aspects of experiential reality available to it and selected by it. History has no simple basic element at all analogous to the natural scientific element, whether that is conceived in terms of atomics or energetics; what history has had from the very beginning is compound units in which in each case a whole series of psychological occurences of an elemental sort is massed together with certain natural conditions to form a unity or totality of life." (Troeltsch, *Probleme*, 32–33; *cf.* 61). "The empirical logic of history constitutes its objects by means of a unit of meaning realizing itself in essence in them, and accordingly it contracts large human groups and large periods of time into individual units of meaning for the creation of which events otherwise psychologically understandable and transparent are united, to be sure without such a meaning being completely and exclusively realized" (*ibid.*, 116–117). "Dissolution of nature into numbers – that is the 'meaning' of modern natural science..." (and, as the result of that statement) "only on the basis of Pythagorean metaphysics could one arrive at the assumption that one had opened up the 'meaning' of the world thus" (Sombart, *Nationalökonomien*, 116).

110 *Cf.* Huizinga's statement: "When one conceives of an historical unit-through-the-ages, for example the Frenchman, then the idea of that unit, only incompletely represented by the separate object, lies in the summarization of all the phenomena implicated in it together, while the idea of the biological unit Mouse is realized by every mouse by itself" (*Werken*, VII, 53).

111 Sombart, *Nationalökonomien*, 237, *cf.* 93, 340. In this work Sombart bases his concept of social economy on Husserl's and Scheler's phenomenology; like the works of Heidegger, Sombart's book, although covering quite different territory, should be listed under the works of phenomenological 'existential analysis'. *Cf.* Erdmann, *Grundriß*, 729; Troeltsch, *Probleme*, 612 n. 324; Korsch, "Nationalökonomie", especially 445.

112 See Sombart, *Nationalökonomien*, 223–224.

113 'Culture' in the most comprehensive sense of the word – the forms of organized human life. The classifications 'primitive' and 'civilized' have already been discussed as dubious and confusing in this connection. The concept of 'evolutionary stages' plays a villainous rôle here (*cf.* Troeltsch, *Probleme*, 59 & n. 24).

114 Aboetari with complete consistency considers possible a categorical system of mechanical causality for economic forms side by side with a categorical system of causality based on individual motives for 'meta-economic'

forms in the whole of human social life (*Verhouding*, 9 n. 2 last sentence, 207–208, 208 n. 3). This is logically untenable.

115 In other fields of the social sciences the term naturally undergoes an expansion over the activities of religion, power politics, etc.

116 For the structure of the 'ideal type', see Weber, *Wissenschaftslehre*; *Methodology*; and *Theory*, 81 ff. *Cf.* Marianne Weber's words: "Certain events and relations of historical life are united into an internally harmonious cosmos of invented complexes 'which exists nowhere in the invented form, but is utopian'... – constructions in which certain elements of reality are 'imaginatively enhanced' in order thus to perceive and to illustrate concrete phenomena and events in which certain elements of the concept are at work. ... [The ideal type] is neither an historical reality nor a schema into which that reality has to be fitted, but a marginal concept by which reality is measured in order to clarify certain important elements of its content with which it is compared... Thus ideal types, in contradistinction to ordinal concepts, are means of perception, not aims, and because the 'everflowing stream of civilization' constantly furnishes the everlastingly youthful discipline of history with new problems, new ideal types have to be constructed again and again and those already in existence constantly have to be revised anew. Perception of history necessarily remains in constant flux. Because of that it is meaningless to divide history into a closed system of concepts from which reality must be deduced." (*Weber*, 327–328). And see also Gerth and Mills' comments in the introduction to Weber, *Essays*, 59–61.

117 Weber, *Wissenschaftslehre*, 369–370.

118 *Ibid.*, 372.

119 *Cf.* Sombart, *Nationalökonomien*, 92–93.

120 While many of the schemata of economic theory regarding the system of exchange and social and economic relations are constructed with the very simple, pastoral village market in the background (*cf. ibid.*, 301–302), completely different factors play the leading rôle in the commodity exchange market – completely depersonalized transactions taking place for a large part with speculative intent, transactions with a whole world's production classified into systematized, standardized types of commodities.

121 Thus, a separate field of 'political economy of the tropical colony' (Van Gelderen, *Voorlezingen*) or 'dualistic economy' (Boeke, *Economie* and other works) as an autonomous discipline seems to me out of the question. One can speak of the use of economic-historical categories in regard to the 'economic systems' of western Europe–North America–Australia–South Africa (as regions of high and late capitalism), Soviet Russia (as a region of socialistic state [late?] capitalism), and Asia–Africa–South and Central America–Oceania (as colonial and semi-colonial regions). Such divisions are divisions of geography and contemporary history. The essence of the three economic sectors is completely identical, thus for all three the same relationships of theory and

empirical research hold. There are no differences of a fundamental sort, thus no 'capitalistic' economy, no 'communist' economy, no economy of 'the tropical colony'. The division is a practical division for working. The inapplicability for 'Oriental' regions of 'economic laws' bearing the stamp of the modern-capitalistic life of western European and American regions is already an established fact. But, with the further-going transformation of capitalism in the countries of western Europe and in America, with the further development of interventionist, late-capitalistic traits, will the inapplicability of older and newer 'classics' of economics not also become an accomplished fact there before long?

122 These constructions, beginning from the observation of a coal train, lead on thus in various of the 'complexes of meaning' to completely different series, all depending on whether one chooses a coal train on a railroad in Germany, America, or the Soviet Union as a starting point.

123 *Cf.* Sombart, *Nationalökonomien*, 206 ff.

124 The concept of the 'economic system', Sombart's creation, has been taken up everywhere by students of economic history, so that a further listing of references is unnecessary.

125 Sombart, *Nationalökonomien*, 218–219. In such things lies Sombart's genius, and therefore the three volumes of *Kapitalismus* are monumental works of art. There is a close kinship here between Sombart and Zola; *cf.* Sombart's statement: "One only has to read Zola again and again to learn national economy. After all, we are all dilettanti in that discipline when we try to measure up to him." (*Volkswirtschaft*, 74).

126 See the Catalogue of the International Exhibition of Economic History held in the Municipal Museum at Amsterdam, 4 July–15 September, 1929. The works listed are nos 11, 27, 88 (all in the Netherlands), 183 (in Nancy), 193 (in the Netherlands), and 337 (in Wolverhampton) in the catalogue. *Cf.* the articles in *Nieuwe Rotterdamsche Courant* 4 July, 31 July, 10 August, 18 August, 1929. That extraordinary exhibition has intentionally been commemorated by this reference.

127 Bernier, *Travels*; Du Halde, *Description*.

II: TRADE AND THE TRADE ROUTES

1 Rolland, *Beethoven*, 19–20, 73.

2 Reichwein, *China*, 110–119, 158; *cf.* 84–86, 96, 98, 101–104, 106.

3 See Wensinck, "School", 81; Huizinga, "Kern", 98.

4 "Humboldtian universality of knowledge and *Einfühlung*" (Rahder, "Siebold", 26).

5 Edited by Max Müller; *cf.* De Goeje, *Müller*, 20.

6 The characteristic, changing conditions of the time need to be kept in

mind. The discoveries in the humanities in the nineteenth century made a powerful contribution to the world picture, the ideology, of the age – the concept of universal development in history, the concept of evolution and progress. "... the great empires of the ancient world, despite their incessant rivalries, their merciless struggles, were all of them working on the same project: the progress of civilization. History is strewn with the ruins of peoples, religions, empires which have left only their memories behind, but the stages of progress achieved in civilization have never been lost and today we are benefitting from those long ages of effort. Civilization is a torch with a light that grows from century to century, passed on by the most diverse peoples one after the other." (Le Bon, *Civilisations*, 6). "Every race carried this civilization on to a certain level until, exhausted by its efforts, it bequeathed the heritage to another race destined to develop it in its turn" (*ibid.*, 806). "The ideas which are penetrating history more and more are mainly the result of the progress of the natural sciences. Pointing out the all predominating influence of the past on the evolution of human beings, these ideas have shown us that to understand the present state of society and to gain an insight into its future one first has to study its past. There is an embryology of societies just as there is an embryology of animals, and, just as the naturalist today finds the explanation of living beings by studying the forms of their ancestors, the philosopher who wants to understand the genesis of our ideas, our institutions, and our beliefs first of all has to study their earlier forms. Viewed in this way, history, which could seem of little use as long as it limited itself to puerile enumerations of dynasties and battles, today acquires an immense topical importance. It becomes the most important of the sciences, because it is the synthesis of all the others." (*ibid.*, 7); "the formidable law of evolution which directs everything – gods, worlds, empires, and men..." (*ibid.*, 22). Le Bon's work is typical of the evolutionary history of man of which Wells' *Outline* (see the telling quotation from Ratzel which he uses as motto for his introduction) is one of the most recent good examples, and Van Loon's *Mankind* one of the most recent poor, Americanized ones. In our times this set belief in the subjection of the universe to rules and laws has disappeared. The sources are becoming more and more abundant but the discovery of a new grave of an Egyptian pharaoh now enjoys its greatest triumphs as journalistic sensation and humbug. In recent years the *Illustrated London News* has published a regular series of richly illustrated articles, from the hands of many experts, in which both museum possessions and recent archeological discoveries have been discussed. However, in them every trace of general trends, every set belief in 'evolution' has disappeared. What remains is a confusing multiplicity: Negro plastic art, Persian miniatures, Samoyedic ivory carvings, Japanese woodcuts, Hellenistic frescos, ancient Chinese jadework, Chaldean seals, northern European bronze objects. The same tendency repeats itself in other areas of civilization.

7 In strict opposition to the 'Linnaeic' categories of modern American abstract sociological theory and to Vierkandt's categories.

8 History, then, can 'teach', for example, about the development of demagogical *charisma*, about the margins of possibility for existence for a capitalistic industry the existence of which forms a guarantee for all of modern civilization, etc. But what is 'good', 'bad', 'progress', 'retrogression' in such phenomena is not for history to judge. There are valid only the personal opinions (the two of them of equal value) of a Mowrer and a Rosenberg.

9 See above, Chapter One, n. 93.

10 Troeltsch, *Probleme*, 704–705.

11 See Weber, "Agrarverhältnisse im Altertum", in *Sozialgeschichte*, 1–288; Hasebroek, *Trade*, and *Wirtschaftsgeschichte*; Meyer, *Hellenismus*; Rostovtzeff, *History*. *Cf.* also Weber, "Die sozialen Gründe des Untergangs der antiken Kultur", in *Sozialgeschichte*, 288–311; Neurath, *Wirtschaftsgeschichte*.

12 In *System*, and *China*; *cf. Wirtschaft* (see bibliography for parts translated).

13 Professor Schrieke's sketch for Sumatra, "Prolegomena" (a translation of which is to be included in the next volume projected in this series of books) remained unfinished. For his methodological starting point, an ethnological one, see "Prolegomena", 91–94.

14 His editions of Megasthenes, Arrian and the *Periplus*, Ktesias, Ptolemy, the accounts of Alexander the Great's expedition to India, and a collection of other accounts scattered in ancient writings (see bibliography). See also Rawlinson, *Intercourse*; Hirth, *China*; Marshall, *Mohenjo-Daro*.

15 Reinaud, *Relations*; Aboulféda, *Géographie*; Ferrand, *Relations*; Ibn Battuta, *Voyages*; Sulaiman, *Voyage*; Bozorg, *Livre*. Only the most important editions available in translation are mentioned here. Moslem geographical work cannot be separated from historiographic work proper: "In its forms of expression historical thought is completely merged with the fundamental aims of the cultural body of Islamic literature, which after all forms one large encyclopedia!" (Richter, *Geschichtsbild*, 23). See also Weil, *Geschichte*; Von Kremer, *Culturgeschichte*.

16 Hiuen, *Si-yu-ki*; Hoeï-li, *Histoire*; Fâ-hien, *Record*; I-Tsing, *Record*. See also Edkins, *Buddhism*; Davids, *India*.

17 See the lists appended to publications of the society, and the special centennial volume, Lynam, *Hakluyt*. See also Coote & Beazley, "Hakluyt".

18 His book *Cathay*, with its important "Preliminary Essay on the Intercourse between China and the Western Nations Previous to the Discovery of the Cape's Road". The medieval notices also include those of Moslems *en route* to Cathay.

19 See Chau Ju-kua, *Trade*. Of the works of the Moslem Chinese Ma Huan and Fei Hsien ('interpreter' secretaries, as Rouffaer calls them) in the train of the eunuch Cheng Ho, ambassador of the Ming emperor in the South Seas, the parts concerning Indonesia have been published by Groeneveld

in "Notes" (*cf.* Groeneveldt, "Jottings"; Rouffaer, "Malaka", 119 end of n. 1, 159 n. 2). See also Rockhill, "Notes"; Chang, *Trade*, 9, 17–18, 23, 25–26, 28–29, 30 n. 2, 42 n. 1, 43, 51 & n. 5, 94, 101–102. On the pilot books for shipping in Çola and Arabia see also Ferrand, *Empire*, 81 n. 4, 98 n. 2; Ferrand, "K'ouen-louen", 486, 489.

20 See Sprenger, *Postrouten*, xv n. 1, 1 n. 1; Le Strange, *Caliphate*, 11; Von Kremer, *Einnahmebudget*, 22.

21 See Danvers, *Portuguese*; Whiteway, *Power*; Rouffaer, "Tijdperk", "Malaka", and "Artikelen". There are also Portuguese works included in translation in the Hakluyt series. Dutch works have been published in the series "Werken der Linschoten Vereeniging" (Works of the Linschoten Society), and some of them (*e.g.* Van Linschoten's *Voyage*) have been issued in translation in the Hakluyt series.

22 See Rouffaer, "Tochten", 391; Sprenger, *Postrouten*, xviii-xix.

23 (Incorrect. The search dates from the eighteenth century and is a result of maintenance of the Biblical, monogenetic concept of creation and history as opposed to the new data furnished by the Jesuit mission then working in the Orient. See Engemann, *Voltaire*, 105 ff. [Note later added by the author.]) The hypotheses of Von Richthofen and De Groot regarding the original Asian society, the hypothesis of the Egyptian origin of Chinese civilization, etc. Characteristic of this spirit is Metchnikoff's interesting work *Fleuves*, in which, using the literary material of Müller's *Sacred Books of the East* series and the geographical work especially of Réclus, the author gives a schema for the origin and structure of the ancient *oikos* civilizations of the East, based upon the 'laws' of historical evolution. The influence of this book appears to be long-lasting – see *e.g.* H. Roland Holst's comments in *Kunst*, 42–43, (based on Müller and Lyer, *Die Phasen der Kultur* [Phases of Culture]). Metchnikoff's book was also a forerunner of the study of geopolitics.

24 *Cf.* Duyvendak, *Historie*, 30.

25 See Scherer, *Geschichte*; Noël, *Histoire*; and a recent work, Schaal, *Tauschhandel*. *Cf.* also Goetz, *Verkehrswege* – a work based upon Ratzel's *Anthropogeographie*, – and especially the introduction, "Zur Herstellung einer Wissenschaft der geographischen Entfernungen" (Toward Establishment of a Science of Geographical Distances).

26 Even the picture of land trade gives the 'evolution' concept a different direction, however – for two reasons. In the first place land trade – transport by wheel, and travel on foot or horseback as well – underwent practically no change for thousands of years, until steam power and the 'iron road' came in the nineteenth century (see Goetz, *Verkehrswege*, 323 ff., 474, 511, 518). In the second place, the image of 'evolution' is in this case separated from economic development in the narrower sense: the great road and post station systems (in the Persian Empire, the Roman Empire, Bactria, northern India, China) were not set up because of economic interests, but because of interests of

military strategy and bureaucratic administration on the part of governments. The forms in which such an organization are realized are to a large extent identical regardless of whether in the Thurn and Taxis post system of the sixteenth and seventeenth centuries, the post system in the caliphates at the time of Ibn Khurdadhbih (the ninth century), or the *cursus publicus* of the time of Emperor Augustus.

27 "... the following generations of peoples ... [achieved] the realization of what was their historical calling, though for a long time by them not recognized as such – to treat the regions of the earth as one dwelling that should render profit for all, by bringing the regions closer together, especially through better use of time and means of transportation" (Goetz, *Verkehrswege*, 138; see the 'laws' on 317, 349, 440 n. *, 516 n. *, 537 n. *). "The place where the merchant lived was then [in the times of Phoenician trading power] no more the one where the goods he dealt in were stored than it is in modern times; thus it is not necessary to consider the location of the Phoenician towns as the beginning of their trade routes, nor even as ports of transit" (*ibid.*, 114). One should imagine the difference between modern trade (fitted into the exchange system, so that a grain transport ship from the La Plata ports can be ordered from Rotterdam to go directly to Bergen) and Phoenician caravan trade, whether that of a royal caravan (*cf. I Kings* 10: 11, 22) or of a joint-stock company, going on adventure by land or by sea, travelling to the Eastern or Western markets.

28 Heichelheim, "Gesichtspunkte". The key thesis is on pp. 154–155: "As it could not be proved, scholars here justifiably stopped believing in an economic evolution of the world upward, for example in the Darwinian or the Marxist sense, or even in a recurrence in the past of present unique forms of life, as an essential dogma. Since then nearly all the attention of serious research in economic history, now limiting itself, has been centred on the scarcely fifteen hundred years old peculiar and unique development of a special historical structure which can be followed as a unity from its origins in the small area of western and central Europe at the time of the Germanic migrations up to the structure-transforming era of high and late capitalism in the nineteenth and twentieth centuries. Out of humanistic reverence scholars make excursions into the economic history of a second special structure, that of approximately two thousand years of classical Mediterranean civilization, without really daring to bring it in relationship to other structures. Economic history has left the approximately three thousand years of urban civilization in the ancient Orient largely to assyriologists and egyptologists, the immense time and space complexes of the first civilizations to the prehistorians, and Islamic culture to the arabists, although only with the aid of all those cultures do essential traits of the complex of the middle ages and modern times [in Europe] become understandable. Respectful circumlocutions have been made around India, China, even America, as well as around the so-called primitive

peoples. The scholars have with reason seen in all these autonomous and to a certain extent secluded special structures of life, but without reason they have disregarded the interconnections of economic forms and have not taken into account the fact that what there were, were variations of analogous basic economic formations which revealed themselves in an ever-new differentiation and thus formed links in the history of the world more important than all differences."

29 *Ibid.*, 154–159, 159 n. 7.

30 The term 'plough civilization' was introduced by Hahn (*Alter*), who saw its origins in Babylonia and defined its elements as 'breaking' of wild cattle, getting of milk, castration of bulls, a calendar based on a sexagesimal system, a seven-day week, the invention of the wheel, the use of cattle as beasts of burden, the plough, the dominant position of the male in agriculture, the growing exclusively of grain, true irrigated fields, lying not in broad patches but in long strips.

31 The concept of 'agrarian civilization', therefore, does not bring us one step closer to the situation of 'primitive economic man'. See Malinowski, *Argonauts*, x–xi (Frazer), 60–62, *cf.* 84–85, 96–97, 156–157, 166–168, 172–175, 282–288, 516.

32 See *Ordnung*, 20–26. For a criticism of the 'stages of civilization' theories by Sombart see *ibid.*, 6–14.

33 *E.g.* Le Bon's schema, illustrated in regard to India: "...in a single country, unusal in its size, its situation, its history, one can see all the steps of this [evolutionary] ladder of peoples within a short time. The country is India. Whoever has visited it, as we ourselves have done, from its retreats of savagery to its splendid cities, can say that he has traversed a hundred thousand years in time and has lived successively in all the periods of prehistory and history. Indeed in the middle of the impenetrable forests of the Amarkantak Plateau he will have been able to see the Kholar tribes, black-skinned with hideous faces and nearer to the ape than to man, living in caves, without habitations, government, laws, or families, and possessing no weapons except carved stone arrows; to the north, in the mountains of Assam, the Nazas and Khasis, whose special social system is matriarchal and who practice polyandry; to the south, on the Malabar Coast, the Nairs, who also live under a matriarchy, but who are handsome and intelligent and already occupy a higher step on the ladder; in the beautiful mountains of the Nilhiris, the Todas, a pastoral, polygynous, and polyandrous people whose political and social unit is the village; towards the centre, the Bhils, who have reached the level of clan formation; further, the Rajputana states, which represent the warring and feudal epoch; above them, the Islamic states; and finally, the civilized European master..." (*Civilisations*, 22).

34 On '*oikos* civilizations' see Weber, *Theory*, 212–213.

35 "The customs and habits, the forms of speech and thought, the insti-

tutions of state and society of the time ... were at work through all the Germanic, Semitic, and Mongol peoples of the old world who created urban civilizations on this basis up to our own times...; the pluriform agrarian civilizations of the world, ... even into the age of the machine, and even for urban complexes of culture, form the foundations which cannot be thought away, and in case of their disintegration everything is treatened" (Heichelheim, "Gesichtspunkte", 163, *cf.* 163–164, 167–168). Three illustrations from recent times may also be cited here. (1) The danger of the absorption of the revolution in the 'liberated' Russian agrarian civilization after 1917 – the danger has now been averted by the modernization of rural areas under the pressure of the Five Year Plans, and one of the largest complexes of agrarian civilization on earth is disappearing. (2) The danger that the Swaraj Movement in India can form for Indian urban civilization – if through active and passive resistance of the peasants the movement takes on more massive and radical forms under the pressure of agitation than Gandhi may intend, then nationalistic Indian society as well as the higher, and leading, colonial English society will be threatened (see Boeke, *Economie*, 25, and compare Romain Rolland's words: "This medieval conception is apt ... to clash with the volcanic forward march of the human mind..." [*Gandhi*, 42]). (3) The danger the Netherlands East Indies run in the constantly progressing illness of world economy – the so highly renowned power of the *desa* to resist means a drop back into natural economy (or at least to a very far from intensive money economy); it is once again the ancient agrarian civilization, the same as that into which the Western Roman Empire collapsed.

36 Heichelheim, "Gesichtspunkte", 166. See also *ibid.*, nn. 14–18, and for geographical delineation 159 n. 6. A few illustrative data on 'primitive' trade in the agrarian civilization of the Toraja lands are given in Van Vollenhoven, *Adatrecht*, I, 354–355, 360, 365–366, 370, II, 772. See also Weber, *System*, 84.

37 See Malinowski, *Argonauts*, Maps I, III, and V.

38 "The Kula is a form of exchange, of extensive, inter-tribal character; it is carried on by communities inhabiting a wide ring of islands, which form a closed circuit. ... Along this route, articles of two kinds, and these two kinds only, are constantly travelling in opposite directions. In the direction of the hands of the clock, moves constantly one of these kinds – long necklaces of red shell, called *soulava*... In the opposite direction moves the other kind – bracelets of white shell, called *mwali*... Each of these articles, as it travels in its own direction on the closed circuit, meets on its way articles of the other class, and is constantly being exchanged for them. Every movement of the Kula articles, every detail of the transactions is fixed and regulated by a set of traditional rules and conventions, and some acts of the Kula are accompanied by an elaborate magical ritual and public ceremonies. On every island and in every village, a more or less limited number of men take part in the Kula – that is to say, receive the goods, hold them for a short time, and then pass

them on. Therefore every man who is in the Kula, periodically though not regularly, receives one or several *mwali* ... or a *soulava* ... and then has to hand it to one of his partners, from whom he receives the opposite commodity in exchange. Thus no man ever keeps any of the articles for any length of time in his possession [*cf. ibid.*, 94]. One transaction does not finish the Kula relationship, the rule being 'once in the Kula, always in the Kula,' and a partnership between two men is a permanent and lifelong affair. Again, any given *mwali* or *soulava* may always be found travelling and changing hands and there is no question of its ever settling down, so that the principle 'once in the Kula, always in the Kula' applies also to the valuables themselves. The ceremonial exchange of the two articles is the main, the fundamental aspect of the Kula. But associated with it, and done under its cover, we find a great number of secondary activities and features. Thus, side by side with the ritual exchange of arm-shells and necklaces, the natives carry on ordinary trade, bartering from one island to another a great number of utilities, often unprocurable in the district to which they are imported and indispensable there. Further, there are other activities, preliminary to the Kula, or associated with it, such as the building of sea-going canoes for the expeditions, certain big forms of mortuary ceremonies, and preparatory taboos. The Kula is thus an extremely big and complex institution, both in its geographical extent, and in the manifoldness of its component pursuits. It wields together a considerable number of tribes, and it embraces a vast complex of activities, interconnected, and playing into one another, so as to form one organic whole... The Kula is not a surreptitious and precarious form of exchange. It is, quite on the contrary, rooted in myth, backed by traditional law, and surrounded with magical rites. All its main transactions are public and ceremonial, and carried out according to definite rules. It is not done on the spur of the moment, but happens periodically, at dates settled in advance, and it is carried on along definite trade routes, which must lead to fixed trysting places. Sociologically, though transacted between tribes differing in language, culture, and probably even in race, it is based on a fixed and permanent status, on a partnership which binds into couples some thousands of individuals. This partnership is a lifelong relationship, it implies various mutual duties and privileges, and constitutes a type of inter-tribal relationship on an enormous scale." (Malinowski, *Argonauts*, 81–85, *cf.* 176, 187–189, 352, 489 & 510: "... the Kula is a sociological mechanism of surpassing size and complexity, considering the level of culture on which we find it. ... A half ceremonial, half commercial exchange, it is carried out for its own sake, in fulfilment of a deep desire to possess.").

39 See Mannheim, *Ideology*, and *cf.* summary. Mannheim's starting point is not so much that of regular scholarly research as an outgrowth of the 'spiritual crisis' which along with – and for the most part separate from – the economic crisis is now holding sway over western European civilization, one

of the phases in the process of disintegration of modern capitalism, which in its full bloom has become the fate of the nineteenth and twentieth century.

40 "It is not the cold speculation of reason but the shadows created by the aspirations of man which have served as the basis for all political, religious, and social structures" (Le Bon, *Civilisations,* 809). "Older societies were not based on practicality and deliberation regarding it..." (Van Vollenhoven, *Adatrecht,* II, 770–771, *cf.* 772, 776, 789, 800, 803).

41 See especially the pages in Malinowski's work cited in note 31 above, as well as the whole of the introduction to the work.

42 Malinowski, *Argonauts,* 11, 69.

43 See *ibid.*, 10 and n. *.

44 See *ibid.*, xiv, 32, and Map IV.

45 See Weber, *Ethic,* n. 2 on p. 185.

46 See Malinowski, *Argonauts,* 37, 52, 62–63, 69, 154–156, 268, 297, 304, 402 n. *, 464–468.

47 "The economic uses and advantages derived from a canoe are not limited to the *toliwaga* [shipmaster, always a chief or a nobleman]. He, however, gets the lion's share. He has, of course, in all circumstances, the privilege of absolute priority in being included in the party. He also receives always by far the greatest proportion of Kula valuables, and other articles on every occasion. This, however, is in virtue of his general position as chief or headman and should perhaps not be included under this heading. But a very definite and individual advantage is that of being able to dispose of the canoe for hire, and of receiving the payment for it. The canoe can be, and often is, hired out from a headman, who at a given season has no intention of sailing, by another one, as a rule from a different district, who embarks on an expedition. The reason of this is, that the chief or headman who borrows, may at that time not be able to have his own canoe repaired, or construct another new one." (*Ibid.*, 119, see also 57, 91–92, 118–119, 122–123, 158, 197, 208–209, 228, 276, 278, 468, 472–473, 480, 500 n. *).

48 See the passage in the preceding note on shipowning and renting. It is almost impossible to separate Kula and 'ordinary' trade.

49 See Malinowski, *Argonauts,* 1–2, 28–29, 83, 99–101, 282–283, 362–363, 390, 476, 478, 480, 494, 499–500. A part of the Kula takes place overland, another part locally, in the village or the surroundings. The interinsular Kula connections with other peoples, however, are the most characteristic and the most important.

50 Trade must always be viewed within the whole of social and political organizational forms, not as an isolated category.

51 "The main attitude of a native to other, alien groups is that of hostility and mistrust. The fact that to a native every stranger is an enemy, is an ethnographic feature reported from all parts of the world. The Trobriander is not an exception in this respect, and beyond his own, narrow social horizon,

a wall of suspicion, misunderstanding and latent enmity divides him from even near neighbours. The Kula breaks it through at definite geographical points, and by means of special customary transactions. But, like everything extraordinary and exceptional, this waiving of the general taboo on strangers must be justified and bridged over by magic." (Malinowski, *Argonauts*, 345, *cf.* 85).

52 See the references given in n. 46 above.

53 See Malinowski, *Argonauts*, 118, 193, 317, 459, *cf.* 455, 457.

54 See *ibid.*, 469–471.

55 The trade goods: "sago, betel-nut, pig; also the various feathers, especially those of the cassowary and the red parrot; rattan-cane belts, plaited fibre belts; obsidian; fine sand for polishing axe blades; red ochre; pummice stone; and other products of the jungle and of the volcanic mountain ... ... armshells, the valuable axe blades, boars' tusks and imitations; ... wooden dishes, combs, lime pots, armlets, baskets, *wayugo* creeper [a very tough creeper used in lashing canoes], mussel shells and lime spatulae of ebony" (*ibid.*, 502).

56 On the westbound voyage there are at most twelve men per boat, old and young, Kula qualified and unqualified included (see *ibid.*, 197–227, letterpress to Plate Forty, 384); the boats for the eastbound voyage are larger (*ibid.*, 144, 496, 498–499). A trading expedition numbers a few score boats. Each one of the crew carried a 'private' cargo of only a half dozen kinds of merchandise with him (see *ibid.*, 363).

57 See *ibid.*, 55–56, 63–65, 67, 70, 76, 97, 147–148, 152, 160–161, 167, 169, 180, 409, 464–465.

58 Malinowski's research, thus, does not bring new information on the 'primitive economic situation'. His sketch of this society of 'savages' in Melanesia and New Guinea shows that there already there are such complicated forms of economic life in general, and trade in particular, that much of what the history of trade gives as 'later' periods of development in other regions of the world is already present. All of it arose autonomously. Work such as Malinowski's shows clearly how little the categories of a history of trade constructed with only the material of the Mediterranean and Near Eastern world and leaving the rest of the world as a periphery, a field for ethnology, can be applied generally, how much they distort the true picture.

59 See *ibid.*, 514–515.

60 See Huizinga, *Werken*, V, 19.

61 Soustelle, in his "Vie", has attempted to fit the Kula form, and other forms in the economic life of 'primitive' peoples, into the scheme of 'development' in economic history – not without doing violence to the facts. It seems to me an oversimplification when Chang points out as the only possible source of the trade between China and the lands in southern waters, "some sort of coastal trade [existing] between the present Kwantung province and eastern Annam or even more distant places lying south of it at the beginning

of or perhaps before our era" (*Trade*, 1), and "Such relations in their even cruder form must have existed from time immemorial, when some coastal towns or villages began to seek some sort of exchange or communication with their neighbours. In the course of time the routes for such intercourse gradually stretched out from their various centers, along the coasts till they joined each other and thus formed a continuous one." (*ibid.*, 3). The magical and ritual in its relationship to shipping and trade in western Europe is relegated to the field of folklore, not to that of economic history. Is it rightly so? As late as the middle ages, certainly, little of it had worn off. One recalls *e.g.* the Shrine of Our Lady in the Walcheren polder, an object of international pilgrimage for sailors (*cf.* also Weber, *Wirtschaft*, 541).

62 "The Mycenic civilization in the Greek motherland, at least in Tiryns and Mycene itself, presupposed a patrimonial soccage kingship of an Oriental sort, though of much smaller dimensions. The structures there, unequalled until classical times, would have been unthinkable without the application of soccage of subjects. On the eastern border of the area of Hellenic civilization at the time (Cyprus) there even seems to have existed an administration of completely the same sort as the Egyptian, which used its own system of writing for keeping accounts and rolls and thus must have been a patrimonial, bureaucratic store-house administration, while later, in classical times even, the administration in Athens was almost completely verbal, and without records. This soccage civilization, together with its system of writing, later vanished without a trace." (Weber, *Wirtschaft*, 553).

63 "The cities of the ancient world were in the view of their inhabitants – in practice certainly not without importance – first of all arbitrary associations and confederations of people – bound together some of them primarily by ties of blood, some of them, as probably the phratries, by military reasons – which in later divisions of the cities were schematized according to administrative views into ... confederations of aristocratic clans. The Hellenic *synoikismos* ... was based on a clan structure; in the *polis* of the classical world the individual, was a citizen, it is true, but originally after all only as a member of his clan ... and even democracy at first could not make a breach in the system that the citizenry consisted of clans (*gentes*) grouped into phratries which were in turn grouped into phyles, all of them purely personal ritual societies. Democracy could only try by indirect means to render these societies actually dominated by the intermarried aristocracy politically harmless. ... For a legitimate society had to find a basis in the traditional, ritually constructed forms of society – the clan, the society for defense (phratry), the political tribal society (phyle) – or it had to stimulate such a basis." (Weber, *Wirtschaft*, 531–534). On the periodization Aegean-Hellenic see Plantenga, "Boek". Writing on the last days of Cretan civilization, he states: "Then died in great distress a civilization which needs to be given as emphatic consideration as Egyptian and Babylonian, independently and for

its own sake. It was murdered during the migrations lumped together as the Dorian migrations; the Cretans must, with others, have belonged to the 'sea peoples' portrayed on the Abu Simbel reliefs as being destroyed by the fleet of Ramses III. When, in an age as far separated from that heyday as the period of Augustus Caesar is from that of Charlemagne, Greek art then gradually begins to develop, although 'the essentials of artistic tradition had been more completely destroyed than was the case between ancient times and the middle ages' [Rodenwaldt, *Kunst*, 20], Aegean civilization is suddenly no longer an independent culture, but belongs to the 'Greek world'." (Plantenga, "Boek", 85). Plantenga then writes that "'Aegean civilization stands on the eve of Greek history...' according to the author [of the book under review], but with the word 'eve' one does not think of a period several times as long as the 'day' of the art one actually wishes to treat, and of a quite different nature. There are also other points in the text which create a confusion of this sort, *e.g.* the mention of Crete as a bridge between Greece and the Orient. Crete did indeed perform such a function, but in an age when Cretan-Minoan art had already been completely destroyed and the new inhabitants, of another race, had to begin again from the very beginning. It is not the Vaphio chalaces with their unique animal reliefs which stand on the 'eve' of Hellas, but the fresco of Prinias, in which the extremely primitive, schematic riders are shorter than a horse's foot and their heads smaller than the hoof of the steed they sit astride.", (*Ibid.*, 85–86).

64 "The political and economic masters of the country, the landowners, the financiers of trade, and the creditors of the peasants, were *astoi*, urban families..." (Weber, *Wirtschaft*, 555, *cf.* 556, 559, 586).

65 See especially *I Kings* 9.

66 The Phoenician aristocratic city states did not develop any national regime (see Neurath, *Wirtschaftsgeschichte*, 16). Their great flourishing of trade and shipping under foreign domination is completely explainable (see *ibid.*, 25, 28–30). National economic categories are of extremely limited validity for those times.

67 In apposition to the course of events in the Orient, where kingship based on city domination developed into bureaucratic territorial and finally 'world' monarchy, the decisive turn in the social history of Hellas was the development of a martial urban particularism and, as a result, the characteristic type of the *polis*" (Weber, *Sozialgeschichte*, 102).

68 "The typical city of the ancient world, its ruling strata, its capitalism, the interests of its democracy are all in the first place politically and militarily oriented, and all the more so when the aspects typically classical come more to the fore. The overthrow of the [ruling] families and the transition to democracy were conditioned by the change in military technique. It was the hoplite army, self-equipped and disciplined, which bore the brunt of the struggle against the aristocracy, eliminating it first militarily and then

politically... After the creation of hoplite discipline the classical *polis* was ... a society of warriors." (Weber, *Wirtschaft*, 591, 596).

69 "Nowhere in the world has such political patronage been united in the hands of single families, formally purely private. Long before there were monarchies, there existed private ruling powers in other phases held by monarchs only." (*Ibid.*, 600, *cf.* 569, 591, 599).

70 "... that the Hellenic *polis* had to be and only it could be the basis of political organization was maintained by the victorious Macedonians also in the Orient, and thus they brought about the last great extension of that fundamental Hellenic institution" (Weber, *Sozialgeschichte*, 154).

71 See *ibid.*, 83.

72 *Acts* 19: 35–40. See also Meyer, *Schriften*, 164–165.

73 The agrarian civilizations were acquainted with *commenda*. On Java, for example, in the form of the 'peddling contract' (as Van Vollenhoven terms it; in the legal terminology of L. W. C. van den Berg it is the 'native commission contract') by which goods were given to a trader for him to peddle, under the obligation within a certain time either to return and pay the price agreed upon (what more the pedlar had received was for himself), to take the goods back, or – so it seems – part one and part the other (Van Vollenhoven, *Adatrecht*, I, 636–637). It is true there is not (yet) any evidence for the antiquity of this Javanese legal institution, and with it as a proposition one moves into the field of conjectural and hypothetical history so sharply criticized by Van Vollenhoven (*ibid.*, II, 763–764). On the other hand, it may be argued in defense that the institution fits in all its elements into the simple trade forms of an agrarian civilization, that as a type it fits into the series of forms of 'urban' trade known in history, and that it is not being set into an evolutionary schema but given as a characteristic institution in a certain form of civilization.

74 See Weber, *Sozialgeschichte*, 57 ff. Monetary exchange was in no sense a requirement for such trade (*cf.* also *ibid.*, 108–109).

75 The famous Phoenician trade and the early Arab caravan trade also took place in these forms.

76 "The economic quality of the patriciate was thus fluid, and it is only possible to determine the point toward which it gravitated. That point was *rentier*-ship. It should be stressed again and again that the economic reason why the [controlling] families had established themselves in the towns was to be found in the chance for making profit there, and that in any case that was the source the exploitation of which led to the economic power of the urban families. Neither the *eupatride* and patrician of ancient times nor the patrician of the middle ages was a trader, not even a merchant, if one applies the modern concept of an entrepreneur directing an office. Certainly he not infrequently took part in enterprises, but then as shipowner, giver of *commenda* or bottomry, lender at sea risk, leaving the actual work of the voyage, the handling of enterprises, to others, and himself sharing only in the risk and

the profit, though under [special] circumstances also taking part in the intellectual direction of enterprises as an occasional trader. All the important commercial forms of the early ancient period as well as those of the early middle ages, and especially *commenda* and bottomry, were attuned to the existence of such moneylenders, who invested their property only in concrete individual enterprises – many of them, in order to spread the risk – each one of which was settled separately. Of course this is not meant to deny that there existed every imaginable transitional stage in between the patriciate proper and personal trade proper. The travelling trader who received money from capitalists on *commenda* for occasional enterprises could become the director of a large firm operating with *commenda* capital and have factors working for him abroad. Money exchange and banking activities, but also shipping and wholesale trade, could easily be carried on for the account of a patrician who himself lived as a gentleman. And the transition between a capitalist constantly active as an entrepreneur and a person who capitalized on his wealth, otherwise lying fallow, by investing in *commenda*, was by nature also fluid. This is certainly a very important and characteristic point in development. But it is primarily a result of development." (Weber, *Wirtschaft*, 560).

77 Free trades were to be found alongside trades operated by slaves working on their own (*apophora*-bound slaves). Freedmen formed the typically 'bourgeois' groups, the groups pursuing a strictly peaceful economy; they had no rights politically (*cf.* Weber, *Wirtschaft*, 529, 585–587, 594–596, *Sozialgeschichte*, 256–257).

78 "In classical times capitalism was politically oriented to deliveries to the state, state building and state armament, state credit..., expansion by the state and booty in slaves, land, obligations to pay tribute, and privileges for acquisition of and investiture with land and soil, and trade on and deliveries for the subjugated towns. Classical democracy was politically oriented in the same way – the farmers, as long as they remained the core of the hoplite armies, were interested in acquisition of land for colonization purposes, by means of war. The urban lesser bourgeoisie, however, was interested in rents directly and indirectly coming from the pockets of the dependent communities, in buildings erected by the state, in sums for theatre and jury, for distributions of grain, and other things, offered by the state from the pockets of the subjects. The hoplite army consisting mainly of rural landowners would never have allowed the rise of a gild policy of the medieval sort..., if for no other reason than because of its consumer's interest in cheap provisions, and the sovereign *demos* of later Hellenic times, influenced by people with typically urban interests, was evidently no longer interested in such a policy, and in any case probably had no possibility of realizing it." (Weber, *Wirtschaft*, 587–588).

79 "For ancient man the exclusion of the entrepreneurial group from the [controlling] families was completely natural. Not by any means that *e.g.* the

body of Roman senators did not include any 'capitalists'; that was not at all where the opposition lay. The old patriciate of early classical times, especially in Rome, was ... active to the utmost degree as 'capitalists', as moneylenders to farmers, the same as the later senatorial families to political subjects. To become entrepreneur was the only thing forbidden by class etiquette (and sometimes embodied in the law, though its strictness might vary) for what were considered as really eminent families ... in the cities throughout the ancient world. Looking at the practice one sees that 'lust for gain' as a psychological motive was by no means prohibited. The Roman *noblesse de robe*... [was] on the average certainly as possessed of the *auri sacra fames* as any class in history. But what was prohibited was the rational, professional, in this special sense bourgeois, form of profit-making activity, that of working systematically for profit." (*Ibid.*, 560).

80 Goetz's representation of the Mediterranean area at the time of the Roman Empire as an "immense free trade area" in which the law of Rhodes was the general commercial law and "the uniformity of imperial coins everywhere [secured] the possibility of real and rapid business transactions" is too modern and therefore incorrect (*Verkehrswege*, 452, 461, 512).

81 "Let us imagine that coal, iron, and all other minerals, all branches of metallurgy, besides that alcohol, sugar, tobacco, matches, and if possible in general all mass products which are nowadays already to a large extent cartelized were taken over by enterprises ... either directly or *de facto* state-controlled; [let us imagine moreover that] the crownlands and entails and the state-controlled leased lands were multiplied and the Kanitz proposal [of 1894 – see *ibid.*, 290] were carried through consistently; state-controlled workshops and consumers' unions catering to the needs of the army and officials, inland shipping bound to state towing, ocean-going shipping controlled by the state, all railroads, etc. nationalized, moreover *e.g.* cotton imports regulated by international agreements and state controlled, and all these enterprises directed under bureaucratic planning, trade unions 'controlled' by the state, everything else taxable, regulated by innumerable permits of academic and other sorts, the type of peaceful *rentier* made general. Then, under a military, dynastic regime, the state of affairs of the later imperial period would be reached, but on a more perfect basis technologically." (Weber, *Sozialgeschichte* 277–278; *cf.* Charlesworth, *Trade-Routes*, 236–237).

82 "The 'publicans', small craftsmen, and small tradesmen were the bases of money economy in the Orient and the Hellenic world, and it was precisely with the increasing political and economic stability in the west and the contemporaneous regression in capital accumulation that they also finally won the field there" (Weber, *Sozialgeschichte*, 32). There cannot have been any other basis for the Byzantine Empire and its successors the caliphates (*cf. ibid.*, 274).

83 In Rostovtzeff, *History*; Bilabel, *Geschichte*; Becker, "Grundlinien". See also Le Bon, *Arabes*, 212, 401. For Mesopotamia *cf.* Weber's remark: "The continuity of traditional Babylonian economic conditions, which were as little disturbed in their singularity by the Seleucid regime as by the Persians, was only limited by the Parthian regime, which in spite of Hellenistic traits was still a specifically barbaric regime, but as a whole it was preserved without any fundamental change up to the Islamic period" (*Sozialgeschichte*, 186).

84 See Weber, *Sozialgeschichte*, 146; Charlesworth, *Trade-Routes*, 238.

85 "But then, too, most such 'enterprises' remained limited to a maximum of a few dozen workers. The 'working capital' required for a 'factory' was lacking." (Weber, *Sozialgeschichte*, 21, *cf.* also 9, 16–17, 178, 267, 271).

86 "The sale of manufactured products, at least their sale abroad, [had] far too much the character of occasional sale, dependent on innumerable political peripateiae, but most of all, to a degree occurring only rarely in the same way since the late middle ages, dependent on the fluctuations in grain prices; the latitude in the ancient world left over for the masses – and it is their needs that are cared for by modern capitalism – beyond expenses for absolute essentials, their purchasing power for craft products, remained so limited and unstable that no socially powerful gild craft could exist on such a narrow basis, let alone big 'home industries' and even 'factories'" (*ibid.*, 269).

87 See *ibid.*, 10, 16, 33, 59–60, 267, 268 n. 1.

88 *Nahum* 3: 16.

89 See Neurath, *Wirtschaftsgeschichte*, 12, 28, 30, 40, 70 (consular representation), 78. What *Numbers* 20: 17–20 states regarding safe-conduct for throughgoing travellers and caravans was still to be found in Hadramaut in 1931 (see Van der Meulen & Von Wissman, *Hadramaut*, 20–21, 32, 36).

90 *I Kings* 20: 34.

91 According to Demosthenes, Athenian grain imports from the Black Sea region in 355 B.C. amounted to 400,000 *medimnoi*, *i.e.* 575,000 bushels; the wheat and barley yield in Zeeland in 1930 amounted to 2,323,000 bushels. The wheat and barley yield in Attica in the years 318 to 315 B.C. averaged 400,000 *medimnoi*, on around 35,200 acres of sowing-land; the Zeeland wheat yield in 1930, 1,488,000 bushels, was harvested from 34,750 acres of land. The grain shipped from Alexandria in the time of the Roman Empire amounted to 48,000 bushels per year, and made up a third of the total amount used in Rome. The 1930 wheat and barley yield of the provinces Groningen and Zeeland together amounted to approximately 3,490,000 + 2,323,000 = 5,813,000 bushels. (Adapted from figures given in Weber, *Sozialgeschichte*, 150, *cf.* 137 n. 1: figures on Greece; Kötschke, *Wirtschaftsgeschichte*, 34 n. 1: shipments from Egypt; *Verslag*, Table D [Crop Yields]: figures on the Netherlands; Goetz, *Verkehrswege*, 438: consumption in Rome.)

"Whoever got the 'key to land and sea', Alexandria, into his hands could with a small amount of troops hold out against armies and create famine throughout Italy" (Neurath, *Wirtschaftsgeschichte*, 78; *cf.* Weber, *Wirtschaft*, 590, and *Sozialgeschichte*, 273).

92 Weber, *Sozialgeschichte*, 292–293; *cf.* Charlesworth, *Trade-Routes*, 237–238. (See Weber, *Ethic*, 17–25; *History*, 352–364).

93 See Marshall, *Mohenjo-Daro*. *Cf.* Weber's statement: "Money economy developed in India at about the time of the rise of Hellenism in Occidental trade. Oversea and caravan trade with Babylon and later with Egypt existed far earlier. In India, as in Babylon, the procurement of coined money, that is to say in some way signed, later stamped or molded metal blocks of a certain weight remained at first a private affair of the great trader families with a trusted coinage. ...The rulers of the Maurya-Dynasty, including Ashoka, did not yet mint coins of their own. The influx of precious metals from Greece and Rome stimulated the great kings of the early Christian centuries to do so while the old private coins and money ersatz long remained in circulation. In India, as in Babylon, the lack of a state coinage did not hinder the rise of capitalistic trade and political capitalism. From around the seventh century B.C. for a thousand year period capitalism developed and expanded." (*System*, 93, *cf.* 31).

94 Goetz, *Verkehrswege*, 46–47.

95 Mookerji calls it "by far the most important event in the world's history" (*Shipping*, 2)!

96 See Masson-Oursel, *Inde*, 21, 29, 243, 246. McCrindle writes: "The Indians themselves did not write history. They produced, no doubt, a literature both voluminous and varied, and containing works which rank as masterpieces in various departments of Philosophy, Poetry and Science, but within its vast range history is conspicuous by its absence. Their learned men were Brahmans whose modes and habits of thought almost necessarily incapacitated them for the task of historical composition. Absorbed in devout meditation on the Divine Nature or in profound speculation on the insoluble mystery of existence, they regarded with indifference or contempt the concerns of this transitory world which they accounted as unreal, as a scene of illusion, or to use their own expression, as Maya. Hence, they allowed events, even those of the greatest public moment, to pass unrecorded, and so to perish from memory. With regard for instance, to such a memorable episode in the national history as the Macedonian Invasion, scarcely an allusion can be traced in Sanskrit writings. So, too, the existence of a line of Graeco-Bactrian kings ... is a fact that remained unknown until brought to light by modern researches. We are, again, left still in darkness as to the origin and progress of that great revolution by which the Brahmans succeeded not only in overthrowing Buddhism, which had been for centuries the state religion, but even in all but completely extirpating it from the land of its

birth. These, and other instances that might be cited, let us see that so far as the native literature is concerned, the ancient history of India would have remained for ever shrouded in all but impenetrable darkness." (*India*, xii). This is perhaps an oversimplification, but the heart of the matter is that the peculiar character of the Brahmanic priesthood as well as, and at the same time through, its position as the most important element of the class of higher officials brought the 'unhistorical' character of early Indian history, just as the Chinese class of *literati*, as the top bureaucracy of the empire, set the stamp of its humanistic, historical culture on the Chinese tradition. For India, *cf.* also Weber, *System*, 42, 49–50, 72–73, 75, 122, 125, 127; *Religionssoziologie*, II, 318, 353, 359, 364–365; *Wirtschaft*, 239.

97 "The Vedic hero is a castle-dwelling, charioteering, warrior-king with a following in the Homeric manner and with a similar accompaniment of predominantly cattle-breeding yeomen..." (Weber, *System*, 46; *cf.* 71, 77, 83, 124–126); "The ancient Kshatriyas of about the time of Buddha ... were a highly educated estate of urban and castled noble gentes, comparable, in this regard, to the knighthood of Provence in the early Middle Ages" (*ibid.*, 78).

98 See *ibid.*, 79–81, 83, 90, 125; *Religionssoziologie*, II, 253. Megasthenes' mention of royal craftsmen for shipbuilding (Mookerji, *Shipping*, 102) is compared by Weber with the *centuria fabrum* of the Roman aristocratic period (*System*, 99), and the liturgical gild of *navicularii* in the later imperial period (*Wirtschaft*, 558 & 586, and *History*, 136–137).

99 Organization following the example of the Persian Achaemenid Empire has been mentioned as a possibility, but it seems to me that such a thing must be considered out of the question, as being conceived in too modern terms. The bureaucratic organization, as technical 'know-how', was completely dependent on individuals, and if this was true already of 'know-how' in crafts it was all the more so for the bureaucratic 'know-how' of the hierarchical officialdom, which involved not only the organization of the population, but also statistical and other documentary clerical work. What is possible in modern times – *e.g.* in 'primitive' Africa constructing and organizing a railroad system all of which has been imported, or setting up in Europe a complete system of production and sales for American automobiles – was completely impossible in those times. For such things all technical 'know-how' was on the one hand too exclusive, on the other too empirical.

100 Hornell, "Design", especially 226–235, and "Canoes".

101 *Sozialgeschichte*, 35.

102 *Cf.* Weber, *Wirtschaft*, 527, 537.

103 *Cf.* Malinowski, *Argonauts*, 85.

104 The Greek Diodorus makes the interesting comment that in the Patala region the regime was the same as in Sparta – two kings and a senate. The retinues of 'trusty lieges' in Coromandel and Malabar, sharing a common

table with their prince and voluntarily following him even into death, also reveal characteristics typical of an aristocratic regime (see Polo, *Book*, II, 347 n. 5; *cf.* also Elliot on the Pallawas in Mookerji, *Shipping*, 51–52). As such aristocratic regimes are encountered in similar forms under similar circumstances as far east as the farthest reaches of Indonesia, it seems to me every idea of influence from the ancient Western world has to be set aside – such forms arose autonomously.

105 The age-old flow of precious metals to India is well known. Pliny's statement that twenty-five million *sestertia* were drained out of the Roman Empire each year is often quoted (see Weber, *History*, 353; Noël, *Histoire*, I, 54; Mookerji says a hundred million: *Shipping*, 84; Moreland, *Akbar*, 283). That flow of metals took place chiefly because of and through sea trade. Thus the coastal ports attracted the lion's share.

106 *Cf.* Weber, *Wirtschaft*, 558.

107 The Roman settlement in Muziris possessed a temple, one typical for merchants, devoted to Fortune and to Augustus (W. A. Smith in Mookerji, *Shipping*, 129; Charlesworth, *Trade-Routes*, 235). The trading colony of the Greeks in Naucratis and the one of the Syrians in Ostia also lay gathered around a sanctuary (Neurath, *Wirtschaftsgeschichte*, 78, *cf.* 85). Compare Unger, *Middelburg*, 17 on the chapel of the Flemish, Brabanders, and Zeelanders in La Rochelle in the fifteenth century.

108 *Commenda* and bottomry are reported in the *Manava Dharmaçastra* (see Mookerji, *Shipping*, 60–61; *cf.* Weber, *System*, 31, 65–66, 92 and n. 42). The explanation of the regulations Mookerji provides is too modern, however: he misunderstands the nature of such trade and shipping completely in taking the concept of 'national shipping' as a starting point (*Shipping*, 5, 8) and seeing its relation to trade as "the existence and development of a national shipping, feeding and supporting a national commerce" (*ibid.*, 53, *cf.* 43, 256). Such a point of view is basically incorrect. Take the situation in Bantam in 1596: "The merchants who are wealthy in general stay at home, then when some ships are ready to leave they give those going with them a sum of money to be repaid doubly, [the amount] more or less according to the length of the voyages, of which they make an obligation, and if the voyage is prosperously completed then the giver is paid according to the contract, and if the drawer cannot pay the money because of some misfortune then he must give his wife and children in pledge for the whole time until the debt is paid, unless the ship be wrecked – then the former loses the money he lent" (Rouffaer & IJzerman, *Schipvaart*, I, 120; *cf.* Colenbrander, *Coen*, V, 48, 124; for *commenda* in Macassar in 1627 see Tiele & Heeres, *Bouwstoffen*, II, 113). The elements were – on the one hand the merchant, the 'nobleman' of *Luke* 19: 12–13, investing capital intermittently; on the other the pedlar, the 'travelling salesman'; and a great distance between the two groups socially (ruthless debt laws, with peonage for the debtor if he remained in default: *cf.* Kohler,

Commenda, 14). As regards this principal form of trade, the picture in Indonesia in the sixteenth and seventeenth centuries is quite the same as that in the ancient world, the Byzantine and Islamic cultural sphere, and the western European middle ages.

109 Moreland, whose economic thought follows typically liberalist lines (see *Akbar*, 82, 85, 93–94, 160, 166, 168, 174, 227, 243, 279, 282, *Aurangzeb*, 188, 302 ff.), also notes the "comparative insignificance of the middle classes" (*Akbar*, 26–27) – the middle classes, the palladium of nineteenth-century capitalism and classical economic theory.

110 "Gibbon's mordant aphorism that 'the objects of oriental trade were splendid and trifling' is in substance as applicable to the sixteenth as to the second century of our era" (Moreland, *Akbar*, 196).

111 *Cf.* also Pegolotti's statement in Yule, *Cathay*, I, 172.

112 Linschoten, *Voyage*, I, xxvi.

113 "...merchants from Gujarat had their agencies in all the chief commercial centres of the East, at Malacca alone there lived a thousand, and three to four thousand others were constantly *en route* between the two places" (Schrieke, "Prolegomena", 103). *I.e.*, on the one hand the eminent tradesmen of the Gujarati towns, merchants who perhaps had a system of factors carrying on trade overseas (*cf.* De Jonge, *Opkomst*, VII, 3). Patricians such as the 'great Moors' of Surat, the banians of Cambay, the prominent foreigners, especially Persians. Patricians such as the *shahbandar* of Surat Kojah Hassan Ali, chief of the town patriciate – the regents of Surat ("The *shahbandar* and the merchants negotiating at sea", as a seventeenth-century document reads: Colenbrander, *Coen*, I, 206, *cf.* 239, 290), the term regents in this case being a concept equivalent to that in seventeenth and eighteenth-century Holland and Zeeland (for the term, often used there for indicating other groups, *cf.* also *ibid.*, I, 765, II, 111, 177, 200, 238, 305, 355, 358, 383, 504, 550, 593, III, 142, 164, 264, 304, 379, IV, 389, V, 69, 72, 106) – who farmed the city government for twenty *lakh mamudi*, or sixty thousand pounds per year, and from whom the English and Dutch companies borrowed sums in tens of thousands in order to procure money for trade (*ibid.*, I, 91, V, 21–22, 153, 346, 516, 519, 584, 589–590, 596, 598, 738, 770). Patricians such as the Hindu merchant Virji Vora in Surat, the Malaya family in Pulicat (Terpstra, *Westerkwartieren*, 32, 40, 181–182, 204–206, 212–213, 229, 238, 281; Moreland, *Aurangzeb*, 147, 153–156; *cf.* Colenbrander, *Coen*, V, 66), and the merchants of Masulipatnam, who could supply cotton cloth a thousand *corges* at a time (while the Company's total sale in Indonesia in 1619 was a little over three thousand *corges*: *cf.* De Jonge, *Opkomst*, III, 151; Rouffaer & Juynboll, *Batik-kunst*, I, Appendix Three; Colenbrander, *Coen*, I, 580–583). On the other hand the masses of travelling pedlars, "...travellers that come thether [to Malacca] to trafficke with them, and such as with their ships will sayle to China, Moluca, or other places, or

that come from thence..." (Linschoten, *Voyage*, I, 104–105) in the same way as the "thousand 'Frankish' merchants" in Alexandria in 1213 (Schrieke, "Prolegomena", 97) – the fifteen hundred Javanese traders involved in the purchase of spices on Banda, each arriving by ship with his own 'small cargo' (*ibid.*, 123, *cf.* 138), and the Malay traders established "by many thousands" in Macassar in 1625 (*ibid.*, 183). Also typical for the character of craft trade is the brokerage system in the Asian ports known from the tales of *The Thousand and One Nights* as well as from later accounts (see *e.g.* Terpstra, *Westerkwartieren*, 181–182, 214, 224, 225, 253, 286; Colenbrander, *Coen*, V, 592, 755; De Jonge, *Opkomst*, III, 213).

114 See Mookerji, *Shipping*, 103–104, 104 n. 1 (McCrindle), 127–129 (following V. A. Smith); Weber, *System*, n. 28 on p. 103, 93, 96; *cf.* Noël, *Histoire*, I, 63–64.

115 Kanakasabhai, *Tamils*.

116 "The cities lost their initial character as mere princely fortifications (pura, nagara). They acquired – particularly on the sea coasts – a section which in its structure was related to the ancient seat of the prince and its form, like the *mercato* in Italy, the economic market. It was the place where buying and selling occurred comparable to the *Piazza* (*del campo della signoria*), the place at which public summons and tournaments were held. Evidence of these functions is clearly retained in the layout by dual squares in the present day Siena behind the *Palazzo Publicco*, and in the dual form of the castle (kasbah) and the market (bazar) in Islamic cities ... Rich nobles moved into the cities to consume their rents. According to one chronicle only the owners of one kror equalling 100 lakhas (the measuring unit for the great prebends according to the number of village rents they contained) was permitted to dwell in the city. Alongside rent there now appeared the possibility of accumulation of wealth through trade." (Weber, *System*, 93–94). See *e.g.* the plan given by Rouffaer of the way early Jambi was built (Rouffaer "Malaka", 14, *cf.* 16 n. 1, 580) – the *kraton* on a higher arm of land on the south bank, the mosque in the quarter of town to the west, the "*kampong* of the *priyayis*" in the quarter to the east, the trading quarters of the Chinese, Arabs, and 'foreign Indonesians' on the south bank.

117 "Arab merchants" as they are called in Rouffaer, "Portugeezen", 454.

118 See Charlesworth, *Trade-Routes*.

119 See Goetz, *Verkehrswege*, 280, 343 ff., 447 ff.; *cf.* Stüwe, *Handelszüge*, 152–153.

120 See Neurath, *Wirtschaftsgeschichte*, 26–27, *cf.* 73.

121 See Przeworski, "Handelsbeziehungen"; *cf.* Jacob, *Einfluß*, 2–5 & 5 n. 1.

122 See Goetz, *Verkehrswege*, 300 ff., 399–401, *cf.* 458.

123 See Neurath, *Wirtschaftsgeschichte*, 49.

124 See also the data from Strabo in Goetz, *Verkehrswege*, 478.

125 Greek was at that time the trading language in the Indian ports (Hirth, *China*, 11–12).

126 Private trade, trade in transit, shipping and freight services. At the time of Augustus the empire acted as the conqueror at sea, the Roman fleet cleaning the Red Sea of pirates and destroying Aden (see Goetz, *Verkehrswege*, 434 n. *, 435).

127 "The expenditure on them [*i.e.*, the buildings of Palmyra] was made possible by the lucrativeness of a well-organized caravan trade carried on by established companies under the direction of distinguished and magisterial personalities. The independent customs regulation administration, which the community has retained control of, also contributed not a little to the fact that that commercial republic governed by a Greek intelligentsia could make such a victorious bid to surpass other oasis towns." (Goetz, *Verkehrswege*, 417, *cf.* 459–460).

128 See Noël, *Histoire*, I, 65–66, 114, 155,

129 Goetz, *Verkehrswege*, 479–484; Krom, *Geschiedenis*, 42, 65.

130 Thus it is impossible to accept Blink's "Roman pedlars" (Brugmans, *Leven*, I, 272, *cf.* 271).

131 "...international trade in which foreigners took a preponderant if not exclusive part..." (Pirenne, *Mahomet*, 82).

132 Weber, *Sozialgeschichte*, 176–177. In Graßhoff's study *Wechselrecht*, the older historical element is practically completely ignored (see 34–35, 35 n. 1, 61–62, 67, 78 there). His arguments regarding the development of the Arab bill of exchange do not seem very strong to me. And one should not make Moslem equivalent to Arab. How Graßhoff can furthermore say that "The development of Arab law on bills of exchange in the heyday of Arab trade beginning in the eighth century [was] far from every foreign influence..." is not clear to me. After all, there was a strong intermingling and 'internationality' in all the economic and political administrative life of the caliphates. See Fischel, *Jews*, 17–25; *cf.* Huizinga, *Werken*, VII, 175. An accurate preliminary definition of terms is given by Mieli, see the review by Fokker, 310 n. 1.

133 Goetz's argument that the Christianization of Europe was "an important basis for the formation of contacts from people to people ... as the development of such contracts is by no means only dependent on technological and commercial 'know-how', but also on moral factors of the parties involved..." (*Verkehrswege*, 617) is certainly incorrect.

134 Weber, *Sozialgeschichte*, 309; Sombart, *Kapitalismus*, I, Part One, 95–96, 117–120; De Goeje, "Handelsverkeer", 247, 250–252, 256–257, 259, and especially 249, on the sea trade on Sicily and Britain carried on by the archbishop of Alexandria. (A fine account of the nature of this trade is given in Scott's *Ivanhoe*, Chapters Five and Ten; *cf.* also Goetz, *Verkehrswege*, 460.) De Goeje's representation of the Jewish 'trade monopoly' in the Ommayid era

("Handelsverkeer", 253–254, 258) is less clear to me; Massignon's "Islam" gives a different impression. On *commenda* in Moslem trade see Kohler, *Commenda*, 3, 6 & n. 2, 7, 9, 14–16; Graßhoff, *Wechselrecht*, 23–24, 29.

135 See De Goeje, "Handelsverkeer", 250; Brentano, "Volkswirtschaft", *passim*. The 'foreigners' trade' on Byzantium is familiar in the history of medieval European trade through the colonial exploitation carried on by Italian cities. The political martial element in the situation was new; the trade forms were the same as of old (*cf.* Graßhoff, *Wechselrecht*, 69 n. 2).

136 See Weber, *Wirtschaft*, 526–528.

137 See Becker, "Grundlinien", 209–210, 213, and "Steuerpacht", 83, *cf.* 85–86. "... the Arabs [knew but] little about public administration techniques and consequently they remained for more than a century dependent on the native taxation officials..." ("Steuerpacht", 83; *cf.*, on the Sudan, Frobenius, *Kulturgeschichte*, 15). As a result of the nature of bureaucratic machinery, positions were held by all sorts of people: Nestorian monks as officials (see Yule, *Cathay*, I, 103), Jewish publicans (see the story of Aladdin, the 650th of *The Thousand and One Nights*), and court bankers (see Massignon, "Islam"; on Jewish activities in general see Fischel, *Jews*).

138 See Weber, *Sozialgeschichte*, 189.

139 See the farming contract of the vizier Hamid Ibn Abbas (Von Kremer, *Einnahmebudget*, 14–15, *cf.* 65) and the speculations of General, later Sultan, Ahmed Ibn Tulun (Becker, "Grundlinien", 216).

140 See Massignon, "Islam", 3; Becker, "Grundlinien", 218–219.

141 See Massignon, "Islam", *passim*.

142 See Becker, "Steuerpacht", 83; Graßhoff, *Wechselrecht*, 9 n. 1, 68 n. 2.

143 Was there a difference between the two? "The Saracens ... were, then, culturally [so] much superior to the decadent Byzantines that in contrast to Byzantium in that time they represented progress and civilization, while the degenerate Eastern Romans already carried the seeds of dissolution within them..." (Von Kremer, *Culturgeschichte*, I, 225–226).

144 The annual proceeds in money from taxation in the time of the caliphate of Harun al Rashid amounted to five hundred thirty million silver *dirhem*, thus at least five times as much as the Byzantine state income and many times as much as that of any European state (Kötschke, *Wirtschaftsgeschichte*, 489). Le Bon fixes the amount of annual income of the caliphate as two hundred million francs, thus eight million pounds (*Arabes*, 161). According to Massignon's calculations, the amount of the budget for the year 918–919 (the Moslem year 306) ran to 14,829,188 gold *dinars*, thus a thousand million francs, or once again eight million pounds ("Islam", 5 n. 1; *cf.* Von Kremer, *Einnahmebudget*, 23, 38, 41). The annual income of the present state of Iraq, a humble and distant descendant of the Moslem state, however, amounted to as much as fifty-nine million rupees, or nearly four million pounds, for 1927–1928 (*Annuaire statistique de la Société des Nations 1932–1933*). From that

can be seen the comparative lack of intensity of the money economy of the caliphate. And that money economy is supposed to have been one of the most, if not *the* most, highly developed of the time.

145 See Von Kremer, *Culturgeschichte*, I, 265–266.

146 Islam, as the official religion, held the leading position. Moslem law was superimposed on indigenous local and national law; application depended on the political regime. The imperial law of the colonial Roman government was superimposed on national law in the same way (see Van Vollenhoven, *Adatrecht*, III, 293; *Acts* 18: 12 ff.).

147 *I.e.* the members of the central Arabian urban patriciate with their followers, mobilized as warriors of the faith (see Becker, "Grundlinien", 209, 213; Weber, *Wirtschaft*, 253, 270–271, 357–358).

148 See Weber, *Wirtschaft*, 293.

149 See De Goeje, "Handelsverkeer", 266, 268–269; Schrieke, "Prolegomena", 96.

150 See Massignon, "Islam", 7–8.

151 See Stöckle, "Zünfte".

152 See Weber, *Wirtschaft*, 514–601.

153 See *ibid.*, 579.

154 See *ibid.*, 575.

155 Max Weber collected material on the subject, but did not publish it, the work being cut off by his untimely death (see Marianne Weber in Weber, *Religionssoziologie*, III, v).

156 See Weber, *Wirtschaft*, 311–312, 328–330, 336, 339, 350, 360; *cf.* Bouman, "Beschouwingen", 181 ff.

157 See what Stüwe reports as an example of 'factory industry' in Moslem Egypt (*Handelszüge*, 149). Practically every city in the Moslem trading area was acquainted with 'export industry' (*cf.* De Vrankrijker, "Textielindustrie", 158), but it was always a relatively small urban complex of trade or manufactures that was involved, whether there were crafts under free masters, a putting-out industry of the urban patriciate and rich merchant groups, or a free or unfree *ergasterion* owned by the last-named groups. All 'industrial technique' was empirical, that is to say, bound to individuals: colonies of craftsmen brought the art of silk-making to southern Europe (see Rouffaer & Juynboll, *Batik-kunst*, I, 499; Lieber, *Weltwirtschaft*, 40 n. 2: "mass migration of silkworkers to Persia" from Syria; Wiskerke, *Afschaffing*, 29–31: Turgot's measures for the abolition of the French gilds in the royal edict of 12 March, 1776) and the art of glass-blowing to Venice (Le Bon, *Arabes*, 318, 560–561); the art of paper-making was carried to the caliphates – first to Samarkand, later to Baghdad – by Chinese prisoners of war who came under Moslem control in the border warfare (751 A.D.) between the Moslems conquering central Asia and the Chinese defending it (Jacob, *Kulturelemente*, 16–17); in Damascus weapon-forging decayed after the city was conquered by Tamerlane

(1399) because the craftsmen involved were deported to Khorasan and Samarkand (Le Bon, *Arabes*, 556, *cf.* 558: "We may make a general remark on wood, ivory, and metal work among the Arabs [here, again, used to designate all the people of the caliphates] ... that among them the finest work is done with crude tools and that it is very rare..." See also Rouffaer, "Kunst", 592, 596: the craft of forging transferred from Pajajaran to Majapahit in 1301; Weber, *System*, 100 and n. 73; Moreland, *Akbar*, 184–187, and *Aurangzeb*, 136).

158 Export of Indian cotton cloth to the West is certain from the time of the Roman Empire on (Goetz, *Verkehrswege*, 482; Charlesworth, *Trade-Routes*, 61, 68). Export to Indonesia is certain from the fifteenth century on, but can probably be assumed even quite a bit earlier (Rouffaer & Juynboll, *Batik-kunst*, 499, *cf.* 408), which assumption is more than a probability in light of the trade to the West. According to Rouffaer, it was a matter of 'big industry' and 'mass export' (*ibid.*, 422, 521, 523, 528; Krom takes over the terms: *Geschiedenis*, 48). The investigation undertaken in Coromandel in 1901 on Rouffaer's initiative brought to light a traditionally organized craft (*cf.* Weber, *System*, 100–101; perhaps organized according to caste: *cf. ibid.*, 96–99). The most advanced form of 'industrial organization' consisted of the putting-out system, the same at the beginning of the seventeenth century and in 1677 and in the middle of the nineteenth century (Colenbrander, *Coen*, II, 294, 299, 444, V, 580, 592; De Jonge, *Opkomst*, III 213, 283, 346; Rouffaer & Juynboll, *Batik-kunst*, I, 254, 256, 395, 398). But those common craftsmen worked in their villages and city quarters for sales on distant Eastern and Western markets. Traders could go there to direct 'production' themselves (putting-out); a local or other authority, too, could mobilize the craft for his advantage; "sometimes looms might be monopolized to provide cargo for an official speculation" (Moreland, *Aurangzeb*, 134, *cf.* 145); and a ruler could send his agent to commission desired textiles to be made (see Shellabear, *Sejarah*, 206–209). Osöman, an Achinese trader from the state Ië Löböë (Ayer Labu) on the north coast of Sumatra, a dealer in areca-nuts, travelled in 1870 to the *keling* regions, the hinterlands behind Negapattinam, where cotton cloth was manufactured for the Achin market. There he gave his directions regarding a new design he thought would sell well; the *kain Usman* did come on the market, to be imitated by European industry as quickly as possible. What is most important in this regard is the completely traditionalistic picture given by this 'international export industry', this trade, and the 'market' (see Snouck Hurgronje in Rouffaer & Juynboll, *Batik-kunst*, 521). It would be unjust to lay the blame for it on the century of havoc wreaked by the capitalistic textile industry, first from overseas, and then from within India itself – the forms depicted are the traditional ones.

159 See also the quotation from Tamil sources given by Mookerji (*Shipping* 135–137).

160 Terpstra, *Westerkwartieren*, 253.
161 *Ibid.*, 256.
162 *Ibid.*, 263.
163 *Cf.* Linschoten, *Voyage*, I, 267.
164 Colenbrander, *Coen*, I, 696.
165 Terpstra, *Westerkwartieren*, 256.
166 *Ibid.*, 257.
167 *Ibid.*, 240, 242, 244–245, 252–257, 262–263, 271, 284–286; *cf.* Colenbrander, *Coen*, I, 238, 486, 693–696, 721, 753–754, 762, II, 712, 737, III, 6–7, 231, 301, IV, 486; De Jonge, *Opkomst*, III, 284; Polo, *Book*, II, 440 n. 3 (Ibn Battuta). The incoming ship from Suez carried the value of two hundred to three hundred thousand pieces of eight and sixteen to twenty thousand ducats in coin, "besides what was not registered". Here, then, was still the same aspect of Indian trade as in the time of the Roman Empire – Oriental merchandise was bought with coin and precious metals.

168 The lords in the Mogol court also put capital in the eastbound sea trade. When in September, 1619 the Dutch Company captured a few English ships in a sea battle off Tiku, on the west coast of Sumatra, it appeared that there had been on the English ship *The Dragon* "certain Gujarati and some Achinese..., one of which said to have lost the value of about 13000 pieces of eight [around two thousand seven hundred pounds] belonging to the prince Sultan Khurram, the youngest son of the grand mogul in Surat, requests reparation" (Colenbrander, *Coen*, I, 514). "Resolution of the Governor-General and Councillors, 28 December, 1619: Whereas on the English ship *The Dragon* captured before Tiku we have taken a Gujarat named Malinshiary, being a pilot of the prince Sultan Khurram, the youngest son of the grand mogul in Surat, who importunes us much and troubles us to have reparation and retribution for the cloths and other merchandise which were laden in the English ships won by us off Tiku for the account of the aforesaid his prince Sultan Khurram, according to his declaration handed over for that purpose amounting to 13000 pieces of eight, moreover in *The Dragon* the value of 300 pieces of eight for his private account – it has been approved to give him an honourable accomodation at Jakarta until by time and tide the occasion shall present itself that we can transport him back to Surat with our or other ships; and with regard to his request, to announce to him that as his prince or lord is our good friend and we are of the intention to send a fleet to Surat at an opportune time, we ourselves shall settle the affair in amity with his lord..." (*ibid.*, III, 573). The prince Sultan Khurram was the later Grand Mogul Shah Jahan, who ruled from 1628 to 1658 (*cf. ibid.*, III, 1002, V, 847). He was at that time (1620) the farmer of customs at Surat (Moreland, *Aurangzeb*, 276). Another incident: the shah of Persia had sent his ambassadors to the States General of the Netherlands and the king of England accompanied by royal merchants (see *Daghregister 1631–1634*,

39). On the return journey in 1627 the merchant Husain Bey carried a cargo of the value of fifty thousand reals of eight overseas to Batavia. The trade was bad there (perhaps because of obstruction by the Dutch Company); the royal factor appeared later in partnership with the notorious Batavian 'free burgher' Bruystens, who was beheaded soon after (Colenbrander, *Coen*, V, 7–8, 11, 101, 116, 175, 642–645, 753).

169 *Cf.* also Unger, *Middelburg*, 19.

170 Van der Meulen & Von Wissmann, *Hadramaut*, 14–19, 21, 27–29, 33. Unfortunately there are no data given on the organization of the crafts (are there craft gilds?), on shipowning by the urban patriciate, on trade transactions, on slave activities; and little data on trade in money and import trade (see *ibid.*, 228: a weaver from Macalla with one camel and two assistants, in the Wadi Hajr in the interior – a case of a handicraft and peddling combined). If the description of Hadramaut is compared *e.g.* with that of a coastal trading centre such as Bantam in 1596, what is changed is that traditional Asian handicrafts products have been partially replaced by capitalistic factory goods – in the bazaar at Macalla, where crafts were pursued and trade was carried on side by side: "All sorts of sweets were offered for sale at the booths: also the first bright-yellow or deep-red dates, not yet quite ripe, tuberous fruits, spices, the celebrated Humumi tobacco in big bundles consisting of whole dried plants, broad waist-bands, Japanese, Indian and Dutch piece-goods, sugar-loaves and rice, coffee-beans and dried coffee-husks, ginger-root and tea from Ceylon and Java, various kinds of grain, meal and *samn*, sesame oil and kerosene, matches and coffee-cups, djambiyas [daggers] and cartridges" (*ibid.*, 17). In 1623 the small southern Arabian coastal port Keshin was "a spot lying in a bay, about a cannonshot from the shore, around 280 or 300 houses of fair construction big; as regards the people, that is completely black, Arab in descent and Mohammedan in faith. There was no negotiation at all there, and very few folk, the most of whom follow the king, by whom the trade here on this coast is carried on, consisting of aloes of Socotra, some ambergris, frankincense, dragon's-blood; and gum arabic, the which the said king with his ships has carried from divers places, and in turn disposes of to Portuguese and banians [thus still an Indian influence in trade, after a thousand years of Islam in those seas]. We have got a fresh supply of goats and sheep here, and an abundance of fish, but the water that is to be obtained here – being drawn from wells that are between the village and the shore – is brackish" (Terpstra, *Westerkwartieren*, 283, *cf.* 240). See also Polo, *Book*, II, 442, 443 n. 1, 449–450.

171 *Cf.* Weber, *System*, 31; *Religionssoziologie*, II, 375–376.

172 See Von Kremer, *Einnahmebudget*, especially 47 ff.; Ali Ibn Isa (*circa* 800 A.D.) as statesman.

173 "Stitched vessels are still used. I have seen them of 200 tons burden but these are being driven out by iron-fastened vessels, as iron gets cheaper,

except where (as on the Malabar and Coromandel coasts) the pliancy of a stitched boat is useful in a surf [*cf.* Mookerji, *Shipping*, 236 n. 1]. Till the last few years, when steamers have begun to take all the best horses, the Arab horses bound for Bombay almost all came in the way Marco Polo describes" (Sir Bartle Frere); "Some of them do still, standing over a date cargo, and the result of this combination gives rise to an extraordinary traffic in the Bombay bazaar" (Yule: both quotations in Polo, *Book*, I, 117 n. 3; *cf. ibid.*, I, 108, II, 415 n. 4; Ferrand, "K'ouen-louen", XIV, 59).

174 Polo, *Book*, II, 332 n. 1 & subnote †.

175 Moreland, *Aurangzeb*, 85–86, 148–149.

176 The tales in *The Thousand and One Nights* have kept alive the memory of this. See also Weber, *Wirtschaft*, 526; Von Kremer, *Einnahmebudget*, 54 n. 3, 66 n. 3. On India see Moreland, *Akbar*, 70–71; *cf.* Weber, *System*, 31; *Religionssoziologie*, II, 253. On southern Arabia see Terpstra, *Westerkwartieren*, 253.

177 Moreland, *Aurangzeb*, 156, 158.

178 See Goetz, *Verkehrswege*, 346; *cf.* Neurath, *Wirtschaftsgeschichte*, 59; Weber, *Wirtschaft*, 518, 557, 584 (Miltiades), 598; Rostovtzeff, "Commerce" (Apollonius, minister for Ptolemy II Philadelphius of Egypt).

179 See Weber, *Sozialgeschichte*, 235 ff. *Cf. ibid.*, 263; Goetz, *Verkehrswege*, 374–375; Charlesworth, *Trade-Routes*, 103.

180 See Massignon, "Islam", 5; Von Kremer, *Einnahmebudget*, 63.

181 See Jain, *Banking*, 15.

182 In 1622: "It is unbelievable how much the whole coast of China is populated, what an abundant multitude of people and vessels there is everywhere" (Colenbrander, *Coen*, I, 768).

183 See *e.g.* the plans of Suchow in 1247 and Hsianfu in the fourteenth century, with their rows of public and military buildings, regular streets, temples, monasteries, and so forth (Polo, *Book*, II, 182, 193).

184 See Yule, *Cathay*, I, 42, 51–53, 65; Goetz, *Verkehrswege*, 496; Ferrand, "K'ouen-louen", XIII, 456, XIV, 6, 14, 20; Chang, *Trade*, 1–3; Krom, *Geschiedenis*, 61–62.

185 *Cf.* Pelliot, "Itinéraires", 144; review, 460. A stronghold like the Roman Eburacum, Lugdunum, or Sarmizegetusa, then.

186 If Chuanchow is the same as Zaitun. A difference of opinion has arisen on the question whether the famous name Zaitun designated the port Chuanchow or the more southerly port Changchow. See Polo, *Book*, II, 237 n. 2, where Yule assumes that Zaitun is Chuanchow; Chang, *Trade*, 12 n. 4, *cf.* 70 n. 6; Rouffaer & Juynboll, *Batik-kunst*, I, 161, 499; Rouffaer & IJzerman, *Schipvaart*, I, 122 n. 4.

187 See Chang, *Trade*, 7.

188 See *ibid.*, 9, 17–18, 23, 25–26, 28–29, 30 n. 2, 42 n. 1, 43, 51 & n. 5, 58 n. 1, 94, 101–102; Yule, *Cathay*, I, 129–130; Ferrand, "K'ouen-louen",

XIII, 465, XIV, 13–14 (Ma Tuan-lin); *cf.* Krom, *Geschiedenis*, 114, 227, 303, 308 (Chau Ju-kua); Colenbrander, *Coen*, I, 725, 765.

189 See Polo, *Book*, II, Second Book, Chapters LXXVI and LXXVII.

190 See *ibid.*, II, 212 n. 12.

191 "...the garden of Pun-ting-qua. Pun-ting-qua of Pun-shi-cheng, the original owner, had been a wealthy merchant at Canton [the last of the Hong merchants: see *ibid.*, 271], but his government ultimately drained him of his wealth, by compelling him to pay a certain fixed sum for the monopoly of the trade in salt. Falling into heavy arrears, and being unable to raise the amount, this property was sequestrated, and his splendid garden raffled in a public lottery. A notable instance, this, of the danger of becoming too rich in China." (Thomson, *Straits*, 255).

192 See Morse, *Gilds*. According to Wittfogel the Co-Hong of Canton was not a typical Chinese merchant gild (*Wirtschaft*, 710–717).

193 See Wittfogel, *Wirtschaft*, 721–722 & n. 134.

194 Chang, *Trade*. Nor does the introductory chapter of Verhoeven's *Bijdragen* ('Trade and Shipping in Southeast Asia before the Coming of the Europeans') give any consideration to this aspect of the problem.

195 *Cf.* Moreland, *Akbar*, 214.

196 Krause, *Geschichte*, I, 127–128.

197 *Cf.* Lieber, *Weltwirtschaft*, 20.

198 The same sort of trade structure provided the background for Coen's plan of campaign to gain the trade on China by violence, for which a fleet was fitted out in 1622: "It is my opinion that even if Your Excellencies should send ten hundred thousand pieces of eight and more to the king and regents of China as a gift [in the hope of opening up trade in China], nothing would be gained, not because of their ancient regulations, with which they seek to excuse themselves, but mainly out of regard for the inequibly higher damage we cause them by preventing the trade on Manila, which is principally an affair of the Chinese lords. The Chinese say that [the risk of] losing the goods will not make them abandon the trade on Manila, but that if we want to keep them from there we will have to imprison or kill all the people we get hold of in order to make the fear of losing life and property greater for the poor than the hope of making profit, for as long as the poor are not in bodily danger the rich will always venture the goods..." (Coen to the Gentlemen Seventeen, 20 June, 1633: Colenbrander, *Coen*, I, 798, *cf.* IV, 620 n. 1, V, 314 ff.).

199 The "merchant, owner of many ships" mentioned in a Sung Dynasty notice from the tenth century (quoted in Krom, *Geschiedenis*, 228) must have been a merchant gentleman of the patriciate; Conti, in 1440, mentions a similar case (Yule, *Cathay*, I, 175). Eiansan and Wangsan of Changchow, the traders and shipowners with which the commander of the fleet the Dutch Company sent to China in 1622 (see the preceding note) came in contact,

were also such patrician merchants. Wangsan's high position appears from his rôle in the embassy which went to the fleet in the Pescadores from the "Governor-General of the Province Hochow, the Admiral of the Sea, and the Captain of the Army" (Colenbrander, *Coen*, I, 765–767; for the Chinese authorities see *ibid.*, V, 72, 149, 169). Another patrician merchant was the trader Simsou, to whom the Chinese administration awarded the monopoly of Chinese trade on Formosa (perhaps the mandarins had some interest in it themselves) after the establishment of the Dutch Company there. Simsou sent shipments on five junks at a time, delivered hundreds of picul of silk (the turnover ran to eight hundred picul a year, *i.e.* more than two and a half times as much as the total amount carried by the Chinese ships to Bantam each year), and held sums in hundreds of thousands of Company money deposited as necessary advances for the silk (Colenbrander, *Coen*, V, 35, 71, 83, 149, 162, 169, 271, 273, 281, 321–322, 489). There is an interesting case of the equally colossal political-capitalistic occasional trade of a Chinese authority dating from the same period. The pirate Icquan, called to the office of chief mandarin of Amoy and admiral of the South China fleet (it was the last years of the Ming Dynasty: the situation is analogous to the many regimes of 'generals' in recent Chinese history), then (1 October, 1628) closed a three-year contract with the Dutch Company to deliver annually:

1400 picul raw silk at 140 tael (10 tael = 13½ reals; thus 1 tael = £ 3 2s 6d) per picul;
5000 picul sugar at 3 reals per picul;
1000 picul confitted ginger at 4 tael per picul;
5000 pieces silk goods at 14 and 19 mas (1 mas = 1/10 tael = 8d) per piece;

the total for a sum of three hundred thousand reals of eight. In payment the Company was to deliver three thousand picul of pepper (Heeres says two thousand: *Corpus*, I, 216, no. lxxix) at eleven reals per picul, and the remainder (thus 267,000 or 278,000 reals, respectively £ 55,600 or £ 58,000) in cash (Colenbrander, *Coen*, V, 149–150). This would have been a gigantic transaction, but the contract was repudiated by the high authorities of the Company at Batavia (Heeres, *Corpus*, I, 217 n. 2). The total sum spent annually by the Company at that time amounted to from four hundred to five hundred thousand reals, or from around eighty to a hundred thousand pounds (Colenbrander, *Coen*, IV, 321–322, *cf.* I, 603, 663, IV, 482–483). In connection with the private trade and occasional trade of patricians and officials the account of the affair with 'inferior' Chinese lead money ('copper money') which as an enterprise set up by the mandarin of Fukien was exported to Indonesia from the Fukien ports does not seen so incredible as it appeared to Moquette (Rouffaer & IJzerman, *Schipvaart*, I, 122 & n. on Plate Forty-

Five, *cf.* 236). 'Dealing in money' in the form of counterfeiting is as old as coinage itself, and has always belonged to the affairs of early capitalism, carried on by preference by the mighty of the earth.

200 *Cf.* Krom, *Geschiedenis*, 227.

201 See Chang, *Trade*, 10–11, 19, 26, 104. Goods in the sea trade to South China at the end of the first century A.D. were pearls, precious stones, 'rare goods', gold, silk cloth (Ferrand, "K'ouen-louen", XIII, 452–453). Trade in Canton at the end of the tenth century – goods imported: perfumes, rhinoceros horn, ivory, coral, ambergris, strung pearls, steel, tortoise shell, carnelian, shells, rock crystal, woven goods, ebony, sapanwood, etc.; exported: gold, silver, small coins, lead, tin, coloured silk, porcelain (Krom, *Geschiedenis*, 227). Goods in the Chinese trade at the beginning of the sixteenth century: spices, musk, rhubarb, pearls, tin, porcelain, silk, damask, satin, brocade (Yule, *Cathay*, I, 180 n. 2).

202 Ferrand, *Empire*, 4.

203 *Ibid.*, 116.

204 *Ibid.*, 56.

205 Ferrand, "K'ouen-louen", XIV, 41.

206 Ferrand, *Empire*, 108.

207 Rouffaer, "Tochten", 374.

208 *Ibid.*, 382. On the other hand in the thirteenth century and earlier (during the Sung Dynasty) it was forty days from Zaitun to Lanli-poi (Lamuri, northern Sumatra) and sixty days from there to Arabia (Polo, *Book*, II, 300 n. 1).

209 Coedès, *Royaume*, 20–21.

210 Yule, *Cathay*, IV, 92.

211 Rouffaer, "Tochten", 392–394.

212 Colenbrander, *Coen*, I, 68, IV, 726, *cf.* I, 49,

213 What are given in the itineraries are of course averages; in the travel accounts adventure at sea can lead to a highly varied picture of the duration of the voyage.

214 Ferrand, "K'ouen-louen", XIII, 438, XIV, 39–41.

215 *Ibid.*, XIV, 46.

216 Polo, *Book*, II, Third Book, Chapter One. Mookerji remarkably enough makes this description one of Indian ships – a chauvinistic annexation (see Mookerji, *Shipping*, 191–193).

217 "...wherein the merchants greatly abide at their ease, every man having one to himself..." (Polo, *Book*, II, 249). This surely held only for the very richest merchants: the great masses were huddled together by hundreds on the ships.

218 *Ibid.*, II, 252 n. 6; *cf.* Yule, *Cathay*, I, 76 n. 3.

219 See Mookerji, *Shipping*, 28–30, 46, *cf.* 77 n. 4, 177; Ferrand, *Empire*, 154–155.

220 See *e.g.* De Jonge, *Opkomst,* IV, 207, 263–265, V, 115, 230; Colenbrander, *Coen,* I, 733, *cf.* 735.

221 "The numbers carried by Chinese junks are occasionally still enormous. In February 1822, Captain Pearl of the English ship Indiana, coming through Gaspar Straits, fell in with the cargo and crew of a wrecked junk and saved 198 out of 1600 with whom she had left Amoy, whom he landed at Pontianak. This humane acte cost him £ 11,000" (Williams, in Polo, *Book,* II, 256 n. 6). For a picture of such a junk see Plate Thirty-Four in Crawfurd, *History.*

222 See the tale of Sindbad the Sailor, the 427th of *The Thousand and One Nights,* and the plaint of the Jew Isaac of York over his ship's accident in the Gulf of Lyon in Scott's *Ivanhoe,* Chapter Ten.

223 *Cf.* also Graßhoff, *Wechselrecht,* 1–2; Kohler, *Commenda,* 10.

224 All the uncertainties and dangers mentioned in the accounts of pilgrimages by the Chinese Buddhists (and the voyages of the apostles in *Acts* as well) apply just as much, and usually at the same time, to the journeys of the peddling traders.

225 "...the distant trade on adventure..." (Unger, review, 197).

226 *Cf.* Malinowski, *Argonauts,* 92, 515.

III: INDONESIA AND THE TRADE ROUTE

1 See Krom, *Geschiedenis,* 39, 45.

2 *Ibid.,* 39.

3 Research for Indonesia is still in a preliminary stage. See the introduction to Nooteboom, *Boomstamkano*; *cf.* Bertling, in Van Vollenhoven, *Adatrecht,* II, 80.

4 Factual historical material on the Far East begins with the cohesive whole formed by the navigation data of the *Periplus* (the first century A.D.) and the geography of Ptolemy contemporary to it. Even so, it must be pointed out how incongruent the relation between 'scholarship' and reality, and still more between literary tradition and reality, can be. On this see the engaging passage by Ferrand (*Relations,* I, i–iii; *cf.* also Malinowski, *Argonauts,* 232 ff., 291 ff.). That notes on the Far East were recorded by Ptolemy is comparatively a matter of chance (perhaps the Alexandrian geographer collected his information from the Indian colony established in Alexandria: see McCrindle, *India,* xviii; Rouffaer, "Tochten", 364); in any case no direct connection should be made between the appearance of scholarly or literary accounts and the state of general knowledge (which very often would have been the knowledge of sailors and merchants and as such for the most part empirical professional and 'secret' knowledge: see Adriani in Rouffaer, "Malaka", 72 n. 1; Kruyt, "Leven", XXXIX, 147–148, *cf.* "Tengke-offer", 233 n. 1). As late as the seventeenth century, when scholarly knowledge in cartography

and astronomical navigation had already been to a large extent emancipated from navigation as an empirical art bound to individuals, the Gentlemen Seventeen could still write to the governor-general: "In case there are any maps or descriptions providing knowledge of the regions of the Indies in the keeping of Your Excellency or anyone else being in our service in the Indies, then Your Excellency should send at least copies of all of them over to us for the accomplishment of a great general work, lest what many by long industry have collected be lost, as has occurred before" (Colenbrander, *Coen*, IV, 471).

5 An indication of the antiquity of Chinese trade in Indonesia is the Chinese earthenware of the Han Dynasty found in graves in the Lampong region and elsewhere in southern Sumatra and near Sambas on Borneo (see Van Orsoy de Flines' annual reports on the ceramics collection of the Royal Batavian Society, "Verzameling").

6 *Cf.* Krom, *Geschiedenis*, 56, 62.

7 Goods in the sea trade to China, at the end of the first century A.D.: pearls, precious stones, rare goods, gold, silk cloth (Ferrand, "K'ouen-louen", XIII, 452–453). For the period of the T'ang Dynasty, a period of flourishing international trade in southern and southeastern Asia, Chinese accounts list as trade goods from Java in the second half of the ninth century: tortoise shell, gold, silver, rhinoceros horn, and ivory (Groeneveldt, "Notes", 13–15; *cf.* Krom, *Geschiedenis*, 166–167). If one did not know better from elsewhere, one would tend to imagine a wealthy but 'barbaric' trade carried on by a tribe on the coast or a river mouth. These are, however, the trade goods in the ports of the Javanese region then subject to the sea power Çriwijaya, a region with a highly developed patrimonial, bureaucratic regime which was in that period able to produce such monuments as the Barabudur, the Chandi Mendut, and the Sewu complex, monuments worthy of admiration from an administrative, economic point of view (in consideration of the organization of labour) just as much as from an artistic one (*cf.* Krom, *Geschiedenis*, 170–171). Indonesian goods shipped to Arabia in the tenth century: aloes, camphor, sandalwood, ivory, tin, ebony, sapanwood, spices (*ibid.*, 205). Alongside that in the tenth century, as presents from Çriwijaya to the emperor of China: ivory, frankincense, rose water, dates, preserved peaches, white sugar, crystal rings, glass bottles, naphtha, coral, cotton cloth, rhinoceros horn, perfumes, condiments (*ibid.*, 226) – all of them goods typical of the international trade of Çriwijaya in its importing and stapling. In 980 "a foreign merchant from Çriwijaya" arrived in Swatow "with a cargo [!] of perfumes, medicaments, condiments, rhinoceros horn, and ivory" (*ibid.*, 225 – why does Krom make this merchant a 'ship captain' in 985?) Goods in the Javanese ports at the time of the Sung Dynasty: gold, silver, rhinoceros horn, ivory, aloe wood, sapanwood, sandalwood, anice, pepper, areca nuts, sulphur (*ibid.*, 285). Gifts of embassies from Çriwijaya to the emperor of

China in the seventh century: silver, pearls, camphor oil, perfumes, and other products (*ibid.*, 303). Among the materials shipped to Arabia in the twelfth century: tin. (In the thirteenth century Indonesian shipping carried iron from Sofala on the east coast of Africa: *ibid.*, 304.) Goods in the international trade in Indonesia in the thirteenth century: tin, elephants' tusks, pearls, tortoise shell, camphor, aloe wood, lacquered wood, cloves, nutmeg, sandalwood, rose water, gold, silver, porcelain, silk, sugar, iron, brandy, rice, galangal, rhubarb (*ibid.*, 306–307, 309 n. 1, 310; *cf.* Polo, *Book*, II, 264, 272, 284). Trade goods in Indonesia in the fourteenth century: rice, salt, pepper, cotton cloth, parrots, Chinese copper coins, beads, gold, silver, betel nuts, carved woodwork, pearls, cloves, sandalwood, porcelain (Krom, *Geschiedenis*, 398–399). Gifts of embassies from Majapahit to the emperor of China in the last quarter of the fourteenth century: black slaves, pearls, pepper (*ibid.*, 401); gifts of an embassy from the state of Pu-ni to the emperor of China in the thirteen seventies: bird feathers, tortoises (or tortoise shell?), peacocks, camphor, clothing material, incense (*ibid.*, 411); gifts of an embassy in 1377: rhinoceros horn, cassowaries, white monkeys, parrots, tortoise shell, cloves, camphor (*ibid.*, 412; *cf.* Tiele & Heeres, *Bouwstoffen*, II, 177). Trade goods in Indonesia in the fifteenth century: head feathers of the rhinoceros hornbill, *coptis teeta*, lacquered wood, aloe wood, beeswax, benzoin, resin, tin, ebony, pepper, sulphur, cherrywood, sandalwood, sapanwood, diamonds, spices, tortoise shell, parrots, porcelain, musk, silk and other materials, beads (Krom, *Geschiedenis*, 434, 441, 443–444). Goods carried by a Portuguese ship returning from Malacca to Europe: "all the rich wares of China, Maluco, Iava, and all those countries ... (as Silkes, Damaskes, clothes of gold and silver, [costly porcelain] & such like wares)..." (Van Linschoten, *Voyage*, II, 272: the "costly porcelain" of the Dutch original was dropped in the English translation). Compare the gifts given to the Dutch East India Company by embassies of the Negus in the last quarter of the seventeenth century: horses, wild donkeys, ostriches, Ethiopian slaves; in 1697 the ambassador from Ethiopia, an Armenian, stated that Ethiopia wished to trade slaves, gold, ambergris, and ivory for cotton cloth, copper, pepper, tobacco, and gunpowder (*Nieuwe Rotterdamsche Courant*, 22 September, 1935, Morning Edition, Section A, 2).

8 Mookerji, *Shipping*, Chapters Four to Nine; other material quoted by him points to much older data: see 156–157 (Davids) and 72 (Foulkes). *Cf.* Ferrand in Masson-Oursel, *Inde*, 129.

9 "The early growth of her shipping and shipbuilding, coupled with the genius and energy of her merchants, ... the enterprise of her colonists, and the zeal of her missionaries, secured to India the command of the sea for ages, and helped her to attain and long maintain her proud position as the mistress of the Eastern seas..." (Mookerji, *Shipping*, 5, *cf.* 4); "swarms of daring adventurers from Gujarat ports, anticipating the enterprise of the Drakes

and Frobishers, or more properly of the Pilgrim Fathers, sailed in search of plenty till the shores of Java arrested their progress and gave scope to their colonizing ambition..." (*ibid.*, 40–41, *cf.* 49 n. 1); "As far back as the 75th year of the Christian era a band of Hindu navigators sailed from Kalinga, and, instead of plying within the usual limits of the Bay of Bengal, boldly ventured out into the open limitless expanse of the Indian Ocean and arrived at the island of Java. There the adventurous navigators planted a colony, built towns and cities, and developed a trade with the mother country which existed for several centuries..." (*ibid.*, 148); "Artists and art-critics also see in the magnificent sculptures of the Burobudur temple in Java the hand of Bengali artists who worked side by side with the people of Kalinga and Gujarat in thus building up its early civilization..." (*ibid.*, 156); "The whole coast of Farther India from Suvarnabhumi or Burma to China, and also of the islands of the Malay Archipelago, was studded with prosperous Indian colonies and naval stations" (*ibid.*, 171). Mookerji, writing in 1910, made a very free use of historical material. See also Van der Kolff, *Bevolkingsrietcultuur*, 13, 16–17, *cf.* 17–18 (on Chinese influence); Aymonier, *Cambodge*, I, 125; Tiele, "Oosten", 200, 219–220; Snouck Hurgronje, *Achinese*, I, 18.

10 Krom, *Geschiedenis*, 90. Compare such quotations as these: "... a contact ... first of a few trading ships, then of more of them, finally with permanent settlement..." (*ibid.*, 67); "Everything taken together it seems to us most probable that in the course of the first century A.D. trade with the east led to settlement there and as a result of that colonial Hindu states arose, in some cases rather quickly, elsewhere after the course of one or two centuries. The second and third century seems to us the actual age of colonization..." (*ibid.*, 88). According to Krom migration of Indian groups is possible, especially as political emigration (*ibid.*, 89, *cf.* 91), but the whole complex of colonization gives the impression "of a Hinduized society, not of a number of separate Hindu colonies abroad" (*ibid.*, 89). For him the earliest Balinese records, those of the ninth century, "reflect ... a completely autonomous Hindu-Balinese society as it may have developed naturally, parallel with Hindu-Javanese society, and not by Hindu-Javanese" (*ibid.*, 210). For Krom's terminology *cf.* 40–41, 56, 62, 66–67, 69, 77, 82, 88, 94, 100–101, 103, 125, 138–141, 147, 164, 178–179, 220, 236, 410, 436–437, 457 n. 2; see also Van Vollenhoven, *Adatrecht*, II, 133, *cf.* 809.

11 Rouffaer, "Tochten", 366; *cf.* Rouffaer & Juynboll, *Batik-kunst*, I, 306; Rouffaer, "Kunst", 340, 349–351, 408, 413, 427 n. 1, 428, 435, 446, 459, 477, 516, 521, 567, 573, 629, 633, 657. Rouffaer suggests belligerent penetration, however, in his "Malaka", 99 n. 1, 112, *cf.* 517; and his *Industrieën*, 1.

12 Berg, *Hoofdlijnen*, 8–15.

13 Berg's view also goes in this direction: "If we look at the great island region stretching from Ceylon east and southeastwards across the Indian Ocean, finally to become lost in the immeasurable Pacific, we find there an

abundant number of different peoples related in race and related in language. Of their cultures it can be said that they are either still completely primitive or have only recently begun to grow out of primitivism as a result of the penetration of the Westerners. Only here and there, where international trade routes reached part of the region, did a development beyond the primitive also take place in earlier times. One of those areas was Java; as so often, it was there the contact with foreigners which gave the impetus to development, and that development will have remained limited to the circles which had contact with foreigners..." (Berg, *Hoofdlijnen*, 8). In order to refute in advance an argument regarding the concept 'primitive' to be treated below, I should like to point out that trade can be 'barter trade' without one's having to think of 'primitive' forms. Trade, and 'international trade' also, can take place in barter forms; by no means does it need to be connected with money economy. As late as the seventeenth century all sorts of 'money' were in circulation in southern Asian trade, not as 'currency', but simply as a 'means to an end', alongside forms of 'money'-less barter, while coins made from precious and other metals coming from the West as early as the period of the Diadochian states and from the north, from the Chinese Empire, had already been used in trade for many centuries then (see *e.g.* Krom, *Geschiedenis*, 286, 309, 395, 438; Reichwein, *China*, 35 n. *).

14 In Bali, Bone, Banjarmasin, Riau, Siak, and especially Achin. See Colenbrander, *Geschiedenis*, III, 175 ff., 194 ff., 199 ff., 207–208, 233 ff., 237 ff. For salvage rights see Polo, *Book*, II, 385–386; Krom, *Geschiedenis*, 444 (at Pançur).

15 *Cf.* Berg, *Hoofdlijnen*, 9–10; Van Vollenhoven, *Adatrecht*, II, 763, 766, 769–770, 776.

16 Brandes, "Jayapattra" (see Krom, *Geschiedenis*, 47–54).

17 See Krom, *Geschiedenis*, 47–48.

18 *Ibid.*, 54. Compare, from another field, the poor picture the Chinese annals of the Tang Dynasty give of Java (see Groeneveldt, "Notes", 13–15; *cf.* Krom, *Geschiedenis*, 167). It is utterly impossible to recognize from such descriptions the patrimonial, bureaucratic state and the hierarchically organized officialdom the economy and the administrative 'know-how' of which were able to create edifices such as the Barabudur, the Mendut, and the Sewu complex. (*Cf.* also Krom, *Geschiedenis*, 27–28, 227–228, 233–238, 254 n. 4, 284; Ferrand, "K'ouen-louen", XIV, 34.) In the same way when Odoric de Pordenone, travelling overseas from India to China in 1321 and 1322 (see Yule, *Cathay*, II, 9; Krom, *Geschiedenis*, 380) gives a description of the island of Java – "In the neighbourhood... is a great island, Java by name, which hath a compass of a good three thousand miles. And the king of it hath subject to himself seven crowned kings. Now the island is populous exceedingly, and is the second best of all islands that exist. For in it grow camphor, cubebs, cardamoms, nutmegs and many other precious spices. It

hath also very great store of all victuals save wine. The king of this island hath a palace which is truly marvellous. For it is very great and hath very great staircases, broad and lofty, and the steps therefore are of gold and silver alternately. Likewise the pavement of the palace hath one tile of gold and the other of silver, and the wall of the same is on the inside plated all over with plates of gold, on which are sculptured knights of gold, which have great golden circles round their heads, such as we give in these parts to the figures of saints. And those circles are all beset with precious stones. Moreover the ceiling is all of pure gold, and to speak briefly, this palace is richer and finer than any existing at this day in the world..." (Yule, *Cathay*, 151–155) – then it takes some trouble to rediscover in that wondrous fairytale-like and at the same time shabby account the empire of Majapahit as it comes to the fore a good forty years later (1365) in all its pomp and splendour as a patrimonial, bureaucratic state in the Indonesian *Nagarakertagama*.

19 *Cf.* Van Vollenhoven, *Adatrecht*, I, 470, II, 784–785; Krom, *Geschiedenis*, 167 & n. 3, 195 & n. 2; Hunter, *Empire*, 334.

20 *Cf.* Van Vollenhoven, *Adatrecht*, I, 331; Krom, *Geschiedenis*, 201, 202 & n. 1, 247, 267 & n. 3, 314. The magical significance of the metalworking craft is general knowledge.

21 It appears to me that the grounds upon which Krom bases his explanation of the Chinese account regarding Java in the Tang Annals, 674–675, as applying to a regime of tribal chiefs, not one of princes, are not reasonable (see Krom, *Geschiedenis*, 106–107). The regime must have been patrimonial and bureaucratic. Compare other passages in Krom, *Geschiedenis*: 123–124, 128 (the great edifices of the Dieng Plateau – such structures are typical of, and only possible in, a state based on levies and soccage), 148, 159 (where Krom himself points to the apanage system of the 'native states' on Java in modern times, *i.e.*, to typically patrimonial, bureaucratic forms, in order to illustrate the early Javanese situation in the eighth and ninth centuries), 161, 162 ("the refined, detailed organization"), 167, 169, 188, 195, 203 & n. 3, 208. The passage in the Airlangga inscription dating from 1041 in which is mentioned the suppression of "a woman of terrific strength, like a giantess" from the uncivilized regions in the southern part of eastern Java lying outside the area of the empire lead one rather to picture a female tribal chieftain (*ibid.*, 256; *cf.* De Jonge, *Opkomst*, VII, 307–308).

22 *Cf.* Van Vollenhoven, *Adatrecht*, I, 136, III, 4–5, 570–571.

23 See Van Vollenhoven, *Adatrecht*, II, 763–771.

24 *Cf.* Krom, *Geschiedenis*, 317.

25 See Van Vollenhoven, *Adatrecht*, I, 364.

26 See *ibid.*, II, 809.

27 Under the pressure of the modern system of colonial administration and of modern capitalism – two independent forms, separated from each other, each making its influence felt in its own 'autonomous' way – many of these

forms are at long last being disrupted. But the pressures exerted and the influences felt in periods before the modern-capitalistic period were of another sort, different in aim, and much weaker. A single illustration. Palima, in the Buginese region, was a coastal village, an important seat of Bone overseas trade and overseas shipping, the dwelling place of many rich Buginese and Arab traders. In the hinterland, in the lake regions of Wajo, Sopeng, and Bone, maize can be grown on the lands along the lakeshores, which are dry in the time of the western monsoons. The civil service encouraged growing maize as a means of 'increasing prosperity'. (A direct result in such regions lacking an intensive money economy was the probability of more and higher tax assessments in money, the proceeds of which were urgently needed for the activities of the civil service.) From 1922–1923 on maize planting was very strongly encouraged; the maize was shipped to Macassar and sold there through the intermediation of the indigenous trade and shipping mentioned above. It was then brought on the world market (it was a period of rising prices) by the Macassar European trade at a sharply competitive price, especially competitive with the La Plata harvest. In a few years the yield grew to large proportions, with six thousand ton in 1925–1926. (According to another source, in 1904 the export amounted to two thousand five hundred ton; in 1928 a maximum of 219,000 ton was reached; then there came a drop, with 112,000 ton in 1932. The total yield can of course be set at much higher figures: as a comparison, the 1932 maize yield on Java was a million nine hundred thousand ton, the average annual export, 1928–1932, fifty-eight thousand.) The result was that the agency of the Royal Packet Navigation Company, eliminating the Macassar intermediary trade, organized exporting directly from Palima to Europe and America, and alongside that tramp steamers, especially Scandinavian, took part in the direct export. The task of moving the maize down from the highlands by way of the river, at first performed by native boats, was also taken in hand by the Navigation Company, which built warehouses and loading stations on the upper river and began transporting by means of motor launches with long trains of flat-bottomed barges. Bringing the maize down and shipping it out in this centralized way made it possible to close direct insurance contracts for the cargoes, a thing underwriters had not been willing to risk under earlier conditions. The shipping company had less uncertainty, cargo risks could be insured, only a single set of bills of lading was needed. What remained of indigenous intermediary trade became dependent on the shipping company financially. The boom brought an excessive amount of money to the population of the maize-growing areas. The collapse of prices on the world market also affected Buginese maize growing. Export was stopped, the amount of maize grown decreased, the stream of money dried up; the social organization remained, seriously disrupted. And Palima, once the flourishing centre of old, indigenous independent trade and shipping, in the meantime (1929–

1930) became a dying village: the houses were decaying, the ships lay rotting on the beach. (Information from Dr H. J. Friedericy; *cf.* his "Aanteekeningen"). It is clear that such devastating influences were out of the question before the expansion of the power of modern capitalism. There was no world market, no capitalistic wholesale trade, no all-prevailing business cycle, no technical superiority of machine methods, no all-embracing modern administrative bureaucracy. Catastrophes could occur: crop failures, famines, epidemics touching the population, fires affecting houses and ships, war raids, shipwrecks, abduction of the men into slavery, loss of money and goods. But it could not occur that a society was undermined and a communal organization broken to pieces by a world-wide system in a 'peaceful' economic struggle, in a strictly 'legal' sphere, without one irregularity, without one 'social offence', in a stage of 'prosperity' and 'economic development'.

28 See *e.g.* Krom, *Geschiedenis*, 90, 93; Berg, *Hoofdlijnen*, 10–12, 14–15.

29 The state of Achinese civilization at the end of the nineteenth century was called 'primitive' by Snouck Hurgronje (in Van Vollenhoven, *Adatrecht*, I, 222). Where, in such a way, does there remain any criterion for a sharp and meaningful historical and ethnographic definition? Javanese *desa* life is just as much 'primitive' as the culture of Nias. The river city Çriwijaya with its ships and its houses on rafts was 'primitive', but even so it was undoubtedly the 'great power' of southeast Asia. Indian agriculture, Indian cotton block-printing, Chinese mining were 'primitive'. The transport system in western Europe in the eighteenth century was 'primitive'. And the first automobiles and airplanes were 'primitive'. *Cf.* the statement by Huizinga: "The consciousness of owing something contains no absolute material necessity to honour what is felt as an obligation to a fellow-man, an institution or a spiritual power. Ethnologists like Malinowski have shown that the view that in primitive civilizations obedience to the social code is mechanically determined and inescapable, is untenable. Whenever in a community the rules of social conduct are generally observed, therefore, it is through the operation of a genuine ethical impulse. The requirements of control over nature in the form of domination of human nature itself, is then fulfilled." (*Shadow*, 30).

30 See Krom, *Geschiedenis*, 54.

31 Not in the forms encountered today; historical transformations have taken place many times in Indonesia (*cf.* Van Vollenhoven, *Adatrecht*, II, 772–807).

32 Can Ferrand's Kwan-lwan be brought into relation with this (see Krom, *Geschiedenis*, 109–110)?

33 One could say, continuing somewhat boldly the image used a few lines above, that the modelling of pottery is one process, the glazing a second; the two can take place separately from each other.

34 Masson-Oursel's statement: "The social problem ... consists of this in-

definite task: the Brahmanization of a demographic chaos never completely assimilated by the Indo-European élite..." (*Inde*, 247).

35 *Cf.* Masson-Oursel, *Inde*, 14–15, 129–130, 243; Weber, *System*, 83–84, 106, 108, 121–122.

36 As a mission it was not therefore expansive by nature, but rather passive. It was no 'revealed religion' such as the Buddhist and Christian soteriologies. The chief cause of the expansion of the Brahmins was probably rather their material interests – the acquisition of power and incomes (prebends) in new areas, where they through their high position consorted with the princes and lords of the lands on an equal footing. For this possibility of Hinduism see also Snouck Hurgronje, "Politique", 241–242.

37 Weber, *System*, 40. *Cf.*: "However, the struggle for or against acceptance of Hinduism ... generally was led by the rulers or ruling strata; in any case, the strongest motive for the assimilation of Hinduism was undoubtedly the desire for legitimation." (*Ibid.*, 41).

38 *Cf. ibid.*, 83.

39 See Krom, *Geschiedenis*, 56, 66, *cf.* 104 & n. 2, 140–141, 158, 265, 304, 419; Ferrand, *Empire*, 98 n. 2; Poerbatjaraka, *Agastya*, 13.

40 According to Krom the indigenous shipping of the Hinduized states of southeast Asia first held an active part in sea trade in the seventh century (*Geschiedenis*, 113). That does not match with what is said above regarding Indonesian – or Javanese – navigation, however. One may consider the Indonesian shipping of the earliest historical period as 'primitive', as 'proa shipping' in vessels with very limited cargo capacities. (The smallest trading vessels for long distance shipping in Indonesia were of thirty, forty, or fifty ton, with dozens of traders and crew in them: see Rouffaer & IJzerman, *Schipvaart*, I, 71, 98, 132–133; and the list for payments of passes for vessels leaving Jakarta, 12 January, 1621, in Colenbrander, *Coen*, III, 681. On a Spanish caravel of around fifty ton which had sailed from Manila to Macao and was stranded near the Johore River *en route* from Macao to Malacca, there were eighteen Spaniards, seventeen Indian women, and fifty or sixty 'blacks': Tiele & Heeres, *Bouwstoffen*, I, 123–124.) But even so everything known regarding early trade and navigation leads one to accept the existence of 'international trade' and intercommunication across great distances with such small vessels as completely plausible. There is no direct connection between the development of shipbuilding technology and the development of trade. That Krom does make such a connection, incorrectly, so it seems to me, appears from the evidence advanced by him in support of his position regarding Indonesian shipping and international trade – *i.e.* that "large sea-going ships" from Cambodia went from western India to China "with a cargo of mirrors" (*Geschiedenis*, 113 n. 2, *cf.* 120, 160). This is viewed and reported unhistorically. The shipping from the port towns of Normandy, Dieppe and Malo, on western Africa carried on

from around 1550 on, shipping which extended as far as the coast of Angola, took place in 1597 with ships carrying not more than fifty ton (Rouffaer & IJzerman, *Schipvaart*, I, 207 n. 18, II, 372; *cf. Daghregister 1631–1634*, 189–190). One should accept Ferrand's reasoning in regard to Indonesian colonization of Madagascar with the same technological reservation (for Phoenician as well as for Indonesian shipping): "The crossing of the Indian Ocean from one end to the other and in the rough season presupposes a perfect knowledge of the sea in the sailors who undertook it and navigational equipment perfected in comparison to the rudimentary equipment for fishing or coastal shipping – in short the existence of everything necessary for ocean-going shipping. Such a preparation can only be conceived of in a people of a high civilization, a preparation for instance identical with that of the sailors of Hiram, king of Tyre, who went to the mysterious Ophir on Solomon's account" (*Empire*, 152–152; *cf.* his "K'ouen-louen", XIII, 463 n. 1, XIV, 36). In the first Dutch voyage to the East, the ship *Duyfken* (Dovekin), a fifty–tonner, also completed the journey around the Cape. More small ships followed in the later fleets. That the Indonesians should have completed an overseas voyage from Indonesia to Madagascar, even with their small sea-going ships, junks of fifty ton or thereabouts, does not seem at all improbable, therefore. When captured Dutchmen who in 1636 fled from the court of Mataram to the south coast of Java and were able to put to sea there arrived at the Keeling Islands, they found a proa from the Lampong Coast there (De Jonge, *Opkomst*, V, 228–229; *Daghregister 1636*, 173 has another reading, however, giving the island of "Trouw" [Faithfulness] instead of "prauw" [proa]). The statement made in Rouffaer & IJzerman, *Schipvaart*, III, 221 is therefore too absolute.

41 Besides that there is of course the possibility that the initiative for this connection of the ruling groups in Indonesia with India may have originated from the side of the Brahman priesthood.

42 See Paul Pelliot in Ferrand, "K'ouen-louen", XIII, 242 n. 2.

43 See Masson-Oursel's statement: "The complete ignorance of the popular masses..." (*Inde*, 248; *cf.* Weber, *System*, 92). One should not make the mistake of considering the wealth and culture of the merchant gentlemen of the cities as the cultural level of 'the traders'. The merchant gentlemen, usually settled permanently in one place and making up the urban patriciate there, organized into merchant gilds, were the *popolo grosso*. Socially they towered high above the *popolo minuto*, formed by the great mass of traders and craftsmen. To begin from that merchant patriciate in judging the state of trade would be just as incorrect as to judge medieval trade and 'industry' in western Europe only from a Fugger, a Vicko van Gelders, or a John Winchcomb.

44 By ignoring the form of royal and aristocratic trade – *i.e.*, by not realizing the historical content of the category 'trade' clearly enough – Rouffaer makes what is certainly a mistake in allowing 'traders' in their turn to change places

with 'rulers'. In 1346 Ibn Battuta travelled from Zaitun to Samudra in northern Achin in the ruler of Samudra's junk (*cf.* Krom, *Geschiedenis*, 122). Rouffaer suggests that the ruler "was thus himself probably a rich *kojah*, from shipowner later having become a rajah!" ("Tochten", 382). That cannot have been true. Trade and shipowning by rulers is an historical form which constantly appeared in Indonesia. It was not so easy to change from *kojah* to rajah! The position of the ruler and the aristocracy over against the traders in Bantam illustrates that with a large number of instances; compare also the position of the traders received in audience by the ruler of Çriwijaya around 950 (Rouffaer, "Kunst", 568). The description given by Chau Ju-kua of the position of the ruler in regard to trade in a small state on the coast of Borneo in the thirteenth century is just as much characteristic for the situation; it does not seem to me advisable to draw the conclusion from the description which Krom does – that it was "not Hinduized or only defectively so", *i.e.* that it was rather 'primitive' (Krom, *Geschiedenis*, 305, *cf.* 399, 458 n. 1). In the first place because the economic activity described had nothing directly to do with Hinduization; in the second place because Chinese accounts of all 'barbaric countries' were depreciative (*cf.* Ma Huan in 1416 on the Javanese of Majapahit, in Krom, *Geschiedenis*, 444); in the third place because the form was one reappearing everywhere in the coastal principalities where ships called more or less regularly to carry on 'international trade'. It is no great step from the 'primitive' Borneo state Pu-ni of the thirteenth century to the Moslem Samudra of the fourteenth with its similar royal interference in trade and royal shipowning (see Yule, *Cathay*, IV, 96; Krom, *Geschiedenis*, 395), and from there to the Moslem Malacca of the fifteenth century (see Krom, *Geschiedenis*, 438) and the Bantam of the sixteenth and seventeenth centuries. Instructions of the Dutch Company dated 15 June, 1628 for a voyage from Batavia to Arakan for purchasing rice there read: "having come well in Arakan [you] shall deliver our accompanying missive and presents to the king there with the requisite compliments, and with all kinds of services and offices try to obtain His Majesty's favour and assistance as much as possible in the collection of a good quantity of rice..." (Colenbrander, *Coen*, V, 307, *cf.* 309). The officials of the Company were there following the same path as the Chinese merchants in the state Pu-ni and the first Indian traders in their early settlements in Indonesia. Compare the trade on Timor in 1614: "And when one arrives there to trade, one is required according to their ancient custom to give some presents that they call *chiripinang* to their king and his nobles, and then furthermore must agree with them what one will give the king for his *ruba-rubas*, or tolls for his *lonbebata* or anchorage fee, and other such things that they have as their custom which first have to be given to him before any of his subjects is allowed to bring any wood and who then obtain permission from him to sell the wood on the beach, which then is bought for such a low price that they are hardly paid for their labour.

All the other profits come for the king and his principal nobles..." (Tiele & Heeres, *Bouwstoffen*, I, 101, *cf.* II, xxii n. 1). And compare also the embassy of the Illustrious Dutch Company to the court of Siam in 1632: "The thirtieth [of September] the *shahbandar* came for the king to announce to us that we should come to court the next day, in which we still put little faith, but have kept their word and came to fetch us the next day around noon so that we drove in company with them to the court, where we had to wait more than two hours before going in. On going in had to wait another time about an hour on a balustrade, after which I [Caen, member of the Council of the Indies] was called to the inner court alone without any of the merchants being allowed to go along, so that I was led by the *shahbandar* and the interpreter from there up towards the door of the inner court, where we also waited a long time, while they kept lying as though on their faces in front of the door until we were admitted. When I came in it was indicated to me that I should go a little bowed, which was rather difficult as it lasted a good 300 steps, but for them still more uncomfortable for [they] crept on hands and knees through mud and filth all the way up to the steps of the king's house, where we came in after having knelt, and there the councillors of state and mandarins were gathered, all of them lying with their faces on the floor, and there the king appeared from a large gilded window, very richly ornamented with thickly gilded wooden bars..." (Tiele & Heeres, *Bouwstoffen*, II, 223; *cf.* the residents at the Javanese court in the eighteenth century: Van Deventer, *Bijdragen*, I, 29). That ambassadors of foreign rulers combined trading with their ambassadorial duties did not in the least mean that the ambassadors themselves had to be merchants. The nobility were separated from the merchants by just as strict class divisions as were the rulers. Either traders went along with the ambassadors (see *e.g.* Colenbrander, *Coen*, V, 7–8, 31, 101, 116, 175), the ambassadors carried on occasional trade (*ibid.*, V, 539 is after all a case of this), or the embassy sailed on a trading vessel and had nothing directly to do with the merchants also sailing on it. The 'visitation officials' of the government of Majapahit, whose function will have been not only a bureaucratic one but, as 'first and foremost task', a religious one, were forbidden "to carry on personal business at the same time" on their journeys of inspection overseas (Krom's paraphrase of *Nagarakertagama* 16: 1 in *Geschiedenis*, 415). Without doubt the form familiar from everywhere else in economic history, of trade carried on by the religious dignitaries, based on the riches of the monasteries, temples, sanctuaries, and religious foundations, needs here to be detected in the background. The trade the Javenese Majapahit visitation officials carried on must most of the time have been occasional trade. With Rouffaer and Krom alike, everything is vague in this regard. The term 'wholesale trade' which Berg (*Hoofdlijnen*, 14) and Gonggrijp (*Schets*, 12, 17, 47, 57, 59) use for Majapahit also lacks a clear historical context.

45 The list of goods the Grand Mogul Jahangir requested of the English is of sufficient interest to reprint in full:

"The Akbar requests these following goods from England:

Fine swords / knives } with which one can hew on iron.

satin / velvet } of divers colours, but no black...

cloth good and fine, green yellow and crimson,
men's and women's clothing not more than 3 or 4 pieces each one of a different cut,
all kinds of paintings of landscapes and personages painted on cloth with oil paint,
Spanish leather perfumed,
mirrors the size of a man with their frames wrought with leafwork,
Japanese weapons,
parrots and cockatoos and other pretty birds,
2, 3, 4, or 5 copper chandeliers to set candles on, most prettily worked with divers work,
finely wrought glasses, the most authentic, and table service, and everything has to be very pretty and gilded,
glass goglets wrought like those of Mecca, also gilded,
3 or 4 clocks, of metal as well as crystal,
2: 3: 4 corslets with their morions, enamelled as well as engraved with gilt,
pretty, illustrious javelins, iron, like those of partisan, gilded with divers work and silvered and engraved, about 200 pieces,
pretty guns and linlocks, pistols that had to have sturdy matchlocks, for once broken they could not be repaired again,
divers other curiosities of lesser value in our land and very agreeable here,
5 or 6 pair exquisite greyhounds and along with them some strong mastiffs that dare to attack tigers and leopards and fight against them..."

(Terpstra, *Westerkwartieren*, 215; *cf.* Moreland, *Akbar*, 143 & n. 1). One should bear in mind how many 'cultural influences' these objects and their like could exert when brought to a court and there allowed to serve as an example for court artificers. (Early capitalistic England and the rest of Europe were then still producing objects of handicraft art the same as Asia!) Incidentally, it should be borne in mind that the influences in handicraft arts coming from Asia to Europe were more important than the influences in the other direction (see Reichwein, *China*, 39–40, *cf.* 81). Only with the rational organization and machine techniques of modern capitalism was there a superior vitality in the influences transferred from the West the the East. All early 'cultural influences' exerted *via* trade need to be regarded in this same light. The above list should also be compared with the lists of goods in Asian trade given earlier (see Colenbrander, *Coen*, I, 44, 47–48, 237, 283, 333, 378–379, 534, 582, 773, IV, 717, V, 835–836, 842).

46 Compare the trader-intermediary in Krom, *Geschiedenis*, 228 – certainly a merchant gentleman.

47 This does not exclude the fact that both rich merchants and *parvenus* gone out 'on adventure' could hold high posts at the courts, especially in places where because of the mobile 'international' life the posts were not so strictly bound to a certain group and not so deeply rooted in the traditional hierarchy (*e.g.* Bantam) as in the courts of the patrimonial, bureaucratic states (*e.g.* Majapahit), with their more closed societies. 'Government by foreigners' in that sense is a form which has recurred over and over, everywhere.

48 See Krom, *Geschiedenis*, 67–81.

49 "Fleet ascertained falsified pedigrees of princes *en masse* in Southern India as early as the ninth century..." (Weber, *System*, 35, following *Epigraphia Indica*, III, 171; *cf.* Aymonier, *Cambodge*, I, 396).

50 On the Brahmins as transmitters of Indian culture see Krom, *Geschiedenis*, 91–92, *cf.* 81, 87, 124, 148, 163, 313.

51 *Cf.* Berg, *Hoofdlijnen*, 13 n. 1. As has been said above, Berg's view is that of a military subjugation of Java by 'robber barons'. What is important in this connection is the great distance which with the help of the caste system there was between the traders and aristocratic society. And that is doubly or trebly valid for the distance between the Brahmins and the Dravidians carrying on peddling trade.

52 See Westenenk, "Chetti", 1–3.

53 *Geschiedenis*, 92. The more so because of the parallels with the propagation of Islam on Madagascar Krom has taken over from Ferrand (*ibid.*, n. 1).

54 Objections to the rather unconsidered hypothesis on the Dravidian extraction of a Batak tribe, the Sembiring Bataks, were made in the unpublished paper "Het schip in de inheemsche kunstnijverheid" (The Ship in Indigenous Arts and Crafts) read by A. N. J. Thomassen à Thuessink van der Hoop at the seventeenth private meeting of the Philology, Geography, and Ethnology Section of the Royal Batavian Society, 20 June, 1940.

55 Rouffaer & Juynboll, in 1900, in *Batik-kunst*, I, 306 (*cf.* Rouffaer in 1933, in "Kunst", 516); Berg, in 1928, in *Hoofdlijnen*, 11, 14.

56 How one could arrive at this view is not clear to me. Traders from every part of India – and certainly not only Moslems – went their way through all Indonesia and Asia, and westward as well, during the centuries of Islamic domination in southeast Asia and Moslem political power in the Near East and western and southern Asia, and during the period of Portuguese and northwest European colonial control. Faith, trade, and *raison d'état* are

completely separate things: *cf.* the case cited above of the Moslem trader who wanted to travel back to Constantinople by going around the Cape on the ship of the Christian Amsterdam Company in order to elude the blockade of the Moslem ruler of Achin. On southern Indian shipping and instructions for port pilots in the fifteenth and sixteenth centuries see Ferrand, *Empire*, 98 n. 2. On Hindu traders in Moslem Malacca in the fifteenth century see Rouffaer, "Malaka", 167; for the sixteenth century see Schrieke, "Prolegomena", 148; Moreland, *Akbar*, 214, 246. For Hindu traders in the Moluccas in the seventeenth century see De Jonge, *Opkomst*, III, 198–199.

57 For a summary of them see Van Vollenhoven, *Adatrecht*, II, 123–125.

58 *Ibid.*, I, 150, 154, 227, 247–248, 273–275, 279, 282, 284, 286, 289–292, 294, 303, 395, 433, 448.

59 *Ibid.*, I, 352, 371–372.

60 *Ibid.*, I, 383, 395, 432–433. The tradition of the founding of Majapahit is connected with Madurese colonization in eastern Java at the end of the thirteenth century (see Krom, *Geschiedenis*, 352–353, *cf.* 436–437, 441 n. 1, 454, 456 & n. 1: the first and second types of colonization overlap each other).

61 See *e.g.* Van Vollenhoven, *Adatrecht*, I, 469, 509. *Cf.* also the interesting institution of Minangkabau 'consuls' in the Malay state Siak (*ibid.*, I, 297–298; *cf.* Van Vollenhoven, *Droit*, 21 n. 4), and the description of a Mandarese settlement at Lepeloan on Lombok, under Mandarese village authorities but with the position of daughter village to the *desa* Beblanting on Lombok (Goris, "Lombok", 210).

62 *Cf.* Schrieke, "Prolegomena", 131.

63 Van Vollenhoven, *Adatrecht*, I, 134, 135, 311, 314, 372, 433, 457, 470–471, *cf.* 510.

64 *Ibid.*, I, 167, 230–231, 234, 294–295, 314–315, 356, 358, 401, 404, 428. It is possible that the inscription from Bangka dating from 686 contains a reference to a *datuk*, a governor, over Bangka from Çriwijaya (Krom, *Geschiedenis*, 116). The hunting of Papuas for slaves (*cf.* Van Vollenhoven, *Adatrecht*, I, 425) as early as the tenth century appears from the fact that Papua slaves were found on Java then (from the record of the foundation of a Buddhist sanctuary: see Krom, *Geschiedenis*, 223 & n. 1, *cf.* 300). On Papua slaves on Java at the end of the sixteenth century see Rouffaer & IJzerman, *Schipvaart*, I, 197 & n. 3; on Papua slaves for the Moluccas in the seventeenth century see Tiele & Heeres, *Bouwstoffen*, II, 6; on slave hunting see *ibid.*, II, 8. For the Ternatese governors around Ambon, the incessant opponents of the Dutch East India Company in the first half of the seventeenth century, *cf.* Rouffaer, "Kunst", 374 n. 1.

65 *Cf.* "Hindoe-Javanen", 1, 9, 12. Westenenk assumes that there was an expansion of Hindu-Javanese power over southern Sumatra.

66 *Cf.* also Van Vollenhoven, *Adatrecht*, II, 122, III, 583–585.

67 *Cf.* Bertling, review, 350–351.

68 *Cf.* Vogel's statement: "It is certainly astonishing that in the inscriptions of the Pallavas and other southern dynasties no reference whatever is made to the relations which in those days must have existed between Coromandel and the Far East. The explanation probably is that those relations, of which the accounts of the Chinese pilgrims have left us such a valuable record, were of a perfectly peaceful nature. Supposed the powerful Pallava princes of Kancipura had equipped armadas and carried their arms to the remote shores of Campa and Java, may we not assume that their conquests on the far side of the ocean would have been extolled in their praçastis [*cf.* Krom, *Geschiedenis,* 196, 288, 375] with no less effusion than we find lavished on their victories over the Calukyas?" ("Inscriptions", 192). The records of a ruler of Çola give copious accounts of his expeditions of war and plunder against Çriwijaya in 1023–1024 (see Krom, *Geschiedenis,* 249–253), and similarly of an overseas expedition in 1068 (see *ibid.,* 303, *cf.* 337, 364–365, 396, 418, 437, 439). The same is true for pacific, 'official' overseas relations (see *ibid.,* 227–228, 238, 303–304).

69 *Cf.* Krom's words: "Incidentally – this by way of preventing a misunderstanding – no one has held the opinion that there could have been any question of a conquest emanating from India in the sense that the regions overseas became dependencies of a central Indian authority. Every shadow of an indication of that is lacking." (*Ibid.,* 90, *cf.* 100).

70 *Cf. ibid.,* 423.

71 *Cf. ibid.,* 304 & n. 5.

72 In that case Indian customary law, not Hindu scholastic law, would have been transferred to Indonesia. *Cf.* Van Vollenhoven, *Adatrecht,* II, 118–119.

73 *Cf.* Van Vollenhoven's words: "There is neither relationship nor resemblance between Indonesian *adat* law on the one hand and the Indonesian manifestations of Chinese, Arab, and Indian customary law on the other. Here are involved not only divergent legal families from divergent legal basins, but even completely divergent legal clans from widely divergent legal districts [*cf. Adatrecht,* III, 569]; it is not the differences between such sorts of customary law that give reason for surprise, but what is amazing is their points of agreement. It would be conceivable, of course, that the legal systems had influenced each other strongly within Indonesia through inculcation and borrowing – that *e.g.* Javanese *adat* law had had some influence on Javanese-Chinese customary law and Javanese-Arabic some influence on Javanese [Van Vollenhoven is completely silent on Indian law in this regard]. But also that secondary relation, a relation which can be imagined just as well elsewhere in Indonesian regions – for Chinese on Formosa, the Philippines, or Malaya, or for Arabs on Madagascar – remained highly exceptional. The study of such new sorts of customary law therefore has value for Indo-

nesian *adat* law only in this sense – that it demonstrates on other legal materials some of the conclusions to which the preceding survey of the *adat* law of the Indonesians [in *ibid.*, I, 133–755] has already led." (*Adatrecht*, II, 3, *cf.* 12–13, 108, 115–120, 614, 751, 808). Krom's thought goes in the direction of Indian group colonization in central Java in *Geschiedenis*, 176–177, 304, *cf.* 185.

74 *Cf.* Sosro Ningrat, "Huwelijk".

75 *Cf.* Berg, *Hoofdlijnen*, 13 n. 1.

76 At the beginning of the eleventh century, in the time of Airlangga, the following Indians and other foreign traders in eastern Java were mentioned: Calinggalese (a name occuring in the records as early as Pliny: see Westenenk, "Chetti", 2 & n. 1; and remaining in usage up to the present day as *keling*), Cingalese, Dravidians, Kanarese, Chams, Peguans, Cambodians (Krom, *Geschiedenis*, 264–265, *cf.* 183; see also Rouffaer, "Pégon", 371).

77 An inscription from Baros dating from 1088 and written in Tamil mentions a donation to a corporation. The corporation must have been a Tamil-speaking community (Krom, *Geschiedenis*, 304). It seems to me indubitable that what is involved here is a settlement of traders from southern India (the second type listed above) in that traditional trading port.

78 Is the fact that the Arab quarters were also called *pekojan* in colloquial speech (Van Vollenhoven, *Adatrecht*, II, 117) an indication of continuity?

79 Krom, *Geschiedenis*, 141 (see the whole passage, pp. 140–141).

80 *Cf.* the remarkable statement in *ibid.*, 183.

81 See *e.g.* the sixth century Chinese notice given by Ma Tuan-lin of a Malay coastal state lying between Tenasserim and Kedah (according to Pelliot's location): "The king half-reclined on a golden bed in the form of a dragon. The nobles in his retinue are on their knees before him, their bodies erect and their arms crossed in such a way that their hands lie on their shoulders. At his court one sees many ... Brahmins who came from India to profit from his munificence and are much in his favour." (Ferrand, "K'ouen-louen", XIII, 254–255). An Indonesian court; Brahmins from overseas come to the court, are held in great respect because of their sacral magical power and sacral literary knowledge, and enjoy prebends and royal gifts.

82 The dates for the beginning of commercial shipping and cultural influence can be widely separated in time, and were so for Indian trade and Indian cultural influence in Indonesia. Furthermore the fact that traders and disseminators of culture come from the same place does not need to mean a primary link between them. The Brahman hierocracy was 'international' *par excellence.* Did Aryan Brahmins go to Indonesia, or was it the Dravidian Brahmins, who belonged to lower castes? An overwhelming majority of the traders will have come from southern India. The journeys of the Buddhist pilgrims were directed especially toward the Ganges ports, and the Buddhist Çailendra kings of Çriwijaya maintained relations with the Buddhist university at Nalanda (see Krom, *Geschiedenis*, 142–143, 204, *cf.* 119,

139, & especially 247–248). Trade will have continued to follow the old route to the ports of Calingga, Coromandel, Ceylon, and Malabar (*cf. ibid.*, 238 & n. 2).

83 Can Berg's view be revised in this way? For example, the use of war chariots was a part of the military technique of aristocratic societies and patrimonial, bureacratic armies alike, in early China, early India, early Hellas, even in Ireland (see Weber, *History*, 38, *Wirtschaft*, 521, and *Essays*, 255 ff.; *cf. Ezekiel* 26: 10, quoted earlier). Can their use on Java be attributed to military importation from India (*cf.* Rassers, *Pandji-roman*, 62)? In this connection the 'chariots' of the ruler of Wengker in 1035 (see Krom, *Geschiedenis*, 258) seem to me to have been war chariots; for Gajah Mada in battle on his chariot see *ibid.*, 404, and *cf.* Rouffaer (following Castanheda) in Fruin-Mees, *Geschiedenis*, II, 11 n. 1. Kern's assumption regarding the Tamil protagonists at the time of Airlangga (Krom, *Geschiedenis*, 265) is of the same sort. And probably there is another such assumption in the remarkable statement by Chau Ju-kua on the followers of the ruler of Çriwijaya who followed their dead master (and thus probably paymaster) in death on the funeral pyre. The same thing is reported of the southern Indian 'trusty lieges'. Can these men be imagined as a half-feudal, half-slave warrior retinue kept as a bodyguard by the ruler of Çriwijaya, and coming from southern India? (According to Yule's notes the berserker lieges of Malabar bore the name Amuki, supposed to be the source of the word amok or amuck, which came to English *via* Malay: see Polo, *Book*, II, 347 n. 5; *cf.* also Krom, *Geschiedenis*, 414–415). Furthermore it is known that 'Malay' (Indonesian?) mercenaries of Çriwijaya served in Persia and Mesopotamia, under the Sassanids as well as the caliphs (De Goeje, "Sajâbidja"). Warriors serving in foreign countries are no rarity. For the Roman soldiers of the Tamil rulers see above; the Indian troops in Xerxes' army for his Greek expedition are known from Herodotus (see also Mookerji, *Shipping*, 95; Masson-Oursel, *Inde*, 34, 126). Marco Polo mentions 'Saracen' troops kept in his day, the end of the thirteenth century, as mercenaries on Ceylon (*Book*, II, 314); in 1266, there were also Chinese soldiers serving as mercenaries there (Yule, *Cathay*, I, 75). The keeping of 'private armies' by the nobles of the northern Javanese port towns (*cf.* Krom, *Geschiedenis*, 323–324, 334, 377) belongs to the same sort of general form.

84 See Coomaraswamy's interesting material in Weber, *System*, 76; *cf.* Krom, *Geschiedenis*, 129, 159 n. 3, 173, 175.

85 *Cf.* Weber, *Religionssoziologie*, II, 358.

86 *Cf.* Krom, *Geschiedenis*, 68–69.

87 See Weber, *System*, 76, 99; *Religionssoziologie*, II, 281–282, 285, 319 n. 1, 324. Nothing is more natural and more a matter of course, given the level of technique and art (in actuality unseparated from each other) in the periods before that of modern capitalism: handicraft knowledge (and that

does not only include ordinary crafts: architecture and the ornamental arts need just as much to be considered as crafts) was bound to individuals or families and tradition; it was empirical, and not efficiently self-sufficient (*cf.* Goris in Ploegsma, *Oorspronkelijkheid*, 162–163), so that every 'cultural influence' had to be transmitted hand to hand. See also Krom, *Geschiedenis*, 303 n. 4.

88 *Cf.* the two following quotations. "The Christianization [of Russia] emanated from the highest social strata, so that the ideals of Holy Russia were not (as was the case in the nineteenth century) borne by the peasantry, but by the representatives of the highest classes. 'The Russian saints are not the Russian people. The saints are bearers of [the concept of] abnegation of the world, in many respects in direct opposition to the world, that is to say to the life of the people to which they belong. The idealization of Russian life would be out of place here.'" (Review). "The Russian language derives an extraordinary richness from the fact that it has a double origin. It is connected by an unbroken line with Church Slavic, which was imported from Bulgaria around the year 1000. It [Church Slavic] was not only the language of the church, but also, in a larger sense, the written language. Eventually it coalesced with another written language based on Great Russian, especially that of Moscow." (Van Wijk, "Poesjkin", 329–330).

89 In Ferrand, "K'ouen-louen", XIII, 320 n. 1.

90 The mountain temple terrace complex of central Java, where the earliest expressions of Hinduism are to be found, is typical. Undoubtedly Hinduism had been preceded there by a traditional indigenous religion (Krom, *Geschiedenis*, 127–128). In connection with this form one involuntarily imagines an organization such as that of early Mexico and early Peru (*cf. ibid.*, 136–137, 159, 167, 185, 274, 276–277, 287, 379, 386, 419 ff.).

91 *Ibid.*, 130, 164, 254.

92 Krom's speaking of the 'apparent aimlessness' of such plunderings by a 'commercial power' (*ibid.*, 135) shows unhistorical reasoning. Piracy was just as much a normal activity in Asian waters as in the Mediterranean at the time of Hellas' power and the time of the Berber harbour princes (see Ziebarth, *Beiträge*; *cf.* the important passage by Ferrand in "K'ouen-louen", XIII, 321–322). Relations in Oriental international trade should not be rendered in nineteenth-century liberal concepts. Plundering fits completely into the historical picture of peddling trade on the one hand and on the other royal authority with personal trade, occasional trade, monopoly, and naval power all for the benefit of the king's own treasury.

93 Krom, *Geschiedenis*, 113–114, 116–117, 120, 122, 130, 133–135, 141–142, 205, 226, 250, 284, 307; Ferrand, *Empire*, 4–5, 9, 13, 66, 106, 145, 184.

94 The constantly recurring story of the 'treasures of the maharajah', the ceremonial of the bars of gold, and so forth sould be called to mind.

95 Chau Ju-kua, *Trade*, 60.

96 Coedès, "Royaume", 25.

97 See Krom, *Geschiedenis*, 141–142.

98 *Cf.* Schrieke, "Prolegomena", 107–108, 108 n. 15, 110.

99 See *e.g.* De Kat Angelino, *Policy*, II, 97–98, *cf.* 101–102, 112. The term 'semi-feudal' used there is open to a great deal of criticism, however.

100 And furthermore what would be the result of the 'half-breed' theory regarding the transmission of Indian civilization if it were consistently carried through for the countries where the ruling groups and dynasties have a Mongoloid component? There has never been any research done by physical anthropologists on Hindu-Burmese or Hindu-Cambodian elements. It seems to me that for those countries and Indonesia alike the theory is based on a premise which is incorrect historically and sociologically. (The 'half-breed' theory is consistently carried through by Bernet Kempers in *Cultuurstroom*, 7, 9–10, 12, 16; *cf.* Lévi, *Indochine*, I, 49, on Hindu-Khmer admixture.) The Indian 'half-breed' ruler of Langka (Rouffaer, "Malaka", 99) was incidentally very probably Indonesian in ancestry.

101 Krom, *Geschiedenis*, 94.

102 *Ibid.*, 100.

103 *Ibid.*, 148.

104 *Ibid.*, 124–125, *cf.* 147.

105 See Berg, *Hoofdlijnen*, 12; Rouffaer, "Malaka", 455 & n. 3, 457–458, 588. This was true elsewhere as well.

106 The same thing applies against Ferrand's explanation of the legend on the foundation of the state of Cambodia by Brahmins ("K'ouen-louen", XIV, 24 n. 2; *cf.* Krom, *Geschiedenis*, 91–92). There is no reason to deduce a "migration of foreigners" (Ferrand, "K'ouen-louen", XIV, 28 n. 1) from this legend of the hierocracy. *Cf.* also Krom, *Geschiedenis*, 71 point 2.

107 In Indonesia as well as elsewhere in southeast Asia, the hierarchy was composed of Çiwaitic, Wisnaitic, and Buddhist elements: the sacral legitimation of rulers could involve any one of the three, or a mixture of all of them. What sort of hierarchy of groups and sects there was would be difficult to determine. There was of course the possibility of various groups – the lower ranks of priests, hermits, and monks – coming in contact with the population. But that had nothing to do with a process of 'Hinduization'; it was the magical *charisma* of the 'priesthood', rather independent of the dogmatic or ethical content of the 'religion' they claimed to adhere to, which was decisive for the great masses of the people. Another question which has not been faced clearly is that of what proportion of the hierocracy was foreign Indian and what proportion indigenous Indonesian (there are a few comments in Krom, *Geschiedenis*, 107–110, *cf.* 115–120, 126–127, 248). Conversion, even mass conversion of Indonesians to the Hindu religious organizations and sects is possible of course, and admittance to the higher priesthood and its public functions as well. After all, the parallel 'secular' bureaucracy was

manned completely by Indonesians. The 'Indonesianization' of Indian civilization took place within that framework, the Indonesian element weakening the original Indian tradition and transforming it. However, a strengthening of the Indonesian element did not have to have a weakening (in an absolute sense) of the Indian element as a 'natural' result. Related to this question is the question of the Indonesianization of Hindu art in the archipelago. The artificers need to be pictured as having craft skills and passing them on as hereditary family traditions. It is an open question to what extent Indonesians were admitted to the closed groups of such artificers as members or apprentices; furthermore the Indonesians taken in apprenticeship could become representatives of a very 'orthodox' tradition or could introduce a large and important element of indigenous artistic style and skill in the work (*cf.* Krom, *Geschiedenis*, 129, 178, 184, 235, 267, 297, 311, 327). A whole range of possibilities can be imagined here.

108 Schrieke, "Adatgrondenrecht", 153–154.

109 See Krom, *Geschiedenis*, 149–153, 231, 269, 291, 293, 295, 340 & n. 4, 421, 424, 445.

110 *Cf.* Berg, *Hoofdlijnen*, 10–11, 14–15; Krom, *Geschiedenis*, 169, 196, 206–209. Berg's view has been taken over here except for the fact that the 'half-breed' theory, the rise of a ruling class of Hindu-Indonesians, whether of Indonesian and Dravidian or Indonesian and Aryan intermixture – *cf.*: "Immigrating in small numbers, the Indians after all intermixed with only a few indigenous families. It is probable that the Hindus had not brought women along" (Ferrand, "K'ouen-louen", XIV, 202) – has been dropped and an Indonesian (Javanese) society which remained Indonesian in composition from the princely superstructure to the popular basis has been assumed. It appears to me in this connection that the caste system in Indonesia was an affair of the hierocracy rather than of the royal court and higher officialdom. It had only a theoretical, sacral value for the whole social structure. Its very basis of interethnic relations was lacking in that form in Indonesian society. One should remember the caste system was not necessary for a sharp class division. Berg writes: "It seems probable that a caste system such as the one still existing today on Bali was one of the institutions taken over, but even without a strong caste system one might expect that after the Oriental fashion the *kraton* circles would be isolated as much as possible from the rest of the people" (*Hoofdlijnen*, 11; *cf.* Korn in Ploegsma, *Oorspronkelijkheid*, 160). The class taboos elsewhere in Indonesia give evidence of this, and in 'Hindu Indonesia' there is not a trace of the process which resulted from Hinduization in southern India, the thorough organization of all groups of the population in a caste system which was completely dominant socially.

111 "Of course something of the culture of the *kraton* eventually filtered down to the people, but in the main they had still not come very far beyond

the level of primitiveness" (Berg, *Hoofdlijnen*, 11–12). The 'primitiveness' is debatable; here it is to be understood as the complex of Indonesian agrarian civilization. The interests of the people were of course only recorded in documents whenever the interests of the authorities or the hierocracy were involved (*cf.* Krom, *Geschiedenis*, 197–198, 223, 264–265).

112 Krom leaves the economic foundations of the authority and the hierocracy as well as the economic position of the people in the dark. The emphasis could be placed on that economic aspect rather than on the artistic and cultural one. On the one side were the authority and the hierocracy with their massive wealth (practically the whole of early Indonesian records has to do with prebends). On the other was the population burdened with enormous quantities of work, labour on all the royal building activities – by which the interests of the hierocracy were directly served, for each foundation of a new temple meant the creation of a new series of prebends (*cf.* Krom, *Geschiedenis*, 152–153, 170–173, 220, 315, 344, 402) – including clearing of ground and transportation of materials, and besides that all the regular burdens, the maintenance of the rulers and members of the dynasty with their courts, the corps of officials, the hosts of priests and religious dignitaries, the swarms of monks and hermits. Considering the rather small area of land cultivated on Java in that time – the present state of clearance and cultivation on Java is only the result of an immoderate extension during the last hundred years – such a civilization must have been a heavy burden for the Javanese people (see Finot, "Etudes", 224; *cf.* Busken Huet's comment in this regard in *Rembrandt*, II, Part One, 237).

113 Gonggrijp, haunted by the ghost of 'progress', expressed this in a curious way by saying that the organization of the Hindu states was based "on the stationariness of society" (*Schets*, 15–16).

114 See Yule, *Cathay*, I, 123 n. 1.

115 Hornell, "Design", 199.

116 See Krause, *Geschichte*, I, 127, 139, 347–348. Krause's view is incorrect in several places in its details of the history of trade.

117 See Yule, *Cathay*, I, 89–90, 129–130. See also Ferrand's statement: "We know that Chau Ju-kua obtained his information on most of the foreign countries of the west from Persian and Arab seamen" ("K'ouen-louen", XIII, 332; *cf. ibid.*, XIV, 210; Krom, *Geschiedenis*, 227).

118 See Ferrand, *Empire*, 69. The statement that 'Hindu' (Tamil?), Persian, Arabic, and Greek were spoken in Çriwijaya at the beginning of the tenth century (*ibid.*, 54) is debated by Krom as far as Greek is concerned (*Geschiedenis*, 204). Does that apply also to Arabic? On the basis of the facts just mentioned it would seem to me certain that Arabic was spoken there at that time (*cf.* Rouffaer, "Kunst", 570–571, 595).

119 See Groeneveldt, "Notes", 14 n. 4, 101; *cf.* Van der Kolff, *Bevolkingsrietcultuur*, 13 & n. 22, 19 & n. 42.

120 Krom, *Geschiedenis*, 452 & nn. 5 & 6; *cf.* Ravaisse, "Inscription", 668 ff.

121 See Ravaisse's statement on "Moslem colonization" ("Inscription", 670, *cf.* 672 & n. 3, 679, 687, 701–702).

122 At least this appears to me to have been the way the process took place. Schrieke's hypothesis is that Mohammedan traders succeeded in getting a foothold in northern Sumatra ("Prolegomena", 109), but it seems to me that an accurate historical orientation of the category 'trade' must lead to the rejection of such an hypothesis on the establishment of a foreign regime *via* trade. In this regard it also seems to me incorrect for Schrieke to say of the northern Javanese ports that "the traders came primarily from the aristocratic classes, not from the people" ("Prolegomena", 130). This was the pattern, after all: the aristocracy carried on trade, owned ships, and so forth, but the actual trade, the commercial expeditions made overseas with the monsoon winds and the great mass of commercial transactions closed on the long journeys, was carried out by small traders, pedlars, most of them going out on *commenda.* The trade of the aristocracy (and the rich merchant gentlemen) was 'passive', occasional investment of capital. If they carried on personal trade, their ships made the journeys commanded by their *nakodas* and with their factors on board (see Tiele & Heeres, *Bouwstoffen*, II, 393).

123 See Krom, *Geschiedenis*, 426–427.

124 A Malay dynasty (see Ferrand, *Empire*, 184; Rouffaer, "Malaka", 587 ff.).

125 Perhaps it should be pointed out once more that such a flowering of trade had nothing to do with an 'economic development' in the sense of historical progress. It was an increase in the amount of trade, in the number of pedlars and craftsmen.

126 See Krom, *Geschiedenis*, 396–397, *cf.* 140; Schrieke, "Prolegomena", 102 ff., *cf.* 120, 124 ff., 151 (Schrieke's view is not completely the same as that of Becker, "Grundlinien", 216–218); Moreland, *Akbar*, 198–199, 245.

127 On the political unity of the Moslem rulers in Egypt, Arabia, and India, see *e.g.* Danvers, *Portuguese*, I, 186, 212, 241, 280, 287, 303, *cf.* 288–289.

128 *Cf.* Schrieke, "Prolegomena", 144–146; Van den Berg, *Rangen*, 92 n. 3.

129 See Rouffaer, "Tijdperk", 122–123, 134 & n. 1, 192–193, *cf.* 192 n. 31; Krom, *Geschiedenis*, 458; Fruin-Mees, *Geschiedenis*, II, 2, 5 & n. 3, 6 & n. 1, 9–10, 18, 21, 28; Schrieke, "Javanen", *passim*, and his "Prolegomena", 114 ff., 129, 136, 140 ff., 154, 159, 202, 204 (that the keeping of slave bodyguards should be a sign of "impopularity" is a rather weak and distorted thesis).

130 See Lévi, *Indochine*, I, 67, 82.

131 The rebellion, emanating from the coastal town Demak, led to an

inland regime once more in the sultanate of Pajang (*cf.* Schrieke, "Prolegomena", 203); the focal point of the power then succeeding, that of the adventurer and usurper Senopati, lay completely within the old inland territory of the state, the *kraton* of Kota Gede. The antithesis Gonggrijp sees – "... the result of the differences in economic interest between the ruling classes, *i.e.* those of the agrarian Hindu-Javanese states and those of the small states founded more on trade..." (*Schets*, 23–24) – therefore seems to me momentary rather than enduring. The aspirations of the coastal regents and the Moslem Javanese aristocratic families struggling with each other for power were just as much 'agrarian' as those of the ruling prebendal officials of the Hindu-Javanese state. In this case also it is the correct historical orientation of the category 'trade' which is in the long run decisive. Krom points out the possible connection of the Moslem priest-ruler Sunan Giri to a Hindu-Javanese ruler Girindrawarddhana (*Geschiedenis*, 451). To that can be added the fact that in the circle of the priest-ruler of Giri as late as in 1680 there was an 'Ady Patty Tumappel', son-in-law of the *panembahan* (see De Jonge, *Opkomst*, VII, 307). With the establishment of the authority of Mataram the independent Javanese aristocratic families were driven from power and replaced by creatures of the ruler. "This family [that of Senopati] has got to the point that it has overthrown and exterminated nearly all the kings of Java and set other stadtholders of low origin in their place" (Colenbrander, *Coen*, IV, 600).

132 Krom, *Geschiedenis*, 454.

133 See Schrieke, "Prolegomena", 110 n. 17, 150; *cf.* Fruin-Mees, *Geschiedenis*, II, 6.

134 Buddhism, the prophetic, revelatory doctrine of early India, quickly degenerated into passive hierocratic and hierarchical rigidity. Buddhism as it came to be known widely in southeast Asia was just as exclusive as the Brahmanic priesthood, a matter of religious dignitaries and a magical, ritual exploitation of the masses by groups of monks and hermits.

135 "Mohammedan merchants from India, following the age-old path of their Hindu countrymen, settled temporarily or for good in a few places on the coast of these islands. Those small colonies exerted the usual power of attraction, even on Java, although Hinduism had been dominating culture there for centuries. However one should not forget in this regard that Hinduism could not shoot out such deep roots there as in its homeland, outside of which it did not as a rule extend itself, and that Hindu culture did not share its spiritual refinement with the masses considered as belonging to the lower castes, so that under the Hindu regime was exactly the place where for a great majority there could be much reason to seek redemption from its state of humiliation in Islam" (Snouck Hurgronje, "Politique", 241–242). I cannot share the opinion of Schrieke, who speaks of the Javanese traders migrating from Çriwijaya to Malacca as "the Hindu-Javanese traders, wrenched

out of their traditional environment" who then, in their attempt to "create a new [Hindu] commercial centre" in Malacca came in contact with the "fanatically Mohammedan Gujarati" and were thus converted to Islam ("Prolegomena", 110–111, *cf.* 126). For 'Hindu-Javanese traders' one should read traders from the coastal towns and hinterlands of eastern Java dominated by a Hindu-Javanese dynasty, *noblesse de robe*, and hierocracy – something completely different. I cannot see what the traditional Hindu environment may have consisted of, especially in the turbulent, cosmopolitan Çriwijaya. So far as the traditions of the Javanese people were concerned, the Javanese small traders and pedlars in their quarters in Malacca (see Schrieke, "Prolegomena", 111–112), under the authority of Javanese nobles and/or merchant patricians (that is after all the way the 'headmen' must be considered), will have been just as strong and of exactly the same nature in that Moslem town as in the Hindu–Buddhist–Sumatran Çriwijaya. Mme Fruin's comment, with reference to a statement by Schrieke, that "as regards the Javanese – who moved throughout the archipelago filled with self-confidence and the spirit of enterprise and there encountered many a land subjugated to Java, – they must have felt more for Mohammed's fiery teachings than for the calmer and more resigned Çiwaism and Buddhism" (*Geschiedenis*, II, 5) also seems to me of just as little validity. India with its Brahmanic might had known trade power, spirit of enterprise, and unbridled struggle for gain in every form and to the greatest dimensions imaginable. *Cf.* Van Linschoten's "Gusarates and Baneanem... are the subtilest and politiquest Marchauntes of all India..." (*Voyage*, I, 60, *cf.* 252–253, II, 137–138; see also Moreland, *Akbar*, 249–250). The "calmer and more resigned Çiwaism and Buddhism" have never appeared to be a hindrance for any economic struggle, especially in the higher castes. The flaw in reasoning lies in the neglect of sociological orientation of the various religions. Çiwaism and Buddhism were on Java matters of a hierocracy and of mendicant monks, and did not form an element in the economic mentality of the people. For the people, on Java and in India alike, the Buddhist and Çiwaitic religious *virtuosi* (to use a Weberian term), like the later Moslem *virtuosi* – hadjis, *kyais*, and so forth – only bore the *charisma* of their magical power. Furthermore, Islam could lead to all sorts of worldly and otherworldly sects and orders whose way of life and economic mentality were solidly traditional and non-economic: the mystical, pantheistic form in which Islam, especially, manifested itself in Indonesia and was organized into sects there led in that direction. Rinkes sketches the activities of the *walis* on Java in quite another way than the 'missionary' work of traders: "...groups of certain persons under the leadership of one or another respected master... took the initiative for establishing places many of which still exist and which in a number of cases developed to flourishing importance...", and he compares their work in opening up the land with that of the monks in western Europe in the early middle ages (Fruin-Mees, *Geschiedenis*, II,

6 & n. 3). In this argument Islam is given an agrarian basis economically! May one here picture exempted *desas* such as the villages of the pious in Achin, on lands given by the Javanese coastal aristocracy? If so, it would be one more indication of the power of the Javanese aristocracy and the inferior position of Moslem missions. It is clear that the whole question of the sociology of Indonesian Islam in its beginnings needs further investigation.

136 Moslems had travelled through Indonesia and stayed in its ports and on its shores for centuries without having exerted any missionary influence worth mentioning. Only toward the end of the thirteenth century did a wave of proselyting emanate from Gujarat – or should the dimensions of that missionary movement be rendered as much smaller, and the dimensions of the political events discussed above as much larger? The motives for the historic happening have not yet been clearly outlined. Was it a passion for competition aroused by the appearance of Christian missions in Asia under the protection of the Mongol states?

137 "But consider how the Portuguese have made their conquests and peopled their places, likewise in what way the Moors have forced their Moordom into the lands of India and increased and enriched their condition. It has, so we understand, occurred principally by gathering people, whether they came of their enemies or were bought with money. Therewith they have principally established their condition..." (Colenbrander, *Coen*, III, 177: document dated 1622).

138 *Cf.* Rouffaer, "Malaka", 123–124.

139 *Cf.* Moreland, *Aurangzeb*, 73–74.

IV: INDONESIAN TRADE AND THE EUROPEANS

1 Ferrand, "K'ouen-louen", XIII, 489.

2 One should not immediately draw the conclusion that there was an economic superiority of Portuguese trade from the single fact of the gigantic tonnage of the Portuguese Indiamen – sixteen hundred ton and more, up to two thousand, while the voyages from Holland and Zeeland at the end of the sixteenth century and the beginning of the seventeenth were accomplished with ships of from two to four hundred ton as large ships. (The ships on the first Dutch voyage had a tonnage of 460, 460, 260, and 50 ton, thus all together 1230 ton, or less than one ordinary Portuguese carack: see Moreland, *Akbar*, 171, 203, 231; Rouffaer & IJzerman, *Schipvaart*, I, xxxiii, II, 117 n. 1. On ship's tons in the seventeenth century see Moreland, *Akbar*, 235. Most of the Dutch figures are given in lasts, which have here been converted into tons at the ratio of two tons per last: see Colenbrander, *Coen*, IV, 11–13, 19, 65, V, 810–811; De Jonge, *Opkomst*, II, 493.) Aside from the

few royal ships of hundreds of tons – which must have encountered similar Oriental vessels in both Indian and Chinese waters – Portuguese trade in Asia was carried on chiefly in ordinary small ships, foists, and junks of forty or fifty ton. The description Terpstra gives of the worthlessness of Portuguese seamanship is a rather bad caricature (*Westerkwartieren*, 13–14). If a parallel judgement on the Dutch Company were to be pronounced on the basis of a few such facts, then the Company, too, would be found to have lacked any vital strength (*cf.* "Verhaal", 645–654).

3 See Moreland, *Aurangzeb*, 5–6, 9–10, 92.

4 Moreland, *Akbar*, 200–201, 247, *Aurangzeb*, 221–222, 225–226; Tiele & Heeres, *Bouwstoffen*, I, vii, 88–89, 226.

5 See Moreland, *Aurangzeb*, 92, 108, 123, 141, 299.

6 See *ibid.*, 176, *cf.* 59.

7 See Moreland, *Akbar*, 208–209, *Aurangzeb*, 7–8; Van Linschoten, *Voyage*, II, 181–182, 229–230.

8 See Moreland, *Akbar*, 200–201; Van Linschoten, *Voyage*, I, 177, 187–188.

9 See Moreland, *Aurangzeb*, 7, 19, 81, 83, 223. For interesting data on the trade in precious stones carried on in Asia by the Venetians *via* Aleppo, see Van Linschoten, *Voyage*, II, 141, 159, 167, 204–205; *cf.* also Rouffaer, "Malaka", 134 end of n. 1.

10 Just as the model organization of Hohenstaufen Sicily was set up by Frederick II by taking over Moslem bureaucratic methods (see Burckhardt, *Renaissance*, 2–3, *cf.* 45; see also Fitzler, "Handelsgesellschaften", 211, 214, 222–223, 232, 240–242, 249). Massignon has a very important passage on this sort of political-colonial capitalism: "Because of a more serious tendency toward imitation, European Christianity has also taken over in colonial affairs certain types of activity systematized by the Moslem state, the result of its symbiosis with Jewish finance. Even the recruitment of Negro slaves for the American plantations, by force of arms, or *assiento*, inaugurated by the marranos in Spain, is inspired by the methods of the Nakhkhasa of Baghdad and Cairo, and the farming out of large colonial exploitations to banks (the Fuggers of Augsburg in Venezuela) from the sixteenth century on is rather an imitation of the farming out to the Jewish bankers of Baghdad in the tenth century." ("Islam", 11). Nor was the pattern of political-colonial capitalism new in the caliphates, however much it may have developed under Jewish influence. It had already been known in colossal forms in the ancient world. With this pattern, therefore, the Jews did not make any new contribution either to the historical economic forms or the economic mentality.

11 *Cf.* Romein, *Landen*, 68–69.

12 This in contradiction to Colenbrander, *Geschiedenis*, II, 170.

13 The material published in De Jonge, *Opkomst* and Tiele & Heeres, *Bouwstoffen* was selected chiefly from the point of view of colonial political history. Data on economic history have most of the time been neglected

and omitted. There is also still much unpublished from the period of Coen. What is of first importance, then, is research in the unpublished sources.

14 See Colenbrander, *Geschiedenis*, II, 62; *cf.* Rouffaer's term 'trans-shipment point' in "Malaka", 23.

15 "...the whole of Manila, whose welfare and commerce consists only of the trade of the Chinese..." (Tiele & Heeres, *Bouwstoffen*, I, 180: record dated 1617).

16 "... it is certain the Portuguese can govern the people of these lands better than we ... the Portuguese trade here is of a completely different nature from that of the [Dutch] Company... With the Portuguese the affair is completely different, and the native trade of the whole of India is licensed by them, with only a little of the merchandise principally suitable for returning to Portugal being reserved for the king, further drawing their wealth from the tolls, not only of their subjects, but of all the Indian nations that trade along the Indian coast, the Gulf of Persia, the Red Sea, and the surroundings, the which up to now has brought in for them extraordinary treasures more than the burdens of the Indian garrisons" (Van Diemen, writing in 1640–1641, in De Jonge, *Opkomst*, V, 245, 252, 243; *cf.* Van Berchem, writing to Governor-General Both, 16 August, 1614, in Van Dijk, *Jaren*, 39 & n. 1). On the basis of such indications it seems to me it can be accepted that the feudal, political-capitalistic Portuguese regime affected the structure of international Asian trade only slightly.

17 Coen in his imperialistic zeal cherished the plan of taking over the whole of Asian trade, sailing to India, Persia, Arabia, and Africa with Chinese goods and spices and to the Middle East and the Far East with Indian textiles, obtaining the Chinese goods with spices and sandalwood, silver from Japan in turn with Chinese goods, gold from China for Coromandel with spices, goods from Surat with silver from Arabia and gold from Africa, and so on. The one circuit would nourish the other; the return trips to Europe would be financed from the profits of the trade. Every other nation would be run on shore by the shipping of the Dutch 'free burghers' in all those regions. The plan failed miserably, partly owing to the opposition of Company circles in the Netherlands, but chiefly to the complete impotence of the Dutch merchant adventurers in Asia. The marginal notes (probably by Reael: *cf.* Colenbrander, *Geschiedenis*, II, 122) on the 'Points for Regulating and Redressing the State of the Company in the Indies', November, 1623 (Colenbrander, *Coen*, IV, 610 ff.), in which Coen's views were elaborated for the Gentlemen Seventeen, are of interest for their insight into Oriental trade, an insight which it seems to me is present in Coen to a lesser extent than in Reael.

18 See Rouffaer & Juynboll, *Batik-kunst*, I, Appendix III, n. 105; De Jonge, *Opkomst*, II, 405; *cf.* Tiele & Heeres, *Bouwstoffen*, I, 156 & n. 1, 195.

A Portuguese statement gives the following figures on the clove yield:

	"in a good season" (in *bahar*)	"in an ordinary season" (in *bahar*)
Ternate	1200–1600	600–1000
Makian	1600–2000	800–1200
Tidore	800–1000	400–600
Motir	300–400	200–300
Batchan	60–70	20–30

(De Jonge, *Opkomst*, 274–275; for Makian and Batchan *cf. Daghregister 1636*, 219, 220). The estimate of three thousand *bahar* is a liberal one. The Dutch Company never got hold of so much. The Moluccan rulers hampered clove picking out of political motives; because of the limited importation of rice the Moluccas had to ship in more sago and cultivate their own rice, and interlopers of every nation carried away a part of the harvest. The Company's export sometimes amounted to as much as a thousand or fifteen hundred *bahar*, but more often fell below the thousand (De Jonge, *Opkomst*, III, 270; Colenbrander, *Coen*, I, 82, 198, 202, 400–401, 449, II, 257, IV, 638, V, 682; Tiele & Heeres, *Bouwstoffen*, I, 355, II, 112, 175, *cf.* 394).

19 The *bahar* has been fixed at five hundred pounds in the following calculations. The weight of the *bahar* varied rather greatly: the *bahar* used by the Portuguese in the Moluccas was 600 lb., in Banda it was 550, in Bantam 495, in Malacca 530–540, in Macassar 550, in Patani 380, in Kedah 360 ("Verhaal", 413, 415, 512; De Jonge, *Opkomst*, II, 444, 519, 525, III, 195; Tiele & Heeres, *Bouwstoffen*, II, 360, 395; *cf. ibid.*, I, 265, II, xliii n. 2; De Rovere van Breughel, "Bedenkingen", 135 n. 1: *bahars* of 1000 lb.?; De Rovere van Breughel, "Beschrijving", 316: a *bahar* of 375 lb. in Batavia in 1762).

20 See "Verhaal", 504–505; De Jonge, *Opkomst*, II, 261 (1600 *bahar*); Colenbrander, *Coen*, I, 255 (1000–1100), 279 (600), 447 (885), 565 (1000, 1500), 784, 786 (1252), II, 257 (1000–1200), 610 (1000–1200), V, 46–47 (456), 12 (312), *cf.* I, 198, 202, IV, 638; Tiele & Heeres, *Bouwstoffen*, I, 262 (1000), II, 187 (1300), 282–283, 288, 336 (1000).

21 "Verhaal", 512, 514, 516.

22 Colenbrander, *Coen*, IV, 482, *cf.* III, 269, IV, 321–322, 452, 544, 563; see also Tiele & Heeres, *Bouwstoffen*, II, xviii no 1.

23 Colenbrander, *Coen*, III, 269, *cf.* 114.

24 See Sombart, *Kapitalismus*, I, Part Two, 680–681. In my opinion Sombart here commits the mistake already indicated earlier in this study in speaking of this trade as "Arabian trading". *Cf.* also Krause's statement on the "Arabian monopoly" of the spice trade (*Geschichte*, I, 365), Massignon's term "Arab state" ("Islam", 11), and Kohler's use of "the Arabs" (*Commenda:* the title of the work correctly speaks of *commenda* in Islamic law).

25 *Cf.* Horst, "Antwerpen", 333.

26 *Cf.* Schrieke, "Prolegomena", 125. In the fifteenth century a Chinese ship still appeared in the Middle East now and then (Yule, *Cathay*, I, 87–88; *cf.* Van Linschoten, *Voyage*, II, 130).

27 Bantam bags of sixty pounds (Colenbrander, *Coen*, II, 779, *cf.* III, 8).

28 Colenbrander, *Coen*, IV, 482. The amount of pepper imported in Europe per year in the first half of the sixteenth century has been calculated at thirty-five thousand quintals at 105 lb. per quintal, or 3,675,000 lb. or 2,450 ton, most of it being imported through Antwerp (Horst, "Antwerpen", 333–334).

29 The same thing holds for the last years of 'free trade' on the spice islands (see De Jonge, *Opkomst*, III, 385–386; Tiele & Heeres, *Bouwstoffen*, I, 11, 190, 215, 224, II, 344). The most valuable material on the pepper trade seems to me that of 1599, when thirty thousand bags were shipped from Bantam (De Jonge, *Opkomst*, II, 448, *cf.* III, 20). Because all the Dutch fleets and later the English fleets, out of fear and envy of competition, and then the Portuguese called on Bantam, while the focal point of the Chinese staple remained there for the moment, a pepper 'boom' which shoved the normal market picture to the background began in Bantam, with harvests of a hundred to two hundred thousand bags (De Jonge, *Opkomst*, IV, 32; Colenbrander, *Coen*, I, 64, 114, 163, 252, II, 248). The political complications which followed, including the blockade of Bantam, put a stop to the whole trade and caused the market to collapse. The general pepper price on the Indonesian market went up from ten or twelve reals of eight per ten Bantam bags in 1600 to fifty or sixty reals in 1620 (Colenbrander, *Coen*, IV, 533; *cf.* Tiele & Heeres, *Bouwstoffen*, II, 304–305, 320). De Barros gives a yearly export from western Java of 7500 *bahar* of six hundred pounds each, thus three thousand pounds, or seventy-five thousand bags (Tiele, "Europeërs", I, 398).

30 Colenbrander, *Coen*, I, 177. I have not found any total figure for the west coast of Sumatra. The following estimate can be made, however: the seven or eight Indian ships sailing from Achin annually would carry sixteen hundred ton, or forty thousand bags; the personal trade transactions of the ruler of Achin usually involved a total of one to two thousand *bahar*, or eight to sixteen thousand bags (Colenbrander, *Coen*, III, 308, 872).

31 *Cf.* Tiele & Heeres, *Bouwstoffen*, II, 320 (1637).

32 See Rouffaer, "Malaka", 137 n. 4. Borneo pepper was marketed at Martapura.

33 "Verhaal", 527; Colenbrander, *Coen*, I, 77, *cf.* 212, II, 9. See the figures on the sandalwood supply in the petty states on Timor, with twenty, a hundred, a hundred fifty, or two hundred *bahar* available annually, in other states sixty or seventy *bahar* every second year or every three or four years (Tiele & Heeres, *Bouwstoffen*, I, 91–92, *cf.* 20).

34 Colenbrander, *Coen*, IV, 393, 456, 564.

35 De Jonge, *Opkomst*, IV, 27; Colenbrander, *Coen*, I, 68, 115, II, 7–8.

36 "...it is affirmed for a truth, that only from the town of Canton there is yearely carried into India, above three thousand Quintals of Silke, which are sold by waight..." (Van Linschoten, *Voyage*, I, 129). Three thousand quintal at almost a hundred thirty pounds per quintal amounts to two hundred fifty or sixty ton. But notice Van Linschoten's way of saying this: it was not a personal experience.

37 See Colenbrander, *Coen*, IV, 456; *cf.* the comment in the preceding section.

38 *Ibid.*, IV, 456–457.

39 *Ibid.*, IV, 564–565.

40 Which, incidentally, must not be conceived of as a 'big industry' working for a mass market. "Your Excellencies be advised that the porcelains are made very far inland in China, likewise that the assortments ordered by us and the regents hereabouts are commissioned and made after the order with money given before, for all such sorts are not used in China [*cf.* Van Orsoy de Flines, "Verzameling", I, 228]. Now the Chinese have been obliged to export and peddle the lot that was made, notwithstanding how much money [they] have lost therein. Therefore if I am well informed no such lots will be commissioned or shipped any more before the Chinese find a great demand again and are requested for them..." (Coen to the Gentlemen Seventeen, 10 October, 1616: Colenbrander, *Coen*, I, 224–225). On porcelain manufacturing at King-te-chen in northeast Kiangsi and the system of distribution see Wittfogel, *Wirtschaft*, 560–561, 709 n. 77, 758–759; Reichwein, *China*, 24; Van Orsoy de Flines, "Verzameling", I, 230, III, 211–215, 218.

41 *Cf.* Van Orsoy de Flines, "Verzameling", III, 213.

42 'Memorandum of Various Cloths and What Otherwise Is Required From the Coast of Coromandel for the Moluccas, Amboyna, Banda, Java, Jambi, Patani, Siam, and the Netherlands, 16 July, 1619' (Colenbrander, *Coen*, II, 580–583). The amount sold on Java was low because of the disturbances, and has here been increased by six hundred *corges*.

43 De Jonge, *Opkomst*, III, 149 ff.; complete text in Rouffaer & Juynboll, *Batik-kunst*, I, Appendix III.

44 The memorandum of 1619 fixes the capital to be spent by the Company on Coromandel cloth at a hundred twenty thousand reals of eight, or twenty-five thousand pounds; in 1621 it was estimated at around forty-two thousand pounds. The Portuguese trade in Coromandel cloth had an annual turnover of three hundred thousand reals, or sixty-two and a half thousand pounds. In 1623 Coen set the amount to be spent on Coromandel and Gujarati cloth at from £ 42,000 to £ 68,000 (Colenbrander, *Coen*, II, 583, III, 94, Is 690, III, 296, *cf.* I, 666, 668, 670–671 [two to three hundred thousand real,

in total], 698 [Surat: a hundred fifty to two hundred thousand reals], 724 [Surat: eighty thousand reals], III, 211 [Surat: forty to eighty thousand reals], 212, 229, V, 346 [Surat: eighty to a hundred thousand reals], 355, 386, 679). The 'Memorandum of the Cotton Cloth Needed and Serviceable for the Gulf of Siam and Cambodia, Together With What Quantities Wanted There Yearly', dating from 1622 ("Verhaal", 311–317) sets the total market there at 790 *corges*, or 15,800 pieces. The size of the Indian cotton cloths varied. There were sheets of from two to six, seven, or eight fathom (one fathom equalling around five and a half feet). The width was for the most part uniform, probably especially for the Indonesian market, *chara melayu* of five span (one span equalling around eight inches). The processes used also varied: there were plain fabrics, coloured and uncoloured cloths printed with block prints, and cloths worked with a batik process ('painted' cloth).

45 For 'Persian cloth' of wool and velvet see Rouffaer & Juynboll, *Batikkunst*, I, 437 n. 2.

46 See *ibid.*, Appendix III, under 'Patana'.

47 See "Verhaal", 544.

48 Van Eyndhoven in De Jonge, *Opkomst*, IV, 59.

49 In *ibid.*, II, 57 ff.

50 Colenbrander, *Coen*, I, 291, *cf.* II, 481.

51 Grise, Jaratan, and Sedayu possessed at least a thousand vessels of from twenty or thirty to two hundred ton; the Japara ships were larger, two hundred ton and more ("Verhaal", 532, 544, *cf.* 540, where a Japara junk of four hundred ton is mentioned; see also Colenbrander, *Coen*, I, 419, 420, where Japara junks of a hundred twenty ton are listed; the statement in Rouffaer & IJzerman, *Schipvaart*, I, 132–133 is therefore too absolute).

52 See Van der Chijs, *Vestiging*, 161; Colenbrander, *Geschiedenis*, II, 118; Tiele & Heeres, *Bouwstoffen*, I, xlvi & n. 2.

53 See Gonggrijp, *Schets*, 41.

54 The Company's rice ration for soldiers, sailors, and slaves amounted to forty pounds per month (Colenbrander, *Coen*, V, 652); for the Indonesians of a Ternatese embassy at Batavia in 1629 consisting of four *orang kayas*, four freemen, and five slaves, a total allowance was made of thirty-six *gantang* of rice per month, *i.e.*, figuring a *gantang* at thirteen pounds (see De Jonge, *Opkomst*, V, 184), about thirty-six pounds per person per month (Colenbrander, *Coen*, V, 683; *cf.* Tiele & Heeres, *Bouwstoffen*, II, 149). But *cf. Daghregister 1636*, 358, where a ration of ten pounds per person per month is suggested.

55 According to the Information of 1603, a hundred fifty *koyan* of rice per month could be sold to Banda. Assuming this as valid for the four or five months the 'foreign' trade come to Banda lasted (from February to May or June) – the rest of the year only a few *gantang* were sold – and taking into consideration the fact that rice purchases were made *en gros* by the lords, who would provide themselves for a year or a year and a half, then the resultant

average for the whole population of 144 lb. per person does not differ very much from the estimate given in the text. Another figure tends in the same direction. The Information of 1603 gives two ton of rice as a basis for barter for four or five *bahar* of nutmeg on Banda (see Rouffaer & Juynboll, *Batik-kunst*, I, Appendix III, under 'Abdemogon'). That is to say, if the total Bandanese nutmeg crop, around four thousand *bahar*, had been exchanged for rice, there would have been at best two thousand ton obtained, and the number becomes even smaller if one figures in a Moluccan *bahar* of six hundred pounds. However, nutmeg was also used to trade for cotton cloth, sago, and Chinese products. The estimate made on the basis of consumption (960 ton) therefore gains in probability (*cf.* Tiele & Heeres, *Bouwstoffen*, I, 216: data for 1617).

56 *Cf.* with this estimate the eight thousand ton of rice the ruler of Mataram was bound to deliver to the Dutch Company by the contract of 28 February, 1677 (De Jonge, *Opkomst*, VII, 81 Article Eight; *cf.* Colenbrander, *Geschiedenis*, II, 173). By 1677 Malacca and the independent Javanese port towns had been subdued, and East Indonesia had become a 'dead region'. If those circumstances are taken into consideration, it seems to me that the estimate for around 1600 bears with the data for 1677 fairly well.

57 There are a few figures on the spice shipping. In 1599 forty junks from East Indonesia were awaited at Jaratan – sixty according to another account (De Jonge, *Opkomst*, II, 404, 409; what has been said on early Company data above also applies here). If the other Javanese ports and the Malay and Indian shipping in Indonesia are taken into account, it appears to me that these figures reflect the actual situation and that the figures on the shipping of foodstuffs fit in with them reasonably well. The figure in Rouffaer & IJzerman, *Schipvaart*, III, 193 is certainly too low a total. *Cf.* also Tiele & Heeres, *Bouwstoffen*, I, xxxiv.

58 In "Verhaal" the tonnage of the Portuguese royal ship to China and Japan was estimated at a thousand to twelve hundred ton. Alongside that came the shipping of Portuguese merchant adventurers, most of them with light ships of two hundred ton. ("Verhaal", 585).

59 Moreland, *Akbar*, 235–236.

60 "180, 190, 200 tuns ... and even this is probably an exaggeration..." (*ibid.*, 232).

61 *Ibid.*, 236–237.

62 Trade on Achin came above all from the ports of northwest India and Arabia. Around 1600 the town Dabhol was especially important for its trade on Indonesia. See De Jonge, *Opkomst*, II, 495, III, 339; Colenbrander, *Coen*, I, 60, 205, 241, 635, 680, 695, 737, 778–779, II, 160, 215, 351, 353, 712, III, 110, 380, 619–620, V, 31. The commissioners of the Zeeland fleet of 1601 went from Achin to Cambay with 'letters of favour' to the authorities there from the ruler of Achin (De Jonge, *Opkomst*, II, 487, *cf.* 496, III, 170 & n. 1).

63 For Coromandel trade on the Middle East see Terpstra, *Westerkwartieren*, 252, 284, 286.

64 See Rouffaer & IJzerman, *Schipvaart*, I, letterpress to Plate Seventeen; *cf.* Rouffaer, "Pégon", 371; Tiele & Heeres, *Bouwstoffen*, II, 308, 360.

65 In 1596, shortly before the arrival of the Amsterdam fleet at Bantam, five junks had left there for China, according to another account seven (Rouffaer & IJzerman, *Schipvaart*, III, 17); and there were eight or nine large ships each year (*ibid.*, III, 25). In 1614 there were six Chinese junks in Bantam, in 1615 five, in 1616 three, and every year three or four went to Bantam, five or six others to Jambi, Japara, and Jaratan, one or two to Ligor, and twenty to thirty to Manila. In 1622 three junks went from Changchow to Batavia, eight to Patani, two to Grise, and two to Bima, and seventeen small ones to Tonkin. (Colenbrander, *Coen*, I, 65, 68, 184–186, IV, 726; De Jonge, *Opkomst*, IV, 27). Certainly there must have been a large number of fishing boats and small coasters included among the seventy junks sunk in 1614 in the storm off the Chinese coast. That the overseas trade was small is apparent from the fact that when the ships trading on Patani were sunk on the return trip in 1614 in the storm, people in Patani did not expect any junks in 1615 (Colenbrander, *Coen*, I, 129).

66 There were Chinese ships of "at least a thousand ton" at Patani (De Jonge, *Opkomst*, II, 493); in 1637 there were seven junks, each one four to six hundred ton, off Batavia (*ibid.*, V, 230). The figures in Rouffaer & IJzerman, *Schipvaart*, I, 122, II, 384, & III, 193 are in my opinion too low.

67 'Sea-going trade' as 'junk trade', if one prefers, to be distinguished from 'coastal trade', or 'proa trade'. Gonggrijp's term 'proa trade' (*Schets*, 24, 42) has reference to the ocean-going trade of the junks and other large ships (*cf.* Rouffaer, "Malaka", 383, 403). It can be seen from the tonnage given that the ships were small in size. Measured by modern criteria the world trade of southeast Asia in its heyday was carried on with ships the size of fishing boats and small coasters.

68 Possibly Persian silk taken to Lisbon by way of the Levant and Genoa, Venice, or Marseilles. *Cf.* Colenbrander, *Coen*, IV, 488–489; Tiele & Heeres, *Bouwstoffen*, I, 114.

69 One should notice the housing of these 'wholesale traders' in valuable high-quality products which they meted out again by the ell. Their shops – one should call to mind the shops typical of the Moslem bazaar – were at the same time their warehouses. Alongside trade, on the same basis, were the handicrafts (*cf.* the following pages in Van Linschoten, *Voyage*).

70 Van Linschoten, *Voyage*, I, 228–229. The phrases placed in brackets were in the original Dutch but omitted by the English translator.

71 *Xaraffos*: from Arab *çarraf.* The Dutch text does not read Christian Jews, but Indian Christians.

72 *Ibid.*, 231.

73 *Ibid.*, 256–257.

74 Schrieke, "Prolegomena", 103.

75 Danvers mentions Hindus in Malacca in 1511 (*Portuguese*, I, 228).

76 *Cf.* Rouffaer, "Malaka", 167, 408–409, 414 n. 3.

77 *Cf. ibid.*, 383.

78 *Description*, 20 recto (Rouffaer & IJzerman, *Schipvaart*, II, 24).

79 Rouffaer & IJzerman, *Schipvaart*, I, 84 n. 23, 108 & n. 19, II, 25 n. 3.

80 Van der Chijs, *Vestiging*, 38; Schrieke, "Prolegomena", 123.

81 *Cf.* De Vrankrijker, "Textielindustrie", 153–154.

82 In 1636 three ships from Coromandel carried five hundred packs of cloth to Achin (Tiele & Heeres, *Bouwstoffen*, II, 307); in 1679 a Danish ship carrying freight from India to Bantam transported a hundred Coromandel traders and six hundred packs of cloth (De Jonge, *Opkomst*, VII, 11; *cf.* Colenbrander, *Geschiedenis*, II, 81).

83 A pack of cotton cloth from Coromandel had an average market value of twenty-six to twenty-eight pounds (see Colenbrander, *Coen*, I, 753, 777). Thus a trader with three or four packs carried a cargo of eighty to a hundred fifteen pounds, *i.e.*, around four hundred to five hundred fifty reals of eight, and ninety or a hundred traders carried a cargo the same value as that of the usual Dutch Company ship on a return voyage. *Cf.* also Jan Huyghen van Linschoten's plans for trading in the Far East with two or three hundred ducats at five shillings per ducat, and the Gujarati 'factor' of a Mogol prince with a cargo worth three hundred reals. Figuring silk as a hundred to a hundred fifty reals per picul (see Colenbrander, *Coen*, I, 67), sugar at four reals (*ibid.*, 68), cloves at forty reals per *bahar*, mace at fifty reals, nutmeg at nine reals (De Jonge, *Opkomst*, II, 451) pepper at one or two reals per bag, porcelain at eight or ten reals per *corge* (see Colenbrander, *Coen*, IV, 564), one can gain some idea of the amount of goods handled by the pedlars and the size of the combined return cargoes. That such a trade was possible was due to the high rates of profit, on the average two or three hundred per cent., often four or five hundred. That such rates of profit were possible was due to the dispersion and isolation of the small markets and the dimensions of trade.

84 Here are some notes on the Chinese trade. "... these small pedlars, who take money on interest and bottomry in China and go trading to Bantam and Patani with it, have to sell dearer or cannot remain solvent..." (Colenbrander, *Coen*, I, 167). "... they are poor seamen, and therefore a profitable trade will never be conducted with them at Bantam, Patani, or any place further away. We have to come near to them, and the nearer the better it will be for the Company..." (*ibid.*, 367). The commentary has to do with the marketing policy of the Dutch Company. What it amounts to here is that the "excellent Chinese trade" was a matter chiefly of "small pedlars" and "poor seamen". The costliness of Chinese merchandise is expressed among other ways in the figures on the loot in ships taken as prizes by the Dutch – the value of seven

ships trading on Manila which were seized was at the highest (but official) estimate set at more than fifty thousand pounds (Colenbrander, *Coen*, 493; *cf.* Tiele & Heeres, *Bouwstoffen*, I, 182 n. 1). The hundreds of Chinese to be found on the ships trading on Manila and Bantam consisted not only of merchants and pedlars but also of emigrants who were voyaging to Chinese colonies in Indonesia and who in many cases had had to give themselves in indenture for the expenses of travel and equipment: "the Chinese who come each year by thousands from China have to care for their freight and costs [and] often pawn their body therefor..." (De Jonge, *Opkomst*, V, 263); "Three hundred Chinese have gone with the Chinese junk that was here. We let them go free and unhindered, for [we] are certain that for them next year fifteen hundred others will come from China..." (Batavia, 1620: Colenbrander, *Coen*, I, 574–575). A Chinese ship carrying food supplies to Manila in 1616 was seized by the Company fleet and taken to Bantam. "As the Chinese with the junk conquered by the *Black Lion* have jumped overboard and run away in large groups numbering 80 each day and the rest are also resolved to it through fear so they said that they will be used on galleys or otherwise for slaves in Amboyna or Banda, notwithstanding that it has been attempted to turn them away from that wrong opinion with all good reasons, [they] still persist stubbornly and desperately thereby, it is approved, in order to avoid further accidents as well as the scandal of the Chinese and Javanese in Bantam, that the aforesaid captured Chinese shall be given their choice that those who remain voluntarily shall keep their goods in order to be able to benefit from them to their own advantage as free persons in Amboyna or Banda, and those who are not disposed to do such shall have all their goods taken prize and be set on shore here..." (Resolution of the President and Councillors of the Lodge of Bantam, 4 March, 1617: Colenbrander, *Coen*, III, 391).

85 After all there were great merchants, merchant gentlemen, among the Chinese traders, such as those who went to Bantam with cargoes thirty or forty thousand reals of eight in value (in 1615: Colenbrander, *Coen*, I, 167), while the total value of the cargo of the fleet of five junks in which the traders had arrived was estimated at three hundred thousand reals (*ibid.*, II, 7–8). (One should consider that *e.g.* the total purchase value of the spices exported from Banda each year, a trade in which hundreds of traders took part, amounted to around eighty thousand reals.) But such merchant gentlemen did not leave their imprint on trade as a whole. That was done by the many small traders and pedlars.

86 The Mierecomaldi of Coromandel referred to in the letter of 12 August, 1621 to the director for the Coromandel Coast – "As much as Mierecomaldi has coming for his opium is promised his servant... ... do not permit any goods to be sent hither with the Company's ships again for him or others..." (Colenbrander, *Coen*, III, 74; *cf. Daghregister 1631–1634*, 334–335) – appears to me to have been a merchant gentleman who sent his 'servant' (factor,

perhaps slave) out with goods to trade, shipping them on a Company ship.

87 The insight into Oriental trade mentioned earlier had to do with the various plans brought up in Company circles during Coen's stay in Holland on the organization of Asian trade under the suzerainty of the Company (*cf.* also Tiele & Heeres, *Bouwstoffen*, II, ix–x & n. 1). As has been said, Coen strove for complete control of all trade from Aden to Nagasaki. The Dutch shipping carried on by free burghers would drive the other Europeans and the Asians from the seas as traders. The Company would finance its return voyages and posts in Asia with the profits from the trade. Thus a plan completely 'colonial' in its design, by which the Dutch would supplant the 'natives'. Marginal notes written by Reael on the document mentioned develop another plan: a monopoly of the Company in Asia, and no shipping by Dutch free burghers but the encouragement and exploitation of Asian trade by drawing it to Company stapling points such as Batavia. Reael denies that it was possible for Europeans to carry on that trade. The costs were too high for them, the position too base. To the Dutch Company "the friendship, good inclinations, and welfare of the small traders, with and alongside whom it has to negotiate, is of great consequence, as the chief welfare of all large wholesalers consists in this – that their clients, shopkeepers, and small pedlars keep the goods in high repute, make profits, and come back again..." (Colenbrander, *Coen*, IV, 620 n. 1). At the staple points the Dutch needed to give out money on *commenda* and keep goods in stock: "Where money is, there trade is..." (*ibid.*, 641; *cf.* De Jonge, *Opkomst*, V, 195). Reael saw Asian trade primarily as peddling trade which the Company and capital-holding Dutchmen overseas needed to lead as merchant gentlemen and financiers. *Cf.* the statement: "...in all the Indies there cannot be more turned over than is retailed every day, which is the cause of the extraordinary rising and falling in the prices of merchandise, for there are nowhere great or rich, daring merchants to be found such as one encounters in Europe who at the same time have the power and the right to buy up an excellent portion and reserve it for retailing, unless one would want to give such to the Chinese on credit..." (Colenbrander, *Coen*, II, 100). The comment is only half true. If 'the Indies' means the whole of southern Asia, then it is completely untrue; if only Indonesia is meant, then the statement in any case points to the important position of the trade of the Chinese settled there. In proportion to that, Indian, Arab, and Persian trade was probably more mobile and more a "splendid and trifling" peddling trade.

88 Such a case was the pepper 'ring' established in Bantam in 1615 close to the time of the new harvest by the Chinese traders settled there with the complicity and cooperation of the Javanese authorities, which obstructed the market for the pepper trade and tried to set monopoly prices. The course of the affair can be followed in its main outlines from Company sources. As the Company with its military power finally interfered, blockaded the port, and

held up the outgoing ships, Bantam's trade was ruined by the monopoly in the course of events during and after the Jakarta War. Coen's rage at "this heinous monopoly" and his dinning at free trade seem strange when compared to his own policy of monopoly, violence, and destruction. For the tyrant Coen any means was apparently good enough if it could lead to the intended result. The obstruction of the market by Chinese merchants and Javanese nobles should not be accepted simply as a case of 'Oriental misrule'. There was commercial calculation in the devising of the pepper boom. The Chinese from Changchow were just as much victimized and also bought for the monopoly price. An example of occasional trade is given in the situation in 1617, when, with the monopoly still controlling the market, the governor of Bantam forbade all trade and then announced to the Company that if it wanted pepper, "...I [Coen] should order him to buy what we want, for such a price as suits us or for the same price the English and the French might buy. He will, so he says, hold all the pepper available and deliver to us as much as we want..." (Colenbrander, *Coen*, I, 276). There had already been similar occasional trade in Bantam in 1599: the town authorities had fixed the prices "...and when they [the governor and the *shahbandar*] believe that they will gain more in selling than the common folk imagine, they buy the pepper from them, then make agreements with the foreign traders, to whom they have [the pepper] delivered which they had bought from the poor at a lower price the day before. In this way they earn a great deal of money without having to face any risk of loss, or taking any trouble thereunto..." (Van Neck, "Reisverhaal", 264–265). *Cf.* the description of the situation in Patani in 1607: "...the great knavery of the *mantris* who every other day forbid our men the purchase of pepper or something else, seeking to buy up everything themselves in order that thereafter whatever is wanted would have to be got from their hands..." (De Jonge, *Opkomst*, III, 247). On the monopolization of foreign trade at Masulipatnam, see Colenbrander, *Coen*, I, 412, V, 118–119, 384–385.

89 See Colenbrander, *Coen*, III, 158 (a ship to Canton, every other year), V, 157, 535 (a royal ship to Tenassarim); De Jonge, *Opkomst*, VI, 145; "Verhaal", 522; De Jonge, *Opkomst*, V, 146 (captains of the royal junks), 264 (large tonnage of the ships: one junk for Jakarta of six hundred ton); Colenbrander, *Coen*, V, 376; Tiele & Heeres, *Bouwstoffen*, II, lxxx–lxxxi.

90 See Colenbrander, *Coen*, I, 329–330, 419, 551, 606–607, 695, 708, II, 374, III, 57, 649, IV, 83; Tiele & Heeres, *Bouwstoffen*, II, 355.

91 See Colenbrander, *Coen*, III, 931, *cf.* IV, 600. The monopoly continued until the Company took over Javanese trade after 1677 (see De Jonge, *Opkomst*, VI, 172–173, 184 – and the quite remarkable information there dating from 1665–1666 on the "sugar merchants from above out of Mataram along with some others sent down as commissioners to visit the various offices of the governors...").

92 Van der Chijs, *Vestiging*, 30.

93 A letter to Patani, 17 April, 1617, reads: "With respect to the arrack of Sire Maharajah Indra confiscated by the late General Reynst in the Moluccas, the arrest should not be retracted, but lest there arise ill favour there about it Your Excellency shall busy himself with appeasing that *orang kaya* as well as possible provided that there is so much done there that no junks will go to the Moluccas any more..." (Colenbrander, *Coen*, II, 228–229; *cf.* Tiele & Heeres, *Bouwstoffen*, II, 173–174).

94 See Colenbrander, *Coen*, III, 856; *cf.* Tiele & Heeres, *Bouwstoffen*, II, 220.

95 See De Jonge, *Opkomst*, II, 524, IV, 70; Colenbrander, *Coen*, I, 304, 343, 349, 735, II, 383–384, 551, 666, III, 663, IV, 79, V, 70–71, 106–107, 146, 376, 664; Tiele & Heeres, *Bouwstoffen*, I, 4, 169 (*cf.* Colenbrander, *Coen*, II, 415), II, lxxxi, 141, 199–200, 253, 393 (*cf. ibid.*, 224–225, 289, 351–352); Chang, *Trade*, 118. For the Golconda royal trade see Moreland, *Aurangzeb*, 79. With the flourishing of Bantam anew after 1659 (see Colenbrander, *Geschiedenis*, II, 181), the ruler, Sultan Agung, and the lords of the state took a large share in the trade to Manila, China, Japan, Siam, Coromandel, Surat, and Arabia, owning ships and carrying on their own shipping and trade (De Jonge, *Opkomst*, VI, 116, 124, 129, 144, 156, 213, VII, 11, 15, 168, 320).

96 Colenbrander, *Coen*, I, 28, 100, II, 560, 745, 757.

97 Therefore in consideration of the amount it seems to me incorrect to speak as Rouffaer and Krom do of 'mass export', and especially to link that with the term 'big industry'. The Indian textile crafts, which worked for the markets in Farther India, Persia, Arabia, and the east coast of Africa as well as Indonesia, were certainly complexes of handicraft production of large dimensions. Moreland's statement "that the aggregate production was one of the great facts of the industrial world of the year 1600" (*Akbar*, 179) must be endorsed, but it remained handicraft production which was not of decisive importance for the daily needs of a population of millions, and that is after all the criterion for big industry and mass export. That the Indian cotton cloth imported into Indonesia could not meet the daily needs of the population so far as textile goods were concerned is proved in the first place by the total amount imported, about four hundred thousand pieces, and in the second place by the amount of weaving done everywhere in the region, the village, the home where it was used. Perhaps in a few port towns the population was accustomed to being supplied on a somewhat large scale by the import from India, but outside the gates of the town Indonesian home weaving and local weaving regained their importance, and even in the cities there were the royal and noble courts as enclaves of self-sufficient economy maintained by slaves and serfs – *cf.* the interesting material overlooked by Rouffaer & Juynboll (*Batik-kunst*, I, 423) on the women – perhaps slaves – of the young ruler of Bantam out of destitution making batik to sell on the market (De Jonge, *Op-*

komst, IV, 21). And in the third place the prices of cotton cloth also plead against mass sales: the Information of 1603 gives the rate of exchange on Banda in weight units (*kati*, 'Banda pounds') of nutmeg for practically all sorts of cloth. It appears from it that one piece of cloth was traded for an average of twenty *kati* of nutmeg; some sorts were cheaper, many were more expensive. If the total nutmeg yield is set at four thousand *bahar*, *i.e.* twelve hundred thousand *kati*, a total conversion of nutmeg into cloth would have resulted in sixty thousand pieces, *i.e.* three thousand *corges*. As the nutmeg at the same time had to serve for procuring rice, Chinese merchandise, and sago, the half of that, fifteen hundred *corges*, will have been nearer to reality. Thirty thousand pieces of cotton cloth per year for a population of nobles, freemen, and slaves numbering fifteen thousand is still no mass sale, however considerable it may be. And Banda, inhospitable, practically without agriculture, formed relatively one of the most intensively marketed areas. For the other markets home production in weaving played a much larger counter-rôle. The Information also gives the money prices for cloth in Macassar. In my opinion the price list for products imported from India and trans-shipped there for other destinations in Indonesia is also of value for an understanding of the situation in the trans-shipping ports in Java. There were prices there for varieties of cloth from 1s 8d to 2s 8d per piece (ten varieties) 3s 4d to 5s (nine varieties), 5s to 6s 8d (three varieties), 6s 8d to 8s 4d (three varieties), 8s 4d to 10s (four varieties), 10s to 11s 8d (one variety), 11s 8d to 16s 8d (one variety), 16s 8d to £1 13s 4d (three varieties), and more than £1 13s 4d (one variety). In Indonesia at the time the daily wage for agricultural work in Bantam amounted to eight hundred to a thousand cash, *i.e.* about fivepence (Rouffaer & IJzerman, *Schipvaart*, I, 129 & n. 5), the pilot money paid by the first Amsterdam fleet in the Sunda Straits off Bantam, five or six reals, "was a common man's fortune" (*ibid.*, II, 289), the poll tax of the Chinese at Batavia amounted to a real and a half per month (Colenbrander, *Coen*, I, 601; De Jonge, *Opkomst*, V, 263; surely an extraordinary amount: see De Haan, *Oud-Batavia*, I, 76), the Dutch Company paid its seamen and soldiers from fifteen shillings to a pound per month plus maintenance, and the poll tax levies from twenty-two villages in an area already fairly well 'opened up' such as that around Semarang amounted to 561 reals altogether (De Jonge, *Opkomst*, VII, 201–202). The prices for cloth given above must be called high for such a land, then, and they could not have led to mass purchases in a region with such a non-intensive money economy.

98 A few illustrations from Chinese trade. Patani, in 1614: "...if capital and people are duly furnished thither, it will be possible in time to do a very fine trade on Japan from Siam and Patani, and at the same time to obtain the whole rich Chinese trade and as much silk as is desired, contracting with the Chinese without advancing money, if only they [the Company officials] are able to show they have funds, for as the Chinese say, if we should bring much

silk and you do not contract and then do not have any money we would be obliged to take the silk back to China or sell to Your Excellencies at your desire because there are no other buyers here..." (Colenbrander, *Coen*, I, 33). Bantam, 1615: "From the accompanying price list Your Excellency [the Company director at Patani] will see what is current for Chinese wares, or better to say what price they are set at, for most all Chinese wares cannot be sold at any price, so that many merchants are necessitated and resolved to stay here until the coming year..." (*ibid.*, II, 10–11). "Likewise and do not be surprised that the people of the junks are selling better silkware than ours a third cheaper on the market than ours is priced at on the bill, for time and need are law for all such people. I do not think that it will be possible to obtain large quantities from them there [in Ambon], but Your Excellency will understand that the [prices of] goods sent from here last year have been driven up between the English and us to obtain the lot and for certain reasons are inflated, and because we and the English have lacked money this year the Chinese are left with most of their ordinary silk cloth on their hands, so that it is possible to get it for cash more than a hundred per cent. cheaper than last year, and the porcelain for much less even..." (*ibid.*, II, 20–21). In the same year the pepper from Japara, which was regularly bought by the Chinese, found no market because the two junks that had gone to Japara each year had apparently been wrecked (De Jonge, *Opkomst*, IV, 60). Trade on Banda took place in the period of the western monsoons, from February to June; in July, when the wind turned, the traders and ships departed. During the western monsoon nutmeg was dear and cotton cloth cheap, during the eastern monsoon the reverse. There was no trade then: "...so that if someone stayed to winter here on Banda and had the following merchandise with him, he would make an inestimable profit..." (Information of 1603, in Rouffaer & Juynboll, *Batik-kunst*, I, Appendix III). During the western monsoon rice was sold *en gros*, but during the eastern monsoon it was measured in *gantang*. In Bantam the chief trading period was between February and July, and in the period before the harvest (which came in September and later), when trade at Bantam went through a quiet period, pepper was cheaper than after the harvest, in the trading period (Rouffaer & IJzerman, *Schipvaart*, I, 86). In Achin, in 1636: "...various vessels were come to Achin, and more than have been seen in many years, namely:

<table>
<tr><td>3</td><td colspan="2">three from the Coromandel Coast that brought more than 500 packs of cloth on the market</td></tr>
<tr><td>1</td><td>one from Pegu</td><td rowspan="4">All laden with cloth, cotton roucou dyed, etc., and the Dabhol ship brought two fine horses as a gift for the King</td></tr>
<tr><td>1</td><td>one from Surat</td></tr>
<tr><td>1</td><td>one from Dabhol</td></tr>
<tr><td>1</td><td>one from the Malabar Coast</td></tr>
<tr><td>7</td><td colspan="2">seven ships.</td></tr>
</table>

In that way, as has been said, Achin being filled with merchandises so that they have dropped in price by almost the half." (Tiele & Heeres, *Bouwstoffen*, II, 307–308).

99 Rouffaer & IJzerman, *Schipvaart*, I, 83 n. 18.

100 See *ibid.*, III, 197–199, *cf.* lx.

101 *Ibid.*, II, 293.

102 Bantam in 1618: "The linen bag of 50 *kati* of pepper did not weigh more than 47 *kati* on the scales of the King of Bantam, where all the pepper was delivered and weighed to us..." (Colenbrander, *Coen*, II, 386); the Company had "1800 bags of pepper lying ready in the weigh-house to be delivered to us on money advanced..." (*ibid.*, III, 419; *cf.* De Jonge, *Opkomst*, IV, 67). The treaty of the Company's delegates with the ruler of Jakarta in 1610 summarized the composition of the tax on pepper as follows: 5 weights per hundred for the ruler; the toll of *beli-belian* (merchandise) with the *ruba-ruba* (port money) of the king ten reals per hundred weight; *ruba-ruba* for the *shahbandar* two reals per hundred weight; for the clerks two reals per hundred weight; for the weighmasters one real per hundred weight (De Jonge, *Opkomst*, III, 353).

103 Unger, *Middelburg*, 159.

104 See De Jonge, *Opkomst*, III, 161, 183, 252; Colenbrander, *Coen*, I, 76, 188, 351, 678, V, 448; "Verhaal", 520, 590; Rouffaer & IJzerman, *Schipvaart*, I, 150; Rouffaer, "Kunst", 588–589 (on iron as money); Tiele & Heeres, *Bouwstoffen*, I, 12, 35. And see especially the excellent notes in Rouffaer & IJzerman, *Schipvaart*, I, 216–238.

105 In De Jonge, *Opkomst*, VI, 19.

106 See Schrieke, "Javanen". No one has yet set himself to analyzing the 'imperialism' of Majapahit. Did the Javanese coastal cities play a rôle in it, with the same sort of relationship to the central inland state as that of the Greek coastal cities of Asia Minor to the Persian inland state?

107 See Fruin-Mees, *Geschiedenis*, II, Chapters Three, Seven, and Eight.

108 *Cf.* Rouffaer, "Kunst", 340–341; Snouck Hurgronje, "Bantam", 253.

109 The nobles supplied their own troops and warships, and one of the nobles was chosen as campaign commander; the standing army could be reinforced by peasants summoned to arms from the villages, the perhaps heathen mountainous hinterlands, and the Lampong region (see Colenbrander, *Coen*, I, 359, 472; Rouffaer & IJzerman, *Schipvaart*, I, 92, 128, III, 38).

110 See Rouffaer & IJzerman, *Schipvaart*, I, 107, *cf.* 128.

111 On the courts of the nobles see *ibid.*, I, 107–108, II, 28–30 (*Description*, 22 verso–23 verso); Van Neck, "Reisverhaal", 299.

112 See Rouffaer & IJzerman, *Schipvaart*, I, letterpress to Plate Fifteen; Van Neck, "Reisverhaal", 302–303. *Cf.* De Jonge, *Opkomst*, VII, 21; Rouffaer & Juynboll, *Batik-kunst*, I, 432; Tiele & Heeres, *Bouwstoffen*, II, 33,

113 See Rouffaer & IJzerman, *Schipvaart*, I, Chapter Thirty. Such a council

should probably be considered as a Buginese-Macassarese *hadat* council rather than as a Malay council (see Van Vollenhoven, *Adatrecht*, III, 420).

114 "...the nobles do not concern themselves with these things..." (Van Neck, "Reisverhaal", 265).

115 *Cf. ibid.*, 250–251.

116 See Rouffaer & IJzerman, *Schipvaart*, I, Chapter Thirty-One; on land ownership by Malacca merchants see De Barros in Rouffaer, "Kunst", 346.

117 There are reports of slaves working only part of the time for their lords: "Others who serve their lords have cost and clothes and nothing else. ... There are still others who work 6 days for their lord and thereafter 6 days for themselves and their households, whether they are fishers or others..." (Rouffaer & IJzerman, *Schipvaart*, I, 129). And of *apophora*-bound female slaves: "For the women it is the same, some sit at the bazaar and sell all [manner of] wares in order to gain some money, and give a certain sum each day..." (*ibid.*).

118 *Cf. Daghregister 1624–1629*, 149.

119 "...the slaves, craftsmen, and traders sit down at the sides [of the roads], squatting on their heels till the time when the authorities have passed by..." (Rouffaer & IJzerman, *Schipvaart*, I, letterpress to Plate Fourteen). That the nobility did not have any respect for 'bourgeois' elements, even for merchant gentlemen, is shown by the treatment of the rich merchant Simsuan (see below, n. 120): his possessions were seized and he himself was put in the stocks (Colenbrander, *Coen*, I, 116–117; *cf.* De Jonge, *Opkomst*, IV, 32; see also Colenbrander, *Coen*, IV, 85, on the fate of Nakoda Watting). The ruler of Achin had a servant of the Dutch Company thrown to the elephants – and went without punishment (Colenbrander, *Coen*, I, 129; *cf.* Tiele & Heeres, *Bouwstoffen*, I, 127 & n. 1, II, 364). *Cf.* the treatment given to the Hindu merchant gentleman Virji Vora of Surat by the lords of the Mogol court (Moreland, *Aurangzeb*, 153). The distrust of the nobility for the merchant is also clearly shown in a passage of the *Malay Annals* (Shellabear, *Sejarah*, 300).

120 Company sources have preserved a few names: Lak Mui, the 'host' of the Amsterdammers on the first Dutch voyage (Rouffaer & IJzerman, *Schipvaart*, I, 96 n. 20, 158 n. 4, 216 n. 1; Purchas, *Pilgrimes*, III, 503); Simsuan, shipowner and dealer in pepper and sandalwood (Colenbrander, *Coen*, I, 62–63, 69, 78, 116–117, 254, III, 421; *cf.* De Jonge, *Opkomst*, IV, 32); Aytsuan, who in 1616 "had a bad loss of many hundreds" of pounds (Colenbrander, *Coen*, II, 101, *cf.* 98); Limco, a Moslem Chinese and favourite of the governor (*ibid.*, I, 270, *cf.* 327).

121 On Simsuan as owner of ricelands see *Daghregister 1624–1629*, 240.

122 "...have... hirelings and purchased servants that they send in all regions to buy up pepper and other wares, also hiring out the same on some voyages, and to whom they always also give some capital to be employed for their profit" (Rouffaer & IJzerman, *Schipvaart*, I, 125).

123 "As Simsuan, a Chinese merchant residing here, is indebted to the general Company a good lot of pepper and as it appears it will not be possible to collect much of his outstanding debts, it is approved that he shall be ordered and forced to have a good sum of the means sent by him to China brought hither next year to pay us, as also that it shall be publicly declared and announced that if the friends of the said Simsuan be negligent in this we will avail ourselves of whatever persons and goods we may be able to lay hold of at Simsuan's and their cost..." (Resolution of the President and Councillors of the Lodge at Bantam, 1 July, 1616: Colenbrander, *Coen*, III, 367; *cf. ibid.*, I, 734: the English had seized a junk from China in 1622 and the captain sent an epistle to Batavia in complaint, "...as do also various other Chinese residing here who are interested therein...").

124 De Jonge speaks of "Chinese junks the cargo of which was consigned to Chinese traders in Bantam..." (*Opkomst*, IV, xxxviii), but nothing of such a consignment appears from the documents. Until counter-evidence is furnished, it would seem preferable to view the return cargoes as goods shipped back with *commenda* traders returning to Indonesia.

125 See *e.g.* Colenbrander, *Coen*, I, 270.

126 See Rouffaer, "Malaka", 137 n. 2, 138–139, 155 n. 2 under no 47; for a Portuguese origin of this Maluku *cf.* Danvers, *Trade*, I, 330.

127 See Rouffaer & IJzerman, *Schipvaart*, I, 88 n. 1, III, 138; Van Neck, "Reisverhaal", 208; De Jonge, *Opkomst*, II, 410.

128 Rouffaer & IJzerman, *Schipvaart*, I, Plate Eleven at v, *cf.* III, 31.

129 One of them, a Persian, was "principal doctor" in Bantam (Van Neck, "Reisverhaal", 220).

130 The characteristic of the Arab traders at the time of the first Dutch voyage was given as follows: "...the Arab, who carries his trade from one island to the other at sea, in which they are very experienced..." (Rouffaer & IJzerman, *Schipvaart*, I, letterpress to Plate Seventeen at B). There is also mention of Turkish influence in shipbuilding at Lasem in eastern Java (*ibid.*, letterpress to Plate Twenty-Seven).

131 See *ibid.*, I, Plate Eleven at I & Y, II, 24 (*Description*, 20 recto), 25 n. 3, 415 n. 13.

132 The census of Chinese for the poll tax levy in Jakarta in 1620 is accompanied by the commentary: "...how many have gone out to the East to trade and other ways may be hidden is not known to us..." (Colenbrander, *Coen*, I, 601; *cf.* De Jonge, *Opkomst*, V, 224). In an investigation of the outstanding debts of the Company office at Grise in 1616 it "was answered that the debtors had gone hither and thither with junks to seek their maintenance..." (Colenbrander, *Coen*, II, 177).

133 See also De Jonge, *Opkomst*, III, 181.

134 There is no evidence of there having been any gilds of the local inhabitants. For an interesting instance of mass demonstration, showing to what

means the Chinese community could resort, see the action against the Chinese headman Bencon at Batavia in 1620 (Colenbrander, *Coen*, IV, 236–239).

135 The merchants of Jaratan, coming to Bantam with their own spice ships manned by their own slaves (sixty in number) and staying there at the house of Lak Mui, were "wholesale traders", as appears from their possession of ships; with Lak Mui they formed a "company" (see Rouffaer & IJzerman, *Schipvaart*, I, 96–97, II, 42–43 [*Description*, 27 verso–27 recto], 43 n. 1, 44 n. 1).

136 *Ibid.*, I, 122, *cf.* 110, II, 26; Colenbrander, *Coen*, I, 163.

137 There is a description of how "slaves, craftsmen, and merchants" gave homage to the nobles squatting on their heels in the dust of the road. Elsewhere it is said that "The Gentlemen, Citizens, and marchantes have their Gardens, and fieldes without the towne, and slaves for the purpose to labour in them" (*Description* 23 verso [Rouffaer & IJzerman, *Schipvaart* II, 30]). But here there needs to be a sharp distinction made between merchants and merchants. It appears to me that this is not done to a sufficient degree either by Gonggrijp (*Schets*, 43–47) or Fruin-Mees (*Geschiedenis*, II, Chapter Eleven). The social stratification in the Chinese community is not brought clearly enough to light by Mme Fruin: it is untrue that "the Bantam merchants" did not go on journeys, but gave out *commenda* (*ibid.*, 40). The largest share of *commenda* money was given out only by merchant gentlemen, the wealthy and the moneyholders; how should the common man have been able to do it? The idea presented here is based on another reading of the passage "The merchants who are wealthy commonly stay at home..." (Rouffaer & IJzerman, *Schipvaart*, I, 120). Mme Fruin reads from this that the Bantam merchants, all of them, were wealthy. It seems to me one should read that those of the merchants who were wealthy – that being a small minority – stayed at home and gave out their money in *commenda*.

138 There was also trade at two other markets each day, at different places in the town (see Rouffaer & IJzerman, *Schipvaart*, I, 113, II, 415).

139 See Rouffaer & IJzerman, *Schipvaart*, I, Chapter Twenty-One and Plate Twelve.

140 Rouffaer in *ibid.*, II, 415 n. 10.

141 *Ibid.*, II, letterpress to Plate Four.

142 *Ibid.*, I, 113.

143 *Ibid.*, I, letterpress to Plate Twelve.

144 For *commenda* at Bantam see *ibid.*, I, 120–121; it is not clear to what extent the relation described on p. 123 there falls in that category. That the Chinese gave out and took *commenda*, and were thus respectively merchant gentlemen and pedlars, is certain from the material in the preceding sections.

145 *Ibid.*, I, 111.

146 So it seems to me 'ship lords' may be read (*cf.* Rouffaer, "Malaka", 97). The commanders of the large ships, heading a great multitude of pedlars on board ('shipper-passengers', to use Rouffaer's indicative term) and

crew, were persons of power and prestige. *E.g.*, when the Company forbade armed entry into the city of Batavia, "*nakodas* of great junks, prominent ambassadors, and plenipotentiaries" were exempted from the prohibition (Colenbrander, *Coen*, III, 930; *cf. ibid.*, I, 788; De Jonge, *Opkomst*, IV, 274). Appearing along with the merchant gentleman Wangsan in a Chinese embassy was a "ship's captain named Hongtay who is well known in Batavia..." (Colenbrander, *Coen*, I, 765–767).

147 *I.e.*, mercantile exchanges, trade exchanges. 'Exchange' more in the sense of the present-day Amsterdam shipping exchange than of the stock exchange and produce exchange.

148 See Van der Chijs, *Vestiging*, 127–128, 135, 138; Colenbrander, *Coen*, I, 446.

149 See Tiele & Heeres, *Bouwstoffen*, I, xxxviii, 199–200, 202 n. 1, 239–242, 261, II, lxiii, 17, 55, 57, 60–61, 69, 185, 198.

150 See Colenbrander, *Coen*, I, 372, 453, 455, 564, III, 66, 257, 280; "Verhaal", 391–392; Tiele & Heeres, *Bouwstoffen*, I, 154 n. 1, II, xviii, 32, 145.

151 See Colenbrander, *Coen*, I, 625–626, 641, III, 22, 28, 37, 44, 688, 705–706; Tiele & Heeres, *Bouwstoffen*, I, xliii–xlv; *cf.* Van Vollenhoven, *Adatrecht*, II, 792.

152 See Tiele & Heere, *Bouwstoffen*, I, iii, v, 2 & n. 2, 205–206, 229–230, 250, 262, 265, II, viii n. 2, 98 n. 3, 150, 162, 196–197, 203–205, 240, 243–244, 315, 321; Van Vollenhoven, *Adatrecht*, I, 396, *cf.* III, 452–453; Rouffaer, "Pata lima", 361, "Oeliasers", 66, and "Malaka", 537, 541–543, 559.

153 On Banda a general diet of all the people met under the holy tree of Urtatan (Van der Chijs, *Vestiging*, 3; *cf.* Tiele & Heeres, *Bouwstoffen*, I, 157); on Ambon festivals for the whole population were given by the nobles ("Verhaal", 352).

154 "...the proud, haughty Bandanese ... who, having nothing except his nutmeg trees, has to live from them year after year without accumulating any extraordinary surplus, accustomed to being constantly much honoured, not to work, and to eat well..." (Tiele, *Bouwstoffen*, I, 6: dated 1612).

155 "Verhaal", 353.

156 Also interesting – and at the same time instructive on the size of trade – is the information in "Verhaal" on the economic activity of slaves on Ambon: "It happens sometimes that a few of these ... slaves are subtle birds and know how to manage trade. These try to talk to people so that they are believed, so that with time they are credited and become better believed than their masters; for I as well as those before and after me have knowledge that in our books slaves of Capt. Hittu and others, as his brothers, have had debts of more than 20 *bahar* each. In fact, what is more, one of these slaves weighed 25 Portuguese *bahar* of cloves in our lodge in one monsoon, each *bahar* being

600 lb. In sum, some of these slaves are better to be trusted than their masters; having obtained what I have refused Capt. Hittu and the other *orang kayas*..." ("Verhaal", 413).

157 "Verhaal", 350, 352, 354, 378–379, 399, 413.

158 In a time of conflict between the Dutch and an English interloper on Ambon in 1613, it was reported that "...an *orang kaya* Ticos, who is a very proud man and has been long a great ally of ours has hung scales in his quarters and sold and had sold a lot of cloves to the English..." (Colenbrander, *Coen*, I, 12; on Ticos see also Tiele & Heeres, *Bouwstoffen*, I, 328 n. 1, II, 13, 53).

159 On the spice traders of eastern Java going out with *commenda* money see De Jonge, *Opkomst*, II, 451, IV, 3. Javanese shipping was described as "carrying on its trade at many places in passing, buying and selling what seems profitable to it..." (Rouffaer & IJzerman, *Schipvaart*, I, 200).

160 See *ibid.*, I, 131 & n. 9; *cf.* Tiele & Heeres, *Bouwstoffen*, II, 274. The 'shipper-passengers' in many cases took along their wives.

161 Van Heemskerck, the first Dutch trader on Banda (1599) wrote: "I could not wish otherwise than that the nobles here had much merchandise of nutmeg and mace, for everything is in demand by them. Then we would lightly obtain our cargo and at a good price. But there is not much. It all has to be bought from the inhabitants here by the pound..." (Van der Chijs, *Vestiging*, II, 6; *cf.* De Jonge, *Opkomst*, II, 431–432). That this was no acute emergency for Dutch trade, but that trade ran its course pound by pound, is shown in Colenbrander, *Coen*, IV, 31 points 13 & 15; *cf.* Tiele & Heeres, *Bouwstoffen*, I, 325. The incoming trade from the west is described thus: "Where they come (namely where they expect to go home again with the other monsoon), they haul their junks or ships on dry land, the which they know how to perform very properly. First they make little huts pinned together like booths at a fair, where they bring all their merchandise and exhibit it, so that it is an Indian fair: there is nothing better to compare this trading with..." ("Verhaal", 533; *cf.* Tiele & Heeres, *Bouwstoffen*, II, 30, 199, 207, 209, 294–295). The Javanese missionary teachers were recruited by the local nobles from among the traders: "... when the junks are leaving they try to hold some persons to serve them as schoolmasters. When they have something still left from their load or keep with them the goods their departing fellows have left unsold, which they get rid of meanwhile at a great advantage, they have it well and completely paid for at the set time, in which they are assisted by the *orang kayas*, who take care that they were contented according to their wishes ..." ("Verhaal", 360). One notice is of a completely different sort. In ten weeks Van Heemskerck received four hundred *bahar* of nutmeg and a hundred *bahar* of mace from a Javanese named Malein; later Malein delivered three shiploads more of spices ("3 junks with mace, nutmeg, and cloves..."), an amount altogether of more than five hundred

bahar. As there is nothing recorded further of this trader (after all, he would have been a respectable merchant, holding around a quarter of the total crop on Banda), it appears to me that he can better be considered as the agent of a group of small traders who had put their cargoes together in one lot and thus did business with the Dutch (De Jonge, *Opkomst*, II, 441). On Ambon the goods imported – cotton cloth, gongs, etc. – often were not used, but were buried as treasure ("Verhaal", 417; *cf. ibid.*, 490–491; Barbosa in Moreland, *Aurangzeb*, 71 n.; Tiele & Heeres, *Bouwstoffen*, II, 321; Rouffaer, "Kunst", 361–362, 362 n. 1; Van Orsoy de Flines, "Verzameling", III, 207–208, 212): another argument against a mass market for daily needs. *Cf.* also the passage: "...whatever one takes there [to Ambon] to make good profit one must take but little of each sort in order to come off lightly and to sell something else..." ("Verhaal", 451).

162 See De Jonge, *Opkomst*, 427, 429, 436; Colenbrander, *Coen*, III, 631 (the Gujarati quarter on Banda); "Verhaal", 451 (Javanese and Gujarati goldsmiths on Ambon); Van der Chijs, *Vestiging*, 14.

163 *Cf.* Rouffaer, "Malaka", 526.

164 *I.e.*, an average of forty traders per junk. In 1619 there were seventy-eight men taken from two Javanese ships going to Malacca (Colenbrander, *Coen*, III, 549, 554–555); on twenty-two or twenty-three Macassarese junks in 1624 there were five or six hundred men (Tiele & Heeres, *Bouwstoffen*, II, 15). *Cf.* "... [as] they sail in small vessels and have many people on board, each of which does his own private trade, this must therefore lead to thin pickings, for they carry as many people on a junk of 20 ton as we on a ship of 200 ton and more..." ("Verhaal", 509); "We can earn something on the cloth but little or nothing on the rice and thereby [we] make ourselves very odious not only to the Moluccans, Ambonese, and Bandanese, but also to the Javanese, Macassarese, Malays, and other nations, for the bread is taken out of small pedlars' mouths thereby..." (Van der Hagen to the Gentlemen Seventeen, 20 August, 1618, in Tiele & Heeres, *Bouwstoffen*, I, 231).

165 One should compare this with the cargo figures in n. 83 above, and see into how many pieces of cotton cloth it could be converted.

166 See Colenbrander, *Coen*, V, 42–43; Tiele & Heeres, *Bouwstoffen*, I, 230–231, 354, 356, II, i–ii, vii, xxxv, liv, lv n. 2, lxv, 91–92, 105, 116, 119–120, 122, 125, 189–192, 235, 279, 284, 301, 325–326, 346, 367–368, 372, 379. *Cf. ibid.*, 250; Rouffaer, "Pata lima", 361.

167 See Colenbrander, *Coen*, I, 367, 564–565, 599, 750, 784, III, 51, V, 134; Tiele & Heeres, *Bouwstoffen*, I, 348, II, 5, 46 n. 1, 137, 162, 211, 342; *Daghregister 1624–1629*, 378 (galley duty), 379 (relocation).

168 Also tributary to Ternate were *e.g.* Solor (*cf. Daghregister 1636*, 223) and Adonare – more than seven hundred miles away (*cf.* Rouffaer, "Kunst", 381, 394), Buton – five hundred miles away, Sula, Bongko, and Gorontalo (see Tiele & Heeres, *Bouwstoffen*, I, 23, 94–95, II, xxii n. 1, xlvii, 90, 93 n. 2,

109 n. 3, 314), the Kai and Aru Islands (Broersma, "Molukken-Zuid", 57–63), and Poso ("Poso", 463).

169 *Cf.* Tiele & Heeres, *Bouwstoffen*, I, 244.

170 See Colenbrander, *Coen*, I, 21, *cf.* 500, II, 591; De Jonge, *Opkomst*, III, 195–196.

171 See "Verhaal", 359–360, 419, 427, 431; Broersma, "Molukken-Zuid", 54.

172 The religious teachers "are maintained by the support of the *orang kayas*..." ("Verhaal", 360). Towards the time of the western monsoon they were given five and a half pounds of cloves per pupil, "which they collect and then depart for Java again..." (*ibid.*, 361). Of Captain Hittu: "It is so that he is a great Mohammedan, who does much to have his faith spread, so that Hittu is full of Moorish priests working much to spread their sect..." (Tiele & Heeres, *Bouwstoffen*, I, 233).

173 Of the four leading Ambonese noble families, one was of Javanese origin, one from Ceram, and two from the island itself ("Verhaal", 3).

174 See Colenbrander, *Coen*, II, 49, II, 736; Tiele & Heeres, *Bouwstoffen*, I, xxxviii, xlviii, 245–246, 252, 256, 303, 334, II, xliv, 11, 80, 198.

On the Study of Indonesian History

1 Perry, *Culture;* Kruyt, *West-Toradjas.*

2 Rüter, *Spoorwegstakingen.*

3 *Cf.* Massignon, "Islam"; Fischel, *Jews*; Fitzler, "Handelsgesellschaften".

4 *Cf.* Van Vollenhoven, *Adatrecht*, III, 583.

5 *Cf.* *Daghregister 1631–1634*, 37,

6 Thus, for example, the use of such terms as 'big industry' and 'large-scale export' in regard to Coromandel textile handicrafts (Rouffaer & Juynboll, *Batik-kunst*, I, 422, 521, 523, 528; Krom, *Geschiedenis*, 48), an undifferentiated view of 'trade', Krom's incorrect view of the relationship of trade to piracy (*Geschiedenis*, 151 n. 82), etc.

7 Stapel, "Speelman", 16, 19, 72, 115.

8 *Cf.* Weber, *Wirtschaft*, *Religionssoziologie* (for details on English translations see the bibliography below), and *History*.

9 *Onderzoek.*

10 Duyvendak, *Kakean-genootschap.*

11 Kruyt, *West-Toradjas*; Vroklage, *Verhältnisse.*

12 For the records and a report on this suggestion, see the *Jaarboek Koninklijk Bataviaasch Genootschap van Kunsten en Wetenschappen* (Yearbook of the Royal Batavian Society of Arts and Sciences; Batavia), III (1936), 50, 132.

13 Gustaaf Willem, Baron van Imhoff, governor-general, 1743–1750; Godert Alexander Gerard Philip, Baron van der Capellen, governor–general,

1816–1826; Vincent Gildemeester, Baron van Tuyll van Serooskerken (1812–1860), commissioner for tin prospecting at Billiton.

14 Commissie voor 's Rijks Geschiedkundige Publicatiën, Economisch-Historisch Archief, Historisch Genootschap.

The World of Southeast Asia

I

1 Ferrand, "K'ouen-louen", XIII, 489. Astrolabes were also used on the Dutch expeditions to Asia (see Rouffaer & IJzerman, *Schipvaart*, III, 287 n. 3, 288 n. 3, 435 ff., 438).

2 Danvers, *Portuguese*, I, 228.

3 Tiele, "Europeërs", I, 342.

4 *Ibid.*, IV, 425, *cf.* 427.

5 Van Linschoten, *Voyage*, I, 109–110 (the words in brackets were omitted in the English translation).

6 Tiele, "Europeërs", IV, 463, 466, 473, 477. When Magellan was at Cebu eight of his crew were sold to Chinese traders (*ibid.*, I, 415).

7 Chang, *Trade*, 34, 52.

8 Tiele, "Europeërs", IV, 462.

9 Danvers, *Portuguese*, I, 181 n. †.

10 *Ibid.*, 226.

11 *Voyage*, I, 87.

12 Moreland, *Aurangzeb*, 74 n.; *cf. Collecção*, II, 110, VII, 378.

13 Rouffaer, "Kunst", 382.

14 See the various reports by Van Orsoy de Flines on the ceramics collection of the Royal Batavian Society, "Verzameling".

15 IJzerman, *Pomp*, 20. In the following calculations all ship sizes and cargo weights have been figured in tons of fifteen hundred pounds. To convert them into modern short tons of two thousand pounds and compare them with present-day figures would emphasize all the more the smallness of them all. Comparison with seventeenth-century Dutch and other European figures is probably more illuminating. One should consider the Asian types of ships in comparison to the Dutch freighter *par excellence*, the flute, usually of four hundred ton. The big ships of the Dutch Company were usually of eight hundred to a thousand ton. The heavy Portuguese ships, the caracks, amounted to fifteen hundred to two thousand ton.

16 Van Linschoten, *Voyage*, I, 146–147.

17 Tiele, "Europeërs", II, 23. The land route to Aleppo and Egypt continued to be used. Italians and also Dutchmen and Englishmen arrived in India by way of it in the sixteenth century. Van Linschoten cherished

plans to go back to Europe along it, the which would have cost him a hundred ducats, or around thirty-five pounds travelling money (IJzerman, *Pomp*, 8). On factors of Venetian merchants in Goa and Malacca for the trade in jewels see Van Linschoten, *Voyage*, II, 159.

18 Rouffaer & IJzerman, *Schipvaart*, I, 74.

19 *Ibid.*, II, 293.

20 *Kojah*, Persian *chòjah*, a designation of respect for wealthy merchants.

21 Rouffaer & IJzerman, *Schipvaart*, I, 83–84.

22 Van Neck, "Reisverhaal", 254–255.

23 Van der Chijs, *Vestiging*, 26.

24 Heeres, *Corpus*, I, 277.

25 Van Spilbergen, *Reis*, 30.

26 The *bahar* was one of the weights most frequently used for spices in Indonesia, varying from place to place according to custom – 600 lb. in the northern Moluccas, 550 on Banda and in Macassar, 495 in Bantam, 530 to 540 in Malacca, 380 in Patani, 360 in Kedah, and so on.

27 Tiele, "Europeërs", I, 408, II, 22–23, IV, 411–413; De Jonge, *Opkomst*, III, 274–275.

28 Indonesia is the only correct name for the region historically. "To want to approach this world with such terms as 'Our Orient', 'the Netherlands East Indies', 'the Netherlands in the Tropics', and the like is to fail to appreciate the fact that it existed and was alive before a single Dutchman appeared in the tropics" (Colenbrander, *Geschiedenis*, II, 45). For the same reasons the term Netherlands East Indies is justified for the time in which this is being written.

29 *Inferno*, XV: 4 ff.

30 Van Orsoy de Flines, "Verzameling", III, 209.

31 For a summary of the view see Krom, *Geschiedenis*, which considers other parts of the archipelago as well as Java.

32 For a summary see the section "Praehistorie" (Prehistory) by A. N. J. Thomassen à Thuessink van der Hoop, in Stapel, *Geschiedenis*, I, 5–111.

33 Here is not the place to elaborate this point. It is however of great importance for Indonesian history, which could use a little geopolitics alongside archeology and ethnology. Mention may be made of Junghuhn's remark in connection with *sawah* terrace farming (given without further substantiation) that a "culture" of opening up the land and settling it had existed "for thousands of years" (*Reisen*, 413, *cf.* 222). And the American ethnologist Barton, speaking on the impressive *sawah* culture of the Ifugaos, an Indonesian tribe on northern Luzon, said that it was "... a work of tens of centuries. Any calculation must be based on vague and hazardous figures of course, but without any theories to prove, and making due allowance for increased rate of building during peaceful times and for the pressure of the needs of an increased population, from a comparison of the estimated area of voluntary rice-

field building with the areas already constructed, I come to the conclusion that the Ifugaos must have lived in their present habitat for at least 2000 years, and I believe that these figures are too small." (*Law*, 11). The question of Javanese history should be approached in such a way.

34 Groeneveldt, "Notes", 14 n., 101.

35 Krause, *Geschichte*, I, 138–139, 347–349, 365.

36 Krom, *Geschiedenis*, 452 & nn. 5 & 6.

37 Tiele, "Europeërs", II, 53, 56.

38 At first the Mongols did not bind themselves to any of the religions of the lands conquered by them. The popes had hoped for a league with the Mongol rulers for reconquering the Holy Land from the Moslems (see Krause, *Geschichte*, I, 351 ff., 373 ff.). The *Societas fratrum peregrinantium propter Christum*, the forerunner of the *Congregatio de propaganda fide*, was founded by Pope Innocent II in 1252 (*ibid.*, 354).

39 *Cf.* Moreland, *Akbar*, 200–201, and *Aurangzeb*, 92.

40 *f* 6,424,588.20. The capital of the fleet of eight of the thirtheen Amsterdam ships in 1601, the next to the last fleet before the union of the companies, the account of which was settled by the new company, was *f* 1,334,742.76, or around £ 110,000. The 1602 fleet, which sailed out under Van Warwijck on a separate account in accordance with Article Seven of the Company charter, had a capital of *f* 1,738,325, or around £ 145,000 (Van Dam, *Beschryvinge*, I, Part One, 14, 16).

41 Colenbrander, *Geschiedenis*, II, 91.

42 De Jonge, *Opkomst*, III, 134; Mijer, *Verzameling*, 44–45 (§§ 76, 77).

43 Heeres, *Corpus*, I, no xviii.

44 Colenbrander, *Coen*, IV, 506: The Gentlemen Seventeen to the Indies, 4 March, 1621. Coen had already written to the Seventeen on 10 November, 1614: "Banda must be subjugated and we will have to dominate the scene there or it will not amount to anything either on Banda or Amboina" (*ibid.*, I, 79).

45 In that time, before the stringent closing off of their country, Japanese were found everywhere in Indonesia, for the most part in military service. For Japanese in the pay of the Spanish see Colenbrander, *Coen*, I, 180; in the pay of the Dutch Company, *ibid.*, I, 210 ("...Japanese which here [in Bantam] are more respected than our nation"), 301–302, 428, 519, 626, 636, 771, II, 106, 373, III, 59, 952.

46 Heeres, *Corpus*, I, no clxiv.

47 Lalis was abandoned in the same year, but later, in 1647, it was regained from the merchant gentleman Malaya with rights as a fortified lodge (*ibid.*, I, no clxxxii).

48 See the statement of the Gentlemen Seventeen in the General Report of 31 December, 1647 (*ibid.*, I, 490–491, *cf.* 528 n. 5).

49 See *ibid.*, I, no xxxvii.

50 Achin and Mataram "...would always like to establish such a great monarchy here as the king of Spain seeks to do in Europe..." (Coen to the Gentlemen Seventeen, 14 January, 1619: Colenbrander, *Coen*, I, 436). In the treaty on tin from Perak in 1650 there is mention of "the august court of Achin" (Heeres, *Corpus*, I, no cxcii).

51 Most of the pepper shipped by the Portuguese came from India; the export to Persia and the ports of the caliphates also involved Indian pepper primarily. Achin, too, carried on a pepper trade to the northwest.

II

1 *Genesis* 37: 25.
2 *Ezekiel* 27: 23–24.
3 1 *Kings* 9: 26–28.
4 Mookerji, *Shipping*, 93–94.
5 Ferrand, "K'ouen-louen", XIII, 452–453.
6 Krom, *Geschiedenis*, 226.
7 *Ibid.*, 285.
8 *Ibid.*, 401.
9 Colenbrander, *Coen*, V, 309.
10 *Daghregister 1637*, 53.
11 Mookerji, *Shipping*, 129.
12 Schrieke, "Prolegomena", 103.
13 *Description*, 20 recto (Rouffaer & IJzerman, *Schipvaart*, II, 24).
14 Rouffaer & IJzerman, *Schipvaart*, I, 84 n. 23, 108 & n. 19, II, 25, n. 3.
15 Van der Chijs, *Vestiging*, 38.
16 Schrieke, "Prolegomena", 123.
17 Van Dillen, *Karakter*, 129.
18 *Ibid.*, 99.
19 *Ibid.*, 152.
20 See *e.g.* "Verhaal", 533.
21 *Daghregister 1624–1629*, 78.
22 *Ibid.*, 125.
23 *Daghregister 1631–1634*, 15.
24 *Daghregister 1624–1629*, 124.
25 See the reference in the story of Aladdin, in the 650th tale of *The Thousand and One Nights*; see also Fischel, *Jews*, *passim*.
26 Yule, *Cathay*, I, 103.
27 Fischel, *Jews*; Massignon, "Islam".
28 Van Linschoten, *Voyage*, I, 229.
29 *Ibid.*, I, 181.
30 Van Dillen, *Karakter*, 105.

31 *Ibid.*, 161 & n. 11.

32 Colenbrander, *Coen*, I, 167.

33 De Jonge, *Opkomst*, V, 263.

34 *Daghregister 1624–1629*, 130, 139, 147, 150.

35 *Ibid.*, 224, 226, 246.

36 *Ibid.*, 305, 307.

37 *Ibid.*, 224.

38 *Daghregister 1631–1634*, 9.

39 *Daghregister 1637*, 122. It would appear that these are not all of them Chinese as they are called in *Daghregister*. In Inretullus, appearing with two deposits, of fifty and of twenty reals, the Jurutulus (scribe) of the following chapter (§ 2) should be recognized. Chily Kitchel and Sambayangh, too, seem to be Indonesian names.

40 Colenbrander, *Coen*, III, 191.

41 Rouffaer & IJzerman, *Schipvaart*, III, 201, 202, 204, 205.

42 *Ibid.*, I, 121, *cf.* 110, II, 26 (*Description*, 21 recto).

43 Van Dillen, *Karakter*, 90, 207 n. 11; cf. Pirenne, *Pays-Bas*, 204: "The large-scale trade from which the patricians lived..."

44 Colenbrander, *Coen*, I, 167.

45 *Ibid.*, II, 7.

46 *Daghregister 1624–1629*, 240; Colenbrander, *Coen*, I, 62–63, 69, 78.

47 Colenbrander, *Coen*, III, 367.

48 *Ibid.*, II, 101.

49 *Ibid.*, V, 35, 71, 149, 162, 271, 273, 281, 321–322, 489; *Daghregister 1624–1629*, 246.

50 Colenbrander, *Coen*, I, 798.

51 When in 1622 the Dutch Company forbade armed entry into Batavia, "*nakodas* of great junks, prominent ambassadors, and plenipotentiaries" were excepted from the prohibition (Colenbrander, *Coen*, III, 930; *cf. ibid.*, I, 788; De Jonge, *Opkomst*, IV, 274).

52 *Daghregister 1624–1629*, 140.

53 *Daghregister 1631–1634*, 173.

54 *Daghregister 1637*, 26: here, despite the high value, everything in cash.

55 Moreland, *Aurangzeb*, 156; *Daghregister 1631–1634*, 364–365.

56 See *e.g. Daghregister 1631–1634*, 144–145, 334–335, 365; *Daghregister 1636*, 250, etc.

57 "As much as Mierecomaldi has coming for his opium is promised his servant... ...do not permit any goods to be sent hither with the Company's ships again for him or others..." (Colenbrander, *Coen*, III, 74: 12 August, 1621).

58 Rouffaer & Juynboll, *Batik-kunst*, I, Appendix III under 'Masulipatam'.

59 Rouffaer & IJzerman, *Schipvaart*, I, 120. For Macassar *cf.* Tiele & Heeres, *Bouwstoffen*, II, 113.

60 *Cf.* Moreland, *Akbar*, 13.

61 *Daghregister 1624–1629*, 140.

62 *Daghregister 1631–1634*, 64.

63 *Ibid.*, 50–51.

64 *Ibid.*, 69.

65 *Ibid.*, 306.

66 *Ibid.*, 72.

67 *Ibid.*, 242; *Daghregister 1636*, 244; *Daghregister 1637*, 73.

68 *Daghregister 1631–1634*, 53, 215, 365; *Daghregister 1637*, 133, 134; *Daghregister 1640–1641*, 74, 75, 84.

69 *Daghregister 1631–1634*, 57.

70 *Ibid.*, 87; *Daghregister 1636*, 51.

71 *Ibid.*, 51, 250–251.

72 *Ibid.*, 248.

73 Terpstra, *Westerkwartieren*, 271.

74 Resolution of the Governor-General and Councillors, 28 December, 1619: Colenbrander, *Coen*, III, 573, *cf.* I, 514, 722, III, 1002.

75 *Daghregister 1631–1634*, 365.

76 *Daghregister 1636*, 45.

77 Colenbrander, *Coen*, I, 349.

78 *Ibid.*, III, 931.

79 Van der Chijs, *Vestiging*, 30; *cf. Daghregister 1631–1634*, 314.

80 *Daghregister 1624–1629*, 81.

81 Colenbrander, *Coen*, III, 856; Tiele & Heeres, *Bouwstoffen*, II, 220.

82 Colenbrander, *Coen*, I, 304.

83 *Ibid.*, I, 343.

84 *Daghregister 1637*, 236.

85 *Ibid.*, 131.

86 Colenbrander, *Coen*, I, 329–330, 419, 551, 606–607, 695, 708, II, 374, III, 57, 649; Tiele & Heeres, *Bouwstoffen*, II, 355 under 40.

87 *Daghregister 1631–1634*, 146.

88 *Ibid.*, 169.

89 De Jonge, *Opkomst*, III, 247.

90 Van Neck, "Reisverhaal", 264–265.

91 See *e.g. Daghregister 1631–1634*, 152, 249.

92 De Jonge, *Opkomst*, III, 270; Colenbrander, *Coen*, I, 82, 198, 202, 400–401, 449, II, 257, IV, 638, V, 682; Tiele & Heeres, *Bouwstoffen*, I, 355, II, 112, 175, *cf.* 394.

93 "Verhaal", 504–505; De Jonge, *Opkomst*, III, 261; Colenbrander, *Coen*, I, 255 (1000–1100 *bahar*), 279 (600), 447 (885), 565 (1000, 1500), 784, 786 (1252), II, 257 (1000–1200), 610 (1000–1200), V, 46–47 (456), 122 (312), *cf.* I, 198, 202, IV, 638; Tiele & Heeres, *Bouwstoffen*, I, 262 (1000), II, 187 (1300), 282–283, 288, 336 (1000).

94 "Verhaal", 512, 514, 516.

95 *Cf.* Tiele & Heeres, *Bouwstoffen*, II, 320 (1637); De Jonge, *Opkomst*, II, 448, III, 20.

96 Colenbrander, *Coen*, I, 177, III, 308, 872.

97 "Verhaal", 527; Colenbrander, *Coen*, I, 77, *cf.* 212, II, 9 ff.; *cf.* Tiele & Heeres, *Bouwstoffen*, I, 91–92.

98 Colenbrander, *Coen*, IV, 393, 456, 564.

99 De Jonge, *Opkomst*, IV, 57 ff.

100 Colenbrander, *Coen*, I, 291, *cf.* II, 481.

101 Van der Chijs, *Vestiging*, 161; Colenbrander, *Geschiedenis*, II, 118; Tiele & Heeres, *Bouwstoffen*, I, xlvi & n. 2.

102 *Cf.* Gonggrijp, *Schets*, 41.

103 De Jonge, *Opkomst*, IV, 27; Colenbrander, *Coen*, I, 68, 115, II, 7–8.

104 Colenbrander, *Coen*, IV, 456–457.

105 *Ibid.*, II, 580–583. The amount shipped to Java was low because of the disturbances; it has been estimated six hundred *corges* higher here.

106 De Jonge, *Opkomst*, III, 149 ff. The complete text is in Rouffaer & Juynboll, *Batik-kunst*, I, Appendix III.

107 Colenbrander, *Coen*, II, 583, III, 94, I, 690, III, 296.

108 Moreland, *Akbar*, 235–236.

109 *Daghregister 1624–1629*, 12.

110 *Daghregister 1631–1634*, 249.

111 *Daghregister 1624–1629*, 14.

112 *Daghregister 1631–1634*, 53–54.

113 *Ibid.*, 438.

114 *Daghregister 1636*, 69–74.

115 *Daghregister 1637*, 157.

116 *Ibid.*, 43.

117 *Daghregister 1631–1634*, 123.

118 *Ibid.*, 144.

119 *Daghregister 1636*, 50.

120 Terpstra, *Westerkwartieren*, 253, 256.

121 *Ibid.*, 257.

122 *Daghregister 1631–1634*, 312–313.

123 *Ibid.*, 298–299.

124 *Daghregister 1636*, 168.

125 Colenbrander, *Coen*, II, 20–21.

126 Tiele & Heeres, *Bouwstoffen*, II, 307–308.

127 *Voyage*, I, xxvi.

128 Colenbrander, *Coen*, I, 100 (27 December, 1614).

III

1 A time in which illiteracy was still known on a large scale. The Instrument of Pacification of Ambon, 7 June, 1621, is characteristic: alongside Coen, Frederik Houtman, Van Speult, and other Company authorities, three Dutchmen, apparently unable to write, signed with a mark (Heeres, *Corpus*, I, 172 n. 1).

2 Pyrard, *Voyage*, I, 414, 415.

3 *Daghregister 1631–1634*, 148–149. The chief accountant of the ruler of Ternate was a party in a commercial settlement there (Colenbrander, *Coen*, IV, 71); in 1638 the weighmaster of Bantam carried on correspondence with Batavia (*ibid.*, V, 75).

4 *Daghregister 1637*, 119. Notice the institution of indenturing the Chinese merchant's family.

5 *Ibid.*, 131–132.

6 Van der Chijs, *Vestiging*, 6; *cf.* De Jonge, *Opkomst*, II, 431–432.

7 Colenbrander, *Coen*, I, 12.

8 *Daghregister 1637*, 262.

9 *Ibid.*, 263: 20 Surat *man* = 27 Deccan *man*.

10 *Daghregister 1631–1634*, 169, 195; *cf.* Colenbrander, *Coen*, V, 21, 346, 516, 519, 584, 590, 738, 770.

11 Colenbrander, *Coen*, I, 149–150. The contract was repudiated (see Heeres, *Corpus*, I, 217 n. 2).

12 *Daghregister 1624–1629*, 140.

13 Van Dam, *Beschryvinge*, I, Part Two, 138.

14 *Cf.* Colenbrander, *Coen*, I, 188, 266–267 (Chinese and Japanese block silver and American plate silver). The Company most of the time traded in hard money, though sometimes letters of credit and non-cash payment – which were forms also known to the East – were used. "We are uncommonly shy of money, have not more than 16 chests in the general office and in all the ships of the whole fleet. From that the Moluccas, Amboyna, and Banda must be supplied and the Chinese trade satisfied. With what can we buy the pepper from Bantam if we shortly reach an accord? The English on the other hand have 70 chests of money of 4000 reals each lying in our warehouse, and besides that as much money in their ships as they plan to send to the Moluccas, Amboyna, and Banda..." (The governor-general to the Gentlemen Seventeen, 8 January, 1621: *ibid.*, I, 620; *cf.* I, 132, 612, II, 12, 35, III, 579, 793–794, V, 147; and see also § 2 above).

15 *Ibid.*, I, 699–700.

16 *Ibid.*, I, 88, 98.

17 *Ibid.*, I, 666, 678, 711.

18 The governor-general wrote to the Gentlemen Seventeen, 8 January, 1621: "Because of the trouble with the English, the capital here went down

about fifty thousand pounds in two or three years, from which the Company must be deprived of the returns..." (*ibid.*, I, 621). 16 November, 1621, he wrote to them: "The arrival of so many excellent ships as have been sent by Your Excellencies in three successive years on the one hand pleases us much, but still more it saddens us that so little money comes with them. We cannot understand whereon the decisions of your council are founded. How is it possible that such large, excessive amounts as are expended by Your Excellencies there and by us here can be gained with a capital of around five hundred thousand reals (Your Excellencies should figure that your capital is not larger than what is sent out every year)? Because we eat into that every year about two hundred thousand reals, nothing but seven tons of gold is left to be employed on the returns for the homeland..." (*Ibid.*, I, 663).

19 Van Dam, *Beschryvinge*, I, Part One, 364 (Appendix II to Chapter Twelve).

20 Colenbrander, *Coen*, I, 690 (21 January, 1621), *cf.* 700.

21 *Ibid.*, IV, 466, 474, V, 830, 846.

22 *Ibid.*, I, 635, 682.

23 *Ibid.*, I, 689.

24 *Ibid.*, I, 690.

25 *Ibid.*, I, 635, 671.

26 Mansvelt, *Rechtsvorm*, 46.

27 *Ibid.*, 45.

28 Rouffaer & IJzerman, *Schipvaart*, I, 111.

29 *Daghregister 1631–1634*, 306; *Daghregister 1636*, 15.

30 Van Dam, *Beschryvinge*, I, Part One, 366–367.

31 *Ibid.*, I, Part One, 416.

32 "In order to have large repartitions, they [the directors] seek to be sparing of the moneys and hold them here [in Holland], which may be all right for the said year, but they ought to see a bit further and also take care for the years following..." (*ibid.*, I, Part Two, 109).

33 *Ibid.*, I, Part One, 418.

34 Sombart, *Kapitalismus*, II, Part One, 156.

35 Colenbrander, *Coen*, I, 528–529.

36 *Ibid.*, I, 749.

37 *Ibid.*, V, 80.

38 The shipping on Bantam, Malacca, and Krawang has not been included here, as it was only for patrolling and blockading. The defence fleet sailing out to Goa, 26 August, 1636, seven ships and three yachts, and the expedition setting out for Ceram with Governor-General van Diemen on board, 30 December, 1636, nine ships and eight yachts, have also been left out of consideration.

39 The number of voyages undertaken independently from the other

offices was rather small. The Formosa office traded on Farther India and sometimes sent ships directly to India and the Middle East. In general, however, all traffic was centralized at Batavia.

40 For an estimate one can figure yachts and frigates at a hundred ton, flutes at two hundred, and 'ships' at four hundred. In the survey of the Company's shipping there are fifty-two ships, sixty yachts, eighteen flutes, two frigates, one junk, and one sloop to be counted. If there is allowance made for the fact that some ships made more than one trip per year and the actual number is set at two-thirds, then the Company's total Asian commercial fleet in 1636 comes to thirty-five ships, forty yachts, twelve flutes, and a few small vessels – or, with the fleets at sea and the patrol ships added, of around fifty-one ships, fifty-eight yachts, and fourteen flutes. This estimate can be tested roughly by comparing it with the report of the Company's actual naval strength in the Indies at the end of 1636 given in the General Report to the Gentlemen Seventeen, 28 December, 1636 in the manuscript *Indische Brievenboek 1636–1637* ('Book of Outgoing Letters from the Indies', National Record Office, Jakarta). Tested only roughly, because the kinds of ships are specified there only now and then. The report gives a total of eighty-one bottoms, including two yachts, five flutes, four sloops, and one boyer. No specification is given for the other sixty-nine vessels. The same report also mentions seven ships of free burghers in Asia, three of them in Company territory.

41 De Haan, *Oud-Batavia*, I, 91, 97.

42 In 1654 there were two hundred seventy male European free burghers in Batavia (*ibid.*, I, 112).

43 *Ibid.*, I, 126.

44 *Daghregister 1624–1629*, 1.

45 De Haan, *Oud-Batavia*, I, 121–122. On the Chinese wayang see Colenbrander, *Coen*, IV, 216.

46 "The rumours are going strong again that the *susuhunan* means to expand his power [to Bali, which was in turmoil because of the struggle for the throne], apparently in order to fish in those troubled waters. Earlier it was also much rumoured that he would come over to Bantam to bring it to obedience, the which he has ordered the *pangeran* of Jambi to do (who has come in person to do the *susuhunan* homage) as well as the ambassadors of Palembang, who had also appeared there for the same reason, who excused themselves because of their limited power, but were ready to join with the *susuhunan*'s forces..." (The governor-general and councillors to the Gentlemen Seventeen, 24 January, 1652: De Jonge, *Opkomst*, VI, 24). Differently from earlier, Mataram at this time effectively expanded its territory to the Company's frontiers: Javanese border guards lay in military colonies on the east bank of the Krawang River (*cf. ibid.*, VI, 35).

47 'Points and Articles in the Form of General Instructions', the fourth document in Mijer, *Verzameling*, 71–116.

48 *Ibid.*, 76–77.
49 *Ibid.*, 77.
50 *Ibid.*, 79.
51 *Ibid.*, 82.
52 *Ibid.*, 82.
53 *Ibid.*, 82–83.
54 *Ibid.*, 84.
55 *Ibid.*, 84.
56 *Ibid.*, 85.
57 *Ibid.*, 85.
58 *Ibid.*, 86.
59 *Ibid.*, 87.
60 *Ibid.*, 88.
61 *Ibid.*, 92.
62 *Ibid.*, 92.
63 *Ibid.*, 93.
64 *Ibid.*, 99.
65 *Ibid.*, 100.
66 *Ibid.*, 102.
67 *Ibid.*, 85.
68 *Ibid.*, 89.
69 *Ibid.*, 100.
70 Van Goens, "Rapport".
71 *Ibid.*, 159.
72 *Ibid.*, 154.
73 *Ibid.*, 176–177.
74 *Ibid.*, 177–178.

Three Reviews

I

1 Stapel, *Geschiedenis* (see bibliography below).
2 N. J. Krom, "De Hindoe-Javaansche Tijd" (The Hindu-Javanese Period), Stapel, *Geschiedenis*, I, 115–298.
3 A. N. J. Thomassen à Thuessink van der Hoop, "Praehistorie" (Prehistory), Stapel, *Geschiedenis*, I, 5–111.
4 Stapel, *Geschiedenis*, I, 111, *cf.* 93.
5 *Ibid.*, I, 119.
6 *Ibid.*
7 See Gosses, "Volksverhuizing", 15–16, 25–26, 42.
8 Stapel, *Geschiedenis*, I, 136–140.

9 See *e.g. ibid.*, I, 137.

10 In De Jonge, *Opkomst*, IV, 284 ff.

11 *Javaense Reijse.*

12 *Geschiedenis*, 247 ff.

13 Stutterheim, "Bijzettingsgebruiken".

14 See Van der Hoop, in Stapel, *Geschiedenis*, I, 33.

15 See *ibid.*, I, Plates Nineteen to Thirty.

16 *Ibid.*, I, 37.

17 Here, too, restriction in numbers equally applies: up till the amazing growth of the population in the nineteenth century, everything on Java was a matter of small dimensions. It would be possible to arrive at a rough idea of the limited area under cultivation on Java on the basis of eighteenth and nineteenth-century data alone. For example, one is amazed on reading of Junghuhn's routes, which time and again mark the borders of the cultivated plains. It is not only the rhinoceros on Kedung Badak (Junghuhn, *Reisen*, II, 20) which illustrates the extent and virginity of the ancient woods and jungles surrounding the plains. One could probably arrive at a rough calculation on the extent of an early Javanese cultural area, for example by figuring an average of the number of workers estimated as necessary for the construction over a number of years of an important temple complex. The amount of labour a man is able to produce can be measured. It could then be investigated how large the quantity of food for the workers performing soccage service for the ruler will have to have been, and, on the basis of the tithes collected, what area will have been necessary to feed such a mass of workers. At least a few reliable estimates of a quantitative sort could thus be arrived at.

18 Stapel, *Geschiedenis*, I, 92.

19 Krom, *Geschiedenis*, 54.

20 From Tugu, western Java: Stapel, *Geschiedenis*, I, 129.

21 "Gesichtspunkte". Heichelheim's important work *Wirtschaftsgeschichte* is not yet available for consultation here in Indonesia.

22 Krom's view – that in the course of the first century A.D. the trade the Hindus carried on with Indonesia led to their settling there, with the result that, in some cases fairly quickly, in others after the passing of one or two centuries, colonial Hindu kingdoms arose, so that the second and third centuries A.D. appear to be the real age of colonization (*Geschiedenis*, 88) – seems to me to present the problem in far too simple terms, both sociologically and technologically.

23 *Geschiedenis*, 81.

24 Lassen in Poerbatjaraka, *Agastya*, 11.

25 Masson-Oursel, *Inde*, 247.

26 Which – I believe I am warranted in stating – took place without trade playing a preponderant rôle.

27 In my dissertation, "On Early Asian Trade", I have attempted to give such an interpretation to the significant Kunyarakunja inscription of 732 A.D. on the Changgal stone (see Krom, *Geschiedenis*, 123 ff.). In his lecture at the meeting of the All-Indian Oriental Conference at Trivandrum, Stutterheim brought forward the thesis that the designation does not imply any indication of an Indian region at all, but that a sacral replica of the holy Indian river country was created in the topography of a certain region in central Java. Such a legitimizing replica will have had as its aim "that one created a place that could be recognized by the souls of the royal forefathers, the ancestors from India whose line ascended to the heroes of the Ramayana and Mahabharata, in order that contact could be maintained with them in the manner and for the purpose known to us from the study of Hindu-Javanese chandi's" ("Relations", 82). However, just as many southern Indian dynasties secured from the Brahman priesthood a patent of their high-ranking royal ancestry without having originated from northern India (as 'colonists' or 'immigrants') themselves one can without doing violence to Stutterheim's thesis imagine an Indonesian court with a Javanese dynasty granting the Agastya priesthood the enjoyment of the rich prebends in exchange for the legitimizing investiture of a sacral consecration of the ruling family. The break-neck hypothesis of traders–colonies–peaceful penetration–foundation of states–higher civilization can then be put aside.

28 "The Brahmin is the one who knows how to assure the protection of the higher powers and at the same time the one who is able to give aid and counsel through all sorts of skills; it is no wonder that the Indonesian chiefs, hearing by rumour or observing by neighbouring tribes how great the value of such a magician must be, do their best to acquire that advantage for themselves. The one wants to hold his own with the other, the Brahmins appear in larger numbers, and besides performing what they have been invited for, they naturally form the nucleus for a constantly further expanding Hindu civilization" (Krom, in Stapel, *Geschiedenis*, I, 138). On reading this possibility sketched by Krom one can only comment that there are no reasons for viewing the stage of Indonesian civilization at the time, and especially that of Java, at the level of chiefs and tribes (*cf.* "tribal chiefs", *ibid.*, I, 141). What fragments of that civilization immediately come to the fore from the documents of the Brahmanic chancellory scribes point toward a world of princes, sacral heads of trains of officials, rulers over large regions, toward a complete apparatus of administration and authority, used and perpetuated by the priests for their own benefit (lust for prebends). That such an indigenous civilization must have taken ages to gestate is a thesis which does no violence to the picture.

29 Krom, in Stapel, *Geschiedenis*, I, 142.

30 An analysis of the types of towns in early Indonesia would provide valuable material for the calculation of the possibilities for social and economic

development in the course of history. In earlier periods the city existed in Indonesia in various forms and thus the development must have a history: the picture of the towns of the sort Bantam and Tuban were around 1600 assures that. Bastiaans' study of the Batatos in early Gorontalo – in which he uses the concept "the early city Gorontalo" ("Batato's", 23), it seems to me completely justifiably, though without further definition – contains valuable elements, probably also for towns of the Bantam type. The writers of the seventeenth-century reports, so much closer to the East of their day, viewing it less as exotic, much more as ordinary, as an environment akin to their own (*cf.* the comments in my article reviewing Du Perron's anthology of Company poetry: see above, p. xix), everywhere on their voyages quite correctly spoke of towns where in more presumptious modern terminology there would only be mention of *kampongs*, a row of *kedais*, or something of the sort. Their eyes were more accustomed to the dimensions and forms of the contemporaneous East. It is no doubt possible to construct an apposition between the coastal towns and the *kraton* towns of the states in the interior, even though a port town like early Surabaya probably included various elements of the *kraton* town. Even taking into account the lust for piracy and booty which was a normal corollary phenomenon to trade in those days (one should consider not only Greece, but also the overseas expansion of Portugal, in many ways still so traditional) and would thus give a military and imperialistic character to coastal towns, however, it seems to me less than correct when Krom remarks that: "Çriwijaya ... was the first state of the archipelago which we see develop into a great power, a maritime and commercial power exerting a strong authority outward, and of which we can observe a consistent policy, applied in a grand style" (in Stapel, *Geschiedenis*, I, 150). This overlooks the fact that the large states of the interior with their agrarian basis and their extremely conservative patrimonial bureaucracy could very well be great powers and could also carry on a consistent policy, though through the nature of their social and political structure adjusted to a static conservatism. Imperial China can offer a parallel example here. How later on, in the fourteenth century, the great expansion of Majapahit then took place is a question of itself. Does one there have to do with phenomena of later development? Did the initiative emanate from a new *noblesse de robe* emerging with the former head of the royal bodyguard elevated to regent of the empire, Gajah Mada, or was it the coastal towns and their nobility that took the initiative, under supervision of the royal seat? Or did Majapahit usurp overseas areas where influence of the Javanese coastal towns already existed? The aristocratic Tubanese family Aria Teja mentioned by Schrieke ("Javanen") which apparently – in a later period, it is true – had overseas interests in the Philippines as well as Pati Unus' sea expedition to Malacca in 1512–1513 point in such a direction.

31 Rouffaer & IJzerman, *Schipvaart*, I, 120.

II

1 C. C. Berg, "Javaansche Geschiedschrijving", II, 5–148; C. Wessels, "Portugeezen en Spanjaarden", II, 149–221; H. Terpstra, "Franschen en Engelschen", II, 223–272, en "De Nederlandsche Voorcompagnieën", II, 273–475.
2 F. W. Stapel, "De oprichting der Vereenigde Oostindische Compagnie", III, 5–44, and "De Nederl. Oostindische Compagnie in de zeventiende eeuw", III, 45–522.
3 See Stapel, *Geschiedenis*, III, 511, 513–514 (Stapel).
4 See *e.g.* Danvers, *Portuguese*, I, 228.
5 See Tiele, "Europeërs", I, 340.
6 *Wirtschaftsgesinnung*, a Weberian term.
7 Stapel, *Geschiedenis*, II, 160.
8 Tiele, "Europeërs", I, 408, II, 22–23, IV, 411–413.
9 *Cf.* Stapel, *Geschiedenis*, II, 423.
10 The voyages of the first companies, and a survey of the times of arrival in various parts of Indonesia.
11 Stapel, *Geschiedenis*, II, 473, 474.
12 Unger, *Middelburg*, 134 ff.
13 Nanninga Uitterdijk, *Handelshuis*.
14 See Unger, *Middelburg*, 138, regarding Caignart.
15 Rycklof van Goens, governor-general, 1678–1681; Cornelis Janszn Speelman, governor-general, 1681–1684.
16 "De Compagnie en de Inlander", Stapel, *Geschiedenis*, III, 509–522.
17 Stapel, *Geschiedenis*, III, 371, *cf.* III, 365.
18 Joannes Camphuys, governor-general, 1684–1691.
19 Stapel, *Geschiedenis*, III, 426.

III: THE EIGHTEENTH CENTURY IN INDONESIAN HISTORY

1 The volume bears the sub-title "De Nederl. Oostindische Compagnie in de achttiende eeuw" (The Dutch East India Company in the Eighteenth Century).
2 Du Bois, *Vies*.
3 De Jonge, *Opkomst*.
4 Colenbrander, *Geschiedenis*, II.
5 Stapel, *Geschiedenis*, IV, 7.
6 Huizinga, *Werken*, VII, 93. See also Romein, *Erflaters*, III, 68.
7 *Cf.* Blok, *Geschiedenis*, III, 371, 427.
8 Stapel, *Geschiedenis*, IV, 7.
9 See above, "The World of Southeast Asia: 1500–1650".
10 Remarkably enough, the break does not occur with the appearance of

Portuguese and Spanish outposts overseas; fitted into the course of Oriental history, they only increased the polyphony for the moment with one theme more.

11 Not so contemporary eighteenth-century writings. The Age of Enlightenment for the most part honoured Far Eastern civilizations as highly advanced, though the reason for its esteem was exclusively a political-philosophical and speculative-historical one, and one not very much based upon a comparative evaluation of the material civilization of the Eastern lands and that of Europe. See the list of writings on the Orient used by Voltaire given in Engemann, *Voltaire*, 143–146. Regarding Voltaire's view on India, see *ibid.*, 30–31, 36–37. The Islamic world was brought to the stage in Voltaire's dramas *Zaïre* and *Mahomet*, the Chinese in *l'Orphelin de la Chine*, the Peruvian American in *Alzire* (*ibid.*, 80–82). Voltaire's comparison of Frederick the Great and Emperor Ch'ien Lung was also in this spirit: "*Sire, vous et le roi de la Chine, vous êtes à présent les deux seuls souverains qui soient philosophes et poètes. Je venais de lire un extrait de deux poèmes de l'empereur Kien-long, lorsque j'ai reçu la prose et les vers de Frédéric le Grand*" (Voltaire to Frederick the Great, 27 July, 1770, reprinted *ibid.*, 91 and n. 1).

12 Figures alone have proved that up to 1798 France was indisputably the richest country of Europe, and in spite of every apocalyptic picture the England of 1790, with its powerful abundance of statesmen and intellectuals, proved to be able to carry on a victorious twenty-five years' war with France and to build up a world empire: see Sombart, *Kapitalismus*, II, 954–955, and Knowles, *Revolutions*, 3.

13 A report from Indo-China in the *Bataviaasch Nieuwsblad* for 31 July, 1940 recalls the construction of the great transversal highway from south to north, the *Route Mandarine*, the present *Route Coloniale N. 1*, as a work of "earlier times, when the land was still at the mercy of the despotism of its princes and chiefs". Here is a typical example of the just-mentioned erroneous way of looking at Oriental affairs. From the historical point of view, this work of the Indo-Chinese mandarin bureaucracy is a technical and organizational achievement of the first order.

14 Duyvendak, *Wegen*, 301, 302.

15 *Cf.* Takizawa, *Penetration.*

16 Feenstra Kuiper, *Japan*, xiv–xv, 85–86.

17 *Cf.* Weber, *China*, 54–55 and n. 60; Engemann, *Voltaire*, 34 and nn. 1–3, 108.

18 In 1721: Honjo, "Population", 65.

19 Boeke, *Dorp*, 40.

20 Sombart, *Kapitalismus*, II, 1046.

21 De Jonge, *Opkomst*, XII, vi–vii.

22 Gonggrijp, in his *Schets*, seems to imply just this: "The influence of the Company's power outside the Moluccas and Java remained trifling. In this

book, therefore, the economic history of the other outer provinces, which had little significance, may be disregarded" (*ibid*, 74).

23 One can – probably – assume an interinsular civilization. There were no great cultural differences between the courts of Sumatra, Java, and the eastern islands, so it appears.

24 Stapel, *Geschiedenis*, III, 511, 513–514.

25 Wisse, *Compagnie*, 11, 53–54.

26 The sketch by Snouck Hurgronje in his *Achehnese*, 120 ff., remains of the highest value for research on the harbour principalities.

27 Gonggrijp merely accepts the retardation of the Indonesian populace as established, without going into any detail regarding the time it began. It is ominous that such a comment finds place as early as in his observations on the period under discussion: "The people of Sumatra have in practice noticed little of the monopoly system. It is of importance for this to be stated, for scholars, seeking after the influence of a foreign domination of the Indonesian peoples, will tend to attribute all their retardation to what was bad in the European administration. That is, however, a great delusion at work. The flight which European civilization has taken in the four centuries since 1500 is without parallel. The retardation of so many Oriental peoples is chiefly the simple result of the fact that in their civilizations the forcé for powerful development was not active. A glance at the Oriental peoples who have not known any domination by Europeans can convince us of this. Not only the Javanese, whose freedom of trade and movement were truncated, were retarded; so many other peoples also lost ground, relatively speaking, in economic and other fields, because the expansive Westerner pressed forward at so fast a tempo." (*Schets*, 74–75).

28 Colenbrander, *Geschiedenis*, II, 319.

29 Boulger, *Raffles*, 90–91.

30 Leyden, quoted in *ibid.*, 93.

31 *Ibid.*, 91.

32 One should not raise the objection of lack of statistical data too quickly: the economic history of Europe has been and still is studied on a fragmentary basis. The problem is primarily one of correct evaluation of source materials and their special significance. The *Daghregisters*, for example, would with complete tabulation gain a significance comparable to that of the toll figures for the Sound (see Bang & Korst, *Tabeller*; for an analysis of the figures related to Dutch trade see Kernkamp, "Nederlanders").

33 Van Hogendorp, *Berigt*, 60. A *koyan* of from 3400 and 3500 to 4000 lb. (*ibid.*, n. 1).

34 But how is the information of a yearly import into Java of ten thousand ounces of gold from other parts of Indonesia reported by Van Hogendorp (*Berigt*, 104–105) to be evaluated?

35 Rouffaer & Juynboll, *Batik-kunst*, 306–307, 426.

36 *Ibid.*, 307.
37 *Ibid.*, 426.
38 Hazeu, *Letterkunde*, 18.
39 Romein, "Stijl".
40 *Ibid.*, 184.
41 Colenbrander, *Geschiedenis*, II, 232. See Article Six of the treaty.
42 Sombart, *Kapitalismus*, II, 1008–1009.
43 Van Oudermeulen's memorandum in Van Hogendorp, *Stukken*, 171–172. *f* 2,700,000 and 5,000,000 respectively, at twelve guilders to the pound (*ibid.*, 187).
44 *Cf.* Gonggrijp, *Schets*, 59–60, 63–65.
45 Colenbrander, *Coen*, IV, 432.
46 Raffles, *History*, I, xxxii–xxxiii.
47 See Mansvelt, *Handelshuizen*. The Dutch colonial government re-established in 1816 closed a cash money loan with the Danish Insurance Company of Batavia (Resolution of 24 December, 1816, no 20), and others with the Messrs Thalmann (15,000 copper [?] rupees), Siberg (a former governor-general – 22,000 Spanish piastres), and Garok Manok (an Armenian? – 7,000 silver rupees).
48 Van Hogendorp, *Berigt*, 84.
49 Quoted in Boulger, *Raffles*, 329.
50 De Jonge, *Opkomst*, X, lxxxv.
51 See Van de Wall, *Buitenplaatsen*.
52 See De Loos-Haaxman, *Rach*.
53 Bataviaasch Genootschap van Kunsten en Wetenschappen.
54 Nederlandsche Handel-Maatschappij, N.V.
55 Busken Huet, *Rembrandt*, II, Part Two, 436. Busken Huet makes the comment regarding the seventeenth century, but in this case, too, the continuity which carried the development of things on deep into the eighteenth century has to be taken into consideration. *Cf. ibid.*, II, Part One, 280, n. 2.
56 Van Hogendorp, *Berigt*, 93, 104, and elsewhere.
57 *Bijlagen Staten-Generaal*, 247.

Bibliography

ASS — *Archiv für Sozialwissenschaft und Sozialpolitik* (Journal of Social Science and Social Policy)

BEFEO — *Bulletin de l'Ecole Française d'Extrême Orient* (Bulletin of the French School of the Far East)

BKI — *Bijdragen tot de Taal-, Land- en Volkenkunde van Nederlandsch-Indië uitgegeven door het Koninklijk Instituut voor Taal-, Land- en Volkenkunde* (Contributions to the Philology, Geography, and Ethnology of the Netherlands East Indies Published by the Royal Institute for Philology, Geography, and Ethnology)

ENI — *Encyclopaedie van Nederlandsch-Indië* (Encyclopedia of the Netherlands East Indies). First edition, The Hague, four volumes, 1896–1905; second edition, The Hague, four volumes plus four supplementary volumes, 1917–1939

Gids — *De Gids: Algemeen Cultureel Tijdschrift* (The Guide: General Cultural Journal)

JBG — *Jaarboek van het Koninklijk Bataviaasch Genootschap van Kunsten en Wetenschappen* (Yearbook of the Royal Batavian Society of Arts and Sciences)

Klio — *Klio: Beiträge zur alten Geschichte* (Clio: Contributions to Ancient History)

KS — *Koloniale Studiën* (Colonial Studies)

KT — *Koloniaal Tijdschrift* (Colonial Journal)

MNZG — *Mededeelingen vanwege het Nederlandsch Zendelinggenootschap* (Communications of the Dutch Missionary Society)

MZGW — *Vroegere en latere mededeelingen voornamelijk in betrekking tot Zeeland, uitgegeven door het Zeeuwsch Genootschap der Wetenschappen* (Earlier and Later Communications Chiefly Relating to Zeeland, Published by the Zeeland Society of Sciences)

SJ — *Schmoller's Jahrbuch für Gesetzgebung, Verwaltung und Volkswirtschaft im Deutschen Reich* (Schmoller's Yearbook for Legislation, Administration, and Economy in the German Empire)

TBG — *Tijdschrift voor Indische Taal-, Land- en Volkenkunde uitgegeven door het Koninklijk Bataviaasch Genootschap van Kunsten en Wetenschappen* (Journal of Indonesian Philology, Geography, and Ethnology Published by the Royal Batavian Society of Arts and Sciences)

TG — *Tijdschrift voor Geschiedenis* (Historical Journal)

TP — *T'oung Pao: Archives pour servir à l'étude de l'histoire, des langues, de la géographie et de l'ethnographie de l'Asie Orientale* (T'oung Pao: Archives for the Study of the History, Philology, Geography, and Ethnology of Eastern Asia)

Bibliography

Composite names beginning with words such as Van, De, and so forth have been placed in alphabetical order under the surname proper rather than under such words. For example, M. J. de Goeje is listed under G, and J. A. van der Chijs under C.

Aboetari, *Verhouding:* — Aboetari, *De verhouding van de koloniale tot de theoretische economie* (The Relation of Colonial Economy to Economic Theory). Dissertation, Rotterdam School of Economics. Rotterdam, 1932.

Aboulféda, *Géographie:* — Aboulféda, Edmadeddin-Ismael, *Géographie* (Geography). Translated and edited by Joseph Toussaint Reinaud. Three volumes, Paris, 1848–1873.

Amonn, "Dynamik": — Amonn, Alfred, "Die Probleme der wirtschaftlichen Dynamik" (Problems of the Dynamics of Economy), *ASS*, XXXVIII (1914), 83–114.

Aymonier, *Cambodge:* — Aymonier, E., *Le Cambodge* (Cambodia). Three volumes, Paris, 1900–1904.

Bang & Korst, *Tabeller:* — Bang, Nina Ellinger, and Knud Korst, editors, *Tabeller over Skibsfart og Varetransport gennem Øresund 1497–1660: Udarbejdede efter de bevarede Regnskaber over Øresundstolden* (Tables on the Shipping and Transport of Goods Passing through the Sound, 1497–1660: Compiled from the Extant Sound Toll Accounts). Two volumes, Copenhagen, 1906, 1933.

Bang & Korst, *Tabeller:* — Bang, Nina Ellinger, and Knud Korst, editors, *Tabeller over Skibsfart og Varetransport gennem Øresund 1661–1783 og gennem Storebælt, 1701–1748: Udarbejdede efter de bevarede Regnskaber over Øresundstolden og Bælttolden* (Tables on the Shipping and Transport of Goods Passing through the Sound, 1661–1783, and through the Great Belt, 1701–1748: Compiled from the Extant Sound and Great Belt Toll Accounts). Volume One, Copenhagen, 1930.

Barton, *Law:* — Barton, Roy Franklin, *Ifugao Law.* University of California. Publications in American Archaeology and Ethnology, XV, Part One. Berkeley, 1919.

Bastiaans, "Batato's": — Bastiaans, J., "Batato's in het oude Gorontalo, in verband met den Gorontaleeschen staatsbouw" (Batatos in Early Gorontalo in Connection with the Structure of the Gorontalese State), *TBG*, LXXIX (1939), 23–72.

Ibn Battuta, *Voyages:* — *Voyages d'Ibn Batoutah* (Travels of Ibn Battuta). Arabic text with a translation by C. Defrémery and B. R. Sanguinetti. Four volumes, Paris, second edition, 1874–1893.

Becker, "Grundlinien": — Becker, C. H., "Grundlinien der wirtschaftlichen Entwicklung Aegyptens in den ersten Jahrhunderten des Islam" (The Course of Egyptian Economic Development in the First Centuries of Islam), *Klio* (Clio), IX (1909), 206–219.

Becker, "Steuerpacht": — Becker, C. H., "Steuerpacht und Lehnswesen: Eine historische Studie über die Entstehung des islamischen Lehnswesens" (Tax Farming and Feudal Tenure: An Historical Study of the Origins of the Islamic Feudal System), *Der Islam* (Islam), V (1914), 81–92.

Berg, *Hoofdlijnen:* — Berg, C. C., *Hoofdlijnen der Javaansche litteratuur-geschiedenis* (Main Currents in Javanese Literary History). Inaugural lecture, University of Leiden. Groningen, 1929.

Van den Berg, *Rangen:* — Van den Berg, L. W. C., *De Inlandsche rangen en titels op Java en Madoera* (Native Ranks and Titles on Java and Madura). The Hague, second edition, 1902.

Bernet Kempers, *Cultuurstroom:* — Bernet Kempers, A. J., *De Indische cultuurstroom* (The Flow of Indian Culture). Inaugural lecture, University of Leiden. The Hague, 1934.

Bernier, *Travels:* — Bernier, Fr., *Travels in the Mogul Empire A.D. 1656–1668.* Revised edition, edited by A. Constable. Constable's Oriental Miscellany, I. Westminster, 1891. (Translation by J. Brock of *Voyages de Fr. Bernier contenant la description des Etats du Grand Mogol, de l'Hindoustan, du Royaume de Kachemire*... Two volumes, Amsterdam, 1709, 1710.)

Bernstein, *Geschichte:* — Bernstein, E., *et al.*, editors, *Die Geschichte des Sozialismus in Einzeldarstellungen* (Sketches of the History of Socialism). I, Part One, Stuttgart, 1895.

Bertling, review: — Bertling, C. T., review of F. A. E. van Wouden, *Sociale structuurtypen in de Groote Oost* (Types of Social Structure in East Indonesia), *KS*, XIX (1935), Part Two, 346–354.

Bijlagen Staten-Generaal: — *Bijlagen Handelingen der Staten-Generaal, Tweede Kamer, Zitting 1939–1940* (Supplements to the Proceedings of the States General, Second Chamber, Session 1939–1940), subject 4, no 76 (Memorandum in Reply to the Provisional Report of the Second Chamber Regarding the 1940 Budget of the East Indies).

Bijlagen Volksraad: — *Bijlagen Handelingen Volksraad, Zittingsjaar 1929–1930* (Supplements to the Proceedings of the People's Council, Session 1929–1930), subject 99 (Contract with the Royal Packet Navigation Company).

Bilabel, *Geschichte:* — Bilabel, Fr., *Geschichte Vorderasiens und Aegyptens vom 16. Jahrhundert vor Christus bis auf die Neuzeit* (History of Asia Minor and Egypt from the Sixteenth Century B.C. up to Modern Times). Bibliothek der klassischen Altertumswissenschaften (Library of Studies in Classical Antiquity), III. Heidelberg, 1927.

Blink, "Opkomst": — Blink, H., "Opkomst en ontwikkeling van den boerenstand in Nederland" (Rise and Development of the Farmer Class in the Netherlands), in Brugmans, *Leven* (see below), I, 264–331.

Bloch, *Kämpfe:* — Bloch, Leo, *Soziale Kämpfe im alten Rom* (Social Conflicts in Ancient Rome). Aus Natur und Geisteswelt (Of the Natural and the Spiritual World), XXII. Leipzig, second edition, 1908.

Blok, *Geschiedenis:* — Blok, P. J., *Geschiedenis van het Nederlandsche volk* (History of the Dutch People). Four volumes, Leiden, second edition, 1912–1915.

Van Blom, "Marx": — Van Blom, D., "Van Marx tot De Man: n.a.v. Hendrik de Man: De psychologie van het socialisme" (From Marx to De Man: Reflections on Hendrik de Man's *De psychologie van het socialisme* [The Psychology of Socialism]), *Gids*, XCII (1928), Part Two, 81–94.

Blumberger, *Beweging:* — Blumberger, J. Th. Petrus, *De nationalistische beweging in Nederlandsch-Indië* (The Nationalist Movement in the Netherlands East Indies). Haarlem, 1931.

Boeke, *Dorp:* — Boeke, J. H., *Dorp en desa* (Village and *Desa*). Leiden, 1934.

Boeke, *Economie:* — Boeke, J. H., *Dualistische economie* (Dualistic Economy). Inaugural lecture, University of Leiden. Leiden, 1930.

Du Bois, *Vies:* — Du Bois, J. P. I., *Vies des Gouverneurs Généraux, avec l'abrégé de l'histoire des Etablissemens Hollandois aux Indes Orientales* (Lives of the Governors-General: With an Abridged History of the Dutch Establishments in the East Indies). The Hague, 1763.

Bolkestein, *Leven:* — Bolkestein, H., *Het economisch leven in Griekenlands bloeitijd* (Economic Life in the Golden Age of Greece). Volksuniversiteits Bibliotheek (Folk University Library), XXV. Haarlem, 1925.

Le Bon, *Arabes:* — Le Bon, Gustave, *La civilisation des Arabes* (Arab Civilization). Paris, 1884.

Le Bon, *Civilisations:* — Le Bon, Gustave, *Les premières civilisations* (The First Civilizations). Paris, 1889.

Boulger, *Raffles:* — Boulger, Demetrius Charles, *The Life of Sir Stamford Raffles*. London, 1897.

Bouman, "Beschouwingen": — Bouman, P. J., "Eenige beschouwingen over de historische betrekkingen tusschen godsdienst en kapitalisme" (Some Observations on the Historical Relations between Religion and Capitalism), *De Economist* (The Economist), LXXXI (1932), 181–198.

Bozorg, *Livre:* — Bozorg, *Livre des merveilles de l'Inde par le Capitaine Bozorg, fils de Chahriyâr de Râmhormoz* (Book of the Marvels of India, by Captain Bozorg, son of Shahriyar of Ramhormuz). Edited by P. A. van der Lith and translated by L. Marcel Devic. Paris, 1883.

Brandes, "Jayapattra": — Brandes, J. L. A., "Een Jayapattra of acte van ẹene rechterlijke uitspraak van Çaka 849" (A *Jayapattra*, or Instrument of a Court Decision, of 849 *Çaka*), *TBG*, XXXII (1889), 98–150.

Brentano, *Gilds:* — Brentano, Lujo, *On the History and Development of Gilds and the Origin of Trade-Unions*. London, 1870. (Also published as General Introduction to Toulmin Smith and Lucy T. Smith, editors, *English Gilds: Their Statutes and Customs,* A.D. *1389*. Early English Text Society, Original Series, XL. London, 1870.)

Brentano, "Volkswirtschaft": — Brentano, Lujo, "Die byzantinische Volkswirtschaft" (Byzantine Economy), *SJ*, XLI (1917), 569–614.

Broersma, "Molukken-Zuid": — Broersma, R., "Land en volk in Molukken-Zuid" (Country and People in the Southern Moluccas), *KT*, XXV (1936), 42–71.

Brugmans, "Geschiedenisonderwijs": — Brugmans, I. J., "Hooger Geschiedenisonderwijs in Nederlandsch-Indië" (The Teaching of History on the University Level in the Netherlands East Indies), *TG*, XLVIII (1933), 281–289.

Brugmans, *Leven:* — Brugmans, H., editor, *Het huiselijk en maatschappelijk leven onzer voorouders* (Home Life and Social Life of Our Ancestors). Two volumes, Amsterdam, 1913, 1915.

Burckhardt, *Renaissance:* — Burckhardt, Jacob, *The Civilization of the Renaissance in Italy*. London, new edition, 1944. (Translation by S. G. C. Middlemore of *Geschichte der Renaissance in Italien*. Stuttgart, second edition, 1878.)

Burgess, *Guilds:* — Burgess, John Stewart, *The Guilds of Peking*. Columbia University Studies in History, Economics, and Public Law, CCCVIII. New York, 1928.

Busken Huet, *Rembrandt:* — Busken Huet, Cd, *Het land van Rembrandt: Studiën over de Noordnederlandsche beschaving in de zeventiende eeuw* (The Country of Rembrandt: Studies in Dutch Civilization in the Seventeenth Century). Two volumes in three parts, Haarlem, third edition, 1898.

Chang, *Trade:* — Chang, T'ien Tse, *Sino-Portuguese Trade from 1514 to 1644: A Synthesis of Portuguese and Chinese Sources*. Dissertation, University of Leiden. Leiden, 1933.

Charlesworth, *Trade-Routes:* — Charlesworth, Martin Peter, *Trade-Routes and Commerce of the Roman Empire*. Cambridge, 1924.

Chau Ju-kua, *Trade:* — Chau Ju-kua, *His Work on the Chinese and Arab Trade in the Twelfth and Thirteenth Century, entitled Chufan-chï*. Translated and annotated by Friedr. Hirth and W. W. Rockwell. Saint Petersburg, 1911.

Chen, *Confucius:* — Chen Huang-Chang, *The Economic Principles of Confucius and His School*. Columbia University Studies in History, Economics, and Public Law, XLIV & XLV. Two volumes, New York, 1911.

Van der Chijs, *Vestiging:* — Van der Chijs, J. A., *De vestiging van het Nederlandsche gezag over de Banda-eilanden (1599–1621)* (The Establishment of

Dutch Authority over the Banda Islands [1599–1621]). Batavia, 1886.

Coedès, "Royaume": — Coedès, George, "Le royaume de Çrivijaya" (The Empire of Çriwijaya), *BEFEO*, XVIII (1918), vi, 1–36.

Colenbrander, *Coen:* — Colenbrander, H. T., and W. Ph. Coolhaas, editors, *Jan Pietersz. Coen: Bescheiden omtrent zijn bedrijf in Indië* (Jan Pietersz. Coen: Documents Concerning His Activities in the Indies). Seven volumes, The Hague, 1919–1953.

Colenbrander, *Geschiedenis:* — Colenbrander, H. T., *Koloniale geschiedenis* (Colonial History). Three volumes, The Hague, 1925.

Collecção: — *Collecção de Noticias para a Historia e Geografia das Nações Ultramarinas, que vivem nos Dominios Portuguezes* (Collection of Data on the History and Geography of Overseas Peoples Living in the Portuguese Dominions). Seven volumes in nine parts, Lisbon, 1812–1841.

Coote & Beazley, "Hakluyt": — Coote, Charles H., and Charles Raymond Beazley, "Hakluyt, Richard", *Encyclopedia Britannica* (Eleventh Edition), XII, 828–829.

Crawfurd, *History:* — Crawfurd, J., *History of the Indian Archipelago: Containing an Account of the Manners, Arts, Languages, Religions ... of its Inhabitants.* Three volumes, Edinburgh, 1820.

Daghregister: — *Daghregister gehouden int Casteel Batavia vant passerende daer ter plaetse als over geheel Nederlandts-India* (Daily Record Kept at Batavia Castle of Happenings at that Place and throughout the Netherlands East Indies). Thirty-one volumes published, Batavia and The Hague, 1888–1931.

Van Dam, *Beschryvinge:* — Van Dam, Pieter, *Beschryvinge van de Oostindische Compagnie* (Description of the Dutch East India Company). Edited by W. F. Stapel. Rijks Geschiedkundige Publicaties (State Historical Publications), LXIII, LXVIII, LXXXVIII. Three volumes, The Hague, 1927–1943.

Danvers, *Portuguese:* — Danvers, Fred. Ch., *The Portuguese in India.* Two volumes, London, 1894.

Davids, *India:* — Davids, T. W. Rhys, *Buddhist India.* London, 1903.

Delbrück, *Kriegskunst:* — Delbrück, Hans, *Geschichte der Kriegskunst im Rahmen der politischen Geschichte* (History of the Arts of War in the Setting of Political History). Seven volumes, Berlin, 1900–1936.

Description: — *Description of a Voyage made by Certaine Ships of Holland into the East Indies: With their Adventures and Successe: Together with the Description of the Countries, Townes, and Inhabitantes of the Same: Who set forth on the Second of Aprill 1595, and returned on the 14. of August, 1597.* London, 1598. (Translation by W. P. of *Verhael vande Reyse by de Hollandtsche Schepen ghedaen naer Oost Indien: Haer avontuer ende succes...* Middelburg, 1597.)

Van Deventer, *Bijdragen:* — Van Deventer, S., *Bijdragen tot de kennis van het landelijk stelsel op Java: Op last van Z. Exc. den Min. van Koloniën, J. D.*

Fransen van de Putte, bijeenverzameld (Contributions to the Knowledge of the Rural System on Java: Collected at the Order of His Excellency the Minister of Colonial Affairs, J. D. Fransen van de Putte). Three volumes, Zalt-Bommel, 1865–1866.

Diehl, *Venise:* — Diehl, Charles, *Une république patricienne: Venise* (Venice: A Patrician Republic). Paris, 1918.

Van Dijk, *Jaren:* — Van Dijk, L. C. D., *Zes jaren uit het leven van Wemmer van Berchem, gevolgd door: Iets over onze vroegste betrekkingen met Japan: Twee geschiedkundige bijdragen* (Six Years from the Life of Wemmer van Berchem, Followed by Some Remarks on Our Earliest Relations with Japan: Two Historical Contributions). Amsterdam, 1858.

Van Dillen, *Karakter:* — Van Dillen, Joh. Ger., *Het economisch karakter der middeleeuwsche stad: I – De theorie der gesloten stad-huishouding* (The Economic Character of the Medieval Town: I – The Theory of the Closed Town Economy). Dissertation, University of Amsterdam. Amsterdam, 1914.

Duyvendak, *Historie:* — Duyvendak, J. J. L., *Historie en Confucianisme* (History and Confucianism). Inaugural lecture, University of Leiden. Leiden, 1930.

Duyvendak, *Kakean-genootschap:* — Duyvendak, J. P., *Het Kakean-genootschap van Seran* (The Kakean Society of Ceram). Almelo, 1926.

Duyvendak, *Wegen:* — Duyvendak, J. J. L., *Wegen en gestalten der Chineesche geschiedenis* (Paths and Persons in Chinese History). The Hague, 1935.

Edkins, *Buddhism:* — Edkins, Jos., *Chinese Buddhism: Sketches Historical, Descriptive, Critical.* London, 1880.

Engemann, *Voltaire:* — Engemann, Karl Walt., *Voltaire und China: Ein Beitrag zur Geschichte der Völkerkunde und zur Geschichte der Geschichtsschreibung sowie zu ihren gegenseitigen Beziehungen* (Voltaire and China: A Contribution to the History of Ethnology and the History of Historiography and to their Interrelationship). Dissertation, University of Leipzig. N. p., 1932.

Erdmann, *Grundriß:* — Erdmann, Joh. Eduard, *Grundriß der Geschichte der Philosophie* (Outline of the History of Philosophy). Revised and continued to the present time by Ferd. Clemens. Berlin, 1930.

Fâ-hien, *Record:* — Fâ-hien, *A Record of Buddhistic Kingdoms: Being an Account by the Chinese Monk Fâ-hien of his Travels in India and Ceylon (A.D. 399–414) in Search of the Buddhist Books of Discipline.* Translated and annotated by James Legge. Oxford, 1866.

Feenstra Kuiper, *Japan:* — Feenstra Kuiper, J., *Japan en de buitenwereld in de achttiende eeuw* (Japan and the Outside World in the Eighteenth Century). Werken uitgegeven door de Vereeniging Het Nederlandsch Economisch-Historisch Archief (Works Published by the Society "The Dutch Economic-Historical Archives"), III. The Hague, 1921.

Ferrand, *Empire:* — Ferrand, Gabriel, *L'empire sumatranais de Çrivijaya* (The Sumatran Empire of Çriwijaya). Paris, 1922.

Ferrand, "K'ouen-louen": — Ferrand, Gabriel, "Le K'ouen-louen et les anciennes navigations interocéaniques dans les mers du Sud" (Kwan-lwan and the Early Overseas Voyages in Southern Waters), *Journal Asiatique* (Asian Journal), Eleventh Series, XIII (1919), 239–333, 431–492, XIV (1919), 5–68, 201–241.

Ferrand, *Relations:* — Ferrand, Gabriel, editor and translator, *Relations de voyages et textes géographiques arabes, persans et turcs relatifs à l'Extrême-Orient, du VIIIe. au XVIIIe. siècle* (Arab, Persian, and Turkish Travel Accounts and Geographical Texts of from the Eighth Century to the Eighteenth Relating to the Far East). Two volumes, Paris, 1913, 1914.

Finot, "Etudes": — Finot, L., "Les études Indochinoises" (Indo-Chinese Studies), *BEFEO*, VIII (1908), 221–233.

Fischel, *Jews:* Fischel, Walter Joseph, *Jews in the Economic and Political Life of Mediæval Islam.* Royal Asiatic Society Monographs, XXII. London, 1937.

Fitzler, "Handelsgesellschaften": — Fitzler, Hedwig M. A., "Portugiesische Handelsgesellschaften des 15. und beginnenden 16. Jahrhunderts" (Portuguese Trading Companies of the Fifteenth and Early Sixteenth Centuries), *Vierteljahrsschrift für Sozial- und Wirtschaftsgeschichte* (Quarterly for Social and Economic History), XXV (1932), 209–250.

Fokker, review: — Fokker, A. A., review of A. Mieli, *La science arabe et son rôle dans l'évolution scientifique mondiale* (Arab Science and Its Rôle in the Evolution of World Science), *TBG*, LXXX (1940), 309–313.

Franke, *Geschichte:* — Franke, Otto, *Geschichte des Chinesischen Reiches: Eine Darstellung seiner Entstehung, seines Wesens und seiner Entwicklung bis zur neuesten Zeit* (History of the Chinese Empire: A Sketch of Its Origins, Its Nature, and Its Development up to the Present Time). Four volumes, Berlin, 1930–1949.

Freud, *Civilization:* — Freud, Sigmund, *Civilization and Its Discontents.* International Psycho-Analytic Library, XVII. London, 1930. (Translation by Joan Riviere of *Das Unbehagen in der Kultur.* Vienna, 1930.)

Freud, *Future:* — Freud, Sigmund, *The Future of an Illusion.* International Psycho-Analytic Library, XV. London, 1928. (Translation by W. D. Robson-Scott of *Der Zukunft einer Illusion.* Leipzig, 1927.)

Friedericy, "Aanteekeningen": — Friedericy, H. J., "Aanteekeningen over adat en adatrecht bij de Bonesche prauwvaarders" (Notes on *Adat* and *Adat* Law Among the Proa Sailors from Bone), *KT*, XX (1931), 490–504.

Frobenius, *Kulturgeschichte:* — Frobenius, Leo V., *Kulturgeschichte Afrikas: Prolegomena zu einer historischen Gestaltlehre* (Cultural History of Africa: Prolegomena to a Morphology of History). Zurich, 1933.

Fruin-Mees, *Geschiedenis:* — Fruin-Mees, W., *Geschiedenis van Java* (History of Java). Two volumes, Weltevreden, second edition, 1925.

Fueter, *Historiographie:* — Fueter, Ed., *Geschichte der neueren Historiographie* (History of Modern Historiography). *Handbuch der mittelalterlichen und neueren Geschichte* (Manual of Medieval and Modern History), edited by G. von Below and F. Meinecke, I. Munich, second edition, 1925.

Fukuda, *Japan:* — Fukuda, T., *Die gesellschaftliche und wirtschaftliche Entwicklung in Japan* (Social and Economic Developments in Japan). Münchener Volkswirtschaftliche Studien (Munich Economic Studies), XLII. Stuttgart, 1900.

Gedenkboek: — *Gedenkboek 1908–1923 Indonesische Vereeniging* (Memorial Volume of the Indonesian Association, 1908–1923). N.p., [1924].

Van Gelder, "Bailleul": — Van Gelder, H. A. Enno, "Bailleul, Bronkhorst, Brederode" [Three Dutch noble families], *Gids,* C (1936), Part Two, 204–220, 348–375.

Van Gelderen, *Voorlezingen:* — Van Gelderen, J., *Voorlezingen over tropisch-koloniale staathuishoudkunde* (Lectures on the Economy of the Tropical Colony). Haarlem, 1927.

De Goeje, "Handelsverkeer": — De Goeje, M. J., "Internationaal handelsverkeer in de middeleeuwen" (International Trade in the Middle Ages), *Verslagen en Mededeelingen der Koninklijke Akademie van Wetenschappen, Afdeeling Letterkunde* (Reports and Communications of the [Dutch] Royal Academy of Sciences, Literary Section), Fourth Series, IX (1909), 245–269.

De Goeje, *Müller:* — De Goeje, M. J., *Notice sur la vie et les travaux de Max Müller* (Account of the Life and Works of Max Müller). Publications de l'Institut de France (Publications of the Institute of France). Paris, 1902.

De Goeje, "Sajâbidja": — De Goeje, M. J., "De Sajâbidja" (The Sayabija), *Feestbundel van taal-, letter-, geschied- en aardrijkskundige bijdragen ter gelegenheid van zijn tachtigsten geboortedag aan Dr. P. J. Veth, oud-hoogleeraar, door eenige vrienden en oud-leerlingen aangeboden* (*Festschrift* of Contributions in the Fields of Philology, Literature, History, and Geography Presented to Dr P. J. Veth, Emeritus Professor, by Some Friends and Former Students...; Leiden, 1894), 10–12.

Van Goens, *Javaense Reijse:* — Van Goens, Ryckloff Volkertsz., *Javaense Reijse: Gedaen van Batavia over Samarang na de koninckliјke hoofdplaats Mataram, door de Heer N. N. in den Jare 1656: Waerinne den wegh uijt Samarangh na Mataram mitsgaders de zeden, gewoonten en regeringe van den Sousounan groot-machtichste Koninck van 't Eijland Java, nauwkeurigh worden beschreven* (Javanese Journey: Made from Batavia by Way of Semarang to the Royal Capital of Mataram by the Gentleman N. N. in the Year 1656: Wherein the Way from Semarang to Mataram, as well as the Morals, Customs, and Government of the Susuhunan, Mighty King of the Island of Java are Accurately Described). Dordrecht, 1666. (Reprinted under the title "Reijsbeschrijving van den weg uijt Samarangh nae de koninck-lijke hoofdplaets Mataram, mitsgaders de zeeden, gewoonten en de re-geringe van den Sousouhounan, grootmachtigste koningk van 't eijlant Java" [Itinerary of the Way from Semarang to the Royal Capital Ma-taram, as well as the Morals, Customs, and Government of the Susu-hunan, Mighty King of the Island of Java], *BKI*, IV [1856], 307–350.)

Van Goens, "Rapport": — Van Goens, Rijckloff Volkertsz., "Rapport van Van Goens" (Van Goens' Report; edited by P. A. Leupe), *BKI*, IV (1856), 141–180.

Goetz, *Verkehrswege:* — Goetz, Wilhelm, *Die Verkehrswege im Dienste des Welt-handels: Eine historische-geographische Untersuchung* (The Trade Routes Serving World Trade: A Historical-Geographic Study). Stuttgart, 1888.

Goetz, *Werdegang:* — Goetz, Walter, editor, *Der Werdegang der Menschheit in Gesellschaft und Staat, Wirtschaft und Geistesleben* (The Development of Mankind in Society and State, Economy and Cultural Life). Ten volumes, Berlin, n. d.

Gonggrijp, *Schets:* — Gonggrijp, G., *Schets eener economische geschiedenis van Nederlandsch-Indië* (Outline of an Economic History of the Netherlands East Indies). Haarlem, 1928.

Goris, "Lombok": — Goris, R., "Aanteekeningen over Oost Lombok" (Notes on East Lombok), *TBG*, LXXVI (1936), 196–248.

Gosses, "Volksverhuizing": — Gosses, I. H., "De groote volksverhuizing" (The Great Migrations), *TG*, LI (1936), 5–42.

Granet, *Civilisation:* — Granet, Marcel, *La civilisation chinoise* (Chinese Civi-lization). L'évolution de l'humanité (The Evolution of Mankind), XXV. Paris, 1929.

Graßhoff, *Wechselrecht:* — Graßhoff, R., *Das Wechselrecht der Araber: Eine rechtsvergleichende Studie über die Herkunft des Wechsels* (Arab Law on Bills of Exchange: A Study in Comparative Law on the Origins of the Bill of Exchange). Berlin, 1899.

Groeneveldt, "Jottings": — Groeneveldt, W. P., "Supplementary Jottings to the 'Notes on the Malay Archipelago and Malacca Compiled from Chinese Sources'", *TP*, VII (1896), 113–134.

Groeneveldt, "Notes": — Groeneveldt, W. P., "Notes on the Malay Archi-pelago and Malacca Compiled from Chinese Sources", *Verhandelingen van het Bataviaasch Genootschap van Kunsten en Wetenschappen* (Proceedings of the Batavian Society of Arts and Sciences), XXXIX (1880), i–x, 1–144. (Reprinted in *Miscellaneous Papers Relating to Indo-China and the Indian Archipelago.* Two volumes, London, 1888.)

Grousset, *Histoire:* — Grousset, René, *Histoire de l'Extrême Orient* (History of the Far East). Annales Musée Guimet (Annals of the Guimet Museum). Paris, 1929.

De Haan, *Oud-Batavia:* — De Haan, F., *Oud-Batavia: Gedenkboek uitgegeven door het Bataviaasch Genootschap van Kunsten en Wetenschappen naar aanleiding van het driehonderdjarig bestaan der stad in 1919* (Early Batavia: Memorial Volume Published by the Batavian Society of Arts and Sciences on the Occasion of the Tercentenary of the City in 1919). Two volumes and one volume illustrations, Batavia, 1922–1923.

De Haan, review: — De Haan, J. C., review of Charles Diehl and Georges Marçais, *Le monde oriental de 395 à 1081* (The Oriental World from 395 to 1081; G. Glotz, editor, *Histoire du Moyen Age* [History of the Middle Ages], III), *TG*, LII (1937), 294–295.

Hahn, *Alter:* — Hahn, Ed., *Das Alter der wirtschaftlichen Kultur der Menschheit* (The Age of Human Economic Culture). Heidelberg, 1905.

Du Halde, *Description:* — Du Halde, J. B., *Description géographique, historique, chronologique, politique etc. de l'empire de la Chine et de la Tartarie chinoise* (Description of the Geography, History, Chronology, Politics, etc. of the Empire of China and of Chinese Tartary). Four volumes, The Hague, 1736.

Hartmann, *Kapittel:* — Hartmann, Ludo Moritz, *Ein Kapittel vom spätantiken und frühmittelalterlichen Staate* (A Chapter on the Late Ancient and Early Medieval State). Stuttgart, 1913.

Hasebroek, *Trade:* — Hasebroek, Joh., *Trade and Politics in Ancient Greece.* London, 1933. (Translation by L. M. Fraser and D. C. Macgregor of *Staat und Handel im alten Griechenland: Untersuchungen zur antiken Wirtschaftsgeschichte.* Tübingen, 1928.)

Hasebroek, *Wirtschaftsgeschichte:* — Hasebroek, Joh., *Griechische Wirtschafts- und Gesellschaftsgeschichte bis zur Perserzeit* (Greek Economic and Social History up to the Persian Era). Tübingen, 1931.

Hatta, "Indonesië": — Hatta, Mohammad, "Indonesië vrij: Pleitrede voor de Haagse Rechtbank 9 Maart 1928" (Free Indonesia: Plea Before the Hague Court of Justice, 9 March, 1928), *Verspreide Geschriften* (Collected Writings; Amsterdam, 1952), 209–308.

Hazeu, *Letterkunde:* — Hazeu, G. A. J., *Oud en nieuw uit de Javaansche letterkunde* (Old and New in Javanese Literature). Inaugural lecture, University of Leiden. Leiden, 1921.

Heeres, *Corpus:* — Heeres, J. E., and F. W. Stapel, editors, *Corpus Diplomaticum Neerlando-indicum: Verzameling van politieke contracten en verdere verdragen door de Nederlanders in het Oosten gesloten; van privilegebrieven, aan hen verleend* (Corpus Diplomaticum Neerlando-Indicum: Collection of Political Contracts and Other Treaties Concluded by the Dutch in the Orient and of Letters of Privilege Granted Them). *BKI*, LVII (1907), LXXXVII (1931), XCI (1934), XCIII (1935), XCVI (1938). Five volumes, The Hague, 1907–1938. Final volume out of series, The Hague, 1955.

Hegel, *Weltgeschichte:* — Hegel, Georg Wilhelm Friedrich, *Philosophie der*

Weltgeschichte (Philosophy of World History). Edited by Georg Lasson. Two volumes, Leipzig, second edition, 1917, 1923.

Heichelheim, "Gesichtspunkte": — Heichelheim, Fritz M., "Welthistorische Gesichtspunkte zu den vormittelalterlichen Wirtschaftsepochen" (The Pre-Medieval Economic Periods from the Point of View of World History), *SJ*, LVI (1932), Part Two (special number in honour of Werner Sombart), 154–195.

Heichelheim, *Wirtschaftsgeschichte:* — Heichelheim, Fritz M., *Wirtschaftsgeschichte des Altertums vom Paläolithikum bis zur Völkerwanderung der Germanen, Slaven und Araber* (The Economic History of Ancient Times from the Paleolithic Age to the Germanic, Slavic, and Arab Migrations). Two volumes, Leiden, 1938.

Hirth, *China:* — Hirth, Friedr., *China and the Roman Orient: Researches into Their Ancient and Mediæval Relations as Represented in Old Chinese Records.* Leipzig, 1885.

Hirth, *Porcelain:* — Hirth, Friedr., *Ancient Porcelain: A Study in Chinese Mediæval Industry and Trade.* Munich, 1888.

Hiuen, *Si-yu-ki:* — Hiuen Tsiang, *Si-yu-ki: Buddhist Records of the Western World.* Translated by Samuel Beal. Two volumes, London, 1884. (Also translated into French as *Mémoires sur les contrées occidentales* [Accounts of Western Countries]. Stanislas Julien, editor, *Voyages des pèlerins bouddhistes* [Travels of Buddhist Pilgrims], II, III. Paris, 1857, 1858.)

Hoeï-li, *Histoire:* — Hoeï-li, and Yen-Thsong, *Histoire de la vie de Hiouen-Thsang et de ses voyages dans l'Inde depuis 629 jusqu'en 645* (History of the Life of Hiuen-Tsiang and His Travels in India from 629 to 645). Stanislaus Julien, editor, *Voyages des pèlerins bouddhistes* (Travels of Buddhist Pilgrims), I. Paris, 1853.

Van Hogendorp, *Berigt:* — Van Hogendorp, D., *Berigt van den tegenwoordigen toestand der Bataafsche bezittingen in Oost-Indië en den handel op dezelve* (Report of the Present Condition of the Batavian Possessions in the East Indies and the Trade Thereon). Delft, 1800.

Van Hogendorp, *Stukken:* — Van Hogendorp, D., *Stukken raakende den tegenwoordigen toestand der Bataafsche bezittingen in Oost-Indië en den handel op dezelve: Met memorie van B. van der Oudermeulen* (Documents Concerning the Present Condition of the Batavian Possessions in the East Indies and the Trade Thereon: With a Memorandum by B. van der Oudermeulen). The Hague, 1801.

Honjo, "Population": — Honjo, E., "The Population and its Problems in the Tokugawa Era", *Bulletin de l'Institut International de Statistique* (Bulletin of the International Institute of Statistics), XXV (1931), 60–82.

Hornell, "Canoes": — Hornell, James, "The Outrigger Canoes of Indonesia", *Madras Fisheries Bulletin,* XII (1920), 43–44.

Hornell, "Design": — Hornell, James, "The Origins and Ethnological Significance of Indian Boat Design", *Memoirs of the Asiatic Society of Bengal*, VII (1918–1923), Number Three (1920), 139–256.

Horst, "Antwerpen": — Horst, W. A., "Antwerpen als specerijen-markt" (Antwerp as a Spice Market), *TG*, LI (1936), 333–336.

Huan K'uan, *Discourses:* — Huan K'uan, *Discourses on Salt and Iron: A Debate on State Control of Commerce and Industry in Ancient China.* Translated and edited by Esson McDowell Gale. Dissertation, University of Leiden; Sinica Leidensia, II. Leiden, 1931.

Huizinga, "Kern": — Huizinga, J., "Kern en de taalwetenschap" (Kern and Philology), *Pallas Leidensis MCMXXV* (Leiden, 1925), 93–101.

Huizinga, *Shadow:* — Huizinga, J., *In the Shadow of To-morrow: A Diagnosis of the Spiritual Distemper of Our Time.* London, 1936. (Translation by J. H. Huizinga of *In de schaduwen van morgen.* Haarlem, 1935.)

Huizinga, *Werken:* — Huizinga, J., *Verzamelde Werken* (Collected Works). Nine volumes, Haarlem, 1948–1953.

Hunger, "Geschenken": — Hunger, Jr, F. W. F., "Sociaal-economische en ceremonieele geschenken op Bali" (Social-Economic and Ceremonial Presents on Bali), *KT*, XXV (1936), 420–423.

Hunter, *Empire:* — Hunter, William Wilson, *The Indian Empire: Its History, People, and Products.* London, 1882.

IJzerman, *Pomp:* — IJzerman, J. W., editor, *Dirck Gerritsz. Pomp, alias Dirck Gerritsz. China, de eerste Nederlander die China en Japan bezocht, 1544–1601: Zijn reis naar en verblijf in Zuid-Amerika, grootendeels naar Spaansche bescheiden* (Dirck Gerritsz. Pomp, alias Dirck Gerritsz. China, The First Dutchman to Visit China and Japan, 1544–1604: His Voyage to and Stay in South America, Mainly from Spanish Documents). Works of the Linschoten Vereeniging (Linschoten Society), IX. The Hague, 1915.

I-Tsing, *Mémoire:* — I-Tsing, *Mémoire composé à l'époque de la grande dynastie T'ang sur les religieux éminents qui allèrent chercher la loi dans les pays d'Occident* (Account Written at the Time of the Great Tang Dynasty on the Eminent Divines Who Went to Seek the Law in the Lands of the West). Translated by E. Chavannes. Stanislas Julien, editor, *Voyages des pèlerins bouddhistes* (Travels of Buddhist Pilgrims). Paris, 1894.

I-Tsing, *Record:* — I-Tsing, *A Record of the Buddhist Religion as Practised in India and the Malay Archipelago (A.D. 671–695).* Translated by J. Takakusu. Oxford, 1896.

Jacob, *Einfluß:* — Jacob, Georg, *Der Einfluß des Morgenlands auf das Abendland, vornehmlich während des Mittelalters* (The Influence of the Orient on the West, Especially During the Middle Ages). Hanover, 1924.

Jacob, *Kulturelemente:* — Jacob, Georg, *Östliche Kulturelemente im Abendland* (Oriental Cultural Elements in the West). Berlin, 1902.

Jain, *Banking:* — Jain, Laksmi Chandra, *Indigenous Banking in India.* New York, 1929.

Jaspers, *Weber:* — Jaspers, Karl, *Max Weber.* Tübingen, 1926.

De Jonge, *Opkomst:* — De Jonge, J. K. J., and M. L. van Deventer, editors, *De opkomst van het Nederlandsch gezag in Oost-Indië: Verzameling van onuitgegeven stukken uit het Oud-Koloniaal Archief* (The Rise of Dutch Authority in the East Indies: A Collection of Unpublished Documents from the Old Colonial Archives). Twenty volumes, Amsterdam and The Hague, 1862–1895.

Junghuhn, *Reisen:* — Junghuhn, Fr., *Topographische und naturwissenschaftliche Reisen durch Java* (Topographical and Scientific Travels on Java). Edited by C. G. Nees von Essenbeck. Magdeburg, 1845.

Kanakasabhai, *Tamils:* — Kanakasabhai, Pillai, *The Tamils Eighteen Hundred Years Ago.* Madras, 1904.

Kantorowicz, *Frederick:* — Kantorowicz, Ernest, *Frederick the Second: 1194–1250.* Makers of the Middle Ages. London, 1931. (Translation by E. O. Lorimer of *Kaiser Friedrich der Zweite.* Berlin, 1927.)

De Kat Angelino, *Policy:* — De Kat Angelino, A. D. A., *Colonial Policy.* Two volumes, The Hague, 1931. (Translation of *Staatkundig beleid en bestuurszorg in Nederlandsch-Indië.* Two volumes in three parts, The Hague, 1929–1930.)

Kautsky, *Vorläufer:* — Kautsky, Karl, *Die Vorläufer des neueren Sozialismus* (The Forerunners of Modern Socialism). Four volumes, Stuttgart, sixth edition, 1921.

Kernkamp, "Nederlanders": — Kernkamp, G. W., "Nederlanders op de Oostzee" (The Dutch on the Baltic Sea), *Vragen des Tijds* (Questions of the Day), XXXV (1909), Part Two, 65–96.

Knowles, *Revolutions:* — Knowles, Lilian Charlotte Anne, *The Industrial and Commercial Revolutions in Great Britain during the Nineteenth Century.* Studies in Economics and the Political Sciences, LXI. New York, new edition, 1927.

Kohler, *Commenda:* — Kohler, Jos., *Die Commenda im islamitischen Rechte: Ein Beitrag zur Geschichte des Handelsrechts* (*Commenda* in Islamic Law: A Contribution to the History of Commercial Law). Würzburg, 1885.

Van der Kolff, *Bevolkingsrietcultuur:* — Van der Kolff, G. H., *Bevolkingsrietcultuur in Nederlandsch-Indië: Een landbouweconomische studie* (Smallholders Cane Cultivation in the Netherlands East Indies: A Study in Agrarian Economy). Dissertation, Wageningen Agricultural University. Nijmegen, 1925.

Korsch, "Nationalökonomie": — Korsch, Karl, "Sombarts 'verstehende Nationalökonomie'" (Sombart's 'Understanding National Economy'), *Archiv für die Geschichte des Sozialismus und der Arbeiterbewegung* (Archives for the History of Socialism and the Labour Movement), XV (1930), 436–448.

Kotwicz, "Mongoles": — Kotwicz, Wladyslaw, "Les Mongoles promoteurs de l'idée de la paix universelle" (The Mongols as Promotors of the Idea of World Peace), *La Pologne au VIIe congrès international des sciences historiques* (Poland at the Seventh International Historical Congress; Warsaw, 1933), I, 199–204.

Kötschke, *Wirtschaftsgeschichte:* — Kötschke, Rud., *Allgemeine Wirtschaftsgeschichte des Mittelalters* (General Economic History of the Middle Ages). Georg Brodnitz, editor, *Handbuch der Wirtschaftsgeschichte* (Manual of Economic History), II. Jena, 1924.

Krause, *Geschichte:* — Krause, Friedrich Ernst August, *Geschichte Ostasiens* (History of East Asia). Three volumes, Göttingen, 1925.

Von Kremer, *Culturgeschichte:* — Von Kremer, Alfred, *Culturgeschichte des Orients under den Chalifen* (Cultural History of the Orient Under the Chalifs). Two volumes, Vienna, 1875, 1877.

Von Kremer, *Einnahmebudget:* — Von Kremer, Alfred, *Über das Einnahmebudget des Abbasiden-Reiches vom Jahre 306 H. (918–919)* (On the Budget of Incomes of the Abbasid Empire for the Year 306 H. [918–919]). Vienna, 1887.

Krom, *Geschiedenis:* — Krom, N. J., *Hindoe-Javaansche geschiedenis* (Hindu-Javanese History). The Hague, second edition, 1931.

Kruyt, "Leven": — Kruyt, Alb. C., "Een en ander aangaande het geestelijk en maatschappelijk leven van den Poso-Alfoer" (Some Remarks on the Spiritual and Social Life of the Alfurese of Poso), *MNZG*, XXXIX (1895), 2–36, 106–153, XL (1896), 7–31, 121–160, 245–282, XLI (1897), 1–52.

Kruyt, "Tengke-offer": — Kruyt, Alb. C., "Een tengke-offer bij de Poso-Alfoeren" (A *Tengke* Offering Among the Alfurese of Poso), *MNZG*, XXXIX (1895), 230–236.

Kruyt, *West-Toradjas:* — Kruyt, Alb. C., *De West-Toradjas op Midden-Celebes* (The West Torajas on Central Celebes). Verhandelingen der Koninklijke Nederlandsche Akademie van Wetenschappen, Afdeeling Letterkunde (Proceedings of the Dutch Royal Academy of Sciences, Literary Section), New Series, XL. Four volumes and one volume illustrations, Amsterdam, 1938.

Lavisse, *Histoire:* — Lavisse, Ernest, and Alfred Rambaud, editors, *Histoire générale du IVe siècle à nos jours* (General History from the Fourth Century to Our Day). Twelve volumes, Paris, 1893–1901.

Lee, *China:* — Lee, Mabel Ping-Hua, *The Economic History of China.* Columbia University Studies in History, Economics, and Public Law, XCIX, Part One. New York, 1921.

Lette, *Grondbezit:* — Lette, Joh. Rud., *Proeve eener vergelijkende studie van het grondbezit in Rusland zooals dit zich heeft ontwikkeld tot de Russische revolutie, en op Java* (A First Comparative Study of Land Ownership in Russia, as Developed up to the Russian Revolution, and on Java). Dissertation, University of Leiden. Leiden, 1928.

Lévi, *Indochine:* — Lévi, S., editor, *Indochine* (Indo-China). Two volumes, Paris, 1931.

Lieber, *Weltwirtschaft:* — Lieber, Alfred, *Frühmittelalterliche Weltwirtschaft* (Early Medieval World Economy). Dissertation, University of Amsterdam, 1938. (In typescript, University of Amsterdam Library.)

Ligthart, *Bodem:* — Ligthart, Th., *et al.*, editors, *De Indische bodem* (The Indies Soil). Weltevreden, 1926.

Van Linschoten, *Voyage:* — *The Voyage of John Huyghen van Linschoten to the East Indies: From the Old English Translation of 1598.* Edited by Arthur Coke Burnell and P. A. Tiele. Works of the Hakluyt Society, LXX, LXXI. Two volumes, London, 1885. (Translation of *Itinerario: Voyage ofte schipvaert van Jan Huygen van Linschoten naer Oost ofte Portugaels Indien 1579–1592.* Edited by H. Kern. Works of the Linschoten Vereeniging [Linschoten Society], II, Parts One and Two. Two volumes, The Hague, 1910.)

Van Loon, *Mankind:* — Van Loon, H. W., *The Story of Mankind.* London, 1922.

De Loos-Haaxman, *Rach:* — De Loos-Haaxman, J., *Johannes Rach en zijn werk* (Johannes Rach and His Work). Batavia, 1928.

Lynam, *Hakluyt:* — Lynam, Edward, editor, *Richard Hakluyt and His Successors: A Volume Issued to Commemorate the Centenary of the Hakluyt Society.* London, 1946.

McCrindle, *India:* — McCrindle, J. W., editor, *Ancient India as Described in Classical Literature: Being a Collection of Greek and Latin Texts Relating to India, Extracted from Herodotus, Strabo, Diodorus Siculus, Pliny, Aelian, Philostratus, Dion Chrysostom, Porphyry, Stobaeus, the Itinerary of Alexander the Great, the Periêgêsis of Dionysius, the Dionysiaka of Nonnus, the Romance History of Alexander and Other Works.* Westminster, 1901.

McCrindle, J. W., editor, *Ancient India as Described by Ktêsias the Knidian: Being a Translation of the Abridgement of His 'Indika' by Phôtios, and of the Fragments of That Work Preserved in Other Writers.* Calcutta, 1882.

McCrindle, J. W., editor, *Ancient India as Described by Megasthenês and Arrian: Being a Translation of the Fragments of the Indika of Megasthenês and of the First Parts of the Indika of Arrian.* Calcutta, 1877.

McCrindle, J. W., editor, *Ancient India as Described by Ptolemy: Being a Translation of the Chapters Which Describe India and Central Eastern Asia in the Treatise on Geography Written by Klaudios Ptolemaios.* Calcutta, 1885.

McCrindle, J. W., editor, *The Commerce and Navigation of the Erythraean Sea: Being a Translation of the Periplus Maris Erythraei ... and of Arrian's Account of the Voyage of Nearkhos ...* Calcutta, 1879.

McCrindle, J. W., editor, *The Invasion of India by Alexander the Great as Described by Arrian, Q. Curtius, Diodoros, Plutarch and Justin: Being Trans-*

lations of Such Portions of the Works of These and Other Classical Authors as Describe Alexander's Campaigns in Afghanistan, the Panjâb, Sindh, Gedrosia and Karmania. Westminster, new edition, 1896.

Malinowski, *Argonauts:* — Malinowski, Bronislaw, *Argonauts of the Western Pacific: An Account of Native Enterprise and Adventure in the Archipelagoes of Melanesian New Guinea.* With a preface by Sir James George Frazer. Studies in Economics and the Political Sciences, LXV. London, 1922.

Mannheim, *Ideology:* — Mannheim, Karl, *Ideology and Utopia: An Introduction to the Sociology of Knowledge.* International Library of Psychology, Philosophy, and Scientific Method. London, 1936. (Translation by Louis Wirth and Edward Shils of *Ideologie und Utopie.* Schriften zur Philosophie und Soziologie [Essays in Philosophy and Sociology], III. Bonn, second edition, 1930).

Mannheim, *Man:* — Mannheim, Karl, *Man and Society in an Age of Reconstruction: Studies in Modern Social Structure.* London, 1940. (Translation by Edward Shils of *Mensch und Gesellschaft im Zeitalter des Umbaus.* Leiden, 1935.)

Mannheim, summary: — Mannheim, Karl, summary of a lecture, *Algemeen Nederlandsch Tijdschrift voor Wijsbegeerte en Psychologie* (General Dutch Journal of Philosophy and Psychology), XXVII (1934), 39.

Mansvelt, *Handelshuizen:* — Mansvelt, W. M. F., editor, *De eerste Indische handelshuizen* (The First Indies Trading Firms). Mededeelingen Centraal Kantoor voor de Statistiek (Communications of the Central Bureau of Statistics), CLXVIII. Batavia, 1938.

Mansvelt, *Rechtsvorm:* — Mansvelt, W. M. F., *Rechtsvorm en geldelijk beheer bij de Oost-Indische Compagnie* (The Juridical Form and Financial Administration of the Dutch East India Company). Amsterdam, 1922.

Marshall, *Mohenjo-Daro:* — Marshall, John, *Mohenjo-Daro and the Indus Civilization: Being an Official Account of Archæological Excavations at Mohenjo-Daro Carried Out by the Government of India Between the Years 1922 and 1927.* Three volumes, London, 1931.

Massignon, "Islam": — Massignon, Louis, "L'influence de l'Islam au moyen âge sur la fondation et l'essor des banques juives" (The Influence of Islam During the Middle Ages on the Establishment and Growth of Jewish Banks), *Bulletin d'études orientales, Institut Français de Damas* (Bulletin of Oriental Studies, French Institute of Damascus), I (1931), 3–12.

Masson-Oursel, *Inde:* — Masson-Oursel, Paul, *et al.*, *L'Inde antique et la civilisation ancienne* (Early India and Ancient Civilization). Paris, 1933.

Meijer Ranneft, summary: — Meijer Ranneft, J. W., summary of letters read at a meeting of the directors of the Batavian Society of Arts and Sciences, *JBG*, III (1936), 29.

Metchnikoff, *Fleuves:* — Metchnikoff, Léon, *Les grandes fleuves et les civilisations historiques* (The Great Rivers and the Historic Civilizations). Paris, 1889.

Van der Meulen & Von Wissmann, *Hadramaut:* — Van der Meulen, D., and H. von Wissmann, *Haḍramaut: Some of its Mysteries Unveiled.* Leiden, 1932.

Meyer, *Hellenismus:* — Meyer, Ed., *Blüte und Niedergang des Hellenismus in Asien* (The Flowering and Decline of Hellenism in Asia). Berlin, 1925.

Meyer, *Schriften:* — Meyer, Ed., *Kleine Schriften zur Geschichtstheorie und zur wirtschaftlichen und politischen Geschichte des Altertums* (Brief Studies in Theoretical History and the Economic and Political History of the Ancient World). Halle an der Saale, 1910.

Mijer, *Verzameling:* — Mijer, J., editor, *Verzameling van instructiën, ordonnanciën en reglementen voor de Regeering van Nederlandsch-Indië, vastgesteld in de jaren 1609–1836* (Collection of Instructions, Ordinances, and Regulations for the Administration of the Netherlands East Indies, Issued in the Years 1609–1836). Batavia, 1848.

Mookerji, *Shipping:* — Mookerji, Radhakumud, *Indian Shipping: A History of the Seaborne Trade and Maritime Activity of the Indians from the Earliest Times.* London, 1912.

Moreland, *Akbar:* — Moreland, William Harrison, *India at the Death of Akbar: An Economic Study.* London, 1920.

Moreland, *Aurangzeb:* — Moreland, William Harrison, *From Akbar to Aurangzeb: A Study in Indian Economic History.* London, 1923.

Moreland, *System:* — Moreland, William Harrison, *The Agrarian System of Moslem India: A Historical Essay.* Cambridge, 1929.

Morse, *Gilds:* — Morse, Hosea Ballou, *The Gilds of China: With an Account of the Gild Merchant, or Co-Hong, of Canton.* London, 1909.

Müller, *Books:* — Müller, F. Max, editor, *The Sacred Books of the East.* Translated by various Oriental scholars. Fifty volumes, Oxford, 1879–1910.

Muller, *Eeuw:* — Muller, P. L., *Onze Gouden Eeuw: De Republiek der Vereenigde Nederlanden in haar bloeitijd* (Our Golden Age: The Republic of the United Netherlands in its Florescence). Leiden, fourth edition, 1927.

Nanninga Uitterdijk, *Handelshuis:* — Nanninga Uitterdijk, J., editor, *Een Kamper handelshuis te Lissabon 1572–1594: Handelscorrespondentie, rekeningen en bescheiden* (A Kampen Trading Firm at Lisbon, 1572–1594: Commercial Correspondence, Accounts, and Documents). Zwolle, 1904.

Van Neck, "Reisverhaal": — "Reisverhaal van Jacob van Neck (1598–1599)" (Journal of the Voyage of Jacob van Neck [1598–1599]; edited by H. T. Colenbrander), *Bijdragen en mededeelingen van het Historisch Genootschap te Utrecht* (Contributions and Communications of the Historical Society at Utrecht), XXI (1900), 194–329.

Neumann, *Weltstellung:* — Neumann, Carl, *Die Weltstellung des byzantinischen Reiches vor den Kreuzzügen* (The World Position of the Byzantine Empire Before the Crusades). Leipzig, 1894.

Neurath, *Wirtschaftsgeschichte:* — Neurath, Otto, *Antike Wirtschaftsgeschichte* (Ancient Economic History). Aus Natur und Geisteswelt (Of the Natural and the Spiritual World), CCLVIII. Leipzig, third edition, 1926.

Noël, *Histoire:* — Noël, Octave, *Histoire du commerce du monde depuis les temps les plus reculés* (History of World Trade from the Earliest Times). Three volumes, Paris, 1890–1906.

Nooteboom, *Boomstamkano:* — Nooteboom, Chr., *De boomstamkano in Indonesië* (The Trunk Canoe in Indonesia). Dissertation, University of Leiden. Leiden, 1932.

Onderzoek: — *Onderzoek naar de mindere welvaart der inlandsche bevolking op Java en Madoera* (Investigation into the Diminishing Prosperity of the Native Population on Java and Madura). Twelve volumes in eighteen parts, Batavia, 1905–1914.

Van Orsoy de Flines, "Verzameling": — Van Orsoy de Flines, E. W., "De keramische verzameling" (The Ceramics Collection), *JBG*, I (1933), 225–230; II (1934), 122; III (1936), 206–218; IV (1937), 173–179; V (1938), 159–166; VI (1939), 140–147; VII (1940), 108–114; VIII (1941), 141–149; IX (1941–1947), 111–120.

Pareto, *Manuel:* — Pareto, Vilfredo F. D., *Manuel d'économie politique* (Manual of Political Economy). Translated by Alfred Bonnet. Bibliothèque internationale d'économie politique (International Library of Political Economy), XXXVIII. Paris, 1909.

Pelliot, "Itinéraires": — Pelliot, Paul, "Deux itinéraires de Chine en Inde à la fin du VIIIe siècle" (Two Itineraries from China to India at the End of the Eighth Century), *BEFEO*, IV (1904), 132–413.

Pelliot, review: — Pelliot, Paul, review of Friedr. Hirth and W. W. Rockwell, editors, Chau Ju-kua, *Trade* (see above), *TP*, XIII (1912), 446–481.

Perry, *Culture:* — Perry, W. J., *The Megalithic Culture of Indonesia.* Publications of the University of Manchester, CXVIII (Ethnological Series, III). Manchester, 1918.

Pijper, *Fragmenta:* — Pijper, G. F., *Fragmenta Islamica: Studiën over het Islamisme in Nederlandsch-Indië* (Islamic Fragments: Studies on Islamism in the Netherlands East Indies). Leiden, 1934.

Pirenne, *Mahomet:* — Pirenne, Henri, *Mahomet et Charlemagne* (Mohammed and Charlemagne). Paris, third edition, 1937.

Pirenne, *Pays-Bas:* — Pirenne, Henri, *Les anciennes démocraties des Pays-Bas* (The Early Democracies of the Netherlands). Paris, 1922.

Plantenga, "Boek": — Plantenga, J. H., "Een nieuw boek over de oude beschaving" (A New Book on Ancient Civilization: review of A. N. Zadoks-

Josephus Jitta, *Antieke cultuur in beeld* [Ancient Civilization in Pictures]), *Gids*, C (1936), Part One, 77–94.

Pleßner, *Geschichte:* — Pleßner, Mart., *Die Geschichte der Wissenschaften im Islam als Aufgabe der modernen Islamwissenschaft* (The History of Islamic Scholarship as a Subject for Modern Islamic Studies). Philosophie und Geschichte (Philosophy and History), XXXI. Tübingen, 1933.

Ploegsma, *Oorspronkelijkheid:* — Ploegsma, N. D., *Oorspronkelijkheid en economisch aspect van het dorp op Java en Madoera* (The Originality and the Economic Aspect of the Village on Java and Madura). Dissertation, University of Leiden. Leiden, 1936.

Poerbatjaraka, *Agastya:* — Poerbatjaraka, Lesya, *Agastya in den Archipel* (Agastya in the [Indonesian] Archipelago). Dissertation, University of Leiden. Leiden, 1926.

Polo, *Book:* — Polo, Marco, *The Book of Sir Marco Polo the Venetian Concerning the Kingdoms and Marvels of the East.* Translated and edited by Henry Yule. London, third edition, revised by Henri Cordier, 1903.

"Portugeezen": — "Portugeezen in den Maleischen Archipel" (The Portuguese in the Malay Archipelago), *ENI* (second edition), III, 454–462.

"Poso": — "Poso (Posso)", *ENI* (second edition), III, 462–464.

Przeworski, "Handelsbeziehungen": — Przeworski, St., "Die Handelsbeziehungen Vorderasiens zum vorgeschichtlichen Osteuropa" (The Trade Relations of Asia Minor with Prehistoric Eastern Europe), *La Pologne au VIIe congrès des sciences historiques* (Poland at the Seventh International Historical Congress; Warsaw, 1933), I, 83 ff.

Pyrard, *Voyage:* — *The Voyage of François Pyrard of Laval to the East Indies, the Maldives, the Moluccas and Brazil.* Works of the Hakluyt Society, LXXVI, LXXVII, LXXX. Two volumes in three parts, London, 1887–1890. (Translation by Albert Gray assisted by H. C. P. Bell of *Voyage de François Pyrard de Laval: Contenant sa navigation aux Indes Orientales, Maldives, Moluques, Brésil ...* Paris, 1619.)

Raffles, *History:* — Raffles, Thomas Stamford, *The History of Java.* Two volumes, London, 1817.

Rahder, "Siebold": — Rahder, J., "Het ontslag van Jhr. Dr. Ph. F. B. von Siebold" (The Discharge of Jonkheer Ph. F. B. von Siebold), *Jaarboekje voor geschiedenis en oudheidkunde van Leiden en Rijnland* (*Leidsch Jaarboekje*) (Yearbook of the History and Archeology of Leiden and Environs), XXV (1932–1933), 26–50.

Von Ranke, *Weltgeschichte:* — Von Ranke, Leopold, *Weltgeschichte* (World History). Nine volumes, Leipzig, 1881–1888.

Rassers, *Pandji-roman:* — Rassers, W. H., *De Pandji-roman* (The *Panji* Romance). Dissertation, University of Leiden. Antwerp, 1922.

Rathgen, "Volkswirtschaft": — Rathgen, Karl, "Japans Volkswirtschaft und Staatshaushalt" (Japan's National and Political Economy), *Staats- und socialwissenschaftliche Forschungen* (Studies in Political and Social Science), X (1891), 1–785.

Ratzel, *Anthropogeographie:* — Ratzel, Friedrich, *Anthropogeographie* (Human Geography). Two volumes, Stuttgart, third edition, 1909, 1912.

Ravaisse, "Inscription": — Ravaisse, P., "L'inscription coufique de Léran à Java" (The Cufic Inscription of Leran on Java), *TBG*, LXV (1925), 668–703.

Rawlinson, *Intercourse:* — Rawlinson, H. G., *Intercourse Between India and the Western World from the Earliest Times to the Fall of Rome.* Cambridge, 1916.

Reichwein, *China:* — Reichwein, Adolf, *China und Europa: Geistige und künstlerische Beziehungen im 18. Jahrhundert* (China and Europe: Intellectual and Artistic Relations in the Eighteenth Century). Berlin, 1923.

Reinaud, *Relations:* — Reinaud, Joseph Toussaint, editor, *Relations de voyages faits par les Arabes et les Persans dans l'Inde et la Chine dans le XIIe siècle de l'ère chrétienne* (Accounts of Journeys Made by Arabs and Persians in India and China in the Twelfth Century A.D.). Two volumes, Paris, 1845.

Review: — Review of G. P. Tedotow, *Sviatie drevni Rusi* (The Saints of Early Rus), *Nieuwe Rotterdamsche Courant,* 5 November, 1935, Section A, 1.

Richter, *Geschichtsbild:* — Richter, Gust., *Das Geschichtsbild der arabischen Historiker des Mittelalters* (The View of History of Medieval Arab Historians). Tübingen, 1933.

Rockhill, "Notes": — Rockhill, W. W., "Notes on the Relations and Trade of China with the Eastern Archipelago and the Coasts of the Indian Ocean During the Fourteenth Century", *TP*, XV (1914), 419–447, XVI (1915), 61–159, 236–271, 374–392, 435–467, 604–626.

Rodenwaldt, *Kunst:* — Rodenwaldt, Gerh., *Die Kunst der Antike: Hellas und Rom* (Ancient Art: Hellas and Rome). Propyläen-Kunstgeschichte (Propyläen History of Art), III. Berlin, 1927.

Roland Holst, *Kunst:* — Roland Holst-van der Schalk, Henriëtte, *Over dramatische kunst: Een studie* (On Dramatic Art: A Study). Rotterdam, 1928.

Rolland, *Beethoven:* — Rolland, Romain, *Beethoven: With a Brief Analysis of the Sonatas.* London, 1917. (Translation by Constance Hull of *Vie de Beethoven.* Paris, 1903.)

Rolland, *Gandhi:* — Rolland, Romain, *Mahatma Gandhi: The Man Who Became One with the Universal Being.* London, 1924. (Translation by Catherine D. Groth of *Mahatma Gandhi.* Paris, 1924.)

Romein, *Erflaters:* — Romein, Jan Marius, and Annie H. M. Romein-Verschoor, *Erflaters van onze beschaving: Nederlandse gestalten uit zes eeuwen* (Testators of Our Culture: Dutch Figures of Six Centuries). Four volumes, Amsterdam, 1938–1940.

Romein, *Landen:* — Romein, Jan Marius, and Annie H. M. Romein-Verschoor, *De lage landen bij de zee: Geïllustreerde geschiedenis van het Nederlandsche volk van Duinkerken tot Delfzijl* (The Low Countries by the Sea: Illustrated History of the Dutch People from Dunkirk to Delfzijl). Utrecht, second edition, 1941.

Romein, "Stijl": — Romein, Jan Marius, "Byzantijnse stijl: Een poging tot karakteristiek" (Byzantine Style: An Attempt at Characterization), *Het onvoltooid verleden* (The Past Imperfect; Amsterdam, second enlarged edition, 1948), 173–184.

De Roover, review: — De Roover, Raymond, review of Hans van Werveke, *De Gentsche stadsfinanciën in de Middeleeuwen* (The Finances of the Town of Ghent During the Middle Ages), *TG*, LI (1936), 89–91.

Rostovtzeff, "Commerce": — Rostovtzeff, M., "Foreign Commerce of Ptolemaic Egypt", *Journal of Economic and Business History*, IV (1931–1932), 728–769.

Rostovtzeff, *History:* — Rostovtzeff, M., *The Social and Economic History of the Roman Empire*. Oxford, 1926.

Rouffaer, "Artikelen": — Rouffaer, G. P., "Encyclopaedie-artikelen" (Articles for *ENI*), *BKI*, LXXXVI (1930), 191–215.

Rouffaer, *Industrieën:* — Rouffaer, G. P., *De voornaamste industrieën der inlandsche bevolking van Java en Madoera: Aanhangsel tot het overzicht van den economischen toestand der inlandsche bevolking van Java en Madoera door Mr C. Th. van Deventer* (The Leading Crafts of the Native Population of Java and Madura: Supplement to the Survey of the Economic Condition of the Native Population of Java and Madura). Koloniaal Economische Bijdragen (Contributions to Colonial Economics), I, Part A. The Hague, 1904.

Rouffaer, "Kunst": — Rouffaer, G. P., "Beeldende kunst in Nederlandsch-Indië" (The Plastic Arts in the Netherlands East Indies), *BKI*, LXXXIX (1932), 321–658.

Rouffaer, "Malaka": — Rouffaer, G. P., "Was Malaka emporium vóór 1400 A.D., genaamd Malajoer? En waar lag Woerawari, Mā-Hasin, Langka, Batoesawar? Met terreinschetsen van Djambi, oud-Singhapoera, en de Djohor-rivier" (Was Malacca an Emporium Called Malayur Before 1400 A.D.? And Where Were Wurawari, Mā-Hasin, Langka, and Batusawar Located? With Maps of Jambi, Early Singapore, and the Johore River), *BKI*, LXXVII (1921), 1–174, 359–604.

Rouffaer, "Oeliasers": — Rouffaer, G. P., "Oeliasers" (People of Uliasa), *ENI* (second edition), III, 65–66.

Rouffaer, "Pata lima": — Rouffaer, G. P., "Pata lima, Pata siwa", *ENI* (second edition), III, 360–361.

Rouffaer, "Pégon": — Rouffaer, G. P., "Pégon", *ENI* (second edition), III, 371–372.

Rouffaer, "Schilderkunst": — Rouffaer, G. P., "Schilderkunst" (Pictorial Arts), *ENI* (first edition), III, 559–561.

Rouffaer, "Tijdperk": — Rouffaer, G. P., "Het tijdperk van godsdienstovergang (1400–1600) in den Maleischen Archipel: wanneer is Madjapahit gevallen?" (The Period of Religious Transition [1400–1600] in the Malay Archipelago: When Did Majapahit Fall?), *BKI*, L (1899), 111–199.

Rouffaer, "Tochten": — Rouffaer, G. P., "Tochten, oudste ontdekkings-" (The First Voyages of Discovery), *ENI* (first edition), IV, 363–395.

Rouffaer & IJzerman, *Schipvaart:* — Rouffaer, G. P., and J. W. IJzerman, *De eerste schipvaart der Nederlanders naar Oost-Indië onder Cornelis de Houtman, 1595–1597: Journalen, documenten en ander bescheiden* (The First Voyage of the Dutch to the East Indies, Under Cornelis de Houtman, 1595–1597: Journals, Documents, and Other Papers). Works of the Linschoten Vereeniging (Linschoten Society), VII, XXV, XXXII. Three volumes, The Hague, 1915–1929.

Rouffaer & Juynboll, *Batik-kunst:* — Rouffaer, G. P., and H. H. Juynboll, *De Batik-kunst in Nederlandsch-Indië en haar geschiedenis* (The Art of Batik in the Netherlands East Indies and Its History). With text in Dutch and German. Publicaties van 's Rijks Ethnographisch Museum (Publications of the State Museum of Ethnography), Series Two, I. Two volumes, Haarlem, 1900.

De Rovere van Breughel, "Bedenkingen": — De Rovere van Breughel, J., "Bedenkingen over den staat van Bantam" (Observations on the State of Bantam), *BKI*, V (1856), 110–170.

De Rovere van Breughel, "Beschrijving": — De Rovere van Breugel, J., "Beschrijving van Bantam en de Lampongs" (Description of Bantam and the Lampong Region), *BKI*, V (1856), 309–362.

Rüter, *Spoorwegstakingen:* — Rüter, Adolf Johann Cord, *De spoorwegstakingen in 1903: Een spiegel der arbeidersbeweging in Nederland* (The Railway Strikes in 1903: A Mirror of the Labour Movement in the Netherlands). Dissertation, University of Leiden. Leiden, 1935.

Schaal, *Tauschhandel:* — Schaal, Hans, *Vom Tauschhandel zum Welthandel: Bilder vom Handel und Verkehr der Vorgeschichte und des Altertums* (From Barter Trade to World Trade: Sketches of Trade and Transportation in Prehistory and Ancient Times). Leipzig, 1931.

Schaeder, "Ausbreitung": — Schaeder, Hans Heinrich, "Ausbreitung und Staatengründungen des Islam vom 7. bis 15. Jahrhundert" (The Spread of Islam and the Foundation of the Islamic States from the Seventh to the Fifteenth Century), Goetz, *Werdegang* (see above), III (1932), 213–248.

Scherer, *Geschichte:* — Scherer, H., *Allgemeine Geschichte des Welthandels* (General History of World Trade). Two volumes, Leipzig, 1852–1853.

Schrieke, "Adatgrondenrecht": — Schrieke, B. J. O., "Uit de geschiedenis van het adatgrondenrecht: De theorie van het zoogenaamde 'vorstelijk eigendomsrecht'" (From the History of *Adat* Land Law: The Theory of the So-Called 'Royal Proprietary Rights'), *TBG*, LIX (1920), 122–190.

Schrieke, "Javanen": — Schrieke, B. J. O., "Varium: Javanen als zee- en handelsvolk" (Varium: The Javanese as Seafaring and Trading People), *TBG*, LVIII (1919), 424–428.

Schrieke, "Prolegomena": — Schrieke, B. J. O., "Prolegomena tot eene sociologische studie over de volken van Sumatra: I (A: Historisch Gedeelte)" (Prolegomena to a Sociological Study of the Peoples of Sumatra: I [A: Historical Section]), *TBG*, LXV (1925), 90–207. (To be published in English translation in B. Schrieke, *Indonesian Sociological Studies*, the second volume of this series, under the title "Shifts in Political and Economic Power in the Indonesian Archipelago in the Sixteenth and Seventeenth Century".)

Schumpeter, *Wesen:* — Schumpeter, Jos. Alois, *Das Wesen und der Hauptinhalt der theoretischen Nationalökonomie* (The Nature and Chief Contents of Economic Theory). Leipzig, 1908.

Shellabear, *Sejarah:* — Shellabear, W. G., editor, *Sejarah Malayu, or The Malay Annals.* Malay Literature Series, IX. Two volumes, Singapore, second edition, 1910.

Smith, *History:* — Smith, Vincent A., *The Early History of India: From 600 B.C. to the Muhammadan Conquest.* London, third edition, 1914.

Sneller, *Walcheren:* — Sneller, Zeger Willem, *Walcheren in de vijftiende eeuw* (Walcheren in the Fifteenth Century). Dissertation, University of Utrecht. Utrecht, 1916.

Snouck Hurgronje, *Achehnese:* — Snouck Hurgronje, C., *The Achehnese.* Two volumes, Leiden, 1906. (Translation by A. W. S. O'Sullivan of *De Atjèhers.* Two volumes, Batavia, 1893, 1894.)

Snouck Hurgronje, "Arabie": — Snouck Hurgronje, C., "L'Arabie et les Indes néerlandaises" (Arabia and the Netherlands East Indies), *Verspreide Geschriften* (Collected Writings), IV (The Hague, 1924), Part Two, 97–114. (Translation of *Arabië en Oost-Indië.* Inaugural lecture, University of Leiden. Leiden, 1907.)

Snouck Hurgronje, "Bantam": — Snouck Hurgronje, C., "Nieuws over Bantam?" (News About Bantam?), *Verspreide Geschriften* (Collected Writings), IV (The Hague, 1924), Part One, 249–256.

Snouck Hurgronje, "Politique": — Snouck Hurgronje, C., "Politique musulmane de la Hollande" (Moslem Policy of the Netherlands), *Verspreide Geschriften* (Collected Writings), IV (The Hague, 1924), Part Two, 221–306. (Translation of *Nederland en de Islam.* Leiden, second edition, 1915.)

Soekarno, *Indonesië:* — Soekarno, *Indonesië klaagt aan! Pleitrede voor den landraad te Bandoeng op 2 December 1930* (Indonesia Accuses! Plea Before the Bandung Local Court, 2 December, 1930). Amsterdam, 1931.

Sombart, *Future:* — Sombart, Werner, *The Future of Capitalism.* Berlin, 1932. (Translation of *Die Zukunft des Kapitalismus.* Berlin, 1932.)

Sombart, *Kapitalismus:* — Sombart, Werner, *Der moderne Kapitalismus: Historisch-systematische Darstellung des gesamteuropäischen Wirtschaftslebens von seinen Anfängen bis zur Gegenwart* (Modern Capitalism: Systematic Outline of the History of European Economic Life from its Origins to the Present Day). Three volumes, Munich: Volumes One and Two, third edition, 1919; Volume Three, first edition, 1928.

Sombart, *Nationalökonomien:* — Sombart, Werner, *Die drei Nationalökonomien: Geschichte und System der Lehre von der Wirtschaft* (The Three Economies: History and System of the Study of Economics). Munich, 1930.

Sombart, "Objekt": — Sombart, Werner, "Objekt und Grundbegriffe der theoretischen Nationalökonomie" (Subject and Basic Concepts of Economic Theory), *ASS,* XXXVIII (1914), 647–661.

Sombart, *Ordnung:* — Sombart, Werner, *Die Ordnung des Wirtschaftslebens* (Planning of Economic Life). Enzyklopaedie der Rechts- und Staatswissenschaften (Encyclopedia of Law and Political Science), edited by G. Kohlrausch *et al.,* XXXV. Berlin, second edition, 1927.

Sombart, *Quintessence:* — Sombart, Werner, *The Quintessence of Capitalism: A Study of the Modern Businessman.* London, 1915. (Translation of *Der Bourgeois: Zur Geistesgeschichte des modernen Wirtschaftsmenschen.* Munich, 1913.)

Sombart, *Sozialismus:* — Sombart, Werner, *Der proletarische Sozialismus ("Marxismus")* (Proletarian Socialism ['Marxism']). Two volumes, Jena, 1924. (Tenth revised edition of *Sozialismus und Soziale Bewegung,* of which the sixth edition translated by M. Epstein as *Socialism and the Social Movement.* New York, 1909.)

Sombart, *Volkswirtschaft:* — Sombart, Werner, *Die deutsche Volkswirtschaft im 19. Jahrhundert und im Anfang des 20. Jahrhunderts: Eine Einführung in die Nationalökonomie* (German Economy in the Nineteenth and Early Twentieth Centuries: An Introduction to Economics). Berlin, 1927.

Sombart, "Wandlungen": — Sombart, Werner, "Wandlungen des Kapitalismus: Auslandanleihen, Kredit und Konjunktur" (Developments in Capitalism: Foreign Loans, Credit, and Market Trends), *Schriften des Vereins für Sozialpolitik* (Papers of the Social Policy Society), CLXXV (1928; Proceedings of the Social Policy Society, Zurich, 13–15 September, 1928), 23–41.

Sosro Ningrat, "Huwelijk": — Sosro Ningrat, "Het huwelijk bij de Kodja's" (Marriage Among the *Kojahs*), *BKI,* L (1899), 695–702.

Soustelle, "Vie": — Soustelle, J., "La vie économique chez les peuples primitifs" (Economic Life Among Primitive Peoples), *Le Monde: Hebdomadaire international,* cxcviii (19 March, 1932).

Speck, *Handelsgeschichte:* — Speck, E., *Handelsgeschichte des Altertums* (History of Ancient Trade). Three volumes in five parts, Leipzig, 1900–1906.

Van Spilbergen, *Reis:* — *De reis van Joris van Spilbergen naar Ceylon, Atjeh en Bantam: 1601–1604* (The Voyage of Joris van Spilbergen to Ceylon, Achin, and Bantam: 1601–1604). Works of the Linschoten Vereeniging (Linschoten Society), XXXVIII. The Hague, 1933.

Sprenger, *Postrouten:* — Sprenger, A., *Die Post- und Reiserouten des Orients* (The Post and Travel Routes of the Orient). Abhandlungen für die Kunde des Morgenlandes herausgegeben von der Deutschen Morgenländischen Gesellschaft (Contributions to the Knowledge of the Orient Published by the German Oriental Society), III, No 3. Leipzig, 1864.

Stapel, *Geschiedenis:* — Stapel, F. W., editor, *Geschiedenis van Nederlandsch Indië* (History of the Netherlands East Indies). Five volumes published, Amsterdam, 1938–1940.

Stapel, "Speelman": — Stapel, F. W., "Cornelis Janszoon Speelman", *BKI*, XCIV (1936), 1–222.

Stein, *Geschichte:* — Stein, Ernst, *Studien zur Geschichte des byzantinischen Reiches vornehmlich unter den Kaisern Justinus II und Tiberius Constantinus* (Studies in the History of the Byzantine Empire, Especially Under the Emperors Justinus II and Tiberius Constantinus). Stuttgart, 1919.

Stier, *Pergamonaltar:* — Stier, Hans Er., *Aus der Welt des Pergamonaltars: Geburt, Blüte und Schicksale der hellenistischen Kultur* (From the World of the Pergamon Altar: The Rise, Flowering, and Fate of Hellenistic Culture). Berlin, 1932.

Stöckle, "Zünfte": — Stöckle, Albert, "Spätrömische und byzantinische Zünfte: Untersuchungen zum sogenannten ἐπαρχικὸν βιβλίον Leos des Weisen" (Late Roman and Byzantine Gilds: Studies on the So-Called Eparchikon Biblion of Leo the Wise), *Klio* (Clio), Ninth Supplement (1911).

Le Strange, *Caliphate:* — Le Strange, G., *Lands of the Eastern Caliphate: Mesopotamia, Persia, Central Asia, from the Moslem Conquest to the Time of Timur.* London, 1905.

Stutterheim, "Bijzettingsgebruiken": — Stutterheim, W. F., "Iets over prae-Hinduïstische bijzettingsgebruiken op Java" (Remarks on Pre-Hindu Burial Practices on Java), [*Verslagen en*] *Mededeelingen der Koninklijke Nederlandsche Akademie, Afdeeling Letterkunde* ([Reports and] Communications of the Dutch Royal Academy of Sciences, Literary Section), New Series, II (1939), 105–140.

Stutterheim, "Relations": — Stutterheim, W. F., "Note on Cultural Relations Between South-India and Java", *TBG*, LXXIX (1939), 73–84.

Stüwe, *Handelszüge:* — Stüwe, Friedrich, *Die Handelszüge der Araber unter den Abassiden durch Afrika, Asien und Osteuropa* (The Trading Expeditions of the Arabs Under the Abassids Through Africa, Asia, and Eastern Europe). Berlin, 1936.

Sulaiman, *Voyage:* — *Voyage du marchand arabe Salaymān en Inde et en Chine, rédigé en 851: Suivi de remarques par Abu Zayd Hasan (vers 916)* Travels of the Arab Merchant Sulaiman in India and China, Written in 851: Followed by Remarks by Abu Said Hasan [circa 916]). Les classiques de l'Orient (The Classics of the East), VII. Paris, 1922.

Takizawa, *Penetration:* — Takizawa, Matsuyo, *The Penetration of Money Economy in Japan and Its Effects upon Social and Political Institutions.* New York, 1927.

Terpstra, *Westerkwartieren:* — Terpstra, H., *De opkomst der Westerkwartieren van de Oost-Indische Compagnie (Suratte, Arabië, Perzië)* (The Rise of the Western Quarters of the Dutch East India Company [Surat, Arabia, Persia]). The Hague, 1918.

Thomson, *Straits:* — Thomson, J., *The Straits of Malacca, Indo-China and China, or Ten Years' Travels, Adventures and Residence Abroad.* London, 1875.

Tiele, "Europeërs": — Tiele, P. A., "De Europeërs in den Maleischen Archipel" (The Europeans in the Malay Archipelago), *BKI*, XXV (1877), 321–420 (Part One: 1509–1520); XXVII (1879), 1–69 (Part Two: 1529–1540); XXVIII (1880), 260–340 (Part Three: 1541–1555), 395–482 (Part Four: 1556–1578); XXIX (1881), 153–214 (Part Five: 1578–1599); XXX (1882), 141–242 (Part Six: 1598–1605); XXXII (1884), 49–118 (Part Seven: 1606–1610); XXXV (1886), 257–355 (Part Eight: 1611–1618); XXXVI (1887), 199–307 (Part Nine: 1618–1623).

Tiele, "Oosten": — Tiele, P. A., "Het Oosten vóór de komst der Portugeezen" (The East Before the Arrival of the Portuguese), *Gids*, XXXVIII (1874), Part Three, 193–242.

Tiele & Heeres, *Bouwstoffen:* — Tiele, P. A., and J. E. Heeres, editors, *Bouwstoffen voor de geschiedenis der Nederlanders in den Maleischen Archipel: Tweede Reeks (Buitenbezittingen) — De opkomst van het Nederlandsch gezag in Oost-Indië: Verzameling van onuitgegeven stukken uit het Oud-Koloniaal Archief* (Materials for the History of the Dutch in the Malay Archipelago: Second Series [Outlying Possessions] — The Rise of Dutch Authority in the East Indies: A Collection of Unpublished Documents from the Old Colonial Archives). Three volumes, The Hague, 1886–1895.

Treub, *Hoofdstukken:* — Treub, Marie Willem Frederik, *Hoofdstukken uit de geschiedenis der staathuishoudkunde* (Chapters from the History of Political Economy). Haarlem, fifth edition, 1930.

Troeltsch, *Probleme:* — Troeltsch, Ernst, *Der Historismus und seine Probleme* (Historicism and Its Problems). *Gesammelte Schriften* (Collected Writings), III. Tübingen, 1922.

Troeltsch, *Thought:* — Troeltsch, Ernst, *Christian Thought: Its History and Application.* London, 1923. (Translation of *Der Historismus und seine Überwindung* [Historicism and Its Triumph]. Berlin, 1924).

Tsur, "Betriebsformen": — Tsur, Nyok-Ching, "Die gewerblichen Betriebsformen der Stadt Ningpo" (The Forms of Industrial Enterprise in the City of Ningpo), *Zeitschrift für die gesammte Staatswissenschaft* (Journal of the Political Sciences), Thirtieth Supplement (1909).

Unger, *Middelburg:* — Unger, W. S., *Middelburg als handelsstad (XIIIe tot XVIe eeuw)* (Middelburg as a Trading Town [The Thirteenth to the Sixteenth Century]). *MZGW.* Middelburg, 1935.

Unger, review: — Unger, W. S., review of Fritz Rörig, *Mittelalterliche Weltwirtschaft: Blüte und Ende einer Weltwirtschaftsperiode* (Medieval World Economy: The Flowering and Decay of a Period of World Economy), *TG,* L (1935), 197–199.

"Verhaal": — "Verhaal van eenige oorlogen in Indië, 1622: Uit het Archief Van Hilten" (Account of Some Wars in the East Indies, 1622: From the Van Hilten Records), *Kroniek van het Historisch Genootschap te Utrecht* (Chronicle of the Historical Society at Utrecht), XXVII (1871), 497–617, 621–658.

Verhoeven, *Bijdragen:* — Verhoeven, F. R. J., *Bijdragen tot de oudere koloniale geschiedenis van het eiland Formosa* (Contributions to the Early Colonial History of the Island of Formosa). Dissertation, University of Leiden. The Hague, 1930.

Verslag: — *Verslag over den landbouw in Nederland over 1930* (Report on Agriculture in the Netherlands in 1930). Verslagen en Mededeelingen van de Directie van den Landbouw, Departement van Binnenlandsche Zaken en Landbouw (Reports and Communications of the Directorate of Agriculture, Ministry of Internal Affairs and Agriculture), 1931, II. The Hague, 1931.

Vissering, *Currency:* — Vissering, W., *On Chinese Currency, Coins, and Paper Money.* Leiden, 1877.

Vogel, "Inscriptions": — Vogel, J. Ph., "The Yūpa Inscriptions of King Mūlawarman, from Koetei (East Borneo)", *BKI,* LXXIV (1918), 167–232.

Van Vollenhoven, *Adatrecht:* — Van Vollenhoven, C., *Het adatrecht van Nederlandsch-Indië* (The *Adat* Law of the Netherlands East Indies). Three volumes in four parts, Leiden, 1918–1933. (English translation in preparation.)

Van Vollenhoven, "Administratief recht": — Van Vollenhoven, C., "Omtrek van het administratief recht" (Outline of Administrative Law; with a summary in French), *Verspreide Geschriften* (Collected Writings), I (Haarlem, 1934), 63–91.

Van Vollenhoven, *Découverte:* — Van Vollenhoven, C., *La découverte du droit indonésien* (The Discovery of Indonesian Law). Etudes de sociologie et d'ethnologie juridiques (Legal Studies in Sociology and Ethnology), XIII. Paris, 1933. (Translation by N. Pernot of *De ontdekking van het adatrecht.* Leiden, 1928.)

Van Vollenhoven, *Droit:* — Van Vollenhoven, C., *Du droit de paix: De iure pacis* (On the Laws of Peace). The Hague, 1932.

De Vrankrijker, "Textielindustrie": — De Vrankrijker, A. C. J., "De textielindustrie van Naarden" (The Naarden Textile Industry) *TG*, LI (1936), 152–164, 264–283.

Vroklage, *Verhältnisse:* — Vroklage, B. A. G., *Die sozialen Verhältnisse Indonesiens, eine kulturgeschichtliche Untersuchung: I – Borneo, Celebes und Molukken* (Indonesian Social Relations, A Study in Cultural History: I – Borneo, Celebes, and the Moluccas). Ethnologische Bibliothek Anthropos (Ethnological Library Anthropos), IV, i. Munster, 1936.

Van Vuuren, "Prauwvaart": — Van Vuuren, L., "De prauwvaart van Celebes" (Celebes Proa Shipping), *KS*, I (1916–1917), Part One, 107–116.

De Waard, "Walcheren": — De Waard, C., "De rand van het eiland Walcheren in 1546" (The Coastline of the Isle of Walcheren in 1546), *MZGW*, LVII (1912), 129–158.

Van de Wall, *Buitenplaatsen:* — Van de Wall, V. I., *Oude Hollandsche buitenplaatsen van Batavia* (Old Dutch Manor Houses of Batavia). Deventer, second edition, 1943.

Weber, *China:* — Weber, Max, *The Religion of China: Confucianism and Taoism.* Glencoe, Illinois, 1951. (Translation by Hans H. Gerth of *Gesammelte Aufsätze zur Religionssoziologie*, I, 276–536.)

Weber, *Essays:* — *From Max Weber: Essays in Sociology.* International Library of Sociology and Social Reconstruction. London, 1948. (Translation by H. H. Gerth and C. Wright Mills of *Gesammelte Aufsätze zur Religionssoziologie*, I, 207–275, 395–430, II, 396–415; *Gesammelte Aufsätze zur Soziologie und Sozialpolitik*, 484–486; *Gesammelte Aufsätze zur Wissenschaftslehre*, 524–555; *Wirtschaft und Gesellschaft*, III, 631–678, 753–757.)

Weber, *Ethic:* — Weber, Max, *The Protestant Ethic and the Spirit of Capitalism.* New York, 1930. (Translation by Talcott Parsons of *Gesammelte Aufsätze zur Religionssoziologie*, I, 17–206.)

Weber, *History:* — Weber, Max, *General Economic History.* New York, first edition, 1927. (Translation by Frank H. Knight of *Wirtschaftsgeschichte.*)

Weber, *Judaism:* — Weber, Max, *Ancient Judaism.* Glencoe, Illinois, 1953. (Translation by Hans Gerth and Don Martindale of *Aufsätze zur Religionssoziologie*, III.)

Weber, *Law:* — Weber, Max, *Max Weber on Law in Economy and Society.* Cambridge, Massachusetts, 1954. (Translation by Edward A. Shils and Max Rheinstein of *Wirtschaft und Gesellschaft*, 1–20 [abridged], 368–513, 603–618, 660–665 [abridged].)

Weber, *Methodology:* — Weber, Max, *The Methodology of the Social Sciences.* Glencoe, Illinois, 1949. (Translation by Edward A. Shils and Henry A. Finch of *Gesammelte Aufsätze zur Wissenschaftslehre*, 451–502, 146–290.)

Weber, *Religionssoziologie:* — Weber, Max, *Gesammelte Aufsätze zur Religionssoziologie* (Collected Essays in the Sociology of Religion). Three volumes, Tübingen, first edition, 1920–1921. (For parts translated see *China, Essays, Ethic, Judaism, System.*)

Weber, *Sozialgeschichte:* — Weber, Max, *Gesammelte Aufsätze zur Sozial- und Wirtschaftsgeschichte* (Collected Essays in Social and Economic History). Tübingen, 1924.

Weber, *Sozialpolitik:* — Weber, Max, *Gesammelte Aufsätze zur Soziologie und Sozialpolitik* (Collected Essays in Sociology and Social Policy). Tübingen, 1924. (For part translated see *Essays.*)

Weber, *System:* — Weber, Max, *The Hindu Social System.* Minneapolis, 1950. (Translation by Hans Gerth and Don Martindale of *Gesammelte Aufsätze zur Religionssoziologie,* II, 1–32, 48–109, 113–133.)

Weber, *Theory:* — Weber, Max, *The Theory of Social and Economic Organization.* Toronto, 1947. (Translation by A. M. Henderson and Talcott Parsons of *Gesammelte Aufsätze zur Wissenschaftslehre,* 503–523; *Wirtschaft und Gesellschaft,* I.)

Weber, *Weber:* — Weber, Marianne, *Max Weber: Ein Lebensbild* (Max Weber: A Sketch of His Life). Tübingen, 1926.

Weber, *Wirtschaft:* — Weber, Max, *Wirtschaft und Gesellschaft* (Economy and Society). *Grundriß der Sozialökonomik* (Outline of Social Economy), III. Tübingen, second edition, 1925. (For parts translated see *Essays, Law, Theory.*)

Weber, *Wirtschaftsgeschichte:* — Weber, Max, *Wirtschaftsgeschichte: Abriß der universalen Sozial- und Wirtschaftsgeschichte* (Economic History: An Outline of a General Social and Economic History). Munich, second edition, 1924. (For translation see *History.*)

Weber, *Wissenschaftslehre:* — Weber, Max, *Gesammelte Aufsätze zur Wissenschaftslehre* (Collected Essays in the Theory of Knowledge). Tübingen, 1922. (For parts translated see *Essays, Methodology, Theory.*)

Weil, *Geschichte:* — Weil, Gust., *Geschichte der Chalifen nach handschriftlichen Quellen* (History of the Caliphs: After Manuscript Sources). Three volumes, Mannheim, 1846–1851.

Wells, *Outline:* — Wells, H. G., *The Outline of History: Being a Plain History of Life and Mankind.* London, definitive edition, 1924.

Wensinck, "School": — Wensinck, A. J., "De oostersche school" (The Oriental School), *Pallas Leidensis MCMXXV* (Leiden, 1925), 77–92.

Westenenk, "Chetti": — Westenenk, L. C., "De Chetti" (The Chetty), *KS,* VI (1922), Part Two, 1–17.

Westenenk, "Hindoe-Javanen": — Westenenk, L. C., "De Hindoe-Javanen in Midden- en Zuid-Sumatra" (The Hindu Javanese in Central and Southern Sumatra), *Handelingen van het Eerste Congres voor de Taal-, Land- en Volkenkunde van Java, Solo, 25 en 26 December 1919* (Proceedings of the

First Congress for the Philology, Geography, and Ethnology of Java, Solo, 25 and 26 December, 1919; Weltevreden, 1921), 1–39.

Whiteway, *Power:* — Whiteway, R. S., *The Rise of Portuguese Power in India: 1497–1550.* Westminster, 1899.

Van Wijk, "Poesjkin": — Van Wijk, N., "A. S. Poesjkin (1799–1837)" (A. S. Pushkin: 1799–1837), *Gids*, CI (1937), Part One, 327–354.

Wilhelm, *Wirtschaftspsychologie:* — Wilhelm, Richard, *Chinesische Wirtschaftspsychologie* (Chinese Economic Psychology). Schriften des Weltwirtschafts-Instituts der Handels-Hochschule Leipzig (Publications of the Institute for World Economy of the Leipzig School of Commerce), V. Leipzig, 1930.

Wiskerke, *Afschaffing:* — Wiskerke, Corn., *De afschaffing der gilden in Nederland* (The Abolition of the Gilds in the Netherlands). Dissertation, Rotterdam School of Economics. Amsterdam, 1938.

Wisse, *Compagnie:* — Wisse, Adr., *De Commercie-Compagnie te Middelburg van haar oprichting tot het jaar 1759* (The Middelburg Trading Company from its Foundation up to the Year 1759). Dissertation, University of Leiden. Utrecht, 1933.

Wittfogel, "Ursachen": — Wittfogel, K. A., "Die natürlichen Ursachen der Wirtschaftsgeschichte" (Natural Causes of Economic History), *ASS*, LXVII (1932), 466–492, 579–609, 711–731.

Wittfogel, *Wirtschaft:* — Wittfogel, Karl August, *Wirtschaft und Gesellschaft Chinas: Versuch der wissenschaftlichen Analyse einer großen asiatischen Agrargesellschaft* (Chinese Economy and Society: A Preliminary Scholarly Analysis of a Large Asian Agrarian Society). Schriften des Instituts für Sozialforschung an der Universität Frankfurt am Main (Publications of the Institute for Social Research of the University of Frankfurt on Main), III. Leipzig, 1931.

Yule, *Cathay:* — Yule, Henry, editor, *Cathay and the Way Thither: Being a Collection of Medieval Notices of China.* New edition, revised by Henri Cordier. Works of the Hakluyt Society, Second Series, XXXIII, XXXVII, XXXVIII, XLI. Four volumes, London, 1913–1916.

Ziebarth, *Beiträge:* — Ziebarth, Erich, *Beiträge zur Geschichte des Seeraubs und Seehandels im alten Griechenland* (Contributions to the History of Piracy and Sea Trade in Ancient Greece). Hamburgische Universität: Abhandlungen aus dem Gebiet der Auslandkunde (University of Hamburg Publications in the Field of Foreign Studies), XXX. Hamburg, 1929.

Glossary

Weights and measures given in metric or earlier Dutch units and sums given in florins by Van Leur have here and elsewhere in the volume been converted to their British equivalents.

Glossary

adat: customary law.
apophora: wage earned by slaves to be turned over to their masters.
bag: measure of weight, one half picul or one sixth *bahar*.
bahar: measure of weight, three picul or six bags, equivalent to 360–600 lb. (*cf.* pp. 136, 369 n. 19, 391 n. 26).
balang: large, swift-moving boat propelled by paddling.
cash: lead coin from China circulating in southeast Asia, one thousandth tael, in Indonesian also *keping*.
chandi: grave monument, grave temple.
charisma: term used by Weber to denote the magical quality of an extraordinary person, leader, or ruler claiming authority and leadership on its basis.
commenda: form of trading association entered into for carrying out one sea voyage: a producer or exporter of goods turned them over to another person who took them abroad and sold them for a share in the profits, the expenses of the voyage being divided between the two in agreed proportion, and the original shipper bearing the risk.
coptis teeta: root of *coptis teeta Wall.* used as medicine.
corge: a score.
daimio: Japanese feudal vassal, practically an independent lord.
datching: Chinese-type small steelyard.
datuk (besar): prince, high-ranking official.
desa: village community, especially on Java.
dirhem: Near Eastern measure of weight, equivalent to approximately 48 grains; small silver coin.
ducat: gold coin equivalent to about 9s, or silver coin somewhat less than half that value.
ergasterion: large workshop.
fondaco [plural *fondachi*]: quarter of town inhabited by one foreign 'nation'.
gantang: measure of weight, equivalent to 13–17 lb.; measure of capacity, equivalent to one or two gallon.
gaukang: representation and symbolization of the vital spirit of a regional community in southern Celebes in a particular object of supernatural qualities.
kain: piece of cloth.

kampong: non-European quarter of town, more usually village.

kati: measure of weight, one hundredth picul, equivalent to around 1⅓ lb.

kedai: selling booth.

keling: foreign(er), especially Calinggalese, (person) from the Coromandel Coast.

koja(h): rich foreign merchant (*cf.* p. 293 n. 4).

kota: (fortified) town.

koyan: large measure of weight, some thirty to forty picul, equivalent to 3000–5000 lb.

kraton: enclosed royal residence.

Kula: pattern of commercial and ceremonial 'potlatch' forms of trade between tribes of southeastern New Guinea and adjacent islands (*cf.* pp. 54–56).

kyai: 'grandfather', religious teacher or leader.

ladang: high land used for dry-field farming.

lakh: one hundred thousand.

ling(g)a: phallic-shaped monument of marble or other stone for worship of Çiwa.

literati: term used by Weber, class of (mostly noble) persons, well-trained in the classics, comprising the administrative officials of the Chinese Empire.

lontar: palm leaf (of *Borassus flabelliformis*) used as writing paper.

ma(h)mudi: silver coin, equivalent to around 7d.

man: maund, measure of weight, equivalent to 20–26 lb.

mantri [or *menteri*, *cf.* mandarin]: (high) official, minister.

maona [plural *maone*]: joint undertaking of merchants from an Italian town, sometimes state-chartered; predecessor of joint-stock company.

nakoda: master of Asian trading ship.

oikos: term used by Weber, organization of specialized unfree labour in *ergasteria* of lords.

orang baik: 'the good man', the common man.

orang kaya: 'the rich man', patrician or nobleman.

pachul: sort of hoe used in Indonesia.

pagoda: southern Indian gold coin, equivalent to around 10s.

pancado: body consisting of most prominent merchants of the five imperial cities of Japan.

panembahan: 'object of devout reverence', exalted title of, among others, the ruler-priest of Giri.

pangeran: governor; more usually prince, title of member of ruling family.

panglima: representative of (Achinese) ruler in lands under his suzerainty.

patola: kind of figured Gujarati cloth woven from silk threads of various colours.

peculium: property legally belonging to head of family, but actually to another member of the family or a slave.

pekojan: Indian or Arab quarter of Indonesian town (*cf. kojah*).
picul: measure of weight, one hundred *kati* or one third *bahar*, equivalent to 120–200 lb.
priyayi: gentleman, official.
pujangga: man of letters, learned scholar.
pusaka: venerated heirloom.
real (of eight): gold dollar which could be divided into eight pieces; silver dollar having the value of one piece of a gold dollar, or about 6½d.
ronin: waveman, homeless, lordless *samurai*.
roucou: salmon-coloured dye prepared from *Bixa Orellana L.*
sawah: irrigated ricefield.
shahbandar: water bailiff, harbour master.
ship's ton: *cf.* ton.
susuhunan: Javanese royal title.
tael: measure of weight, especially for precious wares, equivalent to around 1⅓ oz; monetary unit, equivalent to about 6s 8d.
ton: here ship's ton of 1500 lb. (*cf.* pp. 366 n. 2, 390 n. 15).
tumenggung: noble title sometimes awarded to regents.
virtuoso: term used by Weber, person initiated into sacral and other religious knowledge.
wangkang: Chinese-type oceangoing junk.
wayang: (shadow) play performed by puppets or living actors.
zamorin: title of Hindu sovereign of Calicut and surroundings.
zemindar: Mogol district governor and tax farmer.

Index

In the index below, which by no means pretends to be exhaustive, references to authors have been included only in cases where their work has been cited, or discussed at some length, by Van Leur. For full details on books and articles referred to in the index by short keywords, see the bibliography above.

Index

SELECTED STUDIES ON INDONESIA

The post-war changes in Indonesia have served to arouse the interest of the world at large in that important area. In contrast with the general interest, however, a large part of the scholarly works on Indonesia are available only in Dutch, to most scholars a 'secret' language. It is for this reason that in 1948 a committee, since 1950 affiliated with the Royal Tropical Institute at Amsterdam, was established in the Netherlands for the purpose of editing in English translation a series of studies on Indonesia written primarily by Dutch scholars.

The members of the committee at the time the present volume was planned are listed on the face-title page. At the time of going to press the committee consisted of the following members:

Other volumes in this series are:

2 *B. Schrieke*, INDONESIAN SOCIOLOGICAL STUDIES: SELECTED WRITINGS, PART ONE. The late Professor Schrieke (1890–1945) was one of the first in his field to recognize the need for a scientific approach to the problem of acculturation. In this volume, together with a brief general article on the subject 'Some Remarks on Borrowing in the Development of Culture' (1927), are three special studies: 'The Shifts in Political and Economic Power in the Indonesian Archipelago in the Sixteenth and Seventeenth Century' (1925), 'The Causes and Effects of Communism on the West Coast of Sumatra' (1928), and 'The Native Rulers' (1928). x + 313 pp. *Published 1955.*

3 *B. Schrieke*, INDONESIAN SOCIOLOGICAL STUDIES: SELECTED WRITINGS, PART TWO. RULER AND REALM IN EARLY JAVA. Professor Schrieke concentrated a large part of his research during the last years of his life on a series of detailed studies emphasizing the continuity in Javanese social and cultural history. This volume contains a translation of the manuscript as it was left behind on his death, plus two closely related shorter studies: 'Disruption and Continuity in Javanese Historiography' (posthumously published in 1950) and 'The End of Classical Hindu-Javanese Culture in Central Java' (1941). xii + 491 pp. *Published 1957.*

4 THE INDONESIAN TOWN: STUDIES IN URBAN SOCIOLOGY. This volume is designed to provide an introduction to urban development in Indonesia. It contains an introductory survey of studies in the field, a general essay 'Town Development in the Indies' (1938), and three specialized studies: 'The Living Conditions of Municipally Employed Coolies in Batavia in 1937' (1939), 'Differential Mortality in the Town of Bandung' by W. Brand (1940), and 'Kuta Gede' by H. J. van Mook (1926). xxxvi + 379 pp. *Published 1958.*

5 BALI: STUDIES IN LIFE, THOUGHT, AND RITUAL. Taken in conjunction with the extensive introductory essay written especially for this volume by J. L. Swellengrebel, the ten studies contained in it constitute a veritable handbook to Bali. The studies are: 'The Religious Character of the Village Community', 'The Temple System', and 'Holidays and Holy Days', all by R. Goris; 'The Consecration of a Priest' by V. E. Korn; 'The State Temples of Mĕngwi' and 'Pĕmayun Temple of the *Banjar* of Tĕgal' by C. J. Grader; 'The Festival of Jayaprana at Kaliangĕt' by H. J. Franken; 'The Irrigation System in the Region of Jĕmbrana' by Grader; 'The Position of the Blacksmiths' by Goris; and 'The Village Republic of Tĕnganan Pĕgĕringsingan' by Korn. xiv + 434 pp. *Published 1960.*

6 INDONESIAN ECONOMICS: THE CONCEPT OF DUALISM IN THEORY AND POLICY. The theory of economic dualism advanced by the late Professor J. H. Boeke (1884–1956) was and is the subject of heated debate. Presenting the pros and cons of the debate in their many ramifications, this volume contains a long introductory essay by the editors, together with four studies by Boeke ('Social and Economic Needs', 'Dualistic Economics', 'Objective and Personal Elements in Colonial Welfare Policy', and 'Village Reconstruction') and nine by other Dutch economists of the last half century: 'Colonial Economics and Theoretical Economics' and 'Value Curves and the Lowest Level of the Indies Economy' by G. Gonggrijp; 'The Economics of the Tropical Colony' by J. van Gelderen; 'Remarks on "Dualistic Economics"' by E. P. Wellenstein; 'Brown and White Economy: Unity in Diversity' by G. H. van der Kolff; 'A Welfare Policy for the Indies' by C. Th. van Deventer; 'The Government's Native Economic Policy' by D. H. Burger; 'Overpopulation and the Emancipation of the Village' by Th. A. Fruin; and 'Cooperation and Social Structure in the Village of Chibodas' by H. ten Dam. xii + 443 pp. *Published 1961.*

Second edition 1967

7 *G. J. Resink*, INDONESIA'S HISTORY BETWEEN THE MYTHS: ESSAYS IN LEGAL HISTORY AND HISTORICAL THEORY. In a series of methodological essays and monographic studies, most of them published in journals over the past fifteen years, Professor Resink (1911–) has cleared away much of the deadwood that tended to obstruct the view of Indonesia's history. This volume collects fourteen of his articles in translation. *In the press.*

8 BALI: FURTHER STUDIES IN LIFE, THOUGHT, AND RITUAL. A second collection of studies complementing those in Volume Five, this volume contains contributions by I Wajan Bhadra, C. J. Grader, R. Goris, F. A. Liefrinck, and J. L. Swellengrebel. *In preparation.*

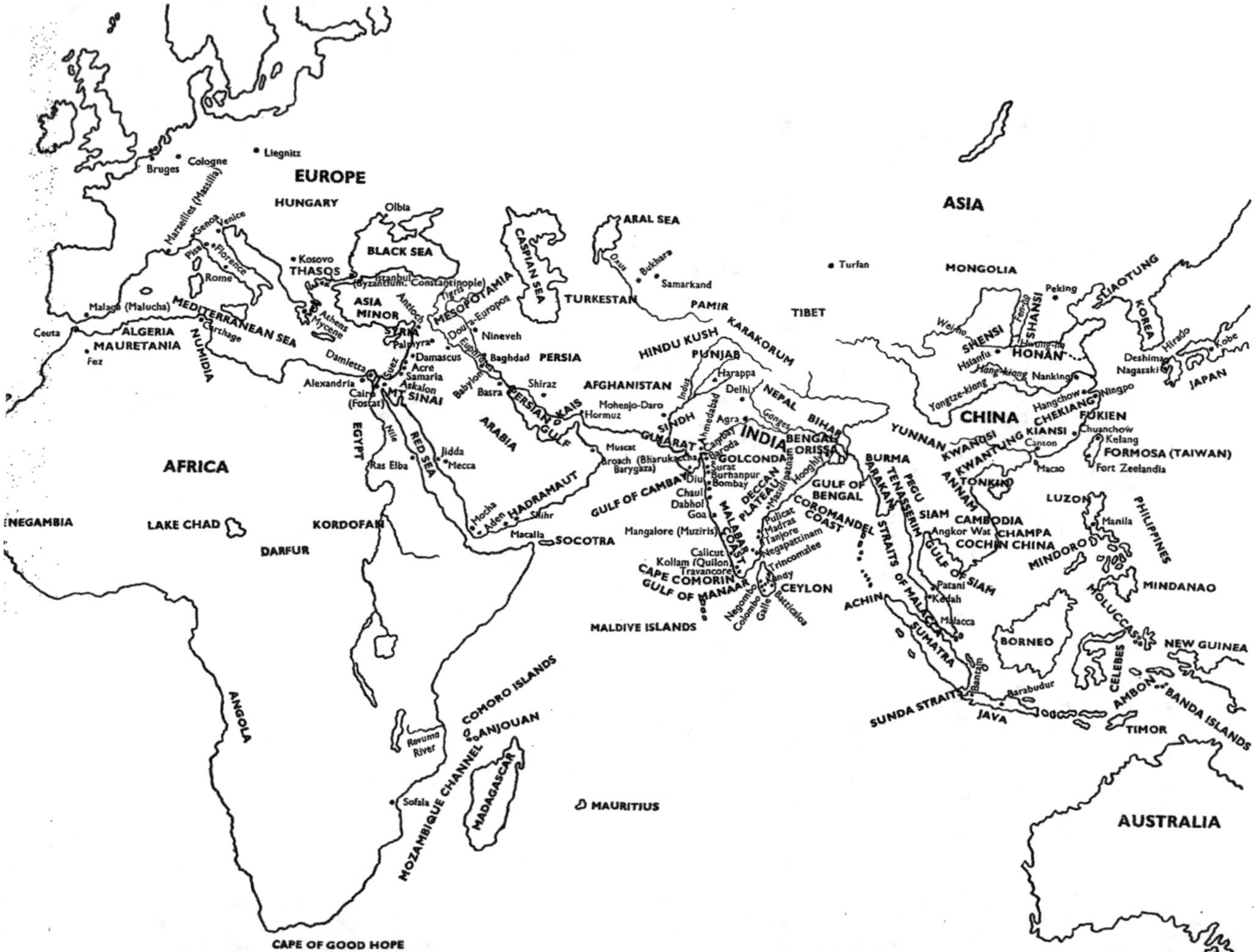
EUROPE
ASIA
AFRICA
AUSTRALIA
Bruges
Cologne
Liegnitz
HUNGARY
Marseilles (Massilia)
Genoa
Venice
Pisa
Florence
Rome
Kosovo
THASOS
Athens
Mycene
Olbia
BLACK SEA
Istanbul (Byzantium, Constantinople)
ASIA MINOR
Antioch
SYRIA
Palmyra
Damascus
Acre
Samaria
Askalon
MT. SINAI
Suez
Damietta
Alexandria
Cairo (Fostat)
EGYPT
Nile
Ras Elba
RED SEA
Jidda
Mecca
ARABIA
Mocha
Aden
HADRAMAUT
Shihr
Macalla
SOCOTRA
MESOPOTAMIA
Tigris
Euphrates
Doura-Europos
Nineveh
Baghdad
Babylon
Basra
PERSIA
Shiraz
PERSIAN GULF
KAIS
Hormuz
Muscat
CASPIAN SEA
ARAL SEA
Oxus
Bukhara
Samarkand
TURKESTAN
PAMIR
KARAKORUM
HINDU KUSH
AFGHANISTAN
Mohenjo-Daro
Indus
SINDH
PUNJAB
Harappa
Delhi
Agra
Ahmedabad
GUJARAT
Cambay
Baroda
Broach (Bharukaccha, Barygaza)
GULF OF CAMBAY
Diu
Surat
Burhanpur
Bombay
Chaul
Dabhol
Goa
Mangalore (Muziris)
Calicut
Kollam (Quilon)
Travancore
CAPE COMORIN
GULF OF MANAAR
MALABAR COAST
DECCAN PLATEAU
GOLCONDA
INDIA
NEPAL
Ganges
BIHAR
BENGAL
ORISSA
Hooghly
Masulipatnam
Pulicat
Madras
Tanjore
Negapattinam
Trincomalee
Kandy
CEYLON
Negombo
Colombo
Galle
Batticaloa
COROMANDEL COAST
GULF OF BENGAL
MALDIVE ISLANDS
TIBET
Turfan
MONGOLIA
Mauritania
Malaga (Malucha)
Ceuta
Fez
ALGERIA
MAURETANIA
NUMIDIA
Carthage
MEDITERRANEAN SEA
NEGAMBIA
LAKE CHAD
KORDOFAN
DARFUR
ANGOLA
CAPE OF GOOD HOPE
Sofala
Revuma River
MOZAMBIQUE CHANNEL
COMORO ISLANDS
ANJOUAN
MADAGASCAR
MAURITIUS
BURMA
ARAKAN
PEGU
TENASSERIM
SIAM
STRAITS OF MALACCA
ACHIN
Patani
Kedah
Malacca
SUMATRA
SUNDA STRAITS
Bantam
JAVA
Barabudur
GULF OF SIAM
Angkor Wat
CAMBODIA
CHAMPA
COCHIN CHINA
ANNAM
TONKIN
YUNNAN
KWANGSI
KWANTUNG
CHINA
KIANSI
Canton
Macao
CHEKIANG
FUKIEN
Hangchow
Ningpo
Chuanchow
Kelang
FORMOSA (TAIWAN)
Fort Zeelandia
Yangtze-kiang
Hang-kiang
Nanking
HONAN
Hwang-ho
SHENSI
Hsianfu
Wei-ho
Fen-ho
SHANSI
Peking
LIAOTUNG
KOREA
Hirado
Deshima
Nagasaki
Kobe
JAPAN
LUZON
Manila
PHILIPPINES
MINDORO
MINDANAO
BORNEO
CELEBES
MOLUCCAS
NEW GUINEA
AMBON
BANDA ISLANDS
TIMOR

www.ingramcontent.com/pod-product-compliance
Lightning Source LLC
LaVergne TN
LVHW052215200926
848481LV00001B/110

* 9 7 8 1 5 9 7 4 0 6 0 4 8 *